# CHRONIC
# POLITICS

# CHRONIC POLITICS
## HEALTH CARE
## SECURITY FROM
## FDR TO GEORGE W. BUSH

Philip J. Funigiello

 University Press of Kansas

Published by the University Press of Kansas (Lawrence, Kansas
66049), which was organized by the Kansas Board of Regents and is
operated and funded by Emporia State University, Fort Hays State
University, Kansas State University, Pittsburg State University,
the University of Kansas, and Wichita State University

Library of Congress Cataloging-in-Publication Data
Funigiello, Philip J.
Chronic politics : health care security from FDR to George W. Bush /
Philip J. Funigiello.
    p.   cm.
Includes bibliographical references and index.
ISBN 0-7006-1399-4 (cloth : alk. paper)
1. National health insurance—United States—History.  2. Insurance,
Health—United States—History.  3. Medical policy—United
States—History.  4. Social policy—United States—History.  5. Medical
care—Political aspects—United States—History.  6. Health care
reform—United States—History.  I. Title.
RA412.2.F86 2005
362.1'0425'0973—dc22    2005008587

British Library Cataloguing-in-Publication Data is available.

Printed in the United States of America
10  9  8  7  6  5  4  3  2  1

TO MY GRANDSON, ALEX

# CONTENTS

# ACKNOWLEDGMENTS

In the course of writing this book, I have incurred a debt to many people and institutions whose encouragement and information have enabled me to accomplish my task. Their words and thoughtful comments have been most helpful and greatly appreciated.

The Carl Albert Center at the University of Oklahoma provided a travel grant that enabled me to examine the manuscript collections of several congressional legislators active in the health care debates over the past century. Its holdings are truly an important source of information on American political history, and the professional staff of the center, particularly Todd Kosmerick, deserves recognition for their cooperation and useful suggestions. The Lyndon B. Johnson Foundation, in Austin, Texas, also awarded me a grant that enabled me to further my investigation of health care issues, particularly the evolution of Medicare, at the Johnson Presidential Library. I had conducted research there in the past, and as always, the staff offered generously of their time and suggested fruitful avenues for investigation. The staffs of the Franklin D. Roosevelt Library in Hyde Park, New York, the National Archives in Washington, D.C., and the National Archives II, in College Park, Maryland, also responded with courtesy and professionalism to my inquiries. The Harry S. Truman Presidential Library and the Columbia University Oral History Collection generously made oral history transcripts available to me.

I also wish to thank the Committee on Faculty Research of the College of William and Mary in Virginia for a summer grant that enabled me to travel to my sources and the Department of History whose research leave program facilitated the writing of the manuscript. Professor James P. Whittenburg gave generously of his time whenever I encountered a computer glitch. Roz E. Stearns unflaggingly provided encouragement and technical help throughout the preparation of the manuscript, as did Betty Flanigan.

The staff of the Earl Gregg Swem Library of the College of William and Mary went well beyond the call of duty in helping me to locate materials. I especially wish to express my appreciation to Alan F. Zoellner and Linda F. Templeman, who guided me through the federal documents to locate often obscure citations, and to Hope H. Yelich, Bettina J. Manzo, Mary S. Molineux, and the capable staff of the Reference Division. The interlibrary loan staff graciously attended to my requests to locate materials from other institutions.

Professors Edward D. Berkowitz of George Washington University and Jennifer Klein of Yale University provided close, critical reading of the manuscript. Their suggestions helped me to clarify the issues, sharpen the analysis, and produce a better manuscript. I owe each a debt of gratitude. Professor Jill Quadagno of Florida State University, in the best of scholarly tradition, generously allowed me to read her own forthcoming manuscript on health insurance. Fred D. Woodward, director of the University Press of Kansas, was unwavering in his support and encouragement.

Beyond academe, the confidence and interest of my family and my friends have enabled me to persevere, despite Hurricane Isabel's destruction to my home and, very nearly, to the manuscript. I particularly wish to thank my wife, Joanne, for encouraging me to persevere in the midst of chaos, to Alicia and Brian, for enabling me to put things into perspective, and especially to Alex, whose infectious good nature was an inspiration. Dr. Joseph Wilson, who, like my wife, encouraged me to see the project through to completion, also deserves recognition. He may not agree with all my conclusions, but I don't believe our views about the state of health care are far apart. Finally, a special word of thanks to Otis L. Haislip and Dr. Phyllis Hall, good friends both. Otis was always ready to lend a hand on the too-frequent occasions when the computer was about to devour portions of the manuscript. His knowledge of word processing rescued me from many a miscue, and he deserves credit for assembling the final draft.

# ABBREVIATIONS

| | |
|---|---|
| AALL | American Association of Labor Legislation |
| AARP | American Association of Retired People [former name—now just AARP] |
| ACP | American College of Physicians |
| ACS | American College of Surgeons |
| AFL | American Federation of Labor |
| AFL-CIO | American Federation of Labor–Congress of Industrial Organizations |
| AFSCME | American Federation of State, County and Municipal Employees |
| AHA | American Hospital Association |
| *ALLR* | *American Labor Legislation Review* |
| AMA | American Medical Association |
| AMPAC | American Medical Political Action Committee |
| AP | Associated Press |
| APHA | American Public Health Association |
| BBDG | Blueberry Donut Group |
| CBO | Congressional Budget Office |
| CCMC | Committee on the Costs of Medical Care |
| CEA | Council of Economic Advisers |
| CES | Committee on Economic Security |
| CHIP | Children's Health Insurance Program |
| CIO | Congress of Industrial Organization |
| CNH | Committee for the Nation's Health |
| COBRA | Consolidated Omnibus Budget Reconciliation Act |
| DHEW | See HEW |
| DNC | Democratic National Committee |
| EMIC | Emergency Maternity and Infant Care |
| FDR | Franklin D. Roosevelt |
| FERA | Federal Emergency Relief Administration |
| FSA | Federal Security Agency |
| GAO | General Accounting Office |
| HEW | Department of Health, Education and Welfare |
| HHS | Department of Health and Human Services |
| HIAA | Health Insurance Association of America |
| HIPC | health insurance purchasing cooperative |
| HMO | health maintenance organization |

| | |
|---|---|
| IDC | Inter-Departmental Committee to Coordinate Health and Human Welfare Activities |
| *JAMA* | *Journal of the American Medical Association* |
| LRG | Legal Review Group |
| MAC | medical advisory committee |
| NACHM | National Advisory Commission on Health Manpower |
| NAFTA | North American Free Trade Agreement |
| NEC | National Economic Council |
| NFIB | National Federation of Independent Business |
| NHC | National Health Conference |
| NHI | National Health Inventory |
| NMA | National Medical Association |
| NPMP | Nixon Presidential Materials Project |
| NRPB | National Resources Planning Board |
| OAA | Old-Age Assistance |
| OASDI | Old-Age, Survivors, and Disability insurance |
| OASI | Old-Age and Survivors Insurance |
| PL | Public Law |
| PPO | Preferred Provider Organization |
| RNC | Republican National Committee |
| SMI | supplementary medical insurance |
| SSA | Social Security Administration |
| SSB | Social Security Board |
| TCMC | Technical Committee on Medical Care |
| UAW | United Auto Workers |
| USPHS | U.S. Public Health Service |
| USWA | Steel Workers of America |
| VA | Veterans Administration |
| WPA | Works Progress Administration |

"The only real capital of a nation is its natural resources and its human beings," President Franklin D. Roosevelt told the National Education Association in 1938. "So long as we take care of and make the most of both of them, we shall survive as a strong nation, a successful nation and a progressive nation—whether or not the bookkeepers say other kinds of budgets are from time to time out of balance. . . . Good health and good education must go hand in hand."[1] A century before Roosevelt uttered these words, free public schools were virtually unheard of, and only the most fortunate could send their children to the private institutions of learning. Today, public education is a shared responsibility of local, state, and federal governments. The same may not be said of good health. Even though the federal interest in the secure health of its citizenry is almost as old as it is in education, throughout most of the nation's history the central government has, either through circumstance or choice, played a carefully circumscribed role that is unique among the major industrialized nations. The medical system (or lack thereof) that evolved in the United States over the course of the twentieth century has afforded its clientele both "the world's best" medical care and, in some respects, the worst.

*Health security,* the term that encompasses not only the early reformers' concept of "social insurance" (for covering the costs of hospitalization and physicians' services) but also concern for the individual's total health and well-being, is one of the most pressing political and social concerns of contemporary America. In almost every national election cycle, health insurance and access to medical care emerge as imperatives, and yet just as assuredly, citizens fail to get real policies that fundamentally remedy the problems of the private, employment-based health insurance system that leaves so many uninsured or underinsured.

Historians who venture into this subject must make clear the parameters they have set for themselves. This author makes no systematic attempt to analyze the American health system in a comparative context. To do so would require a different kind of book, one that other scholars have undertaken with varying degrees of success. What this monograph does is to detail the history of health care finance in the United States from the 1930s to the present as a partisan political issue, debated by Congress and considered by the president. It examines the process by which health legislation came about: how interest groups shaped and promoted their interests; how their efforts molded health legislation; how public opinion impacted policy formation; and how the formation of legislation reflected ideas about fairness. This is the kind of political history that has too often been flattened out by the focus on institutionalist or state-structure models that dominates welfare state literature today. My approach reminds us of the importance of key individuals, the real haggling that goes on in Congress just to get a bill together, and the clash of political personalities and agendas that determines the fate of any given bill. This approach may help us to better comprehend why the United States, the wealthiest and most advanced industrial nation, has never guaranteed its citizens health security comparable to that enjoyed by the people of other industrialized countries.

In 1798, Congress established the Marine Hospital System, an early effort to organize and finance the medical care of mariners, but in a young, dynamically capitalistic economy, most Americans regarded the practice of medicine as falling within the private sector and the physician-patient relationship to be a private one. Federal responsibility for financing or intervening in the health care of citizens was viewed as an anomaly. Physicians fostered this perception by invoking the sacred canons of freedom of enterprise, the unfettered marketplace, and the ideology of the self-made man to persuade Americans that market forces should govern the physician-patient relationship.

Medicine in the nineteenth century underwent a transformation similar to that of other workplace activities, such as education, law, and journalism, from an occupation in which any common citizen (often a barber) might engage to a discipline requiring rigorous standards for admission, formal training, and rules for certification. As evidence of the professionalization of medicine, the American Medical Association (AMA), a corporate body formed in 1847, imposed upon physician-members a requirement that patients pay a monetary fee for medical services rendered. By the early twentieth century, the AMA was a presence in virtually every county in the nation and a powerful force in politics. It had successfully elevated the quality of medical training and medical care throughout the country, but it also shielded the physician-patient relationship from external scrutiny and intervention by government, particularly from federal officials.

It was also in the formative years of organized medicine that some Americans who had gone through the economic depression of the 1890s noted that in the transition to an industrial society, large numbers of unemployed Americans, the nonworking poor, and the working poor lacked the protections afforded by social insurance that were in place in the industrialized countries of western Europe, particularly Bismarckian Germany, where the government had extended government-financed health care as a right of citizenship to every person, regardless of class or status.

In the United States, efforts on the part of social reformers and their legislative allies to replicate at the state level the European experience with social insurance were unsuccessful, and until the Great Depression of the 1930s most Americans remained oblivious to the plight of fellow citizens who, for financial reasons, did not have access to fee-for-service medicine. To the extent that these citizens had access to any medical care, it was charity medicine. In 1935, the National Health Inventory, a federally underwritten study of the nation's health, documented systematically and in great detail the numbers of Americans who were ill, the nature of their illnesses, the regional distribution of the sick, and, of profound influence to a capitalistic economy, the cost to the economy in real dollars of illness-related worker absences.

The empirical data that the inventory produced, unlike earlier and mostly anecdotal tales of poor health, and the political agitation of reformers that had culminated in passage of the 1935 Social Security Act also sparked interest in enlisting the federal government to underwrite the financing and management of health care for every American as a right of citizenship. The late 1930s, however, was not a propitious time for further reform. Public apathy, a growing antipathy toward the New Deal and big government bureaucracy, a failure of political will, organized medicine's ability to outspend and outmaneuver health reformers and liberal legislators, and the outbreak of war discouraged further social experimentation by the federal government.

The road to health security continued to be strewn with obstacles in the decades after World War II, as congressional conservatives invoked cold war rhetoric and public doubts about government bureaucracy and nondefense governmental spending to deflect demands for federally underwritten universal health coverage. Congress, with support from the Dwight Eisenhower administration, instead enacted legislation to permit state governments to administer a matching program of federal funds to underwrite health care for the elderly and the indigent. The Kerr-Mills program never fulfilled its supporters' expectations, and after a bitter and protracted conflict with the AMA and its business allies, congressional liberals, working with a liberal Democratic president, enacted Medicare in 1965. That was the legislation that finally allowed the federal government to underwrite the cost of health care to Social Security recipients: a specifically defined category of the population.

Medicare, however, was a limited governmental intervention program, the product of compromise, and fell short of guaranteeing health security to all Americans as a right of citizenship. But it did modify in important ways the traditional physician-patient relationship, as the health care industry in the United States moved from private-sector medicine driven chiefly by market forces toward a mixed system that was unique among the Western industrialized democracies: a much larger, market-driven, employer-based private health system functioning alongside a smaller public system for Social Security beneficiaries.

The bitter political circumstances of Medicare's birth led to an often-fractious relationship between the two components of this mixed system, particularly as medical inflation escalated over the final three decades of the twentieth century. Both the employer-based and the publicly financed components of this mixed system were forced to retrench and to limit accessibility to health care. The relentless pressures to contain costs dramatically transformed health care in the 1980s and 1990s, as the dominant players in medical decision-making progressed from the historic dominance of the medical profession, grounded in the individualized relationship between physician and patient, to the elevation of large, sophisticated, and often-remote entities, motivated by profit. This new environment brought its own share of problems for physicians and patients and did nothing to diminish the numbers of Americans who were without health coverage.

In a nation of finite resources, health care is an issue of politics and public policy, intersecting on questions of cost, coverage, accessibility, and quality. When health care expenditures rose to 14 percent of the GDP in the early 1990s, a financially overburdened federal government slashed Medicare's budget, thereby imperiling the social premises upon which Medicare was originally founded; the private health industry responded to the same inflationary costs by directing Medicare patients to public services and facilities and turning to alternative forms of managed care to rein in costs.

The financial crisis also revived serious interest in addressing the multifaceted problems of the American health care system as one set piece, and this gave impetus to the ill-fated Clinton health proposal of 1993. However, nothing—not retrenchment, not managed care, and not even the return of prosperity—ameliorated the crisis in health care as the century drew to a close. Despite undeniably world-class funding, the very best research facilities, technology that is unparalleled, and the highest standard of medical training, access to medical care remains beyond the reach of more than 40 million Americans, about 16 percent of the population. Another 30 percent—81 million people—may expect to experience at least a thirty-day gap in health coverage over a three-year period. Another 44 percent of workers furloughed in the recession that began in 2001 may expect to go without health coverage for more than a month.[2]

These statistics are chilling; moreover, because of widespread disparities in health costs across state and regional boundaries, where you live continues to affect how many years you live. For large numbers of Americans, health security does not exist. Even those Americans fortunate enough to be able to afford medical insurance are afraid that they are losing or will lose control of both access and choice. Liberals and conservatives, Democrats and Republicans alike, share the onus for not according to every American health security as a right of citizenship. Political partisanship, ideology, rugged individualism, uncritical devotion to impersonal market forces, all too frequently have substituted for pragmatism, purposive cooperation, and community ethos that should have been as much the hallmarks of good health care and health security as they were of the national character. Not surprisingly, then, for this and other reasons, health security—the issues of cost, coverage, accessibility, and quality—remained a topic of heated political discourse in the 2004 presidential election.

To ensure the health security of all citizens, Americans, regardless of their politics or their economic and social standing, must acknowledge that market forces, private enterprise, and government programs have not conferred the health security that we as a people seek. The more than 40 million poor, working poor, and unemployed Americans who fall between the cracks of the existing mixed health care system are the crux of the crisis. Their presence threatens to destabilize the system of health care for all of us. Hence, self-interest and common sense would dictate that the old political rivalries and antagonisms be replaced with a new, cooperative partnership between private and public health care entities, a partnership that is inclusive rather than exclusive. The long-term costs of not acting are bound to be great, whereas a solution to the problem of the medically uninsured will protect the system for those who are covered. A solution that is equitable to all will require a strong leadership working within an enlightened political system and the willing cooperation of entrenched interests to forge a consensus on trade-offs in a way never tried before. This new coalition will have to transcend historic philosophical, political, and economic differences to complete the business first begun a century ago. Otherwise, as Victor R. Fuchs of Stanford University wrote in June 2002, national health insurance will probably come to the United States after a major change in the political climate—the kind of change that often accompanies a war, a depression, or large-scale civil unrest.[3]

# ONE

## BEGINNINGS: THE FEDERAL
## GOVERNMENT & HEALTH
## SECURITY

We have been slow, as a nation, in developing an adequate health program. We have been equally
slow in developing an adequate program of social security, especially with respect to security
against sickness. These are not really two separate conclusions. They are substantially one,
because both the availability of medical services and the achievement of security against
sickness depend in large measure on a method of assuring that people can pay the costs of
medical care. We have not yet developed that assurance.[1]
*Dr. I. S. Falk, Social Security Administration, January 1951*

The United States is the only major industrialized Western nation not to have implemented a national health security program. The reason for this omission stems in large
measure from the hostile political culture that evolved in the formative years of American health policy, beginning with debates over the proper role of government in health
care and the responsibility of the medical community for health care reform, and continuing through the flawed strategies and missed opportunities of Progressive-era reformers and New Dealers to legislate health and sickness insurance laws.

The origin of the movement for health security in the United States dates to the final
decade of the nineteenth century and derives from interest in state-inspired
workmen's compensation practices among the leading industrial nations of Europe. In
both its European and American contexts, health security was subsumed in the more
general term "social insurance," which meant government payment to the individual
to replace wages lost temporarily or permanently. The social distribution of insurance
for individual loss encompassed unemployment, accident, injury, illness, old age, and
death. Over time, these distinct forms of social provision in Europe tended to shade
into one another, but the objectives remained the same: income stabilization for the
worker, maintenance of production for the employer, and the political allegiance of the
working class for the government.[2]

Differing political conditions and institutions in the United States, however, made it
difficult to replicate the European approach to social provision. A strong tradition of free
enterprise, belief in an unfettered marketplace, an ideology that enshrined the self-made
man, a small, nonprofessional civil service, and a decentralized governmental system
that engaged in little direct regulation of the economy or social welfare were still the

norm. Government, particularly at the national level, had little to do with social provision. The general rule was to leave as much to private and voluntary actions as possible. Even organized labor, which had eschewed politics, unlike its European counterpart, and was suspicious of government, feared that social provision might become a substitute for higher wages, shorter hours, and better working conditions.[3]

Despite the unfavorable environment, in 1893 political economist John Graham Brooks, responding to similar dislocations attendant upon industrialization in this country, undertook the first study of social insurance by an American. After a lengthy investigation into Germany's social insurance program, Brooks was favorably impressed with its workings, as well as those of programs in other European nations, including Great Britain, which had included compulsory sickness insurance as part of a general program to protect workers against the chief risks that interrupted the continuity of income. Brooks's report aroused little interest in a nation in which classical liberalism most thoroughly shaped the relationship between state and society. The industrial depression of 1893–1898, however, shook American society to its core, called into question the prevailing tenets of laissez-faire, and rekindled interest in social provision among a small number of reform-minded political economists and labor authorities who worked outside of government and the political parties.[4]

William F. Willoughby's *Workingmen's Insurance* (1898), although influenced by the prevailing laissez-faire attitude of the day, also viewed sympathetically the European program of insurance against accidents. The following year, Dr. Adna F. Weber of the New York Bureau of Labor, inspired by the passage of the 1897 British Workmen's Compensation Act, conducted a detailed study of industrial accidents in this country. Weber's report differentiated workmen's accident compensation from other forms of social provision, but it was John A. Commons, an economics professor at the University of Wisconsin, who argued for an approach to social insurance different from the European practice in which the state undertook to improve the conditions of employment. Commons contended that the employer, rather than the State, should serve as the focal point of social action. The State should regulate employment conditions to prohibit unsocial behavior, but it should not become party to providing social benefits. If an employer caused harm to his worker, he should be required to pay for the consequences of his actions; this eventually became the essence of the 1911 Wisconsin workmen's compensation law. If an employer laid off his employee, Commons also noted, the employer should be required to shoulder some of the costs.[5]

It was but a short step for reformers like Commons to view health provision as more than just an extension of accident compensation. It was inherent in the theory of social solidarity, and they soon broadened their perspective to include occupational diseases endemic to the "dusty trades," such as tuberculosis, lead poisoning, anthrax, and glass-blower's cataracts. The logic of providing compensation for occupational diseases, as well as accidents, was self-evident to Dr. John B. Andrews, secretary of the American Association for Labor Legislation (AALL). Andrews wrote in 1910 that occupational diseases, in select circumstances, might warrant *compulsory* health insurance. Other reformers, meanwhile, reasoned that sickness might also exist entirely apart from the industrial workplace and warrant insurance in its own right. If Americans were willing to adopt workmen's compensation laws to cover industrial accidents, they might also be persuaded to enact health insurance legislation to protect against sickness, which caused poverty and distress among many more families. Again, they took their cue from Europe. Britain's National Insurance Act of 1911 became the model for transforming health insurance in the United States into a major political issue, as American reformers argued that health insurance would not only benefit American workers but also yield handsome profits for employers by creating a healthier, more productive labor force.[6]

The campaign for health insurance coincided with the 1912 election of Woodrow Wilson, during whose presidency the reform movement reached its zenith with the firm establishment of the public-service concept of government. At its center stood the AALL, an organization founded in 1906 by "social progressives," many of whom had studied abroad, to reform capitalism. Composed of native and foreign-born academics, such as economists Richard T. Ely and John R. Commons, statistician I. S. Falk, and political scientist and health reformer Edgar L. Sydenstricker, the organization viewed compulsory health insurance as "the next great step in social legislation." The AALL established the first nationwide Committee on Social Insurance and, in 1913, organized the first national conference on the subject. Out of this meeting came a resolution to work with the states to enact government-sponsored health insurance laws. In November 1915, the Committee on Social Insurance unveiled a model state law calling for health protection for all low-income workers (those earning less than $1,200 annually, except for domestics and casual employees) and their dependents.[7]

The AALL had formulated its case for health insurance in terms of two objectives: to relieve poverty-related illness by distributing to all families the uneven wage loss and medical costs incurred by individual families; and to reduce the total cost of illness and insurance to society through a mixture of effective medical care and monetary incentives for disease prevention. This combination of concerns was typical of social progressives of Wilson's era. In emphasizing the relief of poverty, they appealed to moral compassion; in emphasizing prevention and increased efficiency, they appealed to economic rationality. Social melioration and efficiency not only fitted perfectly into the reform ideology but also reflected the political conditions of a democratic capitalistic society.[8]

The "Standard Bill," as the model state law was known, contained a serious defect, however: women and minorities, who needed protection most, received the least consideration. Political reality and the prevailing economics of sickness and health care had shaped the "Standard Bill." In forming alliances with "sanitarians," the public health reformers of the early twentieth century, AALL members believed they were acting on behalf of a public more interested in preventing poverty and distress than a particular grievance of labor, such as the conservation of human resources. But they also understood that to enact the bill they had to win support from the public and powerful business interests in the various states. This meant persuading them that the AALL was less interested in redistributing incomes than in their stabilization and that the bill would not disturb prevailing labor, gender, or racial patterns.[9]

By 1916, reformers had introduced the "Standard Bill" in the legislatures of New York, Massachusetts, and New Jersey, and the bill had been accorded a favorable reception from the American Medical Association (AMA), the American Hospital Association (AHA), the National Association of Manufacturers, and many labor unions. By 1920, the governors of eleven states had appointed commissions to investigate the subject, and five of those states reported in favor of compulsory health insurance: California, Massachusetts, New Jersey, Ohio, and Pennsylvania. The medical profession, in response to real or exaggerated grievances, had even gone as far as to establish its own committee on social insurance.[10]

But as happened repeatedly over the next several decades, the victory that was close at hand vanished like a mirage. The summer of 1914, which saw the first steps toward drafting the "Standard Bill," also witnessed the guns of August, heralding a world war that delivered a shattering blow to the prevailing meliorist myth that civilization was moving forward, the powerful stimulus to prewar Progressivism. The reformers' expectation that in the aftermath of the war, they would be able to reconstruct society at home as well as abroad proved entirely too optimistic. The stroke that President Wilson suffered created a leadership vacuum at the highest level of government, leaving the nation to lurch violently from war to peace as labor unrest, radicalism, and conservative reaction wracked postwar America. In the backlash against government bureaucracy, wartime regimentation, and the Red Scare, support for the "Standard Bill" evaporated. The state medical societies and the AMA, fearing that government-as-intermediary would intrude on the physician-patient relationship and put government in a strategic role to exercise social, political, and economic power over medical practitioners, retracted their endorsement of the "Standard Bill" and, with the cooperation of the AHA, assumed a posture of implacable opposition to government as an intermediary in the costs of sickness. The severest blow occurred in New York State on April 10, 1919, when its Senate passed a version of the model law only to see it die in the Assembly at the hands of physician-lobbyists and their business allies. By 1921, not a single state legislature had enacted the "Standard Bill."[11]

Even apart from the divisions within Progressivism, the odds of the AALL successfully persuading state legislatures to pass health insurance laws were never very favorable. By war's end, physicians, employers, the insurance industry, and conservative politicians had forged a uniquely powerful and remarkably durable coalition in opposition to government-sponsored health insurance proposals. They were able to agree on where their interests lay, and their unity, economic power, and skillful deployment of the rhetoric of Americanism allowed them to exercise a leverage over government that the health insurance plan's supporters could not match. By contrast, the AALL and its potential allies divided along class, gender, racial, and religious lines.[12]

The collapse of the Progressive-era health insurance movement did not cause the fragmentation of the health care system in the United States, but it did leave the nation with a flawed, private, employment-based health care system that was stronger and less accommodating to change. Meanwhile, health insurance went dormant as a national issue, and the AALL of the 1920s refocused its attention on unemployment and old-age issues. At the level of the states and localities, however, reformers of all stripes—sanitarians, economists, educators, social workers, women's and children's rights activists, and even prominent businessmen who had witnessed the wartime potential of employer-employee cooperation—continued to maintain a lively interest in social issues and to experiment with programs to ameliorate persistent social ills. Their efforts, often modest in scope and lacking in public fanfare, established a baseline for addressing a wide array of future social needs, including old-age pensions, minimum wage legislation, and affordable health care.[13]

Typical of the seeding and cross-fertilization of ideas that percolated below the national level in the interwar period, and perhaps the best-known, was the Committee on the Costs of Medical Care (CCMC). Established in 1927 under the leadership of Dr. Ray Lyman Wilbur, a former president of the AMA, to address the problem of affordable medical care, the CCMC was composed of medical-care-givers, economists, sociologists, and citizens active in the general public welfare. It selected five broad areas of the nation's health for intensive study and, in November 1932, published its reports and recommendations under the title *Medical Care for the American People*. By the time President Herbert Hoover left the White House in 1933, the CCMC's voluminous research had provided the data for many of the ideas that New Dealers and medical specialists drew upon. The research experience also contributed to the development of a cadre of experts in medical economics—individuals like Drs. Michael M. Davis and Nathan Sinai—whose talents and contributions played a significant role in future efforts to promote a federal interest in health insurance.[14]

The CCMC's recommendations for sweeping changes in the organization and financing of American medicine were considered revolutionary at the time, but the committee stopped short of recommending national health insurance, an issue on which there had developed differing views within the group, ranging from advocacy of federally financed universal health coverage, to neutrality on the relative merits of a government versus a privately funded health insurance system, to support of an entirely privately funded health insurance system. The last represented the majority view, on the grounds that the United States, unlike the war-ravaged countries of Europe, enjoyed a higher standard of living and thus had a greater likelihood of making a success of a private, voluntary, employment-based insurance system. That kind of system was also, the majority insisted, more palatable to a nation that prided itself on individual freedom and private enterprise. Most committee members also preferred some form of prepaid and group practice insurance, but there were almost as many opinions on these issues as there were participants. Physicians representing the AMA, however, opposed *all* forms of prepaid insurance plans, fearing they would become the entering wedge for government intervention, and also vehemently opposed group practice, insisting that only the solo fee-for-service practitioner could provide the type of doctor-patient relationship conducive to good care.[15]

Seeking to preserve its hegemony over health care, the AMA savaged the majority's recommendations long afterwards as an "incitement to revolution" and the product of the "great foundations, public health officialdom, social theory—even socialism and communism." Neither Wilbur's credentials nor the CCMC's evidence moderated the medical profession's indignation over the two key recommendations: group practice and prepaid insurance plans. Nor did the AMA accept the argument that specialization, scientific and technological advances, high overhead costs, the growth of paramedical professions, the isolation of physicians in rural areas, and the lack of coordination among general practitioners, specialists, and medical institutions were rendering the existing medical delivery system obsolete.[16]

In emphasizing the need for new financing arrangements to distribute costs more equitably, the CCMC concluded that medical inflation stemmed, not from the average medical costs that confronted the entire population or any subgroup, but from the unpredictable incidence and costs of illness, complicated by the maldistribution of physicians and medical agencies. Because the availability of medical care appeared to be less a function of need and more a function of the individual's or the community's ability to pay, the CCMC majority had recommended adoption of group insurance, taxation, or a combination of both. The AMA, in lieu of proposing a constructive alternative or finding a common middle ground, responded to the majority's recommendations by accusing the group of subverting American values and by reaffirming the sanctity of private practitioner fee-for-service medicine. Its passionate denunciation of the CCMC's recommendations, like that of the AMA's county and state affiliates, derived from the belief that good medical care depended on the patient's freedom of choice and the medical profession's authority, free from governmental or bureaucratic interference, to determine the standards and content of medical care, without which physicians would be reduced to harassed, incompetent salaried bureaucrats akin to public health officials. In this belief, organized medicine was seeking to maintain both the status of the profession and the status quo, to perpetuate the entrepreneurial individualism of the past, and to preserve medicine as an island of private enterprise in a sea of corporate, centralized organization.[17]

Any suggestion of changing the organization, delivery, and financing of medical services, therefore, was bound to ignite a firestorm of controversy. The CCMC's report, coinciding with the onset of the Great Depression, exposed the deep chasm dividing the AMA from its critics. A growing segment of the American public and many academic physicians, disturbed by the inability or unwillingness of their colleagues in private practice to address adequately the medical needs of low-income and rural Americans, were becoming increasingly disenchanted with the AMA, viewing its self-proclaimed altruism as anachronistic and self-serving. To these critics, organized medicine's implacable hostility to group practice, to health insurance, to federal participation in virtually any form, and its unwavering defense of the solo practitioner and fee-for-service medicine were little more than an emotional response to the impersonal forces affecting American society generally.[18]

The divisions within the CCMC over its summary proposals and the dissatisfaction that the report engendered on both sides of the political spectrum foreshadowed the debates over health care—access, affordability, coverage, and quality—that unfolded over the ensuing decades. Still, many of the CCMC's recommendations were forward-looking by contemporary standards and subsequently were incorporated to varying degrees in a number of the private, professional, and government-sponsored health reforms that emerged during this period. Insurance, including the possibility of universal health coverage, was being discussed more frequently in liberal circles, especially as the situation of individuals and families on the bottom rungs of the economic ladder (the 40 million Americans living on family incomes of less than $800 a year), worsened with the collapse of the economy in fall 1929.

As the economic crisis plumbed lower and lower depths, critics of the administration concluded that the constraints of President Hoover's philosophy rendered him incapable of providing leadership, whether it was to establish federal programs to address the needs of the unemployed and the elderly or to underwrite security against sickness. In their quest for a more dynamic approach to the nation's ills, they drew hope and encouragement from Franklin D. Roosevelt's promise of a "New Deal" for the American people.[19] Indeed, the election of a Democratic president in 1932 coincided with a growing belief among reformers that the problem of social insecurity in all of its manifestations was a national one and needed to be addressed through an intensive federal effort. This represented a fundamental shift in contemporary thinking about politics and the federal system to new ideas: that politics could have a creative and transformative character in coordinating social and economic relationships by stimulating new patterns of thought and devising new programs; that the new Democratic majority would encourage political action and interest group organization by previously excluded groups; and that the federal government had to assume greater responsibility for extensive regulation and expanded social welfare provision. This realization gave new currency to the CCMC's health recommendations.[20]

By the time Roosevelt took office in March 1933, the depression had reached its nadir. No group of Americans, except African-Americans, had been victimized more by social insecurity than the aged, of whom there were about 6.5 million over the age of sixty-five in 1930.[21] The overwhelming majority of the elderly were not paupers, but they were more likely to be unemployed, disabled, or sick than younger people. What rendered their plight so desperate was that the United States had no social insurance legislation. In nearly half the states there was no system of old-age pensions; in the rest, pensions were woefully inadequate. The severity of the depression had forced many, if not most, of the elderly into dependency either on their children or on the community in which they lived. It was this dimension of the plight of the elderly that sparked public interest in legislating provisions for old-age security.[22]

The failures of the Hoover policies and the distress caused by the collapse of the local system of poor relief were the primary catalysts in persuading skeptics that the federal government should embark on a positive intervention in the economy. In his message to Congress on June 8, 1934, Roosevelt set security for homes, jobs, and old age as the New Deal's objectives. He followed up on June 29 with Executive Order No. 6757, to establish a cabinet-level Committee on Economic Security (CES), chaired by Secretary of Labor Frances Perkins. Operating under a December 1, 1934, deadline, the CES became the vehicle for framing the Social Security Act of 1935. Roosevelt thus addressed the plight of the unemployed and elderly long before California physician Dr. Francis Townsend began to lobby for old-age pensions.[23]

Less-publicized was the CES's role as the focal point within the administration for addressing problems of cost, coverage, accessibility, and quality of medical care, which continued to exclude millions of Americans from decent care. These structural weaknesses in America's medical system demanded attention from the White House almost from the moment Roosevelt entered office. Edgar Sydenstricker, formerly of the CCMC and research director for the Milbank Memorial Fund, was among the first to call for a New Deal in health for all Americans. Like other reformers, he was cognizant of the close correlation between economic security and good health and between poverty and illness, and of the regional disparities that existed in sound medical and public health protocols. Sydenstricker insisted that the states and localities had failed to address the medical needs of urban and rural dwellers alike, and he called for a reversal of Hoover's policy of relying on voluntary institutions and local and state authorities to the exclusion of the federal government. In Sydenstricker's judgment, health security was part of a comprehensive challenge to the control of economic resources and services by business corporations, insurance company executives, and organized medicine.[24]

The appeal for a New Deal in economic and health security fell on sympathetic ears within the new administration in the person of Josephine A. Roche, whom Roosevelt had appointed assistant secretary of the treasury, with jurisdiction over the U.S. Public Health Service (USPHS). Armed with a Ph.D. in sociology and owner of a Colorado coal mine, Roche belonged to the generation of college-educated women who helped establish a female dominion in early-twentieth-century reform. Like other progressives of her generation, she opposed the waste of human resources and subscribed to the principles of scientific management to achieve greater "efficiency" in society for the benefit of all. A compassionate, humane, and caring individual and a staunch advocate of universal health coverage, she questioned the prevailing assumption that recent declines in the mortality rate translated as improved well-being among Americans. Evidence from a study of 12,000 families by the USPHS and the Milbank Memorial Fund had disclosed an alarmingly high incidence of acute and chronic diseases and serious physical impairments among families on relief rolls. The findings from seven large cities, a cluster of coal-mining communities, and several mill towns, Roche declared, "challenge us to a swift-moving program of conservation of one of our most valued national resources— the health and vitality of our people."[25]

Roche's background gave her ample vision and courage to champion the federal government's responsibility for conserving the health of Americans, especially the poorest third of the nation identified by the president, and Roosevelt encouraged her to do so. The difficulty, however, was that although he was sympathetic to the economic and medical insecurity that haunted the American people, Roosevelt was fundamentally conservative in economic matters and never a proponent of "social medicine."[26] Roche was unable to break through to the president's inner circle of advisers, and this limited her influence over policy making precisely at the time some reformers feared the administration might cave in to pressure from organized medicine and renege on its pledge to include health insurance in the legislative package for economic security. Yale economist Irving Fisher wrote to the president urging him to "make national health, including health insurance, a major part of your policy." In October 1934, a former member of the CCMC urged Democratic Senator Robert F. Wagner of New York to include "an adequate program of health insurance" in the draft of social security legislation and reminded Wagner that "Mr. Roosevelt indicated, some months ago, that he would make health insurance part of his program for economic security." He worried "lest the opposition of the short-sighted, but aggressive, members of the medical profession deter the President from his announced purpose."[27]

With pressure building on the administration, the CES appointed Dr. Edwin Witte of Wisconsin to the position of executive director to oversee studies conducted by its Technical Board and to act as the liaison between the CES, the Technical Board, and the Advisory Council, composed of business, labor, academic, and other nongovernmental officials. Witte was the point man in drafting the social security bill, transforming it from a "conviction" of Franklin D. Roosevelt and his advisers into a "concrete program" in an extremely short period of time. That this was possible was owing, in great measure, to his statesmanship, intelligence, patience, and tireless efforts. He was assisted by Edgar L. Sydenstricker, who headed the study of medical care and health insurance, and I. S. Falk, who served as the latter's associate director.[28]

At the inaugural meeting of the Technical Board on August 10, 1934, Witte defined economic security to include all forms of social insurance to protect the individual against dependency and distress: unemployment insurance, old-age insurance (retirement pensions), public employment, relief, and health insurance. Three days later, the CES affirmed the board's recommendation that health care and health insurance were components of social security, and in September, the board formed committees to examine each component of social security. The Committee on Medical Care (CMC) included Josephine Roche and, in an ex-officio capacity, Arthur J. Altmeyer, assistant secretary of labor. Its overarching policy goal was to break the perceived interrelationship between poverty and sickness by getting health services to the poor who needed them.[29]

Meanwhile, Roosevelt issued a directive to Labor Secretary Frances Perkins to hold a National Conference on Economic Security, including health security, to parallel the deliberations of the CES. However, the impression of some health reformers, including Dr. Nathan Sinai, Louis H. Pink, an insurance executive, and Worth M. Topping of the Federal Council of Churches, was that the CES was divided over whether to include health insurance in social security legislation. Their impression was valid, for a number of committee members were arguing that it was more urgent to assure passage of the basic forms of social insurance (unemployment, old-age insurance, and public welfare assistance). Those members feared that the inclusion of health care coverage would endanger the entire social security package and preferred to postpone it until after the basic social security bill cleared Congress. Administrator Harry L. Hopkins, of the Federal Emergency Relief Administration (FERA), however, believed that health insurance held so high a priority in the total needs of the country that it should be written into the social security bill. With the tide running strongly in support of the New Deal, he insisted that health insurance stood a good chance of passage, perhaps the best chance it would ever have. The issue was unsettled at the time the delegates to the economic security conference assembled in Washington, D.C., on November 14, but once the AMA's delegates and their business allies discovered that the CES was contemplating the inclusion of health insurance, "a considerable clash of views at the round table sessions on unemployment insurance and on medical care" ensued.[30]

Uncertainty over whether to include the health provision dogged the CES, causing it to fall behind its timetable to produce a draft by December 1, the date it had set in order to give the president time to decide whether to include it in his annual message to Congress. In fact, the final version of the economic security bill was not completed until January 15, 1935. Two days later, Roosevelt sent it and a special message recommending swift action to both congressional chambers. The House passed the legislation on April 19 and the Senate, after some delay, two months later, after which the bills went to conference to reconcile their differences. The House accepted the report of the conference committee, which had dropped the provision for national health insurance, on August 8 without a roll-call vote, and the Senate acted favorably the next day.[31]

The Social Security Act that emerged from the conference committee and that Roosevelt signed into law on August 14, 1935, was perhaps the most significant single piece of social legislation passed by the Congress of the United States in the twentieth century, grafting as it did a welfare state on a capitalist foundation. It was symbolic of the very meaning of the New Deal, but as one scholar noted, it also revealed better than any other legislative enactment "the tangled skein of human needs, economic calculations, idealistic visions, political pressures, partisan maneuvering, actuarial projections and constitutional constraints out of which FDR was obliged to weave his reform program." Every aspect of the Social Security Act was a compromise between impossible alternatives, and many of the questions that troubled the framers of the law would reappear a half century later.[32]

One had to admire the framers' legislative creativity, even their artistry, but the Social Security Act also was a curious piece of legislation. It was also surprisingly inept and conservative, even as it reversed historic assumptions about the nature of social responsibility and established the proposition that the individual has clear-cut social rights. Social support for the elderly, for example, was divided into two different programs—Old-Age Benefits and Old-Age Assistance—thus fragmenting the elderly population along class and gender lines. New Deal policy makers, as well as legislators, insisted that the legitimacy of a permanent economic security program depended on its connection to work. Yet by excluding agricultural and domestic workers from the social insurance program, Congress removed about 5 million workers from coverage—half of whom were African American. Not only did the contributory feature, which rested on continuous earnings, disadvantage blacks and women, but with the exclusion of religious and nonprofit workers, even more women were left out. Poor women and African Americans would have to apply for public assistance, eventually structured as means-tested programs for dependents rather than entitlements for citizens. In no other welfare system in the world did the state shirk its responsibilities to those who most needed assistance most. Besides failing to set up a national system of unemployment compensation, the law also failed to address the thorny problem of sickness (and the associated cost of illness), which the federal government's own inventory of the nation's health had documented as the main cause of joblessness, even in normal economic times.[33]

What had happened to the bill's health security provisions? Federal assistance for maternal and child health and aid to the states for crippled children's services sailed through, with little or no opposition, from either house of Congress or the AMA, but health insurance was entirely a different matter. No provisions relating to national health insurance, except vague references to the need for further study, were included at any stage in the drafting of the social security legislation, and the subject received only brief treatment in the CES's final report. Secretary of Labor Frances Perkins later explained that the CES had postponed writing national health insurance into the bill, for fear that opposition from the AMA and its business and congressional allies would kill the entire Social Security Act. Witte, Altmeyer, and Harry L. Hopkins concurred with her explanation. There is no reason to doubt that this was a political decision, but any comprehensive survey of the social insurance field, such as was indicated in the president's message of June 8, 1934, could not ignore health insurance. It was the next step in social security, and its omission marked the beginning of a process that ultimately transformed health security from a broadly conceived social concept into the more narrow category of contributory social insurance for workers.[34]

The CES had devoted a great deal of attention to the health dimension of social security, once Dr. Michael M. Davis, of the Julius Rosenwald Fund, had persuaded Sydenstricker, Falk, and Witte that the Technical Board should investigate public health and health insurance as components of economic security. The decision to do so caused the White House to be inundated with telegraphic protests stirred up by *JAMA* (*Journal of the American Medical Association*), which accused the administration of trying to railroad universal health coverage through Congress without consulting the medical profession. This and similarly orchestrated attacks caused Roosevelt to pay closer attention to the issue, and Witte became the conduit between the White House (in the person of Dr. Ross T. McIntyre, Roosevelt's personal physician) and Sydenstricker and Falk, the CES officials most closely examining health insurance.[35]

To shield the administration from the accusation that the medical profession was being excluded from deliberations over the health insurance component of social security, Witte informed the AMA that the CES would establish a medical advisory committee

(MAC). McIntyre suggested that the CES appoint eminent physicians to the advisory committee who would command the confidence of their peers and not be regarded in a partisan sense as strongly for or against health insurance; that it strive for geographical representation; and that the presidents of the AMA, the American College of Surgeons (ACS), and the American College of Physicians (ACP) have representation. Sydenstricker and Falk drafted the list for Witte, who forwarded the names to Dr. McIntyre for presidential approval.[36]

Once the White House had vetted the list, Secretary of Labor Perkins announced the names in early November 1934. The list immediately drew the wrath of groups close to the inner circle of the AMA. Hundreds of telegrams, principally from Pennsylvania, Ohio, and the Rocky Mountain states, inundated the White House and the CES through the first meetings of the MAC on November 15 and 16, and just as suddenly they ceased. Administration officials decided that the AMA had orchestrated the entire protest.[37]

The MAC, meanwhile, like the delegates to the CES, divided over whether health insurance should be included in social security, who should administer the program, whether it should be mandatory, and how it should be financed. Their split mirrored the divisions within Congress, where a number of widely divergent bills covering health insurance had been circulating. Senator Arthur Capper, a Kansas Republican, sought to establish a health insurance system with federal aid to the states and contributions from the state, the employers, and the employee. Representative Matthew A. Dunn, a Pennsylvania Democrat, had a bill for workers' health insurance that came closest to free medical care. Legislators on both sides of the aisle, however, were not yet ready to include health insurance in social legislation, and each bill was referred to its appropriate committee, where no action was taken.[38]

Fearful that the controversy over health insurance might jeopardize other aspects of the social security package, Labor Secretary Perkins took the unusual step of reassuring the medical establishment that the administration would not strong-arm such a program through the Congress. President Roosevelt also told the physician-delegates to the National Conference on Economic Security that whether health insurance came sooner or later, the government would do nothing to impede the advance of American medicine. Roosevelt's conciliatory remarks made less impact on the physician-delegates than did the threat of a split within the AMA's ranks. A minority of liberal physicians attending the conference were openly critical of both the AMA's lobbying tactics and its tunnel vision on health insurance. Their outspokenness was so serious that AMA president Walter L. Bierring felt compelled to give assurances that the AMA would cooperate with the medical advisory committee. Some members of the CES interpreted his remarks in the most favorable light: that the administration, working through the MAC, might devise a health insurance program acceptable to the AMA. That interpretation proved to be illusory; as Witte suspected, the AMA's conciliatory position had more to do with papering over divisions within its own profession than to any genuine sympathy for universal health insurance, an issue on which doctors and the earlier Coolidge-Hoover-era CCMC had been bitterly divided.[39]

To forestall government intrusion, some AMA delegates to the economic security conference cynically championed and voted to increase funding for public health programs they had hitherto criticized. But even among pro–New Deal physicians, grave reservations persisted about universal health insurance and federal intervention in medicine. These physicians voiced their concerns at every stage of the Technical Board's deliberations and in its final report to the CES. In February 1935, for example, Dr. Harvey Cushing, a Yale neurologist, and Dr. Will Mayo, of Rochester, Minnesota, urged the president not to include federally underwritten health insurance in the social security bill, preferring an alternative proposal to expand existing state oversight of medical care, "such as appeared to be put into effective operation in New York State."[40]

Perhaps the most articulate case against compulsory health insurance from a friendly adversary came from Dr. Hugh Cabot, of Boston, who warned Roosevelt that the leadership of the AMA was "violently opposed to any form of Government supervision." The hostility of the AMA notwithstanding, the case for national health insurance, Cabot argued, did not rest on the claim that the people who would benefit most from it were not receiving medical care, but that the care they received was insufficient, unsatisfactory, and expensive relative to their income. Compulsory health insurance, he insisted, would not remedy the deficiencies of the present system but would "fix the practice of medicine in its present unsatisfactory pattern," discouraging group practice as the preferred method for improving the quality of medical care, diminishing the hospital's role as dispenser of the best scientific medical practices, and doing little to improve the medical care of rural dwellers.[41]

Previous legislative attempts to correct the deficiencies of American medicine had not addressed the fundamental problem of putting within "the reach of substantially the whole part of the country, scientific medicine based on scientific progress and offered by well-equipped, well-organized and well-trained physicians," Cabot also noted. To achieve this goal, Americans would have to ask fundamental questions of their medical delivery system, including whether national health insurance might not more deeply entrench unsatisfactory medical practices. Fearing that it would require "an administrative agency of staggering proportions" and "a financial commitment which may become a large slice of the income of the country," Cabot cautioned against rushing headlong into national health insurance.[42]

Resurrecting an idea that the CCMC had earlier recommended, Cabot proposed creating two five-year pilot programs monitored by a board of eminent (preferably academic) physicians: one in the area served by the Tennessee Valley Authority, "where admittedly there is important lack of complete medical care," and the other west of the Mississippi, where a scattered, largely agricultural population lacked access to competent hospital, laboratory, and specialists' services. The key to the success of Cabot's proposal was that the government would enroll all the physicians within the service area by guaranteeing them a reasonable income in return for delivering first-class medical service, including specialist referrals. The patient would pay only what he or she could afford, with the government covering the physician's income differential. Whatever the outcome, Cabot predicted that government was "certain to become more and more involved in the financing of medical care."[43]

The reservations of pro–New Deal physicians such as Cabot, Cushing, and Mayo became critically important in persuading the president to separate health insurance from the basic economic security legislation. Anticipating such an outcome, Sydenstricker and Falk advised the CES to include in its report to the president a statement (which ultimately appeared on pages 41–43 of the published report) that it intended to recommend health insurance legislation at a later date. This allowed the MAC additional time—until March 1—to hammer out a health insurance program satisfactory to the administration and the AMA. The CES could then issue a second report recommending legislation that Congress might enact before its summer recess.[44]

That scenario and time frame were overly optimistic. Neither the social security bill, whose only reference to health insurance occurred in enumerating the duties of the Social Security Board (SSB), nor the accompanying CES report, with its hint of possible future health legislation, placated congressional opponents of federally underwritten health insurance or the AMA. The report of the House Committee on Ways and Means on the social security bill on April 5, 1935, made a deliberate point of stating that its support for expanding federal assistance for public health services "should not be confused with health insurance." Earlier, the AMA's House of Delegates had also strongly condemned compulsory health insurance and federal intervention in the practice of medicine. But in a cynical and shrewd concession to its more liberal minority, the delegates endorsed voluntary health insurance programs, the very programs they had hitherto shunned. This tactical flexibility, which was a compromise between their ideal of no insurance and the more unpleasant situation of government-sponsored universal insurance, went a long way toward defusing whatever public support existed for federal action.[45]

A few weeks after the March 1 deadline, Sydenstricker and Falk presented the results of their investigation to the CES, recommending that the economic security bill be withdrawn from the congressional hopper and rewritten to provide health insurance financed through a tax on employers and supplemental appropriations from general revenues to assist the states in providing adequate medical services for people in the lowest-income groups. The CES was initially sympathetic to the proposal, until Witte and Thomas Eliot, assistant solicitor in the Department of Labor, who had helped craft the social security bill, argued that amending the legislation to include health insurance at this point would probably doom the entire bill, a judgment the president and his advisers concurred in. The CES delegated Labor Secretary Frances Perkins and Josephine Roche to verify the president's position. Perkins came away from the meeting convinced that Roosevelt's reluctance also stemmed from concerns over jurisdictional disputes within the federal health bureaucracy that he intended to resolve once the social security bill was out of the way. For the moment at least, even the most ardent congressional Democrats accepted the White House's decision to exclude health insurance rather than jeopardize the entire social security bill. To judge from the remarks of Pennsylvania Representative Henry Ellenbogen during the debate on the House bill, however, they certainly intended to pursue the idea when the timing was more propitious.[46]

After passage of the Social Security Act, Sydenstricker and Falk completed their work on the health insurance program, which the CES transmitted to the president on November 6, 1935. Perhaps the most distinguishing characteristic of both the letter accompanying the report and the document itself was ambivalence. While reaffirming the need for "a national health program," their tone was cautious and their recommendations conservative. Calling for "no drastic or hurried Federal action," the CES modestly proposed that Washington provide "[a] small [amount of] financial aid to those states which develop systems of health insurance designed with due regard to necessary safeguards" and recommended further study.[47]

The health recommendations fell short of providing blanket security against the risks of illness, and they would not have met the health needs of every American who needed protection. Neither would they have created a new federal bureaucracy. The expectation was that the modestly funded program would serve, instead, as a starting point, but only in states that had agreed to establish health insurance programs. *Risks to Economic Security Arising out of Illness,* the report that Secretary of Labor Perkins transmitted to the president in January 1936, justifying the need for such a program, received scant publicity and little official notice from the White House. Roosevelt told Dr. John A. Kingsbury that he did not want to give his Republican opponents a ready-made issue until his reelection was secured, and he observed that "next winter [after the presidential election] would be time to take up general health problems from a national point of view." In this manner, Roosevelt managed to placate both proponents and opponents of national health insurance, though not in equal degree, of course.[48]

Long after the event, Roosevelt's supporters remained divided over whether he should have included health insurance in the social security bill. Operating from the premise that Congress would most likely have gone along with it despite opposition from the AMA, I. S. Falk argued that this had been Roosevelt's opportunity to create a national health insurance program and he *should* have seized it. Wilbur J. Cohen, without denying

that the president could have persuaded Congress to accept a bill that included health insurance, believed that the establishment of such a program in 1935 was inopportune.
Unlike the drive for unemployment insurance, Roosevelt discerned public apathy for
writing universal health coverage into the social security bill. In the absence of support
from the media, state and local governments, and middle-class voters for inclusion, the
AMA's organized and emotionally charged opposition to federal health insurance might
well have torpedoed what the president believed were the nation's more pressing economic needs. With unemployment insurance already on the legislative table, Roosevelt
probably concluded that he had bitten off as much as he could chew.[49]

Moreover, the simultaneous enactment of the unemployment insurance, old-age insurance, and public assistance programs together with national health insurance would
have been a stupendous task and a logistical nightmare, with no guarantee that the administration could have achieved a more efficient and economical administration of social and economic policy. Experience with health security issues since 1935 has demonstrated that the mechanics of designing, staffing, and planning a national health
program are vastly more complicated a problem than an old-age pension and disability
insurance program such as Social Security. A program poorly designed and rushed into
operation may well have proven to be worse than no program at all.[50]

The unsuccessful effort to include health care coverage in the social security bill did
not discourage New Deal reformers from continuing to lobby for health security legislation. Even Roosevelt acknowledged that many health initiatives thought at first to be of
an emergency or temporary nature were likely to become permanent and would require
more effective coordination. On October 27, 1936, he issued an executive order establishing the Inter-Departmental Committee to Coordinate Health and Human Welfare Activities (IDC) in accordance with the new Social Security Act, naming Josephine Roche its
chair. The IDC's mandate was to oversee all activities and personnel within the federal
bureaucracy touching on the health and welfare of the public. The appointments of
Roche and assistant director Arthur J. Altmeyer, who had investigated the health and employment components of social security for the CES's Technical Board, provided continuity between the CES and the new committee.[51]

Roosevelt's action was part of his electoral strategy of offering a national progressive
program to bring about a more democratic and decent society, and a belated acknowledgment that consumers of health care had a right to have their interests represented in
the formation of government policy. It was also an attempt to render more palatable the
expansion of federal authority in which New Dealers were engaged. They perceived a
central government with enhanced authority as a vehicle for achieving greater democracy
and equity, for empowering the consumers of medical care, and for mitigating the excessive power of organized medicine and its business allies. Roche's appointment thrust her
into the man's world of medicine, which, in the 1930s, was a sovereign, self-regulating

profession; it symbolized the New Deal's acknowledgment of the woman consumer as the legitimate representative of the public interest—elevated to a new, official level of civic authority. Roche's interest in health security dovetailed nicely with women's established areas of expertise, which included social work and public health.

The president's actions provided a stimulus to reformers who were arguing that health security, including national health insurance, both made good economic sense and was a right of citizenship. In May 1936, Senator Robert F. Wagner, one of the foremost congressional advocates of health security, told a campaign audience, "We must protect Americans against the financial strain of ill health and disease and we must do that soon." He spoke of the need to move to "the inviting field of health insurance" to combat "perhaps the single greatest cause of economic insecurity." Wagner received support from Dr. Thomas Parran, Jr., a member of the CES's medical advisory committee, who told a conference of health care providers that the Social Security Act was "a good start" in protecting and promoting Americans' health. Josephine Roche linked the New Deal's conservation of natural resources to the protection of human resources from waste and inefficiency through affordable health care, adding that, through specific provisions of the Social Security Act, we had "taken our stand as a nation, that human conservation is definitely a charge on government." [52]

The IDC, meanwhile, proceeded to establish in March 1937 a Technical Committee on Medical Care (TCMC) to investigate "how to furnish medical care to people and what part the Federal Government should play in the development of means for adequate medical care, particularly for groups unable to pay for it under existing conditions." It also sponsored conferences on the role of the federal government in promoting access to good health. Although no definite conclusions emerged from these sessions, a consensus developed that a national health program was desirable and necessary, and that the federal government had a responsibility to protect the safety of the individual citizen by making reasonably priced health care accessible. In September, the IDC instructed the TCMC to draft recommendations for such a program. That fall and winter, the TCMC met regularly to develop proposals, reporting in December that there was "ample evidence that preventive services pay large dividends" by saving money on "future costs for curative care." The TCMC sketched out programs to expand maternal, child welfare, and public health services under Titles V and VI of the Social Security Act; care for the medically indigent; disability compensation; grants-in-aid for hospital construction; and a program to provide "Federal stimulation or aid for the development of health insurance and public medical care." The National Health Inventory (NHI), the most comprehensive investigation into the state of the nation's health, provided the statistical data that formed the basis of the technical committee's proposals and were indispensable for New Dealers seeking to document the case for federal implementation of a national health security program.[53]

The NHI dated from June 30, 1935, when the USPHS requested a grant from the Works Progress Administration (WPA) to conduct a national inventory of incapacitating ailments. Little quantitative data existed on the extent of illnesses lasting ninety days or more in duration, a problem that would become "increasingly important because of a probable increase in the percentage of the population which is more than sixty years old." Similarly, no longitudinal study of health in relation to the ability of individuals and families "to remain self-supporting and in other respects to carry on as a useful member of society" existed. The WPA approved the grant application, and President Roosevelt included it in his $58 million relief bill on July 30. The NHI's data became indispensable to New Dealers seeking to document the case for federal implementation of a national health security program.[54]

Press reaction to the announcement of the health inventory was mostly favorable, but there were some critics, such as the *Detroit Free Press,* which pounced on it as another New Deal boondoggle. The Springfield, Illinois, *Sunday News and Leader* endorsed the concept once it was persuaded that it would be conducted efficiently and free of political interference. The competency of its directors, Drs. Lewis R. Thompson and George St. J. Perrott of the USPHS, and the participation of numerous health care professionals reassured the *American Journal of Public Health*'s editor, who predicted that the findings would "serve as a guide for the future." Supporters of the inventory also were conscious of the grant's public policy implications for health care. Josephine Roche viewed it through a political lens as a test of the New Deal itself and told delegates to the annual meeting of the American Public Health Association (APHA) that any divisions among health care reformers as to how to proceed would benefit the opponents of social progress.[55]

Given the high stakes, the USPHS was under the gun to begin the inventory immediately, even before it had worked through various logistical problems. Pressure also emanated from the WPA, which had gained a reputation for doing too little to put people to work and for wasting taxpayers' money, factors that worked to the advantage of the USPHS. WPA administrator Harry L. Hopkins was ready to jettison projects still in the planning stage and to transfer workers with computational and interviewing skills from other relief programs to the health inventory. This offered the USPHS both a challenge and an opportunity. By moving quickly, it could tap into a pool of highly skilled workers, whereas delay risked losing the allotment, the personnel, and the project itself.[56]

Dr. Lewis R. Thompson, the inventory's overall director, immediately tapped into the WPA's labor pool and called on the USPHS's resources and staff to monitor the canvass, collection, and interpretation of data. Dr. George St. J. Perrott, the project director, acted as liaison between the USPHS and the TCMC. By December 1935, the NHI was employing 2,534 workers (all but 21 of whom had come from relief rolls) in sixty-two cities, which exceeded the WPA target of employing about 90 percent from the relief rolls. *Survey*

*Graphic* noted that the staff of field workers was of a caliber that would not have been available to government in ordinary times and described the WPA's appropriation as "a gilt-edged investment."[57]

Nonetheless, the need to act quickly resulted in some initial miscues, which led Perrott, in January 1936, to reconfigure and centralize the administrative structure, clarifying lines of communication to achieve greater efficiency. Field Director Clark Tibbits, meanwhile, worked up an elaborate public relations strategy to enlist the print and radio media, civic organizations, and community leaders to advertise the inventory and to persuade the public to cooperate with the canvassers. Response to national radio broadcasts by Roche and the surgeon general "has been remarkable," Tibbits later reported, noting that, in many localities, "the whole community—professional groups, civic leaders, and the public"—had developed "a real enthusiasm" for the inventory. In trumpeting the public's interest in health matters, the IDC also was fostering government interest in a sector generally reserved for private enterprise.[58]

By 1936, the NHI was in high gear, canvassing nearly 3,000,000 individuals in January alone. The next month, the supervisor for lower New York State noted that 20,000 families in New York City had already been canvassed, prompting the city's health commissioner to declare that data from the survey "should greatly add to the effectiveness of our local program for chronic illness." Besides urban centers, the NHI also made an effort to assess the state of health of rural America, many of whose southern families suffered from pellagra, poor nutrition, or were otherwise just plain ill. The largest rural study was that of Georgia, beginning in July 1935 and conducted jointly by the state's Department of Health, the Georgia Medical Association, and federal officials. Using 1930 census figures, researchers looked at the health of families in 16 of Georgia's 159 counties, representing a cross-section of the rural areas of the state. Collectively, the 16 counties provided a canvass of 12,107 families, or 53,648 individuals. Of the families, 7,119 were white, and the remaining 4,988 families were black. The racial composition, 59.3 percent white and 40.7 percent black, approached very nearly that of rural Georgia as reported in the census.[59]

Cooperation with the Georgia inventory was remarkable; only 8 households in the 16 counties refused to respond to the enumerators' questions. The population sample was composed almost entirely of low-income agricultural families—sharecropper, tenant, owner, and wage laborer—and families whose heads were engaged in businesses of their own or were employed in industry. In determining family income, the canvassers included only cash income. Slightly more than one-half of white families (56.5 percent) and 93.5 percent of black families existed on incomes of $500 or less during the survey year.[60]

The questionnaire employed elicited information about specific living facilities that were thought to have a bearing on general health, the incidence of disabling and chronic illnesses within the household in the past twelve consecutive months, the nature of the disability, the duration of illnesses, the frequency of physician contact, medical services administered, and the family's financial obligations. The fieldwork, commencing in the first week of December, lasted four months, though the tedious process of collating, hand coding, and analyzing the Georgia data carried the NHI staff into January 1937. The staff found that the incidence of illness among a rural population group was not affected to any appreciable extent by race, income variations, the wife's or head of household's educational status, or by occupation. They did find that the respondents required considerably more medical care than they actually received and that illnesses had gone untreated. NHI personnel interpreted the very small number of cases of pellagra and hookworm—reported by a group that was notoriously susceptible to these diseases—as evidence of the lack of adequate medical attention, owing to economic inability to pay for medical care, and the absence of a hospital or local public health facility to provide treatment. They also learned that the size and dispersed population of the counties had made it impossible in many instances to maintain cost-effective public health facilities. When specialized nursing and hospital care were available, the cost was prohibitive.

The rural South thus posed a twofold challenge: to improve the population's economic status and to establish more adequate health facilities. The former was a long-term "complicated socioeconomic problem," but its resolution offered the best hope of improving the health of Georgia's rural citizenry. The latter problem could be ameliorated by forming health districts, building more hospitals and clinics, and redistributing medical costs so that the uneven incidence of illness did not bear disproportionately on the rural population. The report suggested that there was a need for affordable health insurance to give rural dwellers access to better medical care. Although the findings applied most directly to rural Georgia, concern about the adequacy of medical facilities and services extended, with minor variations, to rural populations of other regions of the South and the United States.[61]

In addressing concerns about the availability, accessibility, and affordability of decent health care in rural areas, NHI personnel had emphasized an economic rationale. The contribution of good health to the successful economic rehabilitation of Georgia's low-income farm population justified and, indeed, required federal action and programs. From this perspective, the health data from rural Georgia dovetailed nicely with the New Dealers' broader strategy to modernize the region by bringing it into the twentieth century, within the living standards of the nation as a whole. Meanwhile, the NHI staff completed its canvass, collated the data, and drafted its conclusions, having reached 2.8 million individuals by the end of 1937. A total of 740,000 urban families in 84 cities of 19 states (for a total of 2,660,000 urban dwellers) and 36,000 families in 23 rural counties (for a total of 140,000 rural persons) had been canvassed.[62]

Social worker Mary Ross, who had seen the preliminary data, noted in July 1937 that the link between chronic illness and poverty contradicted the belief that poor health was the result of personal misfortune. She insisted that the inability to pay for medical care gave the chronically ill a claim on public policy. This linkage strengthened the resolve of health care reformers and New Dealers seeking to break the nexus between poverty and sickness, between income, access to care, and health, and who wanted to enlarge the federal sphere of public health to encompass the working poor and the one-third of the nation lacking access to adequate medical care. IDC chair Josephine Roche urged delegates to the APHA's annual meeting that fall "to recognize the problem of the present uneven distribution of medical services and the widespread human needs of today." The poor, she declared, required preventive medical services and health insurance in proportionately larger numbers than those in higher income brackets. New York Governor Herbert H. Lehman told the same audience that "an equal opportunity for health is the right of all citizens of the community, regardless of circumstances, birth, economic conditions, race, creed, or color." APHA delegates responded with a resolution calling on organized medicine and the federal government to "extend public health work to meet modern needs."[63]

For the first time, the nation had answers to the vital questions of who and how many Americans were sick at a given time, the nature of their disability, the extent of medical and nursing care they received, and the link between their economic circumstances and their access to medical care. The findings, coupled with the earlier reports of the CCMC, were invaluable and formed the statistical underpinning of public policy decisions about health care over the next thirty years. On an average winter day, the health inventory disclosed, 6 million Americans (4.5 percent of the population) were unable to work, attend school, or pursue their customary activities due to illness, injury, or gross physical impairment resulting from disease or accident. For persons 65 or over, this translated to one of every eight being disabled, as opposed to one in forty between the ages of 15 and 24. Slightly over 4 percent of those under 15 and between the ages of 25 and 64 also experienced illness. Disability-related illnesses of a week or more cost the nation about ten days annually per person. Chronic disease accounted for six of the ten days of incapacity; acute respiratory illness, for 1.5 of the 6 million disabled persons, and another 2.5 million Americans disabled by rheumatism, heart disease, diabetes, tuberculosis, asthma, nervous disorders, and stomach ulcers. Injuries due to accident accounted for another 500,000 disabled Americans, with acute infectious diseases afflicting nearly 250,000, mostly children, and an equal number of adults and children disabled by appendicitis and stomach and liver diseases.[64]

A significant correlation existed among illness, access to medical care, and annual income. The families canvassed fell into four income groups: those with annual incomes above $2,000 (about 20 percent of the sampling); those whose income ranged between

$1,000 and $2,000 (about 40 percent); those with incomes below $1,000 (another 40 percent), half of whom had received some form of public relief in the year preceding the canvass; and families in the "comfortable" income bracket, earning $3,000 a year or more. Frequency of illness, disabling illnesses, and acute and chromic illnesses were highest among the lowest-income groups, particularly for families on relief. Not only did relief and low-income families suffer more frequent illness, but the average case of their disabling chronic illness was of longer duration, 63 percent longer to be exact. This translated into 15.3 days annually of chronic and acute disability for relief families and 11.7 days for nonrelief families earning under $1,000. Not surprisingly, access to physicians' care and hospitalization was markedly deficient among lower-income groups, even though this was the period when the FERA made some allowance for "medical relief." Nursing care was only marginally better. Private-duty nursing was available to only about 1 percent of the relief cases, although a higher volume of visiting nurse service, 13 percent, was given to relief and low-income groups, compared to 3 percent for "comfortable" families.[65]

The economic and social implications of the survey were clear: the nation's bill for illness and premature death amounted to about $10 billion annually, and illness incapacitated nearly 4 million persons daily. The annual mortality rate from accidents exceeded that of any other industrialized nation, as did the rate of infant mortality. America's poor fell ill much more often, stayed sick longer, and received substantially less adequate medical attention than did affluent middle- and upper-income families. The NHI report acknowledged the high quality of medical care in the United States but asserted, "The advances in national health ... have only limited significance for the poor." With up to one-half of the population too poor to afford the cost of medical care, the NHI staff concluded that group health insurance seemed appropriate for self-supporting individuals, whereas the nonworking and the working poor required "larger financial support" than they were currently receiving.[66]

The results of the inventory elicited a range of reactions, from the *Detroit News's* explicit recognition that the federal government had to play a proactive role in assuring access to decent health care to all Americans as a right of citizenship in order to reconstruct a viable economy and polity, to the AMA's belief that the unfettered private marketplace should decide who gets medical care and for how much, with states and localities filling the gaps only where absolutely necessary. On health insurance specifically, the AMA recognized that it could no longer oppose all-voluntary prepaid insurance programs, although it would do nothing to encourage their development. It did, however, redefine the terms on which it would accept them: as private, decentralized plans that strictly adhered to AMA payment rules, which effectively placed them under physician control. From this vantage point, the AMA argued that the voluntary plans rendered unnecessary federally underwritten health insurance.[67]

Compared to the past, the *Detroit News* noted, the medical community seemed less united on the federal government's role in medicine; the article cited a group of 430 internationally known physicians who had broken ranks with the AMA to call for tax-paid medical service for every needy person. These physicians asserted their commitment to a humane, democratic society and to equity, insisting that every consumer of health care had a right to have his or her interests represented in the formulation of public policy. A "national health policy directed toward all groups of the population should be formulated," the *News* insisted. As public comment on the health inventory waxed strong, the TCMC drew on the data to write its report for the IDC. The technical committee proposed a national health program along the lines suggested earlier, to be financed out of general revenues or social insurance taxes and also to fund federal initiatives to provide cash payments for illness-caused disability. The cost of the program, which would be phased in over ten years, was put at $850 million annually.[68]

Prior to forwarding the report to the White House, the IDC instructed Roche and Altmeyer to request the president to convene a conference of parties that had a stake in health care, including physicians, representatives of organized labor, the American Legion, parent-teacher associations, and similar civic organizations. By empowering the consumers of health care, the New Dealers hoped to institutionalize and protect the public's stake in the conference's outcome. Their presence along with federal sponsorship would counterbalance the predominant influence of the medical establishment and guarantee that issues of access, affordability, and quality of care received a fair hearing. Roosevelt acknowledged the urgency of the health care needs described in the report, but there is no indication that he discussed its content with his cabinet. However, on March 8, 1938, he directed Roche to release the report and an announcement of a national conference to discuss the recommendation for a "National Health Program."[69]

Calling the conference made good political sense. The AMA would most likely oppose it, but a national conference offered the president an opportunity to "test the water," to determine the extent of support within the larger population, a favorite tactic of Roosevelt. Three days later, Roche wrote him a letter describing the report as "the most important result" to emerge from the IDC's deliberations and as "the first complete agreement as to method and program for meeting health needs ever reached by all the Federal agencies working in health and welfare fields." She announced officially on March 26 that the federal government would sponsor a National Health Conference (NHC), to convene in Washington, D.C., from July 18 to July 20. Details of the conference's organization, which Roche described as "the first of its kind ever and marking a new milestone in American medicine," were entrusted to Dr. George St. J. Perrott, with the TCMC's recommendations for a "National Health Program" defining the agenda.[70]

This initiative led to a new round in the reformers' determination to use federal resources to underwrite the health security of Americans, especially the poorest third of the population. The IDC, working with other components of the federal health bureau-cracy, carefully prepared the groundwork for a favorable outcome. It blanketed the pub-lic with statistics from the health inventory to document the nation's poor state of health and the need for the conference; the new surgeon general, Dr. Thomas J. Parran, Jr., testified before a Senate committee that Congress should establish a health security program for all citizens, but particularly for the poor and underprivileged; later, he pur-sued the same theme in a commencement address at Skidmore College, where he enu-merated recent examples of the federal government's concern for health security, in-cluding passage of the Social Security, the National Cancer Institute, and the Venereal Disease Control Acts.[71]

Officials also ensured that the administration's point of view would be effectively rep-resented among the delegates. One IDC official wrote Treasury Secretary Henry Morgen-thau that "breakfast with a 'couple of doctors' these days means promotional work for the July conference on the national health program"; she added that drawing up a represen-tative list of 100 delegates was "a very difficult job." The IDC was vetting the list of ex-perts, she wrote, stressing that "this group must not only 'know their stuff' technically but must also have a broad understanding of the problem of meeting the needs of the low income groups and have a flexible point of view toward working out ways to meet this need." It was easy enough to agree on representatives of the well-organized groups, she declared, but "we want to include the less well-organized since this latter group makes up the bulk of the people we want to reach: the southern tenant farmers and the marginal and low income groups now in no well-knit national organizations." Outside the corri-dors of government, New Dealers also enlisted sympathetic physicians to encourage other like-minded colleagues to participate in the conference. Dr. Michael M. Davis of the Committee on Research in Medical Economics exhorted one Connecticut physician with strong ties to organized labor and social workers to attend: "Participants, not observers, are needed there, especially physicians like yourself who know from their own experi-ence the existence of widespread needs for medical care among the people; who feel these needs keenly and who are prepared to press a demand for action," he insisted. Dr. Davis warned, "The reactionary group within medicine will continue to attempt to blur this issue and to gain delay."[72]

Anticipating opposition from the AMA, the IDC hoped to manage the agenda and guide the proceedings with cooperation from sympathetic physicians. Dr. Hugh Cabot, responding to Roche's invitation to participate in the session on national health needs, predicted that AMA spokesmen would explain away the evidence of medical need and insisted on speaking immediately after them. He outlined the thrust of his remarks: that anyone with medical knowledge and an open mind knew that the issue of need had been settled years ago, and "the only problems now involved are the methods of attacking the needs, which needs are most crying, and what methods shall be applied to attack them."

Given the opportunity to make this argument, Cabot declared, "I think it might be effective." The order of speakers subsequently indicated that Roche had taken Cabot's suggestion to heart.[73]

Still, the IDC sought the AMA's cooperation, hoping its physician-delegates would agree with the premise that an unfilled medical need existed and that improving the nation's health was the highest priority. Since each side wanted to avoid the kind of partisan fight between delegates who sought to enlarge the federal government's presence in health care and those who adamantly opposed its involvement that a resolution of *any* kind might precipitate, IDC officials and AMA leaders agreed in advance that the delegates would not enact any resolutions at the conference's closing session. The struggle for the hearts and minds of the American people continued unabated, meanwhile, as a consensus emerged among New Deal liberals that this was the time to complete the unfinished business of social security: to establish a New Deal in health care for all Americans. One editor, referring to the forthcoming health conference, wrote, "It will be difficult to excuse further delay in pressing for action by Congress and the states to round out the Social Security program with social insurance provision for the sick." Indeed, Senator Wagner was already promoting a New Deal in health with Senate Resolution 265, which called for a national health program. The resolution never emerged from committee.[74]

Undeterred, Roche ratcheted up the pressure on the AMA when she addressed its House of Delegates on June 14. The *New York Times* observed she "politely but firmly" served notice that the government expected the medical establishment to propose a comprehensive program of medical relief. Also for the first time, the newspaper noted, representatives of both the conservative and liberal wings of the profession would engage in public debate, a reference to delegates from the Committee of Physicians for the Improvement of Medicine, a group of 400 liberal, mainly academic physicians referred to as the "medical New Dealers." Their 1937 statement, "Principles and Proposals," acknowledged that health was "a direct concern of the government" and called for a national health policy financed through public funds. Though their manifesto stopped short of explicitly endorsing compulsory health insurance, many who signed the statement of principles did support it. Their dissident presence would shatter the facade of unity that the medical establishment normally presented to outsiders, as did the president of the American College of Physicians (ACP) who, in April 1938, accused the AMA of "political" and "partisan behavior" and of "stand-patism."[75]

On July 18, nearly 175 invited delegates attended the conference's opening session, which Surgeon General Parran hailed as demarcating "the ridge of the hill between the old indifference to health as a matter of national concern and a new understanding that health is the first and most appropriate object for national action." The AMA was represented in force, led by Dr. Irvin Abell, president, and Dr. Morris Fishbein, editor of *JAMA*.

The ACS sent a delegation headed by its president, Dr. Frederic Besley. Dr. Hugh Cabot and Professor John P. Peters of Yale led delegates from the liberal-leaning Committee of Physicians, and various states and cities sent their high-ranking medical officials. William Green of the American Federation of Labor, James R. Carey, head of the United Electrical, Radio and Machine Workers of America, and Donald Henderson, president of the United Cannery, Agricultural, Packing and Allied Workers of America, represented organized labor. Delegates also came from the American Farm Bureau Federation and several of its state affiliates. In all, the participants represented a broad spectrum of opinion, including the consumers of health care.[76]

Roche, Dr. Parran, and Katherine Lenroot, chief of the Children's Bureau, took their cues from the president's message to the delegates that health problems were "public," that "there is need for a coordinated national program of action," and that health care solutions "must be determined with a view to the best interests of all our citizens." Roosevelt also had alluded to health insurance and the inability of millions of Americans to pay for medical health care, but he stopped short of making health insurance a priority. He asked instead for "a comprehensive, long-range program providing for the most efficient cooperation of Federal, State and local governments, voluntary agencies, professional groups, mediums of public information and individual citizens."[77]

Roche then suggested to the delegates that the TCMC's recommendations provided a framework for establishing a national health program. In two major reports, "A General Program of Medical Care" and "Insurance Against Loss of Wages During Sickness," Dr. Martha Eliot presented the case for such a program and identified the categories in which existing health and medical services were deficient: preventive health services; hospital and institutional facilities, especially in rural areas; medical care for the indigent and the working poor; and the treatment of chronic and disabling illnesses of the working population. The TCMC's recommendations to eradicate certain diseases, expand maternal and child health services, provide access to medical care for the indigent and the working poor, and institute an insurance program modeled on the Social Security Act to protect against loss of wages during illness would require federal, state, and local governments to expend an additional $850 million annually, with Washington contributing one-half the cost. Phased in over a decade once the medical infrastructure was in place, such a national health program would reduce needless loss of life and suffering; it was an investment in people that would return major economic and social dividends.[78]

Eliot wanted the delegates to think about how best to achieve these goals, but no sooner had she presented the TCMC's recommendations than the AMA's Dr. Abell denounced them as "impractical," socialistic, un-American, and ignoring the "varying conditions of the States, counties and cities of this country." Defending the highly decentralized system of American medicine, he insisted that change had to be consistent with local needs and the impact of the change on "the individual sick person." Abell's stinging attack provoked a sharp rejoinder from Dr. Hugh Cabot, who brought into sharp relief the fissures that divided the physician-conferees. He assailed the medical establishment's disdain for public health service, and in a slap at fee-for-service medicine that disregarded ability to pay, he likened the prevailing practice of medicine to a "competitive business." The practice of medicine was positively "medieval" in large areas of the country, Cabot insisted, a reference to the AMA's defense of a system that mismatched the supply of physicians with the need for them geographically, to the detriment of doctor and patient. Instead of responding to Cabot's criticisms, AMA Secretary Dr. Olin West launched into a vituperative personal assault on Dr. Cabot, declaring, "I doubt if the medical profession has any more pride in him than he has in the profession."[79]

On that sour note, the conference adjourned on July 20, but not without first affirming the principle of a national health program for all Americans and Roche reading a message of thanks from the president for the conferees' pledge of cooperation. Beyond that, the conferees did not produce any formal resolutions, not even an innocuous one thanking Roche for conducting the conference "splendidly." The latter was ruled out of order, for fear that it would precipitate other resolutions of a more volatile nature. Before the delegates dispersed, however, Roche informed them that the administration intended to implement the TCMC's recommendations, beginning with a request to Congress for a two-year appropriation for matching grants to those states willing to participate in a health security program.[80] With or without the cooperation of organized medicine, the administration appeared ready to embark on a health security program.

American medicine was seemingly on the threshold of a new era, with government joining private medicine to enhance the public's health and provide access to and funding of medical care for the needy and working poor. The People's National Health Committee declared the conference marked "a new milestone of progress," and even Dr. Abell pledged the AMA's "whole-hearted cooperation" to bring about better access to affordable medical care. Roche, too, was ecstatic, as she cabled the president:

cannot resist sending you word amazing public support at national health conference for national health program and which is mounting daily as evidenced by press comment. telegrams. and letters. our technicians are working with all speed to develop specific proposals which we expect to have ready for you on your return.

The final sentence of the cable was more restrained, however, and portentous of what was to come:

meanwhile we are following your instructions to make no public comments as to future program.[81]

A more accurate reading of the new partnership with organized medicine came from Dr. Morris Fishbein, the editor of *JAMA*, who was openly skeptical about government's ability to plan and implement a national health program. He reminded his readership that only the AMA's House of Delegates had authority to act on the government's proposal. So fearful was the AMA of a favorable public response to the conference that AMA representatives shortly thereafter quietly approached the IDC with an offer to support each of the TCMC's recommendations, except the one for universal health coverage. They rationalized the exception on the grounds that it would impose a very high financial burden on taxpayers, be abused by patients, and lead to the deterioration of quality medical care. Moreover, government insurance was unnecessary because any physician or hospital would provide care free of charge, as circumstances dictated.[82]

The IDC summarily rejected the AMA's logic as well as its reliance on charity medicine. That September, the AMA's House of Delegates convened in emergency session and approved a series of resolutions. It reversed its long-standing opposition to protection against loss of income due to illness and to cash indemnity insurance plans as vetted by county and state medical societies, and it supported the expansion of public health services for the medically indigent. The delegates also insisted that any necessary federal aid be supervised locally. These resolutions were a clever stratagem to isolate compulsory health insurance from other issues and to enlist support from less conservative organizations, such as the APHA, to bring about the political demise of such a program. The committee to which the physician-delegates had referred the insurance proposal went on record against it, saying, "Your committee is not willing to foster any system of compulsory health insurance," and described the idea as "a complicated bureaucratic system which has no place in a democratic state." Universal health coverage would require "a far-reaching tax system with great increase in the cost of government" and would be susceptible "to political control."[83]

The AMA's worst fears had been well founded, for the consumers of health care left the conference energized and enthusiastically endorsed its goals, reported Ernest K. Lindley of *Newsweek* to Senator Wagner in July 1938. "Although there are many difficult problems to be worked out with reference to health insurance, I am convinced that this whole program is several stages further advanced than anybody realized it was prior to the National Health Conference," he wrote. Wagner responded enthusiastically, saying: "I am going to press the matter in the next session of Congress. I really believe that there is an overwhelming sentiment for it, and it will ultimately be translated into law." Josephine Roche also informed the president on October 12 that "the National Health Program ... has aroused intense interest throughout the country," writing that medical opinion in the country "is more liberal in its view of national health problems than some of their spokesmen had indicated." Altmeyer told delegates to the APHA meeting that the conference had been "a turning point in the health program of the nation" and the "health services must adjust themselves accordingly." The APHA subsequently endorsed the TCMC's report, as did the National Association of Medical Students, the Southern Policy Conference, and other organizations.[84]

The most insightful reaction to the conference, perhaps, came from the Swiss-born Dr. Henry E. Sigerist of Johns Hopkins University, who likened it to the sounding of a tocsin. "It meant," he wrote, "that the period of surveys had come to an end and that, at long last, definite steps were to be taken to remedy an untenable situation." The conference's recommendations should be implemented as a matter of good economics, he observed. The nation was losing $10 billion annually, so it would be much less expensive to spend some money to prevent illness than to spend more money to cure it. Sigerist refuted the hoary accusations of "socialized medicine," which Americans equated with communism. "We should not be afraid of the word, but should recognize that the socialization of services is the logical and unavoidable consequence of the industrialization of the world." He reminded his readers that Americans already had embraced in principle the socialization of medicine, and he pointed to the spending of nearly $800 million annually in state, local, and federally organized public health services, workmen's compensation laws, and various insurance plans for spreading the costs of medical care.[85]

Meanwhile, on December 12, Roche informed the president that the IDC was working on federal legislation to implement a national health security program. A week later, I. S. Falk of the TCMC informed Senator Wagner's legislative assistant that the New York Democrat would be accorded "the 'privilege' of sponsoring the legislation." No longer would Americans need to discuss health security in abstract terms; Senator Wagner's bill would give them a tangible program to correct an important omission in the Social Security Act. The legislation would encourage the kind of group arrangements that health insurance reformers supported and temporary disability compensation along the same lines as the federal-state unemployment insurance system. The question was whether Congress and the American people would accept or reject it.[86]

The national health inventory conducted in 1935–1936, covering almost 800,000 families, was the most comprehensive ever attempted. Its statistical finding, that because of lack of ability to pay, those most in need of medical services were least likely to obtain them, was not unexpected, but it did become the leading source of data that the proponents of a national health security program drew on to break the nexus between access to medical service and ability to pay. The inventory's statistical data were important not only for the first national health conference in 1938, but also for the SSB, which used the data two years later to analyze family composition in New York State. The result of the SSB's investigation had implications for future social service legislation. The USPHS also drew from the health inventory's wealth of information to better understand why so

many draft-eligible young men were failing the Selective Service Board's physical examinations at the outset of World War II. Finally, the data were pressed into service by future
presidents to justify asking Congress to legislate a national health security program.

The inventory and the NHC marked important milestones in the reformers' efforts to
improve the nation's health by backfilling what they perceived to be a significant gap in
the Social Security Act: to expand the power of the federal government to underwrite the
cost of health security for all Americans as a right of citizenship. Insurance was the essential component of national health security, particularly for the bottom third of the
population. The conference also was the vehicle for New Dealers to affirm that the consumers of health care had a right to have their interests represented in formulating public
policy. But neither the reformers nor the delegates at the time knew that the conference
would mark the highpoint of the pre–World War II efforts to persuade the public, the
medical establishment, state and local officials, and the president himself of the need for
a federally financed national health program. For despite the success of the conference in
documenting the economic and societal impact of illness and chronic disease, segments
of the public, particularly middle-class Americans, organized medicine, and the president himself, remained skeptical that "government medicine" was the solution.

The AMA's opposition was based on considerations of economic advantage and intan-
gible fears concerning the freedom and status of the physician. The greater the degree of
federal involvement, implicit in any large-scale financing of medical insurance, the less
presumably would remain of the traditional entrepreneurial individual. Unacknowledged
was the de facto erosion of this individualism, owing to progress in medical science and
technology, specialization, the rising costs of good medical care, and the special problems imposed by the increasing proportion of the aged and chronically ill. These forces
were leading inexorably toward the bureaucratization and centralization of medicine.
The AMA might scuttle a national health program, but it would hardly affect these impersonal forces. Its implacable opposition to "government medicine" also caused it to forfeit the opportunity to help guide those forces rationally and efficiently to ensure in the
process satisfactory remuneration, status, and authority for the physician.[87]

Roosevelt, too, had endorsed the goals of the health conference in a general way, but he
was ambivalent toward national health insurance, as were most Democratic Party regu-
lars. Without a visible public constituency to address, the president stopped well short of
committing himself to any legislation emanating from the IDC, the TCMC, or the health
conference. With Democrats already divided over his economic agenda, his humiliating
legislative defeat in the 1937 "Court-packing fight," his failed purge of conservative congressional Democrats, and a new slump in the economy, Roosevelt thought it might be
better to delay pushing for health care reform, but as Altmeyer recalled, "he never made it
an issue then either."[88]

Josephine Roche also bore a measure of blame for the conference's failure to produce legislative results. She had never invited any of the mass-circulation outlets or any of the radio networks to attend and cover the conference's proceedings. This failure put Roche and her associates at a disadvantage in communicating their message to a larger audience after the conference. An effective base of public support for the conference's work was never established, and for this, Roche must bear responsibility. As chair of the IDC, her duty was to disseminate the conference's message as widely as possible. FDR had shown through his weekly news conferences that the media could be managed for his own purposes, but Roche viewed the popular press as vulgar and avoided it whenever she could. Unfortunately, whether she liked it or not, the health reform movement needed major press coverage.[89]

# TWO

# HOPES DEFERRED:
# CONGRESS, WAR, &
# THE END OF THE NEW DEAL

For all the work that had been poured into it, the National Health Conference, not legislation, was the high-water mark of the health care reform movement in the interwar period. This was not immediately evident in the afterglow of the conference, when reformers and their legislative allies, notably New York Senator Robert F. Wagner, continued to work with the IDC's technical committee in drafting legislation for a national health program. Their efforts eventually ran afoul of a reticent president, a bipartisan congressional coalition of Republicans and conservative Southern Democrats, and a deteriorating international situation that absorbed the nation's energies and put legislative limits on New Deal health care provision. The circumstances that inhibited progress toward universal health coverage also dictated that whatever future changes would occur in the funding and delivery of medical health care, they would take place largely within the private health sector, at least until the advent of Medicare in the mid-1960s. But this situation, too, was not immediately evident in 1938.[1]

The drafting process for the national health security program proceeded into the fall and winter of 1938, with Senator Wagner receiving letters from health professionals who empathized with the need to provide medical care for the indigent and working poor but who also urged him to proceed cautiously. Kentucky's health commissioner wrote comparing favorably the TCMC's work with the British and German national health programs with which he had been acquainted while serving as president of the APHA, but he advised Wagner against rushing headlong into legislation mandating universal health coverage without the infrastructure of medical personnel or the facilities to implement it.[2]

The commissioner's letter was a harbinger of the perilous road that awaited a health program predicated upon transferring the oversight and funding of medical provision to the federal government at the expense of state and local agencies or private-sector medicine. Of greater concern was the aloofness that President Roosevelt began to exhibit following his initial enthusiasm for the National Health Conference's work. On December 20, 1938, after a budget meeting, Roosevelt admonished reporters not to go too far in predicting legislative recommendations based on reports from the IDC. He characterized the reports as the work of a very young child and intimated that he would send them to the Hill for study, but without a recommendation. Roosevelt recognized that health security legislation would be controversial not only among congressional Republicans but also among Southern Democrats, who might see in it the potential to upset race relations and adversely impact the region's traditional labor market.[3]

The president's remarks to the press should have served as a cautionary flag to health reformers, but they went largely unheeded, and on January 15, 1939, Senator Wagner disclosed that he would introduce national health legislation along the lines the TCMC had recommended. Two weeks later, Wagner told a nationwide radio audience that swift congressional action was needed to enable states contemplating their own health programs to have a "clear indication of the help and cooperation" they might expect from Washington. To defuse opposition from critics who feared that health security was a stepping-stone to universal health coverage, Wagner further emphasized that the NHC's recommendations had been the result of a consensus, and that his bill would not impose "a Federal straitjacket" on the states. They would be free to draft their own health programs and "to establish compulsory health insurance if they choose to do so," because experience both here and abroad had demonstrated that voluntary programs "will not reach a sufficient proportion of the people in need of insurance protection."[4]

Though he had not precluded the future possibility of compulsory health insurance, Wagner did not make it a requirement of his legislation, hoping thereby to enhance its chances of passage and to give the states time to evaluate the strengths and weaknesses of their own health programs. But his remarks did imply a significant change in the New Deal's entry into a policy area that hitherto had been left entirely to the private sector, states, and localities or had been only marginally affected by federal action. Wagner was proposing to expand national power and to do so within a structure of "cooperative federalism," which acknowledged the continuing role of the states in the administration of health programs.[5]

IDC chair Josephine Roche applauded Wagner's remarks and predicted that the program would "cost the government millions, but will save the nation billions." Referring to the hidden costs of poor health to the economy and the nation, she insisted the nation could not "attack successfully with small change our present $10 billion problem in health."[6] Her remarks were intended to rally support for Wagner's bill, but they fell short of winning the president's support; on January 23, 1939, Roosevelt forwarded the IDC's data and recommendations to Congress for "careful study," as he had promised, but he did not specifically add his endorsement. Nor did Wagner's national health bill have the endorsement yet of another important component of the federal bureaucracy, the Social Security Board (SSB). For unknown to the TCMC, which was drafting the Wagner bill in late 1938–early 1939, the leaders of the SSB were contemplating changes to the Social Security Act, including insurance for medical care and permanent disability coverage. They dropped the amendments for the moment as being too controversial, but the Farm Security Administration did endorse the Wagner health plan. Unfortunately, it had little credibility with Congress.[7]

*Commonweal,* an opponent of compulsory health insurance, however, did note that the president had not asked a Congress that was growing increasingly critical of the New Deal for immediate action, despite support for a health security program from groups such as the Farmer's Educational and Cooperative Union. A *New York Times* reporter also commented on the president's less-than-fulsome endorsement of national health legislation, saying, "Mr. Roosevelt's health program has been caught in a legislative draft.... The chill imposed upon it will undoubtedly give it a cold which will incapacitate it for this session of Congress—and possibly permanently." Absence of a strong presidential endorsement eventually weighed heavily on the Wagner bill as it wended its way through the legislative process.[8]

Despite the president's reluctance to make health care reform a legislative priority for the forthcoming session of the 76th Congress, this did not discourage Wagner, who, on February 28, 1939, dropped his bill (S. 1620) for a national health program "to conquer this last remaining frontier of social security in America" into the legislative hopper.[9] The legislation was entirely consistent with American precedents, he explained, and, in pursuit of a cooperative federalism, he noted that the day had long since passed when the federal government's responsibility for the health of the population was confined to sanitation, quarantine, and asylums for the insane. S. 1620 embodied the TCMC's recommendations as they had emerged from the National Health Conference, and it contained many points of agreement with the AMA's most recent position on health care, Wagner insisted. The only difference was the issue of health insurance, which Wagner's legislation made an option for the states to adopt or not, as they saw fit.[10]

To launch the national health program, Wagner eschewed a new federal payroll tax (similar to the Social Security tax) and authorized an initial appropriation of $80 million in matching funds, exclusive of any additional sums Congress might appropriate to aid states in constructing needed tuberculosis sanitariums and mental hospitals. Contrary to a fairly widespread impression at the time, S. 1620 did not authorize the federal government to furnish medical services. Beyond setting a uniform minimum standard of care, the bill entrusted the provision of health services to the states, localities, physicians, and hospitals. Each state had the option of limiting its health care plan only to those on relief or of including others more fortunately situated.[11]

The bill vested federal oversight in three agencies: the Children's Bureau, which administered the grants for maternal and child welfare and for services to physically handicapped children; the USPHS, which funded general public health programs; and the SSB, which dispensed funding for medical care for the elderly and disabled.[12] The trifurcation of federal functions had the potential for creating jurisdictional disputes, but Wagner told Dr. Hugh Cabot that his intention was to produce a bill "embodying the broad principles of a national health program, without introducing additional and highly complex problems of Federal administration." He was "confident" that issue could be resolved satisfactorily, either through the 1939 reorganization bill pending before Congress or through "specific Congressional action in the health bill itself."[13] To the extent that Congress modified S. 1620, Wagner was optimistic that it would serve as a barometer of lay and professional opinion, and this would result in a stronger and more comprehensive health program.[14]

Of the various health bills before Congress, Wagner's national health act of 1939 generated the most political and popular support and also the fiercest opposition. In March 1939, the senator received a poignant letter from a black sharecropper and seven of his neighbors. "We, a group of Negro sharecroppers & white workers living in the neighborhood of Oxford, Miss. have heard of your bill for Medical Aid and want to give it our wholehearted endorsement. We have very little medical facilities here and practically no free medical aid so that whenever one of us gets sick it becomes a very serious matter," Gus Uth wrote.[15] He then described the plight of a widow whose two small children had contracted tuberculosis but received no medical care because, according to a nurse, she lacked money or hospital insurance. "The little children were told to lie on their backs for 2 months and then they would be alright." Four months had passed "and they still have fever." Uth also reported that a sharecropping family with five children had contracted TB, and "nothing is being done." Securing free medical care locally was an impossibility, but he promised Wagner that "we will try to get as many people as possible to write to back your bill."[16]

Besides getting support from the poorest of the poor, Wagner's bill garnered support from other constituencies that composed the New Deal coalition. The Committee of Physicians for the Improvement of Medical Care, the "medical New Dealers" who were at odds with the AMA leadership, affirmed their "sympathy with the general purposes of the Wagner bill and with the program of the Technical Committee upon which the bill is based." These dissident physicians had an optimistic and expansive perception of social security, believing that the Social Security Act did not have only the negative function of propping up wage earners when other means had disappeared. It also could be used for positive goals, such as promoting health security through medical care and health insurance for every American. These same physicians wanted locally influential constituents to know that not all doctors toed the AMA line; that there were physicians who would cooperate with them in building a nationwide, community-based program of health service and medical care.[17] Representatives of 133 trade unions, social agencies, welfare groups, and the medical and allied professions, meeting in New York on May 11, 1939, also unanimously endorsed the Wagner bill and wired Surgeon General Parran to urge "early passage of Bill S. 1620 in Congress this session."[18]

Still other liberals endorsed the Wagner bill with modifications. Some wanted to expand its disability provision; others sought more specific language to guarantee minorities access to health care. The editor of the *Journal of the National Medical Association,* speaking on behalf of Negro physicians, was generally sympathetic to Wagner's bill, but asked that it include more specific language to protect blacks and other minorities from discrimination. On May 12, 1939, Wagner presented amendments to that effect and assured the editor that financial allotments in the original language of the bill were determined by health needs and special problems in particular states. "It is my purpose and hope that through these conditions of allotment the urgent health needs of the Negro people will be adequately served," Wagner wrote.[19]

Dr. Michael M. Davis, of the Committee on Research in Medical Economics, was another friendly critic, but he had grave doubts that Wagner's bill would survive the legislative process intact. The tripartite division of jurisdiction "would be administratively unworkable on either federal or state levels," he informed Surgeon General Parran on March 24, 1939. Davis preferred that public health officials administer the program, but he knew that politically important groups, such as labor and public welfare, had little confidence in the ability of the officials and would vie for control of the governmentally funded program of medical care. To avoid such conflict and to retain administrative oversight of the program, public health officials would have had to demonstrate through their current health programs that they were up to the task of administering health care efficiently.[20]

Davis had a second, more substantive concern that would become a major bone of contention whenever the issue of national health care reform came up in the future. The issue of eligibility for coverage was potentially explosive because it had implications that cut across class, gender, and racial lines. "No important law concerning medical care will be passed unless it includes self-supporting people of small means," he insisted. "Wage-earners and farmers will not push large measures for the indigent," many of whom were black and female. Because the jurisdiction of any department administering the national health bill would not be limited to the indigent, he argued, public health rather than welfare officials should administer the program. The surgeon general, however, would have to instruct public health officials to remind their colleagues in welfare that poor health was not the exclusive concern of the indigent.[21]

Whereas the bill's supporters argued over details, its opponents rejected the bedrock principle on which it rested: federal intervention in the private sector. Philadelphia's Board of Trade sent a memorial resolution to both houses of Congress urging them to reject S. 1620 as "state medicine with all the perversions and iniquities which such a paternal policy would encourage."[22] A small businessman from Chattanooga denounced the legislation as "communistic," calling Wagner "the most undesirable alien in a so-called Democracy; a radical charlatan par excellence, a treacherous hybrid ready to attempt to socialize this nation into bankruptcy in an effort to glorify yourself." Mistakenly believing Wagner to be Jewish, he launched into an anti-Semitic tirade against the New York senator for sponsoring the Social Security Act—part of the Jewish conspiracy to control the government. "Your continued efforts will prove futile and will ultimately make you and your race objectionable and obnoxious to Americans," he warned.[23]

The outgoing president of the Medical Society of New York may have been more temperate in his remarks, but he was no less critical, accusing Washington officialdom of deferring to laymen rather than to medical and scientific experts in seeking solutions to health problems. He also targeted for specific condemnation the bill's health insurance provision, despite its voluntary character. The AMA's objection to the Wagner bill also had less to do with its specific content than for what it implied, a foreshadowing of *compulsory* health insurance, the code term for "socialized medicine." Dr. Irvin Abell, AMA president, observed that although S. 1620 contained many positive features, it would be tragic if they were lost in the acrimony over certain aspects of the legislation, a thinly veiled reference to national health insurance, which he derided as a sickness tax.[24]

Meanwhile, the Senate Committee on Education and Labor, which had jurisdiction over the bill, assigned S. 1620 to a subcommittee chaired by Senator James E. Murray, Democrat of Montana. The subcommittee conducted extensive public hearings between April and July and accumulated exhaustive documentation on all aspects of health security, including health insurance. Because the bill assigned responsibility to the SSB for administering federal grants to the states to cover medical and disability compensation, Arthur J. Altmeyer, chairman of the SSB, ironically became the Wagner bill's leading spokesman in the hearings. Altmeyer endorsed the principal objectives of the legislation, but because the SSB had been pursuing another agenda, he refused to express an opinion as to the rapidity with which such a health program might be put into effect. All along, the SSB had been working toward substituting social insurance for welfare as better serving America's needs, thus toward the SSB's becoming the dominant federal agency for social welfare. In its bid to attain jurisdictional control, the SSB argued that health policy was a wage earner's issue and that any changes to it should take the form of amendments to the Social Security Act's old-age pension and unemployment compensation programs rather than through entirely new legislation.[25]

Altmeyer, as chair of the SSB and a leading member of the IDC, had been caught between two opposing allegiances, which explains his less-than-enthusiastic support for the Wagner bill. However, his testimony that a national health program was needed resonated with other groups and organizations interested in health security. The American Federation of Labor (AFL) and the Congress of Industrial Organizations (CIO) temporarily set aside their differences to support the Wagner bill, although they would have preferred a national, rather than state, health insurance program. A national program as a right of citizenship was a theme repeated by the representative of the National Association for the Advancement of Colored People and spokesmen from many farm and urban civic organizations, even though they may have had reservations about specific provisions or omissions in the bill.[26]

The bill's critics, by contrast, highlighted what they perceived were its defects: the trifurcation of federal administrative authority, which appeared to contradict the president's reorganization plan, and its alleged disallowance of federal moneys to care for the needy in voluntary hospitals (a misunderstanding that Wagner immediately clarified).[27] AMA witnesses acerbically questioned the necessity for the legislation, alleging that there were no substantially unmet medical needs (a reference to the charity hospital system) and raising anew the specter of "government control," "bureaucracy," and "dictatorship." Surgeon General Parran informed the White House that what the AMA and its allies really feared was "the great expansion of Federal grants-in-aid provided by the bill," which would presumably diminish the role of the states and localities and inject the federal presence into private-sector medicine in a big way. Organized medicine also worried about Title XIII, which they feared would open the door to compulsory health insurance for wage-earning families."[28] The AMA's opposition notwithstanding, the subcommittee, which included such diverse personal and political points of view as those of Senators Murray; Robert A. Taft, Republican of Ohio; Allen Ellender, Democrat of Louisiana; and Robert M. La Follette, Jr., Republican of Wisconsin, issued a stinging rebuke to the medical establishment. "The evidence on needs, in urban and in rural areas, is overwhelming, as may be evident to anyone who will examine the record," the subcommittee's preliminary report declared. The report substantiated its conclusion with findings from the national health survey and from witness testimony, and then declared that it was "in agreement with the general purposes and objectives of this bill."[29]

The subcommittee's report was a significant political statement, suggesting bipartisan agreement on the fundamental principle of cooperative federalism, that the federal government should assist the states in making preventive and curative medicine more readily available to their citizens. But the devil was in the program's details, which the subcommittee had not yet addressed. The preliminary report, for example, had identified a dozen issues, including determining the formula for dispensing federal grants and squaring their amounts with the financial needs of the states; setting the income ceiling to qualify for medical care; providing support for medical education, research, and public health education; coordinating federal and state jurisdictions; guaranteeing minorities access to health care; dealing with state restrictions on medical services and eligibility, the relationship between official and nonofficial health agencies, unneeded hospital construction, and state use of nongovernmental health facilities.[30]

These unresolved, but substantive, issues required expert guidance, whereas others simply needed clarification. But whatever the bill's shortcomings, the subcommittee had rejected the naysayers' claim that it would bring about "dangerous or revolutionary changes" in medical care, calling these fears "unwarranted." Although the subcommittee exhibited remarkable optimism that the bill could, and would, be improved, the full committee was less sanguine about S. 1620. It said it would need additional time to study the Wagner bill, but it expected to report it out of committee when Congress reconvened.[31]

The Wagner national health bill of 1939 never saw the light of day. The political situation at home and abroad changed on September 1, 1939, when Nazi Germany invaded Poland and World War II began. The United States remained officially neutral, but the president quickly became preoccupied with the conflict in Europe, and with tensions rising in the Pacific, his focus was on gearing up the American economy for national defense. Purely domestic policies of the sort New Dealers had advocated during economic hard times were put on the back burner. The Wagner bill was among the casualties, as was evident late that fall. Roche and Altmeyer went to the White House to ask the president which health measures he wished to include in his 1940 legislative package. Roosevelt approved only hospital construction, from which Altmeyer concluded that "the President had changed his mind about making the National Health Program an issue in the Presidential campaign."[32]

Wagner agreed to sponsor the bill to execute the hospital-building program, even as he and other New Deal liberals lamented the shelving of his ambitious national health program. One health expert criticized the president's decision, saying, "The grotesquely weak substitute recommendation for some additional federal hospitals came as a strange alternative from the man who, at the National Health Conference, had declared, 'it is clear that there is need for a coordinated national program of action,' and who, in 1939, had said that 'good health is essential to the security and progress of the Nation.'" The national health program, she lamented, was lost. "It now smolders beneath the avalanche of defense legislation."[33] The Senate approved the hospital construction bill in spring 1940, but its fate was far different in the House. There, the bill languished in the waning days of the 76th Congress and was eventually shelved "for the duration."[34]

Meanwhile, without presidential backing, Wagner's national health bill died in committee after strong opposition to it by the National Physicians' Committee for the Extension of Medical Service, the political arm of the AMA. It was the only medical group to testify against S. 1620 and also to offer no suggestions for its improvement. Following its lead, the AHA and the American Dental Association retracted their earlier endorsements and also denounced the bill. On July 8, 1939, the AMA president, Dr. Charles Heyd, who was about to embark for Europe, declared that the AMA had killed the bill dead in its tracks. He told reporters the legislation would have resulted in inferior medical service, and then he attempted to soften the AMA's opposition, declaring that federal aid should be restricted only to states where a need for assistance could be demonstrated. He also stated that all federal health activities should be consolidated in a single federal health department.[35]

Heyd's professions were disingenuous, given the AMA's history of denying that any medical needs existed and its drumbeat criticism of federal bureaucracy and dictatorship, but it was President Roosevelt who applied the coup de grâce to the Wagner bill. In a public statement a few days before Christmas, he again announced that he would support a limited experiment in only one of the several phases of the national health program, hospital construction. In mid-January 1940, he sent Congress a formal message requesting federal payment and construction of fifty hospitals in parts of the nation where they were acutely needed. The facilities were mostly located in rural areas and, once built, would be transferred to the states to support and operate.[36]

The president's announcement surprised and disappointed supporters of the national health bill. The IDC recognized immediately that the hospital construction bill would kill Wagner's more ambitious proposal. Even Altmeyer thought, "We would have been able to secure favorable congressional action if the president had actively supported Senator Robert F. Wagner's bill." The *American Labor Legislation Review (ALLR)* castigated the project for "fifty little ... hospitals" as a tremendous letdown.[37] Mary Dublin, of the National Consumers League, wrote to Wagner's legislative assistant on March 4, "We are all thoroughly sick about the President's message on the National Health Program and only hope that nevertheless the Senator will reintroduce the bill."[38]

Paul U. Kellogg, editor of the *Survey,* tried to put the best possible face on the president's action when he wrote to Stephen Early, Roosevelt's press secretary, "The Administration's espousal of hospital building in neglected areas (I'm for that with both feet) may prove to be *not* an alternative, but a *curtain-raiser* to the rounded National Health Program laid down by the president's Interdepartmental Committee to Coordinate Health and Welfare Activities." Kellogg rationalized the president's action by transferring blame to the supporters of the Wagner bill for not having mobilized public opinion and sympathetic organizations to offset the AMA's lobbying. "We need the shove of the President" to get the bill on track again, he wrote, and insisted that if Roosevelt decided to run for a third term and pushed the health bill through Congress, "such a move would be a stroke of statesmanship, epitomizing in a fresh way how he has stood out for the common welfare."[39]

Kellogg's effort to put the best face on the president's action could not undo what had occurred, and there remains much speculation about the reasons for the president's action. Did he pull the plug on the Wagner bill, even in an amended format, because of AMA opposition? Was it because of the cost of running a health security program in the midst of rising defense expenditures? Was he seeking to woo conservatives? These, and other considerations, no doubt contributed to Roosevelt's retreat.

The political climate of the time, most likely, reinforced the president's cautious approach. In the wake of his ill-fated court-packing scheme and the sharp but short-lived recession of 1937, Roosevelt had squandered a great deal of the political capital that he had won in his hugely lopsided 1936 reelection. The intense ideological struggle of late 1937 and early 1938 to define the soul of the New Deal, combined with partisan politics and economic strains, had left the administration weaker and more vulnerable to opposition to extending the New Deal into the realm of medicine, as Wagner's bill proposed.

The AMA and its business allies had shown repeatedly that they were a powerful, well-financed force to be reckoned with, in contrast to liberals and health care reformers. The latter had been unable to agree on the composition of a health security program, whether to tie it to or have it stand apart from unemployment insurance, whether such a program was preferable to simply extending the medical infrastructure to communities that lacked it, how to fund health security, and which agency of government should administer the program. They had also consistently underestimated the high political value that middle-class voters, in particular, put on the sanctity of the doctor-patient relationship. Senator Wagner was on the mark when, asked in 1940 to explain the president's actions, he responded, "This is supposed to be a conservative year." It was, after all, a presidential election year.[40]

The president's lack of positive support for the Wagner bill also sprang from his respect for traditional principles and institutions and his commitment to private enterprise and initiatives, themes that he had first raised in his speech to Congress in June 1934. Two years later, in October 1936, Roosevelt spoke at the dedication ceremony of the Jersey City Medical Center, the third-largest entity of its kind in the United States. He reminded his audience that every major health organization, including the AMA, had endorsed the health provisions of the Social Security Act. "This in itself assures that the health plans will be carried out in a manner compatible with our traditional social and political institutions," he noted, adding: "The overwhelming majority of the doctors of the nation want medicine kept out of politics. On occasions in the past attempts have been made to put medicine into politics. Such attempts have always failed and always will fail."[41]

In other words, the president, while sympathetic to those in need of medical care, was circumspect about encroaching on the prerogatives of private enterprise—the private-sector medical establishment as embodied in the AMA—especially without broad public support for doing so. Extending the supply of medical care was preferable to guaranteeing access to it. Moreover, Roosevelt, like most Americans, believed that American medicine, despite its shortcomings, was highly advanced scientifically and technically compared to other countries, and he was not persuaded of the need to institute wholesale change in a system that functioned reasonably well for most Americans. Roosevelt conceded that the poorest third of the population, who were without political clout, needed health care, but he was content for the moment to have those people cared for by expanding the framework of existing practices and institutions, the hospital charity system and pro bono physicians' services.[42]

Also one cannot overlook the political conditions that defined the limits of New Deal liberalism. Support for the Wagner bill from southerners as diverse as Kentucky's health commissioner, black sharecroppers, and poor white farmers was testimony to the success of progressive New Dealers who held out the possibility of a healthier and more productive life to those usually excluded from public-policy making. The New Dealers saw

the politics of health security as part of a broader challenge to the control of economic resources and services by business corporations, insurance company executives, and organized medicine. They also recognized that the South, as the country's poorest and least
modernized region, had the most to gain from a national health security program. The
tragedy was that the Wagner bill ran afoul not only of congressional Republicans but also
of the president's strategy of winning legislative support from the southern wing of his
own party by not interfering in race relations and the region's low-wage labor force.

The 1935 Social Security Act had consciously excluded agricultural and domestic
workers, who were predominantly black and southern. The Wagner bill, however, had the
potential to make health care a right of citizenship. Nationalizing health care standards
would have posed a threat to the status quo, requiring the president to marshal all of his
considerable resources and the support of a unified bureaucracy. Neither was available to
the bill's supporters. Roosevelt refused to commit to the legislation, and the SSB regarded
it as a rival to its bid for bureaucratic supremacy.[43]

The outbreak of war in Europe also undermined the national health bill. War provided
the Keynesian jump start that a still economically depressed America desperately
needed. The Roosevelt administration's commitment to being the "arsenal of democracy" led to the expenditure of billions of dollars for armaments. After the fall of France
in June 1940, Congress appropriated in one fell swoop more money than the nation had
spent in toto on World War I. As employment picked up, factories worked overtime, and
Americans had spending money for the first time in a decade, anxieties about health care
lessened. Deficit spending fueled consumer demand and revived production, which
might have carried the nation into full economic recovery had there not been a war to
fight after the Japanese attack on Pearl Harbor on December 7, 1941. War-induced prosperity thus made it difficult for reformers to persuade Americans, particularly middle-
class Americans, of the urgency for health care reform.[44]

The war had a long-term "ratcheting effect" in expanding the American state. The
Roosevelt administration's management of the government, the economy, and society
built on the expanded state action of the 1930s to transform the federal bureaucracies
into a powerful national apparatus. The state's response to wartime demands resulted in
growing intervention in the consumer economy and substantive changes in the means of
public administration. Social provision, the regulation of labor-management relations,
public finance, and the procurement of the necessary resources to fight the war, all experienced the expansion and deepening of national state authority.[45]

Broad popular support for the war effort validated the president's actions, as Roosevelt
reached out to individuals, organizations, and associations that New Dealers had previously held at arm's length. Business elites entered the federal government, particularly
the war-related agencies. They tended to favor wartime policies at odds with the strong-
est reformist tendencies of the New Deal, yet their involvement also had an important

unintended consequence: it weakened the unqualified opposition that business executives had so often expressed toward the New Deal. Agreements among government, management, and labor also allowed a massive expansion of unions during the war, but
labor's cooperation with the Roosevelt administration proved to be a mixed blessing. It
allowed for wage increases to be contained in fringe benefits and in the structure of
compensation-wages for overtime, and it helped unions grow. By the end of the war, labor
had become an accepted partner in a pluralist American government. But union leaders
had also become increasingly estranged from their rank-and-file membership, particularly over the "no strike" pledge, and were more vulnerable to an increasingly unfriendly
administration and Congress, which supported "work or fight" legislation. By the end of
the war, organized labor had been reduced to an interest group like any other and was no
longer a potential force for social-democratic change.[46]

Contrary to expectations, the president's lack of enthusiasm for the Wagner bill and
the onset of war did not end efforts to establish a national health security program. Nor
did it curtail the promotion of labor- and state-sponsored health insurance plans or
dampen schemes to use federal revenues to finance medical care for welfare recipients
and the medically indigent. Indeed, government-sponsored health security continued to
be a hotly debated topic, as in a 1942 radio forum that one professional journal described
as "a verbal free-for-all."[47] Health security, which had begun ten years before as an idea,
was not a fad, as critics alleged, but a true social movement, declared Dr. Nathan Sinai,
professor of public health at the University of Michigan.[48]

Despite a series of setbacks—the defeat of the national health bill and the hospital
construction bill and the president's decision to terminate the IDC and the transfer of its
functions to defense welfare agencies—the concept of health security continued to grow,
and progressive liberals worked under the most trying circumstances to keep the issue
before the public and the politicians. With an eye fixed on the peace that would follow the
war, the progressive liberals emphasized the importance of renewing democracy at home
to make the fight for democracy abroad worthwhile. They strove to influence states and
localities to fill gaps in health care, and they encouraged unions to include health care
coverage in their collective bargaining with employers. They were creating a sense of
raised expectations, of entitlement, of a belief in the capacity of the postwar state to better people's lives and thereby serve the national interest.

The transformations that occurred in the American state not only reshaped the political landscape but also had consequences for new efforts at progressive liberal reform. The federal government expanded its wartime involvement in health care, directly and indirectly, by supporting health programs that were not intrinsically linked
to the family-wage model of contributory social insurance that the SSB preferred. By
1943, federal programs sponsored by the Children's Bureau, the Farm Security Administration, or other agencies were covering more than 800,000 people for some kind of

medical care service and actively promoted local health experiments, which the policy makers who were their designers and directors hoped would become models for national health policy after the war.[49]

These efforts met with some success, as health care reformers, liberal legislators, and the recipients of the war-induced health benefits leveraged the nexus between consumer demand, patriotism, and nationalism. The State of Washington underwrote the cost of providing medical, dental, hospital, nursing, and pharmaceutical services, as well as eyeglasses and hearing aids, for its 62,000 recipients of old-age pensions.[50] Rhode Island legislators enacted the first compulsory state health insurance law on April 29, 1942. Known as "cash sickness insurance" because it did not provide for medical care directly, it was nevertheless described by the *ALLR* as "a significant step in the recognition by a state of its responsibility to require cash compensation for unemployment due to sickness." The American Federation of Hosiery Workers (part of the CIO) negotiated with hosiery manufacturers in 1943 "one of the most comprehensive health and accident coverage programs" for its members.[51]

A New Deal in health care had become part of democracy's unfinished agenda. The "medical New Dealers," organized labor, the National Farmers Union, and social workers perceived the war, not as an obstacle to social reform, but as an opportunity to advance reform. They publicized, promoted, and lobbied for comprehensive health care legislation as part of the nation's first line of defense. Utilizing preliminary data from the Selective Service Law of 1940, George St. J. Perrott, one of the lead investigators in the National Health Inventory, and his associate, Rollo H. Britten, a senior statistician in the USPHS, wrote that physical examinations of the initial pool of a million inductees revealed "a serious state of ill-health of American youth." Linking health security with national security, they predicted that if the United States found itself in a shooting war, it would have to divert its energies from mobilization of the armed forces to providing remedial medical care, a situation that would compromise both military and industrial manpower needs. "Many of the impairments could have been prevented by more extended public health programs during the period of growth of these individuals," the authors concluded, and they emphasized "the need for further development of such programs in the future." The alarmingly high number of rejections, Perrott hoped, "will promote the planning of future health services for children and adolescents to the end that future generations of young men may have the maximum possible health and vigor."[52]

Perrott's finding, that the pool of 1 million draftees contained almost 40 percent who were physically unfit for military duty, came as no surprise to First Lady Eleanor Roosevelt. Returning from a lecture tour of the South and the Midwest, she had seen firsthand the economic and social weakness of a nation mobilizing for war, and she hoped the sorry Selective Service figures would "give impetus to the movement for a comprehensive and nationwide health program." She reminded the president that genuine national security encompassed not only guns but also good health, better housing, work training, and equal opportunity.[53] SSB chairman Arthur J. Altmeyer drew a similar link between national and health security in July 1941 in testimony before a House committee, when he declared: "Our immediate problem is national security, but no nation can be stronger than its people. . . . In peace or in war, we cannot afford to do less than our utmost to strengthen the place of health security in the 'seamless web' of our national life."[54]

Altmeyer's testimony, with its references to Great Britain and to Sir William Beveridge's recently completed plan for alleviating postwar poverty by providing a cradle-to-grave social security system for all British subjects, was also intended to assert the SSB's right to be the lead agency in this country for social welfare programs. But his proposals, that Congress amend the Social Security Act to include health insurance and disability payments and to liberalize the formula upon which federal grants were awarded to the states for public health services, precipitated an outburst from conservative legislators. Southern Democrats saw the proposals as a ploy to interfere with the region's racial and labor arrangements; the AMA accused Altmeyer and the SSB of attempting to impose a foreign, socialistic plan on America.[55] Dr. Morris Fishbein, the editor of *JAMA*, told health insurance underwriters that an "American Beveridge Plan" would cost $15 billion annually.[56] Those fears strengthened when, on January 14, 1942, a reorganized National Resources Planning Board (NRPB), which was investigating the link among economic security, health, and nutrition, endorsed a unified, comprehensive system of social insurance that included universal health coverage. Congress responded first by cutting off the agency's funding and then abolishing it altogether in 1943.[57]

In fact, although neither the White House nor the Congress could afford to ignore the medical aspects of national security, they stopped well short of embracing a national health program along the lines of either the NRPB report or the Beveridge Plan. Congress, instead, included in the "First Deficiency Appropriation" bill of late 1942–early 1943 the sum of $1.2 million to establish a program of emergency health services for dependents of servicemen in the lower four pay grades. Some liberals purported to see the Emergency Maternity and Infant Care (EMIC) program included in that bill, even though it was limited in scope, a precedent for facilitating passage of a national health security system in the postwar period.[58]

Their optimism was strengthened when, as the tide of battle turned in favor of the Allies, postwar reconstruction problems received more attention from the administration. On January 7, 1943, President Roosevelt, alluding to the Four Freedoms for which the democracies were fighting, observed that Americans at home and at the front were "wondering a little about the third freedom—freedom from want," which became popularly interpreted as the promise of abundance for all Americans after the war. In words that touched the mood of the day, he declared that Americans wanted assurance against the evils of all major hazards—"assurance that will extend from the cradle to the grave." For the first time, the president appeared to be asking Congress for a comprehensive social insurance system. On August 14, 1943, the eighth anniversary of the Social Security Act, he followed up with a call to extend Social Security coverage to farmers, agricultural laborers, small businessmen, and the self-employed and to include "the serious economic hazard of ill health."[59]

In the wake of the report on the health status of Selective Service inductees, Altmeyer's lobbying before Congress, the NRPB recommendation, the Beveridge Plan, and Roosevelt's own rhetoric, health security, like other social security issues, stimulated public discourse and thus remained at the forefront of the nation's wartime domestic agenda. Even insurers sought to capture the political resonance of the New Deal's economic bill of rights by linking it to commercial enterprises and the marketplace—an effort that bore fruit as the number of persons covered by hospital insurance increased from 1 million before the war to 8.5 million by 1944. Liberals hoped that the president's words would finally muster congressional support for the broad range of progressive proposals in the form of postwar veterans' benefits.[60]

There was actually little reason for such optimism. The president's rhetoric was part of a larger strategy to retain executive control of postwar planning and to secure the labor vote in advance of the 1944 presidential election campaign. The 1942 congressional elections had registered a national swing against the New Deal, as Republicans gained forty-six seats in the House and nine in the Senate. Democratic losses outside the South further strengthened that region's position within the party. Conservative Southern Democrats and their Republican accomplices dominated the 78th Congress, standing ready to eviscerate any perceived tampering with race and labor relations, to strike down "nonessential" New Deal agencies (including the NRPB, the Farm Security Administration, the National Youth Administration, and the Civilian Conservation Corps), and to rein in "unnecessary" social experimentation, whether in medical care and child care or in housing.[61]

Conspicuous among these "experiments" was a new proposal to extend health coverage through amendments to the Social Security Act. This approach appealed to Senator Wagner because it allowed him to advance his health program under an umbrella that was broader than the ill-fated 1939 national health bill, and even President Roosevelt appeared initially amenable to amending the Social Security Act.[62] With cooperation from the SSB, technical experts from several government agencies who were familiar with both the British and the Canadian health programs, and input from organized labor, the "medical New Dealers," and representatives of social service organizations, the Wagner-Murray-Dingell bill was assembled in Senator Wagner's office. Wagner sent a copy of the new bill to the president, who wished him "good luck with it." But that was the extent of direct White House involvement in or endorsement of the legislation.[63]

Roosevelt's tepid acknowledgment of the Wagner-Murray-Dingell bill, which became much of the focal point of New Dealers' hopes for the postwar future, lent credence to those who believed he was simply preparing the groundwork for election-year politics. Like the 1939 legislative proposal, the Wagner-Murray-Dingell bill created a dilemma for the president. The war was still his highest priority, the second front in Europe was still a long way off, and Japan remained a formidable adversary. Could he risk alienating the business and social conservatives and their congressional allies whose cooperation and votes he needed for the resources and services with which to conduct the war? Could he risk distracting civilian workers from maintaining the high levels of productivity required to defeat the Axis powers while Congress engaged in an extended debate over the legislation? But could he afford to alienate his liberal supporters by discouraging Wagner's efforts? Roosevelt, in the end, opted for the politically safe route by allowing the bill to go forward, but without White House backing. He thereby pacified the legislation's opponents without discouraging the reformers.

On June 3, 1943, Senators Wagner and Murray introduced the bill (S. 1161) in the Senate, and Michigan Representative John Dingell, Sr., proposed a companion bill (H.R. 2861) in the House. The bills were assigned to the Finance Committee of the Senate and the Ways and Means Committee of the House respectively.[64] The Wagner-Murray-Dingell bill, the health provisions of which were expected to cost $2.5 billion annually by 1955, was the most comprehensive of the wartime health care measures proposed for postwar America.[65] A complex, voluminous bill comprising nearly 200 pages, which touched on many phases of the emerging welfare state, its provisions for medical care were patterned closely after the British health system. The differences between the two systems reflected Britain's more extensive experience and also differences in the customs and governmental organizations of the two countries.[66]

In briefest summary, the Wagner-Murray-Dingell bill was a hybrid that combined traditional employment security provisions with health coverage. It proposed the "single unified system of national social insurance" Altmeyer and the SSB had envisioned. The bill had twelve titles, including extension of old-age pensions to previously excluded groups, such as domestic and agricultural workers; permanent and temporary disability benefits; and maternity leave benefits. It replaced the state-federal unemployment insurance system with a fully national one. Although the bill included a title to increase funding for public assistance to "dependent persons"—the aged, the blind, and children—it left the administration of those programs to the states, again leaving the poor and women out of the social insurance system. Public health measures were gone from the picture. Under the proposed bill, the social insurance program would be funded by a payroll tax: 6 percent from workers' salaries up to $3,000 and 6 percent from employers. Fully one-fourth of the revenues generated would be dedicated to a comprehensive program of medical care, hospital expansion, medical education, and research under the auspices of the surgeon general. The USPHS would handle the technical aspects of the health program, but the surgeon general would be required to consult with the SSB and to have the approval of the head of the Federal Security Administration. Administrative and financial matters would be vested directly in the Social Security Board.[67]

With this bill, the SSB hoped to achieve its long-standing objectives of making contributory social insurance the centerpiece of the welfare state and of running the entire social welfare program by squeezing out other agencies and boards, such as the Children's Bureau with its EMIC program and the NRPB, which wanted to group public assistance, social insurance, and public employment programs under the rubric of "public aid," with no one program being more socially valid than the others. Likewise, the SSB proposed to shunt aside competing ideas about the organization of medical care. The proposed insurance coverage included medical care by general practitioners and specialists, hospitalization, and laboratory costs, but many of its points were written into the law with the expectation that they would be jettisoned at the first sign of opposition. Practitioners, for example, could decide for themselves whether to be remunerated on a fee-for-service, per capita, or salary basis, whereas hospital benefits might be paid on a cash indemnity basis or by the surgeon general approving service contracts. What the bill did not address specifically were possible incentives for supporting the development of group practice plans, health centers, or occupational safety and industrial hygiene programs.[68]

Besides broadening existing programs and extending social security principles into new and controversial fields like health insurance, the most striking feature of the Wagner-Murray-Dingell bill was its intent to nationalize programs that had previously been conceived in terms of federal encouragement to *state* initiative. This centralizing tendency derived from the greater latitude for federal activity that the trend of Supreme Court decisions after 1937 had afforded, and a growing conviction on the part of some New Deal liberals that the wartime experience proved the greater efficiency and comprehensiveness of federal oversight of welfare services.[69]

The Wagner-Murray-Dingell bill marked the start of a new, intensified political debate that continued into the postwar years. When Congress reconvened from its summer recess on September 14, 1943, the battle line between the bill's supporters and opponents was sharply drawn, with rhetoric and money the principal weapons of its opponents. The lineup of forces supporting the legislation was virtually identical with that of the 1939 national health bill: health care reformers, organized labor, the National Farmers Union, social service organizations, and the "medical New Dealers." Even the arguments were familiar: the poor did not have a free choice of physicians, which this bill gave them; doctors' incomes would not be reduced, because those who wanted to continue practicing privately could do so; and standards of medical care would be raised in all regions of the country, because participating physicians would have easier access to specialists, modern equipment, and technical help.[70] William Green, president of the AFL, asserted that the bill was "the fruit of a five-year study by experts on the staff of the American Federation of Labor, which will give the proposed program full sponsorship and support."

Philip Murray, head of the CIO, affirmed that "labor is willing to pay its fair share of the increased amount required for greater benefits" but preferred that the benefits be supported largely "by levies on the swollen incomes and fortunes."[71]

Drs. Channing Frothingham and John P. Peters, spokesmen for the "medical New Dealers," announced in December 1943 that they supported national health security in principle, but they wanted "definite and important changes" written into the bill to reflect the priorities of academic physicians and group practitioners. These included establishing a pilot project with smaller population groups before going nationwide; replacing the mandatory contribution feature with a tax-supported system; strengthening the provisions for group practice and outpatient medical services; affirming the role of specialists in treating certain diseases and illnesses (including diabetes, venereal disease, and mental illness); local administration of the program; and according greater weight in policy-making decisions to the surgeon general's and Social Security administrator's advisory councils respectively. A second prestigious medical body, the Physicians Forum for the Study of Medical Care, endorsed amendments to the legislation to include dental and nursing care and the training of additional specialists in fields such as pediatrics and obstetrics.[72]

Apart from these two organizations, individual physicians who considered the AMA's position on the Wagner-Murray-Dingell bill inflexible and reactionary also endorsed the legislation. One Boston physician told a gathering of social workers that the AMA's authoritarian organizational structure and voting procedures had silenced the voice of liberal and academic physicians from expressing "sound progressive thought." In a devastating critique of the AMA's arguments against changes in the organization and delivery of health care, he asserted that it was salaried physicians and scientists working in university, foundation, and government laboratories, rather than private practitioners, who produced the cutting-edge research that created medical advances.[73] He also cast doubt on the AMA's claim that it served the best interests of the patient and the profession, noting that it had opposed at one time or another the report of the CCMC, the Blue Cross Hospital Plan, the Group Health Association of Washington, D.C. (opposition that the Supreme Court judged to be in violation of the laws of free enterprise), and the encouragement of multispecialty group practice. His plea for the organization's cooperation in writing a better bill fell on deaf ears, as the AMA was wedded to retaining as much of the status quo as it could.[74]

Although health care reformers were sharply divided over the details of the Wagner-Murray-Dingell legislation, they supported it reluctantly in the absence of an alternative. The SSB's power play to gain control of all aspects of social welfare had alienated other federal agencies, whereas several prominent reformers, including Edgar Sydenstricker and Michael M. Davis, who agreed that public financing of health care was a necessary first step, had reservations because the bill made no attempt to restructure the medical delivery system. These more militant voices in the reform camp insisted the bill was too incremental and overly solicitous of organized medicine's interests.[75]

The AMA, meanwhile, had opened an office in Washington in September 1944 to monitor the bill's progress and to coordinate with its political arm, the National Physicians' Committee for the Extension of Medical Service, to kill it.[76] Insurance companies, the Pharmaceutical Manufacturers Association, the AHA, the Catholic and Protestant Hospital Associations, the American Bar Association, and other groups that had been rallied took their cue from *JAMA* editor Dr. Morris Fishbein, who launched a scathing attack on the Beveridge Plan for spawning the "un-American" Wagner-Murray-Dingell bill, which he said threatened private enterprise, elevated the surgeon general to "a virtual 'gauleiter' of American medicine," and created a dangerous bureaucracy that would alter the American way of life.[77]

The AMA's Council on Medical Service and Public Relations, the all-black National Physicians' Committee, and the AMA's business and commercial allies echoed similar themes in defense of the free enterprise system and criticized the interventionist New Deal regulatory state.[78] The Insurance Economics Society of America viewed the degree of government intervention proposed in the Wagner-Murray-Dingell bill as an issue of human rights versus "state slavery." Praising the merits of private voluntary accident and health insurance systems, the society insisted, "We can do a better job than can the federal or any state government." The head of the Federal Life Insurance Company condemned the "socialistic" elements who argued that social problems could be solved "only through the building of another immense Bureau of Political Patroller, serving under the paternal guidance of starry-eyed, impractical professors with the complete domination of the insurance business."[79] *Advertising Age* accused the administration of succumbing to the social service worker mentality that imposed "the constant protection and assistance of the great national government in Washington" on every citizen.[80]

Driving the hostility was the private insurance companies' fear that government-financed health insurance "would cause the elimination of about 80 percent of the business now written by accident and health companies, a 350 million dollar industry." The proposed legislation, one casualty company executive worried, would insure wage earners so fully that there would be no margin left for supplemental policies. What he conspicuously ignored was that private insurance reached only a relatively small percentage of the population and offered only limited protection: a cash benefit to the policyholder, with dependents usually excluded. The individual private policy generally insured against wage loss in the event of temporary disability, but it hardly touched the costs of medical care. Even group insurance, which normally provided the best type of coverage, often did not meet the needs of specific classes of employees or lacked portability. Because premiums varied according to the anticipated rate of claims within a particular group, this type of insurance often was the most expensive for those whose need was greatest. As proponents of the Wagner-Murray-Dingell bill noted, even the Blue Cross Hospital Insurance Plan, with 14 million subscribers, arguably the most successful private voluntary plan, still left 110 million Americans uncovered. Its rate of growth in 1943, the year of the nation's highest national income, had leveled off, a worrisome sign to advocates of health security.[81]

Joining the AMA and the insurance industry in opposition to the bill's mandatory provisions were the leading hospital associations. The AHA adopted as policy in 1942 a request that the Roosevelt administration defer "the inclusion of hospitalization payments in the Social Security Program" and, in lieu of government intervention, encourage the extension of Blue Cross–like voluntary plans and the cooperation of hospitals in developing local nonprofit plans of medical service. Monsignor Maurice F. Griffin, an AHA trustee, condemned the proposed legislation as another "soak-the-rich" scheme.[82]

As debate over the merits of the bill heated up, each side claimed to have the support of public opinion. The vice president of *Hospital Management* cited a Gallup poll that "reduced to an absurdity the fiction of a popular demand for an American Beveridge plan." Sixty-six percent of those questioned had never heard of the British proposal, and only 13 percent were familiar with any of its provisions. Supporters of the Wagner-Murray-Dingell bill retorted that this finding was misleading, because when the questioners asked about health insurance specifically, a considerably different response was elicited. They cited an August 1943 Gallup poll that revealed that 59 percent of Americans favored extending the Social Security system to cover medical and hospitalization expenses; 75 percent of those who supported compulsory health insurance said they would be willing to accept a substantial increase in payroll taxes to finance such a program.[83]

The Committee for the Nation's Health (CNH) analyzed fourteen polls and surveys taken shortly after the introduction of the Wagner-Murray-Dingell bill to illustrate how easily polling data could be manipulated by the wording of the question. Negative responses increased when a survey described federally underwritten health insurance as "government-controlled medicine," "socialized medicine," "compulsory health insurance," or "a new tax for paying people's doctor bills." The approval rating went up when the same plan was presented as "insurance for which the worker helps pay," "a means of providing more low-cost medical care" (not merely paying bills), "a plan supported by the president," or "a method similar to systems already in operation." People, in other words, were generally less prone to recognize issues by names than by descriptive phrases, the CNH concluded. A more accurate picture of informed public opinion would have been attained had pollsters worded their questions around the issue of health insurance.[84]

Meanwhile, organized medicine and its business allies expended huge sums of money to defeat the health provisions. *JAMA* sold more than a million dollars' worth of advertising space to commercial interests allied to the medical profession, a large chunk of which went into lobbying against the bill. The all-black National Physicians' Committee suddenly had seemingly unlimited funds: it bombarded its membership with leaflets propagandizing against the bill, flooded the press with handouts, and distributed more than a million copies of its pamphlet *Abolishing Private Medical Practice*. The bill's supporters did not come near matching their opponents' war chest.

The bill itself lay dormant in committee, a victim of inertia, deep concerns about the efficacy of the New Deal regulatory state, and opposition from Republicans and conservative Southern Democrats. Even liberals hesitated to advance the legislation at a time when the war demanded political harmony and belt-tightening. Few among the Democratic leadership in Congress, including those who insisted on equity in sharing the burden of wartime sacrifices, believed the war should be used to advance a major new reform initiative, particularly when there was little voter support for it.[85] Without Roosevelt's endorsement, the initially high expectations of the legislation's supporters began to give way to dashed hopes. But belatedly and in response, perhaps, to expressions of concern about the general direction of his postwar domestic policies and a forthcoming presidential election campaign, the president inched slowly toward an endorsement of the legislation. On January 11, 1944, in his annual message to Congress, Roosevelt called for an "Economic Bill of Rights" that included "the right to adequate medical care" and "the right to adequate protection from the economic fears of old age, sickness, accident and unemployment." He linked the interests of the consumer, patriotism, and nationalism in concrete language that the ordinary American comprehended by defining the nation's war aims in terms of the economic expectations of its people, which were about security. Economic security included access to decent, affordable health care.[86]

Those reformers and policy makers who saw the expansion of state capacity during the war as an opportunity to implement their particular vision of political economy responded quickly. Eight days later after the president's address to Congress, the SSB called for national health insurance as part of the Social Security system.[87] In mid-August 1944, the Budget Bureau also produced a white paper on full employment that called for higher standards of health care. Then Roosevelt, after his reelection that fall and with the end of the war at last in sight, seemingly set the stage for personal sponsorship of the health security bill. In his budget message of January 1945, he encouraged Americans' sense of entitlement by calling for "extended social security, including medical care," and in his 1945 State of the Union message, he promised to "communicate further" with Congress on this subject.[88]

Encouraged by the president's address, the bill's sponsors submitted a new version of the Wagner-Murray-Dingell bill once the new Congress assembled. As revised, this bill lacked the social insurance provisions pertaining to veterans that the original version had included, but these—minus the health insurance title of the original bill—were incorporated into what became the G.I. Bill of Rights that Congress passed. The presumption was that Roosevelt would press ahead on health insurance once the war was over, and indeed, the SSB had been drafting a special presidential message on health security.[89] Roosevelt never delivered the message. The fall congressional elections had not substantially weakened the conservative coalition in Congress, and the combination of fears of inflation in the economy and adverse military setbacks in late 1944 forced the White House to postpone endorsing the revised Wagner-Murray-Dingell bill. Roosevelt died on April 12, 1945, having neither delivered the SSB's health message nor endorsed the revised health security bill, which also languished in committee.[90]

The onset of World War II and the defeat of the Wagner national health bill and the various versions of the Wagner-Murray-Dingell bill did not signal the "end of reform." Postwar reconversion would put all the old questions of political economy and social structures, including national health security, back on the national political agenda. The New Deal and the war had left legacies of an enlarged state capacity and an expanded sense of entitlement, which created ripe conditions for the activist state of post–World War II America to pursue a new push for comprehensive medical care, including national health insurance.

This legacy was not immediately apparent during the war years, when the huge reservoir of goodwill toward liberal initiatives that President Roosevelt's 1936 electoral victory had forged ran dry by 1942. Democrats retained control of the wartime presidency and Congress, but the latter body's conservative tendencies became more pronounced, as Southern Democrats, fearing that the expansion of state capacity would disturb the region's racial patterns and low-wage labor practices, cooperated with Republicans to repeal many of the New Deal's programmatic achievements and the agencies that supported them. The erosion of congressional support for liberal measures did not occur in a vacuum. It rested on growing popular disaffection with many aspects of the New Deal, particularly taxes, deficits, and the rampant growth of government bureaucracy. In this hostile political environment, Roosevelt could ill afford to alienate organized medicine and its business allies, whose support was essential to waging a successful war.[91] They, in turn, used this dependency to pursue a divide-and-conquer strategy to influence the health reform debate by cultivating legislators who composed the conservative coalition, by smearing the reputations of "liberal" opponents in the Democratic Party, and by playing on the public's fear of an impersonal, alien, and "un-American" bureaucracy.[92]

Health reformers were, perhaps, less surprised by Congress's unwillingness to pass the 1939 national health bill or the Wagner-Murray-Dingell bills than they were disheartened by President Roosevelt's consistent failure to match his rhetorical support for health security, which raised Americans' sense of entitlement, with the political clout to make it a reality. The reformers also failed to acknowledge that the politics of the 1940s differed from the politics of the 1930s, and that conservative opposition alone did not cause the change. By their continued divisions over the course of health care reform, its financing, its rules governing eligibility, and its administration, they were as much to blame as the president.

Some Roosevelt admirers confessed to weariness with certain of the liberal causes for which they and the president had long fought, particularly once the wartime economic boom made them seem superfluous. Others watched with dismay as Roosevelt made increasing concessions to conservatives in the name of the war effort, or as he proved unwilling to take a liberal stance on important policy issues. They refused to accept that he could not push on all fronts and that, on health security, Roosevelt preferred to expand the supply of medical care rather than to guarantee access to it. On this as on other issues, he repeatedly deflected liberal proposals by insisting that "we must start winning the war ... before we do much general planning for the future." His exclusion of leading liberals from his wartime administration signaled that the president's commitment to the New Deal's domestic agenda had cooled, at least until the war was behind him.[93]

The president's death on April 12 created a void in the health reformers' political universe, leaving them to enter the postwar world in search of a new leader who would find a more politically palatable approach that defined a role for government in the funding and delivery of health care within a free market economy, without the bureaucratic tyranny of a totalitarian State. The ill-fated national health bill had been the framework within which health security as a right of citizenship had been fought. Its successor, the Wagner-Murray-Dingell bill, was neither the "socialized medicine" its detractors charged nor the comprehensive attack on ill health that reformers wanted. It was an attempt to accomplish as much as possible under the umbrella of a broadened Social Security law that itself lacked popularity in many quarters.[94] Even its critics initially thought that it might pass congressional scrutiny. Brigadier General Frederick W. Rankin, the departing president of the AMA, predicted that "some form of national health service as an integral function of the state" was on the horizon.[95] But that was not to be. The overwhelming majority of military physicians, upon return to civilian life, engaged in private practice.[96] For them and their business allies—the powerful and wealthy advertisers of drugs, medical and surgical equipment, foods, vitamins, cigarettes, and other tonics and sedatives, the Wagner-Murray-Dingell bill had threatened to change the existing health and sickness economy and to undermine their profits.[97]

A combination of circumstances, then, contributed to the Wagner-Murray-Dingell bill's defeat and, with it, the reformers' best opportunity to go for the grand, comprehensive health plan for the next fifty years, when new crises arising from out-of-control medical costs and the presence of more than 40 million uninsured Americans would force Washington to reexamine the entire health care delivery system and its financing. Until then, reformers of the post–World War II period lobbied for health care reform, with the Wagner-Murray-Dingell bill defining the parameters of the battles over health security and forming the legislative basis of all health insurance bills Congress considered from 1945 to 1950.

The post–World War II period also created new stresses within the ranks of the prewar health reformers, forcing them to rethink both their vision and their tactics. National health security remained the publicly articulated goal, but the strategy for achieving it came into question. Despite being bloodied, some reformers doggedly adhered to bringing about universal health security with one fell stroke of the federal pen; others, like Edgar Sydenstricker, I. S. Falk, Josephine Roche, Wilbur Cohen, and many of the leaders of organized labor (notably the AFL), were dispirited by the bruising wartime battles over health care reform and believed that the prospect that Congress would enact universal health coverage after the war was remote. They redirected their energies toward the creation of a capitalist private welfare state. Even as they paid lip service to the ideal of universal health coverage as a right of citizenship, they looked for other avenues, such as collective bargaining, to achieve pensions and health care coverage. They believed that the political system could better handle an incremental process. The legislative triumph of health security for the aged in the 1960s seemingly confirmed the correctness of this course of action.[98]

# THREE
## HEALTH, SECURITY, &
## THE COLD WAR, 1945–1951

The postwar political scene that began to unfold in the United States in the fall of 1945 promised to be very different from the prewar period. The FDR era was over, leaving the Democrats leaderless, confused, and badly divided along an ideological fault line just when unity among the major interest groups that had composed the New Deal coalition was most required to confront the pressing problems of demobilization, rampant inflation, labor unrest, civil rights agitation, and the beginnings of the cold war. The Republican Party was also divided ideologically, but after more than twenty years of wandering in the political wilderness, Republicans were determined to recapture control of the national government. Indeed, most Americans assumed that the new political era would be one of Republican dominance, relaxation, and normalcy after the long years of national emergency and crisis. But these hopes were soon frustrated.[1]

Harry S. Truman, who succeeded to the presidency on April 12, 1945, was the symbol of the Democrats' declining fortunes and the natural target of Republican attacks. Entering the Oval Office under incredibly difficult circumstances, Truman responded at first indecisively to the challenge of managing the nation's reconversion from war to peace and quickly angered key elements of the New Deal coalition: liberals, farmers, consumers, and union members. This encouraged conservative Democrats to hope that Truman's moderate views might lead him into their camp, but he never committed himself to their cause. In fact, Truman did just the opposite, and more than Roosevelt, he approached health security as a vital national interest, the social equivalent of economic and military security. Unlike his predecessor in the White House, he made health security a cornerstone of his domestic policy.[2]

Truman's attitude toward health security derived from his experiences prior to and after entering the White House. As a judge in Jackson County, Missouri, he had witnessed firsthand the plight of the poor and underprivileged, the devastation that lack of money to pay for doctor and hospital bills had caused his neighbors. As a young artillery officer in World War I and later as U.S. senator, he had been troubled by the large numbers of young men found physically disqualified for military service.[3] As vice president, he had spoken of his interest in national health security to the highest-ranking officials of the AMA, and though he emphasized his preference for having organized medicine draft such a program, he did not rule out federal participation. The onset of the cold war and the enactment of universal military training further persuaded Truman that the successful implementation of Selective Service depended on the good health of the nation's youth. On February 2, 1945, writing to the AMA secretary, Dr. Olin

West, on the status of the nation's health, Truman voiced the "hope that we can find a practical solution to our problems."[4]

Truman's optimism was misplaced. The more he warmed to the idea, the more adamant the AMA became in its opposition to federal participation in any prepayment program for medical care. It rejected an invitation from Senator Robert F. Wagner to propose modifications to a newly revised national health bill that he, Senator Murray, and Representative Dingell had been drafting. Their efforts came under vicious assault from *JAMA*, which claimed in spring 1945 that the bill had been written without input from the AMA. The accusation precipitated a furious exchange of charges and countercharges until finally, in July, the AMA released its own "Constructive Program for Medical Care." The core of the AMA's fourteen-point proposal left no room for compromise in its call to expand private health insurance plans and in its disavowal of federal participation. It demanded that "revolutionary changes" in health services be postponed while so many physicians were still in the armed forces.[5]

The AMA's intransigence only reinforced Truman's conviction that federal participation in a health security program was a necessity. On May 4, 1945, he spoke to Judge Samuel Rosenman and Budget Director Harold Smith about expanding the Social Security Act's safety net to encompass health security as a right of citizenship. Eleven days later, he requested that Wagner, Murray, and Dingell discuss the Social Security implications of their revised health bill with Judge Rosenman; the following day, he informed the budget director that he would send Congress a message on health care and instructed him to provide material for it to Watson Miller, head of the Federal Security Agency (FSA).[6] Finally, in June, Wagner and Murray introduced their newly revised health security bill (S. 1050) in the Senate, and Dingell offered a companion measure (H.R. 3293) in the House. The president came very close to endorsing the legislation that day, but to the consternation of progressive Democrats, he left himself some wiggle room in speaking of it to reporters.[7]

That summer, Rosenman worked on drafting sections of the president's health message, drawing on the expert knowledge of Arthur Altmeyer, who had produced a lengthy document on Social Security expansion, Wilbur Cohen, and Dr. I. S. Falk of the Social Security Administration (SSA), health reformers such as Dr. Michael Davis of the CNH, and medical philanthropist Mary Lasker. By late July, Rosenman completed a first draft of the health message, shortly before Truman departed for Potsdam.[8] Meanwhile, on September 6, 1945, three weeks after V-J Day, Truman unmistakably revealed his progressive inclinations in a comprehensive twenty-one-point message to Congress. Many of the president's points dealt with the short-term reconversion problems facing the nation, but his message also heralded his administration's determination to expand the welfare programs of the New Deal, and he promised to follow up with specific messages on health, social security, and education.[9] Truman's message garnered few bouquets from congressional conservatives, particularly Southern and rural Democrats, who held seniority on key congressional committees and who steadfastly opposed any urban-based and labor-oriented reform, and Republicans, who sensed victory in the 1946 congressional elections and were in no mood to cooperate with the administration. The Wagner-Murray-Dingell bill quickly became a test of the conservative coalition's determination to obstruct Truman's postwar reform program; conservatives held the bill captive in the Finance Committees of both the House and the Senate.[10]

In a fruitless attempt to circumvent the coalition, health reformers and their congressional allies then pondered a variation of S. 1050, one that did not mention finances and that would, they hoped, be referred to different committees, possibly to Senator Murray's Education and Labor Committee and to a House committee less hostile than Ways and Means. Meanwhile, Wagner, Murray, and Dingell decided to time the bill's reintroduction to coincide with Truman's health message. Though the president was aware that the AMA would oppose federal intervention, he decided to make health security a priority of his domestic agenda. His message to Congress would signal that he no longer intended to woo lawmakers but that he would prod them to act.[11]

Rosenman, meanwhile, continued to revise the president's health message to Congress. In a preemptive strike on October 30, the president publicly upbraided the tax-writing committees of both houses for holding up his legislative agenda. His speech to a national radio audience was intended to forestall a report of the Ways and Means Committee expected to be hostile to developing a national health care program through the Social Security system. Then, on November 12, Rosenman finally sent the completed health message to the White House.[12]

Truman was ready to deliver on his September promise. On November 19, 1945, he sent Congress the first of several messages devoted exclusively to health security. The first part of his message outlined the nation's unmet health needs; the second presented the administration's proposals for their solution. Truman urged Congress to enact a comprehensive health security program by providing federal grants to construct hospitals and other health facilities; to fund medical research and education; to expand public health services; and to address the health needs of mothers and children. However, the heart of the program was the proposal for universal health coverage. To protect against economic insecurity due to illness, Truman wanted Congress to establish two systems of social insurance: one covering loss of wages from sickness and disability, the other providing workers and their dependents comprehensive medical services prepaid through Social Security taxes. To deflect criticism of his health plan, Truman emphasized that consumers of health care would be free to choose their doctors and hospitals and that this was not socialized medicine, because "socialized medicine means that all doctors work as employees of government."[13]

In spirit and content, President Truman's health message was a throwback to Roosevelt and the early days of the New Deal and reflected the vital role that staff assistants such as Rosenman, who were carried over from the Roosevelt administration, played in the formulation of Truman's health policy. But unlike FDR's uncertain commitment, Truman's sponsorship of a national health security program represented a major breakthrough, the culmination of efforts dating back more than a quarter of a century to gain presidential support. Health reformers had, at last, been given a clear presidential mandate. "There are educational hills, organizational swamps, and political rivers to cross," Dr. Michael M. Davis of the liberal CNH declared. "But a presidential message is a milestone, nevertheless, from which past progress may be measured."[14]

Glossed over at the time, but highly significant for the future of health care reform over the next two decades, was the increasingly central role that experts within the federal bureaucracy who had mastered the complexities and politics of benefits, eligibility, taxes, and the administration of public policy would play in lending programmatic substance to the expansion of the post–World War II welfare state. The influence of welfare experts and technicians such as Wilbur Cohen and I. S. Falk, who had received their political scars in the health care battles of the Roosevelt and Truman administrations, were critical to drafting Medicare, in which the principle of federally financed health care coverage would finally be embedded in law.[15]

Public reaction to the president's health message was decidedly mixed, especially on the issue of health insurance. During the war years, no less than 58 percent of Americans polled had favored a tax-supported federal health system. After V-J Day, the response was no longer clear-cut; the peacetime nation was more evenly divided, but health reformers tended to discount the results. The CNH, after analyzing one Gallup poll, concluded, as we have seen, that it "illustrates startlingly how totals can be manipulated by the wording of the question"[16] With postwar savings accounts bulging because of lingering consumer controls, more Americans were now able to participate in private prepayment medical plans. The nonprofit Blue Cross and Blue Shield hospital and surgical expense plans, commercial health insurance coverage, and nonprofit consumer-sponsored medical cooperatives were all expanding accordingly.[17]

Both organized medicine and health reformers were cognizant of these trends, although they drew different conclusions from the figures. One Oklahoma physician wrote his congressional delegation in December 1945 that the president's rationale was faulty and labeled his proposal "Socialized Medicine, pure and simple" and urged that it "meet the ignominious defeat it deserves."[18] The conclusion the Truman administration drew from comments such as this and from the polls was that a vigorous educational campaign was necessary to mobilize public opinion behind the president's program. The effort would require strong executive leadership, unity of purpose, and a great deal of good luck.[19]

The health reform movement of the immediate postwar period lacked all these essentials. The president failed to follow up on his initial and decisive endorsement of a national health security program with the kind of articulate leadership the movement needed to broaden its base of support, particularly among middle- and working-class voters.[20] Except for a few passing references to a "national health program" in 1946, Truman did not express himself publicly enough or often enough to educate the average American to its need. Oklahoma Democratic Senator Elmer Thomas, a foe of the Wagner-Murray-Dingell bill, observed that "so little sentiment has developed in favor of the proposal that no action has been taken."[21] This may not have been entirely Truman's fault, busy as he was trying to cope with the dizzying succession of domestic crises that overwhelmed both the nation and the Democratic Party in the transition to a peacetime economy. But his inaction clearly diminished the possibility of securing health legislation in 1946.

Truman, however, did bear responsibility for his administration's inability to present a united front on the issue. This lack of unity and his seeming inability to handle the problems of postwar conversion and the Soviet Union also contributed to liberals' disillusionment with his administration. In April 1946, prior to the Senate's hearings on the revised Wagner-Murray-Dingell bill (S. 1606) embodying his national health program, dissension over its scope, content, and urgency erupted within the executive branch. Whether to transfer the functions of the Children's Bureau, particularly the Emergency Maternity and Infant Care program, to the FSA, as provided for in the Reorganization Act of 1945, threatened to alienate the same women's organizations whose help the administration needed on health care reform.[22]

Surgeon General Thomas Parran's ardor for national health security had also abated, which future FSA Administrator Oscar Ewing unfairly attributed to his being a physician with an affinity for the AMA.[23] Parran supported federal subsidies for construction of medical facilities and for expanded state systems of public health care, but he did not support funding for compulsory health insurance. This put him at odds with both the FSA and the SSA, which argued that the key to the success of the program depended on the same principle of compulsory enrollment that underpinned the Social Security Act. The chief medical director of the Veterans Administration (VA), Major General Paul Hawley, also opposed compulsory health insurance, for programmatic and philosophical reasons. In a classic turf battle, Hawley feared that the latest version of the Wagner-Murray-Dingell bill would threaten the VA's growing complex of medical facilities and services for disabled veterans, and he declared that American medicine did not need the government to tell it how to solve its problems.[24]

Spearheading the lobbying for the bill was Dr. Michael Davis and the CNH, a small, select group of about 2,100 liberals who lent their support to the administration's health program. About half of the CNH's budget of $50,000 came from the philanthropic Rosenwald family, with the other half coming from Albert D. and Mary Lasker, philanthropists with a long-standing interest in medical research. With Davis at the helm, the CNH provided technical information for sponsors of health legislation, prepared and distributed promotional literature to the news media, coordinated the activities of proponents of national health insurance, and, most important, lobbied still-uncommitted organizations to endorse the administration's health security program.[25]

Given the powerful influence of its opponents, the CNH desperately needed allies, but it could count on the support of only a few national splinter groups whose members represented but a small fraction of their respective fields. In the medical profession, the CNH drew support from small groups of mainly Eastern and academic practitioners, such as the 1,000-member Physicians Forum and the 30-member Committee of Physicians for the Improvement of Medical Care; the dissident Dentists' Committee for the Passage of the Wagner-Murray-Dingell Bill; and the 4,000 black physicians of the National Medical Association. A few industrialists; radical farm organizations; consumer groups; and religious, philanthropic, civil rights, and liberal political action organizations also endorsed the administration's health security program. Organized labor had emerged from the war reduced to a special-interest group rather than a force for social-democratic change. Its postwar militancy caused it to further lose public favor, so that its endorsement of the Wagner-Murray-Dingell bill rang hollow. Despite organized labor's profession of support for universal health coverage, labor leaders continued to bargain with employers for private insurance coverage.[26]

The AMA, meanwhile, had carefully crafted its response to the president's health proposal so as to curry political and popular favor, even as it rejected national health insurance, the key element in the administration's plan. In December 1945, the AMA's House of Delegates endorsed a fourteen-point program for medical care that included the expansion of public health services for the indigent, preventive medicine programs, the extension of voluntary private hospitalization and sickness insurance, and the Hill-Burton "Hospital Construction" bill (S. 191), a measure tracing its origin back to the Wagner health bill of 1939, which would dedicate federal money to building up the medical infrastructure, especially hospitals and training physicians. Then, in February 1946, the AMA launched its own preemptive strike against compulsory health insurance by unveiling its Associated Medical Care Plans, a scheme to promote nationally the private surgical Blue Shield prepayment plans sponsored and controlled by its constituent state medical societies. By offering the public a unified nonprofit health insurance system couched in the rhetoric of social and economic voluntarism as opposed to the regimentation of the war years, the medical establishment hoped to persuade Americans that "a voluntary sickness insurance system developed with features peculiar to the American way of life is better for the American people than a federally controlled compulsory sickness insurance system."[27]

By the time the Senate began hearings on S. 1606 (the Wagner-Murray-Dingell bill), the AMA was neither alone in its determination to defend voluntarism nor without powerful allies. Republican Senator Robert A. Taft of Ohio, the outspoken champion of business interests and strict constructionist of the Constitution, with one eye cast on the forthcoming congressional elections that fall and the other on the presidency, seized on the administration's health proposal to spearhead the reversal of the New Deal, even as Senator Murray, chair of the Education and Labor Committee, invoked his prerogative to schedule hostile witnesses in order to minimize the AMA's influence.[28]

Murray's end-run tactic ran afoul of Taft, the ranking minority member of the committee. Within minutes of the opening gavel, the Ohio Republican and Murray became embroiled in a heated exchange over whether S. 1606 was, in fact, socialistic, particularly after Murray had exhorted witnesses to refrain from using the terms *communistic* or *socialistic* in reference to the administration's health bill.[29] Taft interrupted him, declaring: "I consider it socialism. It is to my mind the most socialistic measure that this Congress has ever had before it." Like the full employment bill, another Murray-sponsored initiative, Taft charged that the national health bill came straight out of the Soviet constitution. Banging his gavel, a startled Murray refused to allow Taft to continue, insisting that Senator Wagner was scheduled to speak first. But Taft persisted, demanding that he be allowed to make an opening statement regarding his intention to sponsor a substitute health bill. When Murray refused to yield, Taft rose from his chair, stalked out of the hearing room, and announced a boycott of the committee's meetings. With Taft's departure went any remaining hope that S. 1606 would attract significant Republican support.[30]

This dramatic and controversial start forced Murray to extend the committee hearings beyond the one month he had originally intended, which benefited the bill's opponents. As the testimony of one pressure group after another soon made clear, the AMA had powerful allies in its assault on S. 1606: the AHA, sponsor of the Blue Cross system of prepayment plans for hospital expenses; Protestant and Catholic hospital associations; the American Dental Association; the American Bar Association; the U.S. Chamber of Commerce; the National Grange; and even the women's auxiliary of the American Farm Bureau Federation. Oscar Ewing of the Democratic National Committee (DNC) believed that the AHA—and most likely the others—feared the retaliatory power of the AMA if it did not testify against the bill.[31] Perhaps the most damaging testimony came from the VA's General Hawley, on May 3, 1946. Despite private assurances that medical and hospital services for disabled veterans would remain untouched, Hawley refused to endorse the administration's proposal.[32]

Though Truman remained outwardly optimistic, there was almost no chance that Congress would enact the national health bill in 1945 or 1946. In the Senate, the hearings had become so politically charged that even liberal members of the Education and Labor Committee backed away from health care reform. In the House, Dingell's companion bill (H.R. 4730) remained bottled up in committee, whose chairman, Democrat Clarence F. Lea of California, a foe of organized labor, was openly hostile to compulsory health insurance. Beyond the Capitol, the League of Women Voters retracted its initial endorsement of universal health coverage, another sign of declining public support, and in mid-June, the FSA dropped the bill from its list of legislative priorities. Off to a rocky start, the postwar drive for national health insurance ended in ignominy, destroyed not only by opposition from its foes in the health and business professions and a lack of public support but also by lack of support by members of the president's own Democratic majority.[33]

A bloodied, but unbowed, Murray announced bravely a few weeks later that he would reintroduce the legislation after Congress's summer recess.[34] That fall, however, Republicans won majorities in both houses of Congress for the first time since 1928, and the party's steering committees in both houses announced that Truman's reform recommendations, including health legislation, would not be on their legislative agenda for the upcoming 80th Congress. AMA leaders breathed a deep sigh of relief, while gloom prevailed among the proponents of health reform. The CNH's Board of Directors asked itself in May of 1947: "Is a committee like this required during these years to spearhead work for a national health program? Will the existence of such a committee justify itself?"[35]

Organized labor also was despondent and no longer believed the administration was capable of enacting a national health security program. CIO leader Walter Reuther declared, "There is no evidence to encourage the belief that we may look to Congress for relief." With that, labor turned its energies toward securing protection against sickness and hospitalization through collective bargaining, a process that returned few dividends. At the end of the decade, only 380 out of 2,200 collective-bargaining agreements contained health insurance agreements. Labor-management contract benefits remained closer to a model of welfare capitalism in which the employment compensation and management-employee attributes adhered to a white-male model of participation in the workforce rather than to a genuine workers' health security program or national health care policy.[36]

Legislative prospects for enacting a health security program looked equally bleak from 1600 Pennsylvania Avenue, but nevertheless, President Truman included a request for national health insurance in his State of the Union Message on January 6, 1947. He renewed the request two days later in his first Economic Report and, on January 10, reiterated the request in his Budget Message. Cognizant of the changed political circumstances, Truman limited his request on each occasion to a few random sentences. Clearly on the defensive, he refused to abandon the fight to add health insurance to Social Security, and he opened the White House to reformers. The CNH rallied behind the president, releasing broadsides documenting the lack of sickness and hospital coverage for the two of every three Americans needing assistance. It painted a sharp difference between the president's health program and the Republicans'.[37]

The administration fought a rearguard action when the 80th Congress convened and the legislative initiative passed to the Republicans. Taft replaced Murray as chair of the Education and Labor Committee. On February 10, 1947, he and other Republican senators introduced a revised version of a health bill they had introduced the year before, which guaranteed that it would receive serious consideration. Written in consultation with AMA officials, the "national health act of 1947" (S. 545) offered a medical welfare system exclusively for the nation's indigent, financed through $230 million annually in federal grants and administered entirely by the participating states. The bill included provisions for periodic physical examinations for schoolchildren, cancer research funds, a national health agency to unify government medical activities, and a national institute of dental research.[38]

Health reformers and their congressional allies objected specifically to the bill's imposition of a means test—a mechanism to screen out individuals or families above a certain level of resources or income—to qualify for medical care. They considered this requirement especially demeaning; it excluded the poor from any voice in the administration and dispensation of medical care, and it contravened the reformers' view of health care as a right of citizenship rather than income. Senator Murray denounced the Republican bill for establishing a system of "relief medicine, through public charity, under monopolistic control," a slam at the AMA; Congresswoman Helen Gahagan Douglas of California told the nation's black physicians that the Republican bill was "an insult to the dignity of our self-supporting, self-respecting American people."[39]

Convinced that only universal coverage could adequately ameliorate the nation's health needs and determined to block the Republicans' woefully inadequate and demeaning "charity" program, the Truman administration supported an alternative measure, the "National Health Insurance and Public Health" bill of 1947 (S. 1320). Introduced by Senators Wagner, Murray, Pepper, Glen H. Taylor, J. Howard McGrath, and Denis Chavez, the Democratic alternative differed from earlier Wagner-Murray-Dingell health bills chiefly in its deference to the concerns of the Budget Bureau and to fears of a so-called health czar and by its extension of coverage to groups beyond the purview of Social Security in 1947: farmers and the self-employed, among whom were racial minorities and women. For the indigent on welfare, various government agencies would pay their premiums. More generous and comprehensive than the Republican bill, S. 1320 did not retreat on either the principles of prepaid health care or universal coverage.[40]

The introduction of the Democratic alternative was preceded by the president's second special health message to Congress, a document marking the opening salvo in President Truman's bid for reelection. White House adviser Clark Clifford had persuaded Truman that his political fortunes in 1948, an election year, depended on articulating a bold, clearly defined liberal position on domestic issues that stood in contrast to the reactionary Republicans. The objective was to short-circuit the presidential ambitions of Senator Robert A. Taft, who was threatening to preempt the health issue, and also to rebuild in advance of the presidential election the liberal coalition of labor, blacks, women, and moderate anti-Communist intellectuals, who had been critical of Truman's handling of the postwar economy and the Soviet Union.[41]

Against this background of political maneuvering, Taft commenced hearings of the Senate Health Subcommittee to consider both S. 1320, the Democratic bill filed on May 20, 1947, and S. 545, the Republican alternative. Two days earlier, President Truman had reiterated his request for national health coverage and, in an oblique reference to the Taft bill, had argued that the Social Security approach was necessary because "the poor are not the only ones who cannot afford adequate medical care." National health insurance, he insisted, would prove "far less costly and far more effective than public charity or a medical dole."[42] On the eve of the hearings, Taft announced that he did not expect Congress to act on any health legislation that session, which lent credence to the Democrats' charge that he had sponsored his national health bill (S. 545) only to gain the AMA's support in his quest for the presidency, and once the hearings began, the hostile tone of Republican Senator Forrest Donnell's interrogation of witnesses favorable to the administration's proposal reinforced this belief.[43]

To no one's surprise, the 1947 hearings were contentious from the start, but it was Senator Murray who registered the sharp opening day protest against the way the Republicans had stacked the hearing schedule in favor of the AMA. Congresswoman Helen Gahagan Douglas also roiled the waters when she testified before the subcommittee that the California witnesses were "spokesmen who speak not for the people of my State but for those groups and forces that over the years have persisted in blocking the enactment of a real health program in the State of California and who now seek to defeat a national health insurance program by giving support to a 'substitute' charity measure." New Jersey Republican H. Alexander Smith afterwards called her statement "regrettable" and one of "questionable ethics." Conservative Democrat Allen Ellender of Louisiana agreed, but his fellow Democrats, Pepper and Murray, praised her statement as an effective antidote to the pro-Taft, pro-AMA California witnesses.[44]

Murray's and Douglas's protests encouraged proponents of the administration's health program to testify on its behalf. Representatives of organized labor, consumer groups, church groups, the National Grange and the National Farmers' Union, cooperative organizations, the American Veterans Committee, the black National Lawyers Guild, and prominent health, medical, and welfare officials spoke to its merits and pointed out the flaws in the Taft alternative. As the hearing wound down to a close in the second week of July, officials from the FSA and the SSA appeared before the subcommittee to testify to the merits of S. 1320 and to criticize the charity principle embedded in S. 545 and the monopolistic control of medicine it gave to the AMA. They emphasized that the Taft bill fell short of a truly *national* health program, was inconsistent with the rest of the social insurance program, and would "lead to serious confusion and waste."[45]

Partisan politics took precedence over health reform as the hearings unfolded. Taft and the Republican leadership viewed both Truman and the Democratic Party as politically vulnerable and attempted to use the administration's health program to turn voters against the Democrats. An aggressive congressional probe into executive influence and red-baiting tactics became the Republicans' weapons of choice. If they could prove that the White House had used taxpayer dollars to lobby for the national health security bill, they might discredit the Democratic leadership. And by associating Truman's compulsory health program with a widespread public fear of Communist subversion within government agencies, they would win control of the White House and Capitol Hill.[46] In this probe, Senator Donnell was the Republicans' point man. He opened the hearings with the startling accusation that the executive agencies of the government were costing the American taxpayer $75 million a year for illicit lobbying "in behalf of a nationwide program of socialized medicine," a charge that inspired the House Subcommittee on Government Publicity and Propaganda to launch a congressional probe in July 1947 into the activities of government agencies, including the USPHS and the SSA. The subcommittee, however, found no evidence to support its "firm conclusion" that "American communism holds this [health] program as a cardinal point in its objectives, and that, in some instances, known Communists and fellow-travelers within federal agencies are at work diligently with Federal funds in furtherance of the Moscow party line in this regard."[47]

Allegations that Communists were behind the administration's health program did not cease but became the dominant theme of the Senate Health Subcommittee's hearings, which degenerated into a witch hunt to uncover the government officials who had authored S. 1320, the "socialized medicine" bill. The witch hunt was due chiefly to the influence of a Republican staff health consultant, Dr. Marjorie Shearon, who had been a subordinate of I. S. Falk in the SSA's Bureau of Research and Statistics, who had a deep antipathy toward her ex-boss. On her departure after nearly eight years of government service, she embarked on a mission to expose Falk as the mastermind of a subversive plot to nationalize American medicine. In 1947, she wrote *Blueprint for the Nationalization of Medicine*, a pamphlet alleging that Falk had masterminded a vast conspiracy from within the SSA to "sovietize" American medicine and branding proponents of national health insurance "Collaborationists, Fellow-Travelers, Appeasers, Satellites, and Gullible Accepters."[48]

Shearon's allegations, the charges of corruption, and Senator Donnell's accusatory line of questioning forced Falk to appear before the subcommittee late in July 1947 to defend himself and the bureau's activities. He cited examples of faulty documentation in her pamphlet and then produced memoranda documenting that Shearon had completely reversed her earlier position when she had expressed dissatisfaction with the initial draft of the 1939 Wagner health bill for *not* containing a provision for national health insurance, for *requiring* a means test, and for extending health care *only* to the poor.[49]

Falk's rebuttal thoroughly discredited Shearon's accusations, but that did not prevent the Republicans from retaliating by slashing the president's budget request for the Bureau of Research and Statistics. Nor did it diminish fears of a Communist conspiracy operating within the federal government. The association of national health security with "socialized medicine" stayed firmly embedded in the public consciousness and in the thinking of legislators of both political parties for more than a decade.[50] Democrats from conservative rural states of the South and Southwest were particularly susceptible to political pressures from their state and county medical societies, which very successfully identified Truman's health program with "socialized medicine." Oklahoma's Democratic congressional delegation, consisting of Carl Albert, Toby Morris, Elmer Thomas, and George Howard Wilson, regularly broke ranks with the administration in response to constituents' demands that they reaffirm their opposition to "government control of health services" and "socialized medicine."[51]

As Taft had predicted, the 80th Congress adjourned for the summer without enacting health legislation, but not before the Democratic sponsors of S. 1320 pinned the blame on the Republicans. Rhode Island Senator J. Howard McGrath left no doubt that the AMA was responsible for the failure to enact a national health program by putting documentation into the record that "reveals the gap between the social and economic point of view of American doctors and the publicity proclaimed by the officials of the AMA." McGrath's reference was to a survey conducted by Raymond Rich Associates, which identified an "urgent need" for the AMA to devise "an adequate program to meet the needs of the American people." The firm then resigned as public relations adviser on learning that the AMA's Board of Trustees had misled its own House of Delegates with respect to its recommendation. Raymond Rich released its report to the delegates directly, noting the trustees' failure to "seek the truth…, to put the public first, and to be adequate to its responsibilities." The trustees' ethical violations helped to plant seeds of doubt that the AMA truly represented the nation's physicians.[52]

President Truman, meanwhile, responded uncharacteristically to the partisan assault on his executive agencies by ignoring it and by remaining above the fray while he was building his platform for the coming presidential campaign. He also made two crucial appointments that firmly entrenched influential proponents of national health security in the leadership of the Democratic Party. In August 1947 he replaced Watson Miller with Oscar R. Ewing, the acting chairman of the Democratic National Committee and politically astute head of the liberal policy-making faction within the administration, as administrator of the FSA. Ewing made the president's health program his top priority and forged closer ties with Michael Davis and the CNH. Truman's second appointment came in October, when he selected Senator McGrath to chair the DNC.[53] The appointments were part of the larger strategy to rebuild the liberal coalition by positioning the administration for positive action on labor, civil rights, health reform, and other issues that appealed to specific blocs of voters who had supported Roosevelt and the New Deal.[54]

Wall Street financier Bernard Baruch, meanwhile, attempted to find a compromise by bridging the gap between the Democratic and Republican versions of health care reform. On November 19, 1947, he told members of the Associated Hospital Service of New York that he supported a mandatory system of private health insurance for those in the upper-income groups and insurance under Social Security for those in the low-income ranks. Baruch's proposal was intended to appeal to businessmen and conservative legislators by compromising on the issue of compulsory national health insurance. It won the endorsement of much of organized labor's leadership when, on February 13, 1948, AFL President William Green wrote to Senators Wagner and Murray recommending that in lieu of one omnibus health bill, they submit a number of individual bills, including a "simpler" insurance measure with restricted coverage.[55]

There was little reason to believe that the AMA would accept Baruch's or any other compromise. In October 1948, Major General Paul Hawley, formerly of the VA and at the time director of the Blue Cross and Blue Shield plans, proposed a voluntary plan through which unions and employers might enter into nationwide contracts for hospital and physician services. He told other Blue Cross and Blue Shield officials that Americans wanted health security, and he urged the medical profession to exercise leadership, warning, "If it does not at once cease its double-talk and double dealing with the voluntary nonprofit prepayment plans, and throw its influence squarely and honestly behind these plans, we are going to have compulsory government health insurance in this country within three years." Despite Hawley's admonition, AMA officials, with the covert assistance of the Oregon and New Jersey leaders of the Blue Shield plans, scuttled his proposal.[56]

With health reform at an impasse, Senator Murray reached out to his conservative Democratic colleagues, Alben Barkley, Lister Hill, George Russell, and other members of the Southern bloc on December 19, 1947, to join in writing a compromise health bill that would present a united Democratic front in the forthcoming presidential campaign. Nothing came of the overture once the president began to push for voting rights and equal employment opportunities for black Americans. Senator Taft, by contrast, confident that he would be the Republican presidential nominee, publicly challenged the Democrats to make national health security an issue in the forthcoming election.[57]

Election-year politics on both sides of the aisle continued to drive the agenda as legislators prepared for the opening of the second session of the 80th Congress. FSA Administrator Ewing raised the possibility of the White House convening a health conference to formulate national health goals. The conference would be an opportunity to focus public attention on health security and give the administration an opportunity to educate Americans to its need, which it had not done in 1945–1946. Ewing coupled the conference idea with two other suggestions: that the president send Congress a new special message emphasizing the differences between his health program and Senator Taft's, and that he designate a "national health week" during which each locality would inventory its health needs. That Ewing's proposals were politically motivated is beyond doubt, for he admitted to Budget Director James Webb on February 25, 1948, that "there is no chance of getting a [health] bill through this year."[58]

President Truman responded positively to the health conference idea, and to keep control of the agenda, he decided that the FSA rather than the communities should propose recommendations regarding the nation's health needs. But Ewing, recognizing that he was dealing with a hostile, economy-minded Congress, arranged instead for the incorporation of a private organization, the National Health Assembly, to sponsor the conference. President Truman welcomed the nearly 800 delegates, meeting in Washington on May 1, 1948, with a lengthy and disjointed, but still-effective, speech in which he asked the participants to formulate a ten-year program to accelerate the nation's progress against disease.[59]

The AMA, which had initially feared that the National Health Assembly would rubber-stamp the administration's demand for a radical national health program, was pleasantly surprised when the final report of the panel on medical care did not contain an endorsement of national health insurance. The administration was disappointed, but tempered its disappointment after the AMA's delegates committed the association to several resolutions: that private insurance, although voluntary, should remain the basic method of financing medical care; that state laws prohibiting nonmedical groups from organizing voluntary health insurance plans should be rescinded; and that the means test—the central feature of the Taft bill—should be discarded.[60]

The assembly's deliberations were followed by a series of events that undermined any momentum toward reform the conference might have generated. The AMA's House of Delegates rescinded the agreement to eliminate the means test that reformers found so distasteful.[61] Then the Brookings Institution released its report on health care, *The Issue of Compulsory Health Insurance,* which had been undertaken at the request of Senator H. Alexander Smith, Taft's colleague on the Labor and Public Welfare Committee. The authors of the report, George W. Bachman, a medical administrator, and Lewis Meriam, an insurance expert, employed statistical analysis to challenge Selective Service data used by President Truman to argue that the relatively poor health of the nation's youth justified establishing a national health security program. The authors found that most Americans enjoyed an exceptionally high level of medical care, and contended that compulsory health insurance would bring a huge federal bureaucracy in its wake, that the program would be more costly than private insurance, and that it would politicize the doctor-patient relationship. The authors further concluded that the country did not have the medical infrastructure of personnel and facilities to make universal health coverage viable.[62]

Health reformers condemned the Brookings report for its factual errors and the authors' biases. At the request of Senators Murray and Pepper, Michael M. Davis, of the CNH, and Dewey Anderson, director of the Public Affairs Institute, drafted a lengthy rebuttal that circulated to more than 600 media outlets as a committee print, authorized by the Labor and Public Welfare Committee, but the damage was irreparable. The AMA declared that national health insurance was unnecessary and unworkable.[63]

A further setback to health care reform occurred in July 1948 at the Democratic national convention, in Philadelphia. Davis and the CNH had lobbied the platform writers to include the specific words *health insurance* in the platform document, but they were unsuccessful. President Truman refused to intercede, probably because his political strategists deemed it unwise for him to force local Democrats to run on an issue that had become so controversial. Instead of the ringing endorsement of national health insurance that Davis and the CNH were hoping for, the party pledged itself only to the enactment of "a national health program for expanded medical research, medical education, and hospitals and clinics."[64]

Truman, mindful of his pledge to liberals and the Wallace wing of the party, made up for the *health insurance* omission in his nomination acceptance speech. He picked up the gauntlet thrown down by Senator Taft who had challenged him to make compulsory national health insurance an issue in the campaign by announcing that he would call the 80th Congress into special session to give the Republicans an opportunity to enact, among other items, their own national health program. Neither the president nor his strategists believed the Republican-controlled Congress could pass national health insurance within the two-week time frame; indeed, the issue had become so controversial that Truman's own party had avoided doing so during its long years of dominance on Capitol Hill.[65]

Once the 80th Congress reconvened, Republicans debated health reform and other issues but accomplished nothing of significance. Their failure to enact the Taft health bill provided Truman with the green light to make the Democrats' health security program a major theme in his reelection campaign. Undaunted, he set out on a 31,000-mile whistle-stop train tour during which he castigated the "do-nothing" 80th Congress. Then, on September 2, 1948, he released FSA Administrator Oscar Ewing's report on national health goals and called on the next Congress to act on its recommendations. *The Nation's Health—A Ten Year Program* was a sharp departure from the report of the National Health Assembly. While acknowledging that the assembly had not recommended health insurance through Social Security, Ewing nonetheless declared, "I have reexamined the whole matter as objectively as possible. . . , and I still find myself compelled to recommend it." Ewing's report immediately drew the ire of the AMA.[66]

In contrast to Truman's blunt style, the Republican presidential candidate, Thomas E. Dewey, ran a restrained campaign, designed to avoid rocking the boat. He refused to respond to the president's statements on health or his exaggerated charges against the 80th Congress. Some of this was deliberate—to promote unity and harmony among all Republicans—but Dewey could not easily condemn a government-sponsored health insurance system without focusing attention on the conflicting and well-publicized position advocated by his running mate, Earl Warren. As governor of California in 1945, Warren had championed a state-sponsored health insurance system over the opposition of the California Medical Association.[67]

In his final major campaign appearance, President Truman promised that Congress would soon enact a national health security program, because "the Democrats are going back in power, and we are going to see that we get it." The widespread publicity the president accorded to health security gave reformers a much-needed boost after their disappointment over the wording of the platform. Shrewd campaigning and some fortunate breaks enabled Truman to revive for a short time in the autumn of 1948 the electoral coalition that had won so many victories for the New Deal. Liberal Senator Claude Pepper, for example, enthusiastically campaigned throughout Florida for the president and helped him rebuff the challenge from Strom Thurmond and the Dixiecrats. By aligning himself with the party's liberal wing and assuming Roosevelt's mantle, Truman achieved electoral success, and his campaign rhetoric foreshadowed the program that was to become the Fair Deal.[68]

Truman interpreted his stunning upset victory and the Democrats' wresting control of Congress from the Republicans as vindication for the New Deal and a mandate for liberalism, thus guaranteeing that health security would move to the forefront of the nation's agenda. That, at least, was the perception of Oklahoma's Democratic Senator Elmer Thomas, a critic of the administration's "socialized medicine" proposal. Thomas attributed the president's victory in Oklahoma and elsewhere to the outsiders in American politics—"the colored voters" and the farmers and wage earners—and he fully expected his liberal colleagues to revive S. 1320. He called on his constituents and those of other "right-thinking" legislators to help dilute the bill's "socialistic" features, conceding that with Democrats in control of the 81st Congress, "it will be up to us to make good" on some form of health legislation because "if we do not recognize the wishes of the persons who supported our programs, then we're doomed to disappointment when the next election occurs."[69]

While anti-administration Democrats were sorting out the meaning of the president's victory, Truman confidently began his new term, believing that it was time for government to fulfill its responsibility to provide health security for the poor and the elderly. As he worked on his State of the Union message in 1949, the president penciled in the expression of his intentions, "Every segment of our population and every individual has a right to expect from his government a fair deal." Whether consciously or not, President Truman had invented the tag "Fair Deal" to distinguish his program from the New Deal. Unfortunately for the administration, the temper of both the country and the Congress proved to be even more conservative over the next four years than during the president's first term.[70] Despite pressure from northern Democrats, labor, and liberal groups for universal health coverage, the opponents of health security recovered quickly from the shock of defeat and, in December 1948, mounted a counteroffensive. The AMA's Board of Trustees rejected any accommodation or compromise on mandatory health insurance and vowed, if necessary, to deplete its financial resources to block such legislation once the

81st Congress convened. To carry through on its threat, the board built up a huge war chest by levying a special $25 assessment on each of its members and engaged the services of the high-powered San Francisco public relations firm Whitaker and Baxter to develop a campaign strategy. To protect itself from retaliation by the White House and the Internal Revenue Service, the trustees dissolved the National Physicians' Committee for the Extension of Medical Service, its primary political action group, so as not to jeopardize the AMA's tax-exempt status.[71]

As the AMA marshaled its resources, public interest in health security peaked during the winter of 1948–1949 in response to two developments: the commencement of national health service in Great Britain and the expectation that the president would again press for national health care legislation. Discussion of the one invariably led to comment on the other. Indeed, the FSA received so many inquiries about national health coverage from the media and private individuals by spring 1949 that it resorted to a form-letter response to keep abreast of its correspondence.[72]

A preponderance of the discussion was decidedly critical, especially in the print media, but individuals motivated by self-interest or personal conviction also wrote to their legislators demanding to know where they stood on the administration's "socialized medicine" bill.[73] One Oklahoma physician wrote to Democratic Senator Robert S. Kerr, a foe of the administration's proposal, to complain against Ewing's becoming "the Czar of medicine under a socialized program." It was not "the American Way of doing things," he declared. In response to one constituent, Senator Elmer Thomas wrote that he had personally witnessed "the socialistic and communistic schemes in practice in Russia," and predicted that Great Britain's Socialist Party would "beggar" its citizens through nationalization of the country's major industries, including health care. Thomas "was not in favor of the program outlined in some of the bills now pending before the Congress." One of the relatively few Oklahomans who did support the president's health care program told Thomas that "the people who voted for you and President Truman in Oklahoma want his Health Insurance Program passed"; he added, "To those of us who know about it, the program is far from being Socialized Medicine." The letter received a courteous response, but it did not change Thomas's position. Once again, the administration could expect opposition from conservative Democrats.[74]

As debate over health policy intensified, President Truman outlined his Fair Deal program in his annual State of the Union message on January 5, 1949. He again recommended "a system of prepaid medical insurance which will enable every American to afford good medical care," to be paid for by a federal payroll tax, and he asked legislators to act "without further delay." He followed up with a similar request in the economic and budget messages sent to the 81st Congress. But over the next six months, whenever reporters inquired about the specific details of the administration's health security program, the president responded in vague generalities. Since his program had not yet received budgetary approval, legislative strategy dictated that he not spell out his proposal in precise detail, a principle the administration routinely applied to this and other legislative proposals. Truman, however, did carefully distinguish between being "generally in accord with" the health security proposal that congressional reformers Murray and Dingell were preparing to file and declaring it an "administration bill." The cost of conducting business this way meant that the president would forfeit use of the press conference to persuade Americans that this health security legislation was not simply a necessity but the *right* of every citizen.[75]

The Murray-Dingell bill of 1949 (S. 5), which was referred to the Senate Committee on Labor and Public Welfare and to the House Commerce Committee, was one of seven health security bills introduced between January and May 1949 and was identical to the measure that the contentious 80th Congress had rejected. Though S. 5 had received less than unqualified presidential backing, the CNH and other health reformers were optimistic that the Senate would give it prompt consideration, but that was not to be.[76] Challenges to the bill arose from a rival anti-administration group of conservative Southern Democrats led by Senator Lister Hill of Alabama, who had not forgiven the president's civil rights initiatives, and from Republicans.

To sidetrack a federally administered system of national health coverage, Hill advocated a bipartisan proposal (S. 1456) that called for federal grants-in-aid to assist states in stimulating the voluntary enrollment of employees and rural dwellers in prepayment plans for hospital and medical care. Hill's bill would have facilitated the purchase of Blue Cross–type health plans for the poor, but it would have left the administration of the program in the hands of the states and also retained the Republicans' means test. S. 1456 had been written with the cooperation of the AHA and was cosponsored by Democrats Herbert O'Conor of Maryland and Garrett L. Withers of Kentucky and Republicans Carl Aiken of Vermont and Wayne Morse of Oregon. Despite administration opposition, Hill introduced his rival bill on March 30 and scheduled hearings before his own subcommittee beginning in May. Two weeks later, on April 14, Senator Taft revived his health care proposal to provide federal funds for medical care for the poor, when he introduced S. 1581, a revised version of the earlier Taft-Smith-Donnell bill.[77]

The task of promoting the president's health program fell primarily to the outspoken Oscar L. Ewing, who made at least a dozen major speeches on its behalf in 1949. In February, the FSA administrator appeared on the radio with the AFL's social insurance director, Nelson Cruikshank, to debate the health issue opposite New Jersey's Republican Senator H. Alexander Smith and the AMA's Morris Fishbein. Meanwhile, in response to criticism from legislators and the medical profession, the administration asked Murray and Dingell to modify their proposal to conform more closely to the health needs outlined in Ewing's 1948 report on national health goals. Working with FSA officials, they drafted the "National Health Insurance and Public Health" bill in early April and submitted it to the White

House for review. Unlike in the past, they also agreed to pursue a more flexible strategy, which would enhance the chances of passage of the noncontroversial features of the bill. On April 22, President Truman renewed his request that Congress enact a national health security program, and three days later, Senator Elbert D. Thomas of Utah introduced the "National Health Insurance and Public Health" bill (S. 1679), with Senators Murray, Wagner, Pepper, Chavez, Taylor, McGrath, and Hubert Humphrey of Minnesota as cosponsors. Representative John Dingell filed the companion bill (H.R. 4312) in the House.[78]

Even as the administration was rewriting its bill, the AMA, following the advice of Whitaker and Baxter, launched perhaps the widest-ranging and most imaginative lobbying campaign of the post–World War II era. In the process, it transformed the socialized medicine issue into a political liability for its sponsors. The objective was to defeat the president's health security program; it accomplished that through the distribution of millions of pamphlets, the widespread use of the press and radio, the mobilization of business and other groups fearful of government intervention, a letter-writing campaign to members of Congress, and organization of speakers' bureaus throughout the country. Whitaker and Baxter's blueprint also called for the AMA to launch a "National Education Campaign" from its Chicago headquarters.[79] By the end of February, the powerful state and county medical societies had received Whitaker and Baxter's "Simplified Blueprint," which outlined the tasks of the local organizations in the fight. Most notable was their adoption and forwarding of resolutions opposing compulsory health insurance to their congressional legislators. The New York State Medical Association jumped the sixty-day lead time for doing so when, in January, it voted its own levy to combat the administration's "socialized medicine" proposal.[80]

"The voluntary way is the American way," the theme of the resolutions, reflected the AMA's other long-range objective: to promote the expansion of voluntary, private health insurance similar to its physician-sponsored and physician-controlled Blue Shield plans. Rapid growth of voluntary plans would make compulsory health insurance unnecessary.[81] In June 1949, the AMA's House of Delegates took the unprecedented step of sanctioning lay-sponsored private health insurance coverage and, to placate physicians who had long objected to his intemperate outbursts, stripped Morris Fishbein of his post as editor of *JAMA*.[82] Other important lobbies lined up against the revised administration health bill, including the major welfare organizations of the Catholic church, which feared that the extension of social insurance would lead to the taxing of religious and charitable institutions, the all-black National Medical Association, the Federation of Women's Clubs, the U.S. Chamber of Commerce, and mainstream farm groups and patriotic organizations.[83] This constellation of opponents was powerful evidence of the effectiveness of Whitaker and Baxter's campaign to link the president's health program in the public mind with socialism and totalitarianism, a fear greatly magnified by the threat of Soviet espionage.[84]

On the other side of the health security debate, the financial resources of the CNH paled into insignificance. The AMA had made available to Whitaker and Baxter a war chest of $1.5 million to spend against the administration's bill, whereas the CNH raised a paltry $104,000, of which about $98,000 went into its working budget. With such limited resources, the best the CNH could do was to distribute its broadsides with special condensations of Ewing's 1948 report to members of Congress and to the liberal media. *ADA World,* the *National Union Farmer,* the *American Druggist,* and a few outspoken legislators such as Hubert Humphrey and Helen Gahagan Douglas attempted to respond to the negative assault on the administration's health program, but too often, their words were lost amid the reams of hostile messages generated by Whitaker and Baxter.[85] Michael Davis confessed that the CNH had encountered difficulty mobilizing supporters and "establishing sufficient outlets for information on the health insurance program so as to combat the distorted and prejudiced attacks being made by the AMA." Outspent, CNH was reduced to mailing each member of Congress a fact sheet—and hoped that it would be read![86]

In this atmosphere of bitter controversy, intense lobbying, charges of socialized medicine, and sharp criticism of both Truman and Oscar Ewing, any person or proposal tarred with the brush of *socialism* immediately became suspect, and health reformers of the early cold war period were never able to rid themselves or their health security programs of that onerous epithet. One insurance executive wrote to Oklahoma Representative George H. Wilson, "For God's sake, I hope you will do everything in your power to stop this insidious drift toward national socialism." Even Oklahoma Representative Toby Morris, a moderate Democrat, equated compulsory health insurance with socialized medicine. Responding to an officer of the Oklahoma State Medical Association, Morris wrote, "I am definitely and positively opposed to socialized medicine and while I believe that great progress can be made in regard to the health of our people, yet I do not at this time believe that compulsory health insurance is the answer." Given such sentiments and the financial resources of his opponents, Senator Murray, not surprisingly, was unable to muster enough votes to report the "National Health Insurance and Public Health" bill (S. 1679) out of committee.[87]

This reduced the field to two bills—the Hill-Aiken proposal (S. 1456) and Taft's "charity" bill—until Senators Ralph Flanders of Vermont and Irving Ives of New York led a group of Senate and House Republicans on May 31, 1949, in offering a third alternative (S. 1970), which did not require recipients to take a means test.[88] The Flanders-Ives bill, like the Hill-Aiken measure, sought a middle ground between Taft's "charity" bill and the administration's national health insurance measure. But unlike Hill-Aiken, it did not have bipartisan sponsorship, which greatly reduced its chance of passage, unless President Truman was willing to support it. This put the fate of the Hill-Aiken proposal squarely in the hands of the administration. If the president wanted some form of health insurance passed in 1949, he would have to compromise, particularly since there was little expectation that the conservative-dominated House Commerce Committee would report out the Dingell bill. Even had it done so, Oklahoma Democrat George H. Wilson, a member of its subcommittee, left no doubt that the Dingell bill would have undergone extensive revision in conference. "With strong administration backing it is almost sure to be reported out of the committee *so it will require careful work to make it as acceptable as possible at that point,*" Wilson wrote.[89]

The White House showed no willingness to compromise, however, as the first session of the 81st Congress wore on. Oklahoma Representative Carl Albert reported in August to a constituent on the status of the Dingell bill, "Frankly, it looks as if this bill has little, if any, chance of being reported out of the committee during the present session of Congress." Albert's assessment was correct. Last-ditch efforts to break the impasse, as when Democratic Senator Paul Douglas offered a substitute to provide coverage for catastrophic illness, went nowhere and merely annoyed the White House. The president would not budge. His pugnacious temperament would not allow him to retreat before his political enemies, but other considerations also compelled him to stick with his bold, anti-AMA health insurance plan. He could not easily shift his support to the Hill-Aiken bill without alienating key elements of the liberal coalition that had contributed to his election. The Hill-Aiken bill, coming so soon after the Taft-Hartley Act, offered nothing to organized labor; quite the opposite, for it contained the means test so repugnant to labor and liberals. Hill-Aiken also opened the door to the expansion of the physician-controlled and hospital-controlled insurance systems, the very thing the AMA was seeking. The White House's intransigence was reinforced by its belief that Congress, after the midterm elections, might be more receptive to the president's original proposal.[90]

Rather than reject the president's health security program in toto, the Senate acted by decoupling and passing four of its seven titles as separate bills, which covered federal aid to medical education; the establishment of medical research institutes; the extension and liberalization of the Hill-Burton Hospital Construction Act, which Congress had passed in 1946; and grants to assist the states in developing and maintaining adequate public health systems. The House, by contrast, approved only the Senate-passed amendment to the Hospital Construction Act, which became law in October 1949.

The administration's national health proposal had been among the most controversial and hardest-fought of all issues before Congress in 1949, but its bill was dead in the water. The Senate added insult to injury when, on August 16, 1949, it also rejected the president's "Reorganization Plan No. 1," which would have upgraded the FSA to cabinet-level status and Oscar Ewing to secretary of welfare. Twenty-three Democrats, of whom twenty represented southern states, joined thirty-seven Republicans to kill the reorganization proposal. Herein lay the president's legislative dilemma. His inability to secure a national health security program was as much due to opposition from within his own party as it was to Republican or AMA opposition. Despite the Democrats' numerical majority in both houses of Congress, the party's conservative southern wing remained overwhelmingly opposed to intrusive bureaucratic government that national health security implied, as well as to any other Fair Deal economic and social program that might benefit urban dwellers, organized labor, consumers, and racial minorities.[91]

The AMA had lobbied hard against the reorganization plan, fearing that Ewing would use his cabinet status to advance national health insurance. One newspaper, critical of the administration, editorialized that Ewing, "the principal advocate of socialized medicine in this country," had been defeated because he had made the FSA "the center of socialistic concepts of the old New Deal and the new Fair Deal." The vote was as much a referendum against Ewing and national health insurance as it was against the president's plan to streamline the executive branch.[92]

That fall, the administration suffered yet another setback after the return from Europe of a sixteen-member congressional fact-finding delegation of the House Health Subcommittee. It had been investigating the health systems of seven European countries, and Oklahoma Democrat George H. Wilson took notes as he went along. Afterwards, he talked about his impressions. In Great Britain, Wilson listened to a Scottish physician in one large London hospital and a member of the staff of King's Hospital, the teaching hospital of London University, give candid assessments of their national health system. On the positive side, he reported, these two physicians noted that the treatment of illness was no longer a matter of financial consideration; a physician could refer a patient for admission to the hospital best suited for treating his or her specific malady, without having to canvass several hospitals as in the past. But among the disadvantages they listed were the centralization of medical services at the ministry level rather than at the local level, which artificially separated hospital, preventive, and physician services; the excessive number of directives from the ministry, which overburdened physicians and administrators with paperwork; the government's failure to expand and modernize hospital facilities to accommodate the increased numbers of patients; the "phenomenal" waiting list for beds, especially at the teaching hospitals; the ban on National Health Service physicians' treating of private patients; a cap on specialists' fees; and delayed reimbursements from the Health Ministry. Both physicians agreed that whether centralization had been appropriate and whether physicians would remain "free" to practice medicine were questions that might take fifteen to twenty years to determine. One, a critic of socialism, declared as a matter of personal preference, "I would have been happier had the scheme *not* embraced the entire population, but rather limit[ed] [itself] to only those below [a] certain income bracket."[93]

For all the flaws of the National Health Service, both physicians also believed that historical circumstances had given Britain no alternative but to move toward such a plan. Two world wars had bled the country dry, leaving British medicine no choice but to abrogate part of its freedom for the common good. Even if there had not been a second conflict, one of the physicians insisted, the government—including a Conservative government—would have been obliged to extend health service to the people. In 1945, British medicine had become a political football, with all parties committed to doing something. The medical profession had concluded that retaining the status quo—keeping the government at arm's length—was not a viable option.[94]

But was the National Health Service a model for the United States? In the words of physicians who were acquainted with the practice of medicine in America, Wilson reported, it was "absurd [to think] that England would be [a] pattern for [the] U.S." Historical and geographical circumstances rendered the American problem "entirely different" from Britain's. The United States was composed of forty-eight diverse states, whereas Britain was "a tight island," which more easily facilitated the implementation of a political decision from the central government. Moreover, each nation had a different civil service tradition, which affected the administration, delivery, and reimbursement of health care. On a subjective note, one physician thought his American counterpart placed a premium on attaining a high salary, but the more important reason not to emulate the British model, he noted, was that Blue Cross plans in the United States were making "splendid progress."[95]

Wilson was "amazed" to discover that the general level of mental and chronic patient treatment in Great Britain was *much higher* than what he had observed in the United States, but as his handwritten summary and marginal notations revealed, he was more inclined to emphasize the British health system's deficiencies and to gloss over its positive features. He wrote, "Had I needed arguments to convince me s.m. [socialized medicine] would not work in US—I found them in Europe"; "more vigorously opposed than before"; "scheme [has] completely nationalized health service in England"; "All hospitals taken over"; "Drs. & Dentists became paid employees"; "Compensation not dependent upon service but rather the #s on "list"[,] so inevitable deterioration of standards"; "Healing arts in England—political football"; "all parties committed"; "even profession recognize[s] it['s] politically impossible to do away with scheme"; [therefore] more important to America to steer away of supposed enticements"; "scrutinize with utmost care"; "Arouse US [against] insidious infiltration of socialistic schemes."[96]

Upon Wilson's return to the United States, radio newsman Walter Cronkite scheduled an interview with Wilson. A list of the questions Cronkite would ask was given to Wilson beforehand. In penciled notations, Wilson jotted down his reservations about Europe's government-run socialized medicine programs. In response to Cronkite's question "What do you think the Congress in this or in the next session is likely to do with the compulsory health program?" Wilson wrote, "At present there appears not even wishful or hopeful thinking for action this year," and the future was equally uncertain. Wilson broadcast his reservations over a national radio network on October 5, 1949, and he reiterated his opposition to "regimented" medicine in speeches in Oklahoma and else-where. He told the Business and Professional Women's Club of Enid, Oklahoma, "If I had my qualms to seek arguments against socialized medicine, I found them in England."[97]

Six days later, on October 11, Dr. Joseph S. Lawrence, director of the AMA's Washington office, and the nine physician-members of Congress invited the entire fact-finding dele-gation to dinner at the University Club in Washington, D.C. Nine of the delegation at-tended. "They were unanimous in condemning the English scheme and in expressing their determined resolution that no such scheme should develop in America if they could prevent it," Lawrence reported. Republicans and Democrats alike shared that opinion. "Representative Wilson," he wrote, "gave us a most interesting account of his observa-tions and I know that he will be glad to tell it to the doctors of Oklahoma." Wilson did plan to tour his district prior to the start of the new session of Congress in January 1950, and he welcomed opportunities to speak with physicians. "We should not miss an oppor-tunity of this kind," declared Lawrence. "We hear and read reports made by people we don't know, but when somebody who is well known to us can tell the story it certainly means a great deal more, and I know that you will find Representative Wilson very help-ful in arousing physicians to the seriousness of the threat of socialized medicine which now hangs over us."[98]

Wilson's hostility to national health security illustrated how difficult it was for the ad-ministration to win the support of members of its own party for this and other health-related issues. The conflict between the White House and conservatives over the "Na-tional School Health Services" bill (S. 1411) was a case in point; it demonstrated how poisoned the congressional atmosphere had become. The bill proposed to make available free physical and medical examinations for children of school age at appropriate inter-vals, with the federal government paying for remedial procedures as needed. The AMA and its conservative allies, fearful that the measure was a liberal plot to bring in social-ized medicine through the back door, opposed its passage. Dr. Lawrence, the AMA lobby-ist, informed legislators on December 16, 1949, that "the House of Delegates naturally ob-jected to the suggestion in the bill that all remedial procedures be provided for *all* children regardless of the financial status of their parents or guardians, on the grounds that it would be initiating a compulsory national health program." The bill was subse-quently defeated.[99]

In an atmosphere of mutual suspicion and distrust, of the AMA's relentless accusa-tions that the Truman administration employed police-state tactics against its constitu-ent medical societies, it was perhaps too much to expect the president to support either the Hill-Aiken bill, a measure that further expanded the AMA's control over health coverage, or the Republican-sponsored Flanders-Ives bill. His options were limited, so it was not surprising that President Truman looked forward to the congressional elections in fall 1950 to remove some of the worst obstructionists on Capitol Hill. Until then, FSA Administrator Ewing wrote to him on January 21, he might consider approving a more limited health program, such as compulsory hospital insurance or catastrophic illness insurance, if there was a reasonable chance that Congress might go along. In the interim, Ewing advised the White House to issue a number of "clarifications" to S. 1679, the "National Health Insurance and Public Health" bill, ranging from greater emphasis on the use of private, voluntary prepayment programs to a refusal to authorize payment of health services "if there is evidence that patients abuse the [national health insurance] system."[100]

The president considered Ewing's advice, but he was reluctant to placate those who argued for a softening of his position, nor did he want to yield to his congressional detractors. His inflexibility ruled out whatever possibility might have existed of enacting a more limited health program on which to build, blending private and public participation. But the president was not alone in bearing blame for the failure to enact a national health security program. The tide of public opinion and important factions within the Democratic Party in 1950 also had swung against the president's legislative proposal. One survey disclosed that Americans of the postwar era were against "socialized" medicine by a 2.5 to 1 ratio. Oklahoma's Democratic Representative George Wilson went as far as to visit the White House to tell the president personally of his opposition to "socialized medicine." Even Jacob M. Arvey, the Cook County, Illinois, Democratic chairman and one of the party's big-city political bosses, openly stated that rank-and-file Democrats were not wedded to the administration's health plan.[101]

The AMA and its Republican allies also contributed to the failure to find a middle ground between a private health program that catered to those who could afford to pay and one that required a declaration of poverty as a precondition of coverage. Organized medicine in 1950 expended more than $2.25 million in a lobbying campaign against the administration's health plan, with Dr. Elmer L. Henderson, its campaign director, accusing the White House of being a "sounding board for the socializers." He stated that 1950 was "Medicine's Armageddon" and warned that "the decisive struggle which may determine not only medicine's fate but whether State socialism is to engulf all Americans—is still ahead of us." The president did, indeed, renew his request for the "National Health Insurance and Public Health" bill in each of his remaining annual messages to Congress, but the outbreak of the Korean War on June 25, 1950, forced Truman to back away from national health legislation and to mute his criticism of the AMA, leaving the administration's bill to languish in the Senate Health Subcommittee, while the House Commerce Committee turned its interest to other matters.[102]

The congressional elections that fall delivered the coup de grâce to national health legislation. Two of its leading proponents, Senator Elbert Thomas and Representative Andrew J.

Biemiller, were defeated, and the CNH found its own existence in doubt. Two of the latter's leading financial sponsors, the Laskers and the Rosenwald family, questioned whether national health insurance should remain the CNH's highest legislative priority, given Congress's unrelenting opposition to it. They wanted to focus instead on passing the less-controversial components of the president's health security program, particularly federal funding for medical education and research. Efforts at compromise failed, and both philanthropic families withdrew their support, leaving organized labor as the CNH's chief financial benefactor. In 1956, the CNH disbanded.[103]

For the first time in five years, *JAMA*'s editors noted, Congress felt no pressure "to look into President Truman's compulsory health insurance suggestions." But this was not taken to mean that organized medicine should—or would—relax its vigilance, declared the AMA president, Elmer Henderson. His warning was prescient, because even as President Truman concluded that he did not have the votes to persuade Congress to legislate his national health plan, Oscar Ewing was driving federal officials from the FSA and the SSA to find an alternative to the "National Health Insurance and Public Health" bill.[104]

# FOUR
## THE POLITICS OF
## INCREMENTALISM, 1951–1960

President Truman's efforts to legislate national health security had not been successful, but neither he nor other health reformers abandoned the fundamental principle on which his efforts rested: to establish public financial responsibility for health care as a matter of public policy. Although he repeated his request in 1950 for Congress to enact universal health coverage, that body failed to take action. Disappointed, the president and the health care reformers shifted the focus of their efforts to a more limited objective: federally underwritten health coverage for the elderly, or Medicare. This represented a retreat from Truman's original proposal, but many liberal politicians believed it was a more legislatively attainable program, one on which future Democratic administrations could build.

Restricting federally financed health insurance to Social Security beneficiaries was not a new idea. Dr. Thomas Parran had first mentioned the possibility in 1937, but New Deal liberals did not actively pursue it, preferring to work for universal health coverage. The idea resurfaced in 1944 at the height of the legislative struggle over the Wagner-Murray-Dingell bill, when Merrill G. Murray, an official of the SSA, raised it, probably without being aware of Parran's earlier suggestion. Murray's proposal also was buried in the files and forgotten until after the 1950 congressional elections.[1]

FSA Administrator Oscar Ewing, convinced that the public would not support national health security because of AMA propaganda, resurrected health insurance for Social Security beneficiaries as a serious legislative proposal in 1950. In doing so, he did not have to search far for an alternative to the sweeping, controversial, and moribund "National Health Insurance and Public Health" bill (S. 1679). I. S. Falk and his staff at the SSA's Bureau of Research and Statistics had been quietly developing an alternative proposal, which they called to Ewing's attention in early December 1950.[2] In a memorandum to Ewing, Falk explained that limiting health insurance to Social Security beneficiaries was attractive for economic and political reasons. Social Security officials had been troubled for some time by the knowledge that as long as the safety net failed to protect against the leading single cause of economic dependency in old age—the high cost of medical care—Social Security could not really fulfill its basic objective. Being less ambitious than a national health plan, insurance for the aged would be less costly and would establish an important precedent for the federal government's financial responsibility for health care. And by focusing the proposal on so demonstrably needy a group of citizens, the possibilities of congressional enactment would be enhanced.[3]

Falk's memorandum coincided with growing federal and public interest in the broad range of problems that afflicted older citizens. The 1950 census, disclosing that the aged composed 8 percent of the population and that only one in six had health insurance, called attention to the unmet health needs of this segment of the population. Commercial insurance companies had considered the elderly to be poor risks, whereas organized labor had made little progress in obtaining health coverage for retired workers through employer-sponsored plans. The often crushing financial burden of health care for the elderly thus fell on their children—the middle-class families who had to pay the hospital bills of their parents while trying to set aside funds for their own children's college education. In August 1950, President Truman's convening of the first National Conference on Aging brought the issue to the forefront of the national agenda.[4]

Partly in response to the medical needs of the aged, the Truman administration and Congress joined forces in enacting the 1950 amendments (Public Law [PL] 81-734) to the Social Security Act, which helped the states to provide medical care for welfare recipients being supported by the four federal-state public assistance programs for the indigent. Prior to this change, the federal government had shared with the states only in payments made directly to welfare clients. Under the 1950 amendments, Washington would share not only in direct payments for living expenses but also in "vendor" payments—payments made by the states to health care providers, rather than to the welfare recipient himself (among whom were the elderly). With federal funds available to cover part of the costs of vendor payments, the states began to provide them on a larger scale than previously.[5]

The 1950 amendments made the Social Security program more popular and helped to change the politics of health security. Contributory old-age insurance, financed through the earmarked payroll tax, became the centerpiece of social provision for the elderly, rather than means-tested public assistance, which was funded through general revenue. The changed law had support because citizens believed their money was paying for a contributory, nonwelfare program. The same mechanism would eventually be used to fund the federal Medicare program. The 1950 amendments also were important to a future Medicare program because they helped to ameliorate long-standing conflicts between federal and state officials. Unlike the 1943 Wagner-Murray-Dingell bill, they did not pose a direct challenge to the state welfare and unemployment compensation programs.[6]

Building on these amendments, Ewing, in spring 1951, broached the idea to President Truman of financing a hospital insurance plan for the aged through Social Security. Truman balked initially, even though he knew that his retreat from universal health coverage might help Democrats in the 1952 political campaign.[7] But after two or three additional meetings, a persistent Ewing persuaded the president to go along with the proposal, and he disclosed the administration's intentions during a press conference that summer. Beyond the glare of the media's spotlight, the administration was also planning for a nonpartisan commission on the nation's health needs, which the administration hoped would provide a rationale for reevaluating its health policy and remove the "socialized medicine" issue from the 1952 elections.[8]

The president established the Commission on Health Needs of the Nation in December 1951, and throughout 1952, he spoke out as never before on health security. Some reformers suggested that as an immediate first step in the direction of national health care, the Social Security Old-Age and Survivors Insurance system (OASI) begin paying for the hospitalization costs of persons retired on OASI old-age pensions and their dependents or survivors. Ewing, for example, put forward this proposal in a February 26 speech to a women's group in New York. Despite Truman's whistle-stop campaigning for health reform, nothing happened. His popularity declining, weary of the war in Southeast Asia, and harassed by charges of subversion and corruption, Truman announced in late March that he would not seek reelection, leaving Senate liberals to continue the fight.[9]

On April 10, 1952, Senators James Murray of Montana and Hubert Humphrey of Minnesota, with very little publicity, filed S. 3001, a bill to provide sixty days of government-financed hospital care for Social Security beneficiaries. Representatives John Dingell, Sr., of Michigan and Emanuel Celler of New York introduced companion bills (H.R. 7484 and H.R. 7485) in the House. The rationale behind the legislation was that the aged had particularly high health care costs (especially for chronic, long-term, or terminal illnesses) and low incomes, but they could not afford the high premium payments required by commercial health insurance companies. The SSA, in its annual report to Congress later that month, also endorsed government-financed health insurance for Social Security beneficiaries, estimating that the initial annual expenditure would be less than two-tenths of 1 percent of taxable payrolls.[10] The *New York Times,* however, accurately predicted that the likelihood of congressional action was remote, especially since the Democratic presidential candidate, Adlai Stevenson, had distanced himself from Truman's Fair Deal.[11]

If federally underwritten health insurance for the elderly was a casualty of election year politics, the issue, nonetheless, refused to go away. On December 18, 1952, shortly before Truman left office, his Commission on Health Needs of the Nation issued its one and only report. Affirming that good health was a basic human right to which millions of Americans were being deprived access, the report concluded that the government would be justified in spending $1 billion a year to improve medical care for all Americans. The report stopped short of recommending national health insurance, but it did devote an unexpectedly large amount of attention to the health needs of the elderly, noting the inadequacy of available private insurance programs and pointedly criticizing eligibility "means" testing.[12]

The commission, under the direction of Dr. Paul Magnuson, a prominent surgeon, a Republican, and an outspoken opponent of national health security, had produced a document that filled a large gap in public understanding of the medical and other problems of the aged, and that provided an important database.[13] The report delighted some people, infuriated others, and surprised a great many who had viewed it as Truman's way of conceding that future federal action on health security was highly unlikely. Its recommendations represented a compromise between the extremes of Taft's "charity" health care proposal and Truman's comprehensive program, and to his credit, the outgoing president accepted the commission's findings but viewed them as further evidence that citizens were looking to Washington for help in meeting their medical needs. The president of the AMA simply condemned the report for fallacious reasoning and contradictory conclusions.[14]

Whatever the truth, the recommendations were moot. Despite Democratic control of both houses of Congress, the politics of stalemate persisted. Truman left office having assimilated many New Deal programs into American life, but his efforts to use the Fair Deal to adapt American liberalism to the new postwar conditions—to transform the political equality of the New Deal into economic and social equality—remained more a promise than a reality. But he did establish a socioeconomic agenda for later Democratic administrations, and in this sense, his efforts to obtain comprehensive health care were more influential than contemporary politicians guessed, helping to pave the way for the enactment of Medicare a decade later.[15]

When Dwight D. Eisenhower entered the Oval Office, AMA President Louis Bauer declared optimistically, "As far as the medical profession is concerned there is general agreement that we are in less danger of socialization than for a number of years."[16] Eisenhower's presidency, in fact, legitimated the New Deal by keeping its basic structure and premises intact during an era of cold war and economic prosperity. Nowhere was this more evident than in the area of Social Security coverage, which Eisenhower expanded in the face of opposition from conservative Republicans.[17] But there were limits to Eisenhower's embrace of Social Security, and one of them was his stubborn refusal, unlike his predecessor, to use this mechanism to facilitate federal financing of health care for the aged and the poor. His opposition to "socialized medicine" may have been related to campaign commitments. For shortly after entering the White House, Eisenhower assured the AMA that he would stay out of medical matters, provided it dropped its opposition to a new cabinet-level post to coordinate the government's health, education, and welfare activities, a post that Truman had tried repeatedly to have established. The AMA relented, and in spring 1953, Congress established the Department of Health, Education, and Welfare (HEW). Oveta Culp Hobby, a renegade Texas Democrat, who was appointed HEW's first secretary, promptly announced that her tenure would inaugurate "an AMA administration."[18]

Yet Eisenhower also had promised during the campaign to help needy citizens meet the cost of medical care, and both Democrats and liberal Republicans were determined to hold the president's feet to the fire.[19] In the end, however, it was the growing numbers of retired persons living extended lives and trying to cope with chronic ailments on restricted budgets that drew public attention to the possibility of government health insurance for the aged. HEW Secretary Hobby, who had disparaged federal intervention as "socialized medicine," came under pressure to devise a Republican substitute for the Murray-Humphrey proposal. Cumbersomely titled "Health Service Prepayment Plan Reinsurance," the Republican bill (S. 3114) envisioned the federal government providing $25 million annually to private insurance companies that risked writing low-cost health insurance policies for low-income groups. The reinsurance plan was reported out of committee for a vote in July, but in a minority report Senator Murray, the former Democratic chair of the Labor and Public Welfare Committee, attacked the bill as "a paltry, puny, picayune proposal" and criticized Eisenhower, who had had access to "free, socialized medical care" almost all of his adult life, "for failing to comprehend the medical needs of the average American family." He condemned the reinsurance bill as a deception to reassure Republican campaign contributors that their "vested interest in the established system of paying for medical care would be protected."[20]

Murray's biting attack helped to kill the reinsurance bill in the Senate, and in the House, Minority Leader Sam Rayburn, angry at Hobby, engineered the bill's defeat on July 13, 1954. In truth, no one other than Secretary Hobby had been enthusiastic about the bill. The CNH and organized labor believed it would delay passage of national health insurance and not induce insurance companies to offer moderate-cost coverage to high-risk groups, like the elderly and chronically ill. The AMA, fearing it would vest extensive regulatory power in HEW, also testified against it, calling the bill the opening wedge toward "socialized medicine" that would lead to federal domination of the insurance field. One constituent of conservative Republican Page H. Belcher of Oklahoma thanked him for voting to send it back to committee, saying, "We need less rather than more government control and meddling into business." Hobby's successor at HEW, Marion B. Folsom, attempted to resurrect variations of the reinsurance bill, but none received sufficient congressional support for enactment.[21] The Eisenhower administration's inability to enact any adequate alternative to health care for the elderly under Social Security ironically reinvigorated the effort of liberal reformers to use the Social Security system and the elderly to establish the principle of government financing for medical care. That resulted, after many roadblocks, in the success of the Social Security approach in 1965.[22]

When the 84th Congress convened in January 1955, Eisenhower was cautiously optimistic that he could persuade Congress to enact a legislative agenda that included the reinsurance bill, but he did expect difficulty. The Democrats again controlled both the Senate and the House, meaning that his administration would have to work closely with the new majority leader, Lyndon B. Johnson, and the new Speaker of the House, Sam Rayburn. Eisenhower anticipated that the Democratic Party's conservative southern wing would often break ranks and vote with the administration, an assessment that proved to

be partially correct, but he also knew that congressional Republicans would have to support the administration more than ever. However, 1955 was the prelude to a new presidential and congressional election year, and the activities of the 84th Congress would be
played out against this backdrop.[23]

The pressure that had been building to use Social Security for purposes other than a
contributory retirement pension plan or to provide payments to widows and orphans
peaked in 1955, when a liberal-labor coalition, led by Senator Clinton P. Anderson of New
Mexico, President Truman's former secretary of agriculture, proposed to give permanently and totally disabled workers their retirement benefit at age fifty-five instead of
sixty-five. The change, which the newly united AFL-CIO endorsed, in effect, provided a
federal subsidy for the permanently disabled, but stopped short of providing for short-
term disability or paid maternity leave.[24] Disability insurance extended far beyond the
relatively small number of disabled workers; it created a precedent, transforming the Social Security system from a narrow retirement and survivors' benefit plan into a vehicle
for broad social welfare schemes. A disability benefits amendment, funded separately
through the 1935 Social Security Act, might become the first in a series of incremental
steps toward attaining the elusive goal of universal health coverage. It was also a good political issue. Democrats saw it serving as a wedge between them and the Republicans.
Forcing the Republicans to vote against the measure would help the Democrats in the
1956 presidential election.[25]

The author of the disability amendment was Wilbur J. Cohen, one of the most dynamic
liberal reformers of the twentieth century and a member of the tax policy community (a
cluster of anonymous but influential bureaucrats, legal scholars, economists, and
interest-group representatives) that included Robert Ball, Andrew Biemiller, Robert
Myers, and others who had helped to reconfigure federal taxation into a mechanism for
earmarking government benefits and managing economic growth. Working in tandem
with legislators who shared their view of tax policy, they established a link between Congress and other parts of the government in the post–World War II period. Cohen had participated in the drafting of the original Social Security Act and had observed how congressional committees had dealt with that legislation. Keenly aware of the centrality of
taxation to postwar liberalism and to social welfare policy, he promoted contributory social insurance as the most generous form of government assistance that could be had and
maintained without provoking a strong conservative backlash.[26]

A master of the complexities and politics of benefits, eligibility, taxes and administration, Cohen was a legislative technician and tactician who sought consensus and strove
to fashion bills that would pass. Cohen was suspicious of grandiose attempts at social
change, including the earlier abortive efforts to bring about national health security in
one fell swoop. He had much more confidence in small steps taken with solid political
backing, insisting that only a system with deep congressional support—no matter how

much had to be compromised to get that support—could become a permanent part of American life. A compromiser by nature, he balanced the idealism and radicalism of other liberal ideologues of his day with a political realism that ultimately produced results. He became one of the key players in the growth of the welfare system; *Time* magazine referred to him as "the salami slicer" in deference to his appetite for expanding programs incrementally. Nowhere was Cohen's mastery of negotiating with Congress, and particularly with the chairman of the tax-writing committee in the House, Wilbur Mills, more apparent than in the tedious and often frustrating efforts over the next decade to achieve Medicare for the aged.[27]

Despite the reservations of Speaker Rayburn, in 1955 the House overwhelmingly passed Cohen's amendment to the Social Security Act to include disability benefits for the permanently disabled. That was not surprising, because from the beginning, Democrats and Republicans alike expected the Senate to be the real battleground. There, acting on a personal request from President Eisenhower, Virginia Democrat Harry F. Byrd, the conservative chairman of the Finance Committee, postponed consideration of the bill for a year. Byrd's action gave AMA lobbyists, who sought to limit disability protection to the truly needy who could be monitored by local welfare authorities, ample time to bring pressure to bear on fence-straddling senators facing reelection. The pressure proved too much for some, such as Majority Whip Earle Clements of Kentucky, who was far more liberal on most issues than Senate Majority Leader Lyndon Johnson. Facing a difficult election battle against a popular Republican opponent, Clements quietly informed his allies in organized labor early in 1956 that he could not endorse the disability benefits amendment and risk the wrath of the AMA.[28] Lyndon Johnson appeared even less likely to support the amendment, but what observers did not know was that the majority leader, after scrutinizing the roster of senators that summer, concluded that there *was* a chance the amendment would be carried in the Senate. Playing his cards close to his vest, Johnson uttered not a word about the disability amendment, while behind a facade of studied indifference, he was conducting a laborious, methodical search for Republican votes.[29]

Johnson's task proved especially daunting because Eisenhower, who sometimes appeared aloof in pressing his legislative agenda, was determined on this issue. The president unleashed a pack of administration officials on Capitol Hill to roam the Senate corridors to line up votes against the disability amendment. But with equal cajolery and promises, Johnson secretly weaned away conservative Republicans, such as William Purtell of Connecticut, Wisconsin's Joe McCarthy, and George W. "Molly" Malone of Nevada.[30]

Malone was the least likely of men to play the hero's role in the enactment of landmark social legislation and would have been near the bottom of any Senate popularity list, but one senator who did not cut him dead was Lyndon B. Johnson. Always looking to convert friendless Republicans into Johnson votes, the Senate majority leader recruited Malone by treating him with elaborate courtesy. Fortunately for Johnson, Malone already was angry at the administration for departing from Republican orthodoxy on foreign aid and for its role in McCarthy's censure, but it was Eisenhower's tight budget, which severely limited mineral subsidies that Nevada's tungsten mine owners needed to balance their books, that strained Malone's relationship with the president to the breaking point. Malone eagerly pledged his vote on the disability amendment to Johnson, provided that the majority leader shepherd Malone's tungsten bill through the Senate. On June 18, 1956, Johnson delivered enough Democratic votes to pass the tungsten subsidy bill; few if any legislators had connected tungsten with the disability bill. On July 17, 1956, Malone repaid the favor when the disability amendment finally came to the Senate floor.[31]

To avoid a confrontation with Senate Republican Minority Leader William F. Knowland of California, Malone remained in the cloakroom, emerging long enough to vote for the amendment and then rushing from the chamber. Knowland had more success with McCarthy, persuading him to change his vote from "aye" to "nay." With the disability amendment about to fail on a tie vote, Johnson reluctantly played his last card; he asked Clements to vote for the amendment, knowing full well that Clements would incur the wrath of the AMA. Clements complied, and the amendment carried, forty-seven to forty-five.[32] Two days after the Senate acted, Eisenhower, with some misgivings, signed into law Malone's mineral subsidy bill. Two weeks later, he signed the Social Security bill with even more misgivings, telling reporters that "we are loading on the Social Security System something I don't think should be there, and if it is going to be handled, should be handled another way."[33]

Although Eisenhower never connected the two totally unrelated proposals, the addition of the disability amendment to the Social Security Act was a trailblazing victory that put Johnson, Cohen, and the strategy of incrementalism squarely in the midst of the struggle for health care reform. As an innovation, the new law was significant; it moved disability coverage from welfare-tainted assistance to the more palatable realm of insurance. According to former Social Security Administrator Charles I. Schottland, the change did not overly alarm conservatives, who believed that state control of disability decisions would take some of the menace from federal extension of the welfare state to cover disability. They also thought it would reenergize rehabilitation of the dropout labor force and work to forestall federal action on Medicare. But these were erroneous assumptions; the disability benefit set the substantial precedent that Cohen, organized labor, and liberal reformers had hoped it would.

The AMA also failed to prevent the expansion of another precedent later that year: the 1950 law giving the federal government the authority under the Old Age Assistance (OAA) program to provide small matching grants to the states for medical vendor payments.[34] Preoccupied with the disability fight, the AMA neglected to counter this serious threat. Other than a letter to the committee expressing its disapproval, it did little to

oppose broadening the vendor repayment bill, leading legislators to believe that organized medicine did not seriously object. The Democratic-controlled Congress quickly
enacted the measure. Both amendments were important because they not only coincided with a growing public awareness of how inadequate health care coverage was for
specific groups, such as the elderly, the poor, or the disabled, but also highlighted how
the inadequacy of such coverage affected the middle class unfavorably. It was this dimension of the problem that would capture the attention of legislators of both parties.[35]

The turning point for health care came in 1956, when it moved from the periphery of
the Eisenhower administration's concerns toward the center of its politics. William Reidy,
a staff member of the Senate Committee on Labor and Public Welfare, was among the first
to recognize that the problems of the elderly were acute and impacted the lives of their
children and grandchildren, and that the condition of the elderly would presage a growing
social crisis and become a major political issue. The time was ripe, he thought, to establish
a new Senate subcommittee on aging and to find a senator who would champion the
needs of the aged—preferably one with high ambitions and little national exposure. This
pointed him in the direction of John F. Kennedy, a Massachusetts Democrat and relatively
low-ranking member of the Labor and Public Welfare Committee, who had presidential
ambitions. Reidy attempted to pass along his idea to Kennedy through Theodore Sorensen, Kennedy's closest associate, but Sorensen did not believe Kennedy would have any
interest in the problems of the elderly. Rebuffed, but unwilling to give up, Reidy approached Kennedy through Ralph Dungan, Kennedy's assistant on the committee's staff.[36]

Kennedy turned out to be very much interested, but he was too busy just then with the
work of the Subcommittee on Labor to take up this new responsibility. However, he did
find time to cosponsor with committee chair Lister Hill an omnibus bill dealing with the
problems of the elderly, the "Senior Citizens Opportunity" bill (S. 3417), drafted by Wilbur Cohen, a former classmate of Reidy's and Kennedy's adviser on Social Security matters. The bill, which Kennedy introduced into the Senate on June 26, 1956, never came to
a vote, but the Senate did pass a resolution to appropriate $30,000 for a study of the aged
and aging. Reidy hoped the study, which Cohen also directed, would lead to the establishment of a subcommittee on aging, but it did not. Instead, Cohen's multivolume report became one more addition to the growing body of data about the elderly.[37]

Medicare, as health insurance for the elderly became known, made little headway in
Congress until organized labor lent its support. Like Cohen, most labor leaders no
longer viewed national health security as an immediately achievable goal. At the same
time, except for a few large unions, such as the United Mine Workers and the United
Steel Workers, the labor leaders' vision of health security and pensions for present and
retiring workers had made little headway in collective-bargaining negotiations. Commercial insurers in tandem with management tightly dictated the terms of health
coverage, whereas most pensions were wholly funded by the employer and controlled by

management. Government-financed health coverage for the aged, therefore, became another important piece of Social Security business in labor's own effort to attain health benefits for workers. It was a logical extension of the collective-bargaining process. After the demise of the "Senior Citizens Opportunity" bill, Nelson Cruikshank, director of the AFL-CIO's Department of Social Security, conferred regularly with Robert Ball, a member of the Social Security tax policy community and one of the top figures in the SSA, and with both Cohen and I. S. Falk from HEW. The fruit of this exchange was a new and greatly expanded bill that, if enacted, would establish the principle of federal responsibility for medical care for the elderly through Social Security.[38]

The new bill gave the elderly sixty days of hospitalization and covered the costs of surgery and care in nursing homes. To counter one of the objections from the AMA, physicians, hospitals, and nursing homes were free to participate in the program or not, and patients were free to choose any of the participating physicians and institutions. The secretary of HEW, who was to administer the program, would have no control over the practice of medicine, the manner in which medical services were rendered, the operation of hospitals and nursing homes, or the selection, tenure, and compensation of physician, hospital, and nursing home personnel. The cost of the program would be underwritten by increasing the amount of income on which Social Security taxes were levied from $4,200 to $6,000 and by increasing the tax rate on employees and employers by one-half of 1 percent—enough to pay the annual cost of the bill, estimated at $800 million.[39]

With bill in hand, Cruikshank and labor lobbyist Andrew Biemiller, another member of the tax policy community and ex-Wisconsin congressional representative who attributed his defeat to the AMA, sought a sponsor. They targeted the chair of the House Committee on Ways and Means, which wrote tax legislation, but Tennessee Democrat Jere Cooper, who was ill and occupied with other legislation, turned them down. So did Wilbur Mills of Arkansas and Noble Gregory of Kentucky, the second- and third-ranking Democrats on the committee. The fourth man down the line was Democrat Aime Forand of Rhode Island, a state where organized labor was important. Forand agreed to sponsor the bill, although he did not truly believe that it would go anywhere. On August 27, 1957, shortly before Congress adjourned, Forand introduced the bill (H.R. 9467). After a reporter for the *Providence Journal* and friend of several influential AFL-CIO leaders wrote articles about the bill's popularity among older Rhode Islanders, Forand grew more enthusiastic about it.[40]

In June 1958, the House Ways and Means Committee, then chaired by Arkansas Democrat Wilbur Mills, opened hearings on the Forand bill, beginning the long, frustrating process that led to enactment of Medicare. A small-town lawyer and graduate of the Harvard Law School, Mills had a keen legal mind that comprehended complex legal and financial details; through his chairmanship of the powerful tax-writing committee of the House, his mastery of the federal tax code and Social Security system, and his relationship with the tax policy community, Mills played a pivotal role in shaping the development of federal social and economic policy. By 1960, he was being routinely described as the second-most-powerful man in Washington.

Mills, regarded as a fiscal conservative, nonetheless supported the government's use of moderate tax reductions to stimulate economic growth, even if the reductions required occasional deficits, but he insisted that liberal policy makers fashion an agenda that was politically and economically within congressional guidelines. This meant an agenda centered around a contributory social insurance program based on pay-as-you-go earmarked taxes and wage-related benefits that would avoid means testing; moderate macroeconomic fiscal policy; and a growth-oriented tax code. He sought affordable federal assistance without a welfare state. There was a certain irony, then, that Mills, who in 1958 and the early 1960s had been determined to keep health care out of Social Security, should become one of the key figures (with Wilbur Cohen, Robert Ball, and Lyndon B. Johnson) in the passage of the Medicare law in 1965.[41]

The first witness to testify before Mills and the Ways and Means Committee on the Forand bill was HEW Secretary Marion Folsom. He explained that the Eisenhower administration opposed the bill because the phenomenal growth of private, voluntary health insurance companies was able to take care of the health needs of the elderly.[42] Folsom's testimony assumed the mantle of authority because of the presence at his side of Charles I. Schottland, the commissioner of Social Security. Other witnesses corroborated Folsom's testimony, with spokesmen for the insurance industry warning that passage of the Forand bill would cut into the sale of insurance.[43]

The testimony of the bill's opponents, however, cast doubt on Folsom's rosy portrayal. On how well the aged were faring under voluntary health insurance, Cruikshank, speaking for organized labor, cited a 1956 USPHS survey that documented that large numbers of the elderly were not benefiting at all. Nearly 6 million of the aged lived in families whose total income was less than $3,000, and seven out of ten of these aged persons had no health insurance whatever. Of the 2.4 million elderly not in families, half had incomes under $1,000, and only one-fifth had any health insurance. As the elderly aged, they became poorer risks; the commercial insurance companies refused to cover them, preferring younger, able-bodied workers, who posed less risk. The sick and the elderly were left to the nonprofit insurance companies, like Blue Cross and Blue Shield, which, in many states, were forced to increase their rates and curtail benefits in order to remain solvent. Cruikshank testified that Americans ranked eleventh in longevity—behind Norway, Sweden, Denmark, the Netherlands, West Germany, Iceland, Canada, Israel, Cyprus, and Japan, all of which had national health security programs. On the cost issue, which insurance spokesmen put at $2.1 billion, the Eisenhower administration's own figures indicated that the bill would cost less than $1 billion annually (HEW put the figure at $800 million) and would not unbalance the budget.[44]

Cruikshank's testimony was to no avail. The Ways and Means Committee never recorded a vote on the Forand bill, and had it done so, the bipartisan coalition of Southern Democrats and conservative Republicans that dominated the committee would easily have prevailed. Likewise, Forand, who wanted to build a record that might eventually lead to government financing of health care for the aged, preferred not to have a roll-call defeat a part of that record. Meanwhile, on August 19, toward the close of the congressional session, an incident occurred that suggested the principle of federal underwriting of health care embedded in the Forand bill might acquire a new lease on life. Senator Kennedy, who had emerged as a leading contender for the Democratic presidential nomination, delivered a speech in the Senate in which he outlined a ten-point program for dealing with the most pressing needs of the elderly. These included increases in Social Security benefits and medical care coverage. The speech served to align the presidential hopeful with liberal thinking and reflected the influence of Sorensen (who had, by now, acknowledged the socioeconomic problems of the elderly and their potential political importance); Myer "Mike" Feldman, a Kennedy staffer; and Wilbur Cohen, who was commuting between the University of Michigan and Washington to work with political figures interested in the health of the aged. The three Kennedy advisers agreed that the plight of the elderly was a major issue and, in Feldman's words, "could come to have a very great effect on the outcome of the presidential election in 1960."[45]

Kennedy believed that the federal government in this time of affluence should expand Social Security benefits so that the aged, like other Americans, could participate in the nation's economic prosperity and not be left behind. His position on social welfare legislation rested on the expectation of rising productivity and higher wages—a stance that he would use in 1960 as a potent campaign issue.[46] After his reelection to the Senate that November, Kennedy sought to shore up his liberal credentials by asking Senator Lister Hill to establish a new subcommittee on aging, with himself as chairman. Kennedy's request postdated a similar petition from Michigan Democrat Pat McNamara, an ardent proponent of medical care for the elderly through Social Security, who was up for reelection in 1960. McNamara was eager for the publicity that came with a committee chairmanship, and when, on February 6, 1959, the Senate authorized the establishment of the new Subcommittee on Problems of the Aged and Aging, Hill appointed McNamara over Kennedy as its first chair. That summer, McNamara initiated a series of well-publicized hearings around the country that helped to raise public consciousness of the issue.[47]

Alarmed by the Forand bill hearings, Kennedy's speech, and the McNamara hearings, the AMA, under the leadership of Dr. Edward Annis, a Miami surgeon, counterattacked. Annis charged that the cause of the elderly had been subverted by a few cheap politicians and labor leaders whose only motive was to secure their own positions. Insisting that the aged had few problems that could not be handled through existing welfare mechanisms, he lobbied legislators either sympathetic to the AMA (such as conservative Republican

Thomas B. Curtis of Missouri, a member of the Ways and Means Committee) or undecided. The AMA also spent a quarter of a million dollars to churn out numerous press releases, canned speeches, and pamphlets attacking the Forand bill. Its heavy-handed intrusion into the fall congressional elections backfired, however. The Democrats gained
forty-eight seats in the House and sixteen in the Senate; the Forand bill received more
publicity than even its backers could have hoped for; and members of Congress grew
even more wary of pressure from the AMA.[48] Burned by the outcome, the AMA revised
its strategy to short-circuit the Forand bill. In December 1958, its House of Delegates
adopted a resolution urging physicians to lower their fees to the elderly. One Rhode Island physician then suggested that Blue Cross–Blue Shield be converted to a "paid up at
sixty-five" plan in order to block "Federal medicine for the aged."[49]

Even as the AMA pursued its attack on the Forand bill, proponents of the measure exploited a congressional decision to increase Social Security benefits, paying for them by
raising the taxable wage base by $600. This left Forand free to focus on health insurance
in the 1959 congressional session. By limiting the coverage provided, Forand reduced
further the increase in payroll taxes imposed on both employees and employers so that
no more than $12 a year would be deducted from anyone's paycheck under his revised
bill.[50] By the time Forand reintroduced his bill, political disarray over health care for Social Security beneficiaries had become both rampant and bipartisan. Eisenhower, the Republican president, opposed it, as did the two Southern Democratic leaders in the House
and Senate, Rayburn and Johnson. The Democratic Advisory Council, whose members
included former president Truman and Adlai Stevenson, endorsed the bill, as did
Eisenhower's former commissioner of Social Security, Charles I. Schottland, and HEW
Secretary Folsom. The last two, who had previously testified against the original bill, later
admitted that they actually had favored it.[51]

At the height of this disarray, HEW's new secretary, Arthur Flemming, a liberal Republican who favored the expansion of health insurance, released a report in spring 1959 on
the subject of hospitalization insurance for Social Security beneficiaries. The report,
which began with a recitation of the arguments against the Forand bill, then cited facts
and figures that made a compelling argument for the legislation. It left no doubt that an
older person who was faced with heavy medical expenses, who had exhausted his savings and, perhaps, had sold his home, was left with few options. Either he could go on
welfare at considerable cost to his community and his self-esteem, or he could delay
seeking any medical care at all until it was absolutely unavoidable or too late.[52]

When the Ways and Means Committee announced in late June that it would hold a
new round of hearings on the Forand bill, shock waves passed through the AMA. Its
headquarters in Chicago sent to each of the association's members a "Legislative
Alert," urging each physician and state and local medical society to write, wire, or telephone their congressional delegations to protest the measure.[53] That July, a tense and

uncomfortable HEW Secretary Flemming led off the hearings. He conceded that the problem of the elderly was real but testified that the administration did not consider the Forand bill to be the appropriate remedy. Like his predecessor, Flemming endorsed voluntary health insurance, but his testimony was contradicted by former commissioner of Social Security Schottland and others, who contended that voluntary insurance "cannot be the answer to the total problem of medical care for the aged." Schottland declared that insurance companies, such as Continental Casualty, had issued health policies for the elderly only out of fear of the Forand bill.[54]

As predicted, representatives of the AMA spoke against the Forand bill. The vice-speaker of the AMA's House of Delegates, a Texan, asserted that no one in his state suffered from lack of proper medical care. He actually meant that no Texan went without a physician provided he or she was willing to become a charity case, a position that critics pointed out was at odds with the "sanctity" of the doctor-patient relationship and the right of a patient to choose his own physician. In most charity wards, patients were treated by any physician who happened to be on duty, and there was no guarantee that a patient would be seen by the same physician twice, which made it difficult to establish a "doctor-patient relationship." His testimony also implied that the AMA segregated patients by class: one level of care for patients who could pay their bills and another for those who could not. The medical director of Baltimore's Sinai Hospital, who oversaw treatment of charity patients, bolstered that impression when he also questioned the speaker's assertion that proper medical care was universally available.[55]

As in 1958, this round of hearings produced no legislation, but it alerted larger numbers of Americans to the inadequacy of medical care for the elderly. The Joint Economic Committee of Congress furthered their concern in its report released in fall 1959, as did Senator McNamara's hearings, which had opened in Washington and then proceeded to a number of cities across the country throughout that summer and fall.[56] Jaded Washingtonians paid little attention to the hearings, but outside the nation's capital, McNamara's subcommittee received extensive press coverage, particularly after the chairman opened the hearings to just about any individual who wished to speak on the subject. In Boston, Pittsburgh, San Francisco, Charleston, Grand Rapids, Miami, and Detroit, the elderly lined up to testify about their inadequate medical care and quality of life. Their words, often emotional and heart-wrenching, captured the headlines and transformed health care for the aged through Social Security into the hot issue in Congress and the nation.[57]

McNamara submitted the subcommittee's report to the Senate in February 1960. Its foremost recommendation—that Congress broaden the Social Security system without delay to provide health coverage for all eligible beneficiaries—was not without controversy. Although congressional Democrats liked to time changes in the Social Security program to coincide with elections, two Republican members of the subcommittee, Senators Barry Goldwater of Arizona and Everett M. Dirksen of Illinois, refused to go along and wrote a dissenting minority report asserting that the problems of the elderly were not fundamentally different from those of other Americans. This statement would come back to haunt Goldwater as the Republican presidential candidate. McNamara tried to ignore the minority dissent, but in March, Eisenhower and the Republican leaders in Congress, opposed to an expansionist Social Security program and believing that federally sanctioned health care for the elderly would encroach on the private sector, announced their opposition to health legislation financed through Social Security. Medical care for the aged was fast becoming the most politically charged domestic issue of 1960, even though most of the election campaign rhetoric and press coverage focused on more glamorous issues, such as the missile gap, Eisenhower's record, and Castro and the fate of the Cuban people.[58]

That spring, the Senate calendar was dotted with health care bills for the aged, as ambitious politicians sought to affirm their liberal credentials. Democratic presidential contender John F. Kennedy cosponsored one bill (S. 2915) that was more limited than the Forand proposal, whereas McNamara introduced "Retired Persons Medical Insurance," a Forand-type bill, based on his subcommittee's report.[59] These initiatives demanded an immediate response from the Republican presidential nominee, Richard M. Nixon, especially after Kennedy jumped on the Forand bill bandwagon. Congressional mail was running two to one in favor of the Forand bill. Nixon and HEW Secretary Flemming went repeatedly to Eisenhower to argue that no Republican candidate could ignore the 16 million voters over sixty-five, nearly 20 percent of the electorate, but Eisenhower would not budge. When a desperate Nixon turned to Republican members of the Ways and Means Committee to devise a modified Forand bill that would be acceptable to the president and to Republican legislators up for reelection, Eisenhower was adamant. A troubled Nixon was forced to watch from the sidelines as the leading Democratic contenders called for passage of the Forand bill.[60]

The Ways and Means Committee agreed finally to a vote on the revised Forand bill. Taken on March 31, 1960, the vote was seventeen against to eight for the bill. Democrats voting to kill the Forand bill were committee chairman Wilbur D. Mills and six other southerners. Ordinarily, this would have consigned the proposal to oblivion, but as grassroots support continued to build, the bill's most enthusiastic supporters sought to revive it. Few Democrats, Kennedy included, believed it would pass, but it served their election-year interest to make the effort.[61]

Labor leader Walter Reuther made the most persuasive argument that the Republicans' failure to push for medical coverage would become a major issue in the fall campaign and would offer Democrats a golden opportunity to swing a much higher percentage of older citizens' votes to the Democratic Party. Reuther's appeal convinced Senate Majority Leader Lyndon B. Johnson, who desperately wanted labor's endorsement for the presidential nomination, to modify his earlier opposition, as did House

Speaker Rayburn. The two Texans saw this as the perfect issue to demonstrate Johnson's legendary talents. In remarks to a visiting delegation of physicians, Johnson warned that, one way or other, something would be done to ease the financial burden of health care for the elderly. With their cooperation, he insisted, "We can work out a solution that will not destroy the traditional doctor-patient relationship; that will preserve the integrity of our doctors; that will maintain our system of free enterprise, and at the same time will lift some of the ever-increasing burden of medical expenses from the shoulders of old folks." Johnson adhered to this position in the ensuing five-year struggle to adopt Medicare.[62]

Johnson lectured the physicians, and Rayburn told fellow Democrat Wilbur Mills that something had to be done for the elderly voter before the fall elections. Mills was opposed to financing health care through Social Security, but he reluctantly agreed to reconsider Forand's bill. That much accomplished, Johnson then turned to an ally and supporter of his presidential nomination on the Finance Committee, Senator Robert S. Kerr of Oklahoma. Kerr, who had a keen interest in the health care of the aged and acknowledged a federal responsibility to "enable low-income groups to secure the necessary health services," had opposed the compulsory nature of previous health care legislation, preferring the income replacement concept of Social Security. In 1956, he had spearheaded a drive in the committee to allow cash payments to permanently disabled persons over fifty—a departure in the types of protection afforded the individual through the social insurance programs of the Social Security Act—and an amendment permitting women to receive Social Security benefits at sixty-two rather than at the age of sixty-five. Now he was drafting an alternative to the Forand bill, one that would, over the next five years, bedevil the advocates of the Social Security approach.[63]

Meanwhile, Eisenhower, after heated debate among his staff, came to a partial acceptance of Nixon's assessment of the political situation, and in early May 1960, HEW unveiled a "Medicare Program for the Aged" bill that crystallized Democratic and Republican ideological differences.[64] Though offering broader coverage than the Forand bill and based on an ingenious method of public funding and private control, the proposal was more expensive, requiring large out-of-pocket deductibles and a much larger bureaucracy.[65] New York Republican Governor Nelson Rockefeller declared it to be fiscally irresponsible and an administrative nightmare; Virginia Democrat Burr Harrison likened it to a Rube Goldberg scheme. The AMA and Senator Goldwater both branded it socialistic, whereas Nixon simply declined to comment on it.[66]

Though no one other than Eisenhower showed any sympathy for the measure, its submission to Congress meant that both parties had accepted the idea that the federal government had an obligation to assist elderly people who were sick and too poor to pay for medical care. This enhanced the chances of some kind of bill passing before the election, and so attention focused on the Ways and Means Committee and Wilbur Mills, whose power and influence would determine the health insurance bill's form and scope for years to come.[67] Within the committee, support for the Forand bill was overwhelmingly negative, led by Mills, who feared health care costs would wreck the Social Security system. Mills also had other reasons for opposing the measure. His district was staunchly conservative, and in the past, physicians and insurance agents had spent time and money on efforts to keep it that way, at least in its attitude toward national health insurance. In 1958, fellow Representative Brooks Hays of Little Rock, to everyone's astonishment, was turned out of office after sixteen years by a physician who had not even been on the ticket but had won after an eight-day campaign for write-in votes. This incident shook Mills, who allegedly promised officials of the state medical society that he would oppose the Forand bill.[68]

On June 3, 1960, as he had promised Rayburn, Mills brought the Forand bill before his committee for a vote, and the committee rejected it once again by the same margin of 17 to 8. With that, Mills produced a compromise health care plan of his own. Patterned on the administration's federal-state matching program, the Mills plan provided less-generous benefits for the aged but gave the states more discretion over the scope of their programs. It extended the medical-vendor payments under the OAA program, permitting the federal government to make open-ended matching grants to the states for medical care for the elderly poor, provided that the states matched the federal funds. Unlike the Forand bill, Mills's proposal would not be financed through Social Security. The Ways and Means Committee quickly approved the measure, and on June 23, the House passed it by a vote of 380 to 23. There it remained when Congress adjourned for the presidential nominating conventions.[69]

Even though there was considerable opposition to the bill among delegates, voters, and medical and insurance company executives, the Democratic platform committee adopted a plank endorsing the principle embodied in the Forand bill.[70] The Republican platform, in contrast, was deliberately vague in its proposal for health insurance for the aged, seemingly endorsing the principle embodied in the Eisenhower bill but leaving unanswered many questions of administration, eligibility, and level of benefits. This vagueness rendered Nixon, the Republican presidential nominee, vulnerable to attack from Democrats. How candidate Nixon could reconcile the administration's bill, relying as it did on commercial carriers and voluntary insurance organizations, with the most recent HEW report virtually conceding that private insurers were not equal to the task was unclear.[71]

While each party was jockeying for position in the forthcoming election, Senator Kerr, the most influential member of the Finance Committee and the key to action on health legislation in the Senate, resolved the controversy his own way. Kerr had little use for Kennedy and recognized that the Massachusetts Catholic had almost no chance of carrying Oklahoma, a solidly Baptist state. But like Kennedy, he knew that health care financing would be one of the major issues in the 1960 elections, which is why he had sought to find a position somewhere between the extremes of Flemming and Forand.[72] In March 1960, a group of influential Oklahoma physicians called on Kerr to voice their opposition to any federal program to finance health care payments. After that meeting, one physician wrote to Wilbur Mills (with copies to Kerr, Senator Mike Monroney, and Representative Toby Morris) that the state's aged population wanted neither a federal handout nor an increase in benefits, but only to maintain an "adequate means of existence." "Forand-type" and "Flemming-type" measures, another physician wrote, were "ill advised," and he thanked Mills for holding the line "for better government along conservative lines."[73]

Kerr believed that the attitude of Oklahoma's medical establishment was unrealistic—that some form of health coverage would be legislated in an election year—and he suggested that the physician-delegates spend a couple of days taking the pulse of Capitol Hill. A few days later, shaken by what they had heard and chastened in their judgments, the physicians asked Kerr's help in drafting a substitute for the Forand bill. This gave Kerr the upper hand with Oklahoma's medical leaders. They had approached him, and he would remind them of their indebtedness at election time. By proposing a substitute bill, he would demonstrate his independence to his conservative constituents, should the Democratic national ticket and the platform prove unsatisfactory on the health issue, as he anticipated.[74]

With these ideological and political concerns in mind, Kerr turned to the ubiquitous Wilbur Cohen for his opinion of Mills's bill as it moved through the House. Cohen explained that Mills had consulted him about his bill but that he had not participated in its drafting, and in fact, he had serious reservations about the legislation. Kerr, who, like most legislators, regarded Cohen as the real expert on social insurance and welfare, promptly invited Cohen to leave his teaching position at Michigan and join his staff in Washington to help draft alternative legislation. Cohen accepted the invitation because he believed that Congress might someday enact medical care for the elderly through Social Security, and he was committed to any incremental step that might lead to national health security.[75]

With Cohen on board, Kerr instructed his staff first to work out a proposal based on how much money the Forand payroll tax would raise and then to determine how many benefits that amount of money would buy. He did this because he knew that most legislation was written in reverse: the author first decided on the benefits desired and then devised a system to fund them. When the staff produced the figures, Kerr, like Wilbur Mills, was convinced that "a medicare program financed through the Social Security payroll tax might bankrupt the Old-Age Survivors Insurance and Disability program." Shaking his head in disagreement, he kept repeating, "To many people, that [Social Security] is the only retirement they have." As the cost of living rose, medical benefits would have to keep pace, and that meant raising the payroll tax. A hard-nosed politician, he concluded: "I'm afraid that in the future . . . the Congress in an election year will put on some added benefits and won't have the guts to increase the payroll tax. . . . Once they do that, they will have destroyed the solvency of the Social Security fund and the federal government will have to step in and make a general appropriation." Kerr's opposition, like Mills's, was to the means, not to the goal, of the bill.[76]

When Congress reconvened after the nominating conventions, candidate Kennedy, eyeing the voters rather than his colleagues, declared that the House and Senate should not adjourn until they had enacted a comprehensive plan to meet the medical needs of the elderly. Kennedy's political advisers, meanwhile, persuaded the sponsors of various medicare bills to unite in support of a plan offered by Senator Clinton P. Anderson of New Mexico as an amendment to the recently passed House Social Security amendments. The Anderson proposal was much like the Forand bill, but it went considerably further; it provided health insurance for the elderly through the Social Security OASI system. With vice presidential nominee Lyndon Johnson's help, the Kennedy people sought to force a test vote to dramatize how large and important an issue health care had become. Even if the Anderson proposal were defeated, Kennedy could still emerge a winner: medical care for the aged would become the clarion call of the Democratic presidential campaign.[77]

Kennedy's maneuver threatened to upstage Kerr, who was up for reelection that fall. He would help the Kennedy-Johnson ticket if he could, but a bill with his name attached to it providing for federal payment of part of the medical expenses of the aged would be a great boost to his campaign. "If I go all out for Jack, I'll lose a hundred and twenty-five thousand Baptists," he explained. "And if I come out for health insurance under Social Security, I'll lose every doctor in the state." Kerr's solution, developed during his conversations with Cohen, was a plan aimed primarily at helping the elderly who were neither poor enough to qualify for welfare nor wealthy enough to pay their necessary medical expenses—a group that had come to be known as the "medically indigent." Such assistance would take the form of federal matching grants to the states, which would administer the programs. Kerr asked Cohen and his staff to draft a bill along those lines, one that stood apart from the Kennedy-Anderson proposal, but that also benefited Oklahoma. In response to Cohen's query whether the AMA would go along with the proposal, Kerr said he would take care of that.[78]

Shortly thereafter, Cohen produced the draft of a new bill. Financed from general revenues, Kerr's plan increased federal "vendor" payments to states under the existing OAA program and established a new federal-state matching program for the elderly medically indigent, who were defined as persons not covered under the OAA program but were judged too poor to meet their medical bills. The plan contained the standard language characteristic of existing public assistance legislation. The federal share was tied to the recipient state's per capita income, meaning that low-income states would receive the greatest assistance. Kerr's proposal incorporated much of the Mills bill, with its funding formula providing preferential treatment for Oklahoma and Arkansas. Almost immediately, the press referred to the plan as the Kerr-Mills bill.[79]

Election-year politics and a keen sense of what Congress would accept governed Kerr's strategy both in the Finance Committee and later in the floor debate. Convinced that the committee's conservative members could not vote down the Social Security approach without producing a substitute and knowing that they generally followed the lead of the chairman, Harry Byrd of Virginia, who was adamantly against tampering with the Social Security payroll tax, Kerr offered an alternative method of financing. He also believed that despite their public posturing for a Forand-type bill, the committee's liberal members (Anderson, Albert Gore, Sr., of Tennessee, and Douglas of Illinois) would settle for any program that introduced the principle of federal financing of health care. To make certain, Kerr also proposed legislation to reduce the age requirement for disability benefits under Social Security, one of Anderson's pet proposals.[80]

Any health plan tied to Social Security financing ran the risk of becoming hopelessly entangled in the Rules Committee. Should the Congress pass such a bill, President Eisenhower would certainly veto it. Knowing this, Kerr stood ready to offer his own health care proposal when the Finance Committee reconvened in August. Democrats, he believed, would have little choice but to cooperate on a bill that actually had the possibility of being enacted into law. With his strategy mapped out, he flew to Chicago to meet with AMA officials. Resorting to every forensic trick he knew to secure their cooperation, Kerr got absolutely nowhere until he told them it was either the Kerr-Mills bill or the Forand bill sooner or later, and probably sooner. AMA leaders finally capitulated; they agreed not to oppose Kerr-Mills outright, but that was as far as they would go.[81]

The critical deliberations began when the 86th Congress reconvened late that summer. With the Finance Committee meeting in executive session, Kerr unveiled his health care plan, which the committee approved on August 13, 1960, by a vote of twelve to five, simultaneously rejecting Senator Anderson's proposal to tie medical care into the Social Security system. Kerr's assurance to the committee that his bill had administration backing, lent credence by his close friendship with Eisenhower's treasury secretary, Robert Anderson, explained its quick acceptance, but when questioned as to the odds of it passing both houses of Congress, he admitted they were only fifty-fifty. "The alternative," Kerr observed, "was no bill at all."[82]

Four days later, on August 17, presidential candidate Kennedy and Senator Anderson introduced their substitute for the Forand bill, and it immediately took center stage in the controversy over government health insurance. It was similar to, but went considerably beyond, the Forand bill, providing 120 days of hospital care, 240 days of nursing home care, or 360 home visits by nurses annually.[83] The expectation was that the Senate majority leader and Democratic vice presidential candidate, Johnson, would push the Kennedy-Anderson bill through Congress, a prospect that aroused conservative and AMA opposition but also enhanced the prospects of the Kerr-Mills proposal.[84]

With senators bitterly divided over the Kennedy-Anderson bill, bipartisan support began to coalesce behind the Kerr-Mills bill, especially after President Eisenhower endorsed it in a news conference.[85] To avert a schism within the Democratic Party, which already was burdened with the task of electing a Catholic president, Cohen persuaded Kennedy's aides Theodore Sorensen and Myer Feldman that the Forand approach was dead and that if Kennedy and his supporters in the Senate insisted on passage of a Social Security–financed program, the Senate's conservative coalition would choose the less-offensive Kerr bill. The confrontation would pit Democrat against Democrat and destroy any hope of getting federal health insurance enacted for years to come. Cohen reiterated the merits of incrementalism: if they approached Kerr-Mills as a rung up the ladder—a way to help the medically indigent, who were one rung from the bottom—the Kennedy camp would have a better opportunity later to add Forand-type coverage. Cohen argued that the two bills, viewed from this perspective, complemented each other; his dispassionate, reasoned, and politically realistic argument won over Sorensen and Feldman, who eventually persuaded Kennedy.[86]

Kennedy's changed position was evident by the time Kerr appeared on the Senate floor to outline the Kerr-Mills plan for his colleagues. One of its merits, he added almost parenthetically, was that it could be implemented as early as October 1, 1960, an observation whose implications every senator in the chamber standing for reelection that November immediately understood. Kennedy, who earlier had said that Kerr-Mills did not go far enough and had promised to fight for his own bill, sat quietly throughout Kerr's speech.[87] He and his advisers had decided that the momentum for Kerr-Mills could not be reversed, and rather than divide the party, the Kennedy forces turned aside pleas from liberals and organized labor that the Democratic leadership enforce party discipline. They turned instead to a parliamentary gambit: to piggyback a Social Security–financed program onto the federal-state cost-sharing principle embodied in the Kerr-Mills plan. This combination would broaden the coverage of each plan and, not incidentally, spare legislators the political pain of having to choose one plan over the other.[88]

The Senate debate foreshadowed the bitterly fought presidential campaign that followed. On August 23, Democrats defeated an amendment by Republican Senator Jacob Javits on a straight party vote; then the Kennedy-Anderson bill, with fifteen cosponsors, came up. Vice President Nixon appeared in the Senate, not to preside, but to round up votes to defeat his rival's bill. Nixon understood that if Kennedy's bill passed and Eisenhower carried out his veto threat, the Republicans would be handing the Democrats their biggest campaign issue. If the Senate derailed the Kennedy-Anderson bill, Nixon could support the Kerr-Mills proposal, which might irritate the AMA but would secure the senior citizen vote for his election. Nixon's strategy prevailed. Senate conservatives defeated Kennedy-Anderson, 51 to 44, with 19 Democrats joining 32 Republicans. An embittered Kennedy, who was standing near Senator Douglas when the vote was announced, remarked that "the Southerners would not support the national needs and declarations of our Party, but would demand their full share of the perquisites and patronage" after the election.[89] Democratic Senator Albert Gore of Tennessee, who was critical of the Kerr-Mills plan, complained that it "sets up a means test ... this is the public charity approach. It erodes the pride of our people to make them go hat in hand to public officials and plead their poverty before receiving any aid."[90]

The Kerr-Mills alternative then passed overwhelmingly, by a vote of 91 to 2, with only die-hard conservatives Barry Goldwater and Strom Thurmond of South Carolina dissenting. The Senate's procedural rules made it impossible, as Kennedy's advisers had intended, to tack their defeated amendment onto the Kerr-Mills plan. Two days later, the House-Senate conference committee accepted the Kerr-Mills bill almost intact, and on September 13, 1960, President Eisenhower signed the Kerr-Mills Act (PL 86–778) into law. But not before one minor hitch threatened to delay the signing ceremonies.[91]

According to rumors circulating on Capitol Hill, the president threatened to veto the bill because of its very generous matching formulas. Eisenhower thought it was unusually favorable to the lower-income states, especially Oklahoma (which under the Kerr-Mills formula received a total of $16 million, with no corresponding increase in state spending) and Arkansas. Kerr quickly intervened with the White House through former Social Security commissioner Charles I. Schottland, who explained to the president that through the complex formula for matching funds, rural-agricultural states with low per capita incomes invariably received a larger percentage of federal matching funds than richer, urban-industrial states. Schottland's explanation was technically correct, but it was also not a coincidence that Southern Democrats who controlled the decisive votes received the most favorable federal matching formulas for their states.[92]

Reflecting upon the legislative battles over health care for the elderly, Senator Anderson never quite understood why Kerr opposed financing it through Social Security, or why the popular Kerr believed that he had to win the political support of Oklahoma doctors to retain his seat in the Senate. Anderson underestimated conservatism's deep roots in Oklahoma, a state essentially southern, rural, Baptist, and deeply suspicious of Washington. Kerr's explanation was straightforward: "I don't get any votes in Boston and New York. Mine all happen to come from Ada and Oklahoma City, Tulsa, Stigler and areas like that," he confided to Wilbur Cohen. To one constituent, he wrote, "I felt that in fairness to the people over 65 I should work for the passage of a bill that could become a law, and not for the passage of a bill that had no chance of ever being of benefit to anybody."[93] However sincere Kerr's motivation was in framing the bill as he did, congressional conservatives endorsed it for other reasons. Fearing the Senate would pass a Forand-like national health insurance measure, Oklahoma Republican Representative Page Belcher voted for Kerr-Mills as "a compromise in order to stop the Forand bill." The AMA and "those of us who are interested in stopping socialized medicine felt that this was the best approach to take."[94]

Oklahoma voters elected Kerr to a third term in fall 1960, but his triumph was bittersweet. The margin of victory was the smallest of his career, prompting Kerr to complain to a friend that despite his efforts on their behalf, the medical profession had proved a fickle ally. "After all I did to save the doctors from themselves, I got only 22% of their votes."[95]

It had taken the better part of the decade for reformers to move health care for the elderly from the periphery to the center of electoral and presidential politics—a lengthy, tedious, and ultimately unsuccessful process that occurred only after Democrats had muted their ideological differences and embraced the issue in a bid to defeat the Republicans and regain control of the White House in 1960. But when congressional Democrats transformed health care for the elderly from a medical concern to a political and presidential issue, what was best for senior citizens from a health standpoint or what was fair to private insurance companies was not always necessarily or solely their concern. As the legislative battles over the Kerr-Mills and Forand bills and the rival presidential ambitions of Democratic Senators Robert Kerr and John F. Kennedy attested, the devil was in the details: whether to vest administrative authority in the states, fund the program through matching grants, and impose the much-despised means test, as the Kerr-Mills bill proposed, or to centralize administrative control at the federal level and tap into the Social Security Trust Fund—the approach that Forand, Anderson, and Kennedy had advocated.

Politics had truly triumphed over principle in 1960. Eisenhower's putative successor in the Oval Office, Richard M. Nixon, had been quick to recognize the political potential of the elderly voter in the presidential campaign, but he was handicapped by the departing president who relied upon the private sector to provide adequate health coverage to the elderly, despite statistical data, government reports, and anecdotal evidence that it was unequal to the task. Neither a frustrated Nixon's attempt to carve out a position on Medicare that would appeal to senior-citizen voters nor Eisenhower's belated embrace of the Kerr-Mills bill to thwart federal intrusion into the health care system returned dividends to Nixon and the Republicans. Instead, enactment of the Kerr-Mills legislation, warts and all, benefited Democrats at the polls. Presidential candidate Kennedy claimed credit for the health care program for the elderly, Democrats regained control of the White House and both houses of Congress, and Kerr and Mills boasted of having defeated national health insurance and having saved Social Security. Even Wilbur Cohen could argue that Kerr-Mills had established a precedent of sorts for a federal role in funding health care. But it also was true that Eisenhower, with support from conservative legislators, physicians, and pharmaceutical and insurance companies, had forced health reformers to scale back their ambitious agenda for national health security in favor of a more modest program that the political process might better handle: namely, health coverage, but only for the elderly recipients of Social Security who were not on welfare but who could not afford the cost of private insurance.

To those legislators and health care reformers for whom comprehensive health security for all Americans was a right of citizenship, Kerr-Mills was a way station on the road to universal health coverage. The need to go beyond Kerr-Mills became evident to them soon enough, as one state after another failed to comply with the law's requirement for attaining federal funds. The *Washington Post*, observing that the congressional intent was not and most likely would not be realized, described Kerr-Mills as "a shabby joke," noting that it provided about $12 a month extra in federal funds for medical costs to about 2.4 million Americans eligible for old-age assistance or relief. An additional 10 million elderly persons would have qualified to receive medical coverage, but *only if* the states had been willing to put up more money and *only if* the recipients had proved themselves too poor to pay their own doctor bills.[96] Given the program's flaws, health care for the elderly would remain a lively political issue in the decade of the 1960s.

# FIVE

## MEDICARE:
## A CONGRESSIONAL
## QUAGMIRE

The election of 1960 was a classic in American politics. It not only attracted the highest rate of voter participation in half a century, marked the emergence of an attractive new personality, and restored the Democrats to power after an eight-year hiatus, but it also initiated a resurgence of American liberalism. Candidate Kennedy's sponsorship of health care reform had helped to shape his political identity, give content to his candidacy, and invest his campaign with a sense of historic purpose. But President Kennedy was dissatisfied with the ineffectual Kerr-Mills health care program for the elderly and quickly aligned his administration with a contributory federal Medicare proposal to cover the health needs of the nearly 14.8 million Americans receiving Old-Age, Survivors, and Disability insurance (OASDI), a move that answered the question of whether his election-year liberalism had been a matter of convenience or conviction. Given the centrality of taxation to Social Security and health coverage for the elderly, President Kennedy's action precipitated a confrontation with Wilbur Mills, the Democratic chairman of the powerful tax-writing committee of the House. The 1960s debate about how to pay for Medicare was more than a narrow, arcane issue, for it raised serious questions about the ability of the Social Security system to withstand the high cost of health care.[1]

Public interest in health care for the elderly persisted after Kennedy's election and was, indeed, fueled by Eisenhower as he was leaving the Oval Office. Eleven days before his departure, Eisenhower, pursuant to a 1958 congressional resolution, convened a White House Conference on Aging. When he signed the resolution into law, few people expected that the conference would be held in the midst of a heated debate over the adequacy of medical coverage for the aged. Since Eisenhower was resolutely opposed to any form of compulsory government health insurance, the assumption was that HEW Secretary Flemming had carefully chosen both the conference's chair and the delegates so that a majority would reflect the administration's views.[2]

The conference *was* stacked, but not the way most observers thought, especially since the AMA's representatives dominated the panel that seemed most likely to take up what the press referred to as Medicare. But with Flemming's approval, the proponents of Medicare took control of the panel that endorsed Kennedy's view that medical care was a fundamental human right and a right of citizenship. Kennedy's position received additional support when both Marion B. Folsom, former Secretary of HEW, and Arthur Larson, Eisenhower's special assistant and favorite political philosopher, also came out publicly for Medicare.[3]

Then, on January 30, 1961, President Kennedy told Congress that "measures to provide health care for the aged under Social Security ... must be undertaken this year," and two weeks later, he sent a special message to the Hill appealing for action to deal with "the harsh consequences of illness." Within a few days, Senator Clinton P. Anderson introduced a new Medicare bill (S. 909), based on the work of the Transition Task Force on Health and Social Security, directed by Wilbur Cohen. The bill was assigned to a hostile Finance Committee. Democratic Representative Cecil R. King of California introduced a companion bill in the House (H.R. 4222), which as a tax measure financed through Social Security went to the Committee on Ways and Means, whose chairman was the powerful and equally hostile Wilbur Mills.[4]

Mills's thinking about taxation, fiscal policy, and social welfare is key to understanding why it took seven years from beginning to end for Congress to enact a federally funded health care program for elderly Americans. Mills comprehended the importance of taxation to postwar liberalism, particularly in the realms of social welfare and economic policy and, together with members of the tax policy community like Wilbur Cohen and Robert Ball, had cooperated in the gradual transformation of federal taxation from a revenue-raising device into a mechanism for earmarking government benefits for specific programs and for managing economic growth. This meant that strong income-transfer programs required sound revenue-raising mechanisms to finance them. Taxes served as that mechanism and, handled appropriately, could guarantee strong political support. Thus, Mills worked closely with the Social Security experts in the tax policy community to ensure that OASI became the centerpiece of U.S. social welfare.[5]

The "pay-as-you-go" earmarked tax system had been essential to the success of Social Security, legitimizing the absence of a means test, and winning broad middle-class and congressional support. It also ensured that Congress would raise enough taxes to cover the cost of annual benefits, and by defending the symbolic link between the Social Security *tax* and the social insurance *benefit,* Congress ruled out the possibility of directly financing Social Security pensions through general revenue. For government officials, this decision strengthened the insurance component of Social Security. Mills was not insensitive to the medical plight of the elderly, but he was committed to protecting this earmarked tax system and pay-as-you-go structure. He also knew that provisions such as Social Security and tax breaks created a sense of entitlement that fueled demands for further liberalization. This attitude put him at odds with Medicare supporters who insisted that by financing health insurance through the Social Security tax, the federal government could ameliorate the problem of elderly health care and avoid socialized medicine. The difficulty with this argument was that the earmarked tax system also constrained Social Security.[6]

The tensions this dynamic produced were evident in the long debate over Medicare. Mills feared that the Social Security tax could not withstand the high cost of health care.

He outlined two dangers to the Social Security system: first, forcing Congress to raise payroll taxes beyond acceptable limits would lead to a constituent and corporate revolt; second, Medicare would weaken the relationship between taxes and benefits by using wage-related revenue to pay for non-wage-related service benefits. For these reasons, Mills believed Congress should reject legislation for a health care program financed through the Social Security system. He was ideally positioned to prevent such a rejection, at least until he could shape the kind of Medicare bill that satisfied his concerns.[7]

Mills's reputation for fiscal integrity, his chairmanship of the Ways and Means Committee, and his willingness to reach out to tax policy experts enabled him to craft the technical substance of a health care bill that eventually gained broad bipartisan support in the fiscal committees of both the House and the Senate. Along the way, he influenced the issues that dominated the health care–tax policy agenda, the policy options that were considered or ignored, and how the Medicare legislation would be packaged for legislators and voters. He brokered compromises on Social Security and health care in a way that appeared to partially validate each interest group's efforts, without committing himself to any particular version of Medicare until the end of deliberations. Mills succeeded because as a committee chair in the pre-reform Congress of the 1960s, he benefited from its hierarchical structure, which insulated him politically, so that he could forge the delicate compromises intrinsic to tax legislation.[8]

The King-Anderson bill that came before Mills reflected largely, but not exclusively, the views of its author, Wilbur J. Cohen, who had worked closely during the transitional period with the SSA's Robert Ball and Nelson H. Cruikshank of the AFL-CIO. Cohen had become an assistant secretary for legislation in HEW, charged with writing the Medicare legislation and shepherding it through Congress. From this post, he was ideally situated to oversee the space where the theoretical concerns of health policy experts converged with the fiscal and political concerns of Wilbur Mills, and the two men, despite their policy differences, had a relationship of mutual respect.[9]

Kennedy's claim that he had a mandate to act on Medicare had a certain legitimacy. A University of Michigan survey in March 1960 showed that a majority of Americans favored federal action to help finance low-cost medical care for the elderly, as did six of every ten Americans sixty-five or older. A Gallup poll revealed that two out of three Americans favored increasing the Social Security levy to provide health insurance to the aged.[10] Support for Medicare through Social Security mounted in proportion to evidence that the Kerr-Mills program was not functioning as its sponsors had hoped. Theoretically, about 10 million Americans might have benefited from the Kerr-Mills program, but the more realistic figure was less than 2 million, chiefly because many states found it difficult to match the federal funds.[11] A Senate Special Committee on Aging reported that only about 112,000 elderly people were receiving any medical assistance under Kerr-Mills after eighteen months of operation, and 60 percent of them resided in New York, Massachusetts, and

California. Moreover, the states' monthly per person expenditure varied widely, from a high of $318.81 to a low of $18.40, and according to region. New York spent an average of $135.48 on medical assistance to cover 26,965 persons; Oklahoma, $239.60 to cover 571 people. No wonder liberal Democrats criticized Kerr-Mills as "uneven, unfair, undignified." Apart from leaders of the AMA, few people were satisfied with the program.[12]

The King-Anderson bill, whose provisions were available to all Social Security beneficiaries sixty-five or older (about 14 million people), by contrast, provided for 90 days of hospital care (with a maximum deductible of $90), outpatient diagnostic services (with a maximum deductible of $20 per service), 180 days of nursing home care, and 240 home visits by nurses and other health care specialists. Its annual cost, which included federal grants for the construction of medical school facilities and for loans to medical students (both of which the AMA opposed), was estimated at $1.5 billion. To pay for the program, the bill increased the Social Security tax on both employees and employers 0.25 percent. Like all other health insurance legislation, the King-Anderson bill specifically prohibited restriction of a patient's choice of physician, interference with medical practice, control over the physician, and violation of patient-doctor confidentiality. The cost of physicians was excluded so that Medicare would not infringe on the jurisdiction of the medical industry, which was dominated by private physicians, and hence might make it past the powerful AMA.[13]

King-Anderson also contrasted with the Kerr-Mills plan in two important respects: the selection of a physician and privacy. The latter plan rarely gave patients freedom of choice in selecting a physician. Kerr-Mills was essentially a welfare program, and welfare patients took what they were given; their physician was whichever intern was on duty when they arrived at a hospital. As for privacy, applicants for Kerr-Mills assistance in many states were potentially subject to having their incomes and assets checked, their homes rifled for evidence of valuable personal property, and their medical record scrutinized by any welfare department clerk. Moreover, because Kerr-Mills vested control over medical care firmly in the hands of local and state politicians who put up the matching funds, the delivery and quality of care were often uneven.[14]

Nonetheless, the AMA denounced King-Anderson as "the most deadly challenge" the medical profession had ever faced, and in February 1961, it renewed its campaign against public financing of health care for the aged. A bureaucratically developed and administered fee schedule for hospitals, nursing homes, and nurses would establish a precedent for regimenting physicians' services, it insisted, and portrayed King-Anderson as coercive and wasteful, like the British National Health Service. The AMA repeated the warning that extending Medicare's benefits to everyone under Social Security regardless of ability to pay would prove ruinously expensive and lead to inferior medical care.

The AMA also established the American Medical Political Action Committee (AMPAC), disguised for tax purposes as an educational division, to influence the outcome of the fall congressional elections. It initially appointed all Republicans to its board of directors, but then it realized that this effectively wrote off the entire South, one of its bastions of support. AMPAC also even enlisted a politically ambitious actor, Ronald Reagan, to prepare a tape describing Medicare as the wedge to State socialism and urging insurance companies to enroll the elderly en masse to undercut King-Anderson. By the end of 1961, forty-six state medical societies, taking their cue from AMPAC, had set up their own political action committees.[15]

What was remarkable was the degree to which the AMA and its allies intruded into the political arena in 1961, 1962, 1963, and 1964 and repeatedly resorted to the same successful tactics. The Metropolitan Life Insurance Company's brokers organized a letter-writing campaign against King-Anderson; in January 1962, the president of Mutual of Omaha wrote Senator Kerr, "You can count on our continued efforts to do everything we may properly do to implement your well-considered legislation, and to continue to do all possible to provide health insurance for the aged in the traditional voluntary way." The Blue Cross Association made "a historic decision" to finance its own program of comprehensive health care benefits for the aged, although it was never able to work out the technical details or inform anyone of the program's benefits.[16]

The AMA's allies in Congress argued that Kerr-Mills had not been given a fair test and insisted that the medical needs of the elderly were best provided at the local level, warning that financing Medicare through Social Security would drive up payroll taxes. Senator Kerr's opposition to King-Anderson was informed by state rather than national concerns; he believed, as a matter of principle, that states and localities could best handle the problem of the elderly uninsured.[17] But it is also true that Kerr represented a state where political and social conservatism was the hallmark of both political parties and legislators paid close attention to their constituents' views. He was under tremendous pressure to oppose King-Anderson. When one Oklahoma state legislator wrote that the King-Anderson bill was "a form of insurance against the health hazards of old age" and "an integral and inescapable aspect of social security and railroad retirement," Kerr replied, "I must in all frankness to you say that at this time my position in this matter has not changed."[18] Page Belcher, the lone Republican representative from the Sooner State, wrote to a family from Bartlesville that he would "never vote for any bill that will lead us into socialized medicine" and assured one physician that he would "continue to oppose any and all of the liberal, wild-eyed, socialistic legislation that comes from the New Frontier." To the medical staff of Enid Memorial Hospital he said, "continue to create public sentiment against this attempt to socialize the medical profession," because it would make his uphill fight a little easier.[19]

The constellation of interests around the Medicare bill was varied, however, which rendered the AMA's hold over its allies never as firm as it would have liked. Thus, the National Council of Churches unexpectedly endorsed Medicare in February 1962, whereas the United Presbyterian Church's General Assembly stopped short of taking the same action, thanks to intensive AMA lobbying. The AMA threatened reprisals against the American Nurses Association if it did not retract its 1958 endorsement of Medicare, and it pressured the AHA to remain neutral on King-Anderson. But it did experience a serious defection when a growing number of academic and salaried physicians, public health doctors, and those who practiced in large urban areas, fed up with the organization's negative tactics, formed the Physicians Committee for Health Care for the Aged through Social Security. Its membership included the president of the Group Health Association of America; New York Hospital's chief physician; the head of medical services at Massachusetts General Hospital; New York City's commissioner of health; two Nobel laureates in medicine; pediatrician Benjamin Spock; and heart surgeon Dr. Michael DeBakey.[20] Organized labor and the National Council of Senior Citizens, a lobbying group built around remnants of the Senior Citizens for Kennedy in the 1960 campaign, supported the physicians committee.[21]

Despite the counterlobbying and President Kennedy's call for action, the King-Anderson bill remained locked in the House Ways and Means Committee.[22] Before Wilbur Mills, its chairman, would entertain any version of King-Anderson, he insisted on statutory assurances that revenue gained from wage-base increases would be earmarked to pay for OASDI, not for health benefits. Otherwise, Mills feared escalating medical costs, combined with voter demand for more generous benefits (once constituents discovered that King-Anderson did not cover the cost of physicians), would create pressure on legislators. Either they would raise Social Security taxes beyond reasonable levels (considered to be 10 percent of the payroll), or they would dip into general revenues to pay for the additional benefits, thereby weakening the distinction between social insurance and welfare. The King-Anderson bill also had technical problems that troubled Mills, such as tampering in a number of areas with the complex actuarial logic that underpinned Social Security, leaving payment of hospital costs open-ended, and awarding benefits to individuals who had retired before paying additional Social Security taxes.[23]

Given these issues, Mills warned that Congress would reject the measure, especially since some legislators were terrified of antagonizing the AMA. He did not support the King-Anderson bill, and he used the power of his committee chairmanship to block it from coming to the floor of the House. Without a majority of the committee to override Mills, the best Kennedy could do was to keep health care for the elderly in the forefront of the national consciousness, flush out its opponents, and continue to lay the groundwork for its eventual passage.

Persuaded that medical care for the elderly was an emerging national issue that the Democrats had failed to address in the 1960 campaign, Kennedy made passage of Medicare a priority item on his 1962 domestic agenda.[24] In doing so, he was responding to the argument of presidential assistant Kenneth O'Donnell and Richard Maguire of the

Democratic National Committee that Medicare was the only issue important enough to minimize the losses that the party in power normally suffered in off-year elections. If the party lost heavily in November, they warned, there would be very little chance of getting any legislation through Congress. Partisan politics, then, converged with the health needs of the elderly in driving the president's decision.[25]

Accordingly, the White House signaled Wilbur Cohen, Robert Ball, and others to fine-tune the King-Anderson Medicare bill for the 1962 congressional session. This meant that they would have to redesign the bill to satisfy Mills's concerns without sacrificing its integrity and to gain the votes of legislators who were wavering. Of the major undecided votes on the Ways and Means Committee, Cohen identified Virginia Democrat Burr Harrison as amenable to persuasion, but Harrison shared many of the same reservations as Wilbur Mills. He wanted to shield the program from financial pressures, tighten eligibility requirements, close gaps that allowed individuals who had never paid into the Social Security system to receive health coverage, and to have hospitals designate private, voluntary Blue Cross plans as their agents. Reimbursements, then, would go from the federal government to Blue Cross rather than directly to the hospitals.[26]

Cohen spent much of the spring and early summer of 1962 making modifications that would satisfy Mills, Harrison, and others to the point that he risked alienating liberals and organized labor. However, he believed that flexibility without sacrificing basic principles was necessary to loosen some Republican votes for the administration's proposal.[27] After intense negotiations with Senators Anderson and Jacob Javits, the liberal Republican from New York, he hammered out a significant agreement on June 28 to include an option for reimbursement to private health insurance plans.[28]

White House advisers, meanwhile, urged the president to take his proposal "to the people" directly, via television, so that reporters would not be able to filter his words. Kennedy had already demonstrated that he was very good at turning television into a major political asset, and he seized the opportunity when the National Council of Senior Citizens scheduled a pro-Medicare rally for May 20, 1962, in Madison Square Garden. Kennedy could hardly ask for a more dramatic setting to ignite a popular demand for Medicare across the country.[29] The White House announced the decision in March that the president would make a nationally televised address at the rally, a decision that took on a new urgency because the King-Anderson bill was again in trouble in the House, where Mills's views on tax matters were accepted unquestioningly. On March 21, Senator Kerr's legislative aide wrote a confidential note to a prominent Tennessee Republican, saying, "I do not think that either the Chairman of the House Ways and Means Committee or the Chairman of the Senate Finance Committee is in favor of the King-Anderson Bill," and "I will be somewhat surprised if we are not able to hold the matter status quo."[30]

As the appointed date drew near, a euphoria began to take hold among Medicare's proponents that Kennedy's speech would actually make the difference between victory and defeat. Democratic congressional leaders told the president they had discerned a groundswell of public support for Medicare during the Easter recess. The report of the President's Council on Aging endorsed King-Anderson, which led the AMA to mount a new propaganda campaign against Medicare in the week before Kennedy's address.[31] Finally, on May 20, Kennedy stood before a capacity crowd of 20,000 older people in Madison Square Garden and a nationally televised audience. Setting aside the prepared text, with which he was dissatisfied, he delivered one of the worst extemporaneous speeches of his career. The president's address fell flat because it did not distinguish between his two audiences. He had the support of the senior citizens in the Garden; what he had to do was to persuade the skeptical TV viewer at home that Medicare was needed now, and this he did not do. The speech failed to arouse grassroots pressure on Congress and, worse, annoyed Wilbur Mills and other legislators, who were unlikely ever to be persuaded by such a rally.[32] Oklahoma Republican Page Belcher criticized the use of taxpayer money and complained, "The handling of this entire propaganda campaign ... is just another example of what lengths this administration will go to cram every kind of socialistic legislation down the throats of every American."[33]

The following day, after the television networks had rebuffed the AMA's demand for equal time for rebuttal, the organization purchased thirty minutes of prime-time television and also rented Madison Square Garden to argue its case. Before a symbolically empty arena, the head of the AMA's speaker's bureau ripped into the King-Anderson bill and extolled the virtues of the Kerr-Mills program. In response to reporters' queries, Kennedy said he "gathered" the AMA had been critical of the Medicare bill, which elicited chuckles from the press corps. Striking a serious note, Kennedy pointed out that the AMA had used similar language to successfully defeat President Eisenhower's private, voluntary reinsurance proposal.[34]

The AMA won the contest in the Garden, but the experience stiffened the president's resolve to press forward with King-Anderson and not to accept a Medicare compromise that did not include Social Security financing. "Social Security is at the heart of the legislation. That isn't a compromise. That'd be—just be giving up on the bill, and we don't plan to do that,"[35] Kennedy told reporters. Quite the contrary. He was encouraged by a report from the consulting firm of John F. Kraft, Inc., to the Democratic Senatorial Campaign Committee that June. In a confidential memorandum to the campaign chair, Senator Vance R. Hartke of Indiana, the consultants concluded, "In short, it appears that no matter where people are asked, their overall reaction is that they like and approve of the idea of providing medical care to people over 65, under Social Security" and paying for it with an increase in payroll taxes. The respondents, however, were not asked specifically whether they favored King-Anderson, because the interviewers believed the reaction would be "entirely 'gut,'" tied to whether the respondents liked or disliked the president and his legislative agenda. The consultants also indicated that criticism of the president's recent handling of the steel crisis "might be less beneficial to Medicare than it would have been in March, though still strongly positive."[36]

As the fight to win public support splashed across the media, Cohen continued to modify the Medicare bill to make it easier for private plans to qualify for federal reimbursement. The changes, he hoped, would free it from the Ways and Means Committee and attract Republican votes. He achieved a modicum of success when, on July 11, Republican Jacob Javits agreed to sponsor the revisions in the Senate and Wilbur Mills signaled House Speaker John McCormack that he would facilitate a resolution of the impasse. Mills suggested that the King-Anderson proposal be attached as a rider to a House-passed bill when it came up for a vote in the Senate, a parliamentary maneuver that would bypass his committee. Once the bill emerged from conference, it would go directly to the floor of the House for a vote.[37]

Kennedy had tried a similar tactic in 1960, but the prospect of success, according to a Gallup poll, appeared no better two years later. But with few other options available, the White House acted on Mills's suggestion when the Senate took up a House-passed public welfare bill. Debate opened in the Senate on a desultory, almost perfunctory note on July 2, but its tenor changed dramatically after Senator Anderson amended the bill to include Medicare. The AMA flew physicians to Washington by the thousands from all over the country, including some in Senator Kerr's private plane, to buttonhole legislators to vote against the amendment.[38]

On three successive Tuesday mornings, July 3, 10, and 17, the president and his advisers held breakfast meetings with legislative leaders to discuss strategy. Lawrence O'Brien, the chief liaison with Congress, reported on July 10 that a Senate head count showed a lineup of fifty-one to forty-nine in favor of the bill, due to switches from their 1960–1961 positions by four liberal Republicans and one moderate Southern Democrat. Doubts were raised almost immediately about the reliability of the head count, which had been taken by Robert Baker, the secretary to Senate Majority Leader Mike Mansfield. O'Brien's head count the following Tuesday revealed at best a tie vote. More ominously, he reported, "Senator Randolph has a problem," referring to West Virginia Democrat Jennings Randolph, whose state faced an unmanageable debt as a result of spending more federal funds on welfare programs than it was legally entitled to spend.[39]

Randolph's problem became the administration's problem. In spite of reassurances from Cohen and HEW Secretary Abraham Ribicoff that the administration would cover the debt, Senator Kerr dangled a more tempting solution: inserting a clause in the welfare bill forgiving West Virginia's indebtedness. Randolph insisted that he had not made up his mind on the matter, but the White House assumed correctly that the quid pro quo was his vote against Medicare. Nonetheless, the administration pulled out all the stops, working through Democratic officials and influential labor leaders in West Virginia to hold on to Randolph's vote. Further complicating an already difficult situation, Arizona's Democratic senator, Carl Hayden, informed the White House that he could be counted on if his vote were really needed. Otherwise, he would cast it against Medicare. Prior to the final vote on July 17, the administration was assured of only forty-eight votes solidly for Medicare. If Randolph and Hayden supported the measure, the vote would end in a tie, which Vice President Johnson would break by casting his ballot in favor of the bill. Instead, the Senate voted fifty-two to forty-eight to table Anderson's amendment, thus taking it out of consideration. Randolph had returned Kerr's favor and Hayden went along with Randolph. Kerr's stratagem had killed Medicare for 1962.[40]

Randolph never explained why he had so little confidence in the Kennedy administration's delivering on its promise, but the AMA and its allies were jubilant.[41] One retired Travelers Insurance executive wrote to Vice President Johnson on July 19 that the president should realize that "he cannot drive the Congress to his ideas and demands, as he could in Boston, Mass., with their ward politics."[42] Kennedy never got over the disappointment of this defeat, although, in response to reporters' questions, he tried to put the best possible face on the defection of twenty-one Democrats. The issue in the November elections, he predicted, would be between those who opposed Medicare and those who were for it. What he left unsaid was that even if the Senate had passed Medicare in 1962, it might still have proved impossible to get the measure out of the Ways and Means Committee or a joint conference committee.[43]

Kerr's stratagem had delayed the passage of Medicare, but it did not stop the momentum; Americans were becoming increasingly aware that most of the elderly were ineligible for the type of private health insurance that was comprehensive enough to fulfill their needs and inexpensive enough to fit their budgets. More ominous for the bill's opponents, the AMA's intrusion into the congressional elections that fall did not return dividends commensurate with the expenditure of its resources. President Kennedy would have a huge Democratic margin to work with in 1963, eighty-two in the House and thirty-four in the Senate.[44] Southern Democrats might not be counted upon to support certain progressive aspects of the administration's legislative program, but not a single seat was lost by a candidate who had spoken out publicly in favor of Medicare, a fact that was not lost on other legislators, who also noted that the AMA was not above turning on even its oldest friends, such as Senator Lister Hill of Alabama.[45] Alabama physicians and the AMA supported his opponent when he came up for reelection. Although he won by a narrow margin, he was deeply embittered by the treatment he had received and, in 1965, voted for Medicare, persuading his junior colleague, Senator John Sparkman, to go along, too.

Of more immediate concern to the administration was the internal dissension that defeat of the Medicare amendment provoked. HEW Undersecretary Ivan Nestingen censured Cohen's strategy of concession and accommodation, accusing him of coddling Wilbur Mills, conceding too much to Harrison and Javits, and having nothing to show for his efforts except an embarrassing public defeat. The better tactic, Nestingen argued, was to confront Mills and other opponents with the facts showing Medicare's popularity and mobilizing public pressure to force critics to pass the bill. Critical of Cohen's private negotiating skills, Nestingen found a sympathetic ear in Senator Pat McNamara and White House operative Kenneth O'Donnell and remained a thorn in Cohen's side until Nestingen's departure from HEW in 1965.[46]

Cohen insisted that Mills would not succumb to that type of pressure. Kennedy agreed and in December 1962 reaffirmed Cohen as the administration's point man in a new push for the King-Anderson bill. HEW's new secretary, Anthony Celebrezze, meanwhile, suggested omitting the "option" provision for the continuation of private insurance from any future bill.[47] This was only one of a number of alternative proposals for King-Anderson circulating on Capitol Hill by spring 1963. Others included Louisiana Senator Russell Long's "catastrophic" plan to pay medical bills exceeding 20 percent of an individual's income. Cohen thought the plan was flawed but, not wishing to antagonize the Louisianan who might one day be appointed to a conference committee on Medicare, offered to help put it into legislative shape. The growing congressional interest in health care, Cohen believed, was a sign that the administration was moving in the right direction, but Cohen also knew that the president would eventually have to deal with the southern wing of the party. No bill would emerge from a conference committee that included Mills, Harry Byrd, Russell Long, or Florida's George Smathers without modifications to the administration's basic proposals.[48] Even the endorsement of Medicare in November 1963 by Senator Javits's organization, the National Committee on Health Care of the Aged, meant little without Mills's imprimatur, and he was still raising objections. Mills told Cohen that hospital insurance should be funded under OASDI through higher tax rates, rather than raising the ceiling on the amount of a person's wages on which Social Security taxes were paid, and suggested that a private, nonprofit insurance agency such as Blue Cross administer the program. But he did promise to conduct hearings on Medicare once he disposed of the omnibus tax bill, which had the highest priority.[49]

Both sides in the Medicare battle used the legislative lull to strengthen their support on the Hill and beyond. The administration offered a number of compromises that the AMA and its allies rejected.[50] The head of the Health Insurance Association of America warned that Medicare would regiment physicians and stifle progress in the delivery and quality of health care.[51] Oklahoma Republican Page Belcher told one constituent, "I sincerely feel any venture by the Federal government into the field of subsidizing medical care is a step toward socialized medicine—socialism which gives away so easily to the evil of communism, and erosion of our American heritage."[52] What puzzled him was why so many businessmen supported Kennedy's election and continued to do so.[53]

That fall, after completion of its work on the tax bill, the Ways and Means Committee reconvened for another round of hearings on health care. The records of the Kerr-Mills program as well as the King-Anderson proposal were up for scrutiny.[54] HEW Secretary

Celebrezze made a powerful plea for the administration's proposal on November 18, 1963, testifying that Americans over sixty-five used hospital care three times more often than those under sixty-five, yet they lived on less than half the income of younger people in similar family situations.[55] The most severely affected, he asserted, were middle- and working-class Americans ineligible for public assistance, who fell through the holes in the safety net and who shouldered the heavy burden of medical expenses with inadequate financial resources. The administration's proposal, he concluded, did away with the means test and was "a logical extension of the present social security program," because "private insurance—no matter how imaginatively conceived and energetically applied—cannot by itself meet the need of the aged for protection against the high costs of medical care."[56]

On November 22, 1963, the fifth day of testimony, as heated words crossed between Democratic Representative Al Ullman of Oregon and a witness representing more than five hundred insurance companies, the committee's chief counsel hurried into the hearing room and whispered to Chairman Mills. Turning pale, Mills interrupted the proceedings to announce that President Kennedy had been shot, and then he adjourned the hearings. At the time of Kennedy's assassination, Medicare legislation remained locked in the Ways and Means Committee, with little prospect of passage.[57]

At that darkest hour, a secretary rushed into Wilbur Cohen's office to tell him about the assassination. Cohen had been poring over a memorandum that he and Henry Hall Wilson, Jr., a member of the White House congressional liaison staff, had drafted at Kennedy's request suggesting ways to accommodate Mills's objections. Cohen and Wilson believed they were on the verge of a breakthrough with the Arkansas Democrat when they got the news. Despite his shock and grief, Cohen worked into the weekend, searching for the way through the congressional maze. On Monday, an hour or so after the funeral, Wilson telephoned Cohen to say that White House aide Larry O'Brien thought Lyndon B. Johnson, the new president, should see the memorandum. Wilson took it to O'Brien, who, on November 26, briefed Johnson on the status of various legislative items. Of Medicare, O'Brien wrote, "Chairman Mills appeared to be willing to work out some compromise next year, and the Administration should continue to press for this legislation in order to get a bill reported out early next year."[58]

Johnson subsequently decided to complete and go beyond the liberal agenda of his Democratic predecessors. Building on the strengths of prosperity rather than the necessities of depression, his blueprint for the Great Society would fulfill all the hopes that had been beyond the reach of the New Deal to guarantee a richer quality of life and a decent standard of living for all Americans.[59] In his first address to Congress, on November 27, 1963, President Johnson called for action on "the dream of care for the elderly."[60] He urged Cohen, Ball, and Myers to design a politically feasible version of King-Anderson. HEW, meanwhile, included hospital insurance for the aged in its legislative agenda for

1964, with the notation that this "will contribute to the attack on poverty." Medicare, like federal aid to education, had become an essential component of the antipoverty program that constituted the keystone of the Great Society.[61]

However, when the 88th Congress convened in January 1964, the administration was no more certain than its predecessor that it could get its Medicare bill through the Ways and Means Committee. Sensing a shift in public sentiment, Mills appeared to have more interest in such legislation, but he remained hostile to the King-Anderson approach of financing Medicare through Social Security. He still feared that hospital costs would rise faster than wages; that taxes would have to be increased to pay for them; and that as costs escalated, it would become more and more difficult to keep the Social Security system solvent. Establishing the actuarial soundness of Social Security tied to Medicare, Larry O'Brien told the president, was absolutely crucial to overcoming Mills's opposition.[62] The administration's other concern was that Mills might report a Social Security bill that did not include Medicare right before the fall congressional elections. This would then put great pressure on the White House to accept the Mills version of Medicare.[63]

Given the uncertainty about Mills's intentions, the White House put little stock in an "exclusive" report that claimed that Mills believed the existing Kerr-Mills health care program was a failure and that he was about to jettison it, or to a *Wall Street Journal* declaration that Medicare was "a good bet to come out of Congress this year." When an AMA lobbyist sought to pin down Mills, he refused to comment, which further contributed to the uncertainty. The only "certainty" was that Mills refused to tell the administration or other policy makers what he wanted. By withholding clear statements about his own position, Mills avoided backing himself into a corner through hasty promises. This gave him room to maneuver around alternative proposals in order to design effective compromises, but it left administration officials like Cohen guessing about his intentions.[64]

Meanwhile, the composition of the Ways and Means Committee remained unfavorable to the White House—either 14 to 11 against Medicare financed through Social Security or 13 to 12 against it. The 10 Republicans and 3 of the 15 Democrats on the committee—Mills, A. Sydney Herlong of Florida, and John C. Watts of Kentucky—opposed the King-Anderson bill, whereas Clark W. Thompson of Texas was undecided.[65] The administration's bill was further jeopardized by the introduction of two liberal Republican versions of health insurance: a Javits bill, which adhered closely to the recommendations of his Committee on Health Care of the Aged and differed only slightly from the King-Anderson bill, and a Lindsay bill, which offered the elderly an option between Medicare and increased cash benefits to purchase private hospital insurance. The latter was the proposal of Representative John Lindsay of New York and contained an idea associated with Nelson Rockefeller, a potential Republican presidential candidate.[66]

Although neither Republican bill elicited much interest, they did suggest that bipartisan momentum was building for some form of health insurance for the elderly, and this made Wilbur Cohen cautiously optimistic that Congress would enact legislation in this session. On January 24, 1964, he, Henry Wilson, and Mills conferred for nearly two hours during which Mills again asked the administration to modify its bill to permit Blue Cross to administer the hospital insurance program; to require proof of retirement for receipt of hospital insurance benefits; to increase the maximum earnings base to a figure above $5,200 a year to assure the actuarial soundness of the hospital insurance program; and to overhaul Kerr-Mills to make it more attractive to the states. After the meeting, Mills dispensed with further public hearings and took his committee into executive session. He indicated privately to Cohen that the committee might report a Medicare bill in late March or April, a schedule that would again allow Democrats to make Social Security an election issue in the fall.[67]

While Cohen took Mills's suggestions under advisement, he, Wilson, HEW Secretary Celebrezze, Elmer Staats of the Budget Bureau, and White House counsel Myer "Mike" Feldman met with the president to vet the health message he would deliver on February 10. Johnson barely glanced at the text before inquiring about their progress with Mills. Cohen responded that the prospect of Mills's reporting out a bill that included hospital insurance was promising. A few hours before the president was to deliver his health address, Cohen briefed the press. "The fundamental principles have been agreed upon . . . that [Medicare] would only cover hospitalization, leaving private enterprise the supplementation of physicians' services," he told reporters. The issues had "worked themselves out." For the first time in thirteen years, Cohen felt confident that Congress would embrace federal underwriting of health care. Responding to a reporter's query as to whether the administration could attain Medicare without Mills's cooperation, Cohen answered tactfully, "Any discussions that did not include Wilbur Mills would not be very important discussions."[68]

That evening, President Johnson informed Americans that he had submitted a budget to Congress that included expending $5.4 billion on health and health-related activities. Medicare, he insisted, was the logical extension of Social Security, because neither private health insurance nor welfare medical assistance offered a comprehensive solution to medical problems of the elderly. He would recommend to Congress a federally sponsored hospital insurance program to protect against the most burdensome costs of serious illness—the costs of hospital and related care. It would provide a foundation upon which to erect complementary private programs and "would not hinder the freedom of choice of doctor, hospital or nurse." The president assured Americans that the program "would not specify the kind of medical or health care. Complete discretion would be vested in the patient and his physician."[69]

The president's address was a significant step toward meeting Mills's objections, but it did not guarantee that the Arkansas Democrat would release Medicare from the committee or send a bill to the floor of the House before Congress's Easter recess. In fact, conservative members of the committee encouraged constituents to write to Mills urging him to hold the line. Oklahoma Republican Page Belcher told one Tulsa resident that without letters such as his, "you can be sure that the King-Anderson Bill would have been out of the Committee long before this time."[70] Belcher did not exaggerate; Johnson was pressing his staff to hammer out the details of a bill with Mills as quickly as possible, one that organized labor could support. But White House staffer Henry Wilson ranked Medicare no higher than "passage probable," which meant the administration still had a lot of work before it.[71]

Although Johnson also talked directly with Mills, the latter gave no assurances. He resumed public hearings on Medicare in April and then took the Ways and Means Committee into executive session during which he used his considerable powers to revise the King-Anderson proposal.[72] Cohen provided expert advice on technical questions almost daily over the next six weeks, as the committee sorted through the complexities of health insurance, Social Security benefit increases, and how to improve the Kerr-Mills program. Demonstrating his command of the actuarial logic behind Social Security, Mills made inordinate demands on Cohen and the SSA staff, requesting memoranda on policy alternatives, cost-benefit analyses of every potential change in the Social Security program, and even a draft of a Medicaid program to provide health coverage for welfare recipients. In his determination to protect the solvency of Social Security and the payroll tax system from open-ended hospital costs, he left no option unexplored.[73]

Henry Wilson's memos to Lawrence O'Brien provide a window into Mills's thinking about the content of Medicare and the politics accompanying the Medicare negotiations. In one, Wilson related that he and Mills had discussed various combinations that the Arkansas Democrat might support, but that so far Mills had "not yet worked out a satisfactory combination." Mills did not foreclose the possibility of bringing a bill to the floor, Wilson reported, and was "strongly toying with a pretty fancy revision of Kerr-Mills with which it would appear to be possible to tie in Social Security." In another memorandum, Wilson cited "pretty strong indications" that Mills had decided to drop nursing home coverage from King-Anderson, to raise the base to $6,000, to increase OASDI benefits by 5 to 6 percent (financing the increase by raising contributions to 5 percent), and to streamline Kerr-Mills by grandfathering in those over seventy-two years of age, subject to a means test.[74]

Mills also concerned himself with the legislative process in the House once the bill left his committee. Many Democratic members, specifically those from New Mexico, Idaho, southern Illinois, rural Pennsylvania, Ohio, Indiana, and Texas, preferred not to record their vote on Medicare just yet, believing their chances for reelection would be enhanced by preserving it as an election issue. But according to Wilson, Mills also wanted "desperately" the support of Kentucky Representative John C. Watts, "and again I'm sure his motive is floor votes rather than fear of a 13–12 vote." Through Wilson, Watts signaled Mills that he "would go with what Mills would." This apparently surprised Mills, who said he'd "get on Watts immediately." Wilson offered to try to persuade Florida Representative A. Sydney Herlong to come on board, but he confessed to O'Brien that he considered that "a pretty hopeless exercise."[75]

As his aides beat the bushes to line up the votes of House Democrats, President Johnson invoked his considerable powers of persuasion to enlist the support of businessmen and lawmakers. He invited officials of the U.S. Chamber of Commerce to the White House for the famous "Johnson treatment," and he reminded fellow Texan Clark Thompson of the 2,500 letters he had written to the latter's constituents in his most recent primary fight. Thompson's conversion narrowed the count in the Ways and Means Committee to thirteen to twelve against Medicare.[76] The mind-numbing process of finding a formula acceptable to Mills, meanwhile, dragged on. Cohen and Mills met on May 5 and May 15 to hammer out a proposal allowing the elderly the option of electing higher cash benefits or hospital coverage. Blue Cross would administer the hospital insurance plan, with hospitals being reimbursed up to 99 percent of their costs. This precluded any private insurance company from becoming the administering agent. Cohen relayed this change to Robert Ball of the SSA, who agreed that this was a brilliant maneuver to quiet objections to private insurance company participation in Medicare from HEW Secretary Celebrezze and labor's Nelson Cruikshank. It also would commit Blue Cross to the program.[77]

The negotiations dragged into June, as Mills juggled alternatives: the number of days and size of the deductible, the age of eligibility, and the percentage increase for old-age benefits. He discarded the means test in favor of an age requirement, sixty-seven for men and sixty-five for women; he refused to go for a base higher than $5,800. Cohen and Wilson offered Mills an additional dozen or more proposals to consider. Cohen accepted Mills's age and base figures, but he thought the package should include a 5 percent old-age benefit increase, forty-five days of hospitalization, two days of deductible, and a twelve-month lead time for HEW to implement the program.[78] Meanwhile, Wilson apprised O'Brien of their efforts to build up political support for Medicare in the committee. He reported that Cohen was "trying to get hold of Senator Smathers to talk to him about pushing Herlong." Mills was discussing Medicare with Watts, Herlong, and Thompson; he was confident of Watts's vote, "but needs more assurance about Herlong." Once Mills had cleared away as many obstacles to the bill as he could prior to the committee's vote, Wilson reported, Mills would give Cohen the go-ahead for King to offer a discharge motion.[79]

The White House was, by now, cautiously anticipating a favorable report from the Ways and Means Committee—which was tantamount to passing Medicare, since the full House rarely questioned a tax bill originating from Mills's committee—and so it shifted its attention to the Senate. White House aide Mike Manatos, who had conducted a roll-call analysis of the Senate's 1962 Medicare vote, wrote on May 20 to O'Brien, "Opponents of Medicare who succeeded . . . in defeating a tabling motion by a 52–48 vote have lost

appreciable numbers by reason of death, defeat, retirement, switches in attitude, etc."
These included Senators Kerr, who passed away in January 1963, and Jennings Randolph
and Carl Hayden, who were now supporting Medicare. "Thus assuming the identical set
of circumstances as in 1962, we could win a Medicare vote by 54–46," Manatos predicted.
Other signs also pointed to a more favorable outcome: Senators Russell, Hill, Sparkman,
and Oklahoma's Mike Monroney now supported Medicare, making it unnecessary to bypass the Finance Committee. Hill wanted to punish Alabama's medical establishment for
deserting him in the last election, and Kerr's death removed the most formidable opponent of Medicare in the Senate. Monroney, who had become the senior Senator from
Oklahoma, was willing to support the administration. "It is reasonable to assume that we
could conceivably add 5 or 6 Southern votes should Medicare pass the House and reach
the Senate floor by way of the Finance Committee," Manatos concluded, but added that if
the Finance Committee proved recalcitrant, "we have a revenue bill on the Senate Calendar which would serve as a vehicle for Medicare."[80]

Two days after writing this memorandum, Cohen, Senator McNamara, and White House
officials accompanied President Johnson to Michigan, where he would deliver the commencement address that included his vision of the Great Society. En route to Ann Arbor,
Johnson asked Cohen about the progress of negotiations with Wilbur Mills, which caused
McNamara to fly into a rage. Unaware that Mills had agreed to discard the much-despised
Kerr-Mills means test, McNamara feared a compromise proposal would retain it and remained skeptical of Cohen's assurances.[81] When they returned to Washington, Cohen immediately set to work mending political fences. He reassured administration economists that
health coverage for the elderly, the expansion of Kerr-Mills, and increasing Social Security
benefits would not act as a drag on the economy or negate the effects of the administration's
tax cut; he assured HEW Secretary Celebrezze that raising the earnings base to $12,000
would fully fund Medicare and any other changes that Mills might propose.[82]

But Mills still was not satisfied, and he continued to experiment with the size of the
deductible, the age of eligibility, and the amount of the cash benefit for Social Security recipients. By June 9, the negotiations had become so intense that Cohen enlisted help from
Speaker McCormack and other congressional leaders to determine what it would take for
Mills to commit. Louisiana Representative Hale Boggs suggested that President Johnson
invite Mills and the Democratic leadership to the White House, but the president had already gone this route. Labor's chief lobbyists, Cruikshank and Biemiller, meanwhile, reported that Mills was still hoping to win over Watts and Herlong before bringing Medicare to a vote in the committee. Shortly thereafter, Mills announced that Watts had
switched, giving the chairman his proxy. The vote in the committee now stood at thirteen
to twelve for the bill, which made it possible for Mills to support Medicare.[83]

Until this point, Mills had not wanted his to be the decisive vote. If the AMA balked, he
could explain his vote by telling the doctors that it enabled him to retain control over the

measure in order to prevent it from becoming more objectionable to them than it already was. But on June 23, the day before the committee was scheduled to vote, Watts unexpectedly withdrew his proxy and informed Mills that he would oppose the bill. Pressure from the AMA, the tobacco industry, and a forthcoming election that November had forced Watts to rescind his proxy. Mills then reversed course, telling Cohen he would not support King-Anderson but a Social Security cash benefit instead. He suggested that the administration either take King-Anderson off the table until the following year or attach to it the Social Security bill once it reached the Senate. At that point, Mills indicated that he might be able to convince the AMA that something stronger would come out of conference and that he would act as a mediator by "watering it down." Visibly upset, King, the House sponsor of Medicare, pulled his request for a committee vote on the bill. He did not want an adverse vote entered into the record, fearing it would become more difficult to revive Medicare at a later date.[84]

Months of delicate political maneuvering, of concession and compromise, had unraveled. Medicare did not proceed to a vote in the Ways and Means Committee or on the House floor. On July 1, 1964, the committee reported out a bill incorporating amendments to the Social Security Act, but as Cohen informed Secretary Celebrezze, it "does *not* include any amendments relating to Medical Assistance to the Aged (the Kerr-Mills program) or any provisions relating to hospital insurance."[85] The administration's only success was to beat back the insidiously clever proposal of conservative Republican John W. Byrnes of Wisconsin to increase Social Security benefits by 6 percent, instead of the previously agreed on 5 percent. Byrnes's amendment violated the bipartisan consensus that had developed in Congress since 1935 that the Social Security tax should never go above 10 percent. It would have brought the tax rate on employees and employers above 9.5 percent, leaving no room for the 0.5 percent required to pay for Medicare should the Senate resurrect it as an amendment to the final Social Security bill. Democratic Representative Al Ullman, who realized the implications of Byrnes's amendment, rallied the committee's pro-Medicare forces, and the amendment ultimately failed on a twelve to twelve tie vote (one liberal Representative being absent and the arch-conservative Bruce Alger of Texas voting against the 6 percent increase). This allowed the committee to report out the Social Security amendments based on the 5 percent increase, which the full House then approved with only eight negative votes.[86]

Medicare's defeat in committee was a serious blow to the administration. On July 9, Larry O'Brien consigned it and immigration legislation to the "impossible" category among thirty-one priority bills for the current legislative session. Adding insult to injury, pressure also emanated from the Senate to drop Medicare. Mike Manatos informed O'Brien on July 13 that Elizabeth Springer, chief clerk of the Finance Committee and a conduit for the views of chairman Harry Byrd, reported that the committee was threatening to hold the House bill with its increase in Social Security benefits hostage, should the administration push to include Medicare in the Senate version. "If the President insists on Medicare," wrote Manatos, "it would force the Committee to hold hearings which would last until October." Springer hoped that "it would be possible to get an agreement with the Administration which would preclude Medicare and allow an August adjournment."[87]

But this kind of deal ran counter to White House thinking and led Cohen and SSA Administrator Robert Ball to propose two options the administration might pursue: one, to add Medicare to the House bill in conference in the hope that Mills would agree to a compromise; the other, to have the Senate pass some modified Medicare measure offering Social Security recipients the choice of accepting the cash benefit increase or health insurance. Cohen thought Mills might accept the latter option without any need for a conference, but he noted that each option brought its own complications. If Medicare were simply added to the House bill, then the cost of the entire package became considerable. Social Security tradition required that future tax rates be written into current legislation, and it was not at all certain that Mills would agree to such an idea. The second approach, besides being very expensive, might also be cumbersome to administer.

At a meeting of the president, Secretary Celebrezze, and pro-Medicare legislators on July 16, Cohen emphasized the importance of obtaining from Mills a commitment to accept either a compromise in conference or a substitute version of Medicare without going to conference. Perhaps mindful of Springer's admonition, neither the president nor O'Brien offered Cohen any useful guidance, but Senator Abraham Ribicoff of Connecticut observed that although an increase in payroll taxes to pay for the benefit increase might put Medicare in a bind, it would be equally difficult for senators to vote against the Social Security increase. Of the two options, Ribicoff favored the second, which achieved health insurance under Social Security, kept the cash benefit increase of the Mills bill for those who preferred it, and made Medicare available to those eligible without it being compulsory. But above all, Ribicoff argued, if the King-Anderson proposal did not survive, it would be a serious setback to pass a Social Security bill without any attempt to include hospital insurance. The pro-Medicare forces, he concluded, had to close ranks, or any agreements reached so far would come undone, as in 1962.[88]

The Senate Finance Committee would not take up the House-passed Social Security amendments until August 6, which gave the administration nearly three weeks to rally its supporters. On July 20, the Democratic caucus met to act on the president's "must" bills in advance of the Democratic National Convention. Rhode Island Senator John Pastore raised the Medicare issue, which sparked heated discussion. Senator Spessard Holland of Florida worried that King-Anderson would be a tough vote for many Democratic senators in an election year and "voiced the hope that nothing would be done about medicare." But Ribicoff's counterargument, that "the increased social security payments proposed by the House if enacted into law mean the death of medicare," carried the day. The

Democratic leadership of the Senate agreed to let the benefit increase die rather than pass the Social Security bill without Medicare.[89]

Ribicoff, White House aide Mike Manatos reported, then brought up the option plan, "which he feels ought to be promoted at this time to allow us to get a foot in the door on medical care for the aged." By the time the caucus meeting ended, Senate leaders were tending toward "the Ribicoff amendment," reasoning that even if it failed, it would make an attractive campaign issue because, unlike King-Anderson, it was voluntary and elective. Still, not every Democratic senator was ready to support the Ribicoff amendment; Holland and others wanted to avoid a recorded vote in favor of any Medicare bill with its higher taxes just before an election. Hollings cited warnings from HEW that the cost of piling Medicare on a 5 percent benefit increase would be too expensive. North Dakota Senator Quentin Burdick was "much concerned about voting for a bill which would increase possible tax on self-employed farmers to as much as $500.00," Henry Wilson noted. Indiana's Vance Hartke likewise said, "It would be a mistake to attempt the option plan on Medical Care as proposed by Ribicoff either in Committee or on the floor." He preferred to make Medicare "a major effort next year—that it should be a program operating from a special fund *not* tied to Social Security."[90] Senators Smathers and Russell Long were sympathetic to the Ribicoff amendment but were worried about the AMA.[91] Their concerns notwithstanding, Ribicoff remained convinced that the administration was "on the verge of a breakthrough," but that it would have to decide whether to work or fight for Medicare on the floor of the Senate.[92]

Henry Wilson, meanwhile, apprised Mills of the Ribicoff amendment to offer Social Security recipients an alternative between hospital insurance and a cash benefit. It surprised Mills "but it didn't bother him," Wilson reported, as long as Social Security's financial solvency was safeguarded. The administration was no longer expecting Mills to take the initiative in promoting Medicare. "I told him that as I understood it, what he needed for conference was a Senate bill which would thoroughly alarm the AMA," Wilson wrote. "He said that was right." When he asked whether the AMA would find the Ribicoff amendment fully as repugnant as King-Anderson, Mills "emphatically stated that it would indeed." He reiterated that the Senate bill should be fully and conservatively financed, using the 1963 wage base and 1965 hospital cost projections. Mills insisted on not knowing the details of the Ribicoff amendment "lest the word get out that he was trying to dictate the Senate bill." But he warned that if there were any doubts about its financial soundness, "the opponents would be in excellent shape to have the conference drop the whole thing." Looking ahead to the conference, Mills hedged his own position by refusing to speculate on what kind of bill might emerge.[93]

A consensus gradually evolved that the administration should fight for Medicare on the Senate floor rather than in the hostile Finance Committee. This strategy was hinted at in Wilson's memorandum of July 23 to O'Brien and in a second undated memorandum, possibly written by Manatos. "The need is not just [to] pass the bill but to do so in so posi-tive a manner and with the active, informed participation of so large a group of Demo-cratic Senators as to have strong effect on both House and conferees," the author of the sec-ond memorandum wrote, and he suggested a campaign orchestrated by a politically savvy senator, such as Hubert Humphrey of Minnesota, instead of HEW's technical experts, as had occurred in 1962. In this scenario, the president would invite several senators from different regions of the nation to the White House to convey his strong desire to pass a Medicare bill. Johnson would then instruct Senator Anderson to champion the bill in com-mittee and on the Senate floor, McNamara to offer anecdotal evidence of the plight of the elderly, and Humphrey to "take on the job of behind the scenes coordinator and master-mind." Johnson himself would act as Humphrey's go-between with southern legislators to demonstrate that support for Medicare came from all regions of the country.[94]

Like a scene from a play, each character's part was sketched out: Anderson, Ribicoff, and Claiborne Pell, drawing on the expertise of Cohen and the Social Security Adminis-tration to offer the justification and technical defense of Medicare; Senators McNamara, Johnston, and Gaylord Nelson, utilizing the resources of the Congressional Research Ser-vices, to explicate the needs of the elderly; Senators Jennings Randolph, Edmond Muskie, and Maurine B. Neuberger to speak to the inadequacies of Kerr-Mills, Blue Cross, and the commercial insurance companies; Paul Douglas, Eugene McCarthy, Albert Gore, and John Pastore, with technical assistance from the SSA's Robert Ball and Robert J. Myers, to address the economics of Social Security and Medicare; Senators Milton Young, Wayne Morse, Lee Metcalf, and Frank Church, coached by the AFL-CIO's Nelson Cruikshank, to expose the AMA's opposition; Senators George McGovern and Quentin Burdick to ad-dress the need to extend Medicare to rural areas; and, finally, Senators Edward V. Long of Missouri and Thomas J. McIntyre of New Hampshire to argue the essential conservatism of the administration's approach. Until the Finance Committee finished its business, this scenario remained just that.[95]

All the while, Wilbur Cohen continued his dialogue with Mills, seeking clues to discern whether the latter would accept the Senate-passed Medicare bill in conference. He ulti-mately concluded that Mills would not, and he told O'Brien on August 13 of three separ-ate reports from Senator Byrd, Representative Philip Burton, and Senator Carl Curtis that "under no circumstances" would Mills accede to Medicare in conference. This meant the Senate would have to pass Medicare in a form that would "give the least grounds for ob-jection to Mills," that is, to offer a voluntary choice between a benefit increase and hospi-tal insurance rather than mandatory coverage for all Social Security recipients.[96]

The Senate Finance Committee, which reported out a largely unchanged version of Mills's Social Security bill a week later, rendered the various scenarios and strategies moot. The King-Anderson amendment went down to defeat by a vote of eleven to six, as did the Ribicoff amendment on a vote of twelve to five. The committee's actions played hob with the administration. Cohen was uncertain whether the amendments would be resurrected and attached to the House bill either on the Senate floor or in conference; he also worried that Senator Russell Long might amend the bill to increase Social Security benefits above the 5 percent figure, an act that would almost certainly doom Medicare's prospects.[97] Long did, indeed, offer his amendment, which threw pro-Medicare forces into disarray. Responding to this new threat, Humphrey, Anderson, and Cohen rewrote the Medicare proposal to include a flat $7 increase in benefits, with Medicare built in on top of that. This revision raised the taxable wage base to $5,600, so that the combined contribution totaled 10.4 percent. On August 31, Senator Gore offered this proposal as a substitute for the Long amendment, and the Senate passed it forty-nine to forty-four (seven not voting) on September 2. The revised Social Security bill then passed on a vote of sixty to twenty-eight.[98]

This marked the first time either chamber had passed a bill embodying the principle of federal financial responsibility for health coverage, however limited it may have been. "Many Southerners who have not previously supported Medicare joined with the five Liberal Republicans and 44 longtime Democratic backers of the bill to produce the phenomenal Senate victory," noted the National Council of Senior Citizens. The political tide was now running with the Democrats, declared the *Charlotte Observer*, a reference to Republican presidential candidate Barry Goldwater, who had cast one of the votes against the amendment, just as he had voted against Kerr-Mills. By successfully making Medicare a campaign issue, Johnson and the Democrats had also "increased the pressure on House members."[99]

The Senate's action irritated the AMA, but it remained confident that its friends would look after its interests once the House and Senate bills went into conference. That confidence appeared to be justified because, of the seven Senate conferees, only Gore and Anderson wholeheartedly supported Medicare. Long and Smathers were questionable, and Byrd and the two Republicans were opposed. Of the five House conferees, King and Boggs, the majority whip, favored the bill, whereas Mills and the two conservative Republicans opposed tying Medicare funding to Social Security.[100]

Each chamber's conferees traditionally functioned and voted as a bloc, defending the position of the body they represented. But since the House had not voted on Medicare, Mills was relatively free to interpret matters as he wanted. The Senate vote required Byrd and the other senators to stand by Medicare—up to a point. Also by tradition, the determination of where that point lies rested with the conferees. White House aide Henry Wilson's tally of House members' votes on a conference bill that included Medicare disclosed 180 "reasonably certain" votes for Medicare, 29 "probable/possible," 222 "against," and 4 seats vacant. The only vote that truly mattered, however, belonged to Wilbur Mills, who spoke with such authority on tax legislation that the House rarely overrode him. Medicare would become law only if Mills accepted a compromise in conference. Knowing this, Cohen went to see Mills on September 10 to discuss the Senate-passed bill, taking with him three proposals: one covering the entire Social Security package; another listing options for the conferees to consider; and a third containing modifications of the public assistance provisions of the House bill. As he so often did, Mills asked lots of questions but refused to commit himself.[101]

The administration had reached the point where it had to decide whether Mills was a problem to be managed or an obstacle to overcome. Could the White House turn parliamentary procedure to its advantage? The resolution of this issue was important, because O'Brien informed the president on September 13 that Mills would move for unanimous consent to take Medicare into conference the next day. Assuming no objection, Mills could then move a resolution referring the bill to the Rules Committee. This strategy was moot, however, because Republican Charles Halleck announced that there would be objection to unanimous consent. That being the case, the administration's strategy should be to have Speaker McCormack ask Representative Cecil King to move for unanimous consent to a resolution that the House take the Senate bill from the Speaker's table and adopt it. This procedure would have the effect of bypassing the conference altogether. Knowing there also would be objection to this procedure, King would then introduce a new resolution to accomplish the same thing. The Rules Committee had already scheduled Medicare on its agenda for September 15, but the fear was that its chairman, Howard Smith of Virginia, would either stall or expedite a Medicare ruling, depending on the political circumstances of the moment.[102]

The Rules Committee could follow any one of three courses: to rule for an uninstructed conference (that is, to let the House conferees follow their own inclinations about what to include in or exclude from a bill after talks, or "horse-trading," with Senate conferees); to rule for a conference instructed to accept or reject Medicare; or to rule for the King resolution and accept the Senate bill. Mills wanted the first option; the second, O'Brien noted, had "no precedent in recent history"; and the Rules Committee was unlikely to vote for the third. Mills, O'Brien wrote, "is vehemently, adamantly opposed to being instructed. He says he won't serve on an instructed conference." He was not the only legislator who felt this way; several pro-Medicare committee chairmen also had told Mills they would vote against an instructed conference. The administration did not have the votes to override them. If the White House wanted to challenge Mills before the conference assembled, O'Brien wrote, "we should decide this today and drive hard to get all of our votes back into town." Even then, he warned, "it will be difficult to turn the doubtful votes for a showdown which we obviously will not carry and would be an encouragement to our enemies and a blow to our friends." Whichever course the administration pursued, O'Brien advised, it should be decided before a meeting with House leaders, scheduled for the next morning.[103]

Rather than risk antagonizing Mills and House members, the administration ceased its efforts to get an instructed conference. On September 14, the House voted without dissent to send its representatives to conference uninstructed.[104] In the Senate, after a colloquy among Long, McNamara, Joseph S. Clark, Gore, and Anderson, that body affirmed its intention to go to conference to work out a medical care program under Social Security. Long had assured his colleagues that he would uphold the Senate's position in favor of Medicare, a change of heart that resulted from a quid pro quo with the administration. "Long wants G.I. Insurance. The president wants Medicare," wrote Manatos.[105]

Long subsequently worked for the Senate's bill in the conference, where deliberations dragged on for nearly a month. Mills had hinted repeatedly that he was prepared to compromise and then, just as quickly, spurned various proposals.[106] Still, Cohen refused to give up. He wrote to O'Brien on September 28 of some technical changes in the Medicare proposal that might satisfy Mills and added: "If Mills accepted some medicare compromise, we could go along with a $5 monthly minimum in the 5 percent cash benefit increases. This would increase benefits an additional $250 million annually."[107]

Mills again refused the offer, leaving Senate Medicare supporters to ride an emotional roller coaster, going from optimism to pessimism. On September 15, Senator Anderson told Manatos of his fear that "the conferees on Medicare are ready to 'gut' us," and he suggested "the House and Senate friends of the program should be ready to filibuster the conference report and kill the measure." But Senator Gore thought Medicare was "the hottest domestic issue in the campaign" and, based on his close personal relationship with Senator Byrd, was confident it would pass. With the conference deadlocked, optimism gave way to despair, and Gore said he would rather kill the entire Social Security bill than agree to a benefit increase without Medicare.[108] Senator Long, by contrast, exuded confidence that a Medicare program would emerge from conference and that he could interest Mills in a version of the Ribicoff amendment, whereby Medicare would function under Social Security but be administered by a Blue Cross–type agency to remove fears of "government control." Long also advised the AMA "not to place itself in a position of total opposition but to realistically face the need of older people." He told its leadership that he could cut a deal with Mills that would put the physicians on record as "for" rather than "against" Medicare.[109]

Mills remained the closed door to Medicare, and many pro-Medicare legislators told Manatos that the president alone held the key to unlocking that door. "Every time I talk to a Senator about Medicare I hear the same line of reasoning—'Has the President talked to Mills? ... He's the only one who can persuade him. ... It's now or never, because when we reach the 10% tax figure as the House bill proposes, Medical Care will never see the light of day.'" Manatos relayed that tale to O'Brien. Johnson, who fully appreciated and respected Mills's base of power in Congress, among fiscal conservatives, and the AMA, saw little point in submitting him to the famous "Johnson treatment."[110]

This reticence left White House operatives with little choice but to turn to parliamentary procedure to end the stalemate. Henry Wilson suggested to O'Brien that if the conferees agreed on a report and the Senate acted first to adopt it, then the House would be confronted with an up-or-down vote. The Senate's action would have discharged the conference, leaving no conferees to instruct. But if the House acted first, the minority could propose a motion to reject and instruct. The question of which chamber acted first was significant only if there was a conference report favorable to the administration. In such an event, Wilson declared, "this could be of very major significance indeed," because based on past actions, Mills would likely shrink from a showdown on the House floor. "I think it's clear that he is under very major heat to get a benefit increase bill adopted, and that he intends to do it." The "crunch," Wilson said, would come over "whether the Senate conferees stand up."[111]

As the administration probed the arcane workings of the conference, it relied on the Senate conferees' holding their ground, while it continued to search for compromises Mills might accept. After a few more weeks of futile negotiations, Anderson, Gore, King, and Boggs were becoming desperate, willing to make almost any accommodation to get a Medicare bill. Mills still procrastinated and forced postponement of a vote. Gore decided that Mills's aim was to secure a vote on the Social Security amendments without Medicare in the belief that the administration would not have the political courage to veto the bill. Once Johnson signed the cash benefit increase, it would be all but impossible to persuade Congress to raise Social Security taxes again the following year to pay for Medicare.[112]

Boggs concurred, and he flatly warned Mills that he might refuse to sign a conference report that did not contain some form of Medicare. This blunt admonition rattled the Arkansas Democrat, who had made a point of avoiding this kind of confrontation, particularly with the majority whip, who wielded considerable power. Gore and Anderson also turned up the pressure; they told Mills they would ask the Senate to reject the conference report unless there was a compromise on Medicare. They spoke confidently, knowing that the administration would back them. Indeed, on September 26, Cohen had written to O'Brien, "If we are not successful in getting any medicare provision in the bill, then we should point out to our supporters in the Conference that the *entire* bill can go over until next year without any major adverse effect on most beneficiaries because we could make the cash benefit increase next year *retroactive* to January 1, 1965."[113]

This was the kind of leverage that would draw Mills's attention. And faced with this unprecedented challenge from his legislative colleagues, Mills reluctantly agreed to consider a compromise. But on October 1, Manatos learned from Senator Anderson that the conferees had adjourned that morning in complete disagreement. On Medicare itself, the only part of the Social Security bill the conference considered, Long, Smathers, Anderson, and Gore voted to uphold the Senate's position, and Byrd abstained; he was opposed to Medicare, but as a representative of the Senate, he felt obliged to support that body's position. Both Republican senators voted against Medicare. On the House side, Boggs and King voted to support the Senate's position; Mills and the two Republican conferees voted against Medicare.[114]

The next day, when the conference committee reconvened, Mills confidently called for a vote on the Social Security cash-increase amendments, without Medicare. The two House Republican conferees immediately sided with Mills, making the vote in the House conference three to two for the bill without Medicare. On the Senate side, the two Republicans voted for the motion, Democrats Gore and Anderson voted against. Byrd temporarily abstained, causing a two-to-two tie. Confident of winning over the other Senate conferees, Mills called for the final vote. Senator Russell Long, who hoped to become majority whip if Hubert Humphrey was elected vice president, and Senator Smathers voted against a Social Security bill without Medicare. Byrd then voted for it. Shocked by the outcome, Mills announced that the conference was deadlocked, and he immediately adjourned it without reporting any bill. Medicare remained firmly entrenched in the legislative quagmire.[115]

By 1964, health care for older Americans was at the forefront of the nation's political agenda, as Democrats of all persuasion saw in the issue an opportunity to regain control of both the White House and Congress. Partisan politics as much as concern for the health needs of the elderly had dictated passage of the earlier Kerr-Mills health care program. But as evidence mounted that the program was not meeting the medical needs of the elderly, because many states were unwilling or unable to appropriate matching funds, health care reformers and their legislative allies turned to the idea of a federalized Medicare program financed through the Social Security trust fund. Some, but not all, reformers believed this approach and this financing mechanism were necessary first steps along the road to universal health coverage.

Despite a congressional majority in both houses of Congress in the early 1960s, Presidents Kennedy and Johnson experienced humiliating setbacks in their efforts to replace the Kerr-Mills program with a federal Medicare program for the elderly. As late as 1964, the King-Anderson Medicare bill remained bogged down in the three most powerful panels in the House (the Rules, Appropriations, and Ways and Means Committees) and in the Finance Committee of the Senate. Wilbur Mills, the most powerful of the committee chairs, skillfully used his knowledge of the tax structure and revenue codes to thwart congressional enactment of such a program financed through Social Security.

Mills feared that open-ended and escalating hospital costs would threaten the solvency of the Social Security system; that Congress would be required to raise payroll taxes beyond acceptable limits to pay for the Medicare program; and that dipping into wage-related revenue to pay for non-wage-related service benefits would weaken the relationship between taxes and benefits upon which Social Security rested. Hence, Mills employed the affirmative and negative powers of his chairmanship to force the Kennedy and Johnson administrations to reshape Medicare legislation continually until he could be sure that the program would not undermine the financial underpinnings of Social Security. As late as fall 1964, Mills remained resolute, turning every White House concession into yet another; he wore down his critics; and he refused to yield in his principled opposition. He was more than just a one-man veto, however, for Mills, who had excellent contacts with the Social Security tax policy community, also encouraged Medicare supporters to negotiate and fine-tune their legislative proposal.

President Kennedy's assassination in 1963 and Johnson's landslide election in November 1964, however, created a new political dynamic that put Mills under increasing pressure and enhanced the odds that Congress would finally enact Medicare legislation.

# SIX

## CROSSING AN IDEOLOGICAL RUBICON

The Democrats went into the election in November 1964 without an increase in the Social Security program's benefits to offer the voter, but with a campaign issue instead. Goldwater, after all, had talked about making Social Security private, and he had voted against Medicare in the Senate. This, Oklahoma Representative Page Belcher noted, and Goldwater's other highly controversial proposals frightened many voters and badly split the Republican party.[1] By election eve, Goldwater had painted himself into a position of splendid isolation, failing even to unite the disparate wings of his own party. The result was a landslide for President Johnson and the Democratic Party, which increased its majority in both the Senate and the House. The following morning, Mills promised reporters that he would be receptive to a Medicare proposal in the coming congressional session.[2]

Ironically, Goldwater's defeat helped pave the way for the 1965 Medicare amendments to the Social Security Act, which the Republican president, Richard M. Nixon, would eventually embrace. Twenty-two percent of the popular vote had been cast by people over the age of sixty, 2 million of whom had switched from the Republican column to the Democratic. Seven of the ten states with the highest percentage of elderly voters were traditionally Republican, but all ten went to the Democrats on November 3. Goldwater was not the only foe of Medicare to go down to defeat: eleven of the fourteen physicians who ran for Congress also lost, and one of the three doctors who won supported Medicare. Pro-Medicare forces were strengthened by the addition of four votes in the Senate and forty-four votes in the House. Equally important, the AMA lost three of its most dependable allies on the Ways and Means Committee after the Democratic Caucus altered the party ratio from fifteen to ten to eighteen to seven. Wilbur Mills acquiesced in the change.[3]

Medicare had moved to the forefront of presidential politics, as Johnson promised repeatedly during the campaign that he would push the 89th Congress to enact the Medicare program that its predecessor had rejected. Johnson clearly believed that the voters had delivered a mandate both for Medicare and for other Great Society programs. So did most of the sixty-nine freshman Democrats elected to the House of Representatives who owed, or believed they owed, their victories to the Johnson landslide, and those incumbents whose shaky seats were retained thanks to Johnson's campaigning on their behalf.[4] But political reality born of years of service in Congress tempered the president's optimism. The mandate could quickly erode, he told aides, and therefore he was determined to enact Medicare during the administration's honeymoon period with the Congress. On November 18, Johnson asked Wilbur Cohen to brief the cabinet on the status of the legislation and instructed him to make Medicare the administration's number one legislative priority. He also requested Mills to make it the Ways and Means Committee's first item of business.[5]

In accordance with his instructions, Cohen and the Social Security team of Robert Ball, Nelson Cruikshank, and HEW's actuaries and lawyers began to rewrite what everyone hoped would be the definitive version of Medicare. Cohen also informed Mills and the Democratic leadership in Congress of the president's insistence that health care for the elderly go to the head of the legislative agenda, designating Medicare as "H.R. 1." With the change of membership in the Ways and Means Committee, he was optimistic this would assure early passage of the bill. By November 24, Cohen had prepared a summary of the bill for the president, Speaker McCormack, Anderson, and King and a letter of authorization from HEW Secretary Celebrezze designating him Medicare's point man.[6] The revised draft retained the three prominent features written into earlier Medicare proposals: it allowed beneficiaries to select one of three hospitalization options; it provided for intermediaries such as Blue Cross to administer the program and allowed private health insurance companies to sell "Medigap" policies (covering costs not included in Medicare coverage) on a nonprofit basis; and it mandated a Social Security benefit increase of 7 percent paid retroactively to January 1, 1965. Anticipating Mills's long-standing objection, Cohen told HEW Secretary Celebrezze that the advantage of retaining a separate hospital trust fund was that the administration "could then say that hospital insurance was financed under social insurance *rather than under Social Security*."[7]

By the end of 1964, the Medicare proposal, as Cohen's biographer has noted, had become primarily a political undertaking. Items in the bill gained currency according to their political appeal rather than their value in advancing the American health care system toward clearly defined goals, such as preventive medicine. This was a bow to political reality, and Cohen recognized the need to establish the medical infrastructure indispensable to successfully launching the Medicare program. Hence, Cohen would also draft legislation as part of the administration's 1965 agenda to expand the number of physicians and hospitals with advanced treatment facilities; include public funding for medical research and services related to heart disease, cancer, and stroke; provide financial support for medical schools and medical libraries; and extend Kerr-Mills coverage to the needy, disabled, blind, and children. Wilbur Mills was especially enthusiastic about the last.[8]

The White House, meanwhile, continued to assess legislative support for the new Medicare push. On December 8, Mike Manatos wrote to Larry O'Brien that with the election of new, liberal Democrats, the Senate would support Medicare even more heavily than it had in the previous session: by a vote of fifty-five to forty-five, he estimated. The House, by which he meant the Ways and Means Committee, was more problematic; the enigmatic Wilbur Mills would determine Medicare's fate. Like the White House's political operatives, Cohen also searched for clues as to how Mills would respond to the new Medicare initiative.

On December 2, Mills had delivered a speech to the Lions Club of Little Rock, Arkansas, which Cohen read carefully, underlining Mills's statement that he could "support a payroll tax for cash benefits." But overall, Mills remained sphinx-like, except to reiterate that he preferred a separate Medicare tax to one combining Social Security and Medicare. At the very least, Mills seemed willing to continue negotiations.[9]

Finally, on December 31, Cohen distributed the latest draft of his proposed "Hospital Insurance, Social Security, and Public Assistance Amendments of 1965." The draft provided one set of basic benefits rather than the earlier option of three choices. It limited inpatient hospital services to a maximum of sixty days, with a deductible equal to the average cost of half a day of hospital care; it covered physician services, such as pathology, radiology, and outpatient diagnostic services associated with hospital care, up to sixty days of posthospital extended care in a nursing home or similar recuperative facility, and up to 240 home health visits a year. The use of the private intermediary to process bills for hospital services, the separate hospital insurance trust fund, the inclusion of complementary private insurance, and the 7 percent across-the-board Social Security benefit increase were carried over from previous drafts. The 1965 amendments constituted the largest, most complicated, and most expensive revisions to Social Security that Congress had been asked to legislate, but Cohen sensed that the pendulum was swinging toward the administration and that the 89th Congress, after years of frustration and failure, would embrace the principle of public financial responsibility for medical care and would silence the critics who denounced federal intervention as the wedge to "socialized medicine."[10]

The year 1965 opened on a promising note: the administration received two endorsements of Medicare, one expected and the other anticipated, but by no means taken for granted. On January 3, the Advisory Council on Social Security recommended a separate payroll tax to finance a $2.2 billion program of hospital care for the aged under OASDI. About the same time, the Associated Press (AP) reported that Wilbur Mills had declared in an interview that if Medicare legislation came before the Ways and Means Committee, he assumed the committee would be able to work something out. If that were so, the AP noted, the "decade-long controversy in Congress over health care for the aged could be settled by mid-1965." The AP story received wide notice, for it seemed to suggest that Mills was beginning to modify his opposition. But in fact, Mills had gone little beyond his remarks to the Lions Club and continued to insist that Medicare be financed separately from the rest of Social Security.[11]

Johnson could have used his 150-vote margin in the House to circumvent Mills altogether to pass Medicare, but he saw no point in antagonizing the powerful chairman of the Ways and Means Committee, whose support he would need to fund other Great Society initiatives. Instead, the White House worked through the normal political process, knowing full well that political circumstances had become much more conducive to passage of a

Medicare law. Democratic support for Medicare was converging with a softening of Republican opposition in response to postelection polls indicating that two-thirds of the voters favored Medicare. Frank T. Bow, a conservative Republican from Ohio, who had introduced a private, voluntary insurance program for the elderly three years earlier, had written a letter to fellow House Republicans attributing the party's November disaster to its stance on Social Security and medical care, and the new minority leader, Gerald Ford, promised a program of constructive opposition, which many interpreted to mean that the Republicans would present an alternative to the King-Anderson bill.[12]

Against this shifting political landscape, on January 7, 1965, President Johnson delivered to Congress a short, powerful message quoting Thomas Jefferson, in which he placed hospital insurance for the aged at the very top of his legislative agenda. The program was needed to close the gap in the Social Security net, he insisted, and should be financed under Social Security "by regular, modest contributions during working years." House Speaker McCormack then announced that Medicare would be Congress's first order of business, and Mills announced that he would present the redesigned Medicare bill to the Ways and Means Committee. The King-Anderson bills of 1965 were designated H.R. 1 and S. 1.[13]

Mills, too, was sensitive to the new political terrain. Two days before the president's speech, White House aide Henry Wilson had spoken with him in order to gauge his intentions for this legislative session. Unlike in previous years, Mills promised Wilson that he would take up Medicare as soon as the Democratic caucus had chosen the three new Democratic members to serve on the Ways and Means Committee; the earliest this would occur was January 20, but more likely toward the end of the month. Mills intended to consider the bill without additional public hearings, but he could not promise this until he put it to the committee. He also told Wilson of his intention to report the Medicare bill to the full House by March 15, a target date Wilson thought would be "most helpful," but about which he was privately skeptical, given Mills's previous record. Larry O'Brien apprised the president of Mills's timetable but added, "We will do everything possible to push up [the date]—hopefully to the first."[14]

Mills's subsequent announcement that the committee would take up the bill stunned AMA leaders who, in a postelection closed strategy session, were already organizing against a new initiative to legislate health care for the elderly. A few days after the president's speech, nearly 200 representatives of the state medical societies convened in Chicago with the leaders of the AMA to reaffirm their opposition to King-Anderson, vowing to lobby Mills and to launch a mail campaign of nearly 7 million pamphlets attacking the administration's bill. As part of their campaign, they would reprint Dr. (later Representative) Walter H. Judd's *Reader's Digest* article critical of Medicare. Then, in a surprise move, they unveiled a new program that would provide greater coverage to the elderly than the administration's Medicare tax plan. The "Doctors' Eldercare Plan," as they called it, would provide federal and state grants to subsidize private health insurance policies for the elderly who wanted them, utilizing the public assistance machinery in place under the Kerr-Mills program.[15]

Despite the AMA's protests, Mills convened the Ways and Means Committee on January 27 to take up the King-Anderson Medicare bill. Other than the chairman, few of its members could follow all the technical details, but Mills pushed them, provision by provision, to keep up with him even as he applied pressure on the policy experts to devise stronger safeguards to protect Social Security. The legislators knew that this time they were writing a law rather than positioning themselves in a political debate or laying the groundwork for future legislation. Medicare legislation would pass this session, barring a political catastrophe; nevertheless, committee members still had to consider its many complex details and how the Republican minority would respond to the King-Anderson bill. Cohen anticipated the Republicans would offer an alternative, particularly after one Republican staff member told him they would not support the more liberal Javits proposal but a commercial insurance–type program.[16]

On February 4, 1965, John Byrnes, the ranking minority member, introduced "Bettercare," a more expansive alternative to the AMA's Eldercare that was a hybrid of social insurance and public assistance. The Byrnes bill emulated a plan that the Aetna Insurance Company had made available to federal employees since 1959. It was a classic indemnity plan in which employees had monthly premiums deducted from their paychecks, and the federal government contributed a percentage of the premium. Cohen, with the support of Robert Myers, chief actuary in the SSA, objected to its voluntary nature and feared its costs would be a drain on the Treasury's general revenues, especially a provision to reimburse physicians and hospitals based on "charges" rather than on "costs" (the elderly were believed to cost less to serve than did younger people). He also faulted the requirement that an elderly person pay for health insurance during his retirement when his income was lowest, unlike King-Anderson, which required an individual to pay for health coverage during his working years so that the policy would be paid up upon retirement. But Cohen conceded that the Byrnes bill had definite appeal.[17] Its financing was straightforward, relying as it did on general revenues and current taxes; it avoided the means test; it had none of the problems of maintaining the large reserves that complicated Social Security financing; it allowed annual budgeting; and it was more generous on a range of benefits, including surgical. Not surprisingly, the five Republican members of the committee immediately endorsed "Bettercare."[18]

Competing with both King-Anderson and the Byrnes alternative was the AMA's Eldercare bill (H.R. 3727), which Florida Democrat A. Sydney Herlong and Missouri Republican Thomas Curtain dropped into the legislative hopper. Designed to derail federal intervention, Eldercare, which was estimated to cost $2.1 billion annually, permitted states to expand their Kerr-Mills program in order to pay the physician and hospital expenses of the elderly poor. Like the Byrnes bill, it relied on state administration and a means test. The difficulty with Eldercare, as Oregon Democrat Al Ullman noted, was that relatively few states had committed the funds to participate in the Kerr-Mills program. There was little reason to believe states could afford the more expensive Eldercare plan. The Herlong-Curtain bill had little support in Congress and died quietly without a committee vote.[19]

Amidst the flurry of bills, Mills announced that the committee would begin the process of writing the legislation that would be sent to the floor of the House. He conducted the committee's sessions with businesslike efficiency, calling a total of 641 expert witnesses to advise him on different provisions of the Medicare legislation and demanding up-to-date statistics from the Social Security Administration. Cohen attended each meeting, giving the administration's response to alternative proposals and supplying the committee with the latest numbers. During the course of the hearings and to the annoyance of some committee members, Mills instructed each witness to restrict his remarks to matters within his specific competence. All the witnesses complied, with the exception of Dr. Donovan B. Ward, the AMA president, and several of his colleagues who appeared on February 8. They simply repeated allegations made in their advertising campaign against health insurance, trusting that the same tactics that had defeated earlier legislative efforts to fund medical care for the elderly would work once again. This was a blunder of the worst sort. Rather than seeking to forge a compromise with the administration that would be least disadvantageous to their interests, their behavior ultimately caused committee members to discount their views.[20]

As one meeting blurred into the next, Mills remained focused on the tax rates that the committee would propose. He wanted the accounts to show that the rates would be 9.5 percent of covered payroll for Old-Age, Survivors, and Disability Insurance (OASDI) and 1 percent for hospital insurance. This was both symbolically and psychologically important to Mills, who had demonstrated his fiscal prudence in the past by fighting to keep the OASDI rate below the impenetrable barrier of 10 percent. Administration officials grew restive, but they kept pressure on the committee to report a bill. On February 16, President Johnson, while accepting the President's Council on Aging's annual report, gave a big boost to the King-Anderson bill by reminding council members and cabinet officials gathered in the White House that there was not a man or woman in the room without a relative or parent who did not need this legislation, and he called on "all Americans to get behind and help us and support prompt enactment of a comprehensive program of hospital care for the aged through Social Security." In case legislators did not get the message, the president announced he would designate May as "Senior Citizens Month."[21]

With the committee sessions dragging into March, Cohen worried that delay would give Medicare's opponents time to regroup for a new assault. But his sense of urgency also meant that consideration of other and potentially less expensive forms of health care provision, such as the Kaiser Plan and other managed-care alternatives, received short shrift.

Cohen was not interested in encouraging cheap care; the Medicare program he was designing rested on quality care for the elderly. Cost reduction, which became central to the health care debate in the closing decades of the century, figured only at the margins of the 1965 debate, when prosperity rather than economic constraint was the order of the day.[22]

On March 2, 1965, Mills finally completed his review of each of the major health insurance bills. Three options were before the committee: Medicare, based on the social insurance approach, offered hospital coverage financed through a higher Social Security tax; Eldercare, built on the public assistance approach, expanded means-tested assistance to the "medically indigent" by relying on general revenue; and "Bettercare," offering voluntary hospital and physician coverage financed through general-revenue appropriations and premium contributions by participants.[23]

During an executive session on March 2, Democrats and HEW experts had difficulty finding flaws in the Byrnes plan. Cohen surprised the committee when he acknowledged that it offered higher benefits than Medicare and at a lower cost to participants—though general revenue would subsidize two-thirds of the program. Mills, who had long opposed financing social insurance through general revenue, suddenly went along with it, rationalizing that medical benefits "differed" from cash benefits and could be paid for as insurance using general revenue. The premium, he noted, would also help contain the cost of the program by imposing a fee on the beneficiary. Mills, in effect, overrode Myers's warning that the cost to the Treasury would rise more quickly than through the administration's contributory plan.[24]

Faced with the test of reconciling three very different proposals, Mills sought a compromise to avert a political disaster. At the heart of the compromise would be a Medicare program that relied on earmarked taxes to distinguish Medicare from welfare, but one that did not threaten the earmarked tax system in place for OASDI. Mills could have said yes or no to the various bills at this stage of the deliberations, but something quite extraordinary happened. Turning to Byrnes, Mills declared that he liked his proposal for a voluntary program whose beneficiaries would help to pay by having small deductions taken from their monthly Social Security checks. As he continued, it became clear that Mills liked the idea, not as an alternative to the administration's Medicare plan, but as a supplement to it. Using the analogy of a three-layer cake, he described the bottom layer as the expanded Kerr-Mills program to take care of the needy; the middle layer was Medicare to cover the costs of hospital, nursing home, and home health care for the elderly who could afford to pay; the top layer was the voluntary supplement to cover physicians' fees, whether in or out of hospital.[25]

With this in mind, Mills turned back to Cohen. "Without any advance notice, Mills asked me why we could not put together a plan that included the administration's Medicare hospital plan with a broader voluntary plan covering physician or other services." The suggestion stunned Cohen, as it did Byrnes and others in the hearing room. It was "the most brilliant legislative move" Cohen had witnessed in thirty years, taking as it did the wind out of the sails of the AMA and the Republican opposition even as it gave the administration basically what it wanted: Medicare for hospital services.[26]

Right then and there it was all over except the details. Mills had launched a $2 billion bill, and the most significant departure in the Social Security laws in a generation was brought about. Once he had recovered from his initial surprise, Cohen seized the moment and agreed to fill in the details by the next morning. As Mills adjourned the committee for the day, Cohen raced from the room. Despite his earlier reservations about the effectiveness of Kerr-Mills, he included it in the revision because it embodied the principle of public financial responsibility for health care that he had advocated for more than a decade. The revised bill, with little more than cursory attention from the Congress that enacted it, transformed in a fundamental way the nature of the Medicare proposal.[27]

Medicare had been conceived primarily as medical insurance for the elderly. One had only to be old to receive benefits. Mills, almost casually, transformed it into an antipoverty program as well, by tacking onto it the Kerr-Mills program, renamed Medicaid. Medicaid would not benefit the old primarily, but the poor, regardless of age and race. It was Mills's attempt to address the maldistribution of medical care in the fee-for-service system by transforming delivery of medical care into an issue of technical economics rather than one of class or race, and to do so without fundamentally altering the capitalistic system of production and consumption. Medicaid became an appendage of the welfare rather than the Social Security system, but it had the potential to affect as many people and cost as much money as Medicare. States that elected to participate in Medicaid would receive federal matching grants to pay medical bills for two classes of citizens: welfare recipients and the medically indigent (defined as the blind, the disabled, the aged, or children in single-parent families who were ineligible for welfare but who could not afford to pay for medical care). Conspicuously absent from Medicaid coverage were the working poor.[28]

That evening, while the technical specialists were writing up the new specifications, Cohen drafted a memorandum for the president. He explained that Mills had become concerned that the Republicans would attack the administration's bill as inadequate and would point out that their approach was more liberal and a better total package. Mills's "three layer cake" bill would be unassailable politically and virtually guarantee that no one would vote against it on the floor of the House. Johnson reacted with surprise and amusement when he read the memorandum, and he said to the aide who had brought it to him, "Just tell them to snip off that name 'Republican' and slip that little old amendment into the bill."[29]

The next day, with the latest draft in hand, Mills embarked on another review of the bill, which led to further revisions. Even then it did not move through the Ways and Means Committee without controversy. Some of the disputes were procedural, but others were substantive. Cohen reported to Larry O'Brien on March 18 that Mills was becoming "increasingly impatient" with Republican Tom Curtis, who had a large number of amendments that he wanted the committee to vote on. When Mills and ranking minority member John Byrnes had to leave a session to attend a White House meeting, the committee continued with its business, leading Curtis to protest the absence of a quorum. This forced Mills to round up a quorum to enable the committee to continue discussing the bill in his and Byrnes's absence. A minor irritant, perhaps, but it suggested that tempers were fraying.[30]

More substantive points of contention were Mills's insistence that all physicians' reimbursements (including the services of radiologists and pathologists but not anesthesiologists) be administered through the voluntary rather than the compulsory health insurance provision; the concerns of administration economists Kermit Gordon and Gardner Ackley that the law might act as a drag on economic growth by siphoning money from the economy; and the issue of civil rights: specifically, whether a hospital that received federal grants in the form of Medicare payments would have to be integrated. The first issue tested Cohen's diplomatic skills in soothing Mills's ruffled feathers; the second was resolved when Johnson instructed HEW Secretary Celebrezze and Treasury Secretary Henry Fowler to tell the economists to pipe down; and the third issue arose only in the Senate Finance Committee. Senator Harry F. Byrd of Virginia asked whether Title VI of the Civil Rights Act of 1964 would apply to Medicare. The administration, after some thought, decided not to include a specific civil rights provision in the bill for fear of jeopardizing its chances of passage, but the issue would resurface during the implementation phase of the Medicare program.[31]

As these and other issues arose, Mills marched the committee methodically through further technical changes until the bill read to his satisfaction. At last, on March 23, the committee voted along strictly party lines (seventeen to eight) to report the Social Security bill, amended to include Medicare, to the full House. Scarcely believing their ears, the Democrats cheered, because now they could take *all* the credit for Medicare. President Johnson, in a White House statement after the vote, described the committee's action as "a tremendous step forward for all of our senior citizens" and called the bill "fiscally sound." He singled out Wilbur Mills for special praise, referred to the committee's action as historic, and expressed the hope that Republicans would join with Democrats in voting for it.[32]

Why Mills decided to bring this particular version of Medicare before the full House for action, when he had throttled in committee every version of health care for the elderly since 1957, has long been a matter of speculation. Mills did so in part because there had been no majority in the committee in the past to support such legislation and in part because previous bills had not met his requirement that the fiscal integrity of Social Security be protected. Mills finally had a bill that he believed would do that. Moreover, neither majority Democratic members of the committee nor presidential administrations had been inclined or able to ride roughshod over the most important committee chairman in the House. Like President Kennedy, Johnson depended on Mills's cooperation to secure passage of all important tax and budget legislation. Political circumstances differed this time. Mills used his authority, knowledge of the tax code, and contacts with the tax policy community to shape the bill to his satisfaction. He was able to forge a bill that put all dealings with physicians, from payment of fees to their relationships with patients, in a separate, voluntary category about which there was no taint of government compulsion. People over sixty-five were free to choose whether to enter this voluntary insurance system. By contrast, the compulsory hospital care features satisfied Mills's requirement that they be paid out of a separate trust fund. Though financed by its own share of the Social Security payroll tax, hospital costs would not jeopardize or adversely affect the trust fund from which were paid other old age and survivors' benefits, thereby protecting the actuarial soundness of the Social Security system. Finally, the changed political landscape influenced Mills's decision. Three electoral campaigns—1960, 1962, and 1964—established a powerful public interest in and support for Medicare legislation, contributed to the defeat or replacement of committee and House members who opposed Medicare, and brought to the forefront a president who vigorously expounded Medicare's necessity to a receptive public.[33]

On March 26, three days after the committee's vote, Johnson, in a carefully choreographed and televised White House press conference, gave a brief summary of the bill's provisions and introduced the Democratic leaders of the House and Senate, who would be instrumental in shepherding King-Anderson through their respective chambers. Present were Mills, Cecil King, House Speaker McCormack, Majority Whip Hale Boggs, and Majority Leader Carl Albert; from the Senate, Anderson, Assistant Majority Whip George Smathers, Majority Leader Mike Mansfield, and Finance Committee Chair Harry F. Byrd attended. Everyone except Byrd spoke glowingly of the measure, prompting Johnson to turn to Byrd, who had opposed every previous bill and could derail this, to apply the famous "Johnson treatment." Before a national television audience, the president smiled at Byrd and said, "I know that you will take an interest in the orderly scheduling of this matter and giving it [a] thorough hearing." Byrd looked at him blankly, whereupon Johnson asked, "Would you care to make an observation?" Byrd gave an evasive reply, whereupon Johnson pressed him. "And you have nothing that you know of that would prevent [the hearings] coming about in [a] reasonable time, not anything ahead of it in the committee?" he asked. "Nothing in the committee now," Byrd answered, shifting uneasily. "So when the House acts and it is referred to the Senate Finance Committee, you will arrange for prompt hearings and thorough hearings?" the president asked again and leaned forward intently. In a barely audible voice, Byrd responded, "Yes." Smiling broadly, the president banged his fist on the desk, stared into the camera lens, and said, "Good!"[34]

The next day, the president sent a personal note of thanks to the bill's sponsor, Representative Cecil R. King. Then, in a mood of great anticipation, the House convened on April 8 to vote on the first national health insurance bill ever to come before it. As predetermined, it came to the floor under a "closed rule," which meant that members could not amend the 296-page bill, but had to vote for or against it in its entirety. Speaking for the committee, Mills outlined its provisions, noting that it included a 7 percent increase in pension benefits (thereby breaking the tradition of keeping total Social Security taxes below the historic benchmark of 10 percent), a voluntary supplemental medical insurance (SMI) program, modifications to the original King-Anderson Medicare bill, and an expanded Kerr-Mills program (Medicaid). The cost was about $6 billion the first year, roughly half of it for Medicare. After Mills sat down, Byrnes, the ranking minority member of the Ways and Means Committee, presented his own separate bill as the Republican alternative. Democrats and Republicans debated the merits of each for several hours, before narrowly defeating efforts to recommit. The House then acted on April 8, passing the administration-endorsed bill (H.R. 6675) by a vote of 313 to 115.[35]

Medicare's opponents were distraught. AMA president Donovan Ward issued a statement highly critical of the legislation, saying it would lead to a decline in the quality of medical care and asked that the Senate Finance Committee substitute Eldercare for the administration's bill. Republican Representative Page Belcher informed a constituent that he had voted against the bill, "as I have always been unalterably opposed to any bill of this nature being financed through the Social Security program." Condemning the bill as the first step toward socialized medicine, he wrote, "I am afraid it will eventually destroy the Social Security Program." Wilbur Cohen, by contrast, spoke about the historical importance of the House's action and wrote a sentimental note to former President Truman. Twenty years after he had participated in drafting Truman's health care message, Cohen wrote, "we are finally coming close to victory." To John Dingell, son of the original cosponsor of the Wagner bill, Cohen noted the poetic justice of the representative's presiding over the Medicare debate in the same chamber where his father had first led the movement to reform health care.[36]

Sentiment aside, Cohen moved swiftly to line up Senate support for the legislation after Byrd announced that Finance Committee hearings would begin later that month. During the two weeks of hearings, the committee amassed more than 1,200 pages of testimony. Unlike his appearance before the Ways and Means Committee, AMA president Donovan Ward forsook the emotional rhetoric of the past and adhered closely to matters that fell within his competence as a physician, but the damage had already been done. The deference once shown to a member of the medical profession who testified before a congressional committee was gone. Senator Clinton Anderson, who presided over many of the committee's sessions, was openly skeptical of testimony from AMA officials.[37]

With AMA opposition neutralized, a new and unexpected threat to the Medicare bill materialized from within the Finance Committee. Senator Russell Long, who had become the majority whip, hinted at broadening the legislation to include payments for prescription drugs and to eliminate co-payments. Cohen strongly protested against further tampering with the bill and enlisted the assistance of White House aide Mike Manatos. On May 13, 1965, after a conversation with Senator Anderson, Manatos alerted Larry O'Brien to the threat of the Long amendments. Both Anderson and the White House believed that Medicare's best chance for passage was to have the Finance Committee report a bill identical to the House's legislation. Anderson agreed to speak to Long "to attempt to persuade him to forget about amendments." The Finance Committee, meanwhile, concluded its hearings on May 19 and adjourned for a week, after which it would go into executive session to write its version of the bill.[38]

That afternoon, Long told reporters that he still intended to amend the House bill. Finance Committee staffer Elizabeth Springer immediately telephoned Manatos that the committee's Democratic members believed Long would do so "solely for the purpose of convincing the doctors and his constituents back home that he made a good try, and when the Committee rejects it he will then be able to say he had to support whatever bill the Committee reports[,] having failed with his amendment." Long's amendment was "complicated and impractical," Springer wrote, and she predicted that the committee would not accept it.[39] Long, nonetheless, strung the committee along for several weeks without actually introducing his amendment, but leaving the impression that the majority whip would not propose revisions that the White House had not approved. On June 16, Manatos, citing Cohen and Elizabeth Springer as his sources, noted that the Finance Committee "is anxious to wind up the mark-up on the Medical Care Bill, and could conceivably do so tomorrow if only Senator Russell Long will offer his amendment and let the Committee vote on it." This step would permit the committee to report the bill to the floor for Senate action the week of June 28, "and we could have a huge signing by July 4th to mark this historic event." If Long continued to procrastinate, the signing would have to be postponed until later in the month. But, Manatos insisted, Long "does not have the votes, and he knows it."[40]

Long finally offered his amendment on June 17, but he departed from the committee's normal procedure of passing around printed copies and simply described the details of his changes from his own copy. The revisions were far more extensive than he had indicated to the press or in his private talks with other legislators. He proposed to provide unlimited coverage for "catastrophic illness," by which he meant illness that was catastrophically expensive, and to pay for this open-ended coverage by a sliding scale of deductibles that a patient paid according to his income. Long's amendment, which would have increased Social Security taxes even higher, threw both the administration and health reformers into a frenzy. The *New York Times* editorialized that the amendment turned the bill into a "monstrosity" that would sink Medicare. It not only required the hated means test and was an administrative nightmare but it would also bust the budget by adding a quarter of a billion dollars more to the administration's own figures. No one could possibly estimate expenditures, the *Times* wrote, if, as Long proposed, hospitals were open to any elderly person for indefinite lengths of stay.[41]

After the most cursory discussion of so drastic a modification of the Medicare bill, which would have transformed Medicare into a catastrophic coverage plan, Long called for a vote. The outcome was seven to six in favor of Long's amendment, until Senator Anderson produced a negative proxy given to him by Senator J. William Fulbright, of Arkansas. That made it a tie, and everyone thought that Long's modifications had been defeated until the wily Louisianan produced his own proxy, also from Fulbright but dated after the Anderson proxy. It appeared that the committee's vote would be eight to six for Long's amendments, but Anderson asked the clerk to allow him to examine this new proxy. It was, indeed, dated more recently, but it concerned an entirely different issue. Later that afternoon, Anderson and Fulbright confronted Long, who declared lamely that there had, perhaps, been a misunderstanding and proposed that the committee take another vote. Anderson accepted the offer, but neither he nor many other senators accepted Long's explanation.[42]

The following day, at a cabinet meeting to discuss the growing crisis in Vietnam, HEW Secretary Celebrezze apprised the president of the goings-on in the Finance Committee. An angry Johnson demanded to know how the "misunderstanding" could have occurred and, after the meeting, telephoned Long to ask, unsuccessfully, that he withdraw his amendments. At the same time, Cohen, Nelson Cruikshank, Elizabeth Wickenden, and officials of the AHA lobbied the committee's Democratic members to reverse the vote. Union leaders from Connecticut were enlisted to inform Senator Abraham Ribicoff of the administration's opposition to the Long amendments. Ribicoff, who viewed Long's amendments from a humanitarian perspective, declined to change his vote.[43]

Sensing an opportunity to defeat Mills's Medicare bill, Republican members of the Finance Committee and AMA lobbyists rallied to support Long's amendments. Their maneuvering came too late to offset the administration's intense lobbying against Long's proposals. The committee took up the first of Long's amendments on June 23, with six Republicans voting for it. Ten Democrats, including Senator Byrd, whom the AMA, in the words of Mike Manatos, had lobbied "with a very hard-sell," voted against it. Byrd voted against the amendment and ultimately against the entire bill because, he told Cohen, "it's a bad amendment to a bad bill." On Long's proposal to provide unlimited care, Democrats Ribicoff and Hartke, who liked the idea regardless of cost, supported the Louisianan, but Republican Senators Thruston Morton of Kentucky and Frank Carlson of Kansas voted with the majority Democrats. That defeated both amendments, although not without the committee first agreeing to add another sixty days of hospital coverage to the House bill (with a $10 co-pay during those additional days). Cohen informed the president of the committee's action, noting that the bill involved "some changes which I believe can be satisfactorily adjusted in Conference." The next day, the committee passed its version of the House bill by a final vote of twelve to five. The most significant aspect of the vote, perhaps, was that six of the twelve senators had never before voted for Medicare: Long, Smathers, Herman Talmadge, Fulbright, Carlson, and Dirksen.[44]

The Senate opened debate on Medicare on July 6 and passed it three days later by a vote of sixty-eight to twenty-one. The delay was occasioned by many senators, eager to claim credit for its passage, tacking on 513 amendments to the bill and $1.5 billion in additional expenditures. Both the amendments and added costs resulted from parliamentary maneuvering and from individual senators' convictions. Long used proxies on the Senate floor to accomplish what he had not been able to get in the Finance Committee; Republicans overloaded the bill, hoping to create a deadlock in the conference committee, anticipating that Mills and the House conferees would never accept the changes. A few senators, like Ribicoff and Hartke, for humanitarian reasons and because labor wanted them, supported the more liberalized benefits; other Democrats, like Oklahoma's Fred R. Harris, remained wedded to improving rather than replacing the Kerr-Mills program. Harris voted against the bill because he believed that disregarding different abilities to pay was the "wrong" approach to medical care for the elderly and, accepting Long's argument, because it failed to provide adequately for the needy, particularly in the event of catastrophic illness.[45]

The two chambers then established their respective conference committees to reconcile differences between the two bills. Negotiations took place on a broad range of Social Security and Medicare issues, with Mills and Wilbur Cohen again playing lead roles. To no one's surprise, Mills excised $1.5 billion from the Senate measure. Cohen moved to safeguard the fiscal integrity of the program and to deflect accusations of preferential treatment by persuading the president not to accept more costly amendments from West Virginia Senator Robert Byrd and Senator Vance Hartke.[46]

One major difference between the House and Senate bills was that Mills had secured passage of a provision in the House bill that allowed physicians and hospitals to retain control over their fees rather than having the government establish a rate structure. Another was his successful effort to keep certain specialists (pathologists, radiologists, and psychiatrists) outside of the hospital insurance program (Medicare). They would be compensated under the voluntary supplementary medical insurance (SMI) section. The AMA had lobbied hard for this change, to which the White House, fearing it would lead to runaway medical costs, objected.[47]

The administration asked Senator Paul Douglas to offer an amendment in the conference that would leave the decision as to how specialists were compensated to the hospitals. Mills led the White House to think that he would accept a compromise, and Cohen immediately drafted a substitute amendment he hoped would free the bill. Radiologists and pathologists, for compensation purposes, would come under the jurisdiction of Medicare, and anesthesiologists and psychiatrists under SMI.

The compromise fell apart when Mills, joined by Boggs, Long, and Smathers, persuaded the conferees to go along with his original proposal. This development prompted one Senate conferee to declare: "It was obviously prearranged. Mills had promised the doctors that he would never put any of them under any compulsory system, and he kept his word." The effect would cost the American people hundreds of millions of dollars and "make a hopeless mess out of normal hospital procedures," he predicted. Mills's deference to the AMA also disappointed Cohen, who recalled that he had had to pledge that "there would be no real controls over hospitals or physicians" and that the conferees' action "of course, will make the AMA happy and the result will be viewed as a defeat for the Administration." Mills made these concessions to the AMA to ensure its tepid support of Medicare, even though they might potentially shackle a future Congress if it decided to control the cost of Medicare. Mills's action reflected the political limits of fiscal conservatism; he would forgo significant cost regulation for the support of this particular interest group. As a legislator, a committee chairman, and a foe of direct government controls on markets, he knew that such compromises were sometimes necessary.[48]

Apart from these setbacks, Medicare emerged from conference on July 21 remarkably unscathed. Oklahoma Republican Page Belcher explained to a constituent: "Of course, the President has a huge majority of his own party in both the House and the Senate and is getting just about anything he asks for. There just aren't enough here to oppose him." Belcher's statement was accurate. On July 27, the House passed the revised conference bill by a vote of 307 to 116, with the Senate following suit the next day, 70 to 24. The bill was then forwarded to the president for his signature.[49]

The scope of the bill that crossed Johnson's desk was far more comprehensive than any of the bills that had led up to it. It provided every person sixty-five or older (excluding retired federal employees, who were covered by the Federal Health Benefits Act) with sixty days of free hospital care, after a standard $40 deductible, and thirty more days of hospital care at a charge of $10 a day. It included twenty days of free nursing home care; eighty additional days at a charge of $5 a day; and one hundred home visits after hospitalization by nurses or other health specialists. It also covered 80 percent of the cost of hospital diagnostic tests, after a $20 deductible for each series. To pay for this, the taxable wage base of the Social Security system was raised to $6,600 a year, and the tax itself was increased by 0.5 percent for both employer and employee.[50]

The voluntary supplement provided for payment of 80 percent of "reasonable charges" for all physicians' services, after a $50 yearly deductible; another hundred home health visits, whether a patient had been hospitalized or not; and the costs of nonhospital diagnostic tests, surgical dressings, splints, and rented medical equipment. To pay for this coverage, people sixty-five or older who wished to participate contributed $3 a month apiece, their contributions being supplemented by about a half-billion dollars a year from the Treasury's general revenues.

On July 30, at the suggestion of Jack Valenti, who played on Johnson's love of the dramatic gesture, the president flew out to Independence, Missouri, to the birthplace of President Truman, and surrounded by those Democratic leaders who were responsible for the bill's passage and veterans (or their heirs) of the early battles for national health security, he signed Medicare into law. Medicare (PL 89-97) was the farthest-reaching amendment to the Social Security Act since 1935.[51] Johnson's tribute to the former president, the first chief executive to advocate publicly for national health security, was a touching one, as he hailed the arrival of a new medical era. "No longer will older Americans be denied the healing miracle of modern medicine. No longer will illness crush and destroy the savings that they have so carefully put away," he declared. So moved was Johnson that he even invented an appropriate passage of scripture, "Thou shalt open thine hand wide unto thy brother, to thy poor, to thy needy, in thy land."[52]

Rather than basking in a job well done, Wilbur Cohen was rattled by the president's speech, because it brought to the forefront an issue that had not been resolved. Cohen worried that the dramatic ceremony would send the wrong message to the AMA and the nation. By identifying Medicare with Truman's national health proposal, they might conclude that Johnson intended to extend it to cover all Americans, not just the elderly. The thought was not far-fetched, for the president had also invoked the memory of John Dingell, Sr., Robert F. Wagner, and James Murray, point men in the earlier crusade for universal health coverage. Cohen thought the president should have emphasized the points he had made privately to AMA officials: that the government would adhere scrupulously to the law, would not interfere in the practice of medicine or in the patient's freedom of choice, and would consult with the medical profession on questions of compensation for services rendered.[53]

That meeting had occurred on July 29 when, with Johnson's signature a foregone conclusion, representatives of the AMA requested a private meeting to discuss implementation of the program, scheduled to be operational on July 1, 1966. Johnson had opened the meeting with a powerful appeal to the physicians to accept and cooperate with the new law; he reminded them that Congress had acted on behalf of the people only after due consideration and after following established constitutional procedures; and he emphasized the provisions that prohibited government from interfering in the practice of medicine and the physician-patient relationship. He also gave his personal assurances and then explained the role of Blue Cross and private insurance carriers (the administrative intermediaries under the law) in determining the definition of "reasonable charges." At the close of the meeting, Johnson asked Wilbur Cohen to work with the physicians to make the program a success.[54]

The White House encounter defused a threatened rebellion by a small minority of the AMA's physician-members who had refused to participate in the Medicare program. The AMA leadership greatly toned down references to Medicare as the opening wedge to "socialized medicine" and began to accommodate itself to the new law. AMA criticism shifted, instead, to the possibility that Medicare might become a way station en route to universal health coverage. "Our next great legislative battle could well concern itself with government participation in the financing of the health care of 175 million people under the age of 65," AMA President James Z. Appel warned the AMA's House of Delegates.[55]

Many Americans in the ensuing decade harbored similar concerns that Medicare would become a stepping-stone to a national health program. One angry physician wrote to House Speaker and fellow Oklahoman Carl Albert in 1975, "If any form of National Health Insurance is passed by any legislature in the near future and incorporates any of the characteristics of Medicare and Medicaid it will be an intolerable abuse of American citizens." Pointing to Medicare's and Medicaid's shortcomings, he insisted that if legislators were unable to reform those programs, "they certainly have no business passing an all inclusive National Health Insurance bill. They are not even ready to consider it."[56]

Senator Clinton P. Anderson, one of the legislative architects of Medicare, did not believe at the time that he was proposing a program that would culminate in national health coverage. Two months before the program went into operation, he told a *Look* magazine interviewer, "I don't foresee Medicare growing into a sweeping program for all ages." Unlike the situation with the elderly, he believed that voluntary, private health providers had done reasonably well in covering working people and their families, and improvements in Title XIX of the Social Security law had rendered as many as 35 million indigent and low-income people eligible for health coverage. "That is quite a sleeper in this law," Anderson explained. "It is the extension of Kerr-Mills, which originally covered only the aged, to all medically needy persons." Anderson's preference was to "maintain a strong private health insurance sector" for workers under the age of sixty-five, and he foresaw no major changes in Medicare over the next five years, which he regarded as a period of testing.[57]

Cohen also gave his own assessment of Medicare in a speech he delivered on August 15 at the ancestral home of Franklin D. Roosevelt, in Hyde Park, New York, on the occasion of the thirtieth anniversary of the enactment of the Social Security law. The 1965 amendments marked the pinnacle of Social Security expansion, he told his audience; they had lived to see Social Security become a factor in the life of every American, either in his capacity as an earner or as the dependent of one. It had grown in scope over the years from limited protection for 60 percent of the workforce to a bulwark for almost every family against the loss of the breadwinner's earnings through retirement, disability, or death.[58] But did this statement mean that he viewed Medicare as a milestone on the road to national health coverage? Not necessarily, at least not in the sense the term was applied in its European or Canadian context. A gradualist by temperament, Cohen later observed that to have gone from Medicare (which covered 20 million people) to national health security (a tenfold increase), in which the state underwrites the organization and financing of virtually every aspect of medical provision for its citizens, would have been a leap into chaos. "Our system of medical organization in this country just could not stand that in one single gulp," he explained. A political pragmatist, Cohen believed that government, through its fiscal power, should complement, not displace, voluntary, private-sector providers in establishing a seamless web of health coverage for Americans.[59]

The high tide in the establishment of the Great Society occurred in 1965. Building on the Civil Rights and the Economic Opportunity Acts of the previous year, President Johnson signed into law the Elementary and Secondary Education Act, the Voting Rights Act, and Medicare. After a half-century and more of debate on whether the United States should adopt a national health program and the form it should take, Medicare, a complex but somehow typically American solution to the problem, was adopted. Unlike European and Canadian models of health security, Medicare stopped well short of government-financed and -administered comprehensive health care. It was a more limited union of private and public effort to extend the safety net for a specific category of Americans: the elderly. Its rationale was to provide a modicum of health security for the expanding middle strata of American society of the postwar period, as its members entered their twilight years after a lifetime of average income and regular employment. And the public, particularly the middle class, bought into the program on the grounds that Medicare would also help their children by relieving the latter of the often financially crushing burden of caring for their parents' medical needs at a time when they also had to set aside funds to pay for their own children's college education.[60]

Medicare was the Great Society's solution to the anxiety of the middle class. It resolved the dilemma by helping to lower out-of-pocket health expenditures of the younger generation and offering higher-quality medical care to the older. In the process, it provided the adhesive that integrated and bound the young middle class and their elderly parents into the growing economy and social service state of post–World War II America, an action of enormous future political and economic consequence. The boundaries of public provision that encompassed the middle class also embraced the poor, for Medicaid, the states' counterpart of Medicare, represented a new determination to breathe life into a hitherto moribund Kerr-Mills program. And, indeed, the government opened wide its hand in distributing benefits under the new health care program. Nearly all aged persons in the country qualified for Medicare's hospitalization benefits, and 96 percent also elected to purchase supplementary physicians' insurance. After a decade of operation, Medicare and Medicaid were financing medical services for 20 percent of the nation's population, the elderly and the medically indigent who had heretofore remained outside the scope of the state, at a cost of $32 billion.[61]

Contrary to the view of its critics, Medicare was in the mainstream of the American tradition. It showed a deep affinity to earlier extensions of the role of the State and the continuing influence of the New Deal and the Fair Deal upon the Great Society. Unlike foreign models of national health coverage underwritten entirely by the State, the 1965 law blended public and private enterprise with federal and state intervention. The law was written thus because, outside the circle of policy experts, Americans were largely unfamiliar with the central government's provision of social insurance, as in Britain and elsewhere. Although Americans accepted the use of the Social Security mechanism to finance health care for the elderly, their most familiar and popular form of State provision, this acceptance coexisted with traditional uneasiness over the prospect of excessive State interference. As private pollsters told President Kennedy, "Most people want to have something done, but have doubts about the method."[62]

The public's ambivalence toward the State merged with the policy makers' approach to institutional change: expand the Social Security system, but limit the extent of federal government control. By dispersing Medicare's authority and hamstringing the development of administrative specialization, the resulting health care program expanded benefits while avoiding the appearance of strong federal control. Congress trusted the largely permanent Social Security bureaucracy to implement the Medicare law in a responsible manner. This should come as no surprise, given that Johnson, like his predecessor in the Oval Office, had relied on the same mainstream economists, technicians, and legislators (Cohen, Ball, Mills, Anderson, King) who had conceded from the start the framework of ideas and practices of the larger political economy.[63]

This framework also defined the contours and content of the administration's extension of social insurance. There is no evidence, for example, that either Johnson or the constellation of legislators and experts who put together the Medicare bill had made any effort to reach out to policy intellectuals on the Left or to more heterodox experts who thought "outside the box" for innovative or more creative solutions. Instead, the questions the policy makers framed were tactical rather than ideological, and the Medicare legislation they wrote simply corrected inequities on the margin of a thriving capitalistic system of production and consumption.[64]

In spite of its popularity, the new Medicare law did, as one scholar has noted, raise serious questions about social insurance and its relation to the payroll tax, questions that would become ammunition for future assaults on Social Security by fiscal conservatives, economists, and left-wing activists. For Mills, in response to pressure from the Social Security faction of the tax policy community, had made significant modifications to social insurance that weakened its distinctiveness from other public expenditure. The compromises were acceptable at the time, Mills believed, because of the layered protections and internal fiscal controls built into the program. But he, Cohen, and the tax policy community never equated Medicare with welfare, because of the absence of a means test, the presence of earmarked moneys, and the number of middle-class beneficiaries.[65]

The Social Security Amendments of 1965, however, did belie the propaganda of the payroll tax as a wage-related premium for a wage-related benefit. Now the revenue would finance service benefits that had no relation to past wages. Congress also compromised on a fundamental Social Security principle when it authorized use of general revenue to finance the SMI portion of the social insurance program. Although the SMI program was voluntary, the amendment created a precedent for using general revenue to pay for social insurance that future legislators would exploit.

Thus, although Mills's achievement in expanding earmarked taxes into the sector of private medicine without destroying OASDI was remarkable, the legislation did raise disturbing questions: Medicare challenged the limited capacities of the payroll tax to finance public welfare; it weakened the myth that payroll tax policies were not relevant to economic growth; and it contradicted the beliefs that general-revenue money could not be used in social insurance and that payroll taxes had to be tied to specific benefits. For the moment, however, these problems were overshadowed by the promise of the new legislation.[66]

# SEVEN

## NO PERMANENT SOLUTIONS: HEALTH CARE IN CRISIS

Public and legislative debate in the 1960s had centered on Medicare, but it was the economic growth of the postwar period that fueled the process of broadening the Social Security safety net. Prosperity enabled the architects of the Great Society to use the power of the federal government in unprecedented ways, and Johnson's electoral landslide victory in 1964 created the window of opportunity to use that prosperity to legislate Medicare as a major component of the Great Society's liberal agenda to improve the welfare of the individual. The principles of public financial responsibility for medical care and safeguarding the integrity of the Social Security system became embedded in the body politic in the 1960s and became mainstream public policy. Over time, the whole political-ideological situation evolved, and practically everyone recognized—with greater or lesser degree of tolerance—the increased role for the federal government in financing, organizing, and delivering health care. Believing that prosperity would continue for the foreseeable future, the authors of Medicare did not challenge hospitals to do better, but to do more to ensure the elderly access.[1]

Wilbur Cohen, as much as anyone, had been responsible for the enhancement of the postwar welfare state with the enactment of the Medicare program. He counted on Medicare's popularity, especially with middle-class voters, to maintain and improve it, but he could not count on or know whether the political system, under either party, would always be benevolent toward Medicare and other Great Society programs. Nor did he foresee that postwar America's prosperity would be severely eroded by war abroad, inflation and domestic turmoil at home, and a political system that would turn against Great Society programs. In the changed economic and political circumstances of the 1970s and 1980s, Medicare itself would be sorely tested, making even less likely the prospect of using it as a springboard for national health security.[2]

While the Johnson administration was forging ahead to implement Medicare on July 1, 1966, pressures were building to enhance the program's role in the Great Society in anticipation of the 1968 presidential election. On March 16, 1966, HEW Acting Secretary Wilbur Cohen wrote the president regarding recent Social Security initiatives. HEW had taken Johnson's remarks to the business community two years earlier at the time of signing the tax-reduction act—that it was good business practice not only to enlarge the economic pie but also to share the slices with every social class—as a cue to explore proposals for broadening Medicare beyond the elderly. HEW had been contemplating the possibility of including in Medicare needy children, disabled workers, and the children of disabled and deceased workers—a total of about 2 million adults and 3 million children.[3]

Cohen, like others within the administration, was concerned that after the 1965 legislative triumphs, the Great Society was losing momentum, and anticipating that Johnson would seek reelection, he asserted that the administration should build on these social programs to breathe new political life into the Great Society. The new HEW secretary, John W. Gardner, agreed. With Medicare five weeks old, Gardner had told White House aides Douglass Cater and Bill Moyers that he was "worried that the Administration is suffering from a feeling in the nation that the domestic program has lost its momentum" and that the "people [would] become preoccupied with selfish problems." The time was ripe, Gardner declared, "to create a 'Spirit of 1976.'" Cater relayed Gardner's remarks to the president, adding that Moyers also had received a memo from the secretary "suggesting ways that you may create the spirit of a new burst of momentum that will carry the nation into the 1970s."[4]

Gardner outlined his ideas before the president's political fortunes collapsed and the economy soured, and both Cater and Moyers thought them to be important enough "to be seriously studied."[5] Johnson may already have been thinking along similar lines, for he instructed his White House staff, including Joseph Califano and Harry McPherson, to work with Gardner on a specific set of recommendations. There were other indications as well. Selig Greenberg, a columnist for the *Nation,* recalled the president's statement on May 23, 1966, that "Medicare need not just be for people over 65" and his off-the-cuff remarks at a bill-signing ceremony in Texas about providing coverage for children under the age of six, beginning with dental and optical care. He cited a *New York Times* editorial that also noted the president's linkage of Medicare and better child health care to universal health coverage. But the editor was puzzled by "the tie up" between "this medical counterpart of Operation Head Start and an old-age insurance plan rooted in the social security principle of employer-employee contributions built over a lifetime." There was "much to be said for a national health insurance plan covering all Americans," the editorial declared, "but it should be considered on its merits—not through patchwork additions to Medicare."[6] Greenberg thought the *Times* had missed the point. "There is indeed much to be said for assaying an all-inclusive national health insurance policy, impractical though it may be politically for the time being," he observed, but what most Americans had yet to realize was that the nation was well along the road to a publicly financed system of medical care for large segments of the population, regardless of age. Greenberg observed that piecemeal progress through legislation (what Cohen called "salami slicing") rather than head-on collision between public and private sectors was "the dominant style of our political system, and experience has shown that it achieves in the long run pretty much the same results." Medicare had been a good example. Title XIX not only set higher standards for state medical programs for those on welfare and for the "medically indigent" elderly, but it also required the states to furnish equivalent services to individuals of all ages who were not sufficiently needy to be on relief but who were unable to pay their medical bills.[7]

We may never know whether Johnson intended to use Medicare as the point of departure for establishing a national health security program. His first priority, in 1965–1966, was to ensure that Medicare got off the ground smoothly; this necessitated having enough professionally trained health personnel available to attend to the elderly without depleting or overburdening the existing supply of physicians, nurses, and medical technicians; assuring that there were sufficient beds in hospitals and other health care institutions to accommodate the elderly; and guaranteeing equal access to Medicare to all elderly Americans regardless of their skin color.[8]

In pursuit of these objectives, Johnson prodded HEW to overcome bureaucratic foot-dragging, and the agency did respond with some very clever stratagems. Medicare, for example, would commence on July 1, 1966, when hospital occupancy was lowest, rather than at the beginning of the calendar year. Cohen knew from conversations with I. S. Falk that the sickness rate from influenza and other diseases for which people were hospitalized was as much as 20 percent higher in winter than in summer. July 1 also was close to the holiday weekend, when physicians and people were away on vacation and fewer individuals were admitted to hospitals. By giving it a lead time of eleven months, HEW had provided Medicare a longer start-up than any other program it administered; it also delayed implementation of the extended-care-facility provision by six months, time enough to enable the basic Medicare program to become operational; and it also placed an official of the AMA on Medicare's Health Insurance Benefits Advisory Council to minimize opposition from the medical establishment.[9] Then, on June 15, 1966, President Johnson summoned a group of the nation's leading physicians and hospital representatives to the White House to urge them to provide strong leadership to ensure the most efficient use of hospital beds and medical personnel and to cooperate in rooting out any malefactors who abused the program.[10]

Johnson specifically addressed the unwillingness of many hospitals in the South to comply with Title VI of the 1964 Civil Rights Act by assigning Medicare hospital beds on a nonsegregated basis. Without equivocation, he articulated the administration's color-blind policy. "In some communities, older people may be deprived of Medicare benefits because their hospitals fail to give equal treatment to all citizens," he observed. "Obey the law," he insisted, noting that 80 percent of hospitals would. To those hospitals that did not comply with the law, Johnson said simply: "You must comply. If you discriminate against *some* older citizens in your community, you wreck the program for *all*. The federal government *will not retreat* from its clear responsibility under the law—and you must not retreat from yours."[11] In the two weeks following this admonition, the administration monitored voluntary compliance. On July 7, HEW's Peter Libassi forwarded to Attorney

General Nicholas Katzenbach and presidential aides Cater and Califano a list of the first hospitals to receive notice of the USPHS's intention to initiate enforcement proceedings. Four days later, Libassi informed them that HEW would notify each hospital (and appropriate state agency) that approval of its application for participation in Medicare had been deferred.[12]

The difficulty of guaranteeing Medicare's smooth implementation in the South was symptomatic of the larger and serious problem of civil rights that had arisen whenever there had been talk of federal involvement in health care. But it was soon overshadowed by the rising costs of health care, which threatened the program itself. Before 1950, most hospitals were nonprofit organizations whose administrators had every incentive to keep costs down, for it was the patient who bore most of the costs. Since 1950, with the availability of private medical insurance, the net price of hospital services began to rise as more patients consumed them. The chief motivation for cost restraint no longer applied, because patients and doctors responded to the relatively low net prices by demanding and delivering a level of care that was better and more expensive than they would otherwise have elected. The added costs were increasingly passed on in the form of higher prices and paid through the painless mechanism of insurance. Medical administrators attempted to please physicians, patients, hospital workers, and trustees by purchasing the latest and most expensive high-tech equipment, adding amenities to patient rooms, raising wages, adding more beds, and opening new wings in a process that fed upon itself to drive hospital costs ever upward.[13]

Medical costs rose 7 percent annually after 1950, in contrast to the overall price level, which increased less than 2 percent a year. Hospital costs accounted for 40 percent of the nation's health bill, putting them at the top of this upward spurt. Physician fees also rose in response to the spread of private health insurance. But because insurance caught on more quickly for hospital than for physician care, inflation in physician fees was less acute, rising at 3 percent annually from 1950 to 1965. Blue Cross and private insurers had wrestled with medical inflation throughout the 1950s, and organized labor also had agonized over the problem, finding that every time a new contract that appeared to bring union members greater coverage was negotiated, the gains were wiped out by rising medical and hospital prices. In the 1950s and 1960s, union leaders had repeatedly asked state governments to cap rising Blue Cross rates and to address the inflation problem, but their pleas met with little success.[14]

With passage of Medicare and its accompanying Medicaid feature, the number of insurable services was poised to increase significantly after 1965, especially since, in the compromise to ensure the legislation's passage, the AMA had successfully lobbied Congress not to impose a cap on medical expenses or alter the way hospitals and physicians conducted their business. Hospital price increases doubled to 14 percent in the year following Medicare's enactment and continued to rise over the next decade, averaging 14 percent annually. Physician fees in the same period rose on average 7 percent annually.[15]

Not only did Medicare continue to increase the cost of medicine for society as a whole, but it also provided far fewer financial benefits for most recipients than citizens at the time commonly believed. For the minority of the elderly who had both long periods of hospitalization and small savings, Medicare was a godsend that fulfilled all of its sponsors' promises, but the average elderly were little better off. True, they were paying only 29 percent of their medical bills directly by 1975 (as compared to 53 percent before Medicare), but their total bills were also much higher. The average beneficiary spent $237 out-of-pocket in the year before Medicare and $390 a decade later. In constant dollars, this amounted to almost exactly the same, except that Medicare did not pay for prescription drugs, eyeglasses, and dental care. Over time, however, the elderly paid increasing out-of-pocket sums for the portion of physician and hospital bills that Medicare did not cover. For example, deductibles for each hospital stay had increased from $40 in 1966 to $104 by 1975, and physician fees had increased on average from $66 to $156.[16]

Medical inflation antedated and continued during the Johnson presidency, but this statement presents an incomplete picture of what was actually occurring. General—and medical—inflation was ratcheted up several notches in the mid-1960s as a consequence of President Johnson's decision to fight simultaneous wars against communism in Vietnam and poverty at home without raising taxes to finance the war abroad and to control inflation at home. Resorting to a dangerous sleight of hand, he decided that he could protect the Great Society only by downplaying the costs of his two-front war and by delaying a tax increase as long as possible.[17] Thus, to protect Medicare's benefits, he was determined to quash medical inflation and thrust that responsibility on physicians and hospital leaders. "Responsible medical society and professional leaders *must* take the lead to prevent unreasonable costs for health services." But not even the powerful economies in 1965, 1966, and the first six months of 1967 could solve the government's budget problems or slow the spiral of inflation.[18]

That medical inflation was moving quickly to the forefront of public and political consciousness was evident in the *Washington Post*'s report that Senator Clinton P. Anderson had inquired whether the administration was giving too many "sweeteners" to hospitals at the expense of health benefits to the aged. The Senate Finance Committee chairman, Russell Long, meanwhile, demanded that administration officials explain the guidelines for reimbursing hospitals for treatment of Medicare patients. Both Anderson and Long were troubled by HEW's inclusion of items in the reimbursement formula (totaling $75 million annually) that amounted to a 2 percent bonus to allowable hospital costs, and that it had done so without informing the committee. They feared it might set a precedent for other federally financed health programs. Despite Wilbur Cohen's assurances that the bonus was a "very, very reasonable, conservative solution" compared to the hospitals' original demands (amounting to a 19 percent bonus), neither Anderson nor Long was satisfied with Cohen's explanation. A clash between congressional Democrats and the White House was averted only after Connecticut Senator Abraham Ribicoff observed that if committee members were to order appreciable changes in the guidelines now, they "probably would cause almost a revolution and confusion within weeks before the plan goes into effect."[19]

If social welfare liberals in the Congress feared that the administration's overly generous reimbursements to the private medical sector were a major contributor to spiraling medical costs, organized medicine had a different reading of the problem. The AMA feared that the government would use inflation as an excuse to keep reimbursements too low. That is how it interpreted HEW's collection of statistical data to determine "reasonable charges" for physician fees. Wilbur Cohen wrote to presidential aide Douglass Cater, "We see no alternative but to try to protect Medicare from inflationary pressures."[20] Five days later, he again noted the president's "concern that physicians may raise their fees during the next few months" and told Cater that he would remind both insurance carriers and the AMA of its reimbursement guidelines. Still, he expected they would protest.[21]

Medical inflation was much in the president's mind as he appeared before the television cameras on June 30 to address the nation on the new health care entitlement. He insisted Medicare was not "an act of charity, but . . . the insured right of a senior citizen." But even as he reminded Americans that his administration had made "more extensive preparation to launch this program than for any other peaceful undertaking in our nation's history," he reiterated his plea to hospitals, physicians, and the elderly to cooperate with the government "to make Medicare succeed." The debate over *whether* to have Medicare was over, the *Christian Science Monitor* wrote. The focus now was on how smoothly and efficiently Medicare functioned; until that was determined, the *Monitor* insisted, the administration should resist pressures to expand the program.[22]

The *Monitor* had put the cart before the horse, for the president was thinking less about expansion than escalating costs. The government's own calculations indicated that medical expenditures were rising faster than the total cost of living.[23] The principal causes of this increase were higher utilization of hospitals (partially attributable to Medicare) and the rising wages of hospital workers and physicians. Johnson responded to this threat with an order to HEW Secretary Gardner in August to launch a quick, but broad, investigation into health costs and to make recommendations for moderating the increases. Gardner told the press that HEW, the Council of Economic Advisers (CEA), and the Labor Department would take a "hard and very quick look" at the problem, but he sidestepped reporters' questions about the measures the government would pursue to rein in medical price inflation. The *Wall Street Journal* was dubious that government officials would come up with a quick fix and interpreted the announcement as an attempt to forestall a congressional investigation into Medicare costs. The problem went beyond Medicare, however, because Medicaid's costs also were escalating. Since Medicaid covered the poor and was financed through general tax revenues, it engendered strong liberal support but equally intense conservative hostility. Johnson had to tread carefully, the *Journal* noted, balancing his need to restrain health costs with his need to retain the political support of liberal Democrats.[24]

In fact, it was fiscally conservative Democrats such as Wilbur Mills, the powerful chair of the Ways and Means Committee, whom the administration had most to fear. Mills was greatly troubled by the rising cost of Medicare, which was partially funded through the same Social Security program that paid for cash benefits. The cost of hospitalization had grown much faster than the portion of revenue allotted to the program, and until Congress addressed this problem, Medicare threatened to strain the earmarked tax system.[25]

The same was true of Medicaid, which Mills referred to as the most expensive mistake of his career and for which Congress had expanded funding along with that of existing welfare programs. Physicians' fees had soared because the states implemented liberal definitions of the "medically indigent." At the root of the problem, Mills believed, was that Congress had forfeited control of general revenues after Johnson succeeded to the presidency. A group of bureaucrats and economists with few ties either to Mills or the tax community had transformed new antipoverty initiatives, such as the Economic Opportunity Act and Medicaid, into entitlement programs in which the poor had an unconditional right to a guaranteed income or benefit from government. This change was at odds with Mills's belief in the principle of opportunity, not entitlement.[26]

Mills's discontent became evident when, on September 10, 1966, White House aide Douglass Cater told the president that "Wilbur Mills will shortly report out recommendations to amend Title XIX of the Social Security Act (Medicaid)." To restrain runaway health costs, Mills was prepared to slash Medicaid funding by placing a ceiling on income levels beyond which federal financial contributions for each state would not go. New York State's Medicaid program, Mills believed, had set excessively generous maximum payments for the poor, many of whom were urban and black. If Mills succeeded in capping incomes, Cater feared, the administration's social and fiscal policies would be put on a collision course, which would spark protests from social welfare liberals that the administration was whittling away Medicaid's promises. Scrambling to avoid a confrontation between the White House, social welfare liberals, and Mills, Cater and Wilbur Cohen suggested that the president "take a positive stand by proposing a floor as well as a ceiling be set for the state Medicaid programs." To qualify for federal Medicaid funding, each state would then be required to meet a minimum as well as a maximum income level. Johnson liked the proposed compromise because it did not directly challenge Mills and offered a balm to liberals. "All of you get on this," he instructed Jake Jacobsen, Jack Valenti, and other White House staffers.[27]

At the same time, Johnson was restraining Medicare's personnel needs. He conceded to Secretary Gardner on September 29 that "the most critical need is in the manpower field" but added, in what was most likely an oblique reference to the growing financial drain of the Vietnam war on all Great Society programs, "because of the budgetary situation, with which you are fully familiar, it is of the utmost importance that we employ ingenuity and imagination to adjust existing programs to meet our urgent health manpower needs."[28]

The fear that runaway health costs would prompt investigation and debate on Capitol Hill also shaped the president's response to a laundry list of future press announcements that HEW Secretary Gardner had forwarded to him on November 5, via White House aide Douglass Cater. The president was in Texas at the time. Of the eleven items touching on HEW's jurisdiction, the president wrote by hand, "No," next to those that involved increased medical expenditures and enlargement of the government's role in health care: any mention of including prescription drugs under Medicare; of providing matching funds for a new, innovative program to underwrite the cost of building privately owned nursing homes for the elderly; and of establishing federally funded training programs to lure retired nurses back into the profession.[29]

Johnson's reluctance to push these initiatives in the 1967 fiscal year indicated his sensitivity to the added strain higher medical costs would impose on a budget already burdened by the escalating costs of the war in Vietnam. If he had any doubts on this score, they were erased by the report on medical costs he had requested earlier from HEW. Compiled by William Gorham, assistant secretary for program coordination, with the assistance of the SSA, the report of February 28, 1967, retraced the causes of the long-run upward trend in medical prices, highlighted the acceleration that occurred from 1966 through January 1967, and extrapolated from the data to project future price movements. The Gorham report recommended government intervention in the marketplace to monitor and moderate price increases and to encourage more efficient use of medical resources. But the report candidly acknowledged in a sobering conclusion that medical inflation would not disappear soon.[30]

One tangible outcome of the Gorham report was HEW's sponsorship of national conferences of medical authorities and public representatives "to discuss ... cooperative efforts to improve medical care services and control medical costs." The SSA played a leading educational role at the first conference, held June 27–28, 1967, by tracing for the delegates the trend in medical expenditures, dissecting how the medical care dollar was spent, and analyzing factors that affected cost increases. Three months later, HEW and the SSA again teamed up to organize a National Conference on Private Health Insurance, which brought together leaders of the major private health insurance companies, purchasers of health insurance, providers of health care, and state insurance regulators. The meeting of September 28–29 explored ways to broaden private health coverage to include more, and presumably less expensive, alternatives to hospital care and to develop suggestions for model state laws encouraging comprehensive coverage.[31] Building on growing public concern, Wilbur Cohen, Gardner's successor at HEW, had initiated a series of regional meetings, the first held in Kansas City on June 26–27, 1967, to give the public a forum in which to discuss new policy initiatives in response to rising costs.[32]

That fall, the National Advisory Commission on Health Manpower (NACHM) issued its own recommendations for curtailing medical costs without diminishing the quality of patient care. Its report of November 21, 1967, proposed sweeping revisions of Medicare and Medicaid payment arrangements in order to provide positive incentives for hospitals and other health care institutions to operate more efficiently; penalties for medical providers that wasted federal funds; money for pilot projects that promised to deliver services more efficiently and economically; state-sponsored periodic reviews of physician licenses; continuing education programs to update medical skills; and the establishment of medical peer-review procedures to guard against fraudulent claims and low-quality care. Former Ford executive J. Irwin Miller, the committee's chair, asserted that if these recommendations were implemented, the administration could anticipate a moderation of health costs, better patient care, and a reduction in future federal spending for health care.[33]

Miller's prediction was exceedingly optimistic and underestimated the complexity of the problem, but President Johnson took the task force's recommendations to heart even as he cautioned the Senate in his health message of March 4, 1968, that they would "not be easy" to carry out. For though the overall cost of living was projected to rise by more than 20 percent between 1965 and 1975, health cost increases would go up nearly 140 percent. The average person would have to pay nearly $400 annually for medical care in 1975, twice what he had paid in 1965. Prescription drug payments would increase by 65 percent, dental bills by 100 percent, physicians' bills by 160 percent, and payments for general hospital services by 250 percent![34]

Under the best of circumstances it would have taken time to realize the savings envisioned by the task force, but time was quickly running out for the president. Johnson had underestimated the expense of the war in Southeast Asia and the extent of the backlash against civil rights and the poverty war, which were stoking white discontent against liberal government. Rather than act to implement the NACHM's recommendations, which would have necessitated additional new appropriations, Congress bolted. The Ways and Means Committee, ruled by Mills's iron fist, held hostage the administration's tax bill (which Johnson had delayed for two years before submitting) to pay for the war until the White House agreed to savage cuts in Great Society spending. Without such cuts, Mills argued, a surcharge to pay for the war would place fiscal policy in a "straitjacket" by limiting the prospects for periodic, stimulative income tax reduction. He would not even consider a hearing on the surcharge until January 1968 at the earliest. Then, amidst a growing turmoil at home against the war and challenges to his renomination in 1968, the president announced on the last day of March 1968 that he would de-escalate the war and withdraw from the presidential campaign.[35]

Lyndon Johnson's triumph as president had been to persuade Congress to enact Medicare as a right of citizenship for older Americans. He then devoted much of his own and the administration's energies to getting this Great Society program off to a successful start. The initial reports were positive. The SSA's nationwide survey of hospitals on July 1, 1966, disclosed that Medicare had little or no effect on hospital admissions or overcrowding, and the president's moral and political leadership had turned aside threats to patients' civil rights.[36] Two years later, Medicare had extended coverage to 20 million Americans sixty-five and over (10 percent of the nation's population) and had paid $8.4 billion in benefits toward their hospital and medical bills (covering 10.6 million hospital stays and 640,000 admissions to skilled-nursing homes). Another 485,000 elderly Americans received home care from a home health agency. A staggering 45 million bills were submitted for medical services under the supplementary medical insurance program, with $21 billion being paid out for these services.[37] The *Philadelphia Inquirer* reported in January 1967 that a majority of Americans favored a federal Medicare plan for the entire population.[38]

Johnson never doubted that the government funding of health care for older Americans was a prudent and popular social investment, but over the next two decades, Medicare's benefits failed to expand, and the program acquired a reputation in Congress and the executive branch as an uncontrollable burden on the federal budget. The reasons were many: the development of supplemental insurance, driven by the limited scope of Medicare benefits, created a market niche for private insurers who dampened political pressures for program expansion; the dominance of fiscal concerns in program policy, which shifted the key issue in Medicare policy from how to enhance the program's limited benefits to how to restrain costs through regulatory and financing reforms; and confusion among the elderly regarding Medicare and the scope of its benefits, which undercut the efforts of advocacy groups to mobilize for benefits expansion.[39]

The satisfaction Johnson had derived from establishing Medicare was tempered by the seriousness of the general—and medical—inflation, aggravated by his decision to wage a foreign war without raising taxes to pay for it. "It is appropriate that the Government—which pays more than 20 percent of the nation's medical bill—take the lead in stemming soaring medical costs," he had told the Senate on March 4, 1968, knowing full well that the government's share of health costs was projected to increase from 26 to 37 percent by 1970 and the nation's total health bill would reach a staggering $100 billion in 1975.[40] That is why he had told HEW Secretary Gardner to use creative, but stopgap, measures to cope with the budget deficit, such as delaying implementation of nursing home care for six months.[41] But runaway medical costs that ate insidiously into the health care dollar and undermined quality patient care, like urban race riots and the war in Southeast Asia, proved to be the least tractable of Johnson's problems and the undoing of his hopes for expanding Medicare. Putting the inflation genie back into the bottle was a task left for Johnson's successor in the Oval Office.[42]

Within four years of Johnson's vacating the Oval Office, the liberal period known as the Great Society had turned into a conservative epoch. By 1970, conservative theorists had thrown down four challenges to liberalism that went largely unanswered: the federal government was unable to set realistic goals and simply resorted to throwing money at social problems; the government could not change the outlook or behavior of lower-class people to respond to the opportunities government offered; broad indignation existed among the real majority of average Americans, who believed that liberal politicians, bureaucrats, and social engineers were encouraging the poor and lower class to violate basic norms of behavior (including abusing Medicaid); and the political consequences of the Great Society's liberal policies had been to transform traditional voters in the South, the suburbs, and elsewhere into durable Republican voters.[43]

Into this milieu had stepped Richard M. Nixon, whose election in 1968 set the stage for the conservative political resurgence that influenced the nation for the next three decades. Nixon coined the term *New Federalism* to herald a long-term Republican effort to trim back the Great Society by devolving some federal responsibilities back to the states. He wanted to move from the categorical grant focus of the Johnson administration (such as Medicare) toward general-revenue sharing with the states, whereas members of Congress generally favored the former, with their detailed provisions and control. Nixon's administration, also in contrast to Johnson's, preferred actions in the private rather than the public sector. But with Democratic majorities in both houses of Congress and economic and medical inflation dogging the nation, Nixon's policy of devolution required legislative flexibility. He would have to assimilate the liberal ideas of a Democratic Congress about entitlement programs but recast them in the process. Remarkably responsible and pragmatic rather than ideological, the Nixon White House did not automatically ignore arguments that might prescribe new federal duties.[44]

Nixon's response to skyrocketing medical costs was to "jawbone," to adopt the rhetoric of crisis, as when, on July 10, 1969, he drew on HEW Secretary Robert Finch's report card on the nation's health care systems to lecture reporters about the country's "massive crisis." "Unless action is taken within the next two or three years . . . we will have a breakdown in our medical system," he warned. Characterizing health care so starkly rejuvenated public interest in national health security, but in Nixon's hands, health policy became a paradigmatic case of the conservative assimilation (and ultimate rejection) of liberal reform. The crisis in health care was both a challenge and an opportunity to get hold structurally of the reins of government spending.[45]

Nixon's interest in health care dated back nearly two decades, so it was not surprising that as president-elect, he established a task force to investigate a system whose quality, quantity, and financial shortcomings were under fire at every level of government. In March 1968, Republican Governor Nelson Rockefeller had asked the New York State legislature to enact his health security bill to control the relentless rise in hospital costs and to provide health coverage to virtually all New Yorkers.[46] In June, to minimize further federal intervention in medical care financing, the AMA's House of Delegates passed a resolution advocating federal income tax credits to pay for insurance premiums and a voucher plan to enable indigent and needy individuals under Title XIX to purchase comprehensive health insurance.[47] Harvard economist Rashi Fein circulated a proposal that would have universalized health insurance (thereby terminating the debt-ridden Medicaid program and the means-test stigma that liberals found so distasteful) by allowing everyone to apply federal tax credits toward its purchase.[48] These and other ideas—restricting funding solely to the indigent, tightening eligibility requirements, defining more precisely "reasonable" medical cost—were assimilated into the task force's findings and presented to President Nixon on January 9, 1969.[49]

Health care expenditures had mushroomed rapidly throughout the postwar period, the task force reported, particularly in recent years, and "the involvement of the federal government in health is now very large." Washington contributed 25 percent of the $53.1 billion spent on health care in fiscal 1968; states and localities, approximately 12 percent; and private care providers, 63 percent. Nonetheless, health costs had risen more rapidly than other costs. From 1966 to October 1968, the medical care component of living costs had increased 15.4 percent and medical care service 19 percent, as compared to a 10.9 percent increase in total living costs.[50] Despite a great deal of new money being poured into the health care industry, output had increased relatively little. The supply of health care had become "highly inelastic," the task force concluded, and it warned that the health sector had to become more efficient and more productive. Pouring additional moneys into the existing system and introducing a new range of benefits would further drive up costs, without increasing output very much.[51] The first priority had to be efficiency and productivity, coordination and simplification, and a careful ordering of objectives rather than creating new benefit programs. That required "firm and effective leadership." Reforms, the task force insisted, should establish a system "capable of yielding very significant savings and improvements in care."[52]

The task force singled out Medicare, Medicaid, and the delivery of health care to the poor as specific problems inherited from the previous administration that Nixon would have to address, but it warned that each of these problems was fraught with political implications. Indeed, even within the task force, "significantly divergent views" had emerged as to which policy options the Nixon White House should follow. Suggestions ranged from making no more than minor administrative adjustments ("until we have had more time to judge its full impact") to implementing as soon as possible a major structural revision of how the nation financed its health care. Medicare's financial woes required more than administrative changes to put it on a solid financial foundation, the report stated, but in the interim, "there will be pressures both within the Congress and without to make changes in the program." Among the policy options being discussed, the report noted, were to replace the payroll tax with general revenues, which would likely lead to a confrontation with Wilbur Mills, and to invite private enterprise to participate more widely in Medicare to help reduce overall programmatic costs. Since Medicare had more financing options than Medicaid, the task force concluded that "any major changes in the Medicare Program should await a policy decision by the incoming Administration."[53]

The task force also highlighted the failure to coordinate civilian, military, and veterans' care as a major contributor to duplication and inflated costs. No federal agency provided "a sense of direction" to the government's endeavors; there was no single point in the vast, sprawling bureaucracy where responsibility for coordinating, setting goals for, evaluating, and planning health care programs was lodged. The task force, turning to the model of several state governments, recommended establishing a separate cabinet-level Department of Health and Welfare to fill the void. To further emphasize the seriousness of the health crisis, the task force strongly recommended that the incoming administration establish a Council of Health Advisers within the executive office to oversee the efficient expenditure of capital through more careful planning and distribution of health facilities.[54]

The report, which had provided the context for Nixon's July 10 warning, also urged the president-elect to include brief references to the health care crisis in the Inaugural and State of the Union Addresses and in a separate message to Congress and, in what became an important policy of the Nixon administration, to name to HEW a well-respected health professional and a strong administrator to the "critical posts" of assistant secretary for health and scientific affairs and director of health services and mental health administration.[55] Few, if any, of the task force's recommendations found their way into Nixon's presidential addresses to Congress, but the report did establish a baseline for the administration's health care policy as explicated in its 1971 white paper, *Toward a Comprehensive Health Policy for the 1970's.*[56]

Medical inflation, however, took a backseat to the Vietnam War, although the media repeatedly raised the issue. Then, in February 1969, a bipartisan coalition of senators, including Anderson, Aiken, Mansfield, and Winston L. Prouty, sponsored a bill "to place rational controls" on the soaring costs of Medicare and Medicaid.[57] Their bill stirred little interest until March 17 when the *Washington Daily News* printed stories critical of rising health costs and disclosed that "huge fees [were] paid to doctors, dentists and other medical practitioners" under government health programs, notably

Medicare. The revelations spurred Senators Anderson, Aiken, and Harrison Williams to call for an exhaustive review of existing programs and new legislation to control Medicare payments. An outraged Anderson was quoted as saying, "I am completely opposed to increasing Medicare taxes until we have tried and applied some common sense controls."[58] Three days later, the administration became proactive on the issue when presidential adviser Alexander P. Butterfield forwarded to John Ehrlichman, President Nixon's chief domestic policy adviser, copies of the press clippings.

President Nixon also had read the story, and sensitive to its political ramifications, he wrote Ehrlichman a note via Butterfield that read simply: "John—I want strong action on this in three days. There is no excuse for us to fail to have a position on such a hot issue."[59] Ehrlichman reported on April 1: "I have learned that of the two programs, Medicaid is by far the worst. It is literally fraught with perils as the states are spending federal money with little or no guidelines or regulations governing their expenditures." Until HEW instituted controls and standards, he advised the president that the administration's position "should be one of concern with an accompanying unwillingness to increase the budget without first finding where the holes are and then plugging them."[60]

Ehrlichman's assessment was not unlike that of Wilbur Mills. In the midst of a Social Security debate later that year over whether retirees' benefits were adequate in light of inflation and whether Congress should adjust the benefits for inflation or institute automatic cost-of-living allowances, which the Nixon administration and the Social Security tax policy community favored, Mills told Wilbur Cohen of his disappointment with the inability of the states to control Medicaid caseloads and expenditures. He disclosed that he was contemplating an amendment to federalize welfare and also told Cohen he opposed indexation because it would bypass Congress's power over Social Security taxation. But what particularly troubled Mills was the rising cost of Medicare, and he reminded Cohen that he had warned both Ball and Myers in 1965 that the Hospital Insurance Trust Fund would be depleted by 1973 unless Social Security taxes were increased. That warning was fast becoming a reality.[61]

The inflationary health costs that were pressuring the Nixon administration to carve out a position on health care, dividing Democratic legislators, and straining Mills's ties to the remnants of the tax policy community that had helped to frame Medicare had breathed new life into demands for national health security. Massachusetts Senator Ted Kennedy called for universal health coverage in December 1969. Ehrlichman called Kennedy's declaration to the attention of White House aide Edmund Morgan on December 17, although he dismissed it as "a demagogic ploy since we can neither afford such a program nor would it be a good thing for the practice of medicine in this country." Still, he asked Morgan to "get with Jeb Magruder and anyone else you think appropriate from HEW or elsewhere." He wanted them to "map a strategy to be carried out over a period of the next year or so to meet the challenge that both Kennedy and Wilbur

Mills pose in this area"; the latter was a reference to media speculation about Mills's presidential ambitions. The administration, Ehrlichman suggested, might stage "expositions" of the failure of the national health program in Britain, distribute press releases providing facts about the "extreme cost of such a plan," and employ other tactics to discredit Kennedy's proposal. In closing, Ehrlichman wrote, "Please let me have a game plan on this from you and Jeb by the end of the year."[62]

In January 1970 there were ominous declarations of a "crisis" in health care, which subsequently became one of the hallmarks of the decade. With the health care industry buffeted by high costs and rapid change, two of the nation's leading conservative journals, *Business Week* and *Fortune,* focused their spotlights on the "$60 billion crisis" in health care and warned that American medicine stood "on the brink of chaos." They portrayed American health care in unflattering terms, particularly in comparison to the national health programs of Western Europe. Their indictments were as harsh as any to be found in the liberal press, which, in order to open the way for Medicare and then to push for further reforms, had sought for many years with limited success to persuade Americans that a health care crisis existed.[63]

"Crisis" was a term that did not simply describe the objective reality of American health care; it transformed that reality by recasting the political agenda, making hard decisions about health care policy seem unavoidable and creating political opportunities for the Republican Party. It also afforded liberals and social welfare activists a new reason to resurrect calls for national health care reform. In July 1970, a newly reorganized Committee for National Health Insurance, chaired by labor leader Leonard Woodcock of the UAW and vice-chaired by prominent Texas heart surgeon Dr. Michael DeBakey, along with medical philanthropist Mary Lasker and the National Urban League's Whitney Young, Jr., put together *Health Security Program: Health Care for All Americans Thru National Health Insurance,* a booklet that used "the problem of skyrocketing costs" and the ineffectual organization and delivery of health services to promote health security through universal coverage.[64]

Senator Kennedy, meanwhile, renewed his call for universal health coverage and returned the issue to the congressional and popular spotlight when, on August 27, 1970, he introduced his health security bill (S. 4323). Michigan Democrat Martha W. Griffiths had earlier introduced a similar bill in the House. The health security bill became the liberal initiative in medical care. The legislation offered free universal health coverage, financed partly from increased taxes and partly from general revenues. It eliminated patient copayments and replaced all public and private health plans with a single, federally operated health coverage system. Though the legislation did not involve any nationalization of facilities or require physicians to work on salary, it did set a national budget, allocate funds to regions, provide incentives for prepaid group practice, and oblige private hospitals and physicians to operate within budget constraints.[65]

The Kennedy-Griffith legislation went nowhere that year, and the two Democrats would reintroduce it in 1971. But Kennedy's political challenge and the continuing medical inflation had forced the Nixon administration to think through its own policy initiative, which focused on "pressure points" in the system that might yield to short-run gains rather than an initial application of heavy-handed or intrusive methods, such as market or medical price controls. "The immediate problem was to train more doctors and subprofessional people, and get away from hospital-dominated care into more efficient systems," Lewis H. Butler, HEW assistant secretary, wrote to Ehrlichman in late 1969, but "ultimately," he thought, "some kind of national health insurance should be enacted." This raised for the first time the intriguing possibility that the Republicans might modify their long-standing opposition to comprehensive health coverage and, under Nixon's leadership, actually embrace it, even as the president shaped and transformed it to his liking.[66]

But that was not to be. On February 5, 1970, Butler, Undersecretary John G. Veneman, and other HEW officials met in Washington with Dr. Paul M. Ellwood, Jr., a Minneapolis physician and director of the American Rehabilitation Foundation. Ellwood was a proponent of the view that reform of the health system had to address its "structural incentives." In rehabilitative, as in other fields of medicine, fee-for-service payment penalized medical institutions that returned patients to health. The financing system, Ellwood contended, ought to reward health maintenance; prepayment for comprehensive care would do so. The alternative to fee-for-service medicine and to centralized governmental financing that Ellwood had in mind was the development of comprehensive health care corporations, similar to the Kaiser plan, which he called "health maintenance organizations" (HMOs). Ellwood suggested that the federal government could begin prepaying for services under Medicare and Medicaid while using its resources to stimulate development of other prepaid plans. The appeal of the health maintenance strategy was that rather than requiring a new government bureaucracy and large public expenditures, it called for stimulating private initiative. In March, Ellwood and his colleagues put the matter starkly: the choice in health policy was between a "health maintenance industry that is largely self-regulating" and "continued or increased federal intervention through regulation, investment and planning."

The concept resonated with Assistant Secretary Butler, and HMOs, when stated in those terms, also made a lot of sense to Republicans, although there were some presidential advisers who were initially cool to the health maintenance strategy. Later that month, HEW Secretary Robert Finch, with White House approval, disclosed that the administration would seek legislative authority for an HMO option under Medicare and Medicaid. When Elliot Richardson succeeded Finch as HEW Secretary in June 1970, he became HMOs' most committed advocate, to the extent that he decided a few months later to divert funds already available under other programs to implement a pilot program even before Congress approved any new legislation.

The Ways and Means Committee, in fact, had been working toward a similar end as part of its effort to expand Social Security. On May 14, it reported out the Social Security Amendments of 1970, which contained provisions to reduce the cost of Medicare, including an option for Medicare beneficiaries to use HMOs; an increase in the portion of Social Security taxes going to the Hospital Insurance Trust Fund; and limitations on physicians' fee increases. The Senate, in December, passed its own version of the amendments, which also included a peer-review system to monitor Medicare services, but Mills delayed final passage of the bill, promising it would be the first item on the agenda in 1971.[67]

Apart from their cost-saving features, HMOs were attractive because they offered Republicans a political (and private-sector) alternative to the Democratic proposal and to Senator Kennedy, who was even then crisscrossing the country holding public hearings on the "health care crisis." Under intense political pressure to respond to what Nixon himself had labeled a "massive crisis," White House advisers concluded that health care would be a major issue in the next election. Kennedy, despite his disavowals, was using the crisis to launch a bid for the presidency in 1972. Therefore, they asked HEW Secretary Richardson to put health care policy on the agenda of the president's Domestic Council. Richardson informed council members on November 5, 1970, that he would take up "the present health status of the American people" and follow it with "a possible Administration initiative in response to the many comprehensive health insurance bills that have already appeared in the Congress." The nation had unmet health needs, the background paper accompanying his memo conceded. Certain groups in the population could not afford medical services, and medical care was unavailable in certain regions of the country. In weighing possible financing options, Richardson declared, council members would have to factor in demands for new services and how best to provide the resources to meet them.[68] Health care, he concluded, "will probably be the most important legislative matter facing the Department of Health, Education and Welfare in the next session of the Congress, and promises to have major impact through 1972."[69]

Five days later, Richardson went before the Domestic Council and identified a broad range of problems troubling the existing health care system, many of which had been singled out by the 1968 task force report.[70] After the meeting, the White House requested that he and his staff draft a message on health care for Nixon to deliver in early 1971. HEW policy analysts immediately set to work writing a long-term "National Health Strategy" to serve as the basis of the Nixon administration's alternative health insurance plan. HMOs were the centerpiece of that strategy, which outlined a new, ambitious, and multifaceted "National Health Insurance Standards" bill. The proposed legislation mandated that employers provide minimum health insurance and pay 65 percent of the premium costs in the first two years. It included a family health insurance plan that offered government-funded coverage for low-income families with children that were not eligible for employer-mandated coverage. It contained a nationally uniform definition of eligibility; continued Medicare coverage for the blind, aged, and disabled; abolished premium payments for low-income elderly; encouraged Americans to join HMOs; expanded and reformed medical education; created a National Health Service Corps to serve rural and urban areas lacking in medical personnel; created a privately funded Health Education Foundation; and expanded research into cancer and sickle-cell anemia.[71]

While HEW analysts were fine-tuning the proposed legislation, Congress reassembled after the Christmas recess. Senator Kennedy and Congresswoman Martha Griffiths immediately reintroduced their national health security bill (S. 3, H.R. 22). In response to the liberal challenge, President Nixon, addressing Congress on February 18, 1971, spoke of his own legislative initiative, the "National Health Insurance Partnership" (S. 1623, H.R. 7741), which Senator Wallace Bennett of Utah and Wisconsin Republican John W. Byrnes formally introduced in their respective chambers on April 22, 1971. The administration's bill emphasized health care delivery through privately run HMOs, the goal being to enroll 90 percent of the population by 1980. Besides funding for HMOs, the legislation required employers to provide a minimum package of standard health insurance benefits for their employees and for the government to pick up coverage for low-income families with children that were not eligible for employment-related insurance. For the first time since the late 1940s, a president—this time a Republican—was requesting Congress to enact a nationally mandated health care program, albeit one that relied heavily on the private sector.[72]

Besides the Kennedy-Griffiths and the Bennett-Byrnes bills, two other major health insurance bills were introduced in 1971. The "National Health Care" bill proposed federal standards for health benefits provided by private insurance companies, whereas the "Health Care Insurance" bill (popularly referred to as "Medicredit") utilized a sliding scale of income tax credits to purchase private health insurance, with federally subsidized insurance for low-income persons. The first had the endorsement of the Health Insurance Association of America (HIAA) and the second the imprimatur of the AMA. With these four bills, American medicine found itself increasingly caught between the concerns of government and business about high costs and social welfare liberals' demands for equality and participation in medical care. This portended a sea change in American medicine: physicians' control over the dispensing of health care would have to be shared, even more than in the past, with outside parties. HEW Undersecretary John G. Veneman stressed this point in remarks to reporters on June 3, 1971: "In the past, decisions on health care delivery were largely professional ones. Now the decisions will be largely political," he declared.[73]

Politics and public policy had become inextricably interwoven. White House aide Edward L. Harper quoted George Romney as stating that "health is going to go up as an issue thanks to the media and Teddy Kennedy." Romney's assessment was correct, for on February 17, 1971, Democratic Representative David R. Obey, who was sponsoring a House bill to cover outpatient prescription drugs under Medicare "without waiting for the issue of national health insurance to be resolved," wrote to House Speaker Carl Albert that the 92nd Congress should give "special attention" to the problems of older Americans, because they were "of special importance to the Democratic Party." President Nixon was "especially vulnerable" where the elderly were concerned, Obey declared. Nixon's actions on their behalf "have been either harsh or hesitant," whereas Kennedy's name was attached to the prescription drug bill in the Senate.[74]

Of the four bills, congressional and public attention focused primarily on the Kennedy-Griffiths and Nixon proposals, thanks to the presidential election in less than a year. Kennedy's disavowal of presidential ambitions notwithstanding, he and Nixon continued taking political potshots at each another over health care. Nixon insisted that he wanted to build on the strengths of the existing system and accused Kennedy of seeking to destroy it. Speaking before the AMA's House of Delegates on June 22, 1971, Nixon declared: "When the government pays all the bills for health care, then the government becomes the only party with a strong interest in restraining costs. And this inevitably means that government officials must approve hospital budgets, set fee schedules and take other steps that would eventually lead to the complete federal domination of our medical system." Kennedy retorted that Nixon's plan relied too heavily on private industry.[75]

Soon after Nixon's speech, the Domestic Council came out with a lengthy document that might well have served as a blueprint for election-year campaigning. On health care, the council reiterated Nixon's warning of a "massive crisis" and said the president's bill "is designed to remedy this health crisis by building on the best elements of our present health care system, and reforming those elements that are not effective." Trumpeting the president's policy initiatives, the document insisted that "the Administration does not plan to nationalize our health care system, because it believes that diversity and freedom of choice are essential to improve health care, and that efficiency and experimentation can be encouraged within the existing framework."[76]

Secretary Richardson reiterated the same themes on October 19, 1971, in congressional hearings that sharply differentiated the administration's bill from the Kennedy-Griffiths proposal. After five weeks of public testimony, House Ways and Means Committee Chair Wilbur Mills gaveled the hearings to a close on November 19, but he decided that the committee would not go into executive session before January 1972. Mills's decision effectively postponed action on health insurance for another year at least. In the interim, President Nixon advanced other components of his health strategy. He signed two bills on November 18 that he had recommended to Congress earlier, the Comprehensive Health Manpower Training Act of 1971 and the Nurse Training Act of 1971. These laws, which replaced institutional grants with a new system of capitation grants, were intended to address the geographic maldistribution of health personnel and the nursing shortage; they represented a shift, not a withdrawal, of federal policy and resources from the previous decade by focusing on areas with special needs rather than on growth in all categories of health personnel.[77]

The administration, meanwhile, continued to prepare its legislative agenda for the 92nd Congress, which was scheduled to convene in January. On January 17, 1972, Peter M. Flanigan, the president's legislative adviser, informed Nixon that Wilbur Mills, who was seeking a 20 percent increase in Social Security benefits to bolster his presidential aspirations, had agreed to make revenue sharing his committee's first order of business. That raised the question of the committee's next item of business. Flanigan reminded the president that "the Administration has generally urged that Health Legislation receive early consideration," but he agreed with White House advisers Ehrlichman, George Shultz, and Clark MacGregor that the president should bump pension reform ahead of health legislation, which was likely to be a long, drawn-out process. Democrats would demand that the president "do more" on health care than he was prepared to request of Congress, and "in the course of the battle, no doubt the Administration position will be made to look parsimonious." Congress might not pass any health legislation in time for the fall elections, he speculated, whereas pension legislation would most likely pass without a bruising battle. Flanigan bolstered his argument by noting that the Domestic Council's appetite for a battle over health legislation had diminished considerably. "However," he cautioned, "the Administration cannot appear to be other than enthusiastic for this legislation and particularly cannot be accused of suggesting to Congress that there be a delay in its consideration."[78]

Election-year politics was again determining the legislative agenda. Nixon took the advice and delayed his health message to Congress until March 2, when he reiterated his intention to build on the existing system's strengths rather than to replace it with a federally owned and operated health care system, as Kennedy had suggested. He also asked Congress to enact the "National Health Insurance Partnership" and the "HMO Assistance" bills, both of which were eventually interred in the Ways and Means Committee, and to reform welfare.[79]

Mills, meanwhile, had dropped out of the presidential race, but in July 1972, he successfully navigated through the House and Senate the largest benefit increase in Social Security history, one that also indexed future increases to the cost of living. A second fateful change also occurred that year in response to Nixon's welfare reform effort. Congress enacted the Supplemental Security Income (SSI) program, which provided a guaranteed income to the needy elderly, blind, and disabled (including those requiring hemodialysis and renal transplantation) and shifted administrative responsibility for these programs from the states to the SSA. The new program established a professional peer-review system and permitted Medicare participants to choose coverage through managed care. These modifications, which Nixon accepted reluctantly, liberalized Social Security financing, strengthened the notion of entitlement, and launched the Social Security program on a long-term path of unprecedented and risky growth.[80]

After Nixon's landslide reelection, legislative liaison Richard K. Cook apprised the president of the status of his health package. Mills had said he simply did not know how we could finance comprehensive health care, preferring instead to concentrate on providing better health care for low-income families. But, Cook noted, this conflicted "with his previously stated intention to combine forces with Ted Kennedy in placing high priority on enactment of a comprehensive health care bill during the 93rd Congress." As long as Mills continued to remain an obstacle, the administration's efforts to pry its health bill out of committee went nowhere in 1972 or in the following year, except for an amendment to the Public Health Service Act earmarking $375 million in federal aid to develop HMOs and specifying the basic services that they had to provide to be eligible for federal funding.[81]

Early in 1973 the administration sent its original proposal back to HEW for revisions, where it remained until the fall. Meanwhile, on October 2, Democratic Senators Abraham Ribicoff and Russell Long introduced a new catastrophic health insurance and medical assistance proposal (S. 2513) as an alternative to the Kennedy-Griffiths bill. The latter, they believed, was too expensive and Americans were "not ready" for it, whereas Medicare, with its newly incorporated end-stage renal disease coverage, provided a model of a universal health insurance system based on catastrophic insurance. On the heels of the Ribicoff-Long bill, Republican Senators Hugh Scott and Charles Percy introduced their own legislation, which relied more heavily on private insurance companies, "but would *add over $20 billion* to the federal budget."[82] Of the two pieces of legislation and "in the absence of a viable competitor," HEW's new secretary, Caspar Weinberger, wrote, the Ribicoff-Long bill had attracted the more favorable attention. This was a reference to the absence of the administration-sponsored proposal, which was only then making its way from HEW to the White House. Anticipating that Congress would take up national health legislation in 1974, Republican leaders in the House and Senate had "impressed upon" Weinberger the urgency of the administration's quickly introducing its revised bill. "I am, therefore, very concerned that we are moving too slowly, and I urge that you seriously consider announcing the Administration's proposal to the public by the end of this year," Weinberger wrote to the president on November 2, 1973, in the memo accompanying HEW's revisions.[83]

The revisions were "consistent with the Administration's concept of the appropriate role of the Federal government," Weinberger informed President Nixon, and represented "a middle-ground position between a complete Federal takeover of the health insurance industry combined with a massive restructuring of the health delivery system, as called for in the Kennedy-Griffiths bill, and minor changes in the insurance and delivery systems, as proposed by others." He then explained why he believed the administration needed to move toward a Republican version of national health insurance: "Central to the Administration's 1974 legislative and budget strategy is the principle that insurance coverage rather than direct grants to providers should be the appropriate vehicle for financing access to health care." Weinberger reminded Nixon that the administration's budget requests had been targeted to contain or to terminate HEW's patchwork of service programs. "While I fully support and have promoted this strategy, the absence of a proposal for NHI has temporarily placed the Administration in a very negative posture in the health area," he argued. National health insurance "continues to be of major importance," and recent developments on Capitol Hill "seem to make it advisable for us to reach agreement on an Administration proposal and announce it by the end of the year."[84]

Weinberger accompanied his presentation of the revised HEW bill with a request to speak directly to the president, and an appointment was scheduled for December 8. Although he did not expect Nixon to approve HEW's bill until after he had received input from the other executive agencies, he hoped that a face-to-face meeting might win Nixon's support for the general principles contained in HEW's proposal. He also hoped to unveil the administration's initiative by the end of the year.[85] Fortunately for Weinberger, he had an ally in White House assistant James Cavanaugh, who briefed President Nixon prior to their meeting. Cavanaugh persuaded Nixon to entrust Weinberger with the task of shepherding the administration's bill through Congress. That meant that he would have to make certain that hearings were held early in 1974, and that the groundwork for the hearings was laid by feeding background material to journalists likely to write sympathetic articles. He also would have to mobilize support for the administration's plan among health groups and members of the key congressional committees, "so that when we do announce the program, we will have as much public support for it as possible." Cavanaugh, however, thought Weinberger should delay formal announcement of the administration's proposal until the president had delivered his State of the Union Message and followed it with a separate health message to Congress in early February.[86]

Nixon followed Cavanaugh's counsel. He endorsed HEW's revised national health insurance proposal over the opposition of cabinet officials who feared a conservative Republican backlash against any national health plan. He also agreed to put health care reform at the top of his 1974 domestic legislative agenda. Two days after meeting with the president, Weinberger disclosed to the media in general terms that the administration would deliver a new health proposal to Congress.

President Nixon formally unveiled the "Comprehensive Health Insurance" bill (S. 2970; H.R. 12684) on February 6, 1974, and urged legislators to act, though he talked compromise. The central feature of the bill was the familiar requirement that employers cover part of the cost of providing their workers with a standard package of health benefits, but in an important shift, employee participation was made voluntary. Employers would be required to cover 75 percent of the insurance costs at the end of a three-year phase-in period. The proposal also called for federally subsidized health coverage for the poor and a revamped Medicare program for the aged. Administration of all programs except Medicare would be left to the states, with private insurers offering policies subject to state regulation.[87]

HEW Secretary Weinberger believed that the single-greatest advantage of the new bill was that the greatly enhanced coverage would replace the dizzying array of categorical grant programs, which ran counter to administration philosophy but which HEW was currently operating. Of greater significance, however, the "Comprehensive Health Insurance" bill covered the entire population and provided far more benefits than had the original 1971 bill. This signaled a major shift in health care policy on the part of the Republican Nixon administration. To many legislators and health policy analysts, the right combination of forces was finally coalescing to break the stalemate that had prevented enactment of comprehensive health coverage for thirty-odd years.[88] The reason for their optimism was that the Democratic leadership of both the House and the Senate also was making health care priority legislation. Indeed, Democrats threatened to steal the spotlight from the Republicans as Senator Kennedy and Representative Wilbur Mills introduced a new health initiative on April 2 that was similar to, but also different from, the administration's bill. Mills announced that his committee would hold hearings on the health insurance proposals beginning April 24, the first legislative hearings on the subject in three years.[89]

Both Republican and Democratic bills were premised on retaining the connection between one's employment status and health benefits, although the Kennedy-Mills bill was a compromise measure that fell far short of national health insurance and was far less generous than the earlier Kennedy-Griffiths bill. By allowing private insurers to make the crucial decisions governing the administration, management, and funding of health coverage, the Democratic bill guaranteed them not only a profitable rate of return but also administrative control of the program. This reflected more the influence of the fiscally conservative Mills than it did Kennedy, who wanted desperately to enact health legislation in this congressional session. As the *New York Times* noted, the decision "to retain the insurance company's role was based on recognition of that industry's power to kill any legislation it considers unacceptable."[90]

With two bills to choose from and each party seemingly willing to compromise, the prospect for a successful legislative outcome appeared brighter than at any time in recent years. In June, a buoyant Kennedy detected "a new spirit of compromise" in the air and hinted that a bill could reach the president's desk that fall. Kennedy, however, had miscalculated. The Democratic bill engendered more controversy than it dispelled. Organized labor and social welfare liberals saw it as a step backward from the original Kennedy-Griffiths legislation, which would have mandated universal coverage. On April 16, the Committee for National Health Insurance, followed by the National Council of Senior Citizens and various consumer groups, refused to endorse the Kennedy-Mills compromise and reaffirmed its support for the original Kennedy-Griffiths bill, which was hastily reintroduced and informally renamed the Griffiths-Corman plan after another key House sponsor, California Representative James Corman. Disappointed and angry, the AFL and the UAW preferred to postpone all action on health care until after the November elections, when they anticipated that the election of additional Democrats would make the 94th Congress "veto proof" and facilitate passage of the Griffiths-Corman proposal.[91]

As liberal support for health reform fragmented, the Ways and Means Committee began hearings on April 24, 1974, and conducted them intermittently through July 9. From the chairman's opening gavel, the hearings developed into a contest between the administration's plan and the Kennedy-Mills approach. HEW Secretary Weinberger, the administration's lead-off witness, noted similarities between the two proposals, but then devoted twenty-five pages of his forty-five-page testimony to a detailed critique of the Kennedy-Mills bill, emphasizing its potential need for a vast, new bureaucracy and other differences: Kennedy-Mills's reliance on a new "regressive" 4 percent payroll tax to finance premiums (unlike the administration's plan, which had private insurers collect premiums directly from employer and employees); its reliance on an independent Social Security agency to run the program (unlike the administration's bill, which vested administrative oversight in the states); and its limitation of the role of private insurance carriers to being financial intermediaries (unlike the administration's plan, which allowed private carriers to process claims and reimburse health providers). In a slap at organized labor, Weinberger accused union leaders of seeking to derail a compromise, and he urged Congress to act on health care that year.[92]

President Nixon followed up on May 20 with a national radio address in which he emphasized that health coverage remained his number one domestic priority and pledged to work with congressional Democrats toward a compromise. Weinberger reiterated the compromise offer the following day before the Senate Finance Committee, which had reopened its own hearings, and again urged action in this legislative session. On May 22, in response to the president's address, Senator Kennedy declared that Democrats were ready to work with the administration, but he insisted that the Kennedy-Mills plan was superior in many respects to the administration's proposal. What both sides ignored was that the normal constituency for each bill had serious reservations. The business sector's support for Nixon's employer-mandate solution, which they deemed a "hidden" tax, had

cooled, whereas organized labor and consumer advocacy groups were implacably opposed to the Kennedy-Mills bill for falling short of providing universal health coverage.
After a month more of political posturing by both sides, Kennedy's optimism that his or
any other health bill would pass during the current legislative session finally tempered.
On June 26, he declared that even if the administration were serious about cooperation,
it probably would take one or two years for Congress to act.[93]

Meanwhile, the pressure on Congress to act that year focused attention on a third
major bill, the Long-Ribicoff proposal. The bill, covering catastrophic medical expenses
for all Americans, establishing a federal program to assist the poor, and giving private insurers incentives to offer standard plans for the nonpoor, had the backing of the majority
of the Finance Committee. Senate watchers expected it to sail smoothly through the Senate unless backers of other proposals could defeat it on the floor. The key question was
whether the House Ways and Means Committee would go along with the Long-Ribicoff
proposal. Surprisingly, it received a warm reception there as well, even though the administration firmly opposed the bill. President Nixon had criticized it earlier, in May, for
covering only catastrophic costs, leaving participants vulnerable to other substantial
health costs. Nixon gained an unexpected ally on June 7, when Mills said that he, too, opposed a bill limited to catastrophic coverage, which he likened to the roof of a home. "We
need the floor and walls along with the roof," Mills said, of the Long-Ribicoff bill.[94]

By the time the Ways and Means Committee had completed its hearings on July 9, momentum for action on health coverage had weakened substantially. The *Wall Street Journal* attributed the cooling off to renewed fears that the huge cost of any of the proposals
would further stimulate inflation. The only hole in the safety net, the *Journal* decided, was
the absence of catastrophic coverage and insurance for the less than 20 million indigent
and working poor who had neither Medicare-Medicaid nor any private coverage. This
problem was not so acute, the newspaper concluded, as to warrant nationalizing the
health care industry.[95]

The newspaper failed to mention that the Watergate scandal had engulfed the White
House that summer, with the prospect of lengthy impeachment proceedings against
President Nixon, and the unwillingness of any of the major sponsors of health care reform to compromise. Watergate discredited Nixon personally, but it also dealt a blow to
the middle ground of the Republican Party, which Nixon had preempted. After Nixon resigned the presidency in early August, conservatives within his party, such as William F.
Buckley and Patrick J. Buchanan, who had both broken ranks with the administration,
freely criticized his policies. Nixon's espousal of national health care, as cabinet members
had feared, gave conservative ideologues another opening to charge the president with
having ignored the mandate of the 1972 election: to reverse big spending by big government and to undo the Great Society programs. Conservatives accused the postelection

Nixon of having betrayed his natural constituency by pandering to liberals who promoted free-spending social programs, such as national health care, in the cynical belief that conservatives had no choice but to support him. That criticism was unfair and a disservice to Nixon's long-standing interest in health issues. By 1974, whatever liberal support he may have had was long since gone.[96]

Had Nixon's imprint not been on the administration's bill and had 1974 not been the year of Watergate, the United States might have had the semblance of a national, but seriously flawed, health program, one that excluded many of the same groups that in 2004 still constituted the ranks of the uninsured. But fate dictated otherwise; moreover, the refusal of organized labor and liberal organizations to accept any compromise in lieu of the original Kennedy-Griffiths health security plan made it impossible to forge an acceptable compromise. The irony was heightened by the shifting position of the commercial health insurance companies. Anticipating a more liberal Congress, they no longer dragged their feet and were ready to support some version of the Long-Ribicoff bill. The big losers were the American people because, just at the point when opposition to national health care was at its lowest point (even if it had not completely melted away, as economist Alice Rivlin believed), no one or any combination of the three leading health proposals was able to command a majority.[97]

It turned out that 1974 was the last moment for the next twenty years when any such program had a serious chance of adoption. Few Americans were aware of it at the time, because prospects for House action on health care appeared to improve in the wake of President Nixon's resignation. Gerald Ford, his successor, importuned Congress on August 12 to pass a health bill. "Why don't we write—and I ask this with the greatest spirit of cooperation—a good health bill on the statute books before Congress adjourns?" Ford urged. The following day, he invited Mills and Long to the White House to discuss the odds of Congress acting on health coverage before it adjourned. A week later, the Ways and Means Committee staff came up with a compromise proposal, drawn up at Mills's direction but not specifically sponsored by anyone.[98]

The August 19 compromise most closely resembled Nixon's plan, but included elements of the rival proposals. The committee worked through the least controversial features of the compromise first, but on August 20, it differed sharply over the compulsory character of the proposal and its financing provisions. By a 12 to 12 vote, the committee rejected the staff's voluntary approach (which had been lifted from the AMA's "Medicredit" proposal). Five Southern Democrats and seven of the ten Republicans voted for the proposal with the AMA feature. The committee then rejected, by 12 to 13, the bill's tax credit provisions, which the staff had borrowed from an HIAA proposal. A short time later, it tentatively adopted by a 12 to 11 show-of-hands vote the compromise employer plan drafted by its staff. However, after an additional hour of squabbling, Mills announced on August 21 that he would not go to the floor with any bill approved by a 13 to

12 margin. With that, he halted the drafting process and scheduled no other action on health care before the November elections.[99]

When the 93rd Congress reconvened on November 18, after the elections, a national health law was no longer at the top of its agenda. The Democratic landslide seemingly justified the liberal-labor coalition's position to postpone action until after the new year, when a new, Democratic-controlled Congress was more likely to enact legislation that reflected its position. In anticipation of the new political landscape, Representative Al Ullman of California had begun to draft a bill, observed House Speaker Carl Albert, the purpose of which was "recognition that health care is an inherent right of each individual and of all the people of the United States." Unfortunately for the social welfare activists and their liberal allies in Congress, their hopes were dashed by early 1975. The first blow came in December 1974, after Mills lost the chairmanship of the Ways and Means Committee after a colorful scandal. The second, and perhaps more significant blow, came in January 1975, when President Ford told Congress he would veto any new spending legislation and instead proposed a tax cut aimed to spur a stagnant economy.[100]

The Nixon presidency coincided with a period of sharp controversy about the proper role of the federal government, the states, and the private sector in the formulation of health care policy. Nixon's administration also coincided with a period of contraction in some ways, often in response to the pressures of inflation, a growing federal debt, and the need to constrain growth in government programs. Unlike its Democratic predecessor, the Nixon administration had serious doubts that the federal government could resolve social and economic problems, and this attitude led to considerable conflict among the branches of government, particularly between a Republican president and a Democratic Congress, over domestic policy, including health care. Nixon's New Federalism described his efforts to move government away from the categorized grant focus of the Lyndon Johnson administration, with its strict congressional oversight, and toward revenue sharing and block grants to the states, but he and his advisers did consider proposals that involved new federal duties, such as leadership in promoting HMOs, the forerunners of managed care.

On balance, and perhaps contrary to the most dire liberal predictions, the Nixon presidency was one of "responsible conservatism" in the health care sector. Most changes involved Medicare and Medicaid and emphasized controlling costs in the face of double-digit inflation; they included protecting the fiscal integrity of the Social Security system, which partially funded Medicare; placing constraints on hospital payments; reviewing medical service to be sure it actually worked; promoting changes in the organization and delivery of health care; upgrading and redistributing health professionals to underserved rural and urban areas; and fostering the development of HMOs. Most of these changes, notably peer review and managed care, had the support of the AMA, which viewed them as alternatives to greater federal intrusion into private-sector health care.[101]

In his 1971 State of the Union message, President Nixon had identified "improving America's health care and making it available more fairly to more people" as one of his six great goals. The fruit of that speech was a plan mandating employers to pay the lion's share of health coverage for employees, a new federal health insurance program for poor families, and federal aid to promote development of prepaid comprehensive care. Advocates of national health insurance, particularly organized labor, denounced the plan for falling short of universal coverage, as did businessmen, who complained that it was a hidden tax, and the plan was never enacted. The liberal alternative, the Kennedy-Mills legislation, which also fell short of universal coverage, was not enacted either. The result was that the nation missed the opportunity to take a giant step toward reforming a costly and inefficient medical delivery system, and perhaps establishing a foundation upon which to build toward universal coverage. The irony of this missed opportunity is that in 1978 many of the leaders of organized labor reversed themselves, publicly embracing employer mandates and other proposals based on commercial insurers' retaining a prominent role. Moreover, in his State of the Union speech in January 1994, a Democratic president—Bill Clinton—declared that his proposed health security bill would use "what works today in the private sector to expand employer-based coverage." He credited President Nixon for initially proposing the idea.[102]

# EIGHT
## HEALTH CARE REFORM:
## THE POLITICS OF NEGLECT
## & REDISCOVERY

Americans of the late 1970s and 1980s experienced wrenching economic, political, and social change as the twenty-five-year postwar economic boom ended. Recessions became more frequent, the rate of economic growth slowed, and the "discomfort" index of unemployment plus inflation rose. The 1970s was the first decade since the Great Depression in which Americans' purchasing power declined. Although the economy rebounded in the early 1980s, the economic policies of the Reagan administration had the effect of redistributing wealth upward. Economic inequality and social polarization grew, widening the gap between rich and poor, whites and people of color, the suburbs and the inner cities. Accompanying the economic changes was a resurgence of political and cultural conservatism. The conservatives of the 1980s not only knew that the federal government did not have the capacity to serve the people, let alone solve major problems, but they also viewed government itself as the root of all problems and worked to repeal the New Deal social welfare system.[1]

The 1980 presidential victory of Ronald Reagan set the dominant mood of the day, but it was his Democratic predecessor, Jimmy Carter, who, by establishing the conditions for the conservative Reagan's triumph, prevented Americans from reforming, much less reconstructing, a health care system that everyone agreed was in crisis. The irony was that Americans of the 1980s, perhaps more than political figures of the day and health policy analysts cared to admit, had become more receptive to universal health coverage than at any time previously, but neither the political establishment nor the experts were able to formulate a workable plan. Americans thus were left to struggle with a broken or, at best, a seriously impaired health care system.

As early as May 1975, President Ford's prospects for retaining the Oval Office were gloomy. Watergate, governmental corruption, and the political carping that followed the collapse of South Vietnam enhanced the political fortunes of his Democratic opponent, Jimmy Carter, a Washington outsider who campaigned both as a fiscal conservative who would restrain government spending and as a social liberal who would fight for the working class. To the surprise of many political pundits, Carter and his running mate, Walter Mondale, a liberal Minnesota Democrat, temporarily revived the New Deal coalition to squeak to victory by a slim 1.7 million votes out of the 80 million cast.[2] The real story of the 1976 election had been the low voter turnout. Alienated by Watergate and the lackluster candidates, only 54 percent of the electorate bestirred itself to vote on election day. Of more concern to health care reformers, the vote had, to a marked degree, fractured along the fault line separating the haves and have-nots and foreshadowed the class politics that dominated the political struggles of the 1980s and transformed health reform into a class issue.[3]

Candidate Jimmy Carter had been sympathetic to universal health coverage, telling the National Press Club in November 1974, "I expect the next Congress to pass a national health insurance law." He added rhetorically: "Is a practical and comprehensive national health program beyond the capacity of our American government? I think not."[4] As the Democratic standard-bearer two years later, the Carter-prompted party platform called for "a comprehensive national health insurance system with universal and mandatory coverage." In part because he promised that as president he would back a national health program, Carter won the support of prominent liberals, including Senator Ted Kennedy, and labor leaders such as Leonard Woodcock of the UAW.[5]

After his election, Carter found himself between a rock—his campaign pledge for national health insurance—and a very hard place—"stagflation." He procrastinated presenting such a proposal to Congress despite promising to do so "within weeks" of his taking office. Yet the campaign pledge did not go away; liberals and labor prodded him to make good on his pledge, and Kennedy insisted that Congress must act on health care "within two years" or wait another generation. Other Democratic legislators and many of President Carter's advisers did not share Kennedy's belief that there was momentum to pass a national health law. Asked where the constituency for national health coverage was, Representative Dan Rostenkowski, chairman of the House Ways and Means Health Subcommittee, said, "I don't see it." HEW Secretary Joseph Califano declared in winter 1977 that the new year would not be a good time to introduce national health legislation. The administration proposed, instead, a scaled-back proposal to rein in hospital costs. Unwilling to wait any longer for a Democratic president and Congress to act, an angry Kennedy introduced legislation similar to the Griffiths-Corman proposal of 1970 that vested the financing, management, and operation of a national health program in the federal government.[6]

Carter's inability to fulfill his campaign pledge midway through his presidency owed less to a failure of interest than to the burgeoning problems that had enveloped his administration when he entered the Oval Office. Liberal Democrats viewed the Nixon-Ford years as an interruption in the normal way of doing business, and with a Democrat back in the White House, they expected spending patterns to return to those of the Johnson years. Carter, however, had inherited from President Ford an almost insurmountable set of domestic and international problems that ran counter to expectations, including a budget deficit, a slowing national economy, high unemployment, inflation, and dramatically escalating health expenditures. Nixon's HMO initiative had failed to put a noticeable dent in medical inflation; the great numbers of new persons joining HMOs never materialized; and the HMOs that were around did little to lower hospital admissions—the main way to save money. Americans also expected the new president to reassert America's global power and to ensure its access to cheap fossil fuels.[7]

In short, the incoming president seemed predestined to failure unless he could get the deficit and inflation under control. Carter's transition team advised that by holding government spending down, the administration would be able to balance the budget by 1981, and it would actually have a surplus of $52 billion. Carter decided that balancing the budget and fighting inflation were vital to the country's interests and that if he angered congressional liberals by limiting social spending, so be it. His fiscal conservatism, however, shocked those who assumed that because of his fervent advocacy of civil rights and social justice, he would favor increased expenditures on government social programs, even if it meant deficit spending. They should not have been surprised, because in one of his campaign statements they had chosen to ignore, Carter had said, "There will be no new programs implemented under my administration unless we can be sure that the cost of those programs is compatible with my goal of having a balanced budget by the end of my first term." This was Carter's rationale for limiting social spending. He felt that to act otherwise was a prescription for economic disaster, and everyone, especially the poor, would suffer.[8]

This philosophy explains Carter's mere lip service to his campaign pledge to legislate a national health system in 1977. His first priority, to reduce the deficit and bring inflation under control, necessitated that he persuade Congress to clamp tight revenue limits on the nation's hospitals. The cost-control plan he submitted, which he touted as a prerequisite to a national health program, turned into a futile three-year fight of increasing bitterness with his fellow Democrats, one that led liberal legislators to believe that Carter wanted to put national health coverage on a back burner. They cited as proof his willingness to ignore a basic legislative principle: to build support for cost cutting, be sure to "sweeten" the harsh new controls with new benefits. The plan's prospects for passage deteriorated after Secretary Califano described hospitals as "bloated" creatures. With liberals and their labor allies already angry, the last thing the administration needed was to have the hospitals and their physician, insurance, and medical business allies complain to Congress that the president's plan would crush the hospitals.

House Democratic leaders wanted to delay a vote on the administration measure, fearing that it would go down to defeat, but Carter insisted on bringing the bill to a vote in late 1979. When the House gutted and then rewrote the bill, White House Press Secretary Jody Powell dubbed the revision "a joke," thereby provoking the liberal-labor coalition to shoot back that the president's efforts to restrain hospital costs were misdirected.[9] He should have turned the cost equation back-to-front, to seek legislation authorizing the federal government to control all sources of payment, not simply hospital revenues. That approach required the kind of unitary national system embodied in the Kennedy-Corman bill, which Carter rejected as unrealistically expensive (conservative estimates pegged it at $30 billion). Health costs had to be curtailed before coverage could be expanded, Carter insisted. He also knew that if the Kennedy-Corman bill passed, primary credit for health care reform would go to the Massachusetts senator, a potential rival for the presidential nomination in 1980.[10]

Carter's conundrum was that he had no viable alternative to the Kennedy-Corman bill, and his use of the budget process to fight inflation put him in serious political trouble with the Democratic constituencies that had elected him to office. Liberals felt betrayed; organized labor, African-Americans, and blue-collar workers saw little difference between Carter's fiscal conservatism and that of the Republicans.

After much public prodding from Kennedy, Carter finally proposed a national health plan in 1979, but it turned out to be much more modest than his supporters had been led to believe. The broad outlines of the plan were first disclosed on July 29, 1978, in a directive to HEW Secretary Califano. Carter stated that any national health plan had to include universal coverage and high-quality health care, with citizens free to choose their doctors, hospitals, and health delivery systems. But he also cautioned that it should include "aggressive" cost-containment measures, not be inflationary, and phased in gradually as economic conditions permitted. Financing would come from multiple sources and include a "significant role" for the private insurance industry, subject to "appropriate" government regulation. As it focused on cost containment, phased-in coverage, and reliance on the private sector, liberal Democrats and their labor allies concluded that Carter's approach to national health could just as easily have been written by Republicans.[11]

If Democratic lawmakers were pleased with the principles embedded in the president's message, few said so. Among the congressional health subcommittee chairmen, only Rostenkowski praised the president's plan. He described it as a "prudent and responsible step," but in a reference to the hospital cost-containment bill, he asked skeptically, "If you can't pass that bill how can you talk about national health insurance?" Organized labor and Senator Kennedy, chairman of the Labor and Human Resources Health Subcommittee, rejected the president's plan and denounced Carter's "failure of leadership."[12] Further annoying the liberal-labor coalition, which was looking ahead to the fall elections, was Califano's unhurried timetable for action. The administration would not introduce the legislation until 1979. The coalition believed this contravened an agreement they had secured from the president: that he would produce both the principles *and a bill* before the elections so that congressional candidates would have to go on record on national health insurance.[13]

Growing dissatisfaction with the president's policies came to a head that December when Democrats gathered in Memphis to address remaining issues relevant to the party's new charter and to rules adopted in the wake of the McGovern election fiasco. It was an event the White House did not want, but could not avoid, fearing that the gathering would become a forum for liberal Democrats to publicly lambaste Carter. Party Chair John White had to call on all his skills to avert a resolution condemning the administration for reducing spending on social programs and combating inflation with joblessness. White forged a compromise resolution that reaffirmed the 1976 platform commitment to national health insurance, but without specifying a starting date.[14]

At the beginning of 1979, White House attention was dominated by foreign and domestic economic crises, whose fulcrum was the cost and availability of energy. The hospital cost-containment bill remained locked up in committees of the House and Senate, and more than six months after Carter's directive to HEW, the administration still had no draft of health reform legislation.[15] With no such bill on the horizon, Kennedy and Representative Henry Waxman of California introduced on September 6 the "Health Care for All Americans" bill. The Kennedy-Waxman proposal (S. 1720, H.R. 5191) conceded that the administration was resistant to a national health program as embodied in the 1970 Kennedy-Griffiths health security bill and would not adhere to the principle of the federal government alone financing, managing, and administering the delivery of health care. Although many of its comprehensive and planning features long associated with Kennedy sponsorship were still recognizable, S. 1720's heavy cost-sharing feature and use of private insurance companies as fiscal intermediaries were closer to the 1974 Kennedy-Mills bill than to the 1970 proposal.[16] The Kennedy-Waxman bill drove a wedge into liberal-labor ranks. Representative James Corman refused to support it because of the inclusion of private insurers as fiscal intermediaries. He accused its sponsors of abandoning the more thoroughgoing reform embodied in the 1970 bill, which had approximated the British-style health care system.[17]

Liberal support for health care reform had already splintered when Carter sent his proposal to Congress late that September. The plan, which featured heavy cost-sharing, called for a two-tier system, one for the poor and aged ("Health Care") to be run by the government; the other, which private insurers administered, for the under-sixty-five, better-off working population.[18] The "National Health Plan" bill (S. 1812) of September 25 ranked with the most cautious and conservative versions of earlier health reform bills and disappointed liberal Democrats and organized labor. The administration's plan, unlike the Kennedy-Waxman bill, was to be implemented over time and was contingent on the health of the economy. Its initial phase was based on the catastrophic health insurance program of Senator Russell Long and required an individual to pay a hefty deductible out of his own pocket before the plan began to pay. Carter's critics read into this a blatant effort to outflank Kennedy on national health by making common cause with the shrewd and powerful Louisianan. However, it was not at all clear how many—if any—of the other features of the administration's bill, particularly the significant structural changes in Medicaid and Medicare, Long actually supported.[19]

With Democrats divided, Congress acted on neither the Kennedy-Waxman nor the administration's bill, and this inaction gave other voices an opportunity to be heard on Capitol Hill.[20] On the Democratic left, but little noticed at the time, California Representatives Ron Dellums and James Corman introduced the "National Health Service" bill (H.R. 21, H.R. 2969), which, had it been taken seriously, might have changed profoundly the public discourse over health coverage. Decrying the failures of Medicare, Medicaid, and private insurance to provide universal coverage or access to satisfactory health care, Dellums argued that only a government-funded, direct-service system could provide efficient, effective, and equitable health care. The Dellums-Corman proposal came closest to calling for a British-style health care system, but few legislators at the time were willing to incur the wrath of the powerful health industry lobby to afford it a fair hearing. Unlike every other proposal, which sought to patch up the existing system, the Dellums-Corman bill offered the only truly radical change for a system in crisis, and its approach became a subtext underlining the political and health care battles of the 1980s.[21]

The Dellums-Corman legislation proved to be no match for a very different perspective on health care reform, which also was making the rounds of Congress. This was the argument put forth by neoclassical economists and their adherents who called loudly for greater reliance on market competition to control health care costs. Prominent among the academic proponents of competition were Alain Enthoven of Stanford University, Martin Feldstein of Harvard, and Clark Havighurst of Duke. They contended that government regulation interfered with market competition and was responsible for the uncontrolled cost inflation; the solution was to remove all barriers to competition among health plans. Through their writings and testimony, market competition began to shape up as a highly visible—and bipartisan—alternative to both national health insurance and President Carter's embattled hospital-cost-containment bill. Democratic Representative Richard Gephardt and Republican David Stockman both embraced competition.[22]

Although the economists differed on the specifics, the common thread running through their approaches was the need to increase price competition among health plans and to make consumers aware of their expenditures through substantial cost-sharing. Tax preferences that encouraged firms and employees to spend needlessly for rising health insurance premiums had to be repealed and government regulation of price, quality, and service capacity discontinued. The economists railed against bureaucratic regulations that encouraged monopoly and increased costs; in their place, the federal government needed to pursue strategies that encouraged price competition. It might, for example, allocate a fixed sum to everyone for health care to motivate consumers to comparison shop for the most efficient plans. Ironically, at the moment when economists were promoting market-oriented proposals to create universal access to health care, public opinion polls showed that Americans were *more,* not less, interested in national health insurance.[23]

By the time Carter left office in 1980, none of the various health reform bills under consideration had emerged from Congress. More ominous were the effects of his budget priorities in the 1979 fiscal year; they initiated the austerity social policies one commonly associates with the most brutal assaults on social programs of the Reagan Revolution. Federal social spending as a percentage of the GNP had declined for the first time in twenty years—to less than half of its level under Presidents Kennedy, Nixon, and Ford.[24] Viewed from this perspective, Carter's defeat in 1980 can hardly be attributed to an expansion of New Deal social programs. His failure to act on his stated commitments to these programs contributed in a major way to both his unpopularity and the image of poor leadership he acquired in the 1980 election.[25] As Arthur Schlesinger indicated, Carter was the most conservative Democratic president since Grover Cleveland. Carter, in the judgment of one political commentator, had "built foundations that would become full-fledged conservative architecture under Reagan."[26]

The fissures in the New Deal consensus that had first appeared around the time of the 1966 midterm elections had opened wider during Carter's troubled administration, although there was no profound demonstration that the New Deal consensus was gone until the election of 1980 brought Republican Ronald Reagan into the presidency. Reagan was the rare exception to the rule that the ideological wings always lose in American politics. Rather than moving to the center, as politicians usually did, Reagan moved the location of the center in his direction, that is, to the right. Under Reagan's leadership, the nation turned away from *any* serious consideration of universal access to health care and toward a single-minded concern with improving national and international economic and military predominance.

Reagan's margin over Carter in the Electoral College was overwhelming, 489 to 49, but he had carried the election with only slightly more than 50 percent of the popular vote.[27] Democrats dismissed the outcome as a fluke, more a defeat for Carter than a victory for the Republicans, but what they failed to comprehend were the reasons for the enormous growth in political absenteeism by the population in general and working-class voters in particular. Contemporary explanations for the high levels of voter apathy, especially among working-class Americans, varied from a continuing sense of disillusionment with government itself—a legacy of Watergate—to the Democratic Party's having turned its back on its traditional base of support. By embracing a fiscal conservatism indistinguishable from the Republicans', the Democratic Party lost its appeal to those at the bottom of the social scale, blue-collar workers and ghetto dwellers. The largest group of nonvoters in 1980 was composed of former Democrats who apparently decided that neither party served their interests.[28]

Reagan's triumph, therefore, may have represented less a resounding victory for conservative Republicans than a self-inflicted defeat by a fractured Democratic Party. But clearly, Ronald Reagan had tapped into anxieties about declining national power and eroding living standards to win the presidency, and he headed toward Washington genuinely believing that he had a mandate to dismantle the liberal welfare state. Reagan's main domestic initiative in 1981 in response to the severe economic crisis was a big, quick, tax cut, which was meant not just to put money into voters' pockets but also to signify that government was going to be reduced. Most Democrats, who had endorsed tax reductions under Carter, also endorsed Reagan's tax cut. After the short, sharp recession, the economy rebounded and entered a period of noninflationary growth. But even the economic revival of the 1980s sparked debate over the cumulative impact of annual federal budget deficits to build up the military and the consequences of economic expansion. For despite his constant inveighing against big spending, Reagan's tax cuts were not matched by budget reductions. When he left office eight years later, his administration had compiled the most extraordinary record of deficits and spending in U.S. history until then.[29]

Moreover, the economic growth of the decade was not distributed evenly. The brutal austerity policies carried out by President Reagan and his successor, George H. W. Bush, benefited only the top 20 or 30 percent of the population and created a "Swiss cheese" economy, full of holes. Reagan proved to be far more conservative on social issues than fellow Republican Richard Nixon, as he abandoned the Nixonian quest for defensible distinctions among the roles of sectors of society and levels of government. His pledge that Washington would still maintain a safety net for those who were truly in need of government assistance rang hollow. The number of people whose total package of income and benefits fell below the poverty level rose during Reagan's tenure, after having declined in the 1970s. The burden of poverty fell disproportionately on female-headed households, minorities, and, especially, children. Only Congress's decision to index Social Security benefits and Medicare, to tie them to increases in the rate of inflation, enabled older Americans, who might otherwise have fallen below the poverty line, to hold their own economically during the Reagan years.[30]

Reagan and his conservative supporters also gave new meanings to many traditional political terms. "Liberal" no longer could refer to a set of government programs that would stimulate the economy, help people to buy new homes and consumer goods, and provide access to quality medical care. "Liberalism" became a code word for supposedly wasteful social programs devised by a bloated federal government that gouged hardworking people and gave their dollars to people who were undeserving and lazy. "Conservative" referred to economic growth through limited government and support for traditional social-cultural values. David Stockman, Reagan's budget director, best explained how this phenomenon occurred. "The Reagan Revolution required a frontal assault on the American welfare state," he wrote. Creation of the huge federal deficit was explicitly aimed at weakening the welfare state, and for the most part, this tactic was successful. Reagan's policies were a clear signal for employers to cut wages and fringe benefits, including health care. Declining workplace coverage, not population growth, accounted for over 90 percent of the 6 million newly uninsured workers.[31]

In reducing public expenditures in the health sector, Reagan was more successful than his British counterpart, Prime Minister Margaret Thatcher, not because Americans were less supportive of those expenditures, but because, in Britain, Thatcher's Conservative Party had to compete with a working-class Labour Party committed to expansion rather than reduction of health expenditures. The Republican Party in the 1980s had no such competition or opposition. Organized labor was no longer a force for social change; it had been reduced to one of many interest groups. The result was that Reagan's health cuts were made with the support of the Democratic leadership in Congress. Democrats, instead of marshaling an all-out response to the Republican rhetoric of opposition to taxes, government, and the liberal welfare state, moved rightward, jettisoning the New Deal and Great Society in their attempt to "out-Reagan Reagan."[32] This left the party's left wing demoralized, which helps to explain the high rate of voter abstention, particularly among the working class, women, people of color, and the poor in the 1980s. Democratic leaders rationalized their abandonment of the party's long-term commitment to make health care a human right on the grounds of an assumed antigovernment mood of the American public. And yet, poll after poll in the 1980s showed that no other federal project consistently enjoyed as much popular support as universal health coverage.[33]

The Democratic Party's strategic move toward the center to attract middle-class voters only confirmed the similarity between the two parties and increased voter apathy in the critical sectors the Democrats needed to win the White House. Thus, presidential candidate Walter Mondale's move rightward in 1984 proved to be a major political blunder. In his speech accepting the nomination of his party, Mondale announced that he would raise taxes if elected, a declaration that alienated both the middle-class and the registered, but unmotivated, voters whom he was trying to win over to the Democratic Party. The better strategy might have been to excoriate President Reagan for signing the Deficit Reduction Act of 1984, to raise $50 billion in taxes, and for signing in each of the two previous years tax increases that weighed most heavily on the working population, the 70 percent of Americans who comprised the middle and working classes. Pursuing this course would have revived the class strategy of the New Deal, clearly demarcated the Democratic Party from the Reagan Republicans, and perhaps have enabled Mondale to snatch victory from the jaws of defeat.[34]

Mondale's futile attempt to out-flank Reagan on the right, just as the high cost of health care emerged as one of the top three concerns of the American voter, contributed to the Democrats' overwhelming defeat in the second of the three presidential contests of the 1980s. Most Americans in 1984 wanted changes in the health care system; the percentage asking for profound changes actually increased rather than decreased. A *Washington Post*/ABC News poll that fall revealed that an unprecedented 75 percent of the respondents believed that "the government should institute and operate a national health program."[35] The Reagan White House, with bipartisan congressional support, cut spending for health care and other social programs while maintaining defense spending at relatively high levels. It reversed the postwar trade-off between defense and human services spending and thereby bankrupted the government by creating such a ballooning deficit (over $220 billion by 1989) that politicians had to rationalize the shift in priorities by arguing that there was no escape from the painful trade-offs: between the right to health care and financial restraint, between the clinical autonomy of physicians and cost containment, between consumer freedom of choice and resource scarcity.[36]

A paradigmatic shift occurred in the thinking about health security among 1980s politicians, businessmen, health policy analysts, and certain sectors of the public, from an idealized end for social justice in which there was a textbook-style government takeover of organization and financing to achieve better efficiency and equity in the health sector to a practical instrument for the enforcement of cost effectiveness in health services production and delivery. The rationale underlying the change of thought was that health costs were rising because people were abusing health services. Government responded to the crisis by focusing on reversing the escalation in health care costs. Equity fell victim to efficiency.[37]

Washington's steps to cut costs during the decade of Republican ascendancy included federal regulation of Medicare reimbursements; new federal subsidies to foster the growth of private HMOs; planning initiatives to reduce the redundant expansion of hospitals and equipment; a shift in hospital reimbursement by Medicare from cost to prospective compensation; and a resource-based relative-value scale, which moderated payments from Medicare patients to physicians. The Reagan administration justified these actions on the grounds of efficiency and competitiveness. State governments followed the federal example. They also limited their health care spending by making fewer people, especially the working poor, eligible for Medicaid and by designing programs to limit the numbers of reimbursable visits to doctors, prescriptions, hospital admissions, and time spent in the hospital. Many states also instituted low levels of allowable fees for physicians treating Medicaid patients, required certificates-of-need, and lowered reimbursement rates for nursing home care. Employers took the federal and state actions as cues to lower the costs of their own health benefits, which had averaged annual increases of 10 to 20 percent, by shifting more of the financial burden onto their workers.[38]

Despite the best efforts of all concerned to lower health care costs, that did not happen, but this failure did not prompt any movement toward broader and deeper reforms or lead to a reconsideration of national health insurance. The existing system, with its many different facets and fragmentation, still appeared to offer many advantages to the public.

Most Americans, fearing that cost control would bring less care, preferred to tinker with a flawed system and favored modest rather than substantial government intervention. Midway through its second term, the Reagan administration could no longer ignore the problems of the health care system. It responded with ad hoc measures, such as the 1986 Consolidated Omnibus Budget Reconciliation Act (COBRA), which required that employers with twenty or more employees who were covered by group health insurance continue that insurance for up to eighteen months after the employee left the company with the former employee paying the full premium, and the Catastrophic Health Care Coverage Act of 1988, the first expansion of benefits to Medicare since 1965.[39]

The Catastrophic Health Coverage Act had risen to the top of the Reagan administration's agenda despite the inhospitable political climate, thanks to the political entrepreneurship of the president's secretary of health and human resources, Otis Bowen, the former chairman of the federal Advisory Council on Social Security. That body had recommended expanding Medicare's hospitalization benefit to an unlimited number of days, eliminating co-payments for hospital and skilled-nursing facility care, and putting a cap on out-of-pocket expenses. After his confirmation as secretary, Bowen pushed catastrophic coverage on his own initiative, not as a broader decision of the administration.[40]

A cadre of administration conservatives, led by Attorney General Ed Meese, and private insurers opposed the idea on ideological grounds, as an unwarranted expansion of the federal government. After considerable discussion, Bowen finally persuaded the president that his plan was administratively simpler than any conservative alternative that preserved a broader role for the Medigap industry. Reagan and some of his political advisers also saw merit in Bowen's idea as a way for Republicans to improve their standing with senior citizens. The idea of adding catastrophic coverage to Medicare found an even more enthusiastic audience in Congress on both sides of the aisle, where concerns over limitations in Medicare coverage also meshed with political motives. The result is that the law that Congress enacted in 1988 expanded substantially on Bowen's proposal and the Reagan administration's desire.

This expansion occurred because the Democrats, who already controlled the House and in 1988 controlled the Senate for the first time since 1980, found themselves in the unusual and discomfiting position of ceding credit for Medicare expansion to the Republicans. Driven by Henry Waxman of California, the chair of the House Committee on Energy and Commerce's Subcommittee on Health, Speaker Jim Wright, and Senator Claude Pepper, Democrats had an added incentive to load additional benefits onto the Bowen proposal. These benefits ranged from prescription drug coverage to hospice care, from care in skilled-nursing facilities to mandates to the states to expand care for the Medicare poor, as well as to expand Medicaid coverage to low-income pregnant women and children.

Democrats, then, saw the bill as a vehicle to pursue liberal social policy aims that had eluded them during the Reagan presidency and to have legislators go on record on improving health care for the elderly. This brought the issue to public attention, and a coalition of liberals and conservatives in both houses of Congress, operating from very different motives, quickly enacted the legislation. The following year (1989), the administration of George H. W. Bush, President Reagan's successor, just as quickly repealed the law. President Bush and Congress took this drastic step in response to protests over the financing of this new benefit and in response to questions about intergenerational equity.

Bowen's plan, to which Republicans and Democrats had assented, rested on the principle of self-financing. Medicare beneficiaries alone were to fund the new benefits through a premium increase. Congress wrote the law this way to get around fiscal and political constraints imposed by the federal deficit, but it represented a major departure from financing a social benefit from earmarked payroll taxes on employers and employees. Moreover, although all beneficiaries paid the same additional amount on their monthly Part B Medicare premiums, higher-income beneficiaries had to pay a supplemental premium for catastrophic coverage, which could go as high as $800 annually. Finally, by the time catastrophic insurance emerged as an issue in the mid-1980s, the belief that the elderly deserved governmental assistance was under attack. Unlike in the 1960s, the elderly were perceived as receiving too much government money and were in better financial shape relative to younger people. As a consequence, for the first time in the program's history, the bill that emerged from the legislative process tied Medicare's premiums to income.

When confronted with opposition from the elderly themselves, who either objected to the tax/premium differential or did not want to trade their existing private coverage for another federal program, the Bush administration requested that Congress repeal the law. This action left many Medicare recipients vulnerable to soaring health costs and left the program with a seriously deficient benefits package. There was a broader gap between Medicare and private health insurance, and Medicare's political constituency was left weaker and more vulnerable to advocates of market-based reforms, who sought to restructure Medicare in order to carve out a broader role for private health plans.

Without a commitment to fundamental and major reform, policy makers of the 1980s could not find solutions to the health care crisis. Politicians and health experts put forth many arguments to explain why this was so, but the lack of resources was the least convincing to the political Left and to the average citizen. For as Dr. Vicente Navarro of Johns Hopkins University, editor of the *International Journal of Health Services*, noted, the United States had spent nearly 11 percent of GNP on health services in 1983. The problem was and continued to be the institutions through which the resources were spent, Navarro insisted. Insufficient coverage and high costs were rooted in the private, for-profit character of American medicine. Even in federal programs whose services were publicly financed but privately delivered, waste was overwhelming. Navarro's comparative analysis of the health systems in the United States, France, and Germany showed that countries with government control of funding and administration of health services had better coverage, lower costs, more equitable distribution of resources, and higher popular satisfaction with those services than those with large for-profit private-sector health services.[41]

Navarro's point bore repetition, given the federal cost-containment policies of the Reagan-Bush presidencies, which focused primarily on regulating costs of hospital services without touching directly on the organization, planning, and delivery of health services or the overall size of for-profit medicine. The latter had grown considerably in the 1980s because of the massive involvement of for-profit hospital chains in health care delivery, facilitated in part by federal policies that paid for but did not regulate those services, and programs such as Medicare. Federal payments went not only to hospitals but also to the web of private professionals, independent contractors, pharmaceutical companies, and medical suppliers in both the private and nonprivate sectors. The size of the for-profit sector, Navarro's research suggested, was at the root of the health care crisis, the characteristic of which was ever-shrinking coverage despite enormous growth of expenditures.[42]

Perhaps because of his Marxist perspective, Navarro's arguments went unheeded among political leaders and health policy analysts, except for Jesse Jackson, who spoke of the need for a national health policy in the 1984 election, but even he did not emphasize it to any serious extent. More aggressive support for such a policy, perhaps along the lines suggested by Navarro, might have helped link Jackson more closely to the elderly, organized labor, the AARP, and other elements in the Rainbow Coalition that he hoped to forge.[43] Instead, Mondale and the Democratic Party establishment dismissed Jackson as a nuisance, abandoned the New Deal and the party's own left wing, and echoed the Republicans' austerity call for cost controls and cost reductions. Mondale's platform was silent on a national health policy, speaking only of the need to reduce government intervention in people's lives. Professor Theodore Marmor of Yale, one of the nation's leading authorities on health care, referred to Jackson as a spoiler, attributing to him a larger role in Mondale's defeat than the facts warranted.[44]

Health care reform remained in limbo until November 1987, when Jackson, in a keynote address to the American Public Health Association, spoke of the need to establish a national health care program, federally funded and administered, that took into account popular participation and public accountability. After seven years of social-spending cuts by the Reagan administration, Jackson called access to health care a moral issue. It was the opening salvo in his campaign for the Democratic presidential nomination in 1988.[45]

The news media and the liberal establishment ignored Jackson's speech, which was part of his broader strategy of going back to the mainstay of the party's support, to reach and unite working people by demanding programs such as universal health coverage and full employment. The nation's social and economic problems, Jackson insisted, had resulted not from a scarcity of resources, as Republicans and Carter-Mondale Democrats had maintained, but from skewed and unjust control over those resources. He cited Canada's national health program, which dated from 1966, to demonstrate that the United States could also afford universal coverage at costs lower than it was now paying for health services. Canadian health expenditures had grown at a slower pace than those in the United States, benefits had expanded, and health indicators had improved more quickly. If Canadians could do it, Jackson asked, why not the United States?[46]

Jackson's new and more strident stance on health care reform reflected Navarro's influence as head of his health task force. They hoped to shift the debate from how much a national health program would cost to who would control the funding and organization of health services. The latter would determine the former. "We wanted to emphasize the power of the federal purse to change and reorganize the private delivery of services to make them more efficient, comprehensive and cost-effective," Navarro wrote. In internal position papers, Navarro showed that a health care system similar to Canada's would save $70 billion a year while providing comprehensive coverage to all Americans.[47]

Until the Michigan primary, Jackson was the only candidate who called for a national health program. Linking the United States with South Africa, the only other major country that did not have a national health policy, and insisting we had "to change company" quickly became the hallmarks of his campaign speeches. When the Michigan ballots were counted, Jackson had won an overwhelming victory, receiving the majority of both black and white votes. The 4.4 million black voters and 2 million white voters had clearly been receptive to his message, and yet the press continued to refer to him primarily as a black leader. Worse still, once it was clear that Jackson was a serious contender for the Democratic presidential nomination, many leading liberals, including Geraldine Ferraro, Mondale's vice presidential partner in 1984, and New York Mayor Edward Koch either ignored or brutally distorted his position. The liberal *New York Times* published a series of articles in April 1988, later picked up by other print and television media, that blasted Jackson's demands as potentially ruinous to the country financially. Near the top of the list was the establishment of a national health program.[48]

The liberal establishment's attacks had consequences not altogether intended. On health care, the attacks forced Jackson's campaign to develop a budget demonstrating that the central problem was not financial resources but the priorities in allocating them. Jackson proposed to finance his health program not through general revenue or payroll taxes but primarily through earmarked taxes that would go into a national health trust fund distinct from the general federal budget. The Michigan victory had also raised voters' expectations, and they wanted Jackson's rivals for the nomination to respond to his proposal. Feeling the pressure, front-runner Michael Dukakis, finally and for the first time, called for a "universal" health program, even though he carefully hedged his demand. Dukakis's health adviser, Dr. David Blumenthal, declared that the Massachusetts governor supported employer-mandated coverage after the budget deficit was resolved and Medicare and Medicaid were expanded. The Dukakis camp saw universal coverage, at best, as a long-range goal; in the interim, the candidate proposed expanding some areas of coverage, an expansion based on federal subsidization of the private sector. Dukakis's views gained credibility when, at his urging, the Massachusetts legislature in April 1988 passed (but never implemented) a universal health care bill to provide basic coverage for all residents by 1992. After examining the fine print, Jackson's health team concluded that the Massachusetts plan was neither comprehensive nor universal, and would remain that way as long as the power of the private insurance industry remained intact.[49]

By the close of the primaries in June, Jackson had received 7 million votes, or 16 percent less than Dukakis. However, through manipulation of the party's rules, Dukakis controlled 800 superdelegate votes, enough to put him over the magic number of 2,000 delegates to win the nomination. This forced the Jackson campaign to carry its fight to the platform committee. The subcommittee drafting the platform had met on June 25–26 and produced a document that disappointed Jackson and his advisers. The Dukakis forces on the committee had resisted Jackson's call for a national health program under federal leadership and substituted a vaguely worded right of all Americans to basic health care, without specifying its extent or what level of government would guarantee that care.[50] Jackson's representatives found the wording to be unacceptable, a continuation of the Reaganomics policy of austerity in softer language, and repudiated the committee's work. They vowed to continue the fight by presenting all Jackson's proposals directly to the convention delegates as minority planks, knowing that this tactic would force a confrontation and lengthy bargaining process with the Dukakis delegates. On July 18, the Dukakis campaign, loath to risk the spectacle of a divided convention on national television, agreed to permit the Jackson delegates to present thirteen amendments directly to the floor of the convention.[51]

The following day the convention opened in Atlanta, with the delegates passing by acclamation several of the Jackson-inspired amendments to the platform document, including the call for a national health program underwritten and administered by the federal government. Once again, the media minimized Jackson's campaign accomplishments, reporting only the three amendments that were not accepted and ignoring the ten that were. Nonetheless, adoption of the health program marked an important turning point. For the first time in nearly a decade, the Democratic Party was returning to its traditional ideological and popular base by committing itself to universal health coverage and rejecting the Republican argument that the United States, the richest country in the world, could not afford to make access to health care a human right. The party's commitment was one that future Democratic administrations could not ignore with impunity. Though the principle was secured, the devil remained in the details of such a program.[52]

Dormant for nearly twenty years except for the efforts of some Democrats on the political margin, national health security had, by the end of the decade, emerged from the shadows as an important, if unresolved, political issue.[53] After one of the dirtiest political campaigns in recent memory, the Republican ticket of George H. W. Bush and Dan Quayle won an overwhelming victory in November. It was the fifth time in the past six elections that the Democratic presidential ticket had lost. Defeat prompted a reassessment of what went wrong. Some Democrats interpreted the loss as proof of the party's need to move to the center by being tough on entitlements and strong on defense; others, mainly left-wing Democrats, argued precisely the opposite. Still other Democrats blamed Dukakis for running an incompetent campaign. One fact that was not in dispute, however, was the continued alienation of many voters from their political institutions. Large numbers of working-class and young Democrats had failed once again to show up at the polls, because they did not think Dukakis and the Democratic Party were responsive to them. As late as the 1992 election, 80 percent of Americans believed that government was run for the benefit of a few big interests, and they were angry.[54]

The outcome of the 1988 election was a vote for the political status quo, but health care issues continued to grab the spotlight. During Bush's first year as president, protests arose from more affluent Medicare patients who had purchased catastrophic insurance coverage on their own, and Congress responded in December 1989 with a bill (H.R. 3607) to repeal the Catastrophic Coverage Act, which President Bush signed. This signal failure to expand Medicare rendered legislators even more skeptical of undertaking major health care reform. In such circumstances, politicians of both parties did what they usually do when they want to avoid making hard decisions or when there is no consensus: they set up a commission to investigate the problem. With the election fiasco behind them, the congressional Democratic majority established the U.S. Bipartisan Commission on Comprehensive Health Coverage. Composed of six senators, six representatives, and three presidential appointees, and chaired by that ancient New Dealer, Senator Claude Pepper of Florida, the commission's chief contribution was to keep concerns about the nation's delivery of health care before the public. When it issued its report in 1990, the recommendations reflected the members' differing views. Vague and ambiguous, they demonstrated just how contentious any debate on health care reform was likely to be.[55]

When the 102nd Congress convened in January 1991, legislators introduced over two dozen health reform bills, including the "HealthAmerica" bill, guaranteeing universal ac-

cess to affordable health care, which Maine's Democratic Senator George Mitchell introduced on June 5. However, not a single bill was enacted.[56] The scope and complexity of
the health system's problems, the absence of a consensus on how best to reform it, powerful opposition from the insurance–medical industry complex, and the Bush administration's bruising experience with catastrophic insurance precluded Congress from taking any action. The momentum for health care reform shifted for the moment to the state
level, where the governor of Pennsylvania named Harris Wofford to replace the late John
Heinz as secretary of labor and industry. This appointment precipitated a chain of events
that would refocus health care reform on the national political agenda.[57]

Wofford, a little-known Democrat, had never been elected to political office when he
decided in spring 1991 to run for the U.S. Senate. A clear underdog, Wofford trailed behind Richard Thornburgh, the attorney general of the United States and a prominent former Republican governor of Pennsylvania, until he derided the attorney general as a
"Washington insider" and made health care reform the centerpiece of his campaign.
Working with James Carville, a political consultant and future Clinton presidential campaign manager, Wofford produced a television ad that said, "If criminals have a right to a
lawyer, I think working Americans should have the right to a doctor." The ad resonated
with Pennsylvania voters, Democrats nationally, and with Americans everywhere. In a
stunning upset, Wofford defeated his Republican opponent by a 10 percent margin. The
exit polls showed that national health insurance was the single-most-important issue determining how Pennsylvanians voted.[58] The political appeal of the health issue spread
quickly beyond the state's borders because businessmen tired of paying high premiums
for employees' health insurance; labor unions fighting to improve workers' pay and
health coverage but seeing the gains wiped out by inflation; physicians faced with loss of
autonomy and malpractice suits and awash in paperwork; insurance companies unable
to match their competitors; and states devoting ever larger percentages of their budgets
to health care costs jumped on the reform bandwagon.[59]

Wofford's campaign was never solely about health care; it was about the frustrations
the voters felt at being so powerless in the face of the ineffectuality of the government in
Washington. But his victory in November had a significant impact on politics everywhere, especially the 1992 presidential race.[60] Democratic candidates at every level saw
health reform as an issue on which President George H. W. Bush and the Republicans
were vulnerable, and they incorporated health care reform as the second-most-
important issue (after jobs) in their own campaigns.[61]

The average American's perception of the health care system's shortcomings, however,
differed very sharply from that of the politicians and experts who actually shaped policy.
To the ordinary citizen, access to and the costs of health care were the primary concerns,
whereas the Bush administration and the Democratic-controlled Congress continued to
support the austerity regimen that was the hallmark of Reagan's federal health policies.

Reducing government intervention in the health sector ran counter to polls showing that Americans favored the very opposite. Two-thirds of Americans supported a tax-financed national health program, and a whopping 84 percent wanted Washington to lead in resolving the nation's health care problems.[62]

The disparity between what government was doing and what the governed wanted had grown very large by the time the 1992 presidential election approached. Surveys and polls continued to reveal the dimensions of the health care crisis. Employers' contributions to health benefits costs had declined during the decade of Republican presidential hegemony, from 80 to 69 percent by 1990, leaving employees to pick up the slack. Average family health costs doubled, as did the fear of being unable to pay medical bills. Government projections of future health costs only magnified workers' concerns: the United States would spend $832 billion on health care in 1992, but nearly 38 million Americans—15 percent of the population—would not have any type of medical insurance; spending would increase to $1.6 trillion by 2000, but 100,000 Americans would lose their insurance every month through "restructuring" (that is, massive job layoffs) by large corporations and by state and local governments. The percentage of Americans who thought the health care system either required fundamental changes or needed to be completely rebuilt, not surprisingly, grew from 75 percent in 1982 to 92 percent in 1991.

Less publicized at the time was the number of the largest 200 *Fortune* business firms (mostly manufacturing and export) that had supported human capital investment initiatives and that were also troubled by the spiraling costs of health care. They had developed different initiatives over the years to combat rising health care expenditures, but few had delivered vastly improved outcomes. Between 1965 and 1991, the cost of their employee health benefits had jumped from 2.2 to 13 percent of salaries and wages. Much of the increase was attributed to the practice of "cost shifting" by governments and hospitals, and the rest was due to intense competition from abroad in both the domestic and international markets. Under pressure to cut costs, in a remarkable turnabout, they began to associate national health care reform with keeping costs down rather than driving them up. At least initially, big business seemed receptive to joining a broad-based health coalition that included the federal government in a comprehensive overhaul of the health care financial system.[63]

By the early 1990s, then, 90 percent of Americans believed there was a crisis in health care. Their frustration, evident in the polls, was not new, but it had reached unprecedented levels. The average American attributed the system's problems to waste, greed, fraud, profiteering, and malpractice. Yet, despite a perceived need for reform, health care remained a dangerous minefield for politicians, for average citizens also viewed health care very personally and judged any attempts at reform on how it affected their life and family. The same polls that disclosed broad-based dissatisfaction also revealed that the people did not want to sacrifice their current health status to expand coverage for the uninsured. They wanted reform, but they were not clear about the kinds of changes they wanted, who would pay for them, or whether the federal government alone should be the engine of change. This, too, was a legacy of the Reagan presidency: Americans were deeply skeptical of government and its ability to solve the health care crisis.[64]

Americans' attitudes were conflicted, whereas politicians of both parties and health policy experts analyzed the high health costs in aggregate rather than in human terms: the impact on the deficit, whether other needs had a higher national priority, the expense of new technology, the growth of the third-party payer system, the graying of the population, rising incomes, and tax subsidies for the poor.[65] Rather than scrapping a broken system, as Jesse Jackson had urged, the experts advocated sensitizing patients to the costs of care and limiting unnecessary care, and they talked about providing access to care for those without coverage. However much they turned over the problem, the result was to shift its sources to the clients who utilized (they would say overutilized) the health system unnecessarily.[66] This, too, was a legacy of the Reagan era. In this context of a system in crisis, William Jefferson "Bill" Clinton, governor of Arkansas, who had limited experience in the complexities of health care reform, announced his intention to run for president on October 3, 1991.

Bill Clinton may not have been familiar with the intricacies of the problem, but he was not without friends and advisers who were prepared to educate him. Anne Wexler, a Democratic lobbyist and public relations executive, introduced Bruce Reed, Clinton's campaign issues director, to Bruce M. Fried, who had run the National Health Care Campaign during the 1980s in a futile attempt to put the issue on the agenda of Democratic candidates. Fried offered to draft a memo on the current thinking of liberal-oriented policy experts and volunteered to bring together a small group of people as consultants. From this encounter was born the Blueberry Donut Group (BBDG), named after the repast Fried served at their Tuesday morning conferences. Its members included Judith Feder, former executive director of the Pepper commission, Marilyn Moon of the Urban Institute, Kenneth Thorpe, University of North Carolina health economist, and seven others—lawyers, physicians, and lobbyists.[67]

While the BBDG was schooling Clinton in the three main options around which health policy analysts had coalesced—namely, the single-payer plan, in which the government, using tax dollars, would be the sole source, or "single payer," of all medical bills; managed competition, in which the essentially private health system would rely largely on market forces of supply and demand (employers would pay a portion of their employees' coverage), and government would have the limited role of setting minimum standards for the benefits insurers would have to pay; and pay-or-play, in which each business would be given a choice of providing insurance for its own employees, with part of the cost deducted from their pay and part paid by the employer, or contributing to a national health insurance fund administered by the government—

two of Clinton's Democratic rivals for the nomination hammered away at the Arkansas Democrat for his lack of a specific health proposal. Senator Bob Kerrey of Nebraska had staked out health care as his main concern in July 1991, when he unveiled a comprehensive proposal that bore a close resemblance to the single-payer system adopted in Canada, Great Britain, and most European countries. Using tax dollars, the governments of those countries were the sole source, or "single payer," of all medical bills. Under Kerrey's proposal, the federal government would set the benefits package and an annual budget, leaving to the states to set physician and hospital fees. Kerrey proposed to pay for universal coverage with a 5 percent payroll tax, a new top-bracket income tax, and higher taxes on cigarettes and alcohol. Private insurance companies opposed the plan because it converted private insurance premiums into taxes, enhanced direct government regulation, and, they claimed, would result in lower-quality care.[68]

Whereas Kerrey staked out the most extreme Democratic position on health care, former Senator Paul Tsongas of Massachusetts adopted the most conservative. Tsongas supported the notion of managed competition, a concept that Stanford Business School economist Alain C. Enthoven had developed and publicized.[69] Building on the ideas of Dr. Paul M. Ellwood, Jr., the Minneapolis physician who had persuaded the Nixon administration of the merits of HMOs, Enthoven had conducted seminar-like meetings at Ellwood's vacation home in Jackson Hole, Wyoming, to educate academics, large corporate employers, insurance company executives, pharmaceutical executives, and heads of some major professional associations in the theory of managed competition. From these meetings emerged the Jackson Hole Plan and its advocates, the Jackson Hole Group.[70]

The Jackson Hole Group wanted to establish a health system that relied largely on market forces of supply and demand. Managed competition would restructure the health care market so that the leverage of insurance companies over consumers would be reduced and cost containment would be achieved with a minimum of direct government controls. Under this essentially private system, employers paid a portion of employees' health care costs; insurance companies vied for the business of large pools of individuals through "health insurance purchasing cooperatives" (HIPCs); and the government restricted its role to organizing the HIPCs and setting minimum standards for care. As with HMOs, the advocates of managed competition assumed that many insurance providers, because of the efficiencies involved, would switch to it. This market-oriented reform concept appealed to conservative Democrats like Tsongas and Tennessee Representative Jim Cooper, to a number of Republicans, to businessmen, and to the media. The quickness with which the national press, following the lead of the *New York Times,* presented managed competition as the *only* solution to the nation's health care crisis was indeed remarkable.[71]

In contrast to Kerrey and Tsongas, Clinton's health care philosophy continued to remain uncertain, although he rejected out of hand Kerrey's single-payer proposal or any

option that vested the federal government with sole authority to organize, fund, and administer national health coverage as too liberal for realistic consideration and inconsistent with his own efforts to forge a new coalition of middle-class voters. This latter point
was especially compelling, for in announcing his candidacy, Clinton exclaimed that the
era of big government was over. He premised his campaign on being a "New Democrat,"
unenamored of big, bureaucratic government and fully aware of the need for spending
discipline. Like other governors, Clinton had seen the exploding costs of Medicaid devour their budgets. Distancing himself from the architects of the Great Society, Clinton's
political base was in the Democratic Leadership Council, a group of moderate-to-
conservative officeholders who had no ties to organized labor, the chief proponent of the
Canadian health plan.[72]

It was not until the Renaissance New Year's weekend of 1992, when Clinton and the
Democrats got together in Hilton Head, South Carolina, to brainstorm important
public policy issues that candidate Clinton engaged the issue of health care reform seriously. After a talk on the subject by Ira Magaziner, a Rhodes Scholar classmate down
from Cambridge, Massachusetts, Clinton asked him to outline what he considered the
best approach to reform. By the end of the month, Magaziner had produced a
managed-competition plan that differed from the one Tsongas had endorsed. Although both proposals allowed physicians, insurers, and hospitals to compete for patients, Magaziner's proposal contained regulatory measures to control costs and ensure quality. These were referred to as "global budgets," a concept that sociologist Paul
Starr of Princeton University had introduced to Magaziner. Clinton became familiar
with the managed-competition theory also in conversations with his California campaign chairman, John Garamendi, the state insurance commissioner. On fund-raising
trips to Los Angeles, Clinton discussed health policy with Garamendi and his deputy
Walter Zelman, who had assembled California's health advisory panel, which included the Stanford proponents of managed competition. Both from New England
and the Pacific coast, then, Clinton acquired an education in managed competition
and global budgeting.[73]

On January 19, 1992, one hour before the Democratic candidates met in Nashua, New
Hampshire, in one of the primary debates, the Clinton campaign issued a white paper on
health care, which candidate Clinton and Bruce Reed had drafted. The position paper advocated the pay-or-play model, which was very popular among Democrats in Congress
because it worked within the existing health care structure. Under pay-or-play, businesses either would help cover the insurance costs of employees or would pay into a national health care insurance fund administered by the government. Federal taxes also
would be tapped to expand coverage to those who were unemployed or not already covered by Medicaid. Short on specifics, Clinton's white paper achieved its political goal. It
thwarted the assaults of Democratic rivals Kerrey and Tsongas.[74]

Even though the position paper was not intended to set forth a coherent plan that candidate Clinton firmly believed in, it ignited an eight-month internal struggle among rival factions of Clinton advisers who were trying to get the candidate to define his approach to health care reform more precisely. Clinton was much too preoccupied with politics during the winter of 1991 and spring of 1992 to worry about these doctrinal debates. By June, his rivals had dropped out of the campaign and his nomination was well in hand; then he began to read daily reports that an independent candidate, Ross Perot, was putting together an army of researchers to draft a platform for his own campaign. Feeling that he was under intense pressure to spell out his own general election campaign proposals before Perot did, Clinton hurriedly ordered Bruce Reed's policy staff in Little Rock to undertake a crash project on a booklet entitled *Putting People First*. The health care section gave Clinton's rival presidential advisers—Fried's BBDG, representing the Democratic establishment in Washington, which favored pay-or-play; and Magaziner, leading the Cambridge-California alliance of managed-competition theorists—an opportunity to test their respective influence on the candidate. In the course of their intellectual battle, the crucial question that emerged was whose numbers could be trusted.[75]

The first hint that candidate Clinton was leaning toward a specific health care option came during an interview at a convention of radio talk show hosts in Washington, D.C. Clinton's response indicated that he was moving away from the play-or-pay system, which he had borrowed at the beginning of the nomination campaign, and toward the new notion of managed competition, which Magaziner, Garamendi, and Zelman advocated. But he was still not ready to fully embrace managed competition. Magaziner's attempt to run roughshod over Fried and the Blueberry Donut Group only poisoned the atmosphere within Clinton's campaign team.[76] That became clear the following day during a conference call with Fried in Washington, Magaziner in Massachusetts, and Clinton in Little Rock. Magaziner produced a set of figures showing how managed competition could be financed, but Fried was skeptical of their authenticity. Clinton also was wary of having Perot or Bush challenge their accuracy. Until the financing was more firmly tested, Clinton leaned toward omitting the health care section in *Putting People First*. Bruce Reed proposed a compromise: retain the outline of the proposal, but eliminate the numbers. The resulting chapter on health care was heavy on rhetoric and short on details; it discussed expanding basic benefits but said little about the most controversial and difficult question, how to pay for these reforms.[77]

Reed's compromise was a respite in the struggle for candidate Clinton's mind. Magaziner had promised in the debates to eliminate hospital paperwork with a single claim form, to end billing fraud, and to prevent pharmaceutical companies from drug price gouging. The savings would slow medical inflation and pay for added coverage. The Fried group remained skeptical. *Putting People First* also called for the establishment of a national board to set an annual medical budget for the entire nation, an idea borrowed from

Kerrey's single-payer plan, and spoke vaguely of "local health networks," the HIPCs or buyers' clubs of managed competition, which would be given "the necessary incentives to control costs." Overall, details of the plan were difficult to decipher, again a reflection of Clinton's own lack of resolve. The only hint that new money might be needed came in a pledge to "phase in business responsibilities, covering employees through the public program until the transition is complete." Once more, the pamphlet lacked an adequate description of what that public program entailed.[78]

Then, on July 15, 1992, Clinton accepted the Democratic nomination in New York's Madison Square Garden, vowing to "take on the health care profiteers and make health care affordable for every family." The acceptance speech consisted of "key themes" rather than specific details, in part because Clinton had still not made up his mind and in part for fear that the reward of getting specific would be outweighed by the risk of offending one or other constituency. As Democratic pollster Stan Greenberg cautioned, voters wanted the health system changed, but they were not certain which changes would help them. This was the crucial question, and voters wanted politicians to be careful in making those changes.[79]

President George H. W. Bush, meanwhile, unveiled his own election-year proposal. Rather than fundamentally changing the health delivery system, Bush coupled an expansion of health insurance through tax credits to cover the uninsured, incentives to save money for future health costs, and reform of the private insurance markets with the pledge that he "would preserve what works and reform what doesn't."[80] Knowing that the Democrats enjoyed a definite advantage on the health issue, Bush and the Republicans decided that they could not afford to allow Clinton to campaign in platitudes. In September, Bush charged that Clinton's plan was the familiar liberal Democratic, big government bureaucratic medicine, with price controls. In October, with money running out for the Medicaid program in Arkansas, the Bush campaign faulted Clinton for being unable to control costs in his own state, much less the United States. Magaziner and campaign aide Atul Gawande, a student on leave from the Harvard Medical School, privately warned the Democratic standard-bearer that the campaign's position on health care was too unstructured to fend off Republican attacks. A poll also showed that Clinton's campaign position on health care was not getting through to the public.[81]

Clinton attempted to parry Bush's criticism by going on the attack. He accused the administration of inaction and, in response to Magaziner's warnings, repositioned himself by merging Democratic positions from left to right and shedding the pay-or-play label, which had come under increasing Republican attack. Bringing everyone into an insurance pool would please the Left; letting private insurers and providers compete for business in that pool would please the Right. Allowing market forces to discipline inflation also would please the Right, but putting a ceiling on overall spending would reassure the Left. Clinton's hope was that in the blend of these opposing views, single-payer advocates (the unions) and managed-competition people (elements of the business community) would find enough common ground to be supportive.[82]

Hard on the heels of staff conferences in Washington and Little Rock, Gawande drafted a memorandum summarizing the internal agreements on policy, which became the text for briefing Clinton on September 22, the date of the first scheduled presidential debate. The memo of understanding provided that all workers and their families would receive health insurance through their jobs, with employers paying most of the premiums. Direct subsidies and a slow phase-in would cushion the economic costs to small business; every American would be covered, with the federal government paying the insurance premium for those outside of the workforce; networks of hospitals, physicians, and other medical professionals would be organized in every community to compete in this expanded health care marketplace, charging flat fees for a standard package of benefits for everyone who signed up. The government would set the top fee but would allow market forces to undercut it; states would organize health insurance purchasing cooperatives (HIPCs or alliances) through which small firms, the self-employed, and other individuals could buy policies at better rates than they would otherwise get. The alliances would put competitive pressure on the health care networks to improve quality and reduce costs. To make certain that the anticipated savings were realized, the federal government would set an overall national health budget and require both insurance premiums and providers' fees to remain under that ceiling.[83]

The memo's concluding statement captured the essence of what Clinton's advisers thought they were offering the candidate and the country: "The plan will secure basic health care as a right for every American and it will take a giant stride in securing a strong economy and the public health." It did not nationalize medicine, but it helped small businessmen and consumers; it sheltered doctors and hospitals from micromanagement, paperwork, and bureaucracy and freed them to care for patients. It was a system in which responsibilities were evenly distributed.[84]

Although he had not personally developed this new version of managed competition, the combination of existing proposals and the creation of new ideas were representative of the personal and political style of Bill Clinton. The candidate who wanted to please everyone had adopted the ultimate compromise. Paul Starr conceded as much when he noted that "a reform plan that combined the security of universal, comprehensive coverage with consumer choice and competition in the delivery of services was, in a sense, the natural byproduct of the Democratic Party that Bill Clinton was trying to put back together."[85]

Clinton unveiled his proposal on September 24, 1992, in a campaign speech to employees of Merck Pharmaceutical Company, in New Jersey, a location campaign managers chose deliberately. New Jersey was a swing state, and the company, whose chairman was an active Democrat, had voluntarily decided to keep prescription drug prices below the inflation rate. Without ever using the term "managed competition," Clinton con-trasted his policy approach with Bush's, whose proposed tax subsidies of private insur-ance companies he castigated as "throwing good money after bad." Clinton stressed that his plan was "a private system. It is not pay-or-play. It does not require new taxes. It will preserve what is best about the present health care system, but it will also incorporate what we have learned about what is wrong." Emphasizing the market aspects of his plan, Clinton added, "We've got to quit having the federal government try to micro-manage health care and instead set up incentives for the private sector to manage the cost down within limits, beyond which we absolutely must not go in spending."[86]

For Clinton, both political rhetoric and policy seemed to be working. The combination of the free-market theory of managed competition and an overall budget-spending ceil-ing threw the Republicans off, as did his focus on villains. Following the political advice of James Carville, Paul Begala, Mandy Grunwald, and Stan Greenberg, Clinton delivered the message that for "the plain folks, it's greed—greedy hospitals, greedy doctors, greedy insurance companies." The candidate was extremely good at exploiting the "us-versus-them" issue, as a new Kaiser Family Foundation–Harris poll in early October disclosed. On Election Day, the final poll in that health issue series disclosed a thirty-four-point Clinton lead over Bush.[87]

Clinton's presidential campaign determined not only the basic substantive approach he would take to health care as president but also the political strategy he would pursue to achieve his reform goal. Still, voters had ranked health care reform only third in impor-tance behind the economy and the budget deficit, and public support for Clinton's spe-cific plan had been even less impressive. When the three alternatives were described to voters, one-third of those polled favored Bush's subsidy plan for insurance and another third the single-payer plan. Only 28 percent picked Clinton's unfamiliar managed-competition scheme with national budget caps. Analyzing the poll, Harvard health ex-pert Robert J. Blendon wrote: "Clinton has a general mandate for health reform which will expand coverage and contain costs. He does not, however, have a mandate for a par-ticular plan and he faces the formidable challenge of building consensus on a specific health program."[88]

There were other warning signs to indicate that Clinton's health policy was not free of pitfalls. That August, Senator Jay Rockefeller of West Virginia had sent the candidate a memo, which Clinton ignored, warning that any assertion that Americans deserved or had a right to health care would run into a dead end once voters asked how much it would cost, who would pay for it, and whether it would require an enormous new bureaucracy. He advised Clinton not to read too much into Wofford's victory and reminded him of the congressional battle over catastrophic insurance. In October, Magaziner also warned Clin-ton that he would have to find a way to bridge the financial gap between managed compe-tition and a single-payer plan without "falling through."[89] The most serious warning came from Atul Gawande immediately after Clinton's victory. Gawande reminded the president-elect of the importance of the health care issue and the challenge the administration faced. Reform was "at once our most ambitious and most treacherous task," he wrote, with success or failure riding on its ability to contain costs. If Clinton successfully reformed health care, it would rank with the monumental enactment of Social Security more than a half-century before and be a testament to the president-elect's ability to bring about needed change in the face of special interests. The political rewards also would be enormous. With a vibrant domestic economy and a strong America abroad, Clinton "could restore a Democratic lock on the middle class." But, Gawande warned, legislating health reform would be enormously difficult, for it involved restructuring spending in a sector that occupied 15 percent of the nation's economy. The risk of defeat was very great. "We will have to take on extremely powerful and entrenched interests, and navigate through a deeply divided Congress (and that's just Democrats)," Gawande cautioned. "The difficulty is compounded by the fact that we have won a mandate for change, but not one for any specific policy." Gawande was repeating exactly the same point made by Harvard's Robert Blendon, the Public Agenda Foundation, and others interested in health care reform.[90]

Clinton paid little heed to the warnings, turning his attention after the election to executive branch appointments and his economic reform package. But he did entrust Judith Feder of the BBDG to lead a team of transition advisers in developing the new administration's health policy initiatives. Feder's transition team, which included Gawande, divided its responsibilities into three functional categories, budget (headed by Kenneth Thorpe from Chapel Hill); policy (composed of Lynn Etheredge and Stuart Altman of Brandeis University); and public affairs (consisting of Chris Jennings, Bruce Fried, Anne Lewis, and Charlotte Hayes, each of whom had connections to Congress, special-interest groups, or grassroots organizations). Cognizant of Clinton's campaign promise to present his health plan to Congress within the first hundred days, the transition staff worked under tremendous pressure, as it sought to lay "the groundwork for introducing a comprehensive health reform bill as early as the end of March with as much backing from the public, Congress and interest groups as could be mustered."[91]

Given the complexity of the health care crisis and the differences over what and how much the health policy team could realistically accomplish, such a time frame was exceedingly optimistic, but as Gawande wrote to Hillary Rodham Clinton and Carol Rasco, assistant to the president for domestic policy, "Our specific goal was to create a sense of momentum for the Clinton plan." To do so, the transition team would have to persuade congressional Democrats to submerge their differences and participate early and often in developing the Clinton proposals, and to reach out to Republicans who might support health care reform.[92] Not an easy task, as congressional Democrats had just gone through a bruising fight over cost containment that pitted managed-competition proponents against single-payer advocates against the champions of play-or-pay. The transition team had to figure out a way to refocus their attention from their pet proposals to how they could best contribute to the president-elect's plan.[93]

Taking their cue from the transition congressional liaison group, Feder's health policy team met with Senate Majority Leader George Mitchell and House Majority Leader Richard Gephardt, their respective staffs, and with key committees to discuss substantive issues arising from the Clinton proposal. "We have had extremely favorable reaction from the Hill," Gawande reported. "They are desperate to get away from the bickering and are grateful to have the executive branch actively seek their views on key aspects of the proposal."[94]

Thus, even before Clinton's inauguration, the transition team was forging ties in both houses with single-payer advocates, with leaders of the Conservative Democratic Forum, and with potentially sympathetic Republicans, whose support Clinton would need. The transition team also was reaching out to professional and advocacy groups, such as the Alliance for Health Reform, to create momentum for the Clinton health plan; in addition it was building ties to organizations such as the League of Women Voters and the March of Dimes and to minority groups that did not often participate in the health reform debate. This outreach strategy was followed to ensure that Clinton's proposal would survive intact as it went through the legislative process; it produced constructive suggestions on issues ranging from the most efficient operation of the HIPCs to meeting children's health needs.[95] Feder's transition team also enlisted the nation's governors in the policy development process. To divert attention from the transition process itself to Clinton's plan, she and her colleagues engaged the media in "an all out communication effort of the kind that will be needed during the first one hundred days." The educational campaign was necessary, Gawande explained, because few reporters, "least of all those covering politics," understood the complexity of health reform. The results, he reported, had been "positive."[96]

On balance, the transition team's efforts to transform a campaign promise into legislation were mixed. On the positive side, the team had conceptualized and identified the major issues of the Clinton health plan; drawn the executive branch agencies (Health and Human Services, Social Security Administration, and Treasury) into the process; initiated the coalition building that would be essential to the plan's passage and implementation; and focused media attention on the proposal. They also had, for the moment, neutralized alternative Democratic health proposals, as key Democratic legislators (with the exception of Pete Stark of California) agreed not to introduce their own reform bills when Congress assembled in January 1993, and divided the traditional opponents of health care reform. Managed competition had split insurers into different factions and divided physicians over global budgeting.[97] At this point in the process, the administration's task was to build on this foundation, Gawande informed Clinton, to draft a bill of particulars spelling out the details of the president's health plan, its administration, and, most important, its financing.[98]

On the negative side, Feder's team had also generated problems that would have to be addressed. Despite its efforts to keep a low profile, ideological differences over the plan's structure and financing between Feder, a proponent of stricter regulation, and managed-competition advocates like Gawande, Lynn Etheredge, and conservative Democrats threatened to shift media spotlight from the proposals themselves to the turf war going on within the transition team. The divisions worsened after Clinton's victory. Feder, supported by Altman and Thorpe, asked Clinton to abandon managed competition or, at least, to rely much more heavily on rate regulation than he preferred. The request angered Etheredge, who accused Feder of trying to nudge Clinton away from the core ideas he had espoused during the campaign. Feder threatened to resign from the team. Clinton's top political advisers rejected Feder's request even before it reached the president-elect, but this did not end the infighting. Indeed, the press continued to speculate over which policy option Clinton would choose in tackling the $800 billion-a-year health care problem.[99]

As the internal fighting spilled over into disputes over how quickly Clinton could achieve the goal of universal coverage with minimal new taxes and also moderate cuts in existing programs, Ira Magaziner emerged as a leading antagonist in the debate. Magaziner insisted that managed competition combined with strict budgetary limits could wring out sufficient administrative and clinical waste to fund universal coverage. In a confidential preliminary budget document Feder and the Washington budget specialists countered that it might be impossible to expand coverage to the nation's 37 million uninsured without substantially increasing the federal deficit, raising taxes, or imposing sharp price controls on medical services. They estimated that to achieve universal coverage by 1997, the earliest date possible, it would cost $270 billion above what the nation was already spending on medical care. Managed competition, they insisted, would take several years to moderate medical inflation, with most of the interim savings accruing to the private sector rather than the federal government.[100]

Feder's budget specialists had, in effect, presented Clinton with a serious political dilemma: how to square his campaign promise to ensure that all Americans had access to health coverage with the promise that his proposal would control health care spending and save Americans $700 billion by the end of the decade. With health care already accounting for 14 percent of the GDP, Clinton found the preliminary figures "distasteful," and instructed the transition team to consider and calculate the cost of a wider array of options.[101]

The results of the reanalysis were not made public, but the budget controversy came to a climax in a disastrous meeting between Clinton and his transition advisers on January 10, 1993, in Little Rock. After reworking their key assumptions about the impact of health reform on the budget deficit and recrunching the numbers, Feder's budget analysts still came in with very high cost estimates. They concluded that the costs of universal coverage would be felt long before significant savings could be achieved from reforms. If universal coverage were phased in over four years, the cost would reach $91 billion by 1998. Since it would take two to three years to establish the HIPCs, the only way to avoid huge additional deficits during the startup period would be to impose "all-payer price controls." Otherwise the gap might blow the federal budget wide open.[102]

When Feder laid out the reworked costs to the president and his aides, they were furious, especially Clinton, who was being told he could not do what he had pledged during the campaign. Instead of reassessing the political and fiscal risks of pursuing his campaign pledge, Clinton summarily dismissed Feder and her colleagues as too conventional in their thinking to give him what he wanted. In January 1993, he appointed a presidential health task force to pick up where the transition team had left off.[103] It was from that point that Ira Magaziner's star as the key player in drafting health reform legislation ascended. He became the chief proponent of managed competition, which prompted some members of the transition team to suspect that he had engineered the meeting to sabotage Feder and the budget specialists in order to seize control over the policy process.[104]

The budgetary debates were not the only policy issue on which the press had focused. Clinton's loss of confidence in Feder and abrupt termination of the team's work also captured attention.[105] The suddenness with which he acted created a public perception that health care reform was not his highest legislative priority after the budget. Worse, his action did not put controversy to rest; it also brought out from the shadows the simmering contest among presidential advisers and executive branch agencies for control of the new administration's health policy. The irony of this competition did not escape the press. Whereas no one in the White House as recently as a year before had wanted to deal with health care reform, now everyone was reaching to grab control of the process. Besides Magaziner, White House Communications Director George Stephanopoulos announced that First Lady Hillary Rodham Clinton would be "closely involved in developing health care policy with the president and she'll be part of those discussions." Carol Rasco, the president's assistant for domestic policy, told associates that she, too, wanted to be involved. Health and Human Services (HHS) Secretary Donna E. Shalala was equally determined to retain health care policy development in her department's portfolio, where it had been traditionally.[106]

In the weeks after the demise of the transition team and the appointment of the new presidential task force, backsliding inevitably occurred among the legislators and constituent groups that Feder and her colleagues had worked so hard to cultivate. Atul Gawande, speaking for the disbanded transition advisers, advised the head of the new task force to shore up the outreach process, "where we have developed good, open relationships," and warned that "many opponents on the left and right are lying low until they see the Clinton proposal specifics, but [they] plan on an all out fight." A few were building grassroots opposition networks; small businesses also remained fiercely opposed to the president's plan. "The proposal's specifics will also determine whether the current splits will continue or opponents unite against extremely tough reforms," Gawande observed. He urged the administration to continue to educate the public, especially middle-class voters, to support the Clinton plan. Apart from health care professionals, he declared, "big business, minority groups, some consumer groups are only beginning to get educated about the ideas in our plan."[107]

Over the next several months, the presidential task force adhered to some, but not all, of Gawande's advice or the advice of others, especially about the need to forge a co-alition of legislators, media, big business corporations, and middle-class voters. Their support would be critical to the administration's successful passage of health care reform. The particular policy process the task force followed, unfortunately, did not allow adequate time to draft a bill that captured accurately and intelligibly the full intent of the administration's proposals, or one that could survive the legislative course relatively unscathed.[108]

The signal failure of President Jimmy Carter and his embattled Democratic administration to manage the economy had given rise to twelve years of Republican control of the White House. Because of double-digit inflation and budget deficits, Carter procrastinated on his campaign promise to offer a comprehensive health plan until late in his administration. The plan he proposed turned out to be very modest and disappointing to liberal Democrats, whose lack of support rendered it dead on arrival on Capitol Hill. Republican conservatives, by contrast, were united behind California Governor Ronald Reagan and had forged a plan both to win the White House in 1980 and to undo the welfare state.

With the Reagan presidency there arrived an end to responsible conservatism and a turn toward a demagogic exploitation of social suspicion and political distrust. Reagan's New Federalism unabashedly portrayed the federal government as the root of most evils and the source of misconceived programs. The federal government, he argued, had undermined individualism and depressed capital accumulation by throwing tax dollars at liberal social programs that depleted federal revenues and taxpayers' wallets. In lieu of government, Reagan and his conservative followers promoted an unfettered market mentality and recklessly employed inflammatory rhetoric to transform generalized social resentments into focused attacks on government and taxes. His huge budget deficits to build up the military acted as a brake on social policy activism, as he invoked the budget shortfalls to turn aside the claims of the disadvantaged of society. Reagan's foray into health care consisted largely of applying the government's regulatory authority to limit hospital reimbursement and physician fees and, for political reasons, to expand Medicare benefits with the 1988 Medicare Catastrophic Coverage Act.

Eight years later, when Reagan left the presidency, the New Deal welfare state remained essentially intact, but his austere social policies had led to an unprecedented transfer of funds from the social sector to the military. Neither Social Security nor Medicare, or any other major social welfare program, had been dismantled, but Reagan had succeeded in redefining the national political agenda and accelerated the conservative insurgency that had been developing for over twenty years. He had redirected the thrust of both domestic and foreign policy, put the Democratic Party on the defensive, and forced conventional New Deal liberalism into a panicked retreat. The impact of his austere social policies bore down most heavily on minorities, women, and children. This was evident particularly in the health care sector, where runaway costs and changes in the welfare laws contributed to the increasing numbers of Americans who could not afford insurance.

By the end of the decade, nearly everyone agreed that the nation's dual public and private system of delivering health care was broken and needed to be reformed. Policy makers and experts were at times concerned about issues of access and quality, but mainly the focus was on cost containment. This problem generated a broad spectrum of proposals that represented the economic or ideological interests of their sponsors. The fact was that neither Republicans nor Democrats were willing to engage the larger issues of health care reform, which would have dropped below the federal radar screen had it not been for Jesse Jackson, the only major political figure to campaign for the national health plan that had been promised, but not yet delivered, by the New Deal. But neither the political establishment nor the media considered Jackson a viable presidential candidate, and they refused to take up his call for universal health coverage, despite polls indicating that a majority of Americans, albeit unclear about the details, wanted the federal government to establish such a program. Paralleling rising public support for national health care reform, which may or may not have been the same as national health insurance, was widespread political alienation. This was manifested in low voter turnout throughout the decade, particularly among key elements of the working class that traditionally supported the Democratic Party. These voters perceived both parties and government in general as nonresponsive to the popular will on health care reform and other issues.

Nonetheless, Reagan's personal popularity helped to ensure the election in 1988 of George H. W. Bush, who viewed himself as a guardian president rather than as an activist. The Bush administration launched no new health policy initiatives of any consequence, but under pressure from the affluent elderly, it did support repeal of the Catastrophic Coverage Act. A new wave of inflation at the end of the decade, huge budget deficits, and a recession in the early 1990s, meanwhile, refocused attention on social issues, as hardships crowded in on blue-collar and other—including middle-class—working Americans. The absence of guaranteed access to health insurance and health services joined the cost issue in a push for major reform of the health care system. As annual medical costs approached the trillion-dollar mark, nearly 40 million Americans were without medical insurance, either by choice or necessity. The Bush administration could no longer afford to ignore the health care system, which many believed was irretrievably broken, and still remain politically viable. Meanwhile, Bill Clinton, the Democratic presidential candidate in 1992, and major Democratic party analysts believed that health care was an issue that could help take back the White House for a Democrat—and an issue that could define Clinton's presidency.

A centrist Democrat who wanted to make a large impact and a policy wonk who perceived the linkages among the nation's multifaceted health problems, candidate Clinton pledged to make universal medical coverage for every American and legal immigrant one of the major public policy initiatives of the first hundred days of his presidency, but he underestimated the complexity, cost, and political hazards of health care reform.

# NINE
## "COMPETITION UNDER A CAP": THE CLINTON TASK FORCE

Clinton entered the Oval Office facing an extraordinarily poor environment for a social policy innovation of the magnitude and complexity of comprehensive health care reform. The election had focused heavily on the federal budget deficit, and many newly elected members of Congress were committed more to deficit reduction than to health care reform. His majority in the Senate, where sixty votes were necessary to break a filibuster, was extremely narrow. If Senate Republicans filibustered his legislative agenda, he would need the support of every Democrat plus three (later four) Republicans to ensure its passage. There was also the equivocal nature of Clinton's mandate and popular support. As he had received only 43 percent of the popular vote, his authority as president was limited, especially when one considers that in the congressional districts captured by Democratic candidates, the president-elect had often trailed behind them. Political wisdom dictated that one did not build bold agendas on small majorities, and Clinton had no majority at all.[1]

But neither Clinton nor most journalists took note of the difficult political environment within which his administration would have to function. Indeed, Clinton envisioned his task as overcoming an era of disillusionment and antigovernment sentiment and renewing a progressive political tradition that had been stalled since the 1960s.[2] Journalists inside the Beltway anticipated a successful first term, capped by the passage of major legislation to reform health care. There was some substance to their expectation, because a recent *New York Times*/CBS News poll had disclosed that fully 66 percent of Americans surveyed, including conservatives and Bush voters, expected Clinton would make progress on health care reform.[3]

On January 25, 1993, less than a week after the inauguration, Clinton confidently gathered cabinet officials, presidential aides, and the First Lady behind closed White House doors to listen to him discuss his health security initiative. His approach would be to utilize managed competition within a budget to square the policy circle that past presidents had found politically insoluble.[4] The White House press corps was then ushered in to hear the president describe "the massive task ahead." It was time, Clinton declared, as he announced the establishment of the President's Task Force on National Health Reform, "to make sense of the American health care system." He told reporters he would have legislation ready for submission to Congress "within one hundred days of our taking office," and then he startled them when he declared that First Lady Hillary Rodham Clinton would be chair of the task force. Clinton further disclosed that Ira Magaziner, who was fiercely loyal to him and who enjoyed his complete confidence, would head a group of policy experts to advise the task force.[5]

Clinton described his wife as "better at organizing and leading people from a complex beginning to a certain end" than anyone else he had worked with. A lawyer by training, Hillary Rodham Clinton was prepared to mix private talks on health policy with public appearances scripted along traditional lines of presidents' wives as she shaped and sold her husband's health care plan. As dramatic as her appointment was, it was fraught with potentially negative consequences. Because she was the president's wife, very few people in the health care debate openly critiqued her ideas and decisions.[6] One Washington lobbyist observed that she was so thin-skinned, she really believed that "if you criticize one page of a 1,342 page bill you're the enemy."[7] Magaziner also proved to be a major liability. He was an "outsider" with no previous Washington experience and was little trusted by either the Washington establishment or the longtime advocates of health care reform. His jealously guarded access to the Clintons frustrated and angered the special-interest groups, legislators, and other members of the administration who expected to participate in reforming the health care system. Magaziner was derisively referred to on Capitol Hill as the "Iratollah," and ultimately, he bore the brunt of criticism for the task force's delay in producing a timely and viable reform bill.[8]

The task force itself was not a novel idea, but the decision to go that route again may have been prompted by Bill Clinton's reluctance to entrust the policy-development process to HHS Secretary Donna Shalala, whose agency represented the "big government" he had campaigned against; moreover, the HHS had not fully embraced the managed-competition and global-budgeting concepts that Clinton wanted. In establishing the task force, Clinton also understood that reforming health care in so short a period of time was an enormous undertaking, fraught with a high probability of failure, but he believed that time was of the essence. If health reform was not achieved in 1993, it would become politicized in 1994.[9]

Clinton's self-appointed deadline was an act of hubris, given the enormous complexity of the task. Neither he nor his closest advisers demonstrated any real grasp of how long it took to achieve fundamental change in Washington, even with determination, tight staff work, and a realistic timetable. The president had the first, but he was sorely lacking in the last two. A three-year time frame might have been more realistic, as Washington insiders Haynes Johnson and David S. Broder noted, but having elevated health care reform and the North American Free Trade Agreement (NAFTA) to the forefront of the nation's agenda after the budget deficit, Clinton did not think he had the political freedom to ask the American public to wait that long. The cost of his miscalculation would be high indeed, the loss of both his keystone program and Democratic control of Congress in 1994.[10]

Competing for the president's closest scrutiny, but ahead of both health care reform and NAFTA, was the huge budget deficit of $4.4 trillion. Despite doubts from Vice President Al

Gore and Treasury Secretary Lloyd Bentsen, Clinton decided to include health care reform in the budget package he would present to Congress in February. This strategy offered the administration certain advantages, notably allowing Congress to consider health reform under special rules governing the budget reconciliation process. These rules limited debate and amendment, made a filibuster very difficult, required only a simple majority in both houses to pass legislation, and suited the president's larger purpose of moving the national government in a different direction, in much the same way Reagan had in 1981 to achieve the huge shift in spending priorities and social policies at the heart of the "Reagan Revolution."[11]

Once the president made this decision, Hillary Rodham Clinton and Magaziner sought to bring the Democratic congressional leadership on board. Mitchell and Gephardt agreed that postponing health care reform until the second year of Congress, an election year, would be a mistake, affording critics plenty of time to mobilize against the administration's plan. Gephardt bluntly told the president on February 3, 1993, that he would have to throw the full force of his political and moral leadership behind the reform package in order to unite congressional Democrats and break the policy deadlock between the party's liberal and conservative wings.[12]

Two weeks later, Clinton delivered his first budget and State of the Union address to a joint session of Congress. Responding to pressure from key advisers and the nation's governors, who insisted runaway medical costs had to be reined in to reduce the federal deficit, he reversed the political priorities of his campaign in a direction that had a potentially devastating impact on health care reform. Over the objections of the First Lady and Magaziner, Clinton's speech focused primarily on the economy, the budget, and taxes. He did make a brief, dramatic policy link between health care reform and budget reduction. He omitted at their request any reference to raising taxes to pay for the type of systemic reform that would permanently resolve the health care crisis.[13] But to make matters worse, the budget cutters had targeted Medicare and Medicaid savings as a way to reduce the deficit by nearly $60 billion, money that both Hillary Rodham Clinton and Magaziner had anticipated preserving to help finance health care reform. Their protests were again unsuccessful, as Clinton slashed $60.3 billion from those accounts.[14]

The initial favorable response to the president's speech created a false sense of optimism among White House advisers, who were pressing Clinton to follow a two-step strategy: win a great budget victory in April or May and follow up immediately with introduction of the health care bill. Not everyone was so sanguine that the president could score an easy legislative victory. White House aide Chris Jennings warned the First Lady on February 22 of danger signals emanating from the Hill. Senate Minority Leader Bob Dole signaled that Republicans would unanimously oppose President Clinton's budget, no matter how he framed it, and hinted that if Clinton wanted Dole as his partner on a bipartisan health care bill, it would have to be as a separate piece of legislation. But the major obstacle to weaving health care reform into the budget reconciliation process was not the Republican minority leader but fellow Democrat Robert C. Byrd of West Virginia, chairman of the powerful Senate Appropriations Committee. A staunch defender of Senate procedure, Byrd unalterably opposed adding anything to the reconciliation bill that was not directly related to deficit reduction. His veto of the White House's grand strategy ought to have been the signal for a fundamental shift on Clinton's part, but the administration ignored it.[15]

Clinton's tactical blunder in proceeding was a harbinger of other mishaps that cost him political capital that spring and diverted his attention from health care reform. The task force itself also became a liability in the politically charged atmosphere of the nation's capital, because it conducted its work in secrecy. By removing the center of the health care debate from normally open Washington channels into the clandestine task force setting and by willfully ignoring the Feder transition team's cost analysis, which Congressional Budget Office (CBO) investigations subsequently confirmed, the president, the First Lady, and Magaziner had embarked down a treacherous road, for they short-circuited conventional policy-making processes in ways that not only created legal problems for themselves but also cut out key legislators and significant parts of the president's own administration, notably the Department of Health and Human Services, where any plan for health care reform normally would have gestated. They also slighted the traditional Washington pattern of political appointees (many with extensive backgrounds in health policy) and policy networks throughout the federal bureaucracy that would have joined career officials in the HHS, the SSA, and the Treasury Department in assembling the options for HHS Secretary Shalala to review and the ideas of think tank authors, academics, congressional staffers, and health care advocacy groups that would have vetted each draft of the bill.[16] By the time the president acted, the policy would have undergone multiple layers of scrutiny and a coalition of support would have been put in place. Instead, what finally emerged from the task force's deliberations was chaotic and contributed to the president's fumbling away his best chance to produce a bill that Congress would enact.[17]

Magaziner, particularly, wanted the specialized expertise of Washington's health care bureaucrats, but he did not want them or any special interests to write the policy or control the process. He chose to rely on outside experts who, pledged to secrecy, would challenge the conventional views of the health care establishment and force them to document their assumptions. This approach minimized the influence of government officials who were on loan to the task force from the executive departments and agencies and ensured the dominant influence of the managed-competition proponents. Magaziner became the conduit for Alain Enthoven, Paul Ellwood, and others of the Jackson Hole group to make their views known to the task force. Not surprisingly, the theoretical framework of the president's task force began as the purest form of managed competition and reflected the views of the large insurance companies, some of the largest employers in corporate America, the pharmaceutical industry, and some other major professional associations. The appointment of Princeton University sociologist Paul Starr to the task force's working groups reinforced the dominant influence of the managed-competition model at the expense of alternative points of view, including the single-payer approach.

Starr had emerged as an influential voice in health care reform after organizing a conference on managed competition in the critical days following the election, when there was a vacuum of knowledge about Clinton's precise intentions. The Princeton conference became the critical forum for explaining the rationale behind "competition within a budget" and served as a paradigm of policy advocacy.[18] Ten of its participants eventually joined the task force's working groups, but it was Starr and Walter Zelman, John Garamendi's deputy, who had appointed managed-competition theorists from Stanford University to California's health insurance advisory panel, who assumed the influential roles of advising Magaziner and playing "devil's advocate" on contentious issues. Together with Magaziner, they worked to make managed competition the cornerstone of the Clinton administration's health care reform.[19]

Magaziner's use of outside experts and marginalization of the executive agencies rekindled the infighting between the managed-competition advocates and the budget-conscious proponents of regulation. This went on in stormy White House clashes among the task force leaders, political advisers, and budget-conscious cabinet heads.[20] Atul Gawande, a managed-competition proponent, found himself ironically on the wrong side of the divide after HHS Secretary Shalala named him, Judy Feder, and Ken Thorpe to be the department's liaison to the task force. After an initial meeting with Magaziner on January 28, Gawande complained to HHS Secretary Shalala that Magaziner "does not appear to see the staffing [of the working groups] as a shared decision" and does "not [have] a very interdepartmental conception." The liaison team, he continued, had "many concerns from today's first meeting of the interagency task force, but the key problems relate to the potential role of government officials in Ira's work plan." Gawande feared that the policy process (and hence the dominance of the managed-competition model) "will be controlled principally by Ira and those who head his working groups for the major substantive areas." The last was a reference to Magaziner's having asked Starr and Zelman to come to Washington.[21]

To the casual observer, HHS's involvement looked important on paper, but in reality, Gawande believed, the liaison team's influence on policy making would be minimal, since Magaziner appeared not to share HHS's budgetary concerns. This was important, Gawande told Shalala, because "the heads for issues such as cost control and expanding coverage will be crucial in driving the policy," and Magaziner was dictating which HHS officials would participate in the policy process and the extent of their participation. "We need to find a way to give Judy [Feder] a stronger voice (and a voice distinct from others weighing in) on all task force matters, not just personnel," he wrote. Until then, the liaison team would proceed on the presumption that "we have a veto—i.e., we won't sign anyone onto HHS payroll without approval from us," even though it "allows us to look as if we are starting right off with a turf battle."[22]

However legitimate Gawande's concerns, their resolution on terms favorable to Magaziner was never seriously in doubt. President Clinton stood firmly behind him, and he and Hillary Rodham Clinton orchestrated the task force's work, named the heads of the working groups, ignored criticism from executive agency heads and from Capitol Hill, and fended off a legal challenge to its closed-doors deliberations. In doing so, they preserved the final decisions on health care reform for the president and themselves. The outcome proved to be dubious at best.[23]

To make matters worse, the huge advisory body that composed the task force's working groups, which the press rarely distinguished from the task force itself, was of a scope and design without precedent, whereas the secret deliberations of the task force and its working groups upset leading Democrats in Congress. To placate them, the White House rendered the working groups as open as possible to Democratic congressional staff, and Hillary Rodham Clinton insisted that more women, minorities, and proponents of the single-payer model, notably Ellen Shaffer, health adviser to Minnesota's Senator Paul Wellstone, be brought into the process to make the groups more representative of society as a whole. Magaziner then added to the numbers by approaching health care reform as though it were an academic exercise. As the working groups encountered new subjects that might be relevant to the president's proposal, he established separate groups to explore them. Eventually, more than 630 people, broken down into eight "cluster teams" and thirty-four "working groups," toiled day and night drafting a slew of policy options and proposals, and another 1,000 people vetted their decisions before finalizing the Clinton plan.[24]

Paul Starr described this extraordinary, burgeoning decision-making process: "The paradigm was a corporate restructuring or technological innovation that required thinking through innumerable options and suboptions and meshing together previously uncoordinated activities and groups into a coherent plan." The scale of the project was "astonishing even to some of us who had long advocated a comprehensive plan, and rather than being scaled back, it expanded" as new planning groups were added to deal with issues not encompassed in the original grand design. The sheer audacity of the effort was symbolized by the periodic "tollgate" meetings of more than a hundred people, held in the majestic Indian Treaty Room of the Old Executive Office Building, that Magaziner convened to review the working groups' progress.[25]

The working groups, like freewheeling graduate seminars, began by examining the full spectrum of policy options that was consistent with the reform framework Clinton had articulated during the campaign. This "broadening" process was followed by a "narrowing" phase, during which the working group analyses were distilled down to a list of specific options for the president and his closest advisers. The working groups did not make the final decisions about the plan's structure, nor did they concern themselves with the politics of their recommendations, but informal input from single-payer advocates did cause the theoretical framework of the task force to evolve from an almost exclusively managed-competition model to a model of state flexibility in which states would choose managed competition or single payer under equal terms and conditions.[26]

Magaziner stood at the center of the whole process. As decisions and issues funneled from the cluster groups to the working groups up to the task force, he framed the policy questions for the president and First Lady, who rendered the hard policy and political choices. He also instituted a strict protocol to guide presidential briefings of the task force's progress, which discouraged outsiders from gaining access under open-government laws and tightly controlled the flow of information to the president in ways that minimized opportunities for individuals other than he and the First Lady to turn Clinton's mind spontaneously toward a policy option other than the one that had survived the chain of command.[27]

Despite Magaziner's tight control over the process, the working groups were far too unwieldy to be effective vehicles for policy formulation. Their main effect was to push Clinton's proposal in the direction of ever greater detail, as they expended two months plowing through position papers that reexamined old issues, reinvented them, and looked at just about every conceivable policy alternative. The assumption apparently was that if they could figure out everything that was possibly wrong with the existing health care system, they would be able to fix it all at once. HHS Secretary Shalala, Deputy Budget Director Alice Rivlin, and CBO Director Robert Reischauer predicted that Magaziner's absurdly huge operation was not a disciplined policy process likely to produce tangible results or win congressional approval, but they believed the Clintons had tied health care reform—and their political fortunes—to Magaziner, choosing to ignore or minimize contrary advice.[28]

As events subsequently demonstrated, the president, in giving Magaziner a free hand, had created a house of cards wherein the removal of any one card would bring down the entire structure. By mid-April, the working groups were still not at all near completing their tasks, despite the president's self-imposed deadline.[29] James R. Ukockis, senior economist at the Treasury Department, graphically summed up the situation: "My reading of the matter is we have a massive case of policy constipation. We are halfway through the 100-day period, and I am unaware of *any* policy choices having been made to narrow the focus of the work." He attributed the logjam to the "presence of too many academics, whose intellectual interest in the policy issues far exceeds their understanding of the needs of a successful policy-making process."[30] The Veterans Administration also contributed to the delay by studiously ignoring requests for data, anticipating that it would be better to preserve its own autonomous health care arrangements.[31]

With critical time slipping away, Magaziner accelerated the pace, driving the working groups furiously even as he centralized the important policy choices in the hands of a smaller coterie of advisers composed of himself, Starr, Zelman, Rick Kronick, and Larry Levitt. While they were framing the policy options, Magaziner assigned a second group of advisers, seasoned political campaigners, to develop a strategy for building public and congressional support for the proposal, and a third group, composed of representatives from OMB and the Council of Economic Advisers (CEA), to analyze the plan's budgetary impact.

Financing and cost containment, the hot topics, dominated the deliberations of the task force's working groups, where debate centered on two forms of managed competition. The pure, or "hard," version reflected the views of Alain Enthoven and the Jackson Hole Group, whose spokesmen were particularly active in the working groups on Governance of the Health System and Global Budgeting. The proponents of the "soft" view took their main point of reference from Paul Starr and Walter Zelman, who argued, mistakenly in the view of one critic, that their approach to managed competition was a compromise that fell somewhere between the hard version and the single-payer system. However nuanced was the Starr-Zelman approach, both versions of managed competition proceeded from certain basic assumptions. They agreed that the crisis in American medicine was attributable to the lack of competition in the health care sector; that workers were not sufficiently cost conscious about health insurance because their coverage was paid for by their employers; that Americans were overinsured and overused health care resources, a tendency encouraged by fee-for-service providers; that health insurance and health care should be integrated into the same health plans; and that the government should discipline workers as consumers and leave the insurance industry to discipline health care providers.

To achieve cost consciousness, the proponents of the hard version of managed competition argued that patients' cost-sharing had to increase, with large employers paying only 80 percent of the cheapest available plan. The government should also tax all health benefits over and above the basic or benchmark plan. (To cushion the impact on large employers the government would lower the minimum wage by 8 percent.) Not only would consumers pay more for their health benefits, but they also would be encouraged to enroll in the cheapest and most cost-effective basic health plan. Health providers would work in managed-care plans controlled by large insurance companies to guarantee that they practiced in the most cautious, prudent, and cost-savings fashion. Competition among insurer-controlled health plans for employers' premiums would result in less-costly premiums. Small employers and individuals, by contrast, would be encouraged to obtain their health coverage through purchasing cooperatives (HIPCs), which would serve as bargaining agencies with insurers. By pooling several small employers, the assumption was that HIPCs would get a better deal.

Under the "soft" version, the integration of health insurance and health care provision in the same health plans remained central to any reform. Most people would be enrolled in these insurer-controlled plans, cost-sharing would be increased, benefits above those of the benchmark plans would be taxed, and small employers in the HIPCs would choose their employees' plans. Large employers would be excluded from the HIPCs, reducing the population of the cooperatives to small employers, individuals, and Medicare recipients. To outside critics of managed competition, like Dr. Vicente Navarro and single-payer advocates, the soft and hard versions of managed competition were differences without distinction. Managed competition, they said, would result in the vertical integration of the health industry under the control of the insurance industry.[32]

From the start of the campaign, there had been no question that the primary financing mechanism would be mandated payments by workers and their employers. Clinton had favored this approach because it built on the existing system of employer-sponsored health insurance and because, if the plan were properly structured, it would not be necessary to raise large, new revenues through taxes. But since he had never set forth the details of the mandate, they inevitably became the subject of heated controversy once Clinton invited members of his political and policy team to the White House to debate the task force's major recommendations.[33]

These sessions usually consisted of Hillary Rodham Clinton, Magaziner, Treasury Secretary Bentsen, HHS Secretary Shalala, National Economic Council (NEC) head Robert Rubin, Laura D'Andrea Tyson, chair of the Council of Economic Advisers (CEA), and Budget Director Leon E. Panetta. The president's economic advisers were deeply skeptical from the outset about the shape the plan was taking, perhaps none more than Treasury officials. Bentsen joined Tyson and Rubin, proponents of the hard version of managed competition, in expressing doubts about the scope of the plan, the savings that would be realized, and the speed with which it could be implemented. Rubin questioned the plan's impact on the budget deficit, the scope of the benefits, whether short-term price controls were needed, the time it would take to phase in universal coverage, whether the consumer would be given a variety of health plan choices, and how medical coverage of millions of uninsured citizens would be financed. Tyson argued that it might be better to encourage people to purchase their own long-term-care insurance than to establish a new, very expensive entitlement with a huge bureaucracy. Other participants suggested that Medicare clients be required to join managed-care programs to qualify for prescription drug benefits. The controversies were sharp, the disagreements vehement, and few policy issues ever seemed to be resolved.[34]

As the debates proceeded, Representative Dan Rostenkowski, chairman of the House Ways and Means Committee, warned on March 3 that Congress was unlikely to pass comprehensive health care reform that year. The influential Illinois Democrat observed that Clinton's health proposal would be too big and too complex to combine with his economic package, but the White House, once again, ignored a warning flag. The task force, meanwhile, moved on to consider a straight employer mandate, which obligated employers to pay for a portion of their workers' health insurance premiums, coupled with subsidies for the poor to replace Medicaid and a possible cap on the total payments required of an individual or family.[35] What emerged from the working group's deliberations was an extremely complicated and controversial premium scheme that left even supporters of the model uneasy, and Magaziner suggesting a payroll tax to fund the plan. He withdrew that idea after Starr informed him that the political consequences of a tax would be disastrous for the administration.[36]

A proposal for a sliding scale for capping premiums that businesses would have to pay, depending on the number of employees, also proved troublesome. Many health policy analysts criticized it as too generous, too complicated, poorly targeted, or potentially distortionary; some feared the cap might induce larger employers to subcontract work to smaller, low-wage firms. Some presidential advisers insisted that a subsidy was necessary to minimize opposition from small businesses and would be less expensive than the alternative of subsidizing all low-wage firms regardless of the numbers of workers.[37] Organized labor and leading members of Congress, however, would most likely oppose a tax cap that put limits on tax-free employer payments for health insurance. Addressing this issue, Starr wrote to Magaziner on May 17: "We might be left with the worst of both worlds, a payroll levy that antagonizes Republicans and conservative Democrats and the grassroots health reform constituencies. My worst fear is that our plan ends up compromising away enthusiastic support from every side."[38]

Requiring employers and employees to contribute to the cost of health insurance was not the only source of financing under consideration, especially since Magaziner's closest advisers estimated that $30–90 billion in new federal spending would be required to pay for new health benefits and to cover the subsidies for individuals and small firms. The funding might come from cuts in the rate of growth in Medicare spending and an increase in the tobacco tax, but other sources of funding, such as a tax on health care providers, a value-added tax, and a tax on wine and other alcoholic beverages, also received consideration. Sensitive to the political liability of the payroll tax, Starr explained that this was the reason why he continually came back "to a premium-based system, financed by cigarette taxes, providers' taxes, and the tax cap." The task force on this, as on other important issues, eventually left the final decision on funding to the president.[39]

Paralleling the debate over funding was the issue of cost containment, which bore heavily on the deficit. Toward the close of the presidential campaign, Clinton had promised to consider restricting the escalating costs of health insurance premiums if competition failed to slow them down. When the CBO reported subsequently that managed competition would not generate the kind of savings needed to guarantee universal coverage and to meet Clinton's budget goals, the task force had to give premium regulation a more prominent place in its deliberations.[40] This led Magaziner to establish another working group to consider the option of imposing short-term controls on medically related wages, prices, and revenues. David Cutler of the CEA reported on February 20, 1993, that the short-term cost-control group had identified six potential policy options, focusing primarily on hospitals and physicians, "since these are the largest components of spending." The options were to implement nationally uniform payment schedules for hospital, physician, and outpatient care; to freeze all health-related prices and control the "ballooning" effect once the freeze was lifted; to change incentives offered providers who minimized costs; to squeeze additional savings from Medicare; to enact certain tax and regulatory changes that encouraged the shift to managed competition to reduce costs in advance of systemic reform; and to cap insurance premiums.[41]

Each option had advantages and disadvantages, which made it difficult for Cutler's group to reach a consensus. Though the group was acutely aware of the negative aspects of price controls, some members refused to rule them out. "The more free-market among us," Cutler reported, preferred the tax and regulatory route toward managed competition, but the short-term cost-control group decided that further study was needed to determine how the administration could keep hospitals or physicians from neutralizing the effects of a price freeze by increasing the numbers of clients they served. Drug price regulation was another concern of Cutler's working group, and there was "a great deal of interest on this issue," but it received slight attention at the time because, Cutler explained, "prescription drug savings are not likely to contribute substantially to health care cost savings."[42]

Because each policy option was a labyrinth fraught with complexities that required more thorough exploration, the short-term cost-control group was unprepared to endorse one policy option over another. Strict price controls remained theoretically an option, but no one in or out of the task force, recalling the experience of the Nixon administration with controls, was enthusiastic to go that route. Alain Enthoven, speaking for the Jackson Hole Group, informed Magaziner, "The consensus was the price control model can't work" and would "demoralize the best (conscientious, conservative, economical) doctors."[43] Treasury officials also voiced their opposition. "If, in fact, we go forward with a price control program justified by, and designed to obtain, maximum budgetary savings, we may well find ourselves in the position of the general in Vietnam who declared with a straight face, 'We had to destroy the village in order to save it.' It was not a successful formula in Vietnam, and it will not be a successful formula in health care," wrote senior Treasury economist James Ukockis.[44]

Paul Starr also weighed in against price controls, but he acknowledged the *threat* of imposing them might intimidate health care providers to rein in costs. On February 7, he wrote to Magaziner, "So I am not against that idea as a 'club' to give the President political leverage—if, indeed, the political advisers think he can get Congress to give him the authority."[45] But price controls would not produce "big budget savings." The real basis for cost containment, he wrote ten days later, was to encourage development of the HIPCs by easing the restraints on HMOs (compared to other insurers) imposed by the HMO Act of 1973. "The HIPCs represent a redistribution of economic power in the health market— it's their funneling of the money (countervailing power) that will actually make it possible to control spending at the regional level." The important thing, Starr insisted, was "to concentrate power and accountability and hold the HIPCs accountable not just for meeting immediate budget targets but also for promoting the long-run changes needed to put health care on a more economically sustainable foundation." Starr's advice was never implemented.[46]

The fault line dividing Clinton's economic and health policy advisers over short-term price controls reemerged in sharp clashes on other subjects. Most economic advisers preferred a relatively bare-bones package of health benefits with high cost-sharing requirements; health policy advisers advocated a more comprehensive package. The differences were often substantive, but sometimes they were attributable to poor or loosely worded communications.[47] The president's economic advisers, including Budget Director Leon Panetta, understood that the chief determinant of costs was the benefit package: the larger the package, the higher the costs. Starr argued that this was not necessarily so and cited Medicare as an example. Health care costs fundamentally reflected consumer demand. Medicare relied on consumer cost-sharing, whereas HMOs reflected an entirely distinct concept: that health expenditures were better controlled by organizations that were fully responsible for them. Noting how semantic confusion could lead to poor policy choices, Starr wrote, "I believe that in this case, our language is a serious barrier to the message this reform has to convey."[48]

Another point over which economic and health policy advisers clashed concerned subsidies to fund universal coverage. The former argued that subsidies burdened the budget and had to be phased in over time, whereas the latter advocated a shorter phase-in period. Starr worried not so much about the phase-in period but that the size of the subsidies would adversely affect cost containment.[49] On March 26 he also questioned the cost of delaying full implementation of universal coverage. He challenged the common assumption that the faster the implementation of reform proceeded, the more it would cost. He argued instead, "The longer universal coverage is delayed, the greater the delay will be in achieving the economies from a single, consolidated insurance system." The same was true of merging health coverage under workers' compensation and automobile insurance into universal coverage. The Clintons ultimately sided with the health policy advisers on these issues.[50]

Compared to the heated disputes over financing and cost containment, other issues such as administration of the plan and the size of the purchasing cooperatives received relatively minor consideration or were not resolved in any satisfactory fashion.[51] Medicare's future, by contrast, received close scrutiny. Starr and Magaziner were extremely hostile to a proposal that Medicare be made available to the nonelderly through the HIPCs, an idea favored by various congressional leaders and outside policy experts. Its appeal was both political and practical, but Starr argued that Medicare's inclusion would provide no incentive to control costs and would undermine the strategy of managed competition. Medicare's entire history, Starr concluded, "should be a lesson on how not to structure a national health program."[52]

Starr's argument carried the day. Policy planners foreclosed the Medicare route to universal coverage, but as one scholar noted, "The 'lesson' that Starr had drawn from Medicare's history was not the only one available."[53] Despite its imperfections, Medicare was the largest and most popular federal health program, favored by many congressional leaders and health policy analysts, and it was the only one whose infrastructure could credibly form the basis for a broader public system. Starr's critique had omitted mention of Medicare's administrative advantages, nor did he consider the political advantages of ensuring that people would be able to purchase an inexpensive fee-for-service plan. Instead, he simply assumed that Americans wanted a drastic reform of the existing health care system by replacing fee-for-service, including Medicare, with managed competition. Medicare did not fit into the carefully balanced framework of incentives that managed-care advocates envisioned. Starr, like Magaziner, ignored the policy critiques of their own Health Professions Review Group, which concluded that "the exclusion of Medicare from the proposal is not sufficiently justified."[54]

Starr did not entertain the possibility that Americans might simply want to reform a system with which they were familiar in order to have greater access to it, or that managed competition might itself rest on questionable assumptions. The premises that Americans were not cost-conscious because they did not pay enough of their own health costs and that insurance companies were best suited to control costs and quality of care were highly questionable. As one critic of managed competition observed, costs were the most frequent cause of Americans' concern about health care, and the advocates of managed competition were improperly accusing the victims for being responsible for problems not of their making. The premise that insurance companies were best suited to control costs and quality of care also was based on dubious evidence. With 82 percent of the delivery system under some form of managed care, contracted by, controlled by, and/or influenced by insurance companies in 1993, the ability of those companies to control costs had proven to be very weak. Cost increases in these managed-care systems, according to one authority, ranged from 16 to 20 percent per year, close to twice the annual rate of inflation in the United States from 1981 to 1997. This failure to control costs (but success in raising profits) was accompanied by an equal failure to improve the quality of care as insurers micromanaged the physician-patient relationship.[55]

Because the presidential task force conducted its business outside the spotlight and members of the working groups were sworn to secrecy, the press had been privy to neither the direction reform was taking nor the process by which decisions were reached. This lack of information resulted in a great deal of speculation, some of it erroneous. The *New York Times* tracked Magaziner and White House spokespersons zealously, seeking to report every word and nuanced sentence uttered about the task force's progress. On March 23, the *Times* noted that the administration was weighing a proposal to dismantle Medicaid and merge low-income people into the same health network that served more-affluent people; on April 6, it quoted Magaziner as saying that the president would not fund his program by taxing the health insurance benefits workers received from employers. A week later, it reported that the White House was weighing a "penalty tax" on physicians and hospitals to constrain spending; two days later, it asserted that hints of a value-added tax offered a rare public peek into the private conflict raging inside the administration over financing the costly new program. On April 26, it insisted that the task force had tentatively decided to let firms employing more than 1,000 workers serve as their own health insurers and bypass the regional insurance pools that were the core of Clinton's plan. On May 8, it quoted Hillary Rodham Clinton as saying that the president's plan would cover the cost of treating people injured on the job or in auto accidents, implying a merger of health, workers' compensation, and the medical portion of auto insurance into one big system. Four days later, it cited Magaziner as saying that the plan would probably guarantee insurance coverage for prescription drugs and long-term care so that elderly people need not impoverish themselves to qualify for nursing-home assistance. On May 21, the *Times* reported that Clinton's advisers had outlined a proposal for sweeping change in the handling of medical malpractice suits whereby individual doctors would be relieved of legal responsibility for negligence, and patients, instead of suing their physicians, would sue insurance companies and HMOs.[56]

What is one to make of these reports? Interest in health care reform was clearly a burning national issue (after deficit reduction), which accounts for the close press coverage. The task force's confidential deliberations, while probably unavoidable, also spurred the media to ferret out whatever tidbits of information it could, including ideas and working papers that were far from settled policy, and to speculate on that body's likely recommendations. Whether the result of good investigative reporting or by design (and there is some evidence of deliberate leaks), issues discussed in confidence—price controls, the level of the premiums, the payroll tax, the caps on large versus small businesses, so-called sin taxes on alcohol and tobacco, the value-added tax, subsidies, and Medicare cuts—quickly found their way into print. If the press's spotlight put the task force in the public eye, it also allowed members of the task force and the administration to use the media to float trial balloons (such as the value-added tax and Medicare cuts) before the public and advocacy groups, which could then be disavowed if they evoked strong protests.

Press reports of a rift between the president's economic and health policy advisers, though accurate, also were planted deliberately, as budget cutters, proponents of managed competition, and single-payer advocates all maneuvered to influence public opinion. What the press's speculation also indicated was that as the administration's self-imposed deadline for drafting legislation approached, neither the task force nor the president had made many final decisions. The administration had seriously underestimated the magnitude of the task.[57] Nonetheless, Hillary Rodham Clinton took to the road to mobilize public support for a plan that remained a work-in-progress, on February 11 holding the first of a series of teach-ins across the country to humanize the health care crisis and to show that the administration was reaching out to the people for guidance in solving a problem that had bedeviled lawmakers for decades. As her campaign hit its stride, her father suffered a stroke, and she returned to Little Rock to maintain a bedside vigil until he died on April 7. This sad event brought the need for health care reform closer to home, but it also interrupted the popular momentum for reform she was seeking to build.[58]

Inside the Beltway, the First Lady had sought to enlist bipartisan congressional support for the president's plan. She focused her effort especially on Rhode Island's Senator John Chafee, a moderate, who earlier had lobbied his fellow Republicans and the Bush administration for phased-in universal coverage, but it was not until April 30 that she met privately with him. Meanwhile, Senate Minority Leader Bob Dole's staff—most likely Sheila Burke—had passed the word that Republicans were not to meet with her. The ostensible reason was that Republicans wanted to get their own reform proposal in order. When Hillary Rodham Clinton finally asked Chafee whether he would work on a bipartisan health care bill, he declined. He confidently predicted that Congress would enact health care reform within the year, but that it would more closely resemble a Republican plan. What the First Lady did not know was that Chafee had little influence with fellow Republicans.[59]

Meanwhile, White House policy making had gone ahead without her.[60] When she returned from Little Rock, she had expected to quickly wrap up the task force's work and to forward the administration's health care proposal to Congress for immediate action, but senior White House advisers objected. They insisted that nothing should distract from the battle of the budget.[61] The congressional fight over Clinton's budgetary recommendations upset the neat timetable Magaziner had formulated for implementing health care reform. Its success depended on certain actions being taken sequentially according to a predetermined schedule so that universal coverage would be in place by July 1995. The budget fight made it increasingly unlikely that Clinton would be able to send the health care reform plan to the Hill by the end of May, as he had promised.[62]

The success of the administration's reform plan had depended on Magaziner's getting the health bill to Congress in time to fit it into the budget so that the legislature could enact the two as one big package before the end of the year. But major unresolved policy issues rendered it impossible to adhere to Magaziner's time line or to integrate health care reform into the budget bill. The White House had little choice but to announce that the health reform plan would not be released before mid-June, a date that proved to be not only exceedingly optimistic but also vexing to the administration. The blanket of secrecy over the task force's deliberations sprang new leaks that caused irreparable damage. The *New York Times* reported on May 3 that health care costs might increase as much as $100 billion a year. Although the story and the figure turned out to be erroneous, the administration spent days trying to clear up the distortion and never repaired all the damage. Magaziner believed that some officials within the administration were deliberately undermining the task force's work.[63]

The delay, however, allowed Kenneth Thorpe's working group to continue crunching the numbers to produce the best possible figures for health care costs and savings. The figures, Magaziner told the First Lady, would not be available for the president to review before May 17; this delay was to give yet another group of economists the opportunity "to further review the numbers and the economic impact analysis of the plan" before making policy decisions. Sensitive about the delay and the *Times*'s inflated figures, Magaziner told reporters: "As I have consistently said, health care numbers are not exact. We believe we have done the best job possible of understanding and researching them."[64]

The assertion may have been correct, but the more important fact was that both the complexity of reforming health care and the disagreements within the working groups had reduced to a guess any meaningful time frame for the task force to complete its work. U.S. Healthcare's chief executive, Leonard Abramson, who served on one of the several audit teams that reviewed the task force's findings, wrote to Magaziner on May 10: "The proposal needs a focus and identity that is presently missing. It tries to straddle the line between free-market competition and governmental bureaucratic regulation, but does neither one well." This was not good policy, he declared, and warned prophetically, "nor will the merits of such a plan be easy to communicate to the American people or Congress." The proposal was too bureaucratic and added additional layers of expense and inefficiency to the system. "The health alliance concept, if it is to be successful, should aim for structuring competition, not stifling it," Abramson advised.[65]

The May 28 report of a second audit team, the Legal Review Group (LRG), further indicated how the convoluted process Magaziner had established delayed making final policy decisions. The LRG met in Washington for three two-day periods between the end of April and the middle of May and conducted telephone conferences with task force members. But no one ever presented it with a detailed set of decisions to review. Its report described contacts with the task force staff as an ongoing, extremely fluid decisional process: "It was not unusual for the Group to hear from different staff members widely varying, sometimes mutually exclusive versions of essential decisions about reform. At the same time, many other fundamental decisions had apparently not yet been made at the times that the Group met." The report concluded that this high level of uncertainty greatly affected the legal review process "in that the exercise became mostly one of attempting to identify particularly troublesome issues in the general directions in which decisions seemed headed." Of nineteen major legal issues affecting health care reform that the LRG identified, only six fell within its purview, and even in those instances, the recommendations reflected a consensus rather than unanimity.[66]

Paul Starr's memorandum on catastrophic insurance also provides evidence on just how far the task force was from completing its work. Writing on May 9, Starr presented a reasoned argument for excluding such coverage, but it was his questions regarding the "other issues" the memo raised that revealed how few major policy issues had been decided and how many more still awaited resolution. "We have apparently gone from one extreme to the other," he observed. The task force talked initially about a premium-based system with federal subsidies for the poor; now it was discussing a state-based payroll system with *no* federal subsidies for the uninsured beyond Medicaid money. The future of Medicare, likewise, remained undecided. Starr questioned why they were devoting virtually all new federal revenue to the elderly. "If we end up with a program that enlarges Medicare and provides only catastrophic fee-for-service coverage for the uninsured, it will be an extraordinary irony," he wrote. "A lot of people will wonder what we've been doing here all this time."[67]

Indeed, "a lot of people" were wondering exactly that! The task force was at a critical juncture, with no viable plan in sight, and the opportunity to reform health care was slipping from Magaziner's (and the White House's) grasp. It was increasingly unlikely that the selling of the president's plan to Congress and the public, especially to the all-important middle-class voter, could occur even within the new time constraints that Magaziner and the White House established. The Clinton administration was committing the same mistakes that had bedeviled earlier attempts at reform, even though the working group on Health Care Communications Policy had advised the task force in February that health care reform had to pass through two distinct phases. In the first, the White House had to retain tight control over its message, making certain that it alone and no one else—whether opponents of reform, legislators, health care advocacy groups, or labor—defined that message. This entailed a proactive strategy to create a constituency for the president's plan and, if necessary, to bypass Congress and appeal directly to the people. Educating the public to the health care crisis, explaining simply and clearly the

CHAPTER NINE

elements of Clinton's plan, anticipating public reaction to it, and explaining how the government would ease the transition to the new health care system were essential components of that strategy.[68]

The second phase would then begin, with Clinton going on national television to explain his plan and to rationalize it in universal terms so that every American understood both the need to spread the pain and the benefits of helping *all* Americans. This meant speaking candidly about how the health care plan enhanced the quality of life individually and collectively and did not deprive an individual or group of a benefit it was already enjoying, avoiding an exclusive focus on the "have-nots" (the 35 million uninsured) and the urge to criticize a group such as the AMA.[69]

In light of the task force's tortuously slow deliberations, missed deadlines, leaks, bureaucratic infighting, and the subsequent legislative history of the Clinton plan, the working group on Health Care Communications Policy's emphasis on "Responsibility" and its conclusion that "we will need both Presidential and Congressional leadership" rang hollow. Because of the interminable delays in producing a health plan the administration lost the public relations battle to persuade Americans that fee-for-service medicine was in crisis. The public wanted reform, but as pollster Stan Greenberg had warned, for most Americans that meant relief from the high costs of medical care. They did not want to assume additional financial burdens to support those without insurance. In this atmosphere, the public came to see the Clinton reform as threatening the security of the middle class, not enhancing it. In the battle for the American mind, Clinton's failure to win this point proved to be disastrous, as his opponents gradually gained the upper hand.[70]

Frustrated by delay, White House advisers and congressional staffers clamored for the details of the plan. They wanted the numbers so that they could determine its feasibility and calculate the odds of enacting legislation before Congress adjourned. But with congressional tensions over the budget escalating and the stakes in the internal battles over health care reform and the NAFTA issue growing larger, some advisers urged the administration to delay action on health care until the fall when, presumably, both the budget and NAFTA issues would be behind them. NEC chairman Robert Rubin, however, hoped to speed the process along by suggesting that the White House stage four internal health policy debates so that the president could hear the differing views. The first debate took place on May 20 and focused on the comprehensiveness of the benefits package and how long it would take to achieve universal coverage. Atul Gawande developed the case for the more-generous package that the task force was contemplating, whereas Len Nichols of the OMB argued for a more-modest package. Kenneth Thorpe, the HHS economist on loan to the task force, provided the numbers. President Clinton, who evinced a sharp grasp of both the economics and the politics of the choices, favored the more-comprehensive package as consistent with his campaign rhetoric, but he left the door ajar to the cost cutters by suggesting that drug benefit and long-term care for Medicare recipients might be phased in more slowly to reduce costs.[71]

Accounts of that highly confidential debate appeared in both the *Washington Post* and the *New York Times*. The Clintons considered the latter's account seriously misleading. Angered over the breach of secrecy, the president canceled the remaining debates. The leaks, the Clintons and Magaziner suspected, were coming from HHS, which had lost the battle to control health care reform. Four days later, Magaziner met with the president to discuss the respective merits of a payroll tax versus an employer mandate to pay for reform, but he observed that Clinton, preoccupied with the budget bill difficulties, demurred. Clinton, the policy wonk, told him simply to continue working on alternative options. That was the last time Magaziner discussed health care reform with the president until August 6. The task force disbanded officially on May 31, the members of the working groups dispersed, and the date for sending the health bill to Congress was pushed back to July, with the door left ajar for a September submission.[72]

It then fell to the core of the White House team—Magaziner and his closest advisers, the political strategists, and the economic analysts—to finish drafting the legislation and develop a strategy for enacting it. This last task was rendered even more difficult because public confidence in the president's ability to overhaul the health care system had plunged dramatically since the heady days of January. Fewer than half of all Americans in June expected the president to make significant progress on health care reform. A new poll in July indicated that most Americans doubted that the as-yet-unreleased Clinton plan would either lower their health costs or improve the quality of care they received. More significant for the future prospects of Clinton's legislation was the outcome of another poll released on September 26, a few days after the president delivered his major address on health care reform to Congress. Sixty-one percent of the respondents professed satisfaction with their present coverage, although 65 percent were not satisfied with its cost. This cast doubt as to whether the American public really wanted a drastic restructuring of health care, as President Clinton believed, or whether they simply wanted lower costs and increased access to the existing fee-for-service system.[73]

Meanwhile, a contentious Congress was still debating the budget bill, prompting Magaziner to send a memo to the senior White House staff (George Stephanopoulos, Mack McLarty, and David Gergen) on July 22 to warn them that unless health policy decisions were made by mid-August, the administration might not get a bill passed in this session of Congress. Further delay, he wrote, would continue to erode support for President Clinton's plan, even as he sought to allay concern that health care might displace the budget deficit as the administration's number one priority.[74] Gergen preferred to delay action on health care reform until 1994, but Magaziner and Hillary Rodham Clinton, supported by political strategists who had an eye on the upcoming midterm congressional elections, contended that delay would be its death knell. Everyone agreed that the midterm elections were a critical test of both the Clinton presidency and whether a Democratic president and a Democratic Congress could unite to create real change. But senior White House advisers fretted more about the future of Clinton's presidency should Congress reject his budget. That fear passed on August 6, when Senator John Kerry cast the vote that created a tie in the Senate on the budget bill. Vice President Gore then cast the tie-breaking vote for Clinton's budget.[75]

The budget fight had shown just how polarized Congress was, and it raised questions about the prospects for enacting the far more controversial health plan. With the budget behind them, senior White House advisers and cabinet officers, thoroughly exhausted and angry, regrouped to discuss health care. Costs were predicted to rise to 17 percent of the entire budget, a sum that drew the president's anger against those who continued to argue that the administration's proposal treated Medicare recipients too harshly. These included Secretaries Bentsen, Shalala, and the economists who were not persuaded by the 17 percent projection and who insisted that the cost-containment measures should be less stringent than Magaziner was proposing. Shalala, particularly, questioned the steepness of the Medicare cuts, whereas Bentsen voiced concern about the size of the benefits package and the tightness of the caps that would be placed on insurance premiums. With his advisers still unable to agree, Clinton delayed making a decision until after Labor Day, though he did instruct Magaziner to work on the plan further.[76]

On August 16, meanwhile, President Clinton went before the National Governors' Association to offer his broad vision for reforming the nation's health care system. The governors' support was critically important, because the states would have major responsibilities for organizing the regional HIPCs. The governors urged maximum flexibility in adapting the program to their states; they wanted to avoid federal efforts to shift the burden of additional costs to them. Before Clinton could deliver his address, he found himself having to defend his plan against accusations that it would crush small businesses. John Motley, vice president and lobbyist for the National Federation of Independent Business (NFIB), the largest small business organization, had preceded Clinton on the podium and had criticized the administration's proposal on the ground that to mandate that all businesses provide insurance for their employees would push thousands of small businesses into bankruptcy and throw the nation into recession. Motley's speech constituted a declaration of war, even before the Clinton administration had put the finishing touches on its plan. Although the business community was not monolithic, it was the voice of the NFIB that would make the deepest impression when Congress finally debated the Clinton health plan.[77]

When Clinton's turn to speak came, he appealed for bipartisan support to achieve reform and then responded directly to Motley's attack. Emphasizing that employers would be given time to phase in their insurance programs and that the government would ease economic hardships by making subsidies available to small firms, Clinton declared, "It just defies common sense to say that we can't maintain the world's finest health care system, bring costs under control and still create jobs." The president was clearly prepared to fight for his program.[78]

However, when the Clintons returned from vacation in early September, Magaziner still had not come up with a draft of the legislation, although health care reform and NAFTA were the major initiatives on the president's agenda that fall. The White House, nonetheless, announced that the president would address Congress on health care on September 22. The date could no longer be postponed, as pressure was mounting on the administration from different quarters. Senate Republicans were threatening to preempt the president with their own health plan, one that phased in coverage to every American by the year 2000 and curbed health costs without resorting to tight government controls. Senate Finance Committee Chair Daniel Patrick Moynihan hinted ominously that he might support the Republican alternative and called the Clinton plan a "fantasy." Columnist Robert D. Novak criticized Clinton for having failed to exercise leadership over a runaway administration.[79]

As the date of the speech to the legislators drew near, Clinton could no longer to delay making the important decisions, yet his advisers were no closer to agreement. Bentsen, Shalala, Tyson, Rivlin, and Panetta continued to argue against price ceilings on insurance premiums, contending that Congress would view them as proxies for the much-despised price controls; they also protested that the alliances were too restrictive and bureaucratic and that the Medicare cuts too extreme; and they warned that Democratic members of the Finance Committee, especially Senators Moynihan and Tom Daschle, who would have to navigate the reform bill around the legislative shoals, would have difficulty defending it. Not hearing any new arguments, President Clinton finally overruled the combined judgment of his economic advisers and cabinet officials and sided with Magaziner. The Clintons evidently accorded greater weight to Magaziner's judgment than to the president's cabinet officials and experts. Bentsen and Shalala decided afterwards that if Magaziner had not actually manipulated the numbers to fit his preformed conclusions, he had massaged them. When Treasury Secretary Bentsen voiced his misgivings to Hillary Rodham Clinton, her only response was to ask that Treasury's staff assist Magaziner in drafting the bill.[80]

On September 22, the president delivered his speech to a joint session of the House and Senate, promising to every American the security of "health care that's always there." Paying tribute to First Lady Hillary Rodham Clinton, titular architect of the plan, Clinton alternated long explanations of policy with forceful, even angry descriptions of health care woes. He called for universal medical coverage for all Americans, including the 37 million poor and working poor without insurance, and he told the assembled legislators that six principles had guided his proposal: security, simplicity, savings, choice, quality, and responsibility. Every American, he promised, would be guaranteed a generous basic package of coverage, negotiated separately in each state by alliances of consumers, insurance companies, and medical groups. Most employers would be required to pay 80 percent of average premiums. Then, in a dramatic gesture, he displayed the prototypical health card that every American would receive, and he asked Congress and the American people to work with him to enact the most sweeping national program since Social Security in 1935.[81]

Clinton's speech had been infused with an almost wartime sense of urgency as he implored the nation to "seize" this magic moment. Unfortunately, he did not follow up with the introduction of legislation embodying the concrete details of his plan. Clinton had no bill to introduce. Instead, the speech encouraged a dynamic in which major groups across the economic, social, and political spectrum, such as labor and senior citizens, were given certain guarantees and then permitted to bargain for more. Republicans and the AMA professed a willingness to cooperate, but then they complained the administration was relying too much on government regulation, which would increase costs. The leading proponent of the hard version of managed competition, Alain C. Enthoven of the Jackson Hole Group, by contrast, criticized the president's reforms for not unleashing enough market forces to contain costs.[82]

The hiatus between the president's speech and the introduction of legislation dragged into October, allowing interest groups to lobby the administration to make last-minute adjustments. The professionals in the congressional Office of Legislative Council, who were to draft the actual bill, complained that Magaziner had to cease making changes so that they could do their work. The Clintons, meanwhile, continued to express frustration at the delay in putting the proposal into legislative shape. All to no avail. HHS Secretary Shalala declared that the legislation would be submitted to Congress in mid-October but then hedged her statement by emphasizing repeatedly that major financing elements were "under review." The process still was incomplete. The *Washington Post* reported that the date might have to be postponed again because "officials are fighting over the financing and have underestimated the complexity of the task." Without a bill on the table, Treasury Secretary Bentsen postponed his testimony before the Senate Finance Committee. A further blow to the administration came when the General Accounting Office (GAO) reported that there was no conclusive evidence that managed-care health plans saved money, because they tended to enroll healthier people, who cost less to treat. The report challenged the very premise of Clinton's proposal that moving more people into managed care and HMO plans would slow health costs.[83]

Procrastination also generated criticism in Congress and triggered a furious struggle for control of the president's yet-to-be-introduced health bill between Democratic Senators Edward M. Kennedy, chair of the Labor and Human Resources Committee, and Daniel P. Moynihan, chair of the Finance Committee. Kennedy, a perennial advocate of national health security, favored speedy passage of the Clinton plan, whereas Moynihan had doubts about both its need and its timing. He did not believe that the existing system was in crisis; he conceded that it had problems, of course, but there was no crisis. Moynihan believed that America had succeeded in providing a health care system that satisfied most people, and those who were satisfied with the quality of their own care were not interested in having less in order to give others more. The Clinton plan, he feared, had the making of a huge corporate state enterprise. Privately, he contended that even the 15 percent who did not have medical coverage were not deprived, a reference to the fact that no one needing emergency care was denied it, even if those with insurance ended up paying hospital costs for those without it. The real crisis was in welfare, Moynihan insisted, and in spite of Clinton's message, he continued to believe that welfare reform was of the most urgent importance. As chair of one of the important money committees, Moynihan's reservations came back to haunt the administration.[84]

Almost three weeks after Clinton had delivered his speech to Congress, a *Washington Post* poll disclosed that large majorities of the American people doubted that he actually had a plan for curing the medical system's ailments. With the president fast slipping in the polls, a beleaguered Magaziner finally ceased negotiating with the interest groups and allowed the drafters of the bill to do their job.[85] The allegedly finished product, which the Clintons ceremoniously delivered to Congress on October 27 in a bid to "relaunch" their campaign for health care reform, was a document of 1,364 pages. A compendium of everything anyone wanted to know about health care, it was technical, highly detailed, and the farthest-reaching domestic program since the Social Security Act of 1935.[86]

Clinton's health security bill provided cradle-to-grave coverage for all Americans. Through the employer mandate, employers and employees split the expense of insurance premiums, with employers picking up 80 percent of the cost. Additional financing came from a tax increase on cigarettes of $0.75 per pack and a 1 percent payroll tax on corporations with more than 5,000 employees. The federal government subsidized the health costs of unemployed Americans and those near the poverty line. To effect cost savings, the legislation pooled people together in the HIPCs, renamed alliances, to "negotiate with health plans for the best insurance price for the people in the alliance and then offer the plan to everyone in the region." Each state decided how the alliance(s) were administered. Businesses with more than 5,000 workers could create their own alliances, but they still had to pay a 1 percent payroll tax to fund medical coverage for the unemployed and underemployed and to live within the established global budget. Other groups, such as unions and the Rural Electric Telephone Cooperatives, were permitted to set up their own alliances. As Clinton had spelled out in his campaign speech at Merck Pharmaceuticals the year before, the legislation placed a cap on the annual increase of insurance premium rates. Hundreds of other proposals ranging from the funding of abortions to malpractice reform cluttered the bill.[87]

Most Americans had difficulty comprehending Clinton's health security bill, but they found it easy to discover its shortcomings in the ways it would affect their own particular interest. The business community was a case in point. In the aftermath of Clinton's election, there had been a high level of business support for health reform, although there were varying views about the role of the federal government. Large corporations wanted government cost-containment regulations that functioned through existing private markets and that did not interfere with their own private health programs. Small businesses favored reforms to help small firms purchase group health insurance, but they were implacably opposed to employer mandates, which they feared would become an entitlement. Clearly, business was disposed toward some degree of government intervention. It would seem almost counterintuitive then to ask why big businesses, with their resources, power, and familiarity with the federal bureaucracy, failed to translate their social-policy goals into political action. The short answer is that big business managers feared specific aspects of the Clinton bill, once they became aware of its devilish details. Underlying their litany of complaints against the plan was their anger that the administration had not taken seriously their concerns and had not drawn on their health expertise acquired in their decades-long struggle to contain health costs, such as transferring more of the burden of costs to employees and retirees, tougher bargaining with insurers and providers, shifting to more-predictable managed-care plans, and promoting "wellness" programs.[88]

What big business managers saw before them was a needlessly complex plan requiring a new federal bureaucracy. They worried that the Clinton plan had the potential to transform managed competition from a private-sector solution to the first step toward a single-payer system, threatening their own interest in the existing job-based health care system. But their inability to translate a general anxiety over health costs into legislation that more closely suited their interests also arose from the internal dynamics of the business community itself. Big business lacked an overarching organization that could speak with one voice, convey one message, and lobby effectively for its collective interests. Small business, by contrast, which did not have direct access to the federal bureaucracy, relied on representative associations (for example, the NFIB) to speak for them. In an age of computers, e-mail, and faxes, the unified voice of small business came through much more clearly than did the diverse messages presented by individual large corporations.[89]

In taking a position on Clinton's health plan, the small business agenda of limited social policy prevailed over that of the larger corporations. The NFIB, the lobbying arm of small businesses, found the administration's reliance on employer mandates, the standard benefits package, the regulations, and the so-called ceilings on employer contributions objectionable, and it joined forces with small insurers and providers to dominate the policy deliberations of the National Association of Manufacturers, the Chamber of Commerce, and the Business Round Table to fight the Clinton proposal.

The health "alliances," they feared, were a way station en route to a fully government-run system, and this raised the issue of trust. The CEOs, whatever the size of their companies, believed that Clinton would not prevent his plan from becoming the stalking horse for a single-payer, government-run system. The Republicans encouraged this belief by framing the plan in ideological terms as an expansion of big, bureaucratic government. When the administration invoked the ideological language of class warfare to mobilize the masses, it was even more difficult for policy experts in the larger corporations, who might have been sympathetic to health reform, to portray the Clinton plan as a technical fix for economic growth.[90]

Organized labor's response to the Clinton health plan took a different tack from the business community's. Labor in the early 1990s was not of a single mind about health care reform. Among unions such as the American Federation of State, County and Municipal Employees (AFSCME), the Steel Workers of America (USWA), and the UAW, the single-payer proposal and the Canadian medical systems attracted widespread interest. The AFL-CIO, led by Lane Kirkland, and the Service Employees International Union, led by John Sweeney, remained committed to a private-sector solution for health care reform. In order to increase the likelihood of building a consensus with other groups, particularly business, Kirkland and Sweeney wanted labor to refrain from endorsing any specific health care legislation. Otherwise, they feared, labor would be marginalized politically, as the debate over health care unfolded.[91]

The showdown over national health care reform had come in late 1990 and early 1991, before Clinton's election, as several unions pushed the AFL-CIO to endorse the single-payer approach. Kirkland and Sweeney resisted, continuing to advocate some variant of the employer-mandate model as most acceptable to business, even though the bond between employer and employees had disintegrated to the point that the definition of an employee was open to question. Kirkland and Sweeney successfully neutralized support within the leadership of organized labor for the single-payer system by bringing the full weight of the AFL-CIO bureaucracy, Senator Kennedy, and the Democratic Party to bear. However, local labor organizers and rank-and-file unionists still preferred the single-payer solution. There matters stood in the weeks leading up to Clinton's election.

Labor was fragmented and tentative just as the health care issue emerged into the national spotlight, but the leaders, at least, were optimistic that business was prepared to be a constructive partner with labor and the state to resolve the problem of escalating health expenditures and the growing number of uninsured Americans. After the election, labor outwardly closed ranks around Clinton on health reform, but beneath the surface divisions persisted among unions and between the leadership and the rank and file. The tensions surfaced during the legislative fight over NAFTA, which the Clinton administration and business supported and labor opposed, and also over the direction that Clinton's health plan seemed to be taking.[92]

The battles over NAFTA and the contours of the health plan left labor debilitated. The unions split over whether to prod Clinton to pursue a bolder agenda on health care than he had promised during the campaign. Labor's leadership—the AFL-CIO, the AFSCME, the UAW, and the USWA—accepted the political landscape that Clinton and the Democratic Party had defined. This meant abandoning the single-payer approach in a bid to influence the course of health reform from inside the Clinton team. Other unions—notably the communications workers, the ladies' garment workers, and the oil, chemical, and atomic workers—were more willing to apply pressure on the administration. As Clinton's health plan slowly took shape, most of the single-payer unions straddled the fence, remaining ostensibly committed to a single-payer solution but increasingly finding something positive to say about the president's proposal. The president of the AFSCME, long an outspoken single-payer advocate, was instrumental in persuading organized labor to go easy on the administration—even after Clinton made NAFTA's passage a top priority.

Labor's close identification with Clinton's agenda created a serious political quandary for itself, one that cast doubts on its stated quest for national health care. At the very moment that it was waging a fierce fight with business and the Clinton White House to turn back NAFTA, it was simultaneously arguing that business and the administration could be relied on as constructive partners in health reform. NAFTA finally passed legislative muster in November 1993, but by then rank-and-file unionists had been alienated by the great lengths to which Clinton had gone to pass a treaty they considered antithetical to their economic interests. In the fallout from the bruising NAFTA fight, the AFL-CIO leadership had to delay its plan to train union activists on how to educate the rank and file about the Clinton health plan. Despite the president's efforts to calm labor's ire, labor's senior officials gradually distanced themselves from their earlier, glowing endorsement of the health security bill.[93]

The Clintons had presented the legislation to Congress on October 27 with great fanfare, but, in truth, the plan remained a work-in-progress. The administration continued to negotiate changes on just about everything, except the principles of universal coverage and cost containment. The final authorized version of the health security bill of 1993 was not formally introduced in the House and Senate until November 20. Congress recessed for the winter shortly thereafter.[94]

Given the importance of health, it was not surprising that President Clinton chose to tackle the issue soon after his inauguration. Nor should it have been a surprise, given his conservative Democratic Leadership Council credentials, his deep ties to the financial sector, and his lack of any solid political or ideological roots, that his health plan relied heavily on employer mandates. More than twenty-five years earlier, the Democrats, organized labor, and other health reformers had fought against President Nixon's health plan and had advocated an alternative proposal based loosely on the Canadian health system and premised on eliminating commercial health insurers and the linkage between employment and benefits. The health security bill of 1993 incorporated this key provision of the Nixon health plan: the employer mandate, which obligated employers to pay for a portion of their workers' health insurance premiums. The irony was that much of organized labor's leadership and many public interest groups and influential Democrats rallied around a reform plan overtly modeled on the previously despised Nixon plan.[95]

Clinton and his task force remained conceptually, rhetorically, and programmatically tied to a dysfunctional, fragmented system that had left more than 40 million Americans without health insurance or underinsured. His plan, unlike other welfare state policies, did not compensate for inequalities in the marketplace, yet Clinton promoted it in market terms, as "guaranteed private insurance." His tortured rhetoric also camouflaged the true role of government. By speaking as if the plan relied solely on competition in the marketplace, he helped to undermine the foundation and rationale for national health care reform and guaranteed security. To bolster people's confidence in the public sector, he should have explained and defended government's role in promoting social justice and economic security. Health security, like economic security, was a legitimate responsibility of the state. Clinton's critics understood better what was at stake, and that helps explain why they relentlessly opposed the "Health Security" bill.[96]

Clinton's rhetoric spoke, unfortunately, of consumers of health services rather than of citizens contributing to a system of shared savings. The marketplace became a metaphor for the health care system, a figure of speech that defined citizens as consumers and health security as a commodity. In doing so, the administration ignored one of the fundamental premises upon which Social Security rested: it was a system of collective responsibility and social cohesiveness. By commodifying health security, the administration undermined social cohesiveness, and understandably, Americans perceived Clinton's health plan in terms of individual gain or loss, instead of viewing health security, like economic security, as a public good. *Security,* as the administration used the term in the context of health, had little political meaning and even less content.

President Clinton fumbled the most important opportunity in a generation to rectify the deficiencies of the health care system. From the outset, he ruled out of consideration a single-payer approach to reform (for example, Minnesota Senator Paul Wellstone's health security bill) in an attempt to deflect the opponents of reform from appealing to public dread of government. In a sanguine view of the future, his administration's bill promised a great deal, but because Clinton did not challenge the traditional linkage between health benefits and jobs, the struggle over employers' inclusion or exemption played out in the task force's deliberations. Indeed, the Clinton health plan linked the future of health care once again to the balance of power in the political economy. The issues in debate were pretty much the same as they had been two decades earlier: how to effect universal coverage and retain the employer mandate; whether to focus initially on the health needs of the middle class or the disadvantaged and those whose links to the labor force were irregular; whether to rely on managed competition or some other mechanism to lower costs and lessen the direct role of government; and how to avoid having cost containment perceived as health care rationing.[97]

The administration would soon discover that its answers to these issues had made it difficult to sell the legislation to Congress, the private sector, and the electorate. By late November 1993, the economic recession had moderated, popular support for action was diminishing, and the long-delayed plan had come under mounting criticism from both the Right and the Left. The health security bill had no coalition to defend it. President Clinton seemed unable to explain it, and Republicans were looking ahead to the next elections.[98]

# TEN
## CLINTON, CONGRESS, & THE
## GREAT HEALTH CARE WAR

Health and Human Services Secretary Donna E. Shalala called President Clinton's initiative to reform health care the last great social policy of the century. Even if this claim was exaggerated, Clinton waged one of the most active and sustained presidential campaigns ever conducted in support of a single social issue, and his was undoubtedly the boldest attempt to establish national health security in the United States. As the health security bill of 1993 worked its way through Congress, Clinton envisioned compromise changes, but the inescapable contradictions that existed between the omnibus policy-planning effort the president had established inside the executive branch and the utterly unmanageable legislative-political processes through which the bill had to navigate before it became law doomed this last serious attempt to bring national health security to all Americans. In the process, Clinton's struggle to legislate health care reform revealed much about the politics of divided government in the late twentieth century: the apparent end of the New Deal–Great Society approach to governance, the collapse of the liberal democratic coalition that had supported it, and the high-stakes politics of health care reform. The forces that derailed this particular legislation also provide insight into the persistent political and policy battle that has derailed health care reform in the post-Clinton era and helps us to better comprehend why national health security has proven to be such a potent idea, but one seemingly impossible to accomplish.

The presidential task force's procrastination in developing the health security bill had been one, albeit a very sharp, tip of an iceberg that threatened to sink the bill and the Clinton administration, but another obstacle was the congressional leaders on whom the president relied to navigate his bill around the legislative shoals. The Democratic leadership was generally skeptical of managed care as embodied in Clinton's reform initiative, and rank-and-file Democrats who might have been more natural allies of the president, such as Congressman Jim Cooper of Tennessee and members of the Conservative Democratic Forum, were of little help to the administration. They, too, either did not share Clinton's goal of universal coverage or did not hold influential positions within the legislative hierarchy. Further contributing to the president's problems were a sizable number of legislators, about fifty-eight in all, who advocated a government-financed national health system, which represented a significant philosophical challenge to Clinton's market-based overhaul of health care. On March 3, 1993, well before Clinton's proposal had become a plan, much less a bill, these Democrats had introduced rival legislation to make health care a guaranteed right for all citizens and illegal aliens.[1]

Thus matters stood in January 1994, when the 103rd Congress reconvened. The president was in the difficult position of trying to gain the support of the powerful committee chairs while not alienating the moderates whose votes he needed to pass the "Health Security" bill. His legislative strategy depended on holding almost all liberal and moderate Democrats, winning a significant number of conservative Democrats, and attracting fifteen to twenty moderate Republicans in the House and eight to ten in the Senate. The strategy's weak point was the lack of consensus on how best to assemble the bipartisan majority: whether to begin from the center by writing a bill that appealed to conservative Democrats and moderate Republicans (and informing liberals that this was the best health care reform bill that could be obtained) or to start from the left and move as far to the center as needed to get a majority.[2]

Mack McLarty, the White House chief of staff, and presidential counselor David Gergen made a clear case for the middle-of-the-road strategy, citing as precedent the legislative histories of Social Security, civil rights, Medicare, and the Reagan administration's catastrophic insurance law. Each had become law by virtue of a bipartisan majority of Senate Democrats and Republicans who represented the powerful consensus of the center, the middle ground where the successful legislative battles were fought and won. A bipartisan solution, McLarty argued, was good public policy and good politics, but other prominent Democrats, including Senator Kennedy and Majority Leader George Mitchell, dissented. They argued that it would be better to cobble together a Democratic majority before approaching moderate Republicans. The Democratic leadership of the House rejected the centrist strategy even more vigorously, preferring first to unite Democrats and then to negotiate with Republicans. If the latter proved as recalcitrant as expected, they would bypass them completely.[3]

Magaziner sided with the "start left, go center" voices, recommending that the president adhere to his reform framework but load it with provisions such as larger HIPCs and more generous benefits to attract congressional leadership support.[4] Once Clinton had the chairs' support, he could scale back his proposal to secure the votes of congressional moderates. The important point, Magaziner and Hillary Rodham Clinton believed, was to achieve a consensus Democratic position no later than spring 1994. This would give the Democratic leadership time to negotiate with Senate Republicans to secure the sixty-one votes needed to break a filibuster and put a bill on the president's desk. Their arguments eventually carried the day, but this "bridge to compromise," which preserved both managed competition and global budgeting, was one that not enough Democrats and no Republicans were willing to cross.[5]

President Clinton also contributed to the failure to enlist bipartisan support for his reform plan when, in his State of the Union Address of January 25, 1994, he promised to veto any bill that did not provide universal coverage, a threat that contradicted an earlier pledge to remain flexible on almost every aspect of reform.[6] Intended to reassure liberal

Democrats that he would not accept a conservative compromise, the veto threat ignored the advice of centrist legislators and health policy analysts who argued that reform should be accomplished carefully and incrementally.[7] The veto pledge not only glossed over fundamental differences within Clinton's Democratic majority, but it also restricted the congressional leadership's maneuverability in forging a compromise bill that would be a significant, if partial, step toward broader coverage and cost controls. The ensuing fallout was a political disaster of enormous consequence for both Clinton and the Democratic Party in Congress.[8]

Some Democratic legislators wanted initially to write the health bill in an ad hoc supercommittee of the senior members of the three major subcommittees of the House with principal jurisdiction over health, but Speaker Tom Foley of Washington discouraged such talk, fearing it would create problems with the committee chairs. Once the supercommittee idea was discarded, only two House committees could write a bill that would pass the House: Ways and Means and Energy and Commerce.[9] John Dingell, Jr., chair of the latter, volunteered to be the point man for the House's effort, even though he personally favored a single-payer, government-run insurance program. But with no public or legislative consensus on the questions of who would pay, how much, and who would get what, Dingell knew it would be a difficult assignment. He also knew that many of the twenty-seven Democrats on his committee, including John Cooper of Tennessee, had ideological or constituency problems with the Clinton plan, which required a united front to pass. Without Republican votes, he would be hard-pressed to win conservative Democrat John Cooper's vote, much less twenty-three of the twenty-seven Democratic votes needed to report out a bill. Despite the obstacles, the administration counted heavily on Dingell to broker a version of the president's plan.[10]

When the health security bill came before his committee, Dingell referred it to California Representative Henry Waxman's Health Subcommittee, with a deadline for action that would enable the full committee to bypass the subcommittee if Waxman could not round up enough votes to report a satisfactory bill. Privately, Dingell thought Clinton might have to settle for a "good start" and the hope that a larger congressional victory and a clearer mandate in 1996 would enable him to enact the rest of his plan.[11] Dingell had cause for concern: on October 6, 1993, Cooper and Iowa Republican Fred Grandy had introduced a bipartisan managed-care bill that did not include an employer mandate and that terminated the employer's unlimited right to deduct the cost of health insurance purchased for his employees, leaving those benefits tax-exempt to the workers themselves. The Cooper-Grandy bill posed a formidable threat to Clinton's plan, because it was a concrete piece of legislation, whereas Clinton's plan still remained just that, a plan. Not only did the Cooper-Grandy bill have the bipartisan support McLarty and Gergen had urged, but with twenty-six Democrats and eighteen Republicans cosponsoring it, it also had momentum. The U.S. Chamber of Commerce endorsed it as a "starting point" in health care reform. What the Cooper-Grandy bill did not have was the endorsement of Dingell or key House Republican leaders, and that eventually proved fatal.[12]

In the interim, as the White House and congressional leaders scurried to line up votes for the administration's proposal, House Minority Whip Newt Gingrich decided that there would be no Republican support for the president's legislation. Gingrich believed that the Democrats, particularly Hillary Rodham Clinton, were philosophically committed to a government-controlled, left-wing vision of America. Pragmatically, he also viewed Clinton's health security plan as a political instrument for scoring Republican victories in the midterm congressional elections and in the presidential election two years later. With control of both Congress and the White House at stake, Gingrich had no interest in compromise and excoriated the administration's bill as symbolic of big government run wild, which required a Republican Revolution to tame it. Gingrich's strategy had the support of his former House colleagues, conservative Senators Trent Lott of Mississippi and Phil Gramm of Texas. The intensity of conservative pressure also extended to any Republican alternative and forced Senate Minority Leader Bob Dole, a presidential hopeful with a long-standing interest in health care, to abandon moderate Republican reformers and to participate in Gingrich's effort to rout the president.[13]

While both sides maneuvered to gain the upper hand, a frustrated Dingell, after several unsuccessful attempts to win over fellow Democrat John Cooper with private concessions, gave up and, in late March, focused his energy on fending off another bipartisan minimalist bill. Introduced by Florida conservatives J. Roy "Doc" Rowland, a Democrat, and Michael Bilirakis, a Republican, the Rowland-Bilirakis bill allowed individuals, including those with serious health problems, to purchase insurance, permitted small employers to form voluntary purchasing groups, expanded community health centers for the indigent, and limited malpractice suits, but it included no provision to pay for these changes and offered no additional coverage of the uninsured.[14] The Rowland-Bilirakis bill picked up seventy cosponsors, half from each party, and by May, it had virtually displaced the Cooper-Grandy bill. For legislators who were opposed to employer mandates, the Rowland-Bilirakis bill was an attractive alternative to Clinton's plan.[15]

After the Easter recess, Dingell directly intervened in the working of Waxman's Health Subcommittee in a desperate attempt to have a majority report something that resembled the White House's proposal. With his own reputation on the line, he made concessions and other backroom deals to line up twenty-two of the twenty-three votes he needed to report a bill. His search for the last vote focused on the problematic Jim Slattery of Kansas. An announced candidate for the governorship of a conservative state that also was the home of presidential aspirant Bob Dole, Slattery came under fire from the National Federation of Small Businesses and two of the state's largest employers, the Hallmark Card Company and Pepsico, which threatened to withhold contributions to his campaign if he voted for Clinton's health security plan. On April 21, Slattery informed Dingell that he would oppose any bill containing an employer mandate.[16]

Neither Dingell's concessions to the small business lobby nor pressure from the White House, Speaker Foley, and health reformers succeeded in winning over Slattery's vote, and a desperate Dingell was forced to turn once again to Congressman Cooper. Dingell offered to provide the votes needed to report the Cooper-Grundy bill as a floor amendment to the administration's bill in exchange for Cooper's vote to report out the president's bill, but Cooper turned down the deal in late May, terming it a "procedural fix" that ignored the substantive issues. Four weeks later, Dingell conceded defeat. He notified Speaker Foley that his committee was at an impasse. Ironically, just as Dingell threw in the towel, the Education and Labor Committee was reporting out two health reform bills: the Clinton plan and a single-payer plan. The bill of the Education and Labor Committee, a liberal bastion unrepresentative of the political composition of the House, also went nowhere.[17]

Health care reform fared no better in the Senate, where the majority Democrats still were wrestling with the strategy of whether to begin from the center to write a bill to attract bipartisan support or to start from the left and move toward the center as needed to get a majority. Unable to resolve the question, Majority Leader Mitchell assigned Clinton's plan to two different committees, each chaired by strong but different personalities who had their own ideas on how best to proceed. The Finance Committee, chaired by Daniel Patrick Moynihan and on which sat Republican presidential hopeful Bob Dole, had primary jurisdiction, but to avoid embarrassing Senator Ted Kennedy, a longtime crusader for universal health coverage, Mitchell also assigned the Clinton plan to the Labor and Human Resources Committee, which Kennedy chaired. This division of the Democrats' energies contributed to the bill's undoing.[18]

The seventeen Democrats and Republicans who composed the Labor and Human Resources Committee were far more liberal than Moynihan's Finance Committee. Kennedy was confident that he could report a bill that contained the essential elements of Clinton's plan and was even willing to convene his committee during the Christmas recess in order to be ready to report a bill to the floor of the Senate on the first day of the new legislative session. But Mitchell knew that the Kennedy committee's track record did not lend itself to optimism; it had reported out health bills in the past, only to see them die on the Senate floor for lack of support. But he also feared that Moynihan, whose doubts about health care reform were well known, would be offended by a preemptive strike and prevailed on Kennedy to hold back.[19]

Kennedy would inevitably collide with Moynihan, who insisted that the Democrats, *before* bringing a reform bill to the floor for a vote, first had to build a consensus for the president's plan by securing a bipartisan supermajority of senators. Only a bipartisan effort would secure passage of health care reform, Moynihan argued, and the best way to attain the eighty votes needed to act was to put unrelenting pressure on Republican Bob Dole. This pressure would deprive Dole of the power to decide what kind of reform would be enacted. Mitchell agreed, but felt he could not impose his will on his fellow Democrats. This left Moynihan free to pursue a deal with Dole, even as the Kennedy-sponsored administration bill moved steadily through the Labor and Human Resources Committee.[20]

The odds of Moynihan's enlisting Dole's cooperation were dubious at best. Despite the minority leader's long-standing commitment to health care reform, he was a presidential contender leading a Senate Republican Party that was more fractious and more conservative than at any time in recent memory. Dole's difficulties with the right wing of his own party became clear on the weekend of March 4 and 5 when Republican members of the Finance Committee caucused privately in nearby Annapolis to formulate a Republican alternative to Clinton's plan. The meeting degenerated into chaos when conservative Republicans, who were neither members of the Finance Committee nor senators, stormed the conference and seized control of the deliberations. Annapolis demonstrated to Dole how precarious his presidential ambitions would be should he enter into any compromise.[21]

In this atmosphere, it was unlikely that a compromise bill would emerge from the Finance Committee, which held its first closed-door session on April 19, 1994, to discuss how to finance the president's program, one of the main issues that divided Democrats and Republicans. Committee Republicans firmly opposed tax increases and requiring employers to pay for the health care reform. As Moynihan feared, the Republican position resonated with many Americans who strongly endorsed the principles of universal coverage and employer mandates but whose support quickly eroded if they thought they would be required to pay more taxes or feared the employer mandates would lead to the loss of jobs. Moreover, committee Democrats were far from united even before Moynihan's doubts about health care reform became public.[22]

As the committee process slowly moved along, opposition to mandates of any form grew. Dole signaled Moynihan privately that he wanted a compromise of some sort, but as he did that, pressure from conservative Republicans mounted. On May 31, six influential conservative activists sent an open letter to Dole and Gingrich, warning that any compromise on behalf of big government would lead to the loss of grassroots support in 1996. The real target of their missive was presidential hopeful Bob Dole, who got the message. On June 11, he raised the specter of a filibuster to kill any legislation requiring employer mandates and threatened to make the issue a focus of the congressional elections in November.[23]

Two days earlier, Kennedy's committee had reported out a strong version of Clinton's plan by a vote of eleven to six, with lone Republican Jim Jeffords of Vermont endorsing it. Calling for universal coverage by January 1, 1998, the Kennedy-sponsored bill came amid mounting evidence that the opponents of reform were better organized, better financed, and more highly motivated than the supporters.[24] The president, nonetheless, remained publicly optimistic as he reaffirmed his commitment to reform and renewed his pledge to veto a bill that did not guarantee universal coverage. Hillary Rodham Clinton reinforced that pledge, telling health care advocates that the president would veto a proposal by Cooper and Senator Dave Durenberger to provide 91 percent coverage. Privately, the Clintons grew increasingly pessimistic that an acceptable bill would emerge from the Senate, even as Magaziner orchestrated a new White House push. In a memorandum to the president, Magaziner urged Clinton to invite Chafee, Durenberger, and Danforth, the moderate Republican members of the Finance Committee, to the White House to inquire whether they would break ranks with their fellow Republicans and bargain in good faith for universal coverage. The political risk in extending the invitation, Magaziner warned, was that they might demand that Clinton disavow his particular plan and accept one that did not include universal coverage. Magaziner's desperate suggestion went nowhere.[25]

Meanwhile, on the same day that Kennedy's committee reported out Clinton's plan, Moynihan introduced his own version of it, knowing Clinton's plan had no Republican support and significant Democratic opposition. The Moynihan bill contained an employer mandate for all businesses with more than twenty workers, extended the mandate to smaller firms unless they voluntarily covered their employees within five years, trimmed Clinton's benefits package, continued to seek extensive new taxes, and levied a tax on health insurance premiums, with the proceeds going to teaching hospitals and academic health centers. This last provision greatly favored his own constituents because of the large concentration of both in New York. On June 14, he and Oregon Republican Robert W. Packwood met with Clinton. Packwood had endorsed mandates in the past but was under pressure from the NFIB to oppose them, and no longer did so. Possibly seeking to curry favor from fellow Republicans against sexual harassment charges, he told Clinton bluntly that the votes for reform were not there—not for mandates, not for universal coverage, not for alliances—and that conservative Republicans were convinced they could win at the polls in November if they did nothing about health care reform.[26]

Clinton's own efforts on June 15 to persuade Republican moderates to compromise also failed. Durenberger, who was monitoring changes in the health care marketplace, insisted that any plan had to recognize the realities of the private sector.[27] Citing statistics, he insisted that Clinton's plan was unworkable and would upset market forces that had drastically reduced the rate of medical inflation over the past two years. Those forces were accelerating, as formerly autonomous hospitals and physicians were hastening to form their own networks of integrated providers rather than wait to be swallowed up by HMOs invading their territories. Business delighted in the new competition, Durenberger noted, citing one survey of large firms that revealed that premium increases had fallen from 14 percent in 1991 to 6 percent in 1994. Market forces, Durenberger reiterated, had reduced pressures for rapid or large-scale reform and cast doubt on the administration's contention that health care was in "crisis."[28]

Even if Durenberger and other moderate Republicans had been inclined to compromise, they would have still had to return to a Senate that was increasingly hostile to bipartisan cooperation, torn by the same ideological warfare that wracked the House. Only now, Republicans other than Gingrich sensed the tantalizing possibility of winning control of Congress by denouncing Clinton's health plan as big government and Democratic liberalism run amok. In this highly charged partisan atmosphere, moderate Republicans were themselves under assault from the party's right wing and special interests urging them not to cooperate. The Health Insurance Association of America (HIAA) was spending $14 million to market the infamous "Harry and Louise" television ads that helped to destroy middle-class Americans' confidence in Clinton's health plan.[29]

The partisan mood of Senate Republicans became manifest on June 29, when Senator Dole offered a minimum standard benefits package that firms would be urged, but not required, to offer workers. Dole's proposal contained no timetable for insuring everyone and no provision for additional federal subsidies to the uninsured until savings first were achieved in Medicare and Medicaid. Although Dole's minimalist proposal was much closer to the Rowland-Bilirakis bill than to anything he, Chafee, or Clinton had originally conceived, it gained the endorsement of forty of the forty-four Republican senators and the major business, health, and insurance lobbies.[30] Its timing coincided with Moynihan's long-awaited bill, and there was some expectation a compromise could be found. But moderate and conservative Republicans immediately dismembered the Moynihan bill, especially the triggered mandates and other features the president wanted. As were the moderate Republicans, Moynihan was caught in the crosscurrent of competing political forces, sponsoring a reform that had no bipartisan support. By a twelve to eight vote on July 2, the Finance Committee reported out Moynihan's bill, but it had been so eviscerated that it failed to meet the president's minimum goal of guaranteeing universal coverage. Even Senator Jay Rockefeller of West Virginia, perhaps the most ardent supporter of health care reform, voted against it. Clinton and Magaziner were totally frustrated with Moynihan and the Finance Committee, realizing that there was no possibility even of a compromise "Moynihan-Dole" reform bill.[31]

After the Finance Committee's action, Democratic congressional leaders joined with the president at a late-night White House meeting on July 21. They warned Clinton that he would have to make real concessions on employer mandates and to small business in order to enact health care reform. He agreed, and Senator Majority Leader George Mitchell, after taking political soundings of the different factions of Senate Democrats, leaders of organized labor, the AARP, consumer groups, and hospital and nursing associations, unveiled the outline of a rescue bill that he would introduce in the Senate to accompany a similar House bill that Majority Leader Gephardt had adapted from the Ways and Means Committee's bill. The bill required employers to provide health coverage to 95 percent of the population by the year 2000, with the remaining 5 percent covered at an unspecified distant date, made a major concession to small business by exempting any employer with twenty-five or fewer employees (the great majority of small firms) from having to provide coverage, and abolished Medicaid, rolling its recipients into the private sector. Mitchell's bill was a last-ditch effort to break out of the impasse and to forge a bipartisan compromise by proposing a voluntary system built on the private insurance market. It also was far less bureaucratic and government intrusive than Clinton's plan and substituted for the president's proposal language from an earlier Chafee health plan.[32]

Mitchell and Gephardt formally introduced their bills (S. 2357 and H.R. 3600) in their respective chambers on August 4, with debate scheduled to begin in the Senate five days later. The president, in an orchestrated response, praised the Mitchell-Gephardt rescue bill, declaring that those who were fighting for universal coverage were fighting for the middle class. But in a prelude to the difficulties that lay ahead, Senator Dole castigated the rescue bill as "warmed-over Clinton," whereas conservative Republicans stepped up their ideological assault, accusing the rescue bill of opening the door to socialized medicine. On August 5, House Speaker Foley informed reporters that he and Mitchell had notified all members of Congress to delay their summer vacations until after the rescue bill came to a vote.[33]

While the Democratic leaders were pursuing the rescue bill, White House strategists turned their attention to a crime bill pending before Congress to which House and Senate conferees had seemingly agreed. Their expectation was that Senate and House leaders, prior to taking their summer break, would rally their Democratic majorities for final action. The House vote on the rescue bill would follow five full days of debate beginning August 15, after passage of the crime bill. In this way, each member of the House would be on record before Congress recessed as either supporting or opposing health care reform. The Democrats' strategy followed this script, until Newt Gingrich struck. Gephardt introduced his bill, but Gingrich attacked not the rescue bill but the crime bill, even though most House and Senate Republicans had voted for separate versions of it months earlier. With help from lobbyists of the National Rifle Association, Gingrich suddenly threw up obstacles to the compromise the conferees had forged. As Gingrich's strategy unfolded, it became clear that he intended to defeat health care reform by blocking the crime bill, which preceded it on the legislative calendar. This parliamentary tactic would preclude a vote on the rescue bill, close down Congress, send legislators back to their home districts, and deny Democrats the opportunity to record a vote on health reform before the fall elections.[34]

Gingrich's ambush relied on exploiting ideological divisions between liberal Democrats, particularly members of the Black Caucus, who wanted to modify the crime bill's tough death penalty provisions, and conservative Democrats, who adamantly opposed its gun control provisions. His bold strategy left Democrats paralyzed and in disarray; not even President Clinton's attempt to appease the liberals by promising to increase spending on some inner-city social programs for youths could persuade Democratic legislators to close ranks. Instead, his offer provided Republicans with further ammunition for denouncing the Democrats' "old-fashioned pork barrel programs."[35] In a bid at damage control, Foley and Gephardt decided on August 11 to bring the crime bill before the full House for debate and a vote, a procedural move to clear the calendar for debate on the health bill four days later. That maneuver failed when the Democratic-controlled House voted it down. Although eleven moderate Republicans voted with the Democrats, fifty-eight conservative and liberal Democrats bolted their party to vote with the opposition Republicans. With this stunning desertion, the Democratic leadership lost control of the House, marking the beginning of the party's unraveling of congressional and presidential power.[36]

After that crushing defeat, senior White House aides Leon Panetta and Harold Ickes went to Foley's Capitol office to meet with House Democratic leaders. After conferring for two hours, they crossed the Capitol to Senate Majority Leader Mitchell's office to resume their deliberations. Emerging four hours later, they made no effort to disguise the enormous defeat they had suffered. They decided to postpone health care indefinitely in the House so that the leadership could reopen negotiations on the crime bill with dissident House Democrats and the few Republicans whose votes would be crucial for passage.[37]

The Senate, meanwhile, passed the crime bill on August 25, but by then, health reform was dead in the water in the House and delay and obstruction continued to hobble it in the Senate. There, the majority Democrats were unable to close ranks in the face of withering Republican opposition. After four days of assaults on Mitchell's rescue bill, the majority leader threatened on August 15 to keep the Senate in round-the-clock session until Republicans agreed to cease the rhetoric and begin voting. Senator Bob Kerrey, convinced that most Nebraskans did not want Congress to do anything about health reform, suddenly broke with the administration, causing other centrist Democrats to scurry furtively into Republican John Chafee's office in search of a bipartisan solution.[38] Three days later, the Democratic leadership's private luncheon degenerated into a sharp clash as Kerrey and Arizona Senator Dennis DeConcini, ignoring the objections of Kennedy, John Glenn, Christopher Dodd, and others, strongly criticized the rescue bill and warned that the party would lose the Senate if it persisted in pushing it to a vote.[39] On August 19, a bipartisan group of middle-of-the-road legislators, self-styled the Mainstream Coalition, led by Chafee and Louisiana Democrat John B. Breaux, produced an alternative to the rescue bill. This new bill financed coverage for 92 percent of the population by imposing taxes on cigarettes, high-cost health plans, and cutting Medicare.[40]

Despite all its flaws, Paul Starr of the presidential health task force characterized the Mainstream Coalition's bill as a historic advance. Though it went far beyond what conservatives would accept, unfortunately, it did not go far enough for liberals. Both sides immediately disavowed the legislation and never accorded it a proper hearing. Magaziner, at that point, concluded that neither the rescue bill nor any other compromise bearing similarities to Clinton's plan would pass muster, and he conveyed his belief to the First Lady. He subsequently informed the president that the administration could no longer count on the support of its own Democratic-controlled Congress. They had lost the battle, Magaziner observed, but they would continue to fight for a compromise.[41]

With Democrats in disarray, neither the Senate nor the House came close to passing a health bill, or even close to voting on one. The Senate Democrats, who outnumbered Republicans by a 22-vote margin, were so bitterly divided that no reform bill of any kind came to a vote. The House, with a Democratic majority of 257 to 176 Republicans, plus 1 Independent (who normally voted with the Democrats), likewise failed to bring a reform bill to a vote. A last-minute appeal from Chafee to win Dole's support for the Mainstream Coalition's bill went nowhere; not a single Republican voted for it or any other compromise bill. As Dick Armey of Texas said, "Why should we be enthusiastic about helping Democrats pull their political fat out of the fire with our ideas?" On August 26, with White House Chief of Staff Leon Panetta at his side, Senator George Mitchell announced that health reform was no longer a possibility in the 103rd Congress, whereupon Republicans moved in for the kill.[42]

Republican opposition had little to do with the substantive issues or merits of the various health bills. Instead, Republicans of all stripes were seized by a growing conviction that the Republican Party, for decades the minority congressional party, was on the verge of a historic electoral victory. That prospect drove everything before it, causing the disparate elements of the Republican coalition, from social conservatives and business lobbyists to talk-radio networks and elected officials, to coalesce as one to kill health care reform. Senator Bob Packwood, according to the *New York Times* and never subsequently denied, declared during the Republicans' closed-door strategy sessions that the task now "was to make sure our fingerprints are not on it."[43]

Clinton's presidency threatened to unravel. Unable to get either health or welfare reform bills through the Democratic Congress or to carry out his campaign pledge for middle-class tax relief, the president and his party became the targets of bitter criticism and suffered a humbling defeat in the November elections. For the first time since 1952, Republicans captured a solid majority of both houses of Congress at the same time. In the aftermath of the Democrats' legislative and electoral defeats, ambitious state initiatives to extend health coverage to more of their own citizens in states such as Florida, Massachusetts, Hawaii, Minnesota, Oregon, and Washington stalled.[44] Facing budget deficits of their own, many state officials followed the lead of

New York's Republican Governor George Pataki in slashing Medicaid costs by more than a billion dollars.[45] Meanwhile, the number of uninsured people continue to grow, straining an already financially burdened health care system. The uninsured were by no means the poorest citizens. In the recession of the early 1990s, many had come from the middle and working classes.[46]

Federal and state electoral returns had signaled a clear repudiation of Clinton and the Democratic Congress, but the politics of health care did not slip quietly away. When the 104th Congress assembled in January 1995, President Clinton, knowing that the new Republican majority would have to wrestle with the same issues he had in order to fulfill its election pledge to balance the federal budget within seven years and to trim the deficit by $245 billion, offered no deficit reduction plan, no welfare reform proposal, and no new health initiative. He left it to the Republicans to propose policies and programs in the expectation that they would be decimated by affected interest groups. As the new majority party, Republicans would have to reverse the campaign rhetoric of denying that a health care crisis existed, which they had indulged in to bring down Clinton's reform plan, and deal with the issue. But to do that entailed a certain political liability, as conservative strategist William Kristol, who had argued previously that there was no health crisis, acknowledged. "There is a risk obviously," he declared in spring 1995. "I'm sure the Democrats are sitting back, thinking, 'We can do to them on Medicare and Medicaid what they did to us on the Clinton health care proposal.'"[47]

Kristol's observation was prophetic of the debate that began almost immediately after Congress convened. Democrats pointed to House Speaker Gingrich's remarks on redesigning Medicare to be more efficient to warn that Republicans would use a balanced-budget amendment to gut it and welfare on the grounds that they consumed too much of the federal budget. Republicans scoffed at the notion, but they conceded that major entitlement programs might have to undergo systemic changes if the $4.7 trillion federal debt was ever to stop growing, much less shrink. This exchange marked the first real skirmish of the new legislative session and was a harbinger of the protracted conflict that characterized the 104th Congress, as both the White House and Republican leaders, each with an eye toward the upcoming presidential election, pitted health reform against a balanced-budget amendment.[48]

Besides adopting a shrewdly passive role, Clinton protected his presidency from being marginalized by bringing into the White House as his chief political adviser Richard "Dick" Morris, a veteran of the political wars and adviser to Democrats and Republicans alike. Concerned that the president was perceived as too liberal, Morris worked to reposition Clinton as the centrist he had claimed to be in 1992. In May 1996, a sober Clinton, reflecting on the defeat of his health plan, declared: "I think I overestimated how much the system could change to deal with all the various challenges in health care in one bite. I think you just have to do it in discrete steps, even though if you do it in discrete steps, when you solve a problem it presents new challenges." Clinton's observation was no doubt true, but in 1995, political considerations were uppermost in his mind. This meant co-opting Republican issues, which ran the gamut from gun control and school prayer to overhauling welfare and balancing the budget. Under Morris's tutelage, a wounded Clinton, who had failed to receive credit for reducing the budget deficit by $500 million in 1993 and who was licking the wounds he incurred in the Health Care War of 1993–1994, recast himself as the protector of Medicare and Medicaid.[49] He also abandoned further budget-cutting efforts as good government but bad politics. This attitude was reflected in the budget he unveiled on February 6, 1995, which put the onus on the Republicans to cut Medicare, welfare, and other politically popular programs in order to fulfill their campaign pledge.[50]

By summer 1995, the budget, welfare, and health care reform had all become intertwined, as Clinton, though virtually all his senior aides advised him that he could not beat the Republicans on the budget issue, adopted a strategy of accepting only incremental change in social programs. He would join the Republicans where possible, but on his own terms. He would support smaller and slower cuts in spending for entitlement programs, including health, even if it required more than seven years to balance the budget, but he would draw a line in the sand against the harshest Republican budget cuts wherever polls showed the public breaking ranks with the Gingrich revolution. This strategy would put Clinton at odds with the Republicans on Medicare cuts but would permit him to claim the role of protector of those Americans who would be affected most drastically by the Republican proposals.[51]

As the president's strategy unfolded, health policy analysts such as Uwe Reinhardt of Princeton University worried that the nation's health care problems would become entangled once again in a bitterly partisan struggle, as each party jockeyed for the high ground.[52] Reinhardt's concern came to pass, as the Republican leadership initiated a new round of debate over health care in an effort to persuade voters that Medicare was in crisis and required fundamental changes in the way its 37 million beneficiaries received their health care. "The debate is oddly familiar to anyone who lived through the Great Health Care War of 1993–1994," one journalist observed, but it also was oddly scrambled, as Democrats and Republicans reversed many of their arguments on costs and managed care. Republicans, particularly, resented having the contradictions called to their attention when Democrats accused them of embarking on a massive exercise in social engineering by forcing millions of elderly Americans with long-standing attachments to the way they received their health care into the HMO era.[53]

Speaker Gingrich followed the Democratic script when, on January 31, 1995, he told hospital administrators that Republicans would revisit health care, especially Medicare, which he described as too bureaucratic, too centralized, and too dominated by Washington, as part of their electoral mandate to balance the federal budget. The proposed constitutional amendment to require a balanced budget by the year 2002 would have "a very profound impact on efforts to reconfigure health programs," he declared. Everything was on the table, except Social Security. Senate Majority Leader Bob Dole, who had voted against the original Medicare bill, echoed Gingrich's comments, albeit less stridently.[54]

In this new political universe, Clinton's sweeping plan for universal coverage was giving way rapidly to the Republicans' insistence on cost cutting and budget balancing. On February 7, Republican members of the Ways and Means Subcommittee on Health confirmed Democratic warnings when they disclosed that affluent Medicare beneficiaries were targets in the hunt for savings. Among options Republicans were exploring were the raising of premiums for upper-income recipients, creation of a Medicheck voucher system that would allow the elderly to buy private benefits, and encouraging more of the elderly to join HMOs. When asked how much they wanted to save, California Republican Bill Thomas, chair of the subcommittee, unabashedly responded, "As much as possible, without any diminution in the quality of care for seniors."[55]

Despite that last qualification, Democratic critics and advocates for the elderly were skeptical, as were some Republicans who recognized that they were stepping onto treacherous political ground. "Medicare needs to be approached with a good deal of caution," said one Republican pollster. "It's a very volatile and exploitable issue and a loser for the Republicans," warned one Republican senator.[56] Veteran Republican Congressman John Kasich of Ohio declared that a balanced budget in seven years required Medicare cuts "unlike any this town has ever seen before" and pleaded for flexibility and an extended timetable, but Gingrich overruled him and cut off further debate.[57] The Republican leadership then proceeded to explore two options: short-term proposals to squeeze immediate savings from the Medicare program and fundamental changes to its basic incentives to slow its long-term growth. One frequently heard suggestion for curtailing costs was to encourage the elderly to join HMOs, despite concerns from health policy analysts about moving Medicare participants into managed care too quickly or into HMOs that lacked adequate regulations, warnings that proved timely.[58]

The president, meanwhile, was positioning his administration to become a major player in this new round of health care debates. On April 18, Clinton signed into law a popular bill to give self-employed individuals the right to deduct some of their health insurance costs on their tax returns.[59] Four days later, Republican leaders escalated their rhetoric, saying that Medicare was in crisis. In what one reporter dubbed "Alice-through-the-looking-glass-time on Capitol Hill," Haley Barbour, chairman of the Republican National Committee (RNC), complained about Medicare's uncontrolled costs. Shortly thereafter, Speaker Gingrich told an audience of senior citizens that Republicans would propose a major overhaul of Medicare to save it for the next generation of Americans. Relying on Americans' short-term political memory, Republican leaders were now in full reverse, as they sought to persuade voters that Medicare's burgeoning costs threatened both the budgetary process and the deficit reduction.[60]

At the same time, Gingrich moved to shore up the Republicans' political flanks. He imposed strict discipline upon Republican rank-and-file members of the House; he attempted to win over or neutralize organizations that had helped to defeat Clinton's health plan; and he tried to co-opt the president by challenging him to make Medicare reform a bipartisan effort. Gingrich's efforts were superseded when Republican legislators decided to defer proposals to restructure Medicare for several months to decouple it from their efforts to slash the deficit. But the health policy analysts' worst fears were realized: Medicare had become a partisan political issue. Serious programmatic and financial decisions on the future of Medicare got lost in the increasingly acrimonious debate between Republicans and Democrats, especially after the *New York Times* reported that Clinton would use the White House Conference on Aging to portray himself as Medicare's defender against budget-cutting Republicans.[61]

On May 1, the White House, responding to Gingrich's bipartisan overture, challenged Republicans to specify how they intended to reconcile budget-balancing and tax-cutting promises with pledges to preserve and strengthen Medicare. White House Chief of Staff Leon Panetta declared that the administration was not interested in a plan to shore up the program unless it also made improvements and extended coverage to the 41 million Americans lacking insurance. Pouncing on the Republicans' decision to excise Medicare from the rest of the budget, Panetta asked: "Are they still committed to balancing the budget by 2002? Are they still committed to this huge tax cut for the wealthy? Are they still committed to doing Medicare cuts outside of health care reform? Where are they at? The only way we can get the answer to that, frankly, is when they present their budget resolution." The Republicans had painted themselves into a corner, Panetta insisted, by promising what they could not deliver.[62]

Panetta's "playing to the audience" and Gingrich's accusation that the White House was engaged in demagoguery to frighten the elderly escalated the political tug-of-war over Medicare on the eve of the conference on aging. At issue were the votes of the 37 million Medicare recipients who would go to the polls in 1996. Republican congressional leaders renewed their invitation to the president to join them in controlling Medicare costs to keep the program solvent; the White House accused Republicans of wanting to balance the budget at the expense of the elderly. On May 3, Clinton promised the more than 2,000 conference participants that he would oppose Republican cuts to Medicare and Medicaid.[63]

Amid the political mudslinging, a few points stood out. As a practical matter, the federal budget could not be balanced in seven years, as the Republicans were promising, without deep cuts in future Medicare spending. Cuts of this magnitude would raise the cost of health insurance to millions of retirees who voted or would reduce the services available to them. The Medicare trust fund to finance hospital bills *was* in danger of running out of money, but in the past, presidents and lawmakers had managed to resolve the shortfall without undermining the program.[64] And Democrats were clearly scoring political points with their argument that the Republicans' Medicare plan would finance tax cuts for the wealthy. Even after Gingrich and Dole proposed to remove Medicare from the budget debate, they would be dogged by having to choose between two bad alternatives: either to break faith with the voters who had made the Republicans the majority party in Congress or to keep their promises to balance the budget and preserve Medicare, even at immense political cost.

Having proudly taken as their slogan in the midterm election "Promises made, promises kept," the Republican leadership found itself pressed by their more ideologically conservative freshman colleagues to bring the budget into balance and to cut taxes, even as the growing furor of senior citizens and the lobbying of hospitals against further Medicare cuts rattled the more senior Republican legislators. The general public supported Medicare as an entitlement that had already been paid for through taxes, reported one poll; it was part of the Social Security safety net. Few Americans believed Gingrich's pledge to curtail Medicare costs over seven years without adversely affecting current enrollees. Neither did a skeptical Washington press corps, which, on May 2, peppered Gingrich and Dole with so many questions relating Medicare to the balanced-budget pledge that they were obliged to cut short their news conference.[65]

To avoid having the party's conservative zealots hold their feet to the political fire, Gingrich and Dole pressed ahead to control the budget. On May 9, Senator Pete V. Domenici, the New Mexican Republican who headed the Budget Committee, announced plans to balance the budget within seven years by cutting $430 billion from Medicare and Medicaid, or 16 percent of the projected $2.7 trillion. The House Budget Committee two days later approved a slightly different version of the bill to wipe out the federal deficit that also called for curtailing health costs.[66]

The Clinton administration forcefully rejected the Republicans' Medicare cuts. Testifying before the Senate Finance Committee on May 9, HHS Secretary Shalala declared that the administration opposed raising the eligibility age for Medicare, increasing premiums and other costs to beneficiaries, and reducing payments to hospitals serving large numbers of poor people. She also criticized the Republican proposal to give the elderly vouchers to buy insurance, saying she saw little value in tax breaks to encourage private savings for medical needs. Private medical savings accounts, Shalala testified, "would appeal to the young, the healthy, and the wealthy, but most of our seniors are none of these." That afternoon, in a joint news conference, Dr. Arthur S. Flemming, HEW Secretary in the Eisenhower administration and an advocate of universal coverage, joined Senator Kennedy and House Minority Leader Gephardt to assail the Republican budget proposals. Flemming pleaded with Republican lawmakers "not to go down in history as the party that destroyed Medicare and Medicaid."[67] Health policy analysts also criticized the proposed cuts and described debate over the Republican remedies as surreal because it was largely over a number, not a detailed set of policies.[68]

The debate took another twist on May 18 when RNC Chairman Haley Barbour concluded "reluctantly" that Republicans would have to "go it alone." His assessment, that Democrats were refusing to cooperate in efforts to restrain Medicare spending, however accurate, was disingenuous. With both the presidency and control of Congress up for grabs in 1996, neither party was eager to work with the opposition to reduce the deficit or to reform health care. Majority Leader Bob Dole attempted to take the issue out of politics so that it would not interfere with his presidential bid by calling for an independent commission to resolve the problem, but the White House countered that Medicare repairs had to be linked to reform of the private health care sector, a proposal Republicans had scuttled the previous year.[69]

President Clinton, meanwhile, in keeping with his new persona as the guardian of Medicare, outlined his own plan to balance the federal budget on June 13. With spending cuts of $1.1 trillion by 2005 under Clinton's proposal, Medicare would grow more slowly and government spending on Medicare would be far less than the Republicans were recommending, with the difference being made up from reductions in corporate subsidies and other domestic spending.[70] His proposal surprised even Democratic lawmakers, who had not expected him to unveil it until the fall. Although it was a far cry from the vast restructuring he proposed in 1993, his spokesmen presented it as the first serious step toward health reform.[71]

The fight shaping up over Medicare promised to be the biggest battle between the new Republican congressional majority and the Democrats. On July 17, 1995, House Republicans, ignoring Clinton, began the arduous process of drafting legislation to make immense changes in Medicare.[72] The leadership wanted to impose annual limits on spending and to give older people a choice among several private health insurance plans as an alternative to the standard federal program. The New York Times editorialized on July 25 that the Republicans were risking serious damage to Medicare by manipulating its financial problems to honor their pledge to balance the budget by 2002.[73] That same day, the president joined Democratic legislators and hundreds of elderly Americans in Washington to mark the thirtieth anniversary of Medicare. Surrounded by an invited audience of senior citizens, including his mother-in-law, Clinton used his weekly radio address from the Oval Office to warn that Republican proposals would slow Medicare spending in order to finance tax cuts for the wealthy. He predicted that it would have pushed a half-million elderly people into poverty by 2002.[74]

In August, Republican leaders took advantage of Congress's summer recess to sell their Medicare overhaul to the electorate, pledging "to preserve, protect and improve" the program even as they proposed to extract $270 billion from it over the next seven years—the sum needed to fulfill the balanced-budget promise. Democrats, following the White House lead, retorted that the Republican prescription would not be painless and accused Republicans of lining up support from the medical insurance industry, which was more concerned with profits than the needs of Medicare recipients.[75] The fight grew even nastier: Speaker Gingrich was to discuss changes in Medicare at an Atlanta meeting, but he fled after Democratic Congressman John Lewis and nearly a hundred trade unionists stormed the hall and angrily accused him of wanting to slash Medicare programs to finance tax cuts for the wealthy. The battle also was fought in the media, as Democrats bought television ads in thirteen states and Republicans purchased radio spots in eleven congressional districts. As mentioned earlier, Clinton had, by the end of the month, added Medicaid to the list of programs he sought to protect from the Republican ax. Slashing Medicaid by $182 billion over seven years could deprive 9 million Americans of coverage by the year 2002, in addition to the 41 million already uninsured.[76]

Former task force consultant Paul Starr echoed the administration's concerns early that September. Sarcastically congratulating Republicans for finally wakening to Medicare's problems, he criticized their tactics. They had denounced the secrecy surrounding the task force two years before, but now they were meeting "behind closed doors" to draft a legislative proposal to vote on only a few weeks after unveiling it, short-circuiting independent analysis of their program's costs and evading "other inconvenient aspects of a long national debate." Republicans who had sounded the tocsin against the president's managed-care proposal in 1993 were resorting to the same policy process.[77]

Starr also criticized the allegedly radical nature of the Republican proposals, particularly the attempt to alter the fundamental principles on which Medicare and Medicaid had been established. Whereas Clinton's reform plan had sought to extend access to health security, the Republican approach retracted rights the elderly already enjoyed. And whereas debate over Clinton's proposal reflected a widespread belief that the system needed reform, Republicans simply assumed that the system was self-correcting and government should emulate the private sector. "Budget plans come and go," Starr observed, but "the historic importance of what is happening [now] is the shift in legal rights." Whereas Clinton's ill-fated reform proposed to give Americans a right to coverage and protection from employers, insurers, and health care providers, Republican plans to convert Medicare into a voucher program and Medicaid into block grants eliminated legal rights to health benefits that the elderly and poor already possessed. This was not reform, Starr insisted, but "reverse reform," and "a radical version of that."[78]

Critics of Clinton's plan had demanded that the administration control costs before extending coverage to the uninsured, Starr noted, but the Republican approach cut costs by *retracting* rights to coverage. Nor did the Republican proposal contain federally mandated provisions to include coverage for individuals with preexisting medical conditions or for the uninsured. A Republican Congress, he observed, evidently has no money for these needs, even though opinion polls disclosed that Americans put a high priority on such reforms. "I cannot believe that reverse reform is what they have in mind," Starr declared.[79]

The more the Republicans' war against taxing and spending collided with the White House's determination to protect health care, the more Medicare continued to be the flashpoint. On September 14, after Congress's return from summer recess, in the course of castigating both President Clinton and a "bankrupt" Democratic Party before the Republican Party caucus, Gingrich unveiled the GOP plan to overhaul Medicare. The proposal cut projected spending by $270 billion, or 14 percent, over two years to slow the growth of Medicare costs, gradually doubled health insurance premiums paid by the elderly, capped malpractice settlements, and encouraged doctors and hospitals to form cooperatives. Other than these items, the plan contained few specific details. Republican leaders conceded under questioning that they had omitted financial incentives to persuade the elderly to join HMOs to avoid being accused of crass commercialism. Nonetheless, Gingrich predicted that millions of elderly Americans would enroll voluntarily in HMOs, saving the government $70 billion annually.[80]

Under questioning from reporters, Gingrich admitted that even a $70 billion annual saving was optimistic, but he insisted that to save $270 billion—the amount needed to bring the budget into balance—Republicans would have to tell the elderly that Medicare was not sustainable in it present form. This was an acceptable political risk, because Gingrich believed absolutely that President Clinton would fold under pressure and accede to the Republicans' budget-balancing cuts in Medicare.[81] Gingrich, in fact, seriously miscalculated the president's reaction. Rather than succumb to pressure, Clinton reiterated his threat to veto Republican cuts in health care, declaring they would have draconian consequences and calling on the elderly to lobby for bipartisan congressional support for modifications that would control costs without harming Medicare recipients. Gingrich and Dick Armey of Texas, the second-ranking House Republican leader, shrugged off the president's response.[82]

Clinton's message resonated with the American people and ultimately it was Gingrich's leadership that was called into question. But as health policy analysts feared, partisan politics once more reared its ugly head. Congressional Democrats refused to offer an alternative to the Republican proposal, choosing instead to state again that the harsh Republican cuts would damage the health system and destroy Medicare. They insisted that physicians would not accept the lower fees outlined in the Republican proposal and reiterated that they would not support Medicare reductions so long as Republicans cut taxes on the affluent (those earning $100,000 annually). House Minority Leader Gephardt threatened to do whatever was necessary to forestall Republican changes in Medicare and accused the party of "timidity" and fumbling an opportunity to put the program on a solid financial footing.[83]

Sparking the Democrats' anger was the Republican leaders' decision to conduct only a single day of hearings on its Medicare bill, a tactic it had derived from the lessons of Clinton's defeat the previous year. Republican leaders wanted to avoid the deluge of details, amendments, and endless debate that had delayed and finally crippled Clinton's health bill. When asked why they were truncating the legislative process, they responded with more than a grain of cynicism that partisanship, sloganeering, and thirty-second television spots had so poisoned the legislative process that Congress could not tackle anything as serious, complex, and emotional as health reform.[84]

With that explanation, on September 22, 1995, the Republican-controlled Ways and Means Committee, without revealing specifics of the legislation, conducted a hearing on the bill euphemistically entitled the "Medicare Preservation" bill (H.R. 2425), a hearing that was quickly disrupted by noisy demonstrations of the elderly. Down the corridor, meanwhile, the Commerce Committee was quietly taking a scalpel to Medicaid spending, cutting it by $182 billion, or 19 percent, over the next seven years. The funds that remained would be turned over to the states minus any federal mandates to guide their disbursement. On the Senate side of the Capitol, Republican members of the Finance Committee unveiled their own version of the bill, which also raised Medicare premiums and encouraged the elderly to shift to HMOs. In an ironic twist, Republican legislators of both chambers had borrowed two of the Democrats' favorite tools of the previous year to rein in costs—fixed budgets and price controls applied to doctors and hospitals—although the Republicans claimed there was a big difference between Clinton's approach and what they were proposing.[85]

House Democrats responded to the truncated hearing by engaging in political theater. They conducted their own hearing on the lawn of the Capitol to illustrate the point that Republicans were excluding them from the policy process and to emphasize their contention that the Republicans were ransacking Medicare to pay for a tax cut for the rich.[86] A more serious challenge to the Republican plan came from another, impartial quarter. In the last week of September, the CBO unveiled its analysis of the Republican proposal and concluded that most of the savings in the Republican overhaul of Medicare would come from increasing premiums and allowing enrollees' payments to health care providers to rise. The CBO projected relatively small savings from HMOs and other forms of managed care, but said the "medical savings accounts," one of the Republicans' favorite cost-cutting measures, would actually cost the government $3.2 billion over seven years.[87]

Even with a Republican Congress as united as was the 104th, the Medicare bills before the two chambers were able to move only so fast, and they soon became engulfed in the larger struggle over budget reform. That issue had acquired a new sense of urgency, as the Republican Congress fell far behind schedule in enacting annual appropriations bills to keep the government running beyond September 30, the end of the fiscal year. The effect of the delay, caused by the time it took to pass some controversial appropriations bills earlier in the legislative session and to implement the Republicans' Contract with America, was to allow the Congress's self-declared deadline for passing the reconciliation bill covering taxing and spending policies for the rest of the government to slip as well. Therefore, both the Republican congressional leadership and the White House would have to agree (no later than September 28) to a continuing resolution that would keep the government solvent and operating until midnight of November 13. This impasse occurred at the height of the Medicare debates and well before September 28. Both parties recognized that a crisis was brewing. If the appropriations were not available by then—and no one thought they could be—Congress would have to pass another continuing resolution and also raise the debt limit. Gingrich decided to use those extensions as leverage to get his way on both the spending bills and the budget as a whole. In doing so, he committed a tactical blunder that the White House and Democratic lawmakers turned turn to their advantage.[88]

With Congress officially in recess, several Democratic senators had remained in Washington to continue their theatrical protest to discredit the Republican legislation. They conducted a pseudo-hearing on October 5 and 6 "to examine Republican proposals to cut Medicare and Medicaid to fund tax breaks for the wealthy." Clinton administration witnesses testified that the cuts were much larger than necessary, and ordinary Americans told nursing home horror stories. The hearings were less than an impartial search for truth, but they and a comparable performance two days earlier staged by House Democrats on the Commerce Committee were the only budgetary hearings conducted since the Republicans had put their proposals for saving $452 billion into legislative language.[89]

The Democrats had a simple explanation for what Senator Paul Sarbanes of Maryland termed "the refusal of the Republicans to hold the kind of hearings that legislation of this magnitude requires." Democrat Jim McDermott of Washington explained, "Their whole strategy from the get-go has been to hold everything back until the last moment and then ram it past people like a 96-mile-an-hour fastball so that no one will ever see what went by them." McDermott's explanation was not technically accurate; the Republicans had conducted extensive hearings since February and had met privately with interest groups to ascertain which approaches might work and which would roil the political waters. Gingrich took careful notes during these sessions and had a good understanding of the complexities of the issues and a sense of what was politically feasible and what was not. Therefore, the Republican plan did evolve, but the Republicans were vulnerable.[90]

There was value to holding congressional hearings, seriously conducted and open not just to carping critics who could hammer away at real weaknesses, like the complexity of Clinton's bill, or invented ones, like the Republican charge that thousands of small businesses would have to shut down if the Clinton plan had passed. Public hearings offered opponents a forum to present alternative views and gave access to media coverage. But the Republicans elected not to run that risk. Ari Fleischer, spokesperson for the Republican majority on the Ways and Means Committee, justified the decision to curtail hearings by claiming that the Republicans were only reflecting the wishes of the American people.[91] In fact, people wanted more than action: they wanted a sense that politicians inside the Beltway were working together. To those outside the Beltway, the atmosphere inside seemed to compel politicians to indulge in hyped-up rhetoric and media grandstanding rather than to engage in a serious public discussion of the issues. When politicians really wanted to do business, they worked behind closed doors. Health care, a big explosive issue, fit that description, but the Republican Congress seemed to have little patience with debate, deliberation, and compromise. No wonder so many Americans felt alienated from big government.[92]

The radical conservatives who controlled the new Republican majority, particularly in the House, viewed extended discussion as unnecessarily complicating, an opportunity for predominantly liberal interest groups to feed their greed. Given their reading of the situation, it is not surprising that House Republicans in a string of party-line committee votes on October 11 turned aside every Democratic assault on their effort to squeeze $270 billion from Medicare. In a contentious daylong session of the Ways and Means Committee, Republican unity held, as the Republican majority rejected Democratic amendments to protect the clients of managed care, to couple medical savings accounts with catastrophic insurance coverage, to require physicians and hospitals forming their own HMOs to secure state licenses, and to prohibit Medicare savings from being used for tax relief. The same scenario played out before the Commerce Committee. At the end of the day, both committees endorsed the Republicans' Medicare legislation and advanced it to the House floor for a vote the following day.[93]

As fallout from the highly visible and emotional fight over the Republican plan radiated beyond the Capital Beltway, the party's public approval rating began to suffer. The AARP, the nation's powerful seniors' lobby, after holding its fire all year while the program was being developed, declared war and initiated a nationwide advertising and mailing blitz against the Republican Medicare plan. "We think $270 billion is too much and seven years is too fast," declared one high-ranking AARP official. The campaign made the 30 million–member AARP the first major lobbying organization to come out against the bill.[94]

Until then, the Republican leadership had kept at bay the powerful medical-insurance lobbyists. But now, they, too, were becoming restless, which caused the leadership to scramble to reassure nervous colleagues that their Medicare plan was not in jeopardy. Republican leaders had cause to be worried. Just days before their Medicare bill was to be brought up in the House, legislators from rural areas, where health care was already inadequate, began to drop away, as did some urban lawmakers from New Jersey, who feared their constituents would be unhappy. Gingrich, Dole, and RNC chairman Haley Barbour scheduled joint appearances before separate caucuses of House and Senate Republicans in a determined effort to hold the party together over the next six weeks when the climactic budget battles, which relied heavily on the Medicare cuts, would occur.[95]

Inevitably, this potential threat meant making compromises, and one compromise led to another. On October 14, Gingrich spent two hours going through the bill's details, making changes to shore up support for it. Rural legislators, for example, received a guaranteed minimum reimbursement to managed-care providers in their districts. To pay for this and other deals, Gingrich squeezed payments to other providers all the more. Insurers, physicians, and hospitals liked specific provisions of the Republican plan, but not others. The AMA wrung three important concessions: the first softened the cuts in fees that doctors could charge fee-for-service patients (a concession one AMA official claimed would be worth billions of dollars); the second eased antitrust laws to permit doctors and hospitals to create their own health plans in competition with traditional insurance companies (a concession that allowed physicians to refer patients to laboratories and other facilities in which they had a financial interest); the third capped malpractice awards at ridiculously low levels. Private hospitals received reimbursement for some local taxes, and manufacturers of prescription drugs and medical devices were granted benefits potentially worth millions of dollars. By the time Gingrich was through making concessions, the AMA decided that the Republican bill was not that bad after all. The *New York Times* editorialized that Gingrich's changes had "made an already bad Medicare bill substantially worse." Never designed to give the elderly high-quality health care, the bill was "less likely to do so now."[96]

Press criticism and the CBO's conclusion that some special-interest provisions would actually increase Medicare expenditures most likely contributed to the Republican leadership's decision to adopt a more combative stance vis-à-vis the administration. This decision followed a new threat from President Clinton to veto the bill. After weeks of verbal sparring with the White House, the Republicans took a giant step toward dismantling decades of Democratic social policy on October 19. They brought the Medicare bill to the House floor and, in keeping with their strategy, cut it loose from the budget reconciliation bill. They clearly did not want Medicare cuts to appear in the same legislation as special-interest tax cuts, thereby providing the Democrats with an obvious target and possibly jeopardizing votes on both bills. As one adviser to Gingrich said prior to the House debate, "They're all very nervous that the argument connecting Medicare with the tax cut has got through." Gingrich, likewise, was worried, for he told political associates, "If we can handle Medicare without getting killed politically, we'll be fine."[97]

Thanks to the Speaker's intense involvement, the House, by a vote of 231 to 201, passed the Medicare legislation with relative ease. Four Democrats had joined 227 Republicans in favor of the bill, and 6 Republicans, 194 Democrats, and 1 Independent voted against it. A week later, the House passed its budget reconciliation bill incorporating the Medicare cuts by a vote of 227 to 203.[98]

Riding roughshod over the legislative process and eschewing compromise with the opposition, the process whereby politicians traditionally forged a consensus, was an unfortunate approach to budgetary and social reforms, observed one *New York Times* commentator. He faulted the pollsters and focus groups for dictating the tactics whereby the new Republican majority approached major legislation with a winner-take-all attitude usually reserved for elections. Compromise, the normal process for conducting business in Washington, had become synonymous with capitulation, he wrote, and this boded ill for future legislative-executive relations.[99] But Norman Ornstein of the American Enterprise Institute noted that there were probably a hundred House Republicans "who believe, deep down, that compromise is a bad thing." With only three weeks left to pass the budget, Medicare, and welfare reform bills and then for the House and Senate to resolve their differences, Republicans were playing a "dangerous end game," he warned.[100]

In this chilling atmosphere, political leaders of both parties had given themselves little leeway to forge a consensus before the debt limit expired on November 12. Clinton hunkered down, rebuked the Republican-controlled House, further entrenched himself as the protector of Medicare, and hinted that the Republicans would be responsible for any shutdown of government resulting from their action. Compromise was clearly not in the cards. Gingrich, too, had said after the midterm elections that though he was "very prepared to cooperate with the Clinton administration," he was "not prepared to compromise." Nor were other Republican leaders, including Senate Majority Leader Dole, who declared, "This will not be an autumn of compromise, make no mistake about it."[101]

Like the Republicans, the Democrats also eschewed compromise and attempted to seize the high ground in anticipation of 1996. Accusing the Republicans of taking a hatchet to Medicare, the centerpiece of Lyndon Johnson's Great Society, Clinton and Democratic lawmakers believed Medicare's cuts would hurt Republicans more than Democrats with the voters, and they were prepared to out-demagogue them. Compromise, the willingness to write a bill that would address Medicare's most serious problems while retaining its best features, was not an option, despite the fraudulent nature of the partisan rhetoric on both sides of the aisle and both ends of Pennsylvania Avenue.[102]

Political commentator Elizabeth Drew's analysis of the Republican plan and Clinton's 1993 proposal made this point very well. The Republicans' $270 billion cut would have allowed Medicare to grow at a rate of 7.2 percent, down from 9.9 percent under existing law; Clinton's proposal would have reduced spending by 6–7 percent. The two plans, in other words, were not very far apart in terms of spending: $289 billion by 2002 versus Clinton's $295 billion. Moreover, Medicare and Medicaid constituted one-sixth of the federal budget in 1995. The administration did nothing to address this problem after initially insisting that health care costs had to be controlled. Democrats, instead, resorted to hyperbole, saying Republicans would eviscerate Medicare.[103] The Republicans' insistence that they were *increasing* spending for Medicare by at least twice the rate of inflation was technically correct, but what they did not say was that a combination of more beneficiaries and increased costs would require $270 billion more to maintain the 1995 level of benefits and services. For Republicans to realize the savings they wanted, Drew noted, they would have to increase premiums and reduce reimbursements to providers.[104]

As important as the much-debated reduction in funding were the policy changes contemplated in the Republican Medicare plan. Chief among them were luring the elderly into HMOs through more "choices" or through a voucher system and allowing them to set up tax-deductible medical savings accounts to pay for certain types of coverage. Clinton's plan also had encouraged enrollment in HMOs, but it never went so far toward dismantling Medicare as did the Republican legislation.[105] Furthermore, the Republican plan avoided what was at the heart of Clinton's health reform: to make medical coverage universal and more certain. Whereas Clinton's plan had stumbled over the complexities inherent in bringing about universal and comprehensive coverage, the Republicans' bill made no pretense of expanding coverage to the uninsured or protecting those with insurance from losing it. The Republican legislation, Drew asserted, was likely to result in a Medicare population of the poorer and the sicker—not the makings of a powerful constituency to protect the program.[106]

Drew's conclusion was self-evident. In lieu of a serious debate about Medicare, the House debate focused on partisan politics: whether the Republican revolution would succeed or whether the Democrats would be able to recapture the glory of the New Deal and the Great Society. The 1996 elections would decide the matter. This explained why the House's two-day debate and speech making had been more tactical than explanatory, more concerned with resonance than with truth. Remarkably lacking in drama or suspense, both parties had tailored their arguments to fit a carefully scripted exercise in serial speech making: Democrats complained about tax cuts for the wealthy and the gutting of Medicare; Republicans insisted their bill would keep the system from going bankrupt.[107]

The dilemma for Republicans, however, was that no matter how often they repeated their mantra about preserving and protecting Medicare, they could not escape the popular perception that their true goal was to decimate Medicare to raise money for their fiscal agenda. They had promised to cut taxes for middle- and upper-income Americans in their Contract with America and to balance the federal budget in seven years, but the contract said nothing about Medicare. Once they became the majority party, Republicans had to find money somewhere to offset the tax cuts and to balance the budget. With Social Security off the table, the only available large pot of money was Medicare. The conclusion was inescapable: the "Medicare Preservation" bill would cut Medicare, not for ideological reasons (as was true of welfare reform) or because Republicans disapproved of the existing program (as with environmental regulations), but purely and simply to raise money to trim the deficit. The Republican legislation neither preserved nor protected anything.[108]

To fend off this type of criticism, Republican leaders eagerly seized on the report the Medicare trustees had issued in spring 1995. The report concluded that the system would go bankrupt by 2002 unless spending was reduced or more revenue was raised. The trustees had issued similar reports for years without Republicans ever expressing anxiety, but now the report became a justification for slashing Medicare spending. As critics noted, the amount of savings the Republicans sought—$270 billion over seven years— was many times what was needed to avert insolvency.[109]

If Republicans were unwilling to confront the facts, so were Democrats. No matter how much they pledged allegiance to Medicare, they could not escape the fact that fundamental changes were necessary for the program to survive. CBO figures, once again, were instructive. Without significant changes, according to CBO estimates, the cost of Medicare would rise to $458 billion, or 18.6 percent of the budget, in 2005, up from $178 billion, or 11.7 percent, in 1995.[110] Yet not a single House Democrat had alluded to the incontrovertible fact that taxpayers could no longer afford to sustain Medicare in its present form. Either they were bereft of new ideas to counter the Republican offensive or, more likely, they were following the White House's lead in playing politics with the issue. In either case, Democratic legislators returned to the same well they had relied on for years: Republicans were playing fast and loose with the elderly.

In the Senate, meanwhile, Republicans racked up another major victory for the "revolution." On September 29, the Finance Committee voted eleven to nine along party lines to approve a Medicare plan similar to that of the House, after first adopting an amendment offered by Democratic Senator Kent Conrad of North Dakota to safeguard the income and assets of spouses of nursing home residents on Medicaid. Hours after the Finance Committee approved the bill, President Clinton assailed its "outrageous provisions," which he insisted would devastate the quality of care for the elderly, particularly those in nursing homes. The debate over nursing home standards went to the heart of the much larger philosophical clash between Democrats and Republicans that former President Reagan had set in motion: whether Washington should set prescriptive standards for the use of federal money distributed to the states.[111] The Senate Finance Committee's bill scrapping Medicare's oversight of nursing homes set the stage for a definitive political clash over the size, shape, and purpose of federal spending.

The full Senate took its own giant step toward implementing the Republican Revolution to clamp down on social spending, cut taxes, and remake government in a more conservative image on October 27. On a fifty-two to forty-seven party-line vote, with all Republicans but one in favor and all Democrats opposed, the Senate approved a balanced-budget plan incorporating Medicare cuts. Every Democratic amendment to cushion the impact of the budget cuts on the poor, the elderly, farmers, and the environment went down to defeat. Speaker Gingrich described the action as "the most decisive vote on the direction of government since 1933." Bill Archer, the Ways and Means Committee chairman, observed that "the time has come to admit that tax and spend has failed." Presidential hopeful Bob Dole agreed, adding, "This will be a radical change in the way this government is operated."[112]

Dole's meaning was clear: the Republican legislation would break sharply with the past by dramatically slowing the growth of federal social programs that had flourished since the New Deal and Great Society. It would return to the states the power that Washington had accumulated since 1933. Democrats did not dispute Dole's reading of Congress's action. Minnesota Representative Martin Sabo succinctly defined the Democratic perspective on the budget bill, declaring that it was about "two very different visions for America's future." He called on his colleagues "to reject a vision of America that seeks to reward those who have already prospered in our economy while imposing burdens on those who have not."[113]

The next step in the Republican Revolution against big government was to incorporate the Medicare cuts into the respective House and Senate budget bills as amendments to the Social Security Act, and to do so under threat of a presidential veto and against the November 13 deadline when the government would run out of money. Clinton had warned on October 19, "I will veto this bill," a threat he renewed during the reconciliation process, when each chamber passed the final budget bill with the Medicare cuts intact.[114] With control of the White House and Congress at stake in little more than a year, neither party was willing to compromise by splitting the difference over the dollars to be saved or the number of years in which to reduce the deficit. Instead, threats and bombastic rhetoric emanated from both ends of Pennsylvania Avenue. The AARP predicted a "high noon" showdown between Clinton and his Republican opponents, but in fact, neither side was rushing to close down the government, fearing condemnation from a public increasingly distraught at Washington officialdom and the political gridlock that had developed over the years.[115]

White House and Republican leaders worked separately and in tandem to avert a crisis, but in drafting a continuing resolution to keep the bureaucracy open, House Republican leaders committed a major blunder. They wrote into the resolution a provision eliminating a scheduled decrease in Medicare premiums, which would then go back up even higher once their Medicare plan went into effect. On November 9, the day after Congress approved the debt limit bill, it also enacted the continuing resolution. Democrat Richard Durbin of Illinois exploited the opposition's vulnerability by accusing Gingrich of seeking "to shut down the government so that he can raise the Medicare premium."[116] Republicans had misjudged the extent of popular support for their action and for believing Clinton would cave in under pressure to sign both the continuing resolution and the debt limitation bills. The president pounced instead; on November 10 he accused the Republicans of raising Medicare premiums, cutting education, and rolling back three decades of bipartisan environmental safeguards, all in the name of a balanced budget. Echoing Sabo, Clinton declared, "I believe this budget debate is about two very different futures for America."[117]

With the November 13 deadline for shutting down the government fast approaching, the reconciliation bill took a backseat. Democrats and Republicans continued to blame each other, and last-minute efforts by Senators Domenici and Dole to forge a compromise with the White House ran afoul of Gingrich and House conservatives led by Richard Armey, who believed their senatorial colleagues were too eager to cut a deal. Democrats as well were in no mood to compromise. Clinton and his aides believed that his message was finally getting through to the public, particularly after public opinion polls disclosed that Gingrich's popularity was on a downward trajectory and the public would blame Congress more than the president if there were no budget agreement. The White House took the gamble. On November 13, the federal bureaucracy closed down. The government of the world's most powerful nation technically ran out of money and closed its doors to all but essential services.[118]

Two days later, a defensive Gingrich floated a new resolution to keep the government operating until December 15. Over the protests of conservative freshman Republicans, who were on the verge of rebellion against his leadership, he dropped the provision to increase Medicare premiums and cited CBO figures to call for a balanced budget within seven years. After intense lobbying, he finally persuaded his colleagues to support the resolution, which carried 277 to 151. Forty-eight Democrats, who had voted at various times for a balanced budget, joined the Republican majority. The desertion of so many Democrats gave Republicans a glimmer of hope that they had the votes to override a presidential veto. Following a lengthy and divisive debate within the White House over whether to risk an override, Clinton signaled he would accept the continuing resolution to keep the government running until mid-December, provided that the language did not suggest that he had sold out his priorities. But he demanded that a minimum of 100 Democrats endorse the agreement. With that settled, the continuing resolution passed on November 19.[119]

Hope for a budget agreement before Thanksgiving proved unrealistic, however. Each side interpreted the bill's provisions differently, with House Republicans insisting that the budget was to be brought into balance within seven years and the administration talking about seven years as a target date. Clinton assigned a key role in the bargaining process to his chief of staff, Leon E. Panetta, a deal broker and known budget cutter. Panetta's efforts to negotiate compromises on Medicare and Medicaid, the issues essential to reaching a budget accord, went nowhere. With each side accusing the other of bad faith, President Clinton vetoed the Republican budget bill on December 6, 1995, as he had promised, calling it "extreme" and "wrong-headed." In a symbolic gesture, he issued the veto with the same pen that Lyndon Johnson had used to sign the amendments to the Social Security Act that created Medicare and Medicaid.[120]

Clinton's action nullified the Republican cuts in Medicare, but it did nothing to remedy the program's fundamental problems. Quite the contrary; at the end of 1995 Medicare's trustees projected bankruptcy for the hospital trust fund in 2001, a year sooner than anticipated. Without sufficient votes to override the presidential veto, Republicans threatened Medicaid guarantees to the poor by adding a little-noticed addition to their welfare bill that was awaiting final action in Congress. A confidential draft of the House and Senate conferees' report, which contained the full text of the reconciliation bill, revealed that Republican negotiators from the two chambers intended to eliminate the guarantee of Medicaid coverage for anyone qualifying for cash assistance under the standards in effect on June 1, 1995. This rewrite of the welfare bill went further in reducing federal guarantees to the poor by severing the link between welfare and Medicaid, which had existed since 1965. The bill narrowed further the states' authority to determine Medicaid eligibility. As with the Republican Medicare plan, elimination of the link between welfare and Medicaid gave Clinton cause to veto the welfare bill.[121]

Having lost the battle of the budget, Republicans then lost political control of the issue when they delivered an ultimatum to Clinton: either agree to a deal or the federal government would be shut down, a position that House Speaker Gingrich, who was under relentless pressure from conservative freshman Republicans, was said to have privately opposed. As the December 15 deadline drew close, efforts to cobble together a compromise failed. Republican hard-liners in the House kept their word, forcing a government shutdown, which continued into the new year. Medicare, like the budget itself, was caught up in the poisoned atmosphere of presidential-election-year politics.[122]

Much of the onus for the political deadlock and subsequent closing down of the government fell on the House Speaker. In believing that Clinton would succumb to political pressure to cut Medicare spending to balance the budget, Gingrich had grievously miscalculated his opponent's determination and fumbled the most important battle of his speakership. As with the Democrats in 1994, the Medicare War, which contributed to the unprecedented closing down of government, turned out to be a political disaster for the Republican Party and for the Speaker personally. It was the crowning blow to the Republican Revolution, which was in shambles as 1995 drew to a close. Public opinion, as the White House anticipated, turned against the Republicans. A *New York Times*/CBS News poll disclosed that 61 percent of Americans believed the president had been more earnest than the Republicans in trying to find a solution to the budget crisis. As one expert on public opinion and health policy observed, "What the Republicans learned, and what the Democrats had already found out, was that each day the debate drags on, the worse your numbers get."[123]

The Republican Revolution began the new year fatally wounded. Not only had the party failed to fulfill its pledge to balance the budget, but it also shouldered the blame for closing down the federal government; House Speaker Gingrich suffered a devastating political defeat as his colleagues forced him to maintain a low profile during the 1996 presidential election campaign. But even though Republican legislators failed to determine the details of health legislation, they did successfully shift the terms of the political debate. Both parties and presidential candidates had come to embrace the philosophy that less government was better and that Americans would have to do with less—which came as a distinct surprise to many Democrats in the Rooseveltian and Johnsonian traditions.

Health reform was one of several policy areas where the effects of the Republican Revolution lingered. Gone was Clinton's rhetoric about a health care "crisis." Gone was the ambitious plan to overhaul the nation's health care system, which had been the centerpiece of his progressivism during his first two years in the White House. The collapse of Clinton's health care initiative dramatized his apparent failure to make government work again. In its place, he had to accepted Congress's substitution of a much more modest Health Insurance Portability and Accountability Act, a bipartisan measure sponsored by Democratic Senator Edward Kennedy and Republican Senator Nancy Landon Kassebaum. The Kennedy-Kassebaum bill, which guaranteed that a person who currently had health coverage through his workplace could change jobs without fear of losing coverage, had been adrift in the legislative process with little hope for passage in winter 1995. Driven by election-year politics, it passed suddenly and overwhelmingly in both houses of Congress. Clinton signed it on August 21, 1996, in time for the fall election. Better than no law, perhaps, the health insurance portability act fell far short of Clinton's universal coverage plan. It did little for the more than 40 million Americans who did not have health insurance and failed to guarantee that coverage would be affordable.[124]

# ELEVEN
## UNFINISHED BUSINESS

The vexatious issue of government involvement in health security did not disappear with Clinton's failed attempt at universal coverage; only the lay of the land changed. Out of the rubble of that collapse, a political consensus emerged: the complex, interlocking nature of health care issues seemed to preclude going for the grand, comprehensive plan that had driven the Clinton administration. But with health expenditures on the rise, the numbers of uninsured Americans growing, and an economic recession beginning in 1999, the political system, dominated nationally by conservative Republicans pursuing an aggressive agenda, was forced once again to address the problems of a market-driven health care industry dominated largely by Medicare and private health providers and insurers. In the quest to balance the regulatory and financial challenges of costs, patients' needs and rights, and the quality of care, political leaders gave new urgency to the issue of how best to divide public responsibilities between the federal government and the states. This question also brought issues of federalism to the forefront.

Post-1994 changes in the health care system were made piecemeal in the effort to balance costs, needs, quality, and patients' rights. Nowhere was this more evident than in 1996–1997, when a Republican-controlled Congress, led by budget-deficit hawks and antigovernment conservatives, eschewed a more liberal social policy in favor of two significant, but limited (and some argued less-than-effective), health care enactments: the Kassebaum-Kennedy Health Insurance Portability and Accountability Act of 1996, making insurance more readily available to millions of working Americans who had either changed employment or lost their jobs as industries downsized, and the Children's Health Insurance Program (CHIP), a federally funded, state-administered program to provide health coverage for low-income children. In endorsing the Kassebaum-Kennedy bill, the Clinton administration, to ensure Republican support, reaffirmed the important roles of the private sector and the market by agreeing to include a pilot project to test the feasibility of medical savings accounts as a private alternative to Medicare.

These more limited measures, coupled with prior expansions of the Medicaid program, temporarily made some difference in the numbers of Americans who received health coverage, but the limits of this approach to the uninsured soon became clear.[1] Simultaneous sweeping changes in federal welfare policy inadvertently increased the number of uninsured children, thereby offsetting some of the gains in coverage from the CHIP legislation. Insurance companies, meanwhile, found ways to skirt the Kassebaum-Kennedy law, either by shunning people with serious medical problems or by levying very high premiums. Federal officials also contributed to blunting the law's effectiveness by assuming that the states would quickly adopt the standards established by the Kassebaum-Kennedy law. When that did not happen, as in California and four other states, the federal government was supposed to enforce the law directly, but the Clinton administration was unprepared to assume this immense new responsibility.[2]

Laws such as the Kassebaum-Kennedy Act and the CHIP program raised the question of whether the federal government should even be launching new policy initiatives that impacted the states without much reference to whether they were prepared to assume additional responsibilities, particularly at a time when Congress and the federal courts were denying states' requests for waivers from the Employment Retirement Income Security Act (ERISA) of 1974 to allow them to regulate and tax the premiums of private insurers' health plans. Underlying the specific issue was a broader debate over "devolution," the practice of the federal government's selectively shifting more authority over federal and joint federal-state programs (for example, Medicaid) to the states, particularly financial responsibility.

Meanwhile, hard on the heels of the Clinton administration's failure to restructure the health care system, the private sector undertook the task, and it did so in a top-down revolution that ignored the preferences of the consumers of health care, who were never asked to vote on the changes.[3] Managed care was the buzzword of the new political landscape, and for a brief time, HMOs slowed increases in health costs. But by 1996 expenditures had begun to rise again. The Kaiser Family Foundation reported that monthly premiums for employer-sponsored health coverage rose by 8.3 percent between spring 1999 and spring 2000, a full 5 percentage points more than the national inflation rate and 4 points more than the rise in workers' earnings.[4] As costs rose, health care consumers complained not only about the higher premiums and co-payments but also about the myriad of rules limiting the services they could receive—what Supreme Court Justice David H. Souter in June 2000 bluntly called "treatment rationing." These complaints created a backlash among consumers, physicians, and politicians against the seemingly unbridled and arbitrary power of the managed-care industry. Businesses in increasing numbers abandoned HMOs for Preferred Provider Organizations (PPOs), doctor networks that agreed to reduced rates for their services, although there was no empirical evidence to believe that PPOs over the long run were better able to offer people the care they wanted at an acceptable cost.[5]

At the same time, Republicans who had been calling for the privatization of Social Security seized on the system's problems to call national attention to the far deeper and more imminently threatening financial problems of Medicare, whose trust fund they predicted would run out as early as 2008. Because the elderly were living longer and medical expenditures were rising more quickly than most other prices, Medicare costs rose faster than Social Security outlays, forcing the political system once again to address the unresolved problems of cost, needs, quality, and patients' rights. Congress, in response to changes required by the 1997 budget law, established the seventeen-member National Bipartisan Commission on the Future of Medicare and Louisiana's Senator John Breaux, a centrist Democrat and critic of Clinton's failed health coverage plan, was named as chair. One goal of the budget law, adopted with bipartisan support, had been to generate savings of $115 billion over five years, to be accomplished by lowering Medicare reimbursements and modernizing the program by opening it to competition from private health plans. The expectation was that the Breaux commission would propose the difficult and politically unpalatable choices needed to ensure Medicare's solvency.[6]

Many of the commission's members wanted to perform the most radical surgery on Medicare since the program's inception, but they soon divided over whether cost-effective competition in managed care could be instituted without compromising patient health, especially when few private companies were willing to offer the services that would save Medicare a lot of money. Ten centrist Democratic and Republican appointees favored scrapping the traditional Medicare program in favor of creating a market of competing public and private plans. Seven liberal Democratic appointees fought to preserve the existing government-run fee-for-service plan, which reimbursed doctors according to a fee schedule (fixed by the government) for nearly any bill they submitted. President Clinton preempted the commission's deliberations when he decided to use the federal budget surplus to shore up both Social Security and Medicare. Clinton also decided to include in Medicare "the greatest growing need of seniors: affordable prescription drugs." Drug costs had risen as much as 15 percent each year since 1994, making it a hot issue that seniors, politicians, physicians, pharmaceutical companies, and health insurers could not ignore.[7]

The commission's rules required eleven votes to forward a proposal to Congress, and this put make-or-break power in the hands of two White House appointees: Stuart Altman of Brandeis University and Laura D'Andrea Tyson of Berkeley, former head of Clinton's CEA. As economists, these two swing voters agreed that competition was needed to modernize a sclerotic system, but as liberals, they made the price of their votes a guarantee of a specific set of benefits, including prescription drug coverage, which would add $20–40 billion a year to the $215 billion Medicare program.[8] As the commission approached its March 1, 1999, deadline for deciding what recommendations to forward to Congress, Chairman Breaux found himself between the proverbial rock and hard place: he agreed to add drug coverage to the commission's recommendations, without specifying the extent of that coverage. Breaux feared that if he conceded too much, he would lose the support of some Republicans, notably conservative Senator Phil Gramm of Texas, who refused to endorse a new benefit before the commission had resolved Medicare's financial difficulties.

Despite Breaux's effort to walk a fine line between liberals and conservatives, the deliberations bogged down in partisan and ideological disputes over money, between

Republicans who wanted to cut costs by having private health plans compete for Medicare contracts and Democrats who wanted a guarantee of benefits and expanded coverage, including prescription drugs. Everyone admitted that reforms were needed, but controlling costs and improving benefits were not easily reconcilable goals.[9]

The March 1 deadline passed with the commission unable to make any recommendations, falling one vote short of the eleven votes needed to approve a final report. Eight Republicans and two Democrats voted for major changes that would have opened Medicare to outside competition, as proposed by Breaux and Republican Representative Bill Thomas of California, chair of the Health Subcommittee of the Ways and Means Committee. Clinton's four appointees voted against the Breaux-Thomas proposals, though two of the four saw some merit in them. Altman believed they did too little to find additional revenue for Medicare or to guarantee affordable drug coverage; Tyson believed the competition would not produce enough savings to solve the program's financial problems. Disheartened, Breaux put the best possible face on the commission's paralysis when he declared, "We have advanced the Medicare debate in a very significant way."[10]

Then President Clinton scuttled the commission's efforts. On March 16, 1999, he publicly criticized the recommendations the commission was about to propose, saying they did not provide an affordable prescription drug benefit; the number of Americans without health coverage would be increased by raising the eligibility age; and seniors who remained in the traditional Medicare program would be penalized by sharply higher premiums.[11] The recommendations also were unacceptable because they did not earmark 15 percent of future budget surpluses for Medicare. Insisting that Medicare needed "substantially new revenues" to provide for the baby boom generation, Clinton promised to devise his own program.

Clinton's program, when finally unveiled, entailed a large-scale shift of general revenue to a program that until then had been financed largely by earmarked payroll taxes. Heavily criticized, it guaranteed that Medicare and prescription drug coverage would become partisan issues in the 2000 presidential campaign.[12] The Breaux commission, meanwhile, caught up in the increasingly bitter political environment, disbanded without endorsing any recommendations. Afterwards, Breaux and Thomas pledged to fight for a government voucher plan to enable Medicare recipients to purchase either public or private health coverage.[13]

Health coverage persisted as a dominant national issue in fall 1998, but this time voter anger in eight primary state elections was directed less toward the federal bureaucrat in Washington than the bureaucrat in managed care, whose dominance evoked consumer protests over whether the millions of Americans in HMOs were getting as good treatment as they wished or as they should. Powerful anecdotal evidence suggested that they were not, and politicians responded to the complaints of middle-class voters by shifting their focus from costs and coverage to quality of care. Congressional candidates, gubernatorial hopefuls, and aspiring state attorneys general rallied behind consumer-protection laws—the so-called patients' bill of rights—that promised to force HMOs to pay for more care, expand patient choice, and require health plans to document how well they treated patients.[14]

Patients' rights legislation had broad support among health policy experts, who said it would make insurance companies accountable for the quality of care they provided. But the experts also knew something the politicians would not say: a patients' bill of rights would almost certainly produce the opposite of what consumers wanted. Rather than expand options, it would drive patients into restrictive types of HMOs that limited patients to a small roster of doctors; by making HMOs publicly accountable for how well they prevented, treated, and cured illness, the law would tighten its grip by imposing on them elaborate record-keeping requirements. Accountability clashed with something else patients valued: choice. A patients' bill of rights law could conceivably displace the old-fashioned fee-for-service health insurance, which left medical choices in the hands of doctors and patients. Under the new legislation, the more freedom patients had to choose doctors, the more difficult it would be for plans to keep track of their doctors and to remedy mistakes. Accountability, then, potentially undermined choice, but it was a tradeoff many health policy experts argued was worth making. The trouble was that politicians in 1998–1999 were promising more choice, not less.

To many Americans, the warnings of the employer and insurer groups, which protested that costs and the number of uninsured would rise if there were tighter regulation of managed-care companies, appeared hypocritical. These were the same groups that had fought like demons to thwart Clinton's plan to insure the uninsured. Nonetheless, the Republican-controlled House of Representatives took seriously the private health industry's arguments to defang the growing patients' rights movement and welcomed the expressed willingness of the HMO Group, a coalition of twenty-five HMOs, to accept limited federal regulation. This derailed a farther-reaching and potentially more costly Democratic bill to permit patients to sue HMOs for malpractice. The patients' rights movement suffered a second crippling blow in November 1999, when United Health Group, the nation's second-largest health insurer, suddenly abandoned the bedrock principle underlying managed care. It announced that physicians, not health plan administrators, would have the final say on which treatments it would cover. This decision cut adrift physician support for a patients' bill of rights.[15]

As lawmakers on Capitol Hill wrestled with Medicare and issues of cost and quality, the deeper and more intractable problem of coverage again appeared. The Kaiser Foundation disclosed in spring 1999 that 44 million people, or 18.4 percent of the population, had no health coverage, an increase of 6 million Americans since 1992, despite the remarkable economic boom of the decade. The nation had created more than 14 million jobs, but most of these were in small businesses that were far less likely than large companies to provide employee health coverage. Judith Feder, the former top health adviser to the Clinton administration, observed: "I wonder what will happen when there's a recession. If low-wage workers are in trouble in good times, where will they be in bad?" Others also wondered whether this number was the best it would ever get.[16]

The greater the number of people without medical coverage, the less politicians seemed to want to talk about, let alone deal with it. The National Coalition on Health Care, a bipartisan group headed by former Presidents Bush, Carter, and Ford, reported in May 1999 on the erosion of health coverage, but the report barely made a ripple. It concluded that the number of uninsured was rising because of fundamental economic and demographic forces that, by themselves, were certain to make the problem worse. Most of the uninsured were employed, but worked in small businesses or in service sectors that did not cover employees or required them to pay so much for health coverage that they could not afford it. The ranks of the uninsured were swollen by growing numbers of the self-employed, part-time, and contract workers and the rising percentage of minorities in the population. The most chilling conclusion, however, was that even if the prosperous economic conditions of the 1990s prevailed for another decade, a projected 52 to 54 million nonelderly Americans (1 in 5) would still be without health insurance. The number would probably increase to 61 million, or 1 in 4 Americans, in a recession. The report cast doubt on the capacity of the private sector to meet the needs of those who were most in need of health coverage. "Despite strong economic growth and low unemployment, employer-sponsored health insurance has continued to erode throughout the past decade," the report declared.[17]

With cost, quality, and access to health care so inextricably linked, and with the number of Americans who were unable to pay their own medical bills threatening to destabilize an already-strained and faltering health care system, one might have expected the presidential candidates of the first election after the millennium to address the issue, especially since the last sentence of the coalition's report declared, "We continue to ignore this problem at our peril." Instead, among the presidential primary contenders of *both* parties, there was silence until aspiring Democratic presidential candidate Bill Bradley belatedly put the issue on the agenda of election-year politics.[18] Calling health security an inalienable right of citizenship as much as the guarantees of "life, liberty and the pursuit of happiness," on September 28, 1999, Bradley unveiled a $65 billion plan to dramatically expand the federal health care system, and he accused his Democratic rival, Vice President Al Gore, of shying away from the challenge to insure all Americans.[19]

Gore responded that Bradley's proposal was "wildly unrealistic," "wildly expensive," lacked effective cost controls, and failed to make health coverage mandatory. He countered with a more limited approach that expanded federal efforts to insure all children and to extend coverage gradually to uninsured adults, but he attached no dollar amount to his plan. Republican primary candidates, by contrast, trotted out the familiar proposals of the past: medical savings accounts, means testing for federally subsidized Medicare premiums, tax incentives for small businesses, tax deductions for health insurance for the self-employed, and deductibility for long-term care. Meanwhile, in the weeks after both parties' nominating conventions, poll after poll disclosed that health care issues, particularly prescription drug coverage, had moved to the forefront of presidential politics.[20]

Congress was unlikely to enact legislation prior to the election, whether it was to help seniors pay for prescription drugs, rein in the costs and practices of HMOs, pass a patients' bill of rights, or amend the antitrust laws to let physicians in private practice form unions to bargain collectively on fees and treatment with health insurance plans.[21] There was no consensus among lawmakers or voters on these issues, particularly at a time when there was a broad perception that Americans were more prosperous than at any previous time in the nation's history. Election-year prosperity masked persistent economic and social problems, however, and the rising tide of prosperity that raised all boats, according to traditional economic wisdom, seemed not to apply to health care or health expenditures. For most people, good health is priceless, which presented political leaders with a conundrum: their constituents refused to accept rationing of medical treatment and did not want to be told that good health had a price. Yet neither lawmakers nor health consumers wanted to pay the higher taxes or higher insurance premiums that access to unlimited health care demanded.[22]

In this environment, the political and popular will to find a solution to the health care problem was lacking. When the Democratic presidential candidate Al Gore outlined his economic vision for America in a speech in Cleveland, he did not even mention health policy. The Republican candidate, Texas Governor George W. Bush, also sought to skip the issue of health care and to avoid scrutiny of his state's record on health care provision.[23] This reticence marked quite a change from 1992, when health cost containment and coverage for all Americans had virtually defined the Clinton-Gore campaign. No one then had doubted that there was a serious health care crisis, even though there was disagreement over how best to solve the problem. But in the post-Clinton, pre–stock market crash era of unrivaled prosperity, when Americans expressed complete confidence in their ability to handle most economic problems, the Gore and Bush campaigns did not want even to address the health care issue, and when they did, both candidates evinced doubt that health cost containment and universal coverage were achievable. Above all, each candidate was determined not to repeat the mistakes that had killed Clinton's plan, but beyond that, neither offered a viable solution to a realistic political and economic problem.[24]

Bush's election in 2000 also brought with it Republican majorities in both the House and the Senate. And with budget projections of a $313 billion surplus, there was some expectation that Congress would act to shore up Medicare, pass a patients' bill of rights, and address other unresolved health care problems, including medical malpractice insurance and prescription drug coverage. Little noticed at the time was the ascendancy of neocon- servatives around the president whose hostility to government bureaucracy and liberal social policies had important consequences for the structure of federalism. These advis- ers were determined to pursue a course of selective devolution in matters of social and health policy.

Devolution was not a new phenomenon when it emerged on the political scene in the 1990s. From 1932 through the late 1960s, the national government had been paramount within the federal system, with the states in a subordinate position. That began to change under Presidents Nixon and Reagan, particularly the latter, who had serious reservations about the federal governance in policy making and who promoted the capacity and legit- imate authority of the states. Reagan's New Federalism proposed to curtail government intervention in the private market and to cut drastically the flow of federal dollars allo- cated for social programs. His expectation was that the states, when confronted with fed- eral retrenchment, would curb social programs even more than required by federal ac- tions. It did not always work as scripted, but the policy change signaled a historic shift in federalism's center of gravity.[25]

As practiced by Republicans, Reagan's New Federalism eroded the postwar consensus that medical care was not like other market goods and that government had a respon- sibility to subsidize—and when necessary, supplement—voluntary health insurance. The erosion of this consensus occurred in two phases. In the first, opponents of government-funded health insurance attacked public programs obliquely, as unre- strained budget breakers that were spiraling out of fiscal control and imposing huge tax burdens on the American public. Although Reagan had treaded lightly around Medicare and Social Security in 1981, Medicaid had been hit hard.

As the 1980s wore on and tax revenues lagged behind spending on mandatory entitle- ment programs, the budget deficit emerged as the primary domestic issue in politics. Concerns about the burden of debt set the stage for growing constraints on federal fiscal capacity in the administrations of Presidents George H. W. Bush and Bill Clinton. In this stark fiscal climate, Medicare, Medicaid, and other nondiscretionary programs came under fire as spendthrift entitlements that undermined productivity and threatened to bankrupt future generations. These complaints emanated not only from conservatives opposed in principle to the welfare state but also from moderate Democrats and Repub- licans, the media, academe, and policy experts, who saw the deficit as a sign that the po- litical system had failed.

The emergence of the deficit as a focal point for attacks on existing programs initiated the second phase in the breakup of the postwar consensus by significantly transforming conservative strategy and rhetoric. Critics of the welfare state moved from indirect at- tacks on government programs as unrestrained entitlements to direct, frontal assaults on the programs themselves. Deficit reduction thus became a mechanism to create a smaller, less-intrusive, less-costly government. The Republicans' budget of 1995 was a good example. It had aimed less at fiscal redistribution than at radically reducing the political capacities of the federal government.

That same budget battle had also demonstrated that conservatives were no longer willing to accept either the rationale or the structure of existing government programs—cutting here, trimming there, but leaving the basic principles intact. Instead, the 1995 budget not only questioned the very foundations of existing programs but also presented coherent alternatives to them, as Republicans sought to reduce spending on them and to put into place policy changes that would prevent spending from rising again.

Therefore, for programs that were run jointly by the federal and state governments, Republicans sought to devolve key elements of fiscal and program authority to the state level, while retaining sufficient federal control to mandate requirements for benefits and eligibility. In effect, the states would assume the financial burden of these programs. Also, wherever possible, the Republicans attempted to put in place mechanisms (for example, vouchers) to allow beneficiaries of programs to purchase private alternatives to government-provided services. The primary purpose of these mechanisms was not budgetary savings but to move people out of social insurance and into private plans.

These components of the Republican strategy came into play in 1995 in the congressional leadership's proposals to restructure Medicare and Medicaid. On Medicare, the strategy aimed to realize $270 billion in savings by 2002, an amount that significantly exceeded the funds needed to place Medicare's Hospital Insurance Trust Fund on a firmer long-term footing. In practice, the most important aspect of the proposal was not to effect budget savings (for there were none) but to bring about major structural changes in Medicare. These included broadening the HMO option, replacing a guaranteed level of coverage with a fixed federal contribution to public and private policies, and creating tax-sheltered medical savings accounts. Critics complained that the proposed changes would weaken traditional Medicare by siphoning off the healthiest subscribers to managed-care plans.

On Medicaid, the Republican goals were, perhaps, even more ambitious. Not only did Republican leaders seek to eliminate the federal entitlement to Medicaid, but they also proposed to convert the program into block grants and to devolve most of the authority to determine eligibility and program structure to the states. The Republican electoral victories in 1994 had swept into office a large new cadre of Republican state governors who, in the flush of economic prosperity, were eager to exchange reduced federal funding for greater control over their Medicaid programs. This would be a popular move politically; in addition, the Republican leadership's expectation was that the states would vigorously limit Medicaid's future growth by dropping people from its rolls and steering them into private plans. But states, in fierce competition with one another for capital and skilled labor, were likely to be sharply constrained in their ability to finance programs for the needy and disadvantaged.

These ambitious proposals had rested upon a historic transformation of Republican leadership and strategy, as well as continued economic prosperity. The conservative wing of the congressional Republican Party had forged this aggressive party agenda, as disclosed by Newt Gingrich in his Contract with America. In the wake of the political fight over Clinton's health security bill, Republicans had shown the drawing power of denouncing taxation and the government as the source of public anxiety and discontent. Conservatives seized on this opportunity to forge links with like-minded lobbies, to set up think tanks, and to appeal to the right-wing media to disseminate their ideas and to recruit conservative candidates for political office in order to initiate an era of conservative governance.

President Bush's actions on health care must be seen in the context of his attitudes and those of conservative Republicans toward government and the State. When they took power, there were indications that the economy, particularly the stock market, was cooling. Then came the attack on the World Trade Center on September 11, 2001, with its extensive loss of life, which delivered a further blow to the economy and diverted the attention of both the White House and the Congress from health care reform to an unpredictable war on terrorism, biomedical warfare, and the anthrax scare. Over the next eighteen months, the economy lost a half-trillion dollars.[26]

With the economy sliding into recession, the announcement that the budget surplus was gone dashed whatever hope of health care reform existed. The worst fears of Judy Feder and other health economists had materialized. The health care system once again was teetering on the brink of systemic failure. At the end of 2002, 41.2 million Americans (14.6 percent of the population) were without health insurance. This figure included not only the poor and the working poor but also an increasing number of educated, middle-class professionals whose livelihoods evaporated as businesses large and small furloughed their workforce. The cost to the nation of caring for these Americans was more than it would have been to pay for their health insurance. The Urban Institute estimated that if the country had provided universal coverage under the existing health system, the cost of the additional care would have amounted to $69 billion, an increase of less than 1 percentage point in the gross domestic product for health spending and an increase of only 3 to 6 percent for total health care spending. This was less than the annual inflation rate of health spending and considerably less than the indirect costs of the uninsured to the economy (estimated at $130–160 billion).[27]

Instead, Americans were already paying the world's highest health care taxes. The federal government was spending $2,604 per capita, the highest of any nation, including those with national health insurance, though only a quarter of the U.S. population was covered by government insurance. Not only were we paying more for less, but we could no longer assert, as the AMA had for decades, that we had the finest health care in the world. In both life expectancy and infant mortality, the United States had sunk below the median for developed countries. The nation was clearly not getting much bang for its bucks.[28]

For the health care consumer lucky enough to have insurance, premiums were higher (from 12 to 40 percent more than in the previous two decades), deductibles greater, and prescription drug prices out-of-sight. For employees who had lost their jobs, COBRA health insurance premiums averaged $225 per month for individuals and $583 for families. Wracked by recession and international uncertainty, many corporate employers—Bethlehem Steel, Polaroid, Ford Motor Company, and TXU, a Dallas-based energy company—dropped health coverage altogether or shifted a larger proportion of the cost to employees.

The Kaiser Family Foundation's 2002 survey of 435 corporations disclosed that a decade-long erosion in retiree health benefits was accelerating and that many current workers might find that health coverage had evaporated by the time they retired. Even when these workers went on Medicare, employers were still left to pay one of the most costly benefits: prescription drugs. To trim costs, 22 percent of the corporations planned to eliminate coverage for future retirees, and among those that said they would continue some level of coverage for retirees, an overwhelming number expected to cut benefits and increase significantly the premiums and co-payments required of retired beneficiaries. The traditional social contract between employer and worker was under attack, and many Americans feared that employment-based health insurance might disappear. Recession, job losses, and relentlessly rising health costs fueled labor unrest. When General Electric demanded that workers pay more for their benefits, its largest U.S.-based union responded with a two-day warning strike in January 2003, its first in more than thirty years.[29]

The plight of the uninsured in large urban industrial states with high unemployment, such as California, Michigan, and Pennsylvania, most often captured media attention, but health care issues pressed equally hard on a state like Virginia, which had a large rural population, was heavily dependent on tourism, service-oriented businesses, and military spending, and confronted the largest budget deficit in its history. The Virginia Health Care Foundation reported that nearly 15 percent of the 7 million Virginians had no health insurance whatsoever, although nearly half had household incomes of at least $30,000 a year.[30] The *Wall Street Journal,* no bastion of liberalism, attributed much of the blame for the health care crisis to the insurance industry, which had jacked up the cost of coverage for everybody to recoup its losses in the stock market and to make amends for having fouled up its pricing practices in the early 1990s. Having seriously underpriced medical malpractice insurance premiums, the industry was trying to discredit the trial lawyers who had won big settlements.

The Bush administration, insurers, and physicians, the *Journal* wrote, simplistically blamed trial lawyers and juries for large malpractice awards and preferred to legislate a cap on such suits rather than to address the issue in its complexity.[31]

With nearly every state on the brink of fiscal insolvency, governors and other public officials attributed the lion's share of their financial woes to Medicaid, the joint federal-state program that guaranteed health care for the nation's poor. Pennsylvania's new Democratic governor declared, "We are, in my view, closer to a health care implosion than most people realize." Louisiana Senator John B. Breaux also worried that the American system of medical care was "collapsing around us," and in a stunning reversal of his earlier opposition, he declared his support for universal health coverage. But unlike the managed-care approach of the Clinton plan, he wanted the government to require every citizen to purchase *private* health insurance, much as automobile drivers were required to buy liability insurance. He did not want a federally run, micromanaged program, but a federally *regulated* program wherein Washington subsidized the premiums based on income and private insurers offered levels of coverage with various deductibles and co-payments (much like the Medigap policies available to Medicare recipients), "but everybody would have to buy at least the basic plan." Government oversight would guarantee that insurers did not scam the system, prevent anyone from buying insurance, or require anyone to pay higher rates because of preexisting conditions. Competition among insurers would control costs and lower rates by forcing everyone into big insurance pools to spread the risks. If Breaux's plan virtually eliminated traditional Medicare and Medicaid, it would presumably give elderly Americans health insurance that physicians would accept.[32]

Breaux's proposal was interesting on several counts: it seemed to resurrect the notion of going for the grand plan—to address health care as a whole—that had been dormant since the Clinton plan, but took it down a different path; it implied that piecemeal "reforms" would no longer suffice to halt the slide into systemic failure; it combined federal oversight with private implementation; it would have maintained the federal/senior, state/junior model of federalism; and it would have profound consequences for older Americans. As a three-term centrist Democrat who often voted with Republicans and brokered compromises between liberals and conservatives, Breaux's dramatic shift made him a potential linchpin in enacting legislation that could change the face of health care in America.

The downside of Breaux's proposal was that if his plan became watered down in the legislative process, Americans might end up with something less than they currently had. That possibility also existed. A Republican president surrounded by conservative advisers, preoccupied with war in Iraq, grappling with a sluggish economy and a budget deficit reminiscent of the 1980s, and trying to ride herd on a Republican Congress fixated on cutting taxes and slashing social spending no matter what, might not be able to ignore the health care crisis, but neither was he likely to pursue health care reform in a way that implied comprehensive planning, government bureaucracy, and liberal social spending. At best, liberals hoped the Bush administration would shore up the existing system, but this expectation was confounded when, shortly after the 2002 midterm elections, the White House began to push seriously for passage of a Medicare reform bill that had many attributes of the conservative agenda. The president wanted health care reform in his pocket before facing the voters again in 2004.

In December, Bush appointed Stephen Friedman, his chief economic adviser, to lead the White House push on Medicare, along with Karl Rove, his chief political aide; HHS Secretary Tommy G. Thompson; and Thomas A. Scully, the Medicare/Medicaid administrator. The team met regularly with the president from December to February 2003. In his State of the Union address in 2003, Bush, who described himself as a "compassionate conservative," announced his intention to redefine Medicare, whose benefits everyone agreed lagged behind those of private health plans. He proposed to create a prescription drug benefit and offer it to patients who were willing to join a new version that relied on managed care. The goal was to slow the growth of Medicare costs over coming decades by attracting patients into a less-expensive system dominated by HMOs. Bush said he would not compel older Americans to leave Medicare and join a private plan, but his proposal contained a variety of popular features—besides drug coverage, a new provision to cover catastrophic medical costs—intended as powerful inducements for patients to switch. This approach would be more viable politically than similar proposals, he believed, because it would not force into managed care any patients in traditional Medicare, nor would it require the extreme changes in Medicare's financial structure that the Breaux commission had contemplated. Left unclear in the president's address was whether the drug benefit would also be extended to those who remained in Medicare and whether joining the new program would always be voluntary. Other than projecting the cost of the revised Medicare program at about $400 billion over the next decade, precise details of the president's proposal remained hazy, but its thrust was to overhaul Medicare along more market-friendly lines.[33]

White House efforts on behalf of Medicare reform paused at the beginning of the Iraq war but intensified later that summer and fall. Almost immediately, Bush's proposal ran into criticism from health reformers who noted its silence on a drug benefit for traditional Medicare clients, the absence of a guarantee that HMOs would have to enroll seniors who got sick a lot, and the question of what to do about long-term care for the elderly. What concerned them was an earlier experiment that had allowed Medicare clients to sign up for HMOs through a plan called "Medicare + Choice." Many of the participating HMOs had quickly closed their doors when they discovered that caring for the elderly was not profitable enough. They also noted that Bush's tilt toward managed care did nothing to strengthen traditional Medicare: it neither covered outpatient drugs (the most cost-effective method for upgrading the quality of care) nor offered disease-management programs (unlike many private insurers), which had shown the ability to upgrade care while lowering costs by up to 30 percent. The president's proposal, they feared, would weaken Medicare by draining it of cash.[34]

Liberals tied Bush's Medicare reform to some of his other dubious and controversial proposals, such as wanting people to place their Social Security savings in the stock market, his school-voucher plan, and cutting funds for impacted school districts even as he called up reservists and career military to active duty. Now he was taking money out of Medicare and turning it over to HMOs and PPOs, which even he did not trust! The contradiction between what he was proposing and the actual situation was not lost on reformers and administration critics. Most private insurers had never been keen on catering to Medicare's clientele. And when Bush declared, "Instead of bureaucrats, trial lawyers and HMOs"—the health care axis of evil—"we must put doctors and nurses and patients back in charge of American medicine," they said he had missed the point. This was precisely what Medicare had done. Despite its shortcomings, Medicare had empowered participants to choose their own physicians.[35]

The administration's assault on Medicare did not stop there. Critics noted that among the major changes it planned to make was one that rendered it more difficult for beneficiaries to appeal the denial of benefits. Disguised as an administrative rule change, the president put forth a cost-saving proposal to decide disputed cases by arbitration, mediation, or by lawyers and hearing officers from HHS rather than by federal administrative law judges. The latter were employed by the SSA and had often ruled that frail, elderly people with severe illnesses were being improperly denied coverage. Consumer groups, judges, the American Bar Association, the Federal Bar Association, health care providers, and Medicare recipients in unison denounced the proposal and the administration's attack on the independence of the judiciary.[36]

If the future of Medicare was in doubt, Medicaid's prospects were even more dismal, as Washington contemplated devolving more of its fiscal responsibility upon the states. Afflicted by their own fiscal crises caused by the recession, almost every state was experiencing difficulty balancing its own budget. Revenue was down, whereas pressure to increase spending was strong. This situation was aggravated by structural weaknesses within their existing tax systems. Revenues fell short of the spending needed to maintain the existing levels of services and eligibility. Any contemplated large federal cuts in social welfare would simply intensify the states' problems.[37]

The National Association of Governors, almost evenly divided between Republicans and Democrats, complained to President Bush that Medicaid, the health insurance program for the poor, was eating up as much as 20 percent of state budgets. They wanted Washington to pick up the entire cost of health care for Medicaid's elderly poor, a figure estimated at $80 billion. Bush's response, that an overhaul rather than a federal bailout was the best way to address escalating Medicaid costs, led many governors to conclude that the president's "cure" would exacerbate their own problems. They pointedly declined to endorse his solution—a promise of more money up front over the next seven years but a severe cut in Medicaid funds thereafter—which locked them into an uncertain financial future. Left to their own devices, Republican and Democratic governors responded to their fiscal woes by knocking people off the Medicaid roster and trimming children's health insurance programs.[38]

Meanwhile, congressional Republicans, who feared that the reform would turn into a political liability in 2004, insisted that all seniors should have access to lower-priced medicines. Bush modified his prescription drug plan to include discount drug cards to those who remained in traditional Medicare, but even this change disappointed health economists. Some feared that in making private insurers a central part of Medicare's future, the government would have to accede to their demands for greater contributions to the cost of care over and above the subsidy for prescription drugs; others criticized the drug benefit as a bonanza for the pharmaceutical and managed-care industries, both huge donors to the Republican Party. They predicted it would give them tremendous negotiating leverage with the government.[39]

Having made the prescription drug concession, the White House left the heavy political lifting on the legislation, that is, brokering the deals to make passage of the bill occur, to the congressional Republican leadership: Bill Frist, Senate majority leader; House Speaker J. Dennis Hastert; and Tom DeLay, House majority leader. The "distancing" strategy was a conscious effort to inoculate President Bush from conservative Republican legislators agitated over a ballooning deficit and the huge expense of the $400 billion bill. Karl Rove, one of the architects of the strategy, knew that any kind of enormous expansion of the entitlement program was going to be an ideological-philosophical problem with congressional conservatives. This strategy allowed the White House to guide the process but also to maintain enough distance when Bush needed to do so. Senator Chuck Grassley of Iowa, chair of the powerful Finance Committee, then announced that Republicans would write new Medicare legislation from scratch.[40]

Both houses of Congress, after five years of deadlock and partisan warfare, seemed suddenly more willing than ever to pass a major overhaul of Medicare and to create a prescription drug benefit for the elderly. The political landscape had shifted abruptly, but what specifically had changed? One difference was in the attitude of the White House. President Bush wanted Medicare reform, including a prescription drug benefit, well in advance of the 2004 elections and was willing to put political capital and money on the table to get it. Though the White House still advocated a greater role for private health plans, it signaled its willingness to compromise on some of its free-market principles. It dropped the unequal drug benefit of its original proposal, which opened the way for bipartisan support, especially in the Senate where some, like Senator Tom Daschle, did not want to seem obstructionist in a cause he had championed for years. Other Democrats and the politically influential AARP saw Medicare reform, however imperfect, as a first step toward bringing Medicare benefits in line with private insurance plans.

The clearest indication that a historic breakthrough was possible came on June 12, 2003, when the leaders of the Senate Finance Committee, Grassley, and Democrat Max Baucus found common ground. They announced that drug coverage would be extended to beneficiaries who remained in the traditional Medicare plan. That was enough to bring centrist Democrats on board, notably John Breaux, who viewed the bill as a compromise between those who trusted government and those who trusted the market. Senator Edward Kennedy's unexpected support split liberal Democratic ranks sufficiently to enable the committee to approve a new Medicare drug bill by the remarkably bipartisan vote of sixteen to five, over sharp and recurring criticism from both the Left and the Right. Liberals argued that it offered only a meager benefit, contained big gaps in coverage (so-called doughnut holes), and pushed many elderly Americans into a strange new world of private health plans with widely varying premiums and benefits. Conservatives argued that the bill created a new, expensive entitlement and contained few of the structural changes required to create the new Medicare marketplace of competing private health plans that would be more efficient than the traditional program.[41]

The road between the Finance Committee and a Rose Garden signing ceremony proved not to be an easy one to travel. On June 20, legislation to remake Medicare cleared critical hurdles at both ends of the Capitol, as the Republican-controlled House and Senate moved toward approval of two sharply different bills to provide drug coverage for seniors and to give private insurers a new role in the program. The House action occurred only after a sharply partisan debate in which Democrats, donning black armbands to mourn Medicare's demise, attacked the Republican-crafted bill as an attempt to privatize Medicare, another step toward devolution. This debate occurred after House Democrats objected to a companion measure to allow some individuals to defray the cost of health insurance and prescription drugs with tax-free dollars accumulated in special savings accounts. The Senate proceedings, by contrast, were more collegial, punctuated by a seventy-one to twenty-six vote to divide $12 billion evenly between health care priorities favored by each party.[42]

A week later, each chamber passed the final version of its respective bill and sent it to conference to reconcile the differences. The delay dashed the president's hope for a speedy July 4 signing ceremony and set the stage for a final battle whose outcome remained very much in doubt. Although the Senate had approved Medicare reform by a large majority (76–21), the House bill squeaked through by a single vote (216–215), with 19 conservative Republicans voting against it despite heavy lobbying from the White House.[43]

President Bush, meanwhile, capitalized on his push to reform Medicare, going to Miami on June 30 to talk about the "historic opportunity we have to modernize Medicare on behalf of America's seniors." But just as Bush's "mission accomplished" speech on May 1 had been a premature declaration of success in Iraq, he had minimized the political and policy obstacles to a Medicare victory. The House and Senate bills had "a lot of commonality," but they also contained significant differences. The House bill was more generous to those whose drug bills were less than $2,000 a year, whereas the Senate bill was more generous to low-income people and had a smaller gap in coverage. Robert Reischauer, president of the Urban Institute, predicted, "There are going to be many whose expectations will be dashed."[44]

Indeed, the joint conference committee itself, which included only two Democrats (Max Baucus and John Breaux) over the protests of the minority party, became a battleground between moderate and conservative Republicans, as the conferees attempted to reconcile differences between the two bills. The negotiations went very slowly over the summer and fall, virtually stalling over the issues of how to design the drug benefit; the levels of premiums, deductibles, co-payments, and other expenses that low-income and elderly Americans should pay; whether to raise or reduce government payments to health care providers; whether to impose a means test on affluent Medicare recipients; whether to pit traditional Medicare against private health plans; and whether to include tax benefits for health care used by younger workers. With an October 17 deadline looming, Representative Bill Thomas of California, chairman of the conference committee, issued a schedule that amounted to a forced march through a thicket of controversy. He also stressed the importance of secrecy.[45]

Outside the conference, the political whirlwind swirled as both the Right and the Left, responding to rumors and unnamed sources, resorted to hyperbole and threats in a desperate attempt to shape the outcome of the negotiations. Conservative legislators, convinced that the $400 billion tax bill would blow the budget, accused their leaders of giving away the store—of being too willing to expand benefits without first reforming Medicare. The White House, they complained, was too eager to make a deal. Liberal Democrats protested that this was the unraveling of Medicare, and Senator Kennedy warned that many Democrats who had supported the Senate bill would withdraw that support if the Republican conferees pushed too hard toward privatization and for tax breaks for personal medical savings accounts. Kennedy feared that only the sickest and poorest would be left in the traditional Medicare program.

Behind the scene and publicly, the Bush administration worked with the leadership to prod the conferees along, taking the highly unusual step for Republicans of encouraging the negotiators to consult with the liberal and politically potent AARP at key points on the drug benefit and the provision to discourage employers from dropping drug coverage for their retired employees. This shrewd move ultimately wedded the AARP to the Republican version of Medicare reform, angered Democrats, and neutralized their allegations that Republicans were out to gut the government-run health insurance program. Meanwhile, the White House reached out to conservatives by urging the negotiators to go in some instances beyond the House and Senate bills: encouraging them to take stronger steps to ensure that PPOs were given sufficient incentives to enroll the elderly, establishing a means test that went significantly beyond the House-passed version, and creating a $12 billion fund to pay private health plans to enroll elderly patients in rural regions where managed care was scarce.[46]

Despite White House lobbying, key issues continued to remain unresolved. On October 28, Republican leaders directed the conferees to settle all items by day's end, with the exception of four major areas of disagreement. Three were key demands of Republicans: proposals for direct competition between Medicare and private health plans, curtailing spending if future cost increases were larger than expected, and establishing tax-exempt medical savings accounts. The fourth was the dispute over whether to allow the importation of brand-name drugs from Canada and elsewhere. Both the pharmaceutical industry, a major contributor to the Republican Party, and the FDA vigorously opposed foreign importations, which were under active consideration by Democratic and Republican governors and mayors alike as a way to trim budget deficits. The Republican leadership eventually scaled back the demand for competition between Medicare and the private plans and, in a gesture to conservatives, included a provision for medical savings accounts for individuals purchasing high-deductible health insurance. This broke the logjam and allowed the conferees to work out a final agreement in mid-November. The changes were presented to the two Democratic conferees (whose input had been minimal) for their signature and then disclosed to the public.[47]

The political battle lines hardened almost immediately thereafter. President Bush gave the legislation his enthusiastic backing, and the head of the AARP asserted that though the bill was not perfect, "the country can't afford to wait for perfect," and he promised "to pull out all the stops to get the bill passed," including a $7 million television campaign. Senator Kennedy led the Democratic opposition, calling the bill a partisan attack on Medicare and predicting it would not pass Senate muster. In a blistering attack on the AARP, he accused its leaders of having undercut the Democrats' efforts to get the best bargain they could.[48]

On November 22, a fiercely polarized House approved the Medicare overhaul bill after an all-night session and an extraordinary display of Republican arm-twisting to muster a majority. The final version of the bill was adopted by a vote of 220 to 215, which generally followed party lines. Sixteen Democrats voted for the measure and 25 conservative Republican legislators voted no. The final tally occurred after a night of high legislative drama, as the roll-call vote, which rarely exceeded twenty minutes, began at 3 A.M. and was held open for nearly three hours, as Republican leaders, the president, and administration officials scrambled to quell a conservative rebellion. For most of the three hours of voting, the legislation appeared headed for defeat, as House Speaker Hastert and HHS Secretary Thompson prowled the aisles searching for potential switches. Two Republicans, C. L. "Butch" Otter of Idaho and Trent Franks of Arizona, yielded to the pressure. "I did not want to vote for this bill," declared Otter, "but I was persuaded that if this bill went down, we would end up with a bigger, more expensive alternative with much less reform."[49]

Within hours of the House vote, the Senate took up the Medicare reform legislation. Despite Kennedy's threatened filibuster, Republican strategists expected passage to go smoothly. Even Kennedy conceded that his was an uphill fight, given that the Democratic leadership did not support blocking a vote for fear of offending senior citizens and that other Democrats had indicated they would vote for the measure. Twenty-two Democrats voted with the majority Republicans against a Democratic filibuster, and on November 25, the Senate voted 54 to 44 to pass the Medicare reform bill, which would take effect in 2006. On December 8, before thousands of cheering supporters, President Bush signed it into law, saying the new drug benefit "will save our seniors from a lot of worry." Critics retorted that the worries were just beginning for Medicare's older and disabled Americans, and speaking for the minority, Senator Daschle promised to revisit the issue the next year.[50]

The long political fight had been about neither the nation's senior citizens nor the drug benefit but how to reshape Medicare for the future and how to allocate federal dollars among special interests. The winners were President Bush; the Republican Party; the AARP; the manufacturers of brand-name prescription drugs (which, unlike the Veterans Administration, won a critical provision from Republicans that prohibited the government from negotiating prices or discounts); the pharmacy benefit–management companies, which negotiated with the drug companies on price; physicians, whose compensation rates for treating Medicare patients increased; rural and small urban hospitals, which received higher payments to compensate for a low volume of patients and a disproportionate share of low-income patients; HMOs and other health insurers, which won business and financial incentives to create alternatives to traditional Medicare; employers, provided they continued to offer their health plans to retired workers; and affluent younger workers, who could establish tax-exempt medical savings accounts.[51]

Among Medicare beneficiaries, some won gains and others lost. The winners were those who faced moderate-to-high drug costs, or who spent more than $5,000 annually on prescription medication, and most low-income seniors ($13,054 for individuals and $17,618 for families). The losers were seniors whose drug costs fell between $2,200 and $3,600 (they would still have to pay their premiums, but Medicare would pay up to $2,200 and then pause, resuming payments only after $3,600 was reached); those who had drug coverage from former employers; those who bought drugs from Canada and abroad; chain drug stores faced with new, sharp competition from mail-order pharmacies; and Democrats. But the biggest losers may well be future taxpayers. Until a tax or some other revenue source is identified, all the benefits are to be financed by borrowing. Projected initially to cost $400 billion over ten years starting in 2006, the Medicare reform was expected to rise in cost after that, as drugs grew more expensive and baby boomers retired. Critics and budget watchers predicted the cost could grow as high as $2.4 trillion over the second and third decade, potentially bankrupting the next generation and gravely damaging the economy.[52]

Since passage of the Medicare reform, allegations of ethical impropriety in the law's passage, a slow and confusing start to the discount card prescription drug program, and a series of other issues have cast doubt on the efficacy of the administration's health care program and have plagued both the Bush White House and Republicans in Congress. The chief actuary of the Medicare program disclosed that Medicare administrator Thomas Scully had threatened to fire him if he had revealed to Congress that the cost of the drug benefit was actually closer to $600 billion than the $400 billion the administration told Congress. The ballooning deficit had forced the White House to put a positive spin on its economic numbers, fearing with good reason that conservative Republicans might not have voted for the reform bill. Although no law was broken, this revelation embarrassed the Bush administration as well as Republican legislators of all stripes and their conservative supporters. The Heritage Foundation's director of health policy studies said, "There's no excuse for what the administration did."[53]

Pharmaceutical companies then raised prescription drug prices by nearly triple the rate of inflation in the first quarter of 2004, just before Medicare began its confusing discount card program, negating much of the savings the president had promised to senior citizens. That action also compromised the AARP, which was threatened with a loss of membership. Meanwhile, the executive branch was cast in the role of playing Russian roulette with the lives of sick people when it was announced that a lottery would be held to choose the 50,000 individuals (from an estimated 500,000 eligible) who would receive oral cancer medication and drugs covering other life-threatening illnesses before 2006. Although the financial and eligibility restrictions of the provision were not directly the fault of the administration (a Republican legislator from Ohio had inserted it in the Medicare bill), the administration went along with it.[54]

Finally, in June 2004, the Supreme Court shielded insurers from big-money malpractice suits in two Texas cases, ruling that patients could not sue HMOs in state courts when their refusal to pay for recommended care had resulted in medical catastrophes. The court, in reaffirming superior federal capacity, said that the federal government, not the states, held sway over insurance regulation, thereby eliminating state legal accountability for managed-care plans that altered, delayed, or denied a physician-recommended course of treatment. The distinction between the two jurisdictions was important because juries in state suits often awarded huge malpractice judgments, whereas a 1974 federal insurance law limited damage awards. The cases had an awkward political wrinkle for the administration. As a presidential candidate in 2000, Bush had praised the Texas statute in question as a model for a national patients' bill of rights, but it was the Bush administration's Justice Department that joined insurers and employers in preempting state jurisdiction when federal control was more favorable to the market.[55]

Democrats, mindful of the 2004 presidential election, were quick to seize on the administration's mistakes, requesting that the inspector general of HHS investigate the intimidation allegation, berating Bush for not forcing the drug makers to roll back price increases, forcing the White House to admit that only one in six seniors would receive the discount card, criticizing its position on HMO malpractice suits, and berating it for paying managed-care programs 8.4 percent more for managed care than it paid for traditional Medicare.[56]

Of all the differences between Bush and John Kerry, the Democratic candidate, health care offered one of the more dramatic contrasts to voters. Bush claimed his health plan empowered consumers. He proposed to offer refundable tax credits to allow low-income Americans to buy health insurance, to form "associate health plans" that would let small businesses band together to get the best insurance rates for their employees, and to limit medical malpractice awards. But his proposals would not reach more than 2–3 million of the 43 million Americans without health insurance, would not cost the Treasury very much (about $60 billion over ten years), and would not work unless the pharmaceutical industry was enjoined from manipulating the marketplace, physicians, and patients with misleading or inaccurate information. Kerry's plan, by contrast, would provide health-related tax credits to small businesses, have Washington pick up 75 percent of health insurance premiums over $50,000 to reduce costs for businesses and their workers, extend Medicaid coverage to all low-income children and their parents, shift responsibility for those costs to Washington and away from cash-strapped state governments, and let workers buy into federal employees' health plans. The Kerry plan would cost $895 billion over ten years and would cover about 27 million uninsured Americans. Other than repealing Bush's tax breaks for Americans earning more than $200,000 annually, Kerry did not say how he would pay for his plan or guarantee access to high-quality, truly unbiased health care to less affluent citizens.[57]

During the campaign, both parties affirmed their commitment to the issues that the polls revealed as priorities among voters. On health care, the polls showed that voters trusted Democrats more than Republicans by a wide margin, and Kerry attempted to capitalize on that perception by making health care a major issue in the election. Republicans successfully blunted that perception, as they shifted the campaign's focus to Iraq, the war on terrorism, and the reaffirmation of moral values. The politics of health security, however, returned to prominence following President Bush's reelection. Emboldened by their success at the polls, President Bush and Republican leaders in Congress interpreted their victory as a mandate to move the nation away from the system of employer-provided health insurance, which covered most working Americans. In its place, they proposed to erect a system in which workers—instead of looking to employers for health insurance—took personal responsibility for protecting themselves and their families. Workers would buy high-deductible "catastrophic" insurance policies to cover major medical needs, then pay routine costs with money set aside in tax-sheltered health savings accounts (HSAs), which Congress had authorized in the 2003 Medicare prescription drug bill and the administration has encouraged with tax breaks and subsidies, despite a record budget deficit.[58]

This component of the Bush administration's approach to health care has been on the conservative agenda for years, but both the president and the congressional Republican leadership put it on the fast track in 2005 because they were confident that the political balance of power in Congress had changed. Supporters of this new health care initiative saw it as part of Bush's "ownership society." They argued that workers and their families would become more careful users of health care if they had to pay the bills and that the lower premiums on high-deductible plans would make coverage affordable for the uninsured and for small businesses. Indeed, more than one-quarter of employers, aware of the potential cost savings to their firms, have said they would likely offer HSAs as an option to employees.

Critics responded that Bush's vision represented at best wishful thinking and at worst a perilous attempt to transform the health care system with less public attention or debate than has surrounded his plan to overhaul Social Security. They insisted the Republican initiative was really an attempt to shift the risks, huge costs, and complex problems of health care from employers to individuals, and warned that people will not get needed care, because they will want to save money. Whichever side prevails, the new direction in national health policy is occurring at a time when questions have surfaced regarding the administration's much touted reform of Medicare. Shortly after Bush's reelection, the White House released budget figures indicating that the Medicare prescription drug benefit will cost more than $1.2 trillion over the decade from 2006 to 2015, not the $400 billion the administration had told Congress. This price increase arose largely from an accounting tactic used to secure votes for the bill's passage. Medicare's actuaries had arrived at their original cost estimates by using a ten-year period that ran from 2004 to 2013, even though the drug benefit did not take effect until 2006. This meant there were almost no program costs for the first two years. The 2006 budget, however, had to take into account the 2006–2015 period, which included 2014 and 2015, when the drug benefit's costs are predicted to escalate ($98 billion in 2014 and $109.2 billion in 2015).

This disclosure prompted criticism from Democrats and even from the Republican chairman of the Senate Budget Committee about the overall veracity of the administration's long-term budget estimates. Medicare, thus, may pose a far more serious budgetary problem in the coming decade and may even overshadow debates over Social Security reform, HSAs, and dismantling the employer-provided health insurance system.[59]

National health security has risen and fallen from the American political agenda over the course of the past hundred years, beginning with Theodore Roosevelt and the Bull Moose Progressive Party, which first advocated a plan in 1912. A recapitulation of the legislative history would only hint at the frustration of advocates of universal health care coverage. The failure of President Clinton's reform plan, even after a decade, continues to hang like a dark cloud over contemporary health care debates. But we should not lose sight of the fact that the issue did reach the national political agenda on five distinct occasions, or that future reformers may, perhaps, learn from past failures. Because health care reaches into every quarter of our society, economy, and public policy, we have to ask ourselves why there was such intense opposition to universal health coverage.[60]

Before responding to this question, we have to remind ourselves that the United States has a quite extensive welfare state; however, unlike that of other nations, it is anchored in the private sector but backed financially and in other ways by government policy.[61] We also have to note that there has been over the course of a century no shortage of obstacles to health reform: the intense opposition of interest groups representing the medical profession, private insurance companies, and the pharmaceutical industry; the antigovernment strain of American political culture; and the fragmented nature of American politics and institutions. Overcoming these obstacles has proven to be so difficult and the historical record of failed reform so dismal that many reformers, policy experts, and lawmakers have argued that without a transformation of the political system, it is simply not possible to establish a system of universal health care in this country.

This conclusion ignores the fact that the episodes of stalemate were not all of the same character. For example, what made the complete unraveling of the Clinton health plan so puzzling was that early in the process there was in Congress a potentially realizable majority for health reform. However, the administration was unable to transform that potential into a legislative majority for its bill, or for any other reform bill. This failure also was true of reform efforts in 1974, when the Republican Nixon administration and many Democrats favored health reform but could not muster congressional majorities (or the support of organized labor) to effect a legislative breakthrough. The impasse over national health reform, then, took a particular form the past two times it appeared on the national agenda: blocked legislation even under conditions of presidential sponsorship and congressional majorities favoring reform.[62]

One obvious reason for the failure of the 1974 and 1993 reform drives was that the proponents of reform could not reach a consensus and unite behind one particular plan. In the 1970s, advocates of comprehensive health care dissipated their energies in support of at least three plans: government-operated health insurance, employer-mandated provisions of private insurance, and catastrophic insurance. In the early 1990s, reformers again divided, this time among single-payer, pay-or-play, and managed-competition proposals. The absence of consensus over which approach to health care reform to adopt and the accompanying failure to enact any legislation obscured the extent to which the different reformers favored many, if not all, of the same goals: universal coverage, quality care, cost containment, reform of private health insurance practices, and a patients' bill of rights. No one proposal attracted a legislative majority in either 1974 or 1993, even though citizen and congressional majorities supported these fundamental principles. Health care reform, then, failed because its advocates disagreed over means rather than ends, whereas the opponents of reform were unified in their opposition, well financed, and willing to commit the resources to block reform.[63]

The nature of American politics reinforced this tendency of the majority favoring reform to fragment into many factions advancing competing proposals and unwilling to compromise. Unlike the Westminster, or parliamentary, system of Great Britain, the institutional structure of the American government separates the election of the executive from the legislative branch. That means the electoral fate of members of Congress is not tied directly to that of the president, and thus they are not required to defer to his policy making. Indeed, the president's authority to compel legislators to support a health plan emanating from the Oval Office, even when his party controls both the House and Senate, is limited. The Clinton administration's fumbling of health care reform illustrated this point: Clinton was unable to persuade Democratic legislators backing different reform bills to unite behind his plan. By September 1994, hardly any congressional Democrat was supporting it, with impunity. This illustrated the failure of the president as leader of his party, but also that the system was rigged against him.

Republican President Bush's Medicare reform in 2004, by contrast, demonstrated both the limits and the reach of executive power, though not necessarily in a way one would recommend as standard operating procedure. To achieve the prescription drug coverage he wanted, Bush allowed the congressional Republican leadership to do the heavy lifting in support of his proposal, but even then, the White House lobbied behind the scenes, going as far as to persuade the House leadership to bend the usual parliamentary procedure on a roll-call vote to line up enough conservative Republican votes to pass Medicare reform. And this was accomplished only after the administration had deliberately misled legislators of both parties about the proposal's true cost!

Ethical considerations notwithstanding, the American political party structure further exacerbated the task of maintaining the unity of health care majorities. In this country, unlike in Great Britain, political parties neither control which candidates run under the party's banner nor provide the bulk of campaign funds to candidates. This situation accentuates the political independence of members of Congress and makes it difficult for the party leadership to line up all their members behind a single party proposal (as would be common in a parliamentary system). Moreover, there has been no party based exclusively on ideology or class in this country (such as a Labor Party) to press for national health reform. Geographical and ideological divisions *within* the two major parties, particularly within the Democratic Party, as the experiences with national health reform of Presidents Roosevelt, Truman, and Kennedy demonstrated, reinforced the difficulties they and party leaders confronted in trying to create a consensus among legislators of their own party for a national health reform proposal emanating from 1600 Pennsylvania Avenue.

The internal structure of Congress also rendered health reform extremely difficult to achieve. Congress is organized along committee lines, often with overlapping jurisdictions. This format disperses power throughout that body, while simultaneously enhancing the power of the chair, who exercises authority over committee staffs, creates and terminates subcommittees, controls the agenda and parliamentary procedure, schedules hearings, and serves as floor manager for committee bills. Five different committees shared primary jurisdiction over Clinton's health plan, and another seven exercised partial jurisdiction. These committees were, in turn, divided into subcommittees. The division of legislative authority increased the likelihood of political splintering, as committee and subcommittee chairs often used their position to advance or block specific bills; this fragmentation increased the number of hurdles that any plan had to surmount (as did the bicameral structure of Congress). A powerful committee chair, such as Wilbur Mills, could often shape legislation to his own liking and determine its fate, which helps to explain why it took so long for the House to pass Medicare legislation. Senator Moynihan, an advocate of welfare reform, in contrast, did not believe health care was an urgent priority even as Clinton was unveiling his health security bill.

All this suggests that the institutional separation of powers within the federal government, the structural weakness of the political party system, and the fragmented composition of Congress created a milieu that was more likely than not to breed political division over national policy proposals. In the case of national health care reform, the legislative histories of the various proposals demonstrated that the conditions of American political life made it very difficult for majorities favoring universal coverage to coalesce around and muster majority votes for one single plan. The dilemma reformers have not yet resolved is how to keep a legislative majority favoring universal coverage from splintering over different approaches to national health reform. So far, they have not succeeded in devising a strategy that builds on their consensus goals, whereas the proliferation of power centers has given platforms to the opponents of reform.[64]

The political system is rigged against reform, but the system includes more than the legislative process. If comprehensive reform did not win strong support from powerful segments of the political elite, neither was it well served by the media elite. The amount of news coverage and interpretation of the health care debate by the liberal press—the *New York Times,* the *Washington Post,* and the *Los Angeles Times*—illustrated how press coverage shifted across time as the debate over Clinton's plan progressed. Journalists were not simply passive recorders of information; their reporting initially told readers *what* facet of the issue to think about, and then they told readers *how* to think about health care reform, as newspapers reflected increasingly the success of small busi- ness–interest groups and their business and congressional allies (for example, Senator Bob Dole) in getting out their message. From mid-September to early October 1993, the press framed Clinton's proposal as a way to provide comprehensive reform of the entire health system. This corresponded with the highest level of public support for Clinton's plan and the lowest opposition. Then from mid-December to late January 1994, there was a sharp increase in news coverage of the secrecy of the presidential task force, which was attributed to heightened activity in the lawsuit against it. Press coverage at the time im- plied that Clinton's plan was possibly illegal.[65]

Similarly, from June 1993 on, the press framed health care reform as a debate over em- ployer mandates. During this time, small businesses through the NFIB had the greatest influence in turning public opinion against the Clinton plan; the NFIB persuaded con- gressional opponents to use the alleged plight of small businesses to turn public and po- litical support against the Clinton plan. Some sentimental attachment to universal cover- age may have existed in the liberal press, but from the first there was little editorializing on behalf of any legislation that would provide it. The *New York Times,* for example, criti- cized the plan's regulatory cost controls, but given that the CBO did not believe that man- aged competition could control costs, Clinton had no alternative to that regulation. Like- wise, the *Washington Post* editorialized in favor of an incremental approach to reform. Passing major reform was not likely without support from the pillars of the liberal press, but President Clinton would not have been able to gain Democratic support in 1993 for small fixes in the insurance market to make life better for already-covered middle-class employees. Instead of explaining the provisions of the plan intelligibly in detail and in all of their ramifications, the media, influenced by opposition interest groups and key polit- ical opponents, have encouraged a structure of public discourse that favored simple ideas over complex ones and the status quo over change.[66]

The other great obstacle to national health reform has been the middle class. Middle-class Americans, imbued with the Protestant work ethic and individualistic values and skeptical of government, have perceived universal coverage in class terms and as a zero-sum game, with winners and losers. Yet health care reformers of the 1990s optimistically believed that the conditions for adopting universal health coverage were better than at any previous time, because middle-class Americans were themselves in jeopardy. This was a change from the past, when reformers appealed to middle-class voters to support change, not for their own benefit, but for the well-being of an ill-defined and politically impotent minority of fellow citizens. To the middle-class taxpayer, the family of the unionized worker, and the elderly protected by Medicare, previous comprehensive health reform proposals had offered too little for too much; the fear of the unknown had a firm grip on middle-class Americans. Clinton and his policy advisers believed they could change middle-class sensibilities when they entered the White House. Employers' efforts to control health expenditures and insurers' practice of screening out high-risk individuals had ripped away some of the middle-class insulation from health costs, which had made it so difficult to construct an alliance for universal coverage that transcended class lines. Middle-class Americans found themselves in the early 1990s increasingly subjected to the financial insecurities that afflicted the working poor and the uninsured, and in the health policy sector at least, they did not see government initiatives as socially divisive or evoking the same negative associations as did the redistributive policies associated with antipoverty programs.[67]

The economic recession of 1989–1991 may have persuaded Americans that the health care system needed to be improved, but it did not necessarily translate government intervention into support for comprehensive health reform. A majority of middle-class Americans agreed that changes were necessary, but they also were satisfied with the quality and accessibility—if not the cost—of the medical care they received. Moreover, few Americans understood the major options for reform that policy makers had been considering and the trade-offs each option entailed. The media had done a poor job of educating them; and not surprisingly, middle-class voters turned against Clinton's plan. They feared they would lose what they already had and were familiar with. Universal coverage also implied egalitarian access, which ran contrary to the middle-class belief that all individuals had interests that could be served only by encroaching on the interests of others, and that one should not reward those who had resisted the processes of organized life in society. Universal health insurance, in other words, rewarded the wrong behavior and the wrong people—those who had not contributed to employer health plans. For those who had paid into the system and were retired, there was Medicare; for those temporarily unemployed, there was COBRA; and for the "deserving" working poor, there was Medicaid. When confronted with the Clinton health plan, middle-class voters were not overly troubled by the plight of the working poor and the uninsured. Commitment to community and social solidarity were not in the forefront of their thoughts and actions.

The immediate short-term challenge for health reformers is to safeguard and maintain existing public efforts in health care from assaults by budget-deficit hawks and anti-government ideologues. The long-term challenge is to build momentum toward universal coverage, a task that requires a substantial investment of political energy and capital in the reconstruction and improvement of existing health programs and, equally important, working with like-minded organizations and movements. Reformers of the twenty-first century will have to build an organizational infrastructure and public philosophy of government on which to rest their renewed campaign for health care reform. They will have to find a way to swing the majority of middle-class Americans behind universal coverage, which does not necessarily have to take the form of a grand plan as Clinton had envisioned it. Winning over the middle class may not be beyond the realm of possibility if the economy stumbles and middle-class anger over insurers' practices and managed care continues to grow. Already there is recognition in some influential quarters that the health care system is urgently in need of a basic overhaul. Senate majority leader Bill Frist, a Republican and a surgeon, told the National Press Club: "I would argue that the *status quo* of health care delivery in this country is unacceptable today. It will further deteriorate unless the [health] care sector of 2004 is radically transformed, is re-created."[68]

Before this happens, everyone—reformers, politicians, drug manufacturers, and citizens—will have to engage in tough discussions and make hard decisions on many fronts. These include reaching some consensus on which of the ever-growing bounty of pharmaceuticals are essential and should be covered by insurance and publicly funded programs; deciding what responsibility patients must shoulder for diseases that take a high toll in dollars and lives, but that are preventable; curbing medical inflation resulting from the lobbying and advertising blitz of the big drug companies, which have distorted medical research, misled physicians, induced patients to clamor for expensive (and potentially dangerous) new medications like Vioxx, fended off less-expensive Canadian imports, and undermined the independence of the Food and Drug Administration; insisting on tort reform that holds physicians accountable for mistakes and negligence but avoids the huge settlements that drive up (and out of medicine) the cost of insurance for all physicians and the bills they send to patients and insurers; exercising common sense in designing prescription care for senior citizens; examining rationally how much care is enough; facing the need to discuss whether people who depend on publicly funded care should settle for some lower level of service than those who help pay their own way; and, perhaps the toughest issue of all, deciding what to do about all the people who work but can't afford health insurance, either because their employers—usually small businesses but increasingly some of the largest and best-known corporations in America—can't afford it or because the employees' share is too costly.[69]

With baby boomers easing gently—if creakingly—into the age when health cares and costs take off, the pressure is on everyone to find realistic solutions. This means getting serious about what it will cost to provide the level of health care we seem to want, and what it will mean to provide it universally, if that is where the nation's values take it.

# NOTES

## ABBREVIATIONS

| | | | |
|---|---|---|---|
| ADA | Americans for Democratic Action | HGD | Helen Gahagan Douglas |
| ADCU | Aid for Dependent Children of Unemployed Families | HSTL | Harry S. Truman Library |
| | | *JAMA* | *Journal of the American Medical Association* |
| *ALLR* | *American Labor Legislation Review* | | |
| CAC-OU | Carl Albert Center, University of Oklahoma | LBJ | Lyndon B. Johnson |
| | | LBJL | Lyndon B. Johnson Library |
| CCC | Civilian Conservation Corps | NA | National Archives |
| COHC | Columbia University Oral History Collection | NA II | National Archives II |
| | | NARG | National Archives, Record Group |
| *CQ* | *Congressional Quarterly* | NPMP | Nixon Presidential Materials Project |
| *CQWR* | *Congressional Quarterly Weekly Report* | OF | Office File |
| FDR | Franklin D. Roosevelt | PPF | President's Personal File |
| FDRL | Franklin D. Roosevelt Library | SM&OF | Staff Member and Office Files |
| GUL | Georgetown University Library | SSB | Social Security Bulletin |
| HCIWG | Health Care Interdepartmental Working Group | WHCF | White House Central Files |
| | | WHSF | White House Special Files |

## INTRODUCTION

1. Samuel I. Rosenman, comp., *The Public Papers and Addresses of Franklin D. Roosevelt*, 13 vols. (New York, 1938–1950), 7: 414–418.

2. The Census Bureau reported on September 28, 2000, that the number of Americans without health coverage had dropped for the first time in more than a decade, to 42 million. The bureau attributed the decline to a tight labor market in a period of prosperity, which caused some employers (who otherwise might not have done so) to offer health coverage as a recruitment incentive. But with the economic recession following September 11, 2001, the unemployment rate went up again and the numbers without health insurance hovered around the 44 million mark. Employers, moreover, shifted a greater percentage of health care costs to their employees and cut health care benefits for company retirees. Robert J. Mills, "Health Insurance Coverage: 1999," U.S. Bureau of the Census, *Current Population Reports* (Washington, D.C., 2000).

3. Victor R. Fuchs, "What's Ahead for Health Insurance in the United States?" *New England Journal of Medicine* 346 (June 6, 2002): 24.

## CHAPTER 1. BEGINNINGS: THE FEDERAL
## GOVERNMENT & HEALTH SECURITY

1.  I. S. Falk, "Health Services, Medical Care Insurance, and Social Security," *Annals* 273 (Jan. 1951): 121. Falk's background and role in health policy formulation are discussed in Jonathan Engel, *Doctors and Reformers* (Columbia, S.C., 2002), 29–33.
2.  I. S. Falk, *Security against Sickness* (New York, 1936), esp. pt. 2.
3.  Marc Karson, *American Labor Unions and Politics, 1900–1918* (Carbondale, Ill., 1958); Paul Starr, *The Social Transformation of American Medicine* (New York, 1982), 240–241.
4.  Senate, John Graham Brooks, "Compulsory Insurance in Germany," *Fourth Special Report of the Commissioner of Labor,* 52d Cong., 2d sess., 1893, Sen. Exec. Doc. 66, 275, Append., 305–358. On the depression of the 1890s, see Douglas W. Steeples and David O. Whitten, *Democracy in Desperation: The Depression of 1893* (Westport, Conn., 1998).
5.  William F. Willoughby, *Workingmen's Insurance* (New York, 1898), 329, 344; Edward D. Berkowitz, *America's Welfare State* (Baltimore, 1991), 30.
6.  John R. Commons et al., *History of Labor,* 4 vols. (New York, 1918–1935), 4: 627–629; Henry J. Harris, *National Health Insurance in Great Britain, 1911 to 1921,* Bull. No. 312, U.S. Bureau of Labor Statistics (Washington, D.C., 1923).
7.  A good introduction to the literature of Progressivism is John D. Buenker and Nicholas Burckel, eds., *Progressive Reform* (Detroit, 1980). Progressivism and health reform are examined in Beatrix Hoffman, *The Wages of Sickness* (Chapel Hill, N.C., 2001), 24–44; Jill Quadagno, "One Nation: Uninsured" (forthcoming); Engel, *Doctors and Reformers,* 11–16; Lloyd R. Pierce, "The Activities of the AALL in Behalf of Social Security and Protective Labor Legislation" (Ph.D. diss., Univ. of Wisconsin, 1963), chaps. 1–2. Wilsonian Progressivism is treated in Arthur S. Link, *Woodrow Wilson and the Progressive Era* (New York, 1954).
8.  Starr, *Social Transformation of American Medicine,* 244–246; Jennifer Klein, *For All These Rights* (Princeton, N.J., 2003), 20, 26, 28, 33.
9.  Klein, *For All These Rights;* John Duffy, *The Sanitarians: A History of American Public Health* (Urbana, Ill., 1990), 244–247, 287.
10.  Maurice B. Hahamovitch, "History of the Movement for Compulsory Health Insurance in the United States," *Social Service Review* 27 (Sept. 1953): 281–287.
11.  Clarke C. Chambers, *Seedtime of Reform: American Social Service and Social Action* (Minneapolis, 1963), 1–25, 157, is definitive on social action in the period 1918–1933. The physicians' defection was attributable to several factors: their rising income during the war, abuses they had experienced under workmen's compensation schemes (which increased their fear of "government medicine"), and their growing confidence that compulsory health insurance could be rebuffed successfully. See Ronald L. Numbers, *Almost Persuaded: American Physicians and Compulsory Health Insurance, 1912–1920* (Baltimore, 1978), 15–18, 36, 61–63, 91.
12.  The elitist reformers, who were mostly white, middle class, and, to an extent, nativistic, were unable to rally the support of women's organizations and African-American and Jewish fraternal and mutual aid societies, which were most likely to work for, and benefit from, the passage of health legislation. Hoffman, *The Wages of Sickness,* chaps. 4–7.
13.  Wilbur J. Cohen Oral History, Columbia University Oral History Collection (COHC), pt. 4, 41; Chambers, *Seedtime of Reform,* passim. Chambers argues persuasively that reformers' efforts bore fruit with the onset of the Great Depression and advent of the New Deal.
14.  The CCMC's sponsorship by private philanthropic foundations is discussed in "The Committee on the Costs of Medical Care," *JAMA* 99 (Dec. 3, 1932): 1951–1952. Its work is brought together in CCMC, *Medical Care for the American People. The Final Report of the Committee on the Costs of Medical*

*Care, Adopted October 31, 1952* (Chicago, 1932), and the summary volume, *The Costs of Medical Care* (Chicago, 1933), ed. I. S. Falk, C. Rufus Rorem, and Martha D. Ring. See also Quadagno, "One Nation: Uninsured," 33–34; William Shonick, *Government and Health Services* (New York, 1995), 268–269; Michael R. Grey, *New Deal Medicine* (Baltimore, 1999), 22–24.

15. The committee's work, including the differing opinions of its members, is discussed in CCMC, *Medical Care for the American People*, 38, 109–134; "The Report of the Committee on the Costs of Medical Care," *JAMA* 99 (Dec. 10, 1932): 2035; Falk, *Security against Sickness*, 7–8; Engel, *Doctors and Reformers*, 16–25; Peter A. Corning, *The Evolution of Medicare*, Research Report No. 29, Office of Research and Statistics, Social Security Administration, DHEW (Washington, D.C., 1969), 25–27.

16. "The Committee on the Costs of Medical Care," 1951–1952.

17. "The Report of the Committee on the Costs of Medical Care," 2035; Roy Lubove, "The New Deal and National Health," *Current History* 45 (Aug. 1963): 78–79, 86.

18. See, for example, James A. Tobey, "Menace to National Health," *Current History* 37 (Dec. 1932): 323–326; Mary Ross, "Shall We Afford Health?" *Survey Graphic* 22 (Mar. 1933): 143–146; John A. Kingsbury, "Health Plan for the Nation," *Survey* 69 (Nov. 1933): 373; Thomas J. Parran, Jr., "Local Health Problems Which Must Be Solved," *American City* 49 (Apr. 1934): 71; Edward L. Bishop, "Public Health at the Crossroads," *American Journal of Public Health* (hereafter cited as *AJPH*), 125 (Nov. 1935): 1175–1180.

19. Hoover's response to the economic crisis is set forth in Herbert Hoover, *The Memoirs of Herbert Hoover: The Great Depression, 1929–1941* (New York, 1952). Scholarly criticism of Hoover's ineffectiveness is in Albert U. Romasco, *The Poverty of Abundance* (New York, 1956); and Gene Smith, *The Shattered Dream* (New York, 1970). Contemporary calls for national action were manifested in Abraham Epstein, "The Older Workers," *Annals* 154 (Mar. 1931): 28–32; Epstein, "Do We Need Compulsory Public Unemployment Insurance? Yes," ibid., 170 (Nov. 1933): 21–33; John A. Kingsbury, "A Program for National Health Insurance," *American Labor Legislation Review* (hereafter cited as *ALLR*), 23 (Dec. 1933): 185–188; Isaac M. Rubinow, "National Health Insurance," in National Conference of Social Work, *Proceedings*, 1934, 376–388.

20. For the transition from Hoover to Roosevelt, see David Plotke, *Building a Democratic Political Order* (Cambridge, UK, 1996), 48–56; and Frank Freidel, *Franklin D. Roosevelt: Launching the New Deal* (Boston, 1973); Daniel Fusfeld, *The Economic Thought of Franklin D. Roosevelt and the Origins of the New Deal* (New York, 1954); James T. Patterson, *America's Struggle against Poverty, 1900–1980* (Cambridge, Mass., 1981), 37–45.

21. Many scholars have written on the impact of the Great Depression on African-Americans. See, for example, John B. Kirby, *Black Americans in the Roosevelt Era* (Knoxville, Tenn., 1980); and Patricia Sullivan, *Days of Hope: Race and Democracy in the New Deal Era* (Chapel Hill, N.C., 1996).

22. Statistics on the unemployed are in U.S. Committee on Economic Security (CES), *Employment and Unemployment, 1929 to 1935* (Washington, D.C., 1936), by Anne Page, National Recovery Administration (NRA), Division of Review, no. 5, pt. B, 13; and Social Security Board (SSB), *Social Security in America* (Washington, D.C., 1937), Pub. no. 20, pt. 1: 58–140, pt. 2: 141–181. Contemporary discussion of the plight of older Americans in particular is in J. Prentice Murphy, "Dependency in Old Age," *Annals* 154 (Mar. 1931): 38–43; Edwin E. Witte, "Old Age Security," *National Municipal Review* 24 (July 1935): 371; "Old Age Security in the Social Security Act," *Journal of Political Economy* 45 (1937): 1; William Green, "Unemployment Undermines Health," *American Federationist* 41 (Feb. 1934): 135; Leo Wolman and Gustav Peck, "Labor in the Economic Structure," in *Contemporary Problems in the United States*, ed. Horace Taylor et al. (New York, 1934), 447–448.

23. Other members of the CES were the secretary of the treasury, the attorney general, the secretary of agriculture, and the head of the FERA. *New York Times*, June 9, 30, 1934; Quadagno, "One Nation: Uninsured," 34–38; Patterson, *America's Struggle against Poverty*, 37–77. For the Townsend movement,

see Alan Brinkley, *Voices of Protest* (New York, 1982), 222–226, 251–257. Klein's *For All These Rights,* 78–115, is insightful on the politics of Social Security.

24.  Edgar Sydenstricker, "Health in the New Deal," *Annals* 176 (Nov. 1934): 131, 134–135, 137; Thomas Parran, Jr., "Health Services of Tomorrow," ibid., 78; Charles Winslow, "The Untilled Fields of Public Health," *Modern Medicine* 2 (Jan. 9, 1920): 138; *New York Times,* Apr. 27, 1934, July 15, 1934; Klein, *For All These Rights,* 145.

25.  *New York Times,* Sept. 15, 1935. Josephine Roche's background is sketched in George Creel, "Up from Riches," *Colliers* 95 (June 15, 1935): 14. Elinor McGinn's "A Wide-Awake Woman: Josephine Roche in the Age of Reform," *Colorado History* 7 (2002), is the standard, but uncritical, biography of Roche. The concept of the female dominion is discussed in Robyn Muncy, *Creating A Female Dominion in American Reform, 1890–1935* (New York, 1991); 28–37. See also Samuel P. Hays, *Conservation and the Gospel of Efficiency: The Progressive Conservation Movement, 1890–1920* (Cambridge, 1959).

26.  For FDR's views on medicine, see Stephen Early to Dr. Spencer T. Snedecor, Sept. 28, 1936, Franklin D. Roosevelt Papers (FDR Papers), President's Personal File (PPF) 528; Phillip E. Buck to Dr. Marvin H. McIntyre, Mar. 12, 1936, ibid., PPF 6222; Early to Dr. Harry H. Kay, Aug. 8, 1936, ibid., Office File (OF), Franklin D. Roosevelt Library (FDRL).

27.  Irvin Fisher to Franklin D. Roosevelt (FDR), June 11, 1934; Nov. 10, 1936, FDR Papers, PPF 431, FDRL; William T. Foster to Robert F. Wagner, Oct. 1, 1934, Robert F. Wagner Papers, SM-460 (1934–1947), Folder: Health Insurance, Georgetown University Library (GUL).

28.  *New York Times,* July 27, 1934; Edwin E. Witte, *The Development of the Social Security Act* (Madison, Wisc., 1962), 21, 24–25, 30–31.

29.  Ibid.

30.  Dr. Nathan Sinai to FDR, Sept. 17, 1934; Louis H. Pink to FDR, Sept. 27, 1934; Worth M. Topping to FDR, Oct. 5, 1934, FDR Papers, OF 103, Folder: Health, 1933–1937, FDRL. See also Witte, *Development of the Social Security Act,* 41–43, 45; Shonick, *Government and Health Services,* 270.

31.  CES, *Report to the President of the Committee on Economic Security* (Washington, D.C., 1935); Witte, *Development of the Social Security Act,* 68–69, 75, 106–108.

32.  SSB, *Social Security in America: The Factual Background of the Social Security Act as Summarized from Staff Reports to the Committee on Economic Security* (Washington, D.C., 1937). The quote is from David M. Kennedy, *Freedom from Fear: The American People in Depression and War, 1929–1945* (New York, 1999), 258–272.

33.  William E. Leuchtenburg, *Franklin D. Roosevelt and the New Deal* (New York, 1963), 132–133; Klein, *For All These Rights,* 104, 135–140.

34.  Marvin H. McIntyre to Dr. Marjorie R. Nesbit, July 2, 1935, FDR Papers, OF 103, Folder: Health, 1933–1937, FDRL; Witte, *Development of the Social Security Act,* viii, 172; *Report to the President of the Committee on Economic Security,* 42–43.

35.  Michael M. Davis, M.D., "The American Approach to Health Insurance," *Milbank Memorial Fund Quarterly* 12 (July 1934): 203–217.

36.  Witte, *Development of the Social Security Act,* 175–179.

37.  Ibid.

38.  "Should a System of Complete Medical Service Be Available to All Citizens at Public Expense?" *Congressional Digest* 14 (Aug.–Sept. 1935): 196–197.

39.  Witte, *Development of the Social Security Act,* 172–173, 181.

40.  FDR replied to Dr. Will Mayo that the New York approach was "worthwhile considering" as a method of "expanding the existing machinery." Dr. Harvey Cushing to FDR, Feb. 4, 1935; FDR to Dr. Will Mayo, Feb. 13, 1935, FDR Papers, OF 103, Folder: Health, 1933–1937, FDRL.

41. Dr. Hugh Cabot, "The Case against Compulsory Health Insurance with Suggestions for Other Experimental Procedures," n.d., copy in the Records of the Inter-Departmental Committee to Coordinate Health and Human Welfare Activities (IDC Records), Box 8, Folder: Plans for a National Health Program, FDRL.
42. Ibid.
43. Ibid.
44. Witte, *Development of the Social Security Act*, 182–185.
45. House, Committee on Ways and Means, *The Social Security Bill*, 74th Cong., 1st sess., 1935, H. Rep. 615, pt. 2, 13; "Show-down Coming on Health Insurance," *Literary Digest* 119 (Feb. 9, 1935): 17.
46. What transpired at this point is somewhat murky. According to Arthur J. Altmeyer, assistant secretary of labor, the president apparently told the CES in June 1935 to submit its report recommending a health program that included health insurance, and he would then decide what to do with it. The committee did so on June 15, while the social security bill was still pending. The letter of transmittal, signed by all members of the CES, said, "Although we realize that a difference of opinion exists as to the advisability of establishing compulsory health insurance, we are convinced ... that the compulsory feature is essential to the accomplishment of the end in view." Secretary of Labor Frances Perkins wrote separately to FDR, "In view of the controversial character of certain phases of the subject, I suggest that the report not be made public until the Social Security Bill, now pending before the Congress, has been enacted into law." After the CES had transmitted its report to the president, Witte received a letter from the committee's medical advisory board recommending that any federal or state legislative action be deferred until the growing experience with voluntary health insurance in the United States and Canada could be analyzed. Arthur J. Altmeyer, *The Formative Years of Social Security* (Madison, Wisc., 1968), 57n. Ellenbogen's remarks are in 74th Cong., 1st sess., *Congressional Record* 79, pt. 13, 1935, 13678. See ibid., pt. 7, 7839, for similar comments.
47. Witte, *Development of the Social Security Act*, 188–189.
48. It was not until 1937, after the Social Security Board (SSB) had been organized, that Roosevelt forwarded a copy of this report with the suggestion that the new board give the subject further study. The SSB assigned Dr. I. S. Falk to work on health insurance. CES to Frances Perkins, Nov. 6, 1935; Dr. John A. Kingsbury to FDR, Nov. 24, 1935; FDR to Kingsbury, Dec. 4, 1935, Perkins to FDR, Jan. 13, 1936; FDR to John Winant, Jan. 14, 1936, FDR Papers, OF 103, Folder: Health, 1933–1937, FDRL.
49. Cohen Oral History, COHC, pt. 4, 50–52, 55–56.
50. Ira Katznelson and Bruce Pietrykowski, "Rebuilding the American State: Evidence from the 1940s," *Studies in American Political Development* 5 (Fall 1991): 312–313.
51. The need to coordinate the various components of health policy within the federal bureaucracy is discussed in J. G. Leukhardt to E. L. Bishop, IDC Records, Box 12, Folder: Corres. re: Reports; Bishop to Leukhardt, July 15, 1936, ibid., Box 11, Folder: Corres. re: Procedural Methods; "Progress Report to President Franklin D. Roosevelt," Feb. 12, 1938, ibid., Box 12, Folder: First Progress Report; "Second Progress Report," n.d., ibid., Box 12, Folder: Second Progress Report, FDRL. A copy of Executive Order 7481 is in ibid., Box 14, Folder: Administration, FDRL. Other members of the IDC were Oscar L. Chapman, assistant secretary of the interior, and Milo L. Wilson, assistant secretary of agriculture. See FDR to Josephine Roche, Aug. 19, 1935, ibid., Box 5, Folder: Corres. with Miss Roche, Aug. 1935–July 1938, FDRL; Arthur J. Altmeyer, "The National Health Conference and the Future of Public Health," *AJPH* 29 (Jan. 1939): 2; Engel, *Doctors and Reformers*, 96–98.
52. Undated campaign speech, copy in Robert F. Wagner Papers, Box 404, Folder: 24 (1936 Speeches), Georgetown University Library (GUL). See also "The Achievement of the Social Security Act," May 6, 1936, speech to the Women's Trade Union League, ibid., Box 406, Folder 1 (1937–1938); J. Joseph Huthmacher, *Senator Robert F. Wagner and the Rise of Urban Liberalism* (New York, 1968), 263–264; *New York Times*, Feb. 26, 1936; Josephine Roche, "Medical Care as a Public Health Function," *AJPH* 27 (Dec. 1937): 1223, 1225.

53. "Members of Technical Committee on Medical Care," n.d.; "Third Progress Report of the Interdepartmental Committee . . . ," n.d., IDC Records, Box 10, Looseleaf Binder: Josephine Roche to FDR, Sept. 27, 1937; "Summary of Work of Technical Committee on Medical Care"; "Summary: Progress Report from the Technical Committee on Medical Care to the Chairman of the Interdepartmental Committee . . . on Federal Participation in a National Health Program," Dec. 17, 1937, ibid., Box 38, Folder: Medical Care, FDRL.

54. FDR to the Secretary of the Treasury, July 26, 1935; memo to Treasury Department and USPHS, "Health Inventory," Feb. 14, 1936; "Press Release," July 30, 1935, Box 4, Folder: Project Alamo, Records of the National Health Inventory, 1935–1936 (NHI), National Archives, Record Group 443 (cited hereafter as NARG 443), Washington, D.C. A copy of Roche's radio address is in IDC Records, Box 26, Folder: Address: National Broadcasting Co., Oct. 14, 1935, FDRL. See also *New York Times,* July 1, 1935.

55. For comments, see *New York Times,* July 17, 30, 1935; Oct. 16, 1935; copies of the letters to both the news and radio media and to professional organizations and news articles are in NHI Records, Box 1, Folder: NHS-Letters Announcing Inventory, 1935–1936; Box 2, Folder: Publicity and Releases, 1935–1938, pts. 1 & 2, NARG 443. See also "National Health Inventory," *AJPH* 25 (Dec. 1935): 1370–1371; Josephine Roche, "Economic Health and Public Health Objectives," *AJPH* 25 (Nov. 1935): 1181.

56. John M. Carmody, "The Federal Works Agency and Public Health," *AJPH* 30 (Aug. 1940): 887–894; *New York Times,* June 30, July 17, 1935.

57. Cf. *The Progress of the Health Survey,* issues 5, 6, and 8 (Nov. 15, 29, 1935; Dec. 5, 1935), NHI Records, Box 2, Folder: Progress of the Health Survey, Nov. 1, 1935–May 21, 1936, NARG 443; *Survey Graphic* 26 (July 1937): 371.

58. Some of the problems of classification, budgeting, and administration are discussed in: Memo, Technical Council to Supervisors in Texas and California, Nov. 18, 1935, "Organization Chart for the Health Inventory Project," n.d., NHI Records, Box 2, Folder: "Central Office Memoranda, Oct. 14, 1935–Apr. 18, 1938"; W. F. Draper to Daniel W. Bell, Feb. 8, 1936, ibid., Box 4, Folder: Project Alamo, NARG 443. The mechanical aspects of gathering and coding the data were conducted on-site, but USPHS's Division of Scientific Research in Washington determined the coverage and type of data collected and did the final tabulations. See L. R Thompson to NHI Staff, Jan. 28, 1936; Field Director to All Supervisors, Dec. 2, 1935, NHI Records, Box 2, Folder: Central Office Memoranda, Oct. 14, 1935–Apr. 18, 1938, NARG 443.

59. For the disbursement of funds to conduct the canvass in the different regions, states, and cities, see NHI Records, Box 4, Folder: Surgeon General's Bi-monthly Reports, Oct. 29, 1935–Dec. 9, 1936, NARG 443. Copies of the field forms and bulletins are in ibid., Box 1, Folder: NHI Field Forms and Field Bulletins, Nos. 1–36, Oct. 17, 1935–Mar. 14, 1936. For the canvass in New York and other cities, see "Uncle Sam Checks Up on Father Knickerbocker's Health," typescript, n.d., ibid., Box 4, Folder: Project Alamo, NARG 443; and *New York Times,* Jan. 23, Feb. 17, 1936.

60. The details of the Georgia study are in NHI Records, Box 1, Folder: Manual: Georgia, Rural, NARG 443.

61. Ibid.

62. In what was surely one of the earliest efforts to gather large aggregate amounts of data and subject them to sophisticated manipulation and interpretation, the findings were coded and correlated over months of painstaking work by a staff that, at its peak, numbered a thousand workers, also on the WPA payroll. The coding task alone required 13,000 "man-months" of labor. Editing, verification, and checking through repeated processes also constituted a vast undertaking. See "The Public's Health," *Survey Midmonthly* 74 (Jan. 1938): 54. See also Grey's *New Deal Medicine* for the rural health programs of the Farm Security Administration; and Mary Ross, "How Healthy Are We? First Findings of the NHI," *Survey Graphic* 26 (July 1937): 374.

63. *New York Times,* Oct. 6, 8, 1937; Roche, "Medical Care as a Public Health Function," 1223.

64. These data and those in the following paragraphs derive from "The Public's Health," 54–55. See also Shonick, *Government and Health Services,* 270–271.

65. "The Public's Health."

66. *New York Times,* Mar. 27, 1938; Peter A. Corning, *The Evolution of Medicare* (Washington, D.C., 1969), 45.

67. *Detroit News,* Jan. 23, 1938, news clipping in NHI Records, Box 2, Folder: Publicity and Releases, 1935–1938, pt. 2, NARG 443; Starr, *Social Transformation of American Medicine,* 273.

68. *Detroit News,* Jan. 23, 1938, NHI Records, Box 2, Folder: Publicity and Releases, 1935–1938, pt. 2, NARG 443; "Report from the Technical Committee on Medical Care," Feb. 10, 1938, Copy A-12, IDC Records, Box 38, Folder: Mary Switzer; "Summary of the Work of the Technical Committee," n.d., ibid., Box 38, Folder: Medical Care; "Summary of the Work of the Technical Committee," n.d., ibid., Box 38, Folder: Medical Care, FDRL; *New York Times,* Mar. 27, 1938.

69. Arthur Altmeyer to E. L. Forster, Mar. 8, 1938, FDR Papers, OF 130, Box 1, Folder: Health, 1938–1939, FDRL; "Meeting of the Interdepartmental Committee with the Technical Committee on Medical Care," Feb. 10, 1938, IDC Records, Box 45, Folder: Proceedings; FDR to Roche, Mar. 8, 1938, ibid., Box 10, Loose-leaf Binder, FDRL.

70. Roche to FDR, Feb. 11, 1938, ibid., Box 38, Folder: Medical Care; Roche to Dr. Thomas Parran, Jr., Apr. 7, 1938, ibid., Box 11, Folder: National Health Conference; press releases re: the forthcoming conference are in ibid., FDRL. See also Engel, *Doctors and Reformers,* 132–139.

71. *New York Times,* Mar. 17, June 7, July 10, 17, 1938.

72. Mary Switzer to Henry Morgenthau, May 20, 1938, IDC Records, Box 38, Folder: Medical Care; "Meeting of the Inter-Departmental Committee," n.d., IDC Records, Box 45, Folder: Proceedings; Dr. Michael H. Davis to Dr. Alice Hamilton, June 15, 1938, ibid., Box 12, Folder: Organizational File; and the various memoranda in Box 5, Folder: Corres. with Miss Roche, FDRL.

73. Dr. Hugh Cabot to Josephine Roche, July 4, 1938, IDC Records, Box 8, Folder: Plans for a National Health Conference, FDRL; *Proceedings of the National Health Conference, July 18–20, 1938* (Washington, D.C., 1939), iii, Box 5, Loose-leaf Binder; Roche to Dr. Irvin Abell, June 22, 1938, ibid., Box 5, Folder: Corres. with Miss Roche, Aug. 1935–July 1938, ibid., FDRL.

74. For Wagner's support of health security, see Roche to Wagner, May 28, 1938; Wagner to Roche, June 7, 22, 1938, Wagner Papers, GF, Box 328, Folder: 14, National Health, 1939–1946, Corres. G-Y; "Senator Wagner's Record on Health Insurance," n.d., ibid., GF, Box 325, Folder: 1, 1938, Campaign Material, GUL; Robert F. Wagner, "A Senate Investigation of Security against Sickness," *ALLR* 38 (June 1938): 77–78; "A National Health Conference," ibid., 38 (June 1938): 75–76.

75. Roche, "Work of the Inter-Departmental Committee on Health and Welfare Activities," June 14, 1938, IDC Records, Box 26, Folder: AMA—June 14, 1938, FDRL; *New York Times,* May 31, 1938; July 19, 1938; Oliver Garceau, *The Political Life of the American Medical Association* (Cambridge, Mass., 1941), 147–152. The quote from ACP president Dr. James B. Means is in "Medical Politicians v. Medical Statesmen," *ALLR* 28 (June 1938): 76.

76. *New York Times,* July 17, 19, 1938; Josephine Roche, "The Worker's Stake in a National Health Program," *ALLR* 28 (Sept. 1938): 125–130.

77. *Proceedings of the NHC,* IDC Records, Box 5, Loose-leaf Binder; "Press Release," July 18, 1939, Box 26, Folder: National Health Conference, FDRL; FDR to Roche, July 15, 1938, FDR Papers, OF 103, Box 3, Folder: Health, 1938–1939, FDRL.

78. *New York Times,* July 19, 1938; Arthur J. Altmeyer, "Progress toward Health Security," *ALLR* 29 (Mar. 1939): 8–9. The complete report, *The Nation's Health,* is in the IDC Records, Box 10, Folder: *The Nation's Health,* FDRL. See also "Printed Program, National Health Conference, July 18–19–20, 1938, Called by the Inter-Departmental Technical Committee on Health and Human Welfare Activities," copy in Wagner Papers, GF, Box 329, Folder: 11, 1938–1946: Health Conference Reports, GUL.

79. *Proceedings of the National Health Conference* (Washington, D.C., 1938), 8, 19–20, 26, 65, 101, 156–157, IDC Records, Box 5, Folder: Plans for a National Health Conference, FDRL. See also *New York*

*Times,* July 20, 1938; Dr. Irvin Abell, "Attitude of the American Medical Association toward the National Health Program," *AJPH* 29 (Jan. 1939): 11–12.

80.  *New York Times,* July 21, 1938. See also "Memorandum to the President regarding the National Health Program," Dec. 15, 1938, and the action of the Committee of Physicians for the Improvement of Medical Care, Nov. 26, 1938, IDC Records, Box 11, Folder: Memo. re: the National Health Program, FDRL.

81.  People's National Health Committee, *The People's Fight for Health and Life,* July 18, 1938, IDC Records, Box 11, mimeographed copy in envelope marked "National Health Conference," FDRL; Corning, *Evolution of Medicare,* 47.

82.  Morris Fishbein, "American Medicine and the National Health Plan," *New England Journal of Medicine,* 220 (Mar. 23, 1939): 495–504. For Fishbein's persistent hostility to government intervention, see Engel, *Doctors and Reformers,* 2–3, 5–8.

83.  Maxine Davis, "Socialized Medicine," *Good Housekeeping* 109 (Aug. 1939): 142; Corning, *Evolution of Medicare,* 48; Altmeyer, *Formative Years of Social Security,* 96; Starr, *Social Transformation of American Medicine,* 276–277.

84.  Ernest K. Lindley to Robert F. Wagner, July 23, 1938; Wagner to Lindley, Aug. 1, 1938, Wagner Papers, GF, Box 328, Folder: 15, National Health Insurance Corres., 1934–1940, GUL; Roche, "Memorandum to the President . . . The National Health Program," Oct. 12, 1938, IDC Records, Box 11, Folder: Memoranda to the President, FDRL; Altmeyer, "The NHC and the Future of Public Health," *AJPH* 29 (Jan. 1939): 1.

85.  Henry E. Sigerist, "The Realities of Socialized Medicine," *Atlantic Monthly* 163 (June 1939): 794, 797, 799–800, copy in Wagner Papers, GF, Box 328, Folder: 7, Health Insurance: Corres., 1930–1938, GUL.

86.  Roche, "Memorandum to the President . . . the National Health Program," Dec. 12, 1938, IDC Records, Box 11, Folder: Memoranda to the President; I. S. Falk to Josephine Roche, Dec. 20, 1938, ibid., Box 5, Folder: Corres., Miss Roche, July, 1938–1939, FDRL.

87.  Roy Lubove, "The New Deal and National Health," *Current History* 45 (Aug. 1963): 86, 117.

88.  Altmeyer, *Formative Years of Social Security,* 96; Starr, *Social Transformation of American Medicine,* 277; James T. Patterson, *Congressional Conservatism and the New Deal* (Lexington, Ky., 1967), passim.

89.  C. Richard Mulcahy, "Working against the Odds: Josephine Roche, the New Deal and the Drive for National Health Insurance," *Maryland Historian* 25 (1994): 15–17.

## CHAPTER 2. HOPES DEFERRED: CONGRESS, WAR, & THE END OF THE NEW DEAL

1.  For a useful survey of conservative opposition to the New Deal, see Mary H. Hinchey, "The Frustration of the New Deal Revival, 1944–46" (Ph.D. diss., Univ. of Missouri, 1965).

2.  Dr. A. T. McCormack to Robert F. Wagner, Jan. 21, 1939, Robert F. Wagner Papers, General Files (GF), Box 3289, Folder: Health Insur., Corres. 1930–1938, Georgetown University Library (GUL).

3.  *New York Times,* Dec. 21, 1938; Jan. 16, 1939.

4.  Robert F. Wagner, "The National Health Bill," *ALLR* 29 (Mar. 1939): 14–17; Jonathan Engel, *Doctors and Reformers* (Columbia, S.C., 2002), 140–186.

5.  On federalism, see Harry N. Scheiber, ed., *The New Deal Legacy and the Constitution* (Berkeley, Calif., 1984), 2, 6.

6.  *New York Times,* Jan. 10, 1939.

7.  House, *Health Security, Message from the President of the U.S. Transmitting the Annual Message on Health Security,* 76th Cong., 1st sess., 1939, H. Doc. 120, 1–24; Almer McCurtain to FDR, Feb. 2, 1939,

IDC Records, Box 8, Folder: Plans for a National Health Program, FDRL; Jennifer Klein, *For All These Rights* (Princeton, N.J., 2003), 147; Michael R. Gray, *New Deal Medicine* (Baltimore, 1999), 68, 152–157.

8. "The Health Program," *Commonweal* 29 (Feb. 3, 1939): 394; *New York Times*, Feb. 3, 1939.

9. Wagner's bill provided for relatively independent state health systems subsidized by Washington; Capper's bill (S. 658) did much the same, but with more stringent federal prescription and control. The various bills reflected a growing belief that some degree of federal intervention was necessary to ensure the health security of all Americans. For the Capper and Wagner bills, see 76th Cong., 1st sess., *Congressional Record* 84, pt. 1 (Jan. 16, 1939): 354; pt. 2 (Feb. 28, 1939): 1976. See also Herbert D. Simpson, *Compulsory Health Insurance in the United States* (Evanston, Ill., 1943), 24–25; J. Joseph Huthmacher, *Senator Robert F. Wagner and the Rise of Urban Liberalism* (New York, 1968), 264.

10. William Shonick, *Government and Health Services* (New York, 1995), 800; Wagner, "The National Health Bill," 13–44.

11. "National Health Act of 1939: A Summary of the Wagner Bill before the U.S. Congress," *AJPH* 29 (May 1939): 568–569.

12. For specific details of S. 1620, see *Congressional Record* 84, pt. 2 (Feb. 28, 1939), 1976–1982.

13. Wagner to Dr. Hugh Cabot, Mar. 17, 1939, Wagner Papers, GF, Box 328, Folder 8, Health Insur., Corres., 1939, GUL.

14. On the significance of the 1939 reorganization bill for a strong executive government, see Ira Katznelson and Bruce Pietrykowski, "Rebuilding the American State: Evidence from the 1940s," *Studies in American Political Development* 5 (Fall 1991): 313–314.

15. Gus Uth to Wagner, Mar. 3, 1939, Wagner Papers, GF, Box 328, Folder 8, Health Insur. Corres., 1939, GUL.

16. Ibid.

17. Michael Davis, "Senators, Doctors and National Health," *Survey* 75 (Sept. 1939): 280; Klein, *For All These Rights*, 240–241.

18. See Harriet Silverman's telegram to Dr. Thomas Parran, May 11, 1939, IDC Records, Box 31, Folder: Resolutions, FDRL.

19. Wagner to John A. Kenney, June 19, 1939, Wagner Papers, GF, Box 328, Folder 8, Health Insur., Corres., 1939.

20. Dr. Michael M. Davis to Parran, Mar. 24, 1939, IDC Records, Box 8, Folder: Plans for a National Health Program, FDRL.

21. Ibid.

22. See the "Memorial Resolution" of George L. Markland, Jr., to both houses of Congress, n.d., ibid., Box 31, Folder: Resolutions, FDRL.

23. Walter H. Adams to Wagner, Mar. 6, 1939, Wagner Papers, GF, Box 328, Folder 8, Health Insur., Corres., 1939, GUL.

24. *New York Times*, Apr. 26, 1939; Maxine Davis, "Socialized Medicine," *Good Housekeeping* 109 (Aug. 1939): 145.

25. Klein, *For All These Rights*, 147–148, 163.

26. Excerpts of Altmeyer's testimony are in "Pledged Action on Health Bill Endangered by Delays," *ALLR* 29 (Dec. 1939): 158–159.

27. Joseph Hirsh, "The National Health Bill, Past, Present, Future," ibid., 112–113.

28. Parran to Missy Le Hand, Dec. 30, 1940, IDC Records, Box 5, Folder: Inter-Office Corres., FDRL; Hirsh, "The National Health Bill," 113.

29. Davis, "Senators, Doctors and National Health," 280.

30. James E. Murray, "The National Health Bill," *ALLR* 30 (Mar. 1940): 11.

31. Ibid.; Parran to Le Hand, Dec. 12, 1940, IDC Records, Box 5, Folder: Inter-Off. Corres., FDRL; *Congressional Record* 84, pt. 10 (Aug. 4, 1939): 10983; Senate, *National Health Program*, 76th Cong., 1st

sess., 1939, S. Rep. 1139; Murray, "The National Health Bill," 11–12; Davis, "Senators, Doctors and National Health," 280.

32.  Peter A. Corning, *The Evolution of Medicare*, Research Report No. 29, Office of Research and Statistics, Social Security Administration (Washington, D.C., 1969), 52.

33.  Kathleen Rivet, "Lost, a National Health Program," *ALLR* 31 (Sept. 1941): 120.

34.  H. A. Wallace (Bureau of the Budget), to Sen. Elbert D. Thomas, Mar. 19, 1940, Wagner Papers, GF, Box 328, Folder 14, National Health, 1939–1946, Corres., G-Y; Huthmacher, *Wagner*, 267.

35.  *New York Times*, July 9, 1939.

36.  Samuel J. Rosenman, ed., *The Public Papers and Addresses of Franklin D. Roosevelt, 1939*, 13 vols. (New York, 1938–1950), 8: 597–599; "Message to Congress," Jan. 18, 1940, IDC Records, Box 7, Folder: Hospital Construction Bill Messages, FDRL. See also Senate, *National Hospital Act of 1940*, 76th Cong., 3d sess., 1940, S. Rep. 1558; House, Committee on Interstate and Foreign Commerce, *Public Health Service, Message from the President of the United States*, 76th Cong., 3d sess., 1940, H. Doc. 604.

37.  "Minutes of the Meeting . . . of Jan. 11, 1940," IDC Records, Box 45, Folder: Proceedings, FDRL; Arthur J. Altmeyer, *The Formative Years of Social Security* (Madison, Wisc., 1968), 261; John B. Andrews, "While Millions Suffer," *ALLR* 30 (Mar. 1940): 3; Huthmacher, *Wagner*, 266–267.

38.  Mary Dublin to Philip Levy, Mar. 4, 1940, Wagner Papers, GF, Box 328, Folder 14, National Health, 1939–1946, Corres. G-Y, GUL.

39.  Paul U. Kellogg to Stephen Early, Jan. 15, 1940, ibid., Folder 9, Health Insur., 1940–1949, Corres., GUL.

40.  See the review of Alan Brinkley's *The End of Reform* in the *New York Times*, Mar. 12, 1996; Huthmacher, *Wagner*, 267.

41.  *New York Times*, Oct. 3, 1936.

42.  Jaap Kooijman, "Just Forget about It: FDR's Ambivalence towards National Health Insurance," in *The Roosevelt Years*, ed. Robert A. Garson and Stuart S. Kidd (Edinburgh, UK, 1999), 30–41.

43.  Ira Katznelson, Kim Geiger, and Daniel Kryder, "Limiting Liberalism: The Southern Veto in Congress, 1933–1950," *Political Science Quarterly* (Summer 1993): 288–289.

44.  Lizabeth Cohen, *A Consumers' Republic* (New York, 2003), 63–64.

45.  Bartholomew H. Sparrow, *From the Outside In: World War II and the American State* (Princeton, N.J., 1996), esp. chaps. 1–2, 4, 6–7.

46.  Ibid.; Nelson Lichtenstein, *Labor's War at Home* (Cambridge, UK, 1982), chaps. 4–6, 8–10; Robert K. Murray, "Government and Labor During World War II," *Current History* 37 (Sept. 1959): 146–152; Andrew A. Workman, "Creating the National War Labor Board: Franklin Roosevelt and the Politics of State Building in the Early 1940s," *Journal of Policy History* 12, 2 (2000): 233–264.

47.  "Is Compulsory Health Insurance in the Public Interest?" *Medical Economics* 20 (Oct. 1942): 42; Wagner's remarks in "Arguments against Allowing the National Defense Program to Check Social Gains," *Congressional Digest* 20 (Apr. 1941): 126–128; Shonick, *Government and Health Services*, 271.

48.  Nathan Sinai, "Present Status of Health Insurance in the United States," *AJPH* 34 (Feb. 1943): 107–108.

49.  Klein, *For All These Rights*, 162.

50.  Washington State Planning Council, Health Section, "Proposed General Principles of a Program for Rendering Medical Care to Needy Persons in the State of Washington," Jan. 13, 1939; Gertrude Sturges to I. S. Falk, Feb. 6, 1939, IDC Records, Box 30, Folder: Resolutions, FDRL.

51.  "Pioneer Health Insurance Law Adopted by Rhode Island," *ALLR* 32 (June 1942): 57. See also Kenneth Close, "Money While You're Sick, Rhode Island's Compulsory Insurance Sickness Law," *Survey* 79 (Dec. 1943): 328–331; for New York, "Health Insurance, Plan for Health Care for All Persons Living or Working in New York City," ibid., 80 (June 1944): 190; James W. Johnson, Jr., "Collective Bargaining and Health Insurance," *American Economic Security* 10 (Apr.–May 1944): 8–10.

52. More than 40 percent of the inductees examined, including youth in the 21–25 age group, who should have been the healthiest, were classified as unfit for general military service. This compared with a rate of about 30 percent rejections in 1917–1918. Rollo H. Britten and George St. J. Perrott, "Causes of Physical Disqualification under the Selective Service Law. Early Indications," n.d., typed report, Record Group 443, Box 12, Folder: Annotated Material, National Health Service, NARG, Washington, D.C.; *American Economic Security;* Perrott, "Physical Status of Young Men, 1918–1941," *Milbank Memorial Fund Quarterly* 19 (Oct. 1941): 344.

53. Doris K. Goodwin, *No Ordinary Time* (New York, 1994), 191, 202.

54. Quoted in Rivet, "Lost, a National Health Program," 120.

55. *Social Insurance and Allied Services,* the formal title of the Beveridge Plan, had been in progress since 1941. Churchill did not disclose its details until March 21, 1943, in a wartime radio broadcast from Chequers. The plan and American reaction to it may be followed in Janet P. Beveridge, *Beveridge and His Plan* (London, 1954); *New York Times,* May 20, 23, 28, 1943; Beulah E. Amidon, "NRPB and Beveridge Reports," *Survey* 79 (May 1943): 141–143; "Who'll Kill the Beveridge Bill?" *New Republic* 108 (May 24, 1943): 699.

56. Roosevelt was keenly aware of Great Britain's health program, as embodied in the National Insurance Acts, long before publication of the Beveridge Report. See Dr. Foster Kennedy to FDR, Jan. 31, 1939, and the accompanying correspondence of Dr. G. C. Anderson, Secretary of the British Medical Association, to Dr. John McCrea, Mar. 29, 1933, and Ross T. McIntire to Kennedy, Mar. 28, 1939, FDR Papers, PPF 5827, Folder: Foster Kennedy, FDRL. Fishbein's attack on the Beveridge plan and the Planning Board's reports are in "Medical Decisions Must Be Made by Medical Men," *Eastern Underwriter,* June 4, 1943, 42.

57. For the report written by Eveline M. Burns, see National Resources Planning Board, *National Resources Development, Report for 1942,* esp. 3, 109–112, 117–118, reprinted as H. Doc. 560, 77th Cong., 2d sess. (Washington, D.C., 1942). See also Katznelson and Pietrykowski, "Rebuilding the American State," 314–316.

58. *New York Times,* Nov. 1, 1942; Mar. 4, 10, 13, 27, 1943; Klein, *For All These Rights,* 166–176. A subsequent appropriation of $4.4 million for the fiscal year 1944 was contained in the Labor–Federal Security Appropriation Act (1944). See Senate, Committee on Appropriations, *Emergency Maternity and Infant Care for Wives of Enlisted Men in the Armed Forces—Additional Appropriation, Fiscal Year 1944,* 78th Cong., 1st sess., 1943, S. Rep. 413.

59. Rosenman, ed., *Public Papers of FDR, 1943,* 13: 30–31; John Morton Blum, *From the Morgenthau Diaries,* 3 vols. (Boston, 1959–1967), 3: 72; FDR to William Green, Nov. 5, 1942, FDR Papers, OF 1092, FDRL. Green was president of the AFL.

60. *New York Times,* Jan. 8, 9, 11, 14, 20, 1943; Mar. 11, 14, 1943; James Rorty, "Health under the Social Security Tent," *Antioch Review* 3 (Dec. 1943): 498; Klein, *For All These Rights,* 212.

61. Among the New Deal agencies eliminated were the WPA, the National Youth Administration (NYA), the Civilian Conservation Corps (CCC), and the NRPB. The wartime impact on New Deal programs of the conservative congressional coalition is examined in John D. Kingsley, "Congress and the New Deal," *Current History* 4 (Mar. 1943): 25–31; Louise Overacker, "Should the New Deal Be Dropped?" ibid., 6 (Feb. 1944): 110–115; John R. Moore, "The Conservative Coalition in the United States Senate, 1942–1945," *Journal of Southern History* 33 (Aug. 1967): 368–376; Roland Young, *Congressional Politics in the Second World War* (New York, 1956).

62. For a succinct comparison of the four leading contemporary proposals for a national plan of medical care and hospitalization (Wagner's 1939 health bill, the 1943 Wagner-Murray-Dingell bill, the 1935 American Association for Social Security health insurance bill, and the 1943 Canadian health bill), see the private memorandum dated Oct. 1, 1943, "Four National Health Bills Compared," by Rose Ehrlich and Dr. Michael M. Davis of the Rosenwald Fund, copy in Wagner Papers, GF, Box 329, Folder 11, Health, Amends., Votes, Reports, GUL.

63. *New York Times,* Jan. 18, 1943; Wagner to FDR, June 13, 1943; FDR to Wagner, June 16, 1943; to William A. Green, Oct. 6, 1943; to Philip Murray, Oct. 19, 1943; "Wagner-Murray-Dingell Bill, 1943," Wagner Papers, GF, Box 329, GUL.

64. "Wagner-Murray-Dingell Bill, 1943"; *Congressional Record,* 78th Cong., 1st sess., vol. 89, pt. 4 (June 3, 1943): 5257, 5354; Corning, *Evolution of Medicare,* 54; Huthmacher, *Wagner,* 292.

65. Frank P. Huddle, "Medical Insurance," *Editorial Research Reports* 1 (Jan. 25, 1944): 76.

66. "Social Security Lifts Its Sights," *Survey Graphic* 32 (July 1943): 283–284.

67. *Congressional Record,* 78th Cong., 2d sess., vol. 90, pt. 1 (Jan. 12, 1944): 84; pt. 7 (Dec. 8, 1944): 9047–9048.

68. Klein, *For All These Rights,* 175–176.

69. Huthmacher, *Wagner,* 293.

70. *New York Times,* June 2, 4, 13, 1943; Aug. 2, 7, 1943; Nov. 4, 20, 1943; Dec. 20, 24, 28, 1943.

71. B. D. McElroy, "Weighing Mr. Wagner's 'Baby,'" *Medical Economics* 21 (Oct. 1943): 93, 97.

72. "The Wagner-Murray-Dingell Bill: An Analysis of Its Health and Medical Features by the Physicians Forum," 1–9, as cited in "The Wagner-Murray-Dingell Bill," *American Journal of Nursing* 44 (Apr. 1944): 52–69.

73. Allan M. Butler, "Medical Freedom and the Wagner Bill," *Medical Care* 43 (Feb. 1944): 12–16.

74. In 1937, the AMA had attempted to restrain the Group Health Association in the District of Columbia, which was operating a health insurance system that failed to meet with AMA approval. Doctors serving with Group Health were expelled from both the local medical society and from the AMA, were excluded from Washington hospitals, and were denied the privilege of consulting with specialists. The District Court of the District of Columbia on April 4, 1941, convicted the AMA and its affiliate, the District Medical Society, of conspiring to restrain trade in violation of the Sherman Anti-Trust Act. The Supreme Court upheld the conviction on January 18, 1943. *Washington Post,* Apr. 5, 1941; Jan. 19, 1943.

75. Michael R. Grey, *New Deal Medicine* (Baltimore, 1999), 157.

76. "The Wagner-Murray-Dingell Bill," *American Journal of Nursing* 44 (Apr. 1944): 52–69; Corning, *Evolution of Medicare,* 55.

77. Morris Fishbein, "Plans for Postwar Medical Service," *Journal of the Missouri State Medical Association* 40 (July 1943): 191–194; McElroy, "Weighing Mr. Wagner's 'Baby,'" 93.

78. "The Wagner-Murray-Dingell Bill," *JAMA* 123 (Nov. 13, 1943): 700; John M. Pratt, *Abolishing Private Medical Practice* (Chicago, 1943).

79. Katherine G. Clark, "Insurance Companies and the Wagner Bill," *Medical Care* 3 (Nov. 1943): 311; Editorial, *Advertising Age* (Feb. 8, 1943); "Brand Describes Group Insurance as Greatest Force to Combat Agitators," *Eastern Underwriter* (June 4, 1943): 38; *New York Times,* June 17, 1943.

80. Editorial, *Advertising Age.*

81. Clark, "Insurance Companies and the Wagner Bill," 303, 310–313; Alton L. Linford, "Dispute over the U.S. Health Insurance Act," *Public Affairs* 7 (Spring 1944): 169.

82. American Hospital Association, *Transactions of the American Hospital Association* 44 (1942): 134; McElroy, "Weighing Mr. Wagner's 'Baby,'" 97, 99; "Catholic Viewpoints with Reference to a National Health Program and the Wagner-Murray Bill," *Hospital Progress* 24 (Nov. 1943): 336.

83. *New York Times,* Feb. 29, 1944; McElroy, "Weighing Mr. Wagner's 'Baby,'" 103; Huddle, "Medical Insurance," 66.

84. CNH, "Opinion Polls on National Health Program," n.d. [193?], Wagner Papers, GF, Box 329, Folder 12, Health Bulletins, GUL.

85. Meg Jacobs, "How About Some Meat?" *Journal of American History* 84 (Dec. 1997): 939.

86. FDR to Henry Wallace, Jan. 10, 1944, FDR Papers, PPF 41, FDRL; Draft Memorandum, Harold D. Smith to FDR, Aug. 6, 1944, NARG 243, Fiscal Division, Bureau of the Budget, National Archives (NA); Rosenman, ed., *Public Papers of FDR, 1944,* 13: 32–42, 457–458, 483–506.

87. Social Security Board, *Eighth Annual Report* (Washington, D.C., 1945).

88. *New York Times,* Jan. 7, 1945.

89. "Proposed National System of Health Insurance," *Christian Century* 62 (Jan. 10, 1945), 37–38; Amy Porter, "Do We Want National Health Insurance?" *Collier's* 115 (Jan. 27, 1945): 20–21.

90. "Sinner to Respected Citizen, Social Security Board Recommends Comprehensive Sickness Insurance," *Journal of Home Economics* 36 (Mar. 1944): 157–159; Corning, *Evolution of Medicare,* 55–56.

91. Alan Brinkley makes this point in his excellent study, *The End of Reform, New Deal Liberalism in Recession and War* (New York, 1995), 139–144, 160.

92. Two of the most influential books warning of centralized bureaucratic power were James Burnham's *The Managerial Revolution* (New York, 1941) and Friedrich A. Hayek's *The Road to Serfdom* (Chicago, 1944).

93. *New York Times,* Dec. 29, 1943; Brinkley, *End of Reform,* 145; James M. Burns, *Roosevelt, the Soldier of Freedom* (New York, 1970), 466.

94. "Medical Care Must Be Complemented by Public Health Measures," *AJPH* 33 (Dec. 1943): 1466–1467; Linford, "Dispute over the U.S. Health Insurance Act," 169; Rorty, "Health under the Social Security Tent," 498.

95. Rankin's remarks are printed in the "Minutes of the Chicago Session of the House of Delegates," *JAMA* 122 (June 19, 1943): 519–520.

96. The Opinion Research Corporation's survey disclosed that 53 percent of physicians in the military indicated a preference for group practice upon return to civilian life. Cf. "The Big Debate," *Time* 44 (Dec. 11, 1944): 70, and Morris Fishbein, "Medical Insurance, Which System Will Guarantee the Best Medical Care?" *Vital Speeches* 11 (Jan. 1, 1945): 190–192.

97. Rorty, "Health under the Social Security Tent," 513.

98. Antonia Maioni concludes in *Parting at the Crossroads: The Emergence of Health Insurance in the United States and Canada* (Princeton, N.J., 1998), 157–158, that American labor abandoned national health insurance in the 1960s when it embraced Medicare, but the evidence suggests this occurred more than a decade earlier, in the immediate postwar years.

## CHAPTER 3. HEALTH, SECURITY, & THE COLD WAR, 1945–1951

1. *Congressional Quarterly* devoted a special issue to the postwar period, "Politics in America—1945–1964: The Politics and Issues of the Postwar Years" (Aug. 31, 1965). See also *Congress and the Nation, 1945–1964* (Washington, D.C., 1965), 1–4; Meg Jacobs, "Pocketbook Politics: Democracy and the Market in Twentieth-Century America," in *The Democratic Experiment,* ed. Meg Jacobs, William J. Novak, and Julian E. Zelizer (Princeton, N.J., 2003), 261–267. Good surveys of the period are Dewey W. Grantham, *The United States since 1945* (New York, 1976), esp. 32–33ff., and William H. Chafe, *The Unfinished Journey: America since World War II* (New York, 1986), chaps. 4–6.

2. For the growing disenchantment of New Dealers with Truman, see Oscar R. Ewing Oral History, 2 vols., 2: 171–172, Harry S. Truman Library (HSTL); Robert J. Donovan, *Conflict and Crisis* (New York, 1977), 107–255; Alonzo L. Hamby, *Beyond the New Deal, Harry S. Truman and American Liberalism* (New York, 1973), 53–85, 121–134.

3. See Oscar R. Ewing Oral History, 34 (COHO); and Truman speech of May 1, 1948, to the National Health Assembly in *Public Papers of the Presidents of the United States: Harry S. Truman, 1948* (Washington, D.C., 1961–1966), 239–241 (cited as *Public Papers: Truman* [with year]).

4. The meeting is recounted in the definitive study of Monte M. Poen, *Harry S. Truman versus the Medical Lobby* (Columbia, Mo., 1979), 54–55. Truman's approach to health policy is also discussed in Jonathan Engel, *Doctors and Reformers* (Columbia, S.C., 2002), chap.7, and Jill Quadagno, "One Nation: Uninsured" (forthcoming), 40–59.

5. "Constructive Program for Medical Care," *JAMA* 128 (July 21, 1945): 883; *New York Times,* July 19, 1945.

6. Exactly when Rosenman and Smith learned of the president's intent is unclear. See Harry S. Truman, *Memoirs,* 2 vols. (Garden City, N.Y., 1955–1956), 1: 483; Poen, *Truman v. Medical Lobby,* 56–57. The FSA was an umbrella organization for several agencies, including the Office of Education, the Public Health Service, the SSA, the Federal Employment Service, the CCC, and the NYA. Congress established the FSA with the Reorganization Plan of 1939.

7. *Public Papers: Truman, 1945,* 32; *New York Times,* June 2, 1945. There is no evidence that Truman, as senator, had participated in drafting the bill, which he characterized as cumbersome and unfocused. See Truman, *Memoirs,* 1: 19.

8. Truman, *Memoirs,* 1: 481–482.

9. Ibid., 1: 481–486; *Public Papers: Truman, 1945,* 263–309.

10. *New York Times,* Apr. 4, 1945; Margaret Hinchey, "The Frustration of the New Deal Revival" (Ph.D. diss., Univ. of Missouri, 1965), 156–174.

11. The day after his September 6 message had stunned conservatives, Truman raised the health issue in a cabinet meeting and referred to the shortage of physicians, the poor distribution of medical centers across the nation, and the statistics on the Selective Service System's draft rejections to argue that the federal government needed to take "radical steps" to upgrade the nation's health. Poen, *Truman v. the Medical Lobby,* 60–61; J. Joseph Huthmacher, *Senator Robert F. Wagner and the Rise of Urban Liberalism* (New York, 1968), 320–321; Walter Millis, ed., *The Forrestal Diaries* (New York, 1951), 93.

12. *Public Papers: Truman, 1945,* 441; Poen, *Truman v. the Medical Lobby,* 62–63.

13. The text of the president's message is in House, *National Health Program,* 79th Cong., 1st sess., 1945, H. Doc. 380, copy in Preston Peden Papers, Box 62, Folder 7, Carl Albert Center, University of Oklahoma (CAC-OU).

14. Dr. Michael M. Davis, "A Milestone in Health Progress," *Survey Graphic* 34 (Dec. 1945): 485.

15. On the role of the technical expert, see Ewing Oral History, 41–42, COHC. Ewing considered Falk an excellent technician but naive in not understanding that health security was a *political* issue, not a medical one. Had Ewing written the health bill instead of Falk, the government would have allowed the pharmaceutical industry to set drug prices to neutralize it in the fight with the AMA—at least until there was evidence of price gouging. Only then would he have had the government intervene. But as the bill read, Ewing thought that Falk had irritated the pharmaceutical industry unnecessarily. See ibid., 79–80.

16. See the results of the Gallup polls between August 1944 and April 1946, in Hadley Cantril, ed., *Public Opinion, 1935–1946* (Princeton, N.J., 1951), 441–443; CNH, "Opinion Polls on National Health Program" [1945?], Robert F. Wagner Papers, GF, Box 329, Folder 12, GUL.

17. Blue Cross membership more than quadrupled between 1940 and 1946, and participation in Blue Shield increased from 370,000 to over 4 million. Commercial insurance policies expanded fivefold in the same period, and cooperative facilities providing comprehensive health services (such as those offered by West Coast industrialist Henry Kaiser) also began to flourish. Franz Goldmann, *Voluntary Medical Care Insurance in the United States* (New York, 1948), 93–187.

18. Dr. L. S. Willour to Hon. Paul Stewart, Dec. 14, 1945, Elmer Thomas Papers, Legis. Ser., Box 61, Folder 44, CAC-OU.

19. Quoted in Elizabeth Wilson, *Compulsory Health Insurance* (New York, 1947), 105.

20. On the failure to educate the public to the need for health security, see Ewing Oral History, 65–66, COHC; Poen, *Truman v. the Medical Lobby*, 67–68.

21. *Public Papers: Truman, 1946*, 1–8, 143, 166. For differing assessments of Truman's commitment to health security in 1946, see Poen, *Truman v. the Medical Lobby*, 68; Ewing Oral History, 1: 140–143ff., HSTL; Lt. R. D. Anderson, MC, to Elmer Thomas, Apr. 3, 1946; Thomas to Anderson, Apr. 8, 1946, Thomas Papers, Legis. Ser., Box 61, Folder 43, CAC-OU.

22. The circumstances surrounding the Reorganization Act and the transfer of the Children's Bureau to the FSA are discussed in the *New York Times*, Jan. 19, 1945; June 13, 1945. See also Agnes W. Brewster and Carl E. Ortmeyer, eds., *Health Insurance and Related Proposals for Financing Personal Health Services: A Digest of Major Legislation and Proposals for Federal Action, 1935–1957* (Washington, D.C., 1957), 34; Marjorie Shearon, *Blueprint for the Nationalization of Medicine* (Washington, D.C., 1947), 21–22; Poen, *Truman v. the Medical Lobby*, 75–81.

23. Ewing conceded, however, that the USPHS provided the FSA with whatever technical information it had requested and noted that lower-ranking staff physicians, such as Dr. George St. J. Perrott, had supported national health insurance. Ewing Oral History, 39–40, COHC.

24. The long-standing differences between the USPHS and the Social Security Board are discussed in Wilson, *Compulsory Health Insurance*, 6. See also FSA, *The Health of the Nation*, June 1, 1946, copy in Helen Gahagan Douglas (HGD) Papers, Box 33, Folder 4b, CAC-OU.

25. The Rosenwald family had also financed Davis's Committee for the Reform of Medical Education (CRME). See Poen, *Truman v. the Medical Lobby*, 83; *New York Times*, June 27, 1946; May 28, 1947.

26. These included Gerard Swope, the retired president of General Electric; James Patton, head of the National Farmers Union; the National Consumers League; the American Jewish Congress; the National Association for the Advancement of Colored People; and the Union for Democratic Action. Representatives of these organizations regularly testified in support of the Truman health security program, but on the whole, their numbers, finances, and public standing were overshadowed by the AMA and its insurance, business, and financial allies. See Senate, Committee on Education and Labor, *National Health Program, Hearings on S. 1606*, 79th Cong., 2d sess., Apr. 2–July 10, 1946, 735, 787–788, 1036, 2650.

27. AMA, *Digest of Official Actions, 1846–1958* (Chicago, 1959), 325–327; Senate, Committee on Education and Labor, *Hospital Construction Act, Hearings ... on S. 191*, 79th Cong. 1st sess., 1945, 137–155; *Congressional Record*, 79th Cong., 1st sess., vol. 91, pt. 1 (Jan. 10, 1945): 158; pt. 8 (Nov. 1, 1945): 10248; pt. 9 (Dec. 10–12, 1945): 11710–11736, 11792–11800, 11930; *Congressional Record*, 79th Cong., 2d sess., vol. 92, pt. 8 (July 30, 1946): 10479–10483, 10522–10523; Morris Fishbein, "The Public Relations of American Medicine," *JAMA* 130 (Feb. 23, 1946): 511.

28. For Taft's view on medical care, see James T. Patterson, *Mr. Republican: A Biography of Robert A. Taft* (Boston, 1972), 192–193, 259, 323, 432, 442–443, 504.

29. These witnesses included Arthur Altmeyer, chairman of the Social Security Board, Fiorello H. La Guardia, former mayor of New York and former president of the U.S. Conference of Mayors, Joseph W. Fichter, chairman of the Joint Subcommittee on Health of the National Planning Association, Dr. Clark Foreman, of the Southern Conference for Human Welfare, Harold L. Ickes, chairman of the Independent Citizens Committee for the Arts, Sciences and Professions, Dr. Allen M. Butler of Harvard Medical School and chief of the Children's Medical Service at Massachusetts General Hospital, Dr. Ernst Boas, of the Physicians Forum, the president of the National Medical Association, and assorted church and social work groups and followed by, among others, labor leaders Philip Murray of the CIO and Martin Hiller of the Brotherhood of Railroad Trainmen. Cf. Senate, *National Health Program, Hearings on S. 1606*. (Summaries of the hearings for Apr. 5, 10–12, 19, 1946; May 3, 1946; June 24, 1946, are in the Peden Papers, Box 62, Folder 7, CAC-OU.)

30. Senate, *National Health Program, Hearings on S. 1606*, 47–52.

31. Ibid., 50, 1689–1695, 1170–1174, 1786–1808, 1020–1025. For the characterization by the president of the Americans for Democratic Action (ADA), see *New York Times*, Dec. 7, 1945. Ewing's view is in Ewing Oral History, 2: 217, HSTL.

32. Senate, *Hearings on S. 1606*, 1383–1384, 1590–1639, 2337–2342. The Elmer Thomas Papers contain numerous critical letters denouncing the administration's compulsory health insurance proposal, comparing its quality to the "socialized medicine" of the military. See, for example, Thomas Papers, Legis. Ser., Box 61, Folders, 7, 43, 45, CAC-OU.

33. A biographical sketch of Clarence F. Lea is in Anne Roth, ed., *Current Biography, 1945* (New York, 1946), 334. See also "The Battle for the Nation's Health," *Nation* 162 (Apr. 20, 1946): 450; *New York Times*, May 4, 1946.

34. *New York Times*, July 10, 1946.

35. Ibid., Nov. 16, 1946. The courts did not sanction labor's right to bargain for health and welfare agreements until several years later, but in 1948, both Reuther's United Auto Workers (UAW) and the United Steelworkers were negotiating and winning precedent-setting contracts containing health and welfare provisions. See Raymond Munts, *Bargaining for Health: Labor Unions, Health Insurance, and Medical Care* (Madison, Wisc., 1967), 9–12. Reuther's observation is in Frank G. Dickinson, "The Trend toward Labor Health and Welfare Programs," *JAMA* 133 (Apr. 26, 1947): 1286.

36. Quoted in Poen, *Truman v. the Medical Lobby*, 94. For organized labor's postwar attitude toward private insurance, see Colin Gordon, *Dead on Arrival: The Politics of Health Care in Twentieth-Century America* (Princeton, N.J., 2003), 63–64, 230–231, 274–284; Alan Derickson, "Health Security for All: Social Unionism and Universal Health-Insurance, 1935–58," *Journal of American History* 80 (Mar. 1994): 1333–1356; Jennifer Klein, *To Secure These Rights* (Princeton, N.J., 2003), 220–235.

37. *Public Papers: Truman, 1947*, 5, 8, 37, 58, 72; CNH, "Do the People of the United States Need a National Health Insurance Program?" Nov. 7, 1947, copy in HGD Papers, Box 46, Folder 14, CAC-OU.

38. A copy of S. 545 is in HGD Papers, Box 33, Folder 4b, CAC-OU. See also "Health Legislation, 80th Congress, Review and Summary," n.d., ibid.; James G. Burrow, *AMA, Voice of American Medicine* (Baltimore, 1963), 348–349.

39. Copies of the testimony against S. 545 and in favor of the administration's alternative (S. 1320) by Michael Davis of the CNH, Albert D. Lasker, Dr. Ernst P. Boas, Andrew J. Biemiller of the ADA, and Dr. John P. Peters, secretary of the Committee of Physicians for the Improvement of Medical Care, in June and July 1948, are in HGD Papers, Box 143, Folder 8, CAC-OU. Murray's characterization is in *New York Times*, June 3, 1948; Wagner's statement is in Senate, Committee on Labor and Public Welfare, *National Health Program, Hearings on S. 545 and S. 1320*, 80th Cong., 1st sess., 1948; for Douglas's characterization of the Taft bill, see Helen Gahagan Douglas, "What Price Medicine, Current Legislation Dealing with Health before the Present Congress," *Journal of the National Medical Association* 40 (Jan. 1948): 14, copy in HGD Papers, Box 131, Folder 1a, CAC-OU.

40. A copy of S. 1320 is in HGD Papers, Box 33, Folder 4b, CAC-OU. Michigan Representative John Dingell introduced the companion bill (H.R. 3548) in the House. For a comparison of the Republican and Democratic bills, see the CNH flyers, "How Do the Two Major National Health Proposals Compare with One Another, *S. 1320 Versus S. 545*," n.d., and "What a National Health Program Would Mean," n.d., in ibid.

41. Eleanor Roosevelt, her son James, Senator Claude Pepper of Florida, Americans for Democratic Action, and labor leaders from the CIO and United Mine Workers, for example, had been seeking to dump Truman from the ticket and replace him with General Dwight Eisenhower, whose political affiliation at the time was unknown. See Ewing Oral History, 1: 143, HSTL; *New York Times*, Mar. 1, 7, 1946; Apr. 5, 1946; Sept. 21, 23, 1946; Nov. 21, 1946; Mar. 25, 26, 1947; Apr. 12, 13, 1947; May 1, 1947; June 6, 1947; Oct. 14, 1947; Julian M. Pleasants, "Claude Pepper, Strom Thurmond, and the 1948 Presidential Election in Florida," *Florida Historical Quarterly* 76 (Spring 1998): 439–472; Gary A. Donaldson, "The

Wardman Park Group and Campaign Strategy in the Truman Administration, 1946–1948," *Missouri Historical Review* 86 (Apr. 1992): 282–294; Susan M. Hartmann, *Truman and the 80th Congress* (Columbia, Mo., 1971), 71–72; Patterson, *Mr. Republican*, 375–378.

42. *Public Papers: Truman, 1947*, 250–252.

43. Poen, *Truman v. the Medical Lobby*, 101–103; Burrow, *AMA*, 349–350; *New York Times*, May 20, 1947; Bernard De Voto, "Doctors along the Boardwalk," *Harper's Magazine* 185 (Sept. 1947): 222.

44. CNH, "Health Legislation, 80th Congress, First Session, Review and Summary," Aug. 4, 1947, copy in HGD Papers, Box 143, Folder 6, CAC-OU; Margaret I. Stein to HGD, June 3, 1947, ibid., Box 33, Folder 4a. See also "Release from Office of Congresswoman Helen Gahagan Douglas," June 6, 1947; Raymond McKelvey, memorandum, "Mr. Reidy in Senator Murray's Office," n.d.; Claude Pepper to HGD, June 9, 1947; James Murray to HGD, June 7, 1947, in ibid.; "Statement to Members of the Subcommittee on Health of the Senate Committee on Labor and Public Welfare, by Rep. Helen Gahagan Douglas, Fourteenth District of California," June 6, 1947, copy in ibid., Box 33, Folder 4b, CAC-OU.

45. CNH, "Hearing Highlights, No. I, Week of May 19–23, 1947"; "Hearing Highlights, No. II, Second and Third Weeks"; "Hearing Highlights, No. III, Fourth and Fifth Weeks," HGD Papers, Box 33, Folder 4b, CAC-OU.

46. Ewing Oral History, 2: 181–182, HSTL. Ironically, the president's 1947 executive order establishing a federal employee loyalty program contributed to the public's fears. See Allan D. Harper, *The Politics of Disloyalty: The White House and the Communist Issue, 1946–1952* (Westport, Conn., 1969).

47. CNH, "Health Legislation, Review and Summary," Aug. 4, 1947, HGD Papers, Box 143, Folder 6, CAC-OU. For the Harness hearings (Forest A. Harness was a Republican Representative from Indiana) and report, see House, Committee on Expenditures in Executive Departments, *Investigation of the Participation of Federal Officials in the Formation and Operation of Health Workshops, Hearings*, 80th Cong., 1st sess., May 28–June 18, 1947; Senate, *Hearings on S. 545 and S. 1320*, 1200ff.; *New York Times*, May 28, 1947.

48. Marjorie Shearon, *Blueprint for the Nationalization of Medicine, Plans to Enchain Medicine by Regulative Interference* (Washington, D.C., 1947), copy in HGD Papers, Box 131, Folder 1b, CAC-OU; Senate *Hearings on S. 545 and S. 1320*, 2219, 2803–2804.

49. When the hearings resumed in January 1948, Falk continued to defend the agency from new accusations. "Notes Prepared by I. S. Falk on *Blueprint for the Nationalization of Medicine*, pub. by Marjorie Shearon," copy in HGD Papers, Box 33, Folder 4b, CAC-OU. Copies of Shearon's memoranda, dated Nov. 2, 12–14, 1938, are in Senate, *Hearings on S. 545 and S. 1320*, 1807–1826.

50. See, for example, the 1947 "Factual Memorandum" of the AMA's lobbying arm, the National Physicians' Committee for the Extension of Medical Service, entitled "The Most Deadly Menace," declaring that the "Moscow dominated Communist Party of the United States" was masterminding the "drive for Compulsory Health Insurance—Socialized Medicine." Copy in Peden Papers, Box 62, Folder 7, CAC-OU. Also see Ewing Oral History, 50–51, COHC, and Wendy P. Posner, "*Common Human Needs:* A Story from the Prehistory of Government by Special Interest," *Social Service Review* 69 (June 1995): 188–225.

51. See, for example, Dr. McLain Rogers to Carl Albert, Oct. 18, 1948; Albert to Rogers, Oct. 21, 1948; June 16, 1950; Albert to V. V. Harris, June 27, 1949, Albert Papers, Legis. Ser., Box 4, Folders 29, 31, 33; Box 14, Folder 75; Elmer Thomas to W. J. Horton, Nov. 30, 1948; Thomas to Judge George C. Crump, Dec. 10, 1948, Thomas Papers, Legis. Ser., Box 71, Folder 24; Box 88, Folder 30, CAC-OU. For pressures on Toby Morris to vote against "socialized medicine" in 1949 and 1950, see Morris to Mrs. Orin C. Darling, Jan. 24, 1949, Morris Papers, Legis. Ser., Box 10, Folder 11, and Box 7, Folders 27–31, CAC-OU.

52. CNH, "Hearing Highlights No. IV, July 9–11," HGD Papers, Box 33, Folder 4b, CAC-OU.

53. Ewing claims that he was not immediately familiar with the national health insurance controversy at the time of his appointment, but that he embraced the drive for national health insurance as a dutiful official of the administration. Ewing Oral History, 1: 145–147, HSTL; and Ewing Oral History, 46–48, COHC. For a different view, see Poen, *Truman v. the Medical Lobby*, 113, 115–116.

54. These issues ranged from legislation to protect the consumer and farmer to the repeal of the Taft-Hartley Act and, especially, civil rights. The inner workings of the Clifford-led group are discussed in Ewing Oral History, 1: 143; 2: 265–268ff., HSTL.

55. Citizens earning above $5,000 annually would be exempt from compulsory social insurance protection, as well as farmers and their families who lived in rural areas where medical facilities and personnel were lacking. *New York Times,* Nov. 20, 1947; Poen, *Truman v. the Medical Lobby,* 117–118.

56. CNH, "Will A.M.A. Block a National Voluntary Health Insurance Plan?" Nov. 18, 1948, HGD Papers, Box 33, Folder 4a, CAC-OU. See also Margaret I. Stein to HGD, Nov. 30, 1948; HGD to Stein, Dec. 10, 1948, ibid.

57. For the AMA's endorsement of the Taft bill, see *The Ten Point National Health Program of the American Medical Association,* reprinted as a pamphlet after appearing in *JAMA* 136 (Jan. 24, 1949): 261–266, copy in Peden Papers, Box 61, Folder 4, CAC-OU. See also *New York Times,* Dec. 26, 1947.

58. The idea for the conference originated with Don Kingsley, the FSA's assistant administrator. Ewing later denied that the conference was politically motivated. Ewing Oral History, 2: 180ff., HSTL; and Ewing Oral History, 36, COHC, but see Poen, *Truman v. the Medical Lobby,* 119–120, for Ewing's letter to Webb.

59. Ewing Oral History, 2: 188–192, 210–213, HSTL; *Public Papers: Truman, 1948,* 117–118, 239–243; *New York Times,* Apr. 18, 1948; May 2–5, 1948; Senate, *National Health Program,* 2400–2420.

60. Editorial, *JAMA* 136 (Mar. 6, 1948): 694; National Health Assembly, *America's Health, a Report to the Nation* (New York, 1949), 191–234; *New York Times,* May 5, 1948; Michael M. Davis, "Who Will Pay the Costs?" *Survey* 84 (June 1948): 191–193; AMA, *Digest of Official Actions,* 330–331.

61. Ewing Oral History, 44, COHC; *New York Times,* Feb. 3, 1948; Poen, *Truman v. the Medical Lobby,* 122–123.

62. George W. Bachman and Lewis Meriam, *The Issue of Compulsory Health Insurance* (Washington, D.C., 1948), 67–70, copy in HGD Papers, Box 131, Folder 1b, CAC-OU.

63. *New York Times,* May 10, 17, 1948; "Galileo Was Right, Brookings Institution Report on Issue of Compulsory Health Insurance," *AJPH* 38 (Sept. 1948): 1275–1276; Michael M. Davis, Letter to the Editor on Nation-wide Compulsory Health Insurance, ibid., 38 (Nov. 1948): 1580–1581.

64. "Cantilevered Roof, Democratic Platform," *Time* 52 (July 19, 1948): 24; Henry Hazlitt, "Democrats' Platform Economics," *Newsweek* 32 (July 26, 1948): 24; "Democrats, Their Convention Was Dreadful, But They Will Survive," *Life* 25 (July 26, 1948): 22; Kirk H. Porter and Donald B. Johnson, eds., *National Party Platforms, 1840–1956* (Urbana, Ill., 1956), 433.

65. *Public Papers: Truman, 1948,* 406–410; Poen, *Truman v. the Medical Lobby,* 126–127.

66. Ewing Oral History, 2: 265ff., HSTL; *Public Papers: Truman, 1948,* 416–421; Oscar R. Ewing, *The Nation's Health—A Ten Year Program* (Washington, D.C., 1948), x–xi, 75–114, copy in HGD Papers, Box 131, Folder 1a, CAC-OU; "AMA Blast on Oscar Ewing's Health Plan," *Newsweek* 32 (Oct. 4, 1948): 45.

67. Ewing Oral History, 2: 178–179, HSTL; "Why Prepaid Medical Insurance? An Analysis of Governor Earl Warren's Recommendation for California," n.d., copy in HGD Papers, Box 143, Folder 5, CAC-OU.

68. Ewing Oral History, 1: 138, HSTL. The 1948 presidential election campaign is discussed in Donovan, *Conflict and Crisis,* 388–439.

69. *Public Papers: Truman, 1948,* 938; Elmer Thomas to W. J. Morton, Nov. 30, 1948; to Judge George C. Crump, Dec. 10, 1948, Thomas Papers, Legis. Ser., Box 88, Folders 29, 30.

70. Cabell Phillips, *The Truman Presidency* (New York, 1969), 103–104, 162–165, 199–200; *Public Papers: Truman, 1949,* 1–7.

71. For the AMA's critique of the Ewing report's endorsement of national health insurance, see Frank G. Dickinson, *An Analysis of the Ewing Report* (AMA, *Bulletin,* no. 69, 1949), and Dr. Joseph S. Lawrence to George H. Wilson, Sept. 29, 1949, George H. Wilson Papers, Box 21, Folder 6, CAC-OU. For Whitaker and Baxter's role, see Ewing Oral History, 2: 213–214, HSTL. The AMA's tax status is discussed in Ewing Oral History, 59, COHC. See also "A Call to Action against Nationalization of Medicine," *JAMA*

138 (Dec. 1948): 1098–1099; "The American Medical Association, Power, Purpose and Politics in Organized Medicine," *Yale Law Journal* 63 (May 1954): 1012.

72. See "National Health Service Act," *Nation* 166 (Feb. 28, 1948): 19; Paul Jones, "Should Bureaucrats Practice Medicine?" *Saturday Evening Post* 220 (May 1, 1948): 144; "Free Care for Britons, Birth to Death Security," *U.S. News* 25 (July 2, 1948): 19; Lester Velie, "Is England's Socialized Medicine Working?" *Collier's* 123 (Mar. 5, 1949): 13–15; Richard H. Fry, "Appraisal of Britain's Welfare State," *New York Times Magazine* (Sept. 25, 1949): 124ff.

73. See, for example, "State Medicine Hasn't Worked Any Miracles," *Saturday Evening Post* (Jan. 1949); "Good Medicine Doesn't Mean Socialism," *Collier's* (Mar. 1949); "Free Medicine, How Much?" *U.S. News* (Apr. 1949); "Shouldn't Doctors Have Rights Too?" *Reader's Digest* (Apr. 1949); "Do You Really Want Socialized Medicine?" *Saturday Evening Post* (May 1949); "England Finds Free Ride Ain't Necessarily So," *Saturday Evening Post* (July 1949). Discussion of the merits and applicability of the British health system to the United States continued into 1950. See, for example, Rebecca West, "Can a Nation Afford Health for All Its People," *Ladies' Home Journal,* 67 (Sept. 1950): 10ff.

74. Dr. R. G. Jacobs to Robert S. Kerr, Jan. 12, 1949, copy in Wilson Papers, Box 20, Folder 22; Elmer Thomas to Mrs. Fred S. Fox, Feb. 23, 1949; Haskell Pruett to Elmer Thomas, Mar. 8, 1949, Thomas Papers, Legis. Ser., Boxes 88, 89, Folders 30, 3, CAC-OU.

75. *Public Papers: Truman, 1949,* 5, 26–27, 226–230; Elmer Cornwell, Jr., *Presidential Leadership of Public Opinion* (Bloomington, Ind., 1965), 168–170.

76. For the president's call for national health insurance in his State of the Union address and an analysis of the seven health bills, see CNH, "National Health Insurance Bills Introduced," Jan. 11, 1949, and Helen E. Livingston, *National Health Insurance, Public Affairs Bulletin,* no. 85 (Washington, D.C., June 1950), x–xiii, copies in HGD Papers, Box 33, Folder 4a; Box 111, Folder 1. A copy of S. 5 is in Andrew J. Biemiller Papers, Box 19, Folder 1, CAC-OU.

77. Senate, Committee on Labor and Public Welfare, *Hospital Survey and Construction (Hill-Burton Act) Amendments, Hearings . . . on S. 205, S. 231, S. 614, Title III of S. 1679, and Title IV of S. 1581,* 81st Cong., 1st sess., 1949. A copy of Taft's bill is in Biemiller Papers, Box 19, Folder 11, CAC-OU.

78. Ewing Oral History, 61–63, COHC. A copy of Truman's message to Congress is in Wilson Papers, Box 21, Folder 13; copies of S. 1679 and H.R. 4312 are in Biemiller Papers, Box 19, Folder 12, and in HGD Papers, Box 85, Folder 9, CAC-OU.

79. "A Simplified Blueprint of the Campaign against Compulsory Health Insurance, National State County," prepared by Whitaker and Baxter, Campaign Directors, Feb. 2, 1949. Copy in HGD Papers, Box 131, Folder 1a. See also Marjorie Shearon, ed., *American Medicine and the Political Scene* 3, no. 17 (Chevy Chase, Md., Apr. 28, 1949), copy in Wilson Papers, Box 21, Folder 10, CAC-OU.

80. See American College of Radiology, "Resolution Opposing Compulsory National Health Insurance," Feb. 4, 1949, HGD Papers, Box 85, Folder 9, CAC-OU; Dr. Louis H. Bauer and Rep. Andrew J. Biemiller, "What Kind of Health Insurance Do You Want?" American Forum of the Air, no. 9 (Feb. 28, 1949), copy of transcript in ibid. For the action of the New York physicians, see *Christian Science Monitor* press clipping, Jan. 25, 1949, in Wilson Papers, Box 21, Folder 5, ibid.

81. See, for example, the letters of Dr. Charles Gordon Heyd (president of United Medical Service, the Blue Shield "doctors' plan") to HGD, Apr. 1, 1949, and Earle V. Grover (president of the Los Angeles Chamber of Commerce) to HGD, Apr. 19, 1949, HGD Papers, Box 85, Folder 9, CAC-OU; Heyd to George H. Wilson, Apr. 1, 1949; Louis H. Pink to Wilson, Apr. 8, 1949, Wilson Papers, Box 20, Folder 5, ibid. Pink was president of the Associated Hospital Services of New York (Blue Cross).

82. Burrow, *AMA,* 413; *New York Times,* June 8, 10, 1949; *Public Papers: Truman, 1949,* 281.

83. *New York Times,* Apr. 18, 1949.

84. See the press clippings from the *Christian Science Monitor,* Jan.–Apr. 1949, Wilson Papers, Box 21, Folder 12, CAC-OU. See also *New York Times,* Apr. 23, 29, 1949; May 2, 15, 1949; June 10–11,

13, 1949. For the hearings, see Senate, Committee on Interstate and Foreign Commerce, *National Health Plan, Hearings . . . on H.R. 4312, H.R. 4313, and H.R. 4918 and Other Identical Bills,* 81st Cong., 1st sess., 1949.

85. For the pro-administration voices, see the correspondence between Margaret Kopp and Helen Gahagan Douglas, Mar. 25, 1949; Apr. 19, 1949; May 18, 1949, HGD Papers, Boxes 85 and 86, Folders 9 and 1, CAC-OU. Also see press clippings from the *Christian Science Monitor,* Feb. 1, 1949; Mar. 3, 1949; *Evening Star* (Washington, D.C.), Feb. 14, 1949; Maurice Mermey, "Opinion Leaders Strongly Favor Truman Health Plan," *American Druggist,* Mar. 1949; Hubert H. Humphrey, "The Case for National Health Insurance," *New York Times Magazine,* May 8, 1949, Wilson Papers, Box 21, Folders 10, 11, CAC-OU.

86. CNH, "Questions Asked by Members of Congress about National Health Insurance," 1945; CNH, "Some Statements and Misstatements about National Health Insurance," n.d.; Dr. Channing Frothingham to Members of Congress, Mar. 11, 1949; Chat Paterson to HGD, Mar. 18, 1949, HGD Papers, Box 85, Folder 9, CAC-OU.

87. Travis T. Wallace to George H. Wilson, June 9, 1949, Wilson Papers, Box 20, Folder 22; Toby Morris to Dr. McLain Rogers, June 14, 1950, Morris Papers, Legis. Ser., Box 4, Folder 21, CAC-OU; Poen, *Truman v. the Medical Lobby,* 161.

88. Richard M. Nixon, Clifford Case, Jacob Javits, and Christian Herter were among the sponsors of S. 1970, which proposed to establish a locally organized and controlled private insurance system with premiums scaled to subscribers' incomes. Federal and state funds would make up any deficiency between the system's cost and the individual subscriber's income. S. 1970 was paired with a companion bill to make the premiums of voluntary prepayment plans tax deductible. Livingston, *National Health Insurance,* xiii.

89. Emphasis mine. For evidence of Southern Democratic support for the Hill-Aiken bill, see David B. Truman, *The Congressional Party* (New York, 1949), 59; George H. Wilson to Dr. Howard Johnson, Mar. 23, 1949, Wilson Papers, Box 20, Folder 24, CAC-OU.

90. Carl Albert to Hon. Grover Flanagan, Aug. 18, 1949, Albert Papers, Legis. Ser., Box 9, Folder 29, CAC-OU; *New York Times,* Oct. 27, 1949; Dec. 8, 1949.

91. Truman's decision to desegregate the armed forces and his insistence that Congress establish a new fair employment practices committee to monitor job discrimination had particularly grated on southerners' sensibilities. *Public Papers: Truman, 1948,* 121–126; Richard M. Dalfiume, *Desegregation of the U.S. Armed Forces, Fighting on Two Fronts, 1939–1953* (Columbia, Mo., 1969), passim; Barton J. Bernstein and Allen J. Madhouse, eds., *The Truman Administration: A Documentary History* (New York, 1966), 108–110.

92. *Public Papers: Truman, 1949,* 310–311; *Congressional Record,* 81st Cong., 1st sess., vol. 95, pt. 9 (Aug. 16, 1949): 11560; Ewing Oral History, 2: 173, HSTL. The quoted editorial is in Poen, *Truman v. the Medical Lobby,* 164.

93. Besides Great Britain, the delegation visited France, Germany, and Sweden. Wilson's handwritten notes of Sept. 13, 1949, are in the Wilson Papers, Box 22, Folder 1, CAC-OU.

94. Ibid.

95. Ibid.

96. Ibid.

97. Cronkite's questions and Wilson's written responses dated Oct. 14, 1949, are in ibid., Box 22, Folder 1; news clipping, "Congressman Speaks Here on Socialized Medicine," *Blackwell Daily Journal Tribune,* Nov. 4, 1949, ibid., Box 21, Folder 18, CAC-OU.

98. Dr. Joseph S. Lawrence to R. H. Graham, Oct. 12, 1949, ibid., Box 20, Folder 25, CAC-OU.

99. A copy of S. 1411 (companion bill H.R. 3942) is in ibid., Box 22, Folder 11, CAC-OU. See also American Parents Committee, Inc., Washington Report on Legislation for Children, "School Health Bill

and the Children's Bureau Budget," Report no. 4 (Apr. 1949), and Dr. Joseph S. Lawrence to Members of Congress, Dec. 16, 1949, in ibid.

100. For the AMA's accusations, see press clippings from *ADA World*, Feb. 16, 1949; *Christian Science Monitor*, Feb. 18–19, 21, 1949; Apr. 25, 1949, in ibid., Box 21, Folder 12; "Statement by the Board of Trustees on Investigations of Medical Organizations," *JAMA* 141 (Oct. 15, 1949): 465; *New York Times*, Aug. 7, 1949; Oct. 16, 1949. For support of the Flanders-Ives bill, see Russell W. Davenport, "Health Insurance Is Next," *Fortune*, Mar. 1950, copy in Wilson Papers, Box 21, Folder 11, CAC-OU. Ewing's memo is in Poen, *Truman v. the Medical Lobby*, 175–176.

101. For the survey and Arvey's remarks, see *Christian Science Monitor*, Mar. 6, 1950; Apr. 19, 1950, clippings in Wilson Papers, Box 21, Folder 12, CAC-OU. For Wilson's meeting with Truman, see George H. Wilson to Dr. William P. La Finned, Feb. 22, 1950; to Dr. and Mrs. Elmer E. Heady, Mar. 28, 1950; to Mrs. L. Earl Weeks, May 25, 1950, ibid., Box 20, Folder 26. For efforts to reelect conservative opponents of health security, see Bruce R. Hinson to Members, Oklahoma Medical Association, n.d., Kay-Noble County Medical Society, *Political Bulletin* (Aug. 1950 [?]); Dr. F. E. Wilson to Dick Graham, Executive Secretary, Oklahoma State Medical Assoc., Aug. 3, 1950, ibid. See also Hamby, *Beyond the New Deal*, 421–422; Donald R. McCoy and Richard T. Ruetten, *Quest and Response, Minority Rights and the Truman Administration* (Lawrence, Kans., 1973), 283–285.

102. "Report of the Coordinating Committee," *JAMA* 147 (Dec. 22, 1951): 1692; Dr. Elmer L. Henderson, "1950—Medicine's Armageddon," n.d., flyer in Wilson Papers, Box 21, Folder 11, CAC-OU; *Public Papers: Truman, 1950*, 9, 29, 46, 54.

103. Poen, *Truman v. the Medical Lobby*, 177–178.

104. "Legislative Notes," *JAMA* 145 (Jan. 20, 1951): 34; "The President's Page," ibid., 145 (Feb. 24, 1951): 567.

# CHAPTER 4. THE POLITICS OF INCREMENTALISM, 1951–1960

1. Peter A. Corning, *The Evolution of Medicare*, Research Report no. 29, Office of Research and Statistics, Social Security Administration (Washington, D.C., 1969), 71; Oscar R. Ewing Oral History, 2 vols., 2: 224, Harry S. Truman Library (HSTL).

2. Corning, *Evolution of Medicare*, 72. Ewing believed that SSA officials refused to contemplate anything less than universal health coverage before 1950, largely owing to the amount of time, labor, and psychic energy they had invested in the president's original proposal: Oscar R. Ewing Oral History, Columbia University Oral History Collection (COHC), 73.

3. Falk's original proposal had included all categories of beneficiaries, the preponderance of whom were the elderly, two-thirds of whom had annual incomes of less than $1,000. I. S. Falk, "Health Services, Medical Care Insurance and Social Security," *Annals* 273 (Jan. 1951): 114–121.

4. See, for example, "What to Do about the Old Folks," *Newsweek* 35 (Mar. 20, 1950): 58; Wilma Donahue et al., "Problems of Aging," *University of Chicago Round Table*, Aug. 13, 1950, 1–16; "Emotional Problems of the Aged," *AJPH* 40 (Sept. 1950): 1140–1142; O. A. Randall, "The Impact of the Aged on the Community," *Jewish Social Service Organization* 27 (Dec. 1950): 212–220; Ethel Shanas and Robert J. Havighurst, "The Challenge of the Aged," *State Government* 24 (May 1951): 133–134. Ewing denied a direct link between the conference and Medicare legislation, observing that although the work of the former would bear on the latter, the decision to convene the conference on aging had proceeded from a different logic and rationale. Ewing Oral History, 83–84, COHC; *New York Times*, June 8, 1950; Aug. 14–16, 1950; Corning, *Evolution of Medicare*, 72–73.

5. The public assistance programs were Old Age Assistance, Aid to Dependent Children, Aid to the Blind, and Aid to the Permanently and Totally Disabled. Cf. Neil R. Peirce, ed., *Congress and the Nation 1945–1964* (Washington, D.C., 1965), 1153.

6. Edward D. Berkowitz, *America's Welfare State* (Baltimore, 1991), 43–56.

7. Ewing, intent on salvaging something from this latest defeat, turned to publisher William R. Hearst, Jr., and Louis Pink, head of New York's Blue Cross hospital-insurance system, for suggestions. Hearst proposed a program less ambitious than universal health insurance and Pink suggested a prepayment program for those over sixty-five, a population cohort for which there was little experience or actuarial data. Their ideas appealed to Ewing, who knew that the administration had been "licked on the big program for national health insurance," but who believed that a more modest proposal might serve as the pilot for a future program and enable the federal government to gain valuable administrative experience. Ewing Oral History, 79–80, 83–84, COHC; *Public Papers of the Presidents: Harry S. Truman, 1951* (Washington, D.C., 1965), 96–99 (cited as *Public Papers: Truman* [with year]); *New York Times,* Jan. 16–17, 27, 1951; Mar. 20, 1951; Apr. 19, 1951; Dec. 5, 1951.

8. Ewing Oral History, 2: 225–226, HSTL.

9. *Public Paper: Truman, 1951,* 655–656.

10. Corning, *Evolution of Medicare,* 73; *Congressional Record,* 82d Cong., 2d sess., vol. 98, pt. 3 (Apr. 10, 1952): 3926–3932, pt. 3 (Apr. 14, 1952): 3998; Ewing Oral History, 2: 196, 215–216, 219–221, HSTL. For the SSA's recommendations, see *Annual Report of the Federal Security Agency, 1951: Social Security Administration* (Washington, D.C., 1952), 28–31; *New York Times,* Apr. 11, 1952.

11. Ewing Oral History, 2: 131, 353, HSTL. See also Bert Cochran, *Adlai Stevenson: Patrician among the Politicians* (New York, 1969), 210–223; Edward P. Doyle, ed., *As We Knew Him: The Stevenson Story by Twenty-one Friends* (New York, 1966), 82–84; *New York Times,* July 31, 1952; Aug. 22, 1952.

12. The report recommended a cooperative state-federal program wherein each state would establish its own health plan (subject to federal approval) with federal matching funds providing the payments for those who could not afford the premiums. Social Security beneficiaries would be covered through payments to the states out of the OASI tax mechanism. See *Building America's Health: Report to the President by the President's Commission on Health Needs of the Nation* (Washington, D.C., 1953), 42–44, 72.

13. The report revealed that since 1900, the number of Americans 65 years old and over had risen from 3 million to more than 12 million, up from 4 to 8 percent of the total population, and would increase to 25 million by 1970. People over 65 were hospitalized twice as long as those under 65 and were incapacitated by chronic illness five times as often. Hospital costs were rising at a steady annual rate of 5–7 percent, but nearly two-thirds of the aged had annual incomes of less than $1,000. The result was that only one in eight elderly couples had any kind of health insurance. Moreover, private carriers considered them bad risks. Even if they were eligible, the premiums were usually too expensive. Compounding the problem, Americans were living longer and retiring earlier, which meant that both their incomes and savings were lower. Ibid., 71–72.

14. *Public Papers: Truman, 1952–1953,* 1166–1167; Richard Harris, "Medicare, Part II," *New Yorker* 42 (July 9, 1965): 31–33. Harris's series of four articles in the magazine remains in many respects the best account of Medicare's history. The articles were published subsequently under the title *A Sacred Trust* (New York, 1966).

15. Ewing Oral History, 2: 228–230, HSTL; *New York Times,* Jan. 7, 1951; Dec. 30, 1951; Nov. 20, 1952; Dec. 29, 1952.

16. For insights into Eisenhower's politicoeconomic policies, see the articles by Charles V. Murphy in *Fortune,* beginning with vol. 48 (July 1953), 75–77, 176–181, and extending to vol. 56 (July 1957), 96–99, 228–231. See also "The President's Page," *JAMA* 150 (Dec. 17, 1952): 1675; "Organization Section," ibid., 1695.

17. Eisenhower's views on Social Security are expressed in a letter to his brother Edgar, Nov. 8, 1954, as quoted in Fred I. Greenstein, *The Hidden-Hand Presidency: Eisenhower as Leader* (New York, 1982), 50. On Eisenhower and health care, see Jill Quadagno, "One Nation: Uninsured" (forthcoming), 59–63.

18. *New York Times,* Aug. 21, 1952; Sept. 15, 1952. For allegations that Eisenhower cut a deal with the AMA, see Harris, "Medicare, Pt. II," 33–34.

19. *New York Times,* Mar. 11, 1954. For the Dingell bill (H.R. 8, later amended and reintroduced as H.R. 6034), see *Congressional Record,* 83d Cong., 1st sess., vol. 99, pt. 6 (July 2, 1953): 7860. The Murray bill (S. 1966) is in ibid., pt. 4 (May 25, 1953), 5415.

20. House, Committee on Interstate and Foreign Commerce, *Health Service Prepayment Plan Reinsurance Act,* 83d Cong., 2d sess., 1954, H. Rep. 2106. Hobby's letter to Rep. Charles Wolverton, Mar. 24, 1954, endorsing the bill is in ibid., 12–13. For Murray's minority report, see Senate, *Federal Reinsurance Service,* 83d Cong., 2d sess., 1954, Sen. Rep. 1798, pt. 2.

21. For the debate and vote on H.R. 8356, see *Congressional Record,* 83d Cong., 1st sess., vol. 100, pt. 8 (July 13, 1954): 10393–10426, and *Congress and the Nation,* 1153. For conservative opposition, see the exchange of letters between Dr. George F. Lull, secretary of the AMA, and Rep. Page H. Belcher, July 13–14, 1954, and Kittie C. Sturdevant to Belcher, July 14, 1954, Page H. Belcher Papers, Box 12, Folder 40b, Carl Albert Center, University of Oklahoma (CAC-OU).

22. Chester J. Pach, Jr., and Elmo Richardson, *The Presidency of Dwight D. Eisenhower* (Lawrence, Kans., 1991), 56.

23. Corning, *Evolution of Medicare,* 105–106.

24. Organized labor simultaneously endorsed a companion bill to reduce the retirement age for women to sixty-two, but according to former commissioner of Social Security Charles I. Schottland, this was mainly a bargaining chip to get what labor really wanted—disability insurance. Charles I. Schottland Oral History, pt. 3: "Social Security Administration and Medicare Project," 96, 101–102, COHC.

25. The origin of the disability amendment is discussed in Clinton P. Anderson, *Outsider in the Senate: Senator Clinton Anderson's Memoirs* (New York, 1970), 262–264. The author has relied on the more detailed account of the legislative maneuvering leading to its passage in Rowland Evans and Robert Novak, *Lyndon B. Johnson: The Exercise of Power* (New York, 1966); James E. Murray, "Health Insurance for All," *Progressive,* June 1957, 6–9; John H. Miller, "Health Insurance for Older Citizens," *American Economic Security* 13 (Dec. 1956): 17–24.

26. Schottland Oral History, pt. 3, 95, 102, COHC. Excellent on all aspects of Social Security and Medicare is the definitive biography of Wilbur J. Cohen by Edward D. Berkowitz, *Mr. Social Security: The Life of Wilbur J. Cohen* (Lawrence, Kans., 1995); the same author's *Robert Ball and the Politics of Social Security* (Madison, Wisc., 2003), 120–138, and Julian E. Zelizer's *Taxing America* (Cambridge, UK, 1998), 9, 12.

27. "The Salami Slicer," *Time* 91 (Apr. 5, 1968): 24–25.

28. Clements's opponent was Thruston B. Morton. Schottland Oral History, pt. 3, 98–99, 103, COHC; Evans and Novak, *LBJ: The Exercise of Power,* 170–171.

29. Evans and Novak, *The Exercise of Power,* 170–171.

30. Ibid., 171–172.

31. Ibid., 172–173.

32. Clements's bid for reelection that fall failed, owing to AMA opposition. Corning, *Evolution of Medicare,* 173; *New York Times,* Nov. 9, 1956.

33. *Public Papers of the Presidents: Dwight D. Eisenhower, 1956* (Washington, D.C., 1958), 638–639 (cited as *Public Papers: Eisenhower* [with year]).

34. In 1950, when federal participation in vendor payments for medical care of public assistance recipients was first authorized, the rule established was as follows: of the first $50 of a state's combined monthly outlays for living expenses and vendor payments for a welfare client, the federal government

would reimburse the state for $30. The formula was revised upward in 1952, 1956, and 1958. Following the 1958 change, the federal share increased to between $41.50 and $46.75 of the first $65 combined outlay for living expenses and vendor payments. In 1960, to induce the states to spend more for medical care for the elderly under the Kerr-Mills health care program, the federal government provided additional matching funds for vendor payments under the Old-Age Assistance (OAA) program. Cf. Senate, Committee on Finance, *Medical Care Vendor Repayments,* 85th Cong., 1st sess., 1957, Sen. Rep. 473; *Congress and the Nation,* 1154.

35. Schottland Oral History, pt. 3, 91, COHC.

36. Harris, "Medicare, Pt. II," 35, 52.

37. *Congressional Record,* 84th Cong., 2d sess., vol. 102, pt. 8 (May 7, 1954): 6189. After earlier rebuffs, reformers finally persuaded Congress to add disability insurance to the Social Security Act in 1956. The Old-Age, Survivors, and Disability Insurance (OASDI) amendment provided total permanent disability compensation for those over fifty years of age who were permanently removed from the workforce. Berkowitz, *America's Welfare State,* 165; Jennifer Klein, *For All These Rights* (Princeton, N.J., 2003), 259.

38. Schottland Oral History, pt. 3, 93–94, COHC; Harris, "Medicare, Pt. II," 35–36; Berkowitz, *America's Welfare State,* 167; Klein, *For All These Rights,* 232–234.

39. Katherine Ellickson, "Toward Proper Health Care," *American Federationist* 64 (July 1957): 12–14.

40. "What Labor Really Wants from You: Interview with Nelson H. Cruikshank," *Medical Economics* 35 (Mar. 17, 1958): 90–95; Harris, "Medicare, Pt. II," 36; *Congressional Record,* 85th Cong., 1st sess., vol. 103, pt. 12 (Aug. 27, 1957): 16173, pt. 12 (Aug. 30, 1957): 16769.

41. On Mills's chairmanship of the committee, see John F. Manley, *The Politics of Finance: The House Committee on Ways and Means* (Boston, 1970); Zelizer, *Taxing America,* 21, 80, 119–120, 155–156, 207, 216–219.

42. The number of people covered by hospitalization policies between 1952 and 1958 had risen from 91 million to 121 million; those covered by surgical insurance, from 91 million to 109 million; and those covered by general medical insurance, from 36 to 72 million. The growth of voluntary health insurance is discussed in Health Insurance Council, *The Extent of Voluntary Health Insurance Coverage in the United States as of December 31, 1956: Final Report on Annual Survey* (New York, 1957); John F. Follmann, Jr., "Four Years of Progress in Voluntary Private Health Insurance," *AJPH* 47 (Nov. 1957): 1381–1389; David D. Allman, "Medicine's Role in Financing Health Care Costs," *JAMA* 165 (Nov. 23, 1957): 1571–1573; "'Preferred' Protection against Health Hazards: Voluntary Health Insurance Guards Twice as Many Americans as a Decade Ago," *Journal of American Insurance* 35 (Oct. 1959): 16–17.

43. Folsom's testimony is in House, Committee on Ways and Means, *Social Security Legislation, Hearings... on H.R. 9467,* 85th Cong., 2d sess., 1958, 3–39.

44. Cruikshank's testimony is in ibid., 368–387, 772ff. See also Jerome Pollack, "A Labor View of Health Insurance," *Monthly Labor Review* 81 (June 1958): 626–630, and Wilbur J. Cohen, "The Forand Bill: Hospital Insurance for the Aged," *American Journal of Nursing* 58 (May 1958): 698–672.

45. One of the formative influences on Kennedy's thinking about health care legislation for the elderly was the report of Wilbur J. Cohen et al., "Attitudes toward Governmental Participation in Medical Care," University of Michigan Subcommittee on Income Maintenance and Social Security of the Coordinating Committee on Social Welfare Research, School of Social Work, March 1960. Copy and notation in Carl Albert Papers, Legis. Files, Folder 17, Box 93, CAC-OU. See also Harris, "Medicare, Pt. II," 55; Berkowitz, *Mr. Social Security,* 121.

46. *Congressional Record,* 85th Cong., 2d sess., vol. 104, pt. 14 (Aug. 19, 1958): 18422–18424; Berkowitz, *Mr. Social Security,* 119–120.

47. Harris, "Medicare, Pt. II," 55; Sherri David, *With Dignity* (Westport, Conn., 1985), 21.

48. "The AMA Defends the 'Liberty Tree,'" *Industrial Union Digest* 3 (Spring 1958): 58–65; Harris, "Medicare, Pt. II," 44, 49–50, 55–58.

49. Alexander A. Jaworski, "How to Fight the Forand Bill," *Medical Economics* 35 (July 7, 1958): 71–77; "The AMA Relents," *Industrial Union Digest* 4 (Fall 1959): 45–53.

50. Harris, "Medicare, Pt. II," 50.

51. Schottland Oral History, pt. 3, 89–90, COHC.

52. The statistics underpinning the report disclosed that 60 percent of all Americans sixty-five years of age and older had annual incomes amounting to less than $1,000 and another 20 percent had between $1,000 and $2,000. Of the best-off among the elderly (i.e., those couples who lived alone in their own homes), about half had incomes of less than $2,000 per year; the other half had incomes of less than $900 per year. Harris, "Medicare, Pt. II," 52.

53. Ibid., 58; "Federal Health Insurance Looms as Election Issue," *Congressional Quarterly Weekly Report* (cited hereafter as *CQWR*) 17 (Aug. 7, 1959), 1075–1076; *New York Times,* July 16–17, 1959; Oct. 21, 1959.

54. Aime Forand, "Health Care for Our Elders," *Industrial Union Digest* 4 (Summer 1959): 3–9; Nelson H. Cruikshank, "Health Delayed, Health Denied," *American Federationist* 66 (Sept. 1959): 16–17; Harris, "Medicare, Pt. II," 58, 60.

55. Harris, "Medicare, Pt. II," 60–61.

56. Congress, Joint Economic Committee, 86th Cong., 1st sess., "Trends in the Supply and Demand of Medical Care," by Markley Roberts, Materials Prepared in Connection with Study of Employment, Growth and Price Levels, Study Paper no. 5 (Nov. 10, 1959).

57. For McNamara's hearings, see Senate, Committee on Labor and Public Welfare, Subcommittee on Problems of the Aged and Aging, *The Aged and the Aging in the United States,* 86th Cong., 1st sess., 1959.

58. Edward T. Chase, "Fight over the Forand Bill," *Reporter* 22 (May 26, 1960): 13–19; and Chase's "Politics of Medicine," *Harper's* 221 (Oct. 1960): 124–131.

59. Harris, "Medicare, Pt. II," 62; Memorandum, Senator Pat McNamara, "Retired Persons Medical Insurance Act," May 1960, copy in Lyndon B. Johnson (LBJ) Papers, White House Central Files (WHCF)-Aides Files (George Reedy), Box 11, Folder: Aging, Forand Bill, Social Security, Lyndon B. Johnson Library (LBJL); *Congressional Record,* 86th Cong., 2d sess., vol. 106, pt. 1 (Jan. 26, 1960): 1238; pt. 8 (May 6, 1960): 9704–9709; "Kennedy Health Bill," *CQWR* 18 (Jan. 29, 1960): 178.

60. Anne H. Morgan, *Robert S. Kerr: The Senate Years* (Norman, Okla., 1977), 190.

61. "Forand Bill Sparks Top Lobbying Campaign," *CQWR* 18 (May 6, 1960): 796–799; *New York Times,* Apr. 10, 1960; Harris, "Medicare, Pt. II," 65–66.

62. Ben McCrary to George Reedy, n.d. (1960?), LBJ Papers, WHCF-Aides Files (Reedy), Box 11, Folder: Aging, Forand Bill, Social Security, LBJL.

63. *Congressional Record,* 84th Cong., 2d sess., vol. 102, pt. 9 (July 12, 1956): 12413; Robert S. Kerr to Dr. Porter Routh, Aug. 21, 1954; "Kerr Press Release," Feb. 2, 1956; Kerr to Dr. Douglas L. Rippeto, Feb. 7, 1956, Kerr Papers, Legis. Files, Boxes 17, 18, 24, Folders: Old Age Care, CAC-OU.

64. This was not the first use of the term "Medicare." In 1956, Congress passed an administration measure providing free medical care to dependents of servicemen that went by that name. *Wall Street Journal,* Mar. 21, 24, 31, 1960; Apr. 6–8, 1960; May 3, 1960.

65. The bill also provided payments for up to six months of hospitalization, physician, surgeon, and dentist fees, one year of care in a nursing home, and X-ray and drug therapy. Single people over sixty-five with annual incomes of less than $2,500 and couples with incomes of less than $3,800 also were eligible upon payment of an annual fee of $24. A comparison of the two bills, with notations, is in House, Democratic Study Group, *Medical Care for the Aged,* Fact Sheet no. 27 (1960), 3–4, 7–10, Albert Papers, Legis. Ser., Box 93, Folder: 17, CAC-OU. See also *Wall Street Journal,* May 5, 9–10, 12, 17, 19, 1960; Anderson, *Outsider in the Senate,* 265.

66. *Wall Street Journal,* May 5, 1960.

67. *Congressional Digest* for March 1960 was devoted entirely to the type of bill that Congress would enact. See, for example, its article examining the merits and drawbacks of adding medical coverage to the Social Security program.

68. Harris, "Medicare, Pt. II," 68–70.

69. Ibid., 70; *Congressional Record,* 86th Cong., 2d sess., vol. 106, pt. 10 (June 22, 1960): 13808–13814, 13826–13828, 13832–13856.

70. Lawrence V. Davis to JFK, Aug. 5, 1960, Wilbur J. Cohen Papers, Box 4, Folder: Letters to JFK, LBJL.

71. Mike Gorman to George Reedy, n.d. [1960?], and Democratic Policy Committee, "Analysis of Republican Platform on Health," copies in LBJ Papers, WHCF-Aides Files (Reedy), Box 11, Folder: Medical, LBJL.

72. Morgan, *Kerr,* 191.

73. Dr. F. C. Lattimore to Wilbur Mills, May 1960, copy in Kerr Papers, Legis. Ser., Box 24, Folder 14, CAC-OU.

74. The Senate Finance Committee, in fact, conducted hearings on the Mills bill on June 29–30, 1960. Senate, Committee on Finance, *Social Security Amendment of 1960, Hearings on H.R. 12580,* 86th Cong., 2d sess., 1960. See also Morgan, *Kerr,* 192.

75. Theodore R. Marmor, *The Politics of Medicare* (Chicago, 1973), 30; Morgan, *Kerr,* 192–193; Harris, "Medicare, Pt. II," 70.

76. Morgan, *Kerr,* 193; Anderson, *Outsider in the Senate,* 266.

77. *New York Times,* July 31, 1960; Morgan, *Kerr,* 193–194; Anderson, *Outsider in the Senate,* 266.

78. David, *With Dignity,* 37; Harris, "Medicare, Pt. II," 70, 72.

79. A copy of the Kerr-Mills bill (along with virtually every report, bill, and proposal relative to government health insurance) may be found in HEW, SSA, *Background on Medicare, 1957–1962* (2 vols., 85th–87th Cong., Baltimore, 1962)), vol. 1 (86th Cong., 1959–1960), LBJ Papers, WHCF-Aides Files (Ervin Duggan), Box 9, LBJL. See also Anderson, *Outsider in the Senate,* 267.

80. *Wall Street Journal,* Aug. 16, 22, 1960; Anderson, *Outsider in the Senate,* 264; Morgan, *Kerr,* 194–195.

81. Harris, "Medicare, Pt. II," 73.

82. "Committee Roundup," *CQWR* 18 (Aug. 19, 1960): 1457; *Wall Street Journal,* Aug. 14–15, 1960.

83. *Congressional Record,* 86th Cong., 2d sess., vol. 106, pt. 12 (Aug. 17, 1960): 545–548; "Health Care Battle to Focus on Anderson Plan," *CQWR* 18 (Aug. 5, 1960): 1371–1372; Anderson, *Outsider in the Senate,* 266; David, *With Dignity,* 26.

84. Harris, "Medicare, Pt. II," 73–74.

85. "The Text of President Eisenhower's Aug. 17 Press Conference," *CQWR* 18 (Aug. 19, 1960): 1470.

86. Harris, "Medicare, Pt. II," 72; Morgan, *Kerr,* 195–196.

87. *Congressional Record,* 86th Cong., 2d sess., vol. 106, pt. 12 (Aug. 15, 1960): 16425–16434; *New York Times,* Aug. 15, 1960; *Wall Street Journal,* Aug. 15, 1960.

88. *Congressional Record,* 86th Cong., 2d sess., vol. 106, pt. 13 (Aug. 23, 1960): 17145–17146, 17157–17176, 17183–17220; *Wall Street Journal,* Aug. 17, 19, 1960.

89. Paul H. Douglas, *In the Fullness of Time* (New York, 1972), 393.

90. Quoted in House, Democratic Study Group, *Medical Care for the Aged,* Fact Sheet no. 27, n.d., copy in Albert Papers, Legis. Ser., Box 93, Folder: 17, CAC-OU.

91. *Congressional Record,* 86th Cong., 2d sess., vol. 106, pt. 13 (Aug. 23, 1960): 17235; Harris, "Medicare, Pt. II," 74.

92. James L. Sundquist, *Politics and Policy: The Eisenhower, Kennedy and Johnson Years* (Washington, D.C., 1968), 307; "Medical Care Changes," *Congressional Quarterly Almanac* (1960), 161; "Press Release on Kerr-Mills," Aug. 31, 1960, Kerr Papers, cited in Morgan, *Kerr,* 196.

93. Schottland Oral History, pt. 3, 110–112, COHC; Kerr to Delbert Davis, Sept. 26, 1960, Kerr Papers, Box 18, Folder: Old Age Care, CAC-OU; Morgan, *Kerr,* 198.

94. Anderson, *Outsider in the Senate,* 266–267; Page H. Belcher to Dr. Carl R. Smith, Mar. 6, 1961, Belcher Papers, Box 70, Folder: 3K, CAC-OU.

95. Quoted in Morgan, *Kerr,* 199.

96. Quoted in *Washington Post,* Aug. 16, 1960.

# CHAPTER 5. MEDICARE:
# A CONGRESSIONAL QUAGMIRE

1. The election is discussed in Theodore C. Sorensen, "The Election of 1960," in *History of American Presidential Elections 1789–1968,* ed. Arthur M. Schlesinger, Jr., 4 vols. (New York, 1971), 4: 3449–3469; and Allen J. Matusow, *The Unraveling of America: A History of Liberalism in the 1960s* (New York, 1984), 3–29. For Kennedy's campaign criticism of Kerr-Mills, see Page H. Belcher to E. A. Guise, May 22, 1961, Page H. Belcher Papers, Box 70, Folder 3F, Carl Albert Center, University of Oklahoma (CAC-OU). See also "Nixon and Kennedy Discuss the Issues," *U.S. News* 48 (May 30, 1960): 119–123; Richard Harris, "Medicare, Part II," *New Yorker* 42 (July 9, 1966): 76–77.

2. The conference chair was former Republican representative Robert W. Kean of New Jersey. Department of Health, Education and Welfare (HEW), *White House Conference on Aging, 1961: Background Paper on Health and Medical Care* (Washington, D.C., 1961).

3. The term *Medicare* had been first applied to a law enacted in 1956 to provide medical care for dependents of servicemen. For Flemming and the conference, see "Membership and Scope of January 9 Conference on Aging," *CQWR* 18 (Dec. 30, 1960): 2014–2015; "Information Kit, Plans and Preparation for the White House Conference on Aging, Scheduled January 1961, at Washington, D.C."; "Fact Sheet: White House Conference on Aging," n.d., Belcher Papers, Box 70, CAC-OU; HEW, *White House Conference on Aging, 1961: Policy Statements and Recommendations, February, 1961* (Washington, D.C., 1961); Senate, Subcommittee on Problems of the Aged and Aging, *The Aged and Aging in the United States: A National Problem, Rept. . . . purs. to* (Jan. 29, 1960), 86th Cong., 2d sess., 1961; Harris, "Medicare, Pt. III," *New Yorker* 42 (July 16, 1966): 35–37.

4. *Public Papers of the Presidents: John F. Kennedy, 1961* (Washington, D.C., 1962), 22, 77–83; *Congressional Record,* 87th Cong., 1st sess., vol. 107, pt. 2 (Feb. 13, 1961): 2058, 2135. See also Jill Quadagno, "One Nation: Uninsured" (forthcoming), 77–98.

5. The role of government, taxes, and the tax policy community in the post–World War II period is discussed in Julian E. Zelizer, "The Uneasy Relationship: Democracy, Taxation, and State Building," in *The Democratic Experiment,* ed. Meg Jacobs, William J. Novak, and Julian E. Zelizer (Princeton, N.J., 2003), 282–294.

6. Julian E. Zelizer's *Taxing America* (Cambridge, UK, 1998), 13, 16–22, 80, 109–110, 141–145, 184, is indispensable for understanding Mills's thinking about Social Security and Medicare.

7. Ibid., 130–132, 198–201, 204, 208–209, 212–239, 275–276, 280–281. See also Edward D. Berkowitz's definitive study, *Robert Ball and the Politics of Social Security* (Madison, Wisc., 2003), 114, 120–121, 126–135, 143.

8. Zelizer, *Taxing America.*

9. Wilbur J. Cohen, "The President's Program of Hospital Insurance for the Aged," n.d., copy in Lyndon B. Johnson (LBJ) Papers, White House Central Files (WHCF)-Aides Files (Richard Goodwin), Box 31, Folder: Office File (OF) Medicare, Lyndon B. Johnson Library (LBJL). Cohen's role is authoritatively discussed in Edward D. Berkowitz, *Mr. Social Security: The Life of Wilbur J. Cohen* (Lawrence, Kans., 1995), esp. 138, 161, 166.

10. For the survey that Cohen directed as professor of social welfare at the University of Michigan School of Social Work, see Wilbur J. Cohen et al., "Attitudes toward Governmental Participation in Medical Care," Subcommittee on Income Maintenance and Social Security of the Coordinating Committee on Social Welfare Research, March 1960; and "Lack of Big Margin in Winning Election No Indication of Public Disapproval of Kennedy Legislative Program," n.d., memorandum in Carl Albert Papers, Legis. Ser., Box 93, Folder 17, CAC-OU. The Gallup poll results were published in "Medical Care for the Aged," *Public Opinion News Service*, June 9, 1961, copy in LBJ Papers, WHCF-Aides Files (Fred Panzer), Box 181, Folder: OF-Medicare, LBJL. See also "Should the Gallup Poll Worry You?" *Medical Economics* 38 (Oct. 23, 1961): 179–180.

11. Under a federal-state matching formula, the law made funds available for the care of persons defined as "medically indigent," i.e., persons who were not indigent but who would become so if they had to pay substantial medical bills. The law also stipulated that each state had to apply a means test before giving assistance to an individual, but left the maximum levels of income and assets up to the states. See "Record of Kerr-Mills Program Crucial to Medicare Debate," *CQWR* 21 (Nov. 15, 1963): 2039–2043.

12. The figures, taken from the committee's report, are contained in the "Democratic National Committee (DNC) 1962 Campaign Kit," copy in Albert Papers, Legis. Ser., Box 93, Folder 16, CAC-OU. The critique of state-funding problems under Kerr-Mills is in HEW Commissioner Robert M. Ball's letter to Vice President Lyndon B. Johnson, Sept. 21, 1962, LBJ Papers, Vice Pres., 1961–1963, Box 185, Folder: 1962 Subj. Files—Social Welfare, LBJL. Also on Kerr-Mills, see Miriam Kerpen and Beverly Liden, "Medical Assistance for the Aged," *Management Record* 24 (Mar. 1962): 26–35.

13. *Congressional Record*, 87th Cong., 1st sess., vol. 107, pt. 2 (Feb. 13, 1961): 2124–2127.

14. Harris, "Medicare, Pt. III," 37–40.

15. See, for example, Axel Krause, "Private Medicare," *Wall Street Journal*, July 16, 1962; Norman C. Miller, Jr., "Doctors and Politics," ibid., July 24, 1962; "For the Aged: The Doctor's Plan," *U.S. News* 52 (Feb. 5, 1962): 67–69; "Same Old Tactics," *Industrial Union Digest* 7 (Spring 1962), 8–18; Michael J. O'Neil, "Siege Tactics of the AMA," *Reporter* 26 (Apr. 26, 1962): 29–32; AMA, *Federalized Health Care for the Aged? A Critical Symposium* (Chicago, 1963).

16. V. J. Skutt, to Robert S. Kerr, Jan. 27, 1962, Robert S. Kerr Papers, Legis. Ser., Box 3, Folder 5, CAC-OU; Harris, "Medicare, Pt. III," 54.

17. See the notations comparing the Kerr-Mills program with the administration's bill as incorporated in S. 909 and H.R. 4222, in Kerr Papers, Legis. Ser., Box 24, Folder 15, CAC-OU. See also Anne H. Morgan, *Robert S. Kerr: The Senate Years* (Norman, Okla., 1977), 223.

18. Harlan Bell to Kerr, Jan. 29, 1962; Kerr to Bell, Feb. 21, 1962; Kerr to Donald Quinn, June 12, 1962; Harry L. Halley to Kerr, July 19, 1962; Kerr to Halley, Aug. 16, 1962, Kerr Papers, Legis. Ser., Box 18, Folder 6, CAC-OU.

19. R. E. Vincent to Belcher, May 16, 1962; Belcher to Dr. Elvin M. Amen, Apr. 3, 1962; Dr. A. W. Jantzen to Belcher, June 20, 1962; Belcher to Jantzen, June 25, 1962, Belcher Papers, Box 70, Folders 3L, 3D, 3C, CAC-OU. See also the letter of Los Angeles physician Dr. Stanley L. Drennan to Belcher, Aug. 21, 1962, ibid.

20. Harris, "Medicare, Pt. III," 46.

21. Ibid., 49–51; James C. O'Brien, "The Elderly Fight for Health Care," *American Federationist* 69 (Feb. 1962): 8–10.

22. For the hearings, see House, Committee on Ways and Means, *Health Services for the Aged under the Social Security System, Hearings . . . on H.R. 4222*, 87th Cong., 1st sess., July 24–Aug. 4, 1961.

23. Lawrence F. O'Brien, *No Final Victories: A Life in Politics—from John F. Kennedy to Watergate* (New York, 1974), 104, 133; Zelizer, *Taxing America*, 217–218.

24. Nora M. Sanborn, of the American Institute of Public Opinion, reporting the results of the September 23 and December 14, 1960, polls to White House aide Fred Panzer, Dec. 14, 1964, LBJ Papers, WHCF-Aides Files (Panzer), Box 181, Folder: Medicare, LBJL.

25. Besides the King-Anderson bill, the administration had great difficulty in getting other important items on its 1961 legislative agenda enacted. See "Administration to Push Medicare Issue in 1962," *CQWR* 20 (Jan. 5, 1962): 19–20; Theodore C. Sorensen, *Kennedy* (New York, 1965), 343; Harris, "Medicare: Pt. III," 51–54.

26. This was not a novel procedure; it closely resembled the billing system that many hospitals already practiced, and it had the additional benefit of distancing the administration's bill from the accusation that it was a form of socialized medicine. See the entire January 1962 issue of *Congressional Digest* entitled "The Controversy over the Administration's New Medicare Plan for the Aged," and "Why Not Let Blue Cross Handle Aged Care?" *Medical Economics* 40 (May 1963): 120–122.

27. Berkowitz, *Mr. Social Security,* 172–173.

28. Robert L. Brenner, "Will Javits Bring on Social Security Medicare?" *Medical Economics* 38 (Nov. 20, 1961): 195–196.

29. For Kennedy's use of television, see David Halberstam's introduction in *The Kennedy Presidential Press Conferences,* ed George W. Johnson (New York, 1978), iv; *Wall Street Journal,* Feb. 27, 1962.

30. Don McBride to Mrs. Louis G. Ost, Jr., Mar. 21, 1962, Kerr Papers, Legis. Ser., Box 18, Folder 6, CAC-OU.

31. See President's Council on Aging, *The Older American,* May 14, 1962, copy in LBJ Papers, Vice President, Subj. File, Box 239, Folder: Social Welfare-Medical Care for the Aged, LBJL.

32. *New York Times,* May 21, 1962. For differing assessments of Kennedy's speech, see Sorensen, *Kennedy,* 343, and O'Brien, *No Final Victories,* 134.

33. O'Brien, *No Final Victories,* 134; Belcher to Perry E. White, June 12, 1962, Belcher Papers, Box 70, Folder 3L, CAC-OU.

34. "The Fight over Medical Care," *U.S. News* 52 (June 4, 1962): 39–41; Johnson, ed., *Kennedy Presidential Press Conferences,* 302–303.

35. *New York Times,* May 22, 1962; Johnson, ed., *Kennedy Presidential Press Conferences,* 304; Harris, "Medicare, Pt. III," 59.

36. The reference was to the president's intervention in forcing the steel industry to roll back price increases. See "Attitudes on Medicare," Memorandum no. 10, John F. Kraft, Inc., to Hon. Vance R. Hartke, June 28, 1962, copy in LBJ Papers, Vice President, Box 185, Folder: 1962 Subject File—Social Welfare, LBJL.

37. Sorensen, *Kennedy,* 343.

38. On the Gallup poll results, see Nora M. Sanborn to Fred Panzer, Dec. 14, 1963, LBJ Papers, WHCF-Aides Files (Panzer), Box 181, Folder: Medicare, and "News Release," Oct. 27, 1962, ibid., Folder: Old Age, Retirement, Medicare, LBJL; *New York Times,* July 2–3, 1962; Harris, "Medicare, Pt. III," 62, 65.

39. O'Brien, *No Final Victories,* 134–135; Berkowitz, *Mr. Social Security,* 174; Harris, "Medicare, Pt. III," 65.

40. "Senate Kills Social Security Health Plan," *CQWR* 20 (July 20, 1962): 1205–1210.

41. In 1964, when the Senate was again preparing to debate and vote on amendments to the Social Security Act, Randolph, who had become a firm supporter of Medicare inclusion, felt the need to explain to President Johnson why he had voted with Kerr. At that time, he wrote, the program of Aid for Dependent Children of Unemployed Families (ADCU) already had lapsed and thousands of West Virginians faced deprivation. The controversy over the Medicare amendment "created an inordinate time loss in the progress of the measure embracing the welfare amendments." Slowness in restoring the ADCU program was intolerable to Randolph. "Consequently, I voted to table the amendment which would have the

effect of further delaying restoration of the ADCU work relief and cash benefit provisions and thereby compound the deprivation of thousands of our people." Jennings Randolph to LBJ, Aug. 5, 1964; O'Brien to Randolph, Aug. 10, 1964; Randolph to O'Brien, Aug. 11, 1964, LBJ Papers, WHCF, President 1963–1969, Legislation, Box 166, Folder: L/WE 6 (Aug. 1964–Mar. 1965), LBJL.

42.  H. Bright Keck to LBJ, July 19, 1962, LBJ Papers, Vice President, 1961–1963, Box 185, Folder: 1962, Subject File—Social Welfare, LBJL.

43.  Sorensen, *Kennedy,* 344; Johnson, ed., *Kennedy Presidential Press Conferences,* 355; Harris, "Medicare, Pt. III," 65.

44.  For the election returns, see *New York Times,* Nov. 4, 1962.

45.  Thousands of physicians benefited directly from the Hill-Burton Act of 1946, which provided federal funds for building and expanding hospitals across the country. In the recent vote on Medicare, Hill not only had sided with the AMA but also had persuaded his fellow Alabaman, Senator John Sparkman, to do so. "Squeakers and Precedents," *CQWR* 20 (Nov. 9, 1962): 2128; *New York Times,* Nov. 7, 1965; Harris, "Medicare, Pt. III," 66, 68.

46.  Wilbur J. Cohen, "Reflections on the Enactment of Medicare and Medicaid," *Health Care Financing Review* 7 (1985 Annual Supple.): 5; Berkowitz, *Mr. Social Security,* 183.

47.  "Here's JFK's Plan for Old Folks—How Good Are Its Chances?" *U.S. News* 54 (Mar. 4, 1963): 76–77.

48.  Cohen thought Long's bill might provide hospitals an incentive to raise costs to the point where medical bills would have to be paid from the Social Security fund. See "Many Interests Involved in Fight over Aged Health Care," *CQWR* 21 (Nov. 22, 1963): 1991–1996; Berkowitz, *Mr. Social Security,* 186.

49.  Berkowitz, *Mr. Social Security,* 186–187.

50.  AMA, *Federalized Health Care for the Aged,* passim; Harris, "Medicare, Pt. III," 70.

51.  See, for example, the interview with "Henry S. Beers," in the *Spectator* 171 (Feb. 1963): 3–11.

52.  Belcher to Mrs. E. L. Hare, Apr. 12, 1963; to Ben Hood, Oct. 2, 1963, Belcher Papers, Box 76, Folders 12a and 12d, CAC-OU.

53.  Belcher to Verl A. Teeter, Apr. 19, 1963; to Sibyl Weems, May 31, 1963; to E. L. Hare, Apr. 12, 1963, ibid., Box 85, Folder 2; Box 86, Folder 8b; Box 76, Folder 12a, CAC-OU.

54.  "Record of Kerr-Mills," 2039–2043.

55.  A copy of HEW Secretary Celebrezze's testimony is in LBJ Papers, WHCF-Aides Files (Richard Goodwin), Box 31, Folder: Medicare, LBJL. See also House, Committee on Ways and Means, *Medical Care for the Aged, Hearings … on H.R. 3920,* 88th Cong., 1st and 2d sess., Nov. 18, 1963–Jan. 24, 1964, 5 vols.

56.  *Medical Care for the Aged,* 1: 1–3ff.

57.  Harris, "Medicare, Pt. III," 71; Berkowitz, *Mr. Social Security,* 187.

58.  O'Brien, *No Final Victories,* 143; Harris, "Medicare, Pt. III," 71; O'Brien to LBJ, Nov. 26, 1963, LBJ Papers, WHCF-Aides Files (Henry H. Wilson), Box 3, Folder: Legis. Prog., 1964–1965, LBJL.

59.  "The New Era in Washington: Its Meaning," *U.S. News* 55 (Dec. 9, 1963): 35–37; *New York Times,* Jan. 16, 1964. See also Bruce J. Schulman, *Lyndon Johnson and American Liberalism* (New York, 1995), 89–90; Doris K. Goodwin, *Lyndon Johnson and the American Dream* (New York, 1991), 219.

60.  The text is reprinted in *Vital Speeches* 30 (Dec. 15, 1963): 1–31.

61.  "Major Issues Involved in HEW Legislative Program for 1964," Dec. 8, 1963, LBJ Papers, WHCF-Aides Files (Wilson), Box 3, Folder: Legis. Prog. 1964–1965, LBJL.

62.  O'Brien to LBJ, Jan. 27, 1964, ibid., WHCF, File LE/IS 1, Box 75, LBJL.

63.  This legislative session would be more complicated because of the likelihood that the administration might also pursue a tax cut. If that occurred, President Johnson did not want the increased payroll taxes for Medicare to stifle the effect of the tax cut on the economy. Berkowitz, *Mr. Social Security,* 212–213.

64.  "Compromise Medicare Bill Due for Debate," *CQWR,* 1964, copy in LBJ Papers, WHCF-Aides Files (Wilson), Box 3, Folder: Medicare, LBJL; *Wall Street Journal,* Mar. 25, 1964; Zelizer, *Taxing America,* 221.

65.  Harris, "Medicare, Pt. III," 78.

66. There were other more subtle differences between the two bills. The Javits bill, for example, unlike the Lindsay bill, had a mechanism to encourage the purchase of supplementary private insurance to cover physicians' bills and other expenses not handled by Medicare. Javits wanted this insurance to be private but nonprofit, and available at low cost. Like Lindsay, he hoped to please both the elderly and private insurance companies by arguing that this approach offered a built-in limit to the expansion of Medicare. The government would be limited to the payment of hospital insurance, not to the payment of physicians' fees. "Social Security Hospital Care," *CQWR* 22 (Jan. 31, 1964): 217; *New York Times*, Jan. 17, 1964.

67. Henry H. Wilson, "Suggestions Made by Mr. Mills in Meeting on Friday, January 24, 1964," LBJ Papers, WHCF-Aides Files (Wilson), Box 3, Folder: Medicare, LBJL; Berkowitz, *Mr. Social Security,* 214.

68. *New York Times,* Feb. 11, 1964; Berkowitz, *Mr. Social Security,* 214–215.

69. Under the program Johnson recommended, senior citizens had the choice of three in-patient hospital benefit plans: 45, 90, or 180 days of hospitalization, with higher deductibles applying in the latter two programs. In addition, benefits would be provided for services received in skilled nursing facilities, for home health services, and for outpatient hospital diagnostic services. The financing would be "soundly funded through the Social Security system." The Social Security contributions of both employers and employees would be increased by 0.25 percent, and the annual earnings subject to Social Security taxes would be increased from $4,800 to $5,200. "Health Message," draft of Feb. 3, 1964, LBJ Papers, WHCF-Aides Files (Wilson), Box 3, Folder: Wilson—Health Message, LBJL; *Wall Street Journal,* Feb. 11, 1964.

70. Belcher to Betty R. Spurgin, Feb. 25, 1964, Belcher Papers, Box 87, Folder 5m, CAC-OU.

71. Wilson to O'Brien, Feb. 17, 1964, and accompanying memorandum, "Prospects of Enactment of Legislation during Remainder of Session," LBJ Papers, WHCF-Aides Files (Wilson), Box 3, Folder: Legis. Prog. 1964–1965, LBJL.

72. "President Talks to Rep. Mills—Hopes to Free Medicare Bill," *Senior Citizens News,* Feb. 1964, copy in Belcher Papers, Box 87, Folder: 5b, CAC-OU; *New York Times,* Feb. 2, 1964.

73. See, for example, O'Brien to LBJ, Apr. 20, 1964, LBJ Papers, WHCF-Aides Files (Wilson), Box 3, Folder: Legis. Repts., LBJL, concerning the committee's discussion about changes in the Kerr-Mills program.

74. Wilson to O'Brien, Apr. 20, 27, 1964, ibid., Box 3, Folder: Medicare, LBJL.

75. Wilson to O'Brien, Apr. 20, 1964, ibid.

76. "President's April 27 Speech to the U.S. Chamber of Commerce," *CQWR* 22 (May 8, 1964): 934–938; Harris, "Medicare, Pt. III," 78, 80.

77. O'Brien to LBJ, May 11, 18, 1964, LBJ Papers, WHCF-Aides Files (Wilson), Box 3, Folders: Medicare and Legis. Repts., LBJL; *Wall Street Journal,* May 25, 1964; Berkowitz, *Mr. Social Security,* 215–216.

78. *New York Times,* May 24, 1964; Wilson to O'Brien, June 8, 1964, LBJ Papers, WHCF-Aides Files (Wilson), Box 3, Folder: Legis. Prog. 1964–1965, LBJL.

79. Ibid.

80. Mike Manatos to O'Brien, May 20, 1964, ibid., WHCF-Aides Files (Manatos), Box 9, Folder: Medicare, LBJL. Johnson, according to one report, was less certain that the principle of financing Medicare through Social Security would be retained in the bill. *New York Times,* June 3, 1964.

81. Berkowitz, *Mr. Social Security,* 216. For the president's speech, see "The Great Society," *Michigan Business Review* 16 (July 1964): 1–3.

82. Berkowitz, *Mr. Social Security,* 216–217.

83. *Wall Street Journal,* June 22, 1964.

84. Watts represented a district in Kentucky in which tobacco was the principal crop. Harris, "Medicare, Pt. III," 80; Berkowitz, *Mr. Social Security,* 218; *New York Post,* June 24, 1964; Zelizer, *Taxing America,* 227–228.

85. Cohen to Celebrezze, July 2, 1964, LBJ Papers, WHCF-Aides Files (Wilson), Box 3, Folder: Medicare, LBJL.

86. Alger explained that since he was opposed to the Social Security system as a matter of principle, his conscience would not have permitted him to vote to amend it. Harris, "Medicare, Pt. III," 82; *New
York Times,* June 25–26, 1964; *Wall Street Journal,* June 25, 1964.

87. O'Brien to LBJ, July 9, 1964, LBJ Papers, WHCF-Aides Files (Wilson), Box 3, Folder: Legis. Prog.
1964–1965; Manatos to O'Brien, July 13, 1964, ibid., WHCF-Aides Files (Manatos), Box 9, Folder: Medicare, LBJL; Berkowitz, *Mr. Social Security,* 218.

88. For Ribicoff's role, see *New York Times,* Aug. 7, 11, 15–16, 18, 1964; Berkowitz, *Mr. Social Security,* 218–220.

89. Manatos to O'Brien, July 20, 1964, LBJ Papers, WHCF-Aides Files (Manatos), Box 9, Folder:
Medicare, LBJL.

90. Ibid.; Wilson to O'Brien, July 21, 1964, ibid., WHCF-Aides Files (Wilson), Box 3, Folder: Medicare;
Manatos to O'Brien, July 28, 1964, ibid., WHCF-Aides Files (Manatos), Box 9, Folder: Medicare, LBJL.

91. Manatos also wrote that this support permitted Smathers to tell the AMA's president that the
administration had the Senate votes for Medicare and that he could save the AMA by urging it to support the option. Manatos to O'Brien, July 25, 1964, ibid., WHCF-Aides Files (Manatos), Box 9, Folder:
Medicare, LBJL.

92. Ibid.

93. Wilson to O'Brien, July 21, 1964, LBJ Papers, WHCF-Aides Files (Wilson), Box 3, Folder: Medicare, LBJL.

94. Berkowitz, *Mr. Social Security,* 220; Wilson to O'Brien, July 23, 1964, LBJ Papers, WHCF-Aides
Files (Wilson), Box 3, Folder: Legis. Prog. 1964–1965, LBJL; "Medicare in the Senate," [1964], ibid.,
WHCF-Aides Files (Manatos), Box 9, Folder: Medicare, LBJL.

95. "Medicare in the Senate."

96. *Wall Street Journal,* Aug. 5, 1964; O'Brien to LBJ, Aug. 10, 1964; Cohen to O'Brien, Aug. 13, 1964,
LBJ Papers, WHCF-Aides Files (Wilson), Box 3, Folders: Legis. Repts. and Medicare, LBJL.

97. *New York Times,* Aug. 15, 1964; O'Brien to LBJ, Aug. 17, 1964, LBJ Papers, WHCF-Aides Files
(Wilson), Box 3, Folder: Legis. Repts., LBJL; *Wall Street Journal,* Aug. 18, 1964; Berkowitz, *Mr. Social Security,* 220–221.

98. O'Brien to LBJ, Aug. 31, 1964, LBJ Papers, WHCF-Aides Files (Wilson), Box 3, Folder: Legis.
Repts., LBJL. For the vote on the Gore amendment, see *Congressional Record,* Sept. 2, 1964, 20660, in
ibid., WHCF-Aides Files (Manatos), Box 9, Folder: Medicare. See also *New York Times,* Sept. 2–4, 1964;
*Wall Street Journal,* Sept. 1, 3–4, 1964.

99. Harris, "Medicare, Pt. III," 83–84; John W. Edelman, "News Release," National Council of Senior
Citizens, *News,* Sept. 7, 1964, 1–2; "Medicare: A Heavy Drain or a National Necessity?" *Charlotte Ob-
server,* Sept. 5, 1964, LBJ Papers, WHCF-Aides Files (Wilson), Box 3, Folders: Medicare and Medicare
News Clippings, LBJL.

100. As a precaution, the AMA planned to launch a $1 million advertising campaign against Medi-
care. *Wall Street Journal,* Sept. 9, 16, 1964; Harris, "Medicare, Pt. III," 84.

101. Cohen memorandum, "Medical Care," Sept. 4, 1964; Cohen to Manatos and Wilson, Sept. 10,
1964, LBJ Papers, WHCF-Aides Files (Wilson), Box 3, Folder: Medicare, LBJL.

102. O'Brien to LBJ, Sept. 13, 1964, ibid.

103. Ibid.

104. National Council of Senior Citizens, *News,* Sept. 16, 1954, copy in ibid.

105. O'Brien to LBJ, Sept. 18, 1964; Manatos to O'Brien, Sept. 15, 16, 17, 1964, ibid., WHCF-Aides
Files (Manatos), Box 9, Folder: Medicare, LBJL.

106. For example, between September 20 and September 23, Cohen, Ball, and Sidney Saperstein, an
SSA lawyer, drafted a proposal involving two elements: the creation of a Medicare trust fund, separate
from Social Security, into which the working population would pay and from which this group would

eventually receive Medicare; and giving the retired population the option of deducting payments for Medicare from its Social Security benefits. The success of the compromise hinged on whether Mills could be persuaded that such a proposal was "in conference." When Mills sought clarification from the House parliamentarian, he was told that the proposal would be subject to "points of order" in the House. Despite the admonitions of Gore, Anderson, Boggs, and Cecil King, Mills was unwilling to ask the Rules Committee for a rule waiving "points of order" in the House debate. On September 24, Cohen and others met with Carl Albert and John McCormack to see whether anything could be done to overcome Mills's objections. Mills would not go along and that ended the discussion. See O'Brien to LBJ, Sept. 23, 1964, LBJ Papers, WHCF, File LE/IS, Box 75; Cohen to Manatos and Wilson, Sept. 10, 1964; National Council of Senior Citizens, *News,* Sept. 15, 1964; Wilson to O'Brien, Sept. 20, 1964; Cohen to O'Brien, Sept. 28, 1964, ibid., WHCF-Aides Files (Wilson), Box 3, Folder: Medicare, LBJL.

107. Cohen added, "To keep Long definitely on our side we can go along with $5 monthly exemption from public assistance in addition to the public assistance increase he has already won in Conference." Cohen to O'Brien, Sept. 28, 1964, LBJ Papers, WHCF-Aides Files (Wilson), Box 3, Folder: Medicare, LBJL

108. Manatos to O'Brien, Sept. 15, 16, 1964, ibid.; *Wall Street Journal,* Oct. 2, 1964; Berkowitz, *Mr. Social Security,* 221.

109. Manatos to O'Brien, Sept. 15, 1964, LBJ Papers, WHCF-Aides Files (Manatos), Box 9, Folder: Medicare, LBJL.

110. Manatos to O'Brien, Sept. 17, 1964, LBJ Papers, WHCF-Aides Files (Manatos), Box 9, Folder: Medicare, LBJL; Goodwin, *Lyndon Johnson and the American Dream,* 301–302.

111. Wilson to O'Brien, Sept. 20, 1964, LBJ Papers, WHCF-Aides Files (Wilson), Box 3, Folder: Medicare, LBJL.

112. Harris, "Medicare, Pt. III," 84–85.

113. Cohen to O'Brien, Sept. 28, 1964, LBJ Papers, WHCF-Aides Files (Wilson), Box 3, Folder: Medicare, LBJL.

114. Manatos to Mike Feldman, Oct. 1, 1964, ibid., WHCF-Aides Files (Manatos), Box 9, Folder: Medicare, LBJL; *New York Times,* Sept. 30, 1964.

115. *Wall Street Journal,* Oct. 5, 1964; *New York Times,* Oct. 1–4, 1964; Harris, "Medicare, Pt. III," 86, 89.

## CHAPTER 6. CROSSING AN IDEOLOGICAL RUBICON

1. Edward D. Berkowitz, *Mr. Social Security: The Life of Wilbur J. Cohen* (Lawrence, Kans., 1995), 222; *New York Times,* Nov. 12, 1964; Page H. Belcher to Donald R. Wilson, Sept. 13, 1964, Page H. Belcher Papers, Box 86, Folder 8c, Carl Albert Center, University of Oklahoma (CAC-OU).

2. *New York Times,* Nov. 4–5, 1965; Wilbur J. Cohen, "Social Security," pt. 4, 63–64, Columbia University Oral History Collection (COHC).

3. *New York Times,* Nov. 6–8, 1965; Richard Harris, "Medicare, Part IV," *New Yorker* 42 (July 23, 1966): 35.

4. *New York Times,* Nov. 19, 1964; Dec. 1–2, 1964.

5. Ibid., Oct. 4, 8, 25, 1964; Nov. 1, 15, 18, 1964; Berkowitz, *Mr. Social Security,* 223.

6. Anthony J. Celebrezze to LBJ, Nov. 25, 1964, LBJ Papers, WHCF-Aides Files (Bill Moyers), OF, Box 1, Folder: Health Care, 1965, LBJL; *New York Times,* Nov. 18, 1964; Dec. 2, 1964.

7. Berkowitz, *Mr. Social Security,* 222–223.

8. Ibid., 225–226.

9. "Mills's Terms for Medicare: Excerpts from Address," *U.S. News* 57 (Dec. 21, 1964): 74; Mike Manatos to Lawrence O'Brien, Dec. 8, 1964, LBJ Papers, WHCF-Aides Files (Mike Manatos), Box 9, Folder: Medicare, LBJL; *New York Times*, Dec. 3, 1964; Berkowitz, *Mr. Social Security*, 225.

10. Berkowitz, *Mr. Social Security*, 226.

11. *The State of the Social Security Program and Recommendations for Its Improvement: Report of the Advisory Council on Social Security, 1965* (Washington, D.C., 1965), 29–33; *New York Times*, Jan. 4, 1965.

12. Wilbur J. Cohen, "Reflections on the Enactment of Medicare and Medicaid," *Health Care Financing Review* 7 (Annual Supplement, 1985): 5; *Congressional Record*, 89th Cong., 1st sess., vol. 111, pt. 5 (Mar. 24, 1965): 5775–5776; Harris, "Medicare, Part IV," 35.

13. A copy of the president's message to Congress of Jan. 7, 1965, *Advancing The Nation's Health*, is in LBJ Papers, WHCF-Aides Files (Richard Goodwin), Box 31, Folder: OF—Medicare, LBJL; *New York Times*, Jan. 8, 1965. See also "Medicare, Other Health Measures Asked by President," *CQWR* 23 (Jan. 8, 1965): 53–56.

14. "The 1965 King-Anderson 'Medicare Bill,'" *Congressional Digest* 44 (Mar. 1965): 75; *New York Times*, Jan. 8, 1965; Henry H. Wilson to O'Brien, Jan. 5, 1965, LBJ Papers, WHCF-Aides Files (Henry H. Wilson), Box 9, Folder: Medicare; O'Brien to LBJ, Jan. 8, 1965, ibid., WHCF-Aides Files (Manatos), Box 9, Folder: Medicare, LBJL.

15. For AMA opposition, see *New York Times*, Jan. 10, 1965; Feb. 7–10, 17, 1965. Its financial outlays for the campaign against the King-Anderson proposal between January and June were reported in ibid., June 22, 1965. See also Walter H. Judd, "Medicine or Medical Care," *Reader's Digest* 86 (Feb. 1965): 97–102.

16. *New York Times*, Mar. 11, 1965; Berkowitz, *Mr. Social Security*, 227.

17. For details of the Byrnes bill, see "Other Health Care Proposals Now Pending," *Congressional Digest* 44 (Mar. 1965): 77; Berkowitz, *Mr. Social Security*, 228; *New York Times*, Mar. 6, 1965.

18. Berkowitz, *Mr. Social Security*, 228–229; Julian E. Zelizer, *Taxing America* (Cambridge, UK, 1998), 238–239.

19. Details of the Herlong bill are in "Other Health Care Proposals Now Pending," 76; *New York Times*, Feb. 9, 1965; and *Congressional Record*, 89th Cong., 1st sess., vol. 111, pt. 6 (Apr. 7, 1965): 7238–7239. For a comparison of the different bills, see "Eldercare v. Medicare," *Time* 85 (Feb. 19, 1965): 22; "Medicare vs. the AMA's Latest Substitute," *Consumer Report* 30 (Mar. 1965): 148–149; and Page H. Belcher to E. L. Tetrick, Mar. 12, 1965, Belcher Papers, Box 105, Folder 9a, CAC-OU.

20. House, Committee on Ways and Means, *Medical Care for the Aged*, 89th Cong., 1st sess., 2 pts., 1965. Ward's testimony is in ibid., pt. 2, 741ff. AMA opposition also is cited in "Should Congress Enact the King-Anderson Bill to Provide More Medical Care for the Aged under Social Security?" *Congressional Digest* 44 (Mar. 1965): 91, 93; Cohen, "Social Security," pt. 4, 24–25; *New York Times*, Feb. 9, 1965; Harris, "Medicare, Part IV," 37–38.

21. Office of the White House Press Secretary, "Remarks of the President to the President's Council on Aging," Feb. 16, 1965, LBJ Papers, WHCF-Aides Files (Goodwin), Box 31, Folder: OF—Medicare, LBJL.

22. Berkowitz, *Mr. Social Security*, 229–231.

23. Zelizer, *Taxing America*, 240.

24. Ibid.

25. Harris, "Medicare, Part IV," 39–40; Edward D. Berkowitz, *Robert Ball and the Politics of Social Security* (Madison, Wisc., 2003), 130–132.

26. Ibid.

27. Cohen, "Social Security," pt. 4, 15.

28. On this point, see Allen J. Matusow, *The Unraveling of America: A History of Liberalism in the 1960s* (New York, 1984), 227.

29. Cohen, "Social Security," pt. 4, 15; Berkowitz, *Mr. Social Security,* 231–232.

30. Cohen to O'Brien, Mar. 18, 1965, LBJ Papers, WHCF-Aides Files (Wilson), Box 9, Folder: Medicare, LBJL.

31. *New York Times,* Apr. 3, 6, 1965; Berkowitz, *Mr. Social Security,* 232–233; Zelizer, *Taxing America,* 242–245.

32. "Wrapping Up the Medicare Bill: House Ways and Means Committee Reports," *Business Week,* July 3, 1965, 25; *New York Times,* Mar. 24, 1965; House, Committee on Ways and Means, *Social Security Amendments of 1965,* 89th Cong., 1st sess., 1965, H. Rep. 213; "Medicare Report Filed in House," *CQWR* 23 (Apr. 2, 1965): 589–590; Cohen to O'Brien (including "Summary of Major Provisions of Social Security Amendments of 1965"), Mar. 19, 1965, and Cohen to LBJ, Mar. 22, 1965, LBJ Papers, WHCF-Aides Files (Wilson), Box 9, Folder: OF—Medicare; Office of the White House Press Secretary, "Statement of the President," Mar. 23, 1965, ibid., WHCF-Aides Files (Goodwin), Box 31, Folder: OF—Medicare, LBJL.

33. See the perceptive column of Tom Wicker in the *New York Times,* Apr. 11, 1965.

34. Office of the White House Press Secretary, "Transcript of the President's Statement," copy dated Mar. 26, 1965, LBJ Papers, WHCF-Aides Files (Goodwin), Box 31, Folder: OF—Medicare, LBJL.

35. Belcher to F. C. Bacon, June 23, 1965, Belcher Papers, Box 105, Folder 9a, CAC-OU; LBJ to Cecil R. King, Mar. 27, 1965, LBJ Papers, WHCF (Legislation, 1963–1969), Box 164, Folder: LE/WE6, LBJL; *New York Times,* Apr. 1, 8–9, 1965; "House Passes Medicare, Social Security Bill," *CQWR* 23 (Apr. 9, 1965): 603–604; "Biggest Change Since the New Deal: Mills's Medicare Bill," *Newsweek* 65 (Apr. 12, 1965): 88–90.

36. *New York Times,* Apr. 9, 27, 1965; Belcher to Mrs. Marvin Bauer, Apr. 9, 1965, Belcher Papers, Box 105, Folder 9h, CAC-OU; Berkowitz, *Mr. Social Security,* 233.

37. Senate, Committee on Finance, *Social Security, Hearings . . . on H.R. 6675,* 89th Cong., 1st sess., 2 pts., 1965, esp. pt. 2, 602–603ff. See also "Dr. Ward's Last Word: AMA Opposition to Medicare Bill," *Time* 85 (May 21, 1965): 28–29; *New York Times,* Apr. 30, 1965; May 12, 1965; Harris, "Medicare, Part IV," 46, 48.

38. "Senate Medical Care, Social Security Hearings Begin," *CQWR* 23 (May 7, 1965): 886; *New York Times,* May 1, 1965; Manatos to O'Brien, May 13, 19, 1965, LBJ Papers, WHCF-Aides Files (Manatos), Box 9, Folder: Medicare, LBJL.

39. *New York Times,* May 19–20, 1965; Manatos to O'Brien, May 20, 1965; LBJ Papers, WHCF-Aides Files (Manatos), Box 9, Folder: Medicare, LBJL.

40. Manatos to O'Brien, June 16, 1965, ibid.

41. Manatos to O'Brien, June 21, 1965, ibid.; *New York Times,* June 18–19, 1965.

42. Harris, "Medicare, Part IV," 50, 52.

43. *New York Times,* June 21, 1965; Wilbur J. Cohen to LBJ, June 17, 1965, LBJ Papers, WHCF-Aides Files (Bill Moyers), Box 1, Folder: OF—Health, LBJL. See also "Russell Long's Capers: Medicare Bill Amendments," *New Republic* 153 (July 3, 1965): 6.

44. "Senate Finance Committee Approves Medical Care Plan," *CQWR* 23 (June 25, 1965): 1236–1237; *New York Times,* June 24, 1965; Cohen, "Social Security," pt. 4, 13; Manatos to O'Brien, June 21, 30, 1965; July 2, 6, 1965, LBJ Papers, WHCF-Aides Files (Manatos), Box 9, Folder: Medicare; and Cohen to LBJ, June 24, 1965, ibid., WHCF-Aides Files (Moyers), Box 1, Folder: OF—Health, LBJL. See also Senate, Committee on Finance, *Social Security Amendments of 1965, Report . . . to Accompany H.R. 6675,* 89th Cong., 1st sess., June 29, 1965, S. Rep. 404.

45. "Senate Amends Medical Care-Social Security Bill," *CQWR* 23 (July 19, 1965): 1320–1323; "More for More: Senate Version of the Johnson Administration's Medicare Bill," *Time* 86 (July 16, 1965): 16–17; *New York Times,* July 7–10, 1965; Harris, "Medicare, Part IV," 52, 54–56, 58–60; Fred R. Harris to A. J. Hayes, Nov. 22, 1965; to E. J. Bottger, Mar. 9, 1965, Fred R. Harris Papers, Box 26, Folders 39 and 37, CAC-OU.

46. "Agreement Reached on Health Care-Social Security Bill," *CQWR* 23 (July 23, 1965): 1411; *New York Times,* July 22, 1965.

47. Zelizer, *Taxing America*, 250–251.

48. Harris, "Medicare, Part IV," 60–61; Berkowitz, *Mr. Social Security*, 234–235; Zelizer, *Taxing America*, 250–251.

49. "Medical Care–Social Security Bill Sent to the President," *CQWR* 23 (July 30, 1965): 1493; Belcher to Edward J. Ash, July 22, 1965, Belcher Papers, Box 105, Folder 9h, CAC-OU; *New York Times*, July 27–29, 1965.

50. For the bill's provisions, see "Medical Care–Social Security Bill Sent to the President," 1493; *New York Times*, July 25, 31, 1965.

51. For the text of the law, see *United States Statutes at Large*, vol. 79, pt. 1 (Washington, D.C., 1966), 286–423.

52. Office of the White House Press Secretary, "Remarks of the President at the Signing of the Medicare Bill," July 30, 1965, LBJ Papers, WHCF-Aides Files (Fred Panzer), Box 381, Folder: Medicare, LBJL; *Public Papers of the Presidents: Lyndon B. Johnson, 1965*, 2 pts. (Washington, D.C., 1965), pt. 2, 813–814; *New York Times*, July 31, 1965.

53. Prior to the meeting, Cohen, at the request of presidential aide Douglass Cater, had drafted a memo briefing the president on the main provisions of the law and highlighting ten points he might wish to emphasize to allay fears of federal interference in the practice of medicine. As Cohen was aware that access to future medical care for millions of elderly Americans would change dramatically, the tone of his memo was one of cooperation. Cohen to Douglass Cater, July 26, 1965, LBJ Papers, WHCF-Aides Files (Cater), Box 65, Folder: AMA Meeting with the President, LBJL; Berkowitz, *Mr. Social Security*, 236.

54. *New York Times*, July 30, 1965; Harris, "Medicare, Part IV," 62.

55. Appel opposed a physician boycott of Medicare, which caused strained relations within the AMA and with other medical-specialty organizations, but he continued to criticize government intervention. See *New York Times*, Aug. 12, 1965; Oct. 4, 1965, and James Z. Appel, "We the People of the U.S.—Are We Sheep?" *JAMA* 193 (July 5, 1965): 26–30.

56. Dr. John R. Oglesbee to Carl Albert, July 3, 1975, Carl Albert Papers, Legislative Series (Legis. Ser.), Box 12, Folder 12: Ways and Means, CAC-OU.

57. Clinton P. Anderson, "The Surprising Facts about Medicare," *Look* 70 (May 17, 1966): 87.

58. "Remarks by Wilbur J. Cohen," Aug. 15, 1965, in LBJ Papers, DHEW, "Administrative History of the Social Security Administration," vol. 7, pt. IVe, Box 17, Tab 42, LBJL.

59. Quoted in Wilbur J. Cohen, "Oral History," 10–11, copy in LBJ Papers, AC 72–26, LBJL.

60. On Johnson's domestic policies, see John A. Andrew III, *Lyndon Johnson and the Great Society* (Chicago, 1998), and Doris Kearns Goodwin, *Lyndon Johnson and the American Dream* (New York, 1976), chap. 8; Matusow, *Unraveling of America*, 227–228; Ira Katznelson, "Was the Great Society a Lost Opportunity?" in *The Rise and Fall of the New Deal Order, 1930–1980*, ed. Steve Fraser and Gary Gerstle (Princeton, N.J., 1989), 185–211.

61. *New York Times*, Aug. 2, 1965; Margaret Weir et al., eds., *The Politics of Social Policy in the United States* (Princeton, N.J., 1988), 267–268.

62. Lawrence R. Jacobs, *The Health of Nations: Public Opinion and the Making of American and British Health Policy* (Ithaca, N.Y., 1993), esp. 216–236.

63. Berkowitz, *Robert Ball and the Politics of Social Security*, 138.

64. Ibid.

65. Zelizer, *Taxing America*, 252–254.

66. Ibid.

## CHAPTER 7. NO PERMANENT SOLUTIONS:
## HEALTH CARE IN CRISIS

1.  Lawrence R. Jacobs, *The Health of Nations: Public Opinion and the Making of American and British Health Policy* (Ithaca, N.Y., 1993), 235–236; Jill Quadagno, "One Nation: Uninsured" (forthcoming), 121–134.

2.  Edward D. Berkowitz, *Mr. Social Security: The Life of Wilbur J. Cohen* (Lawrence, Kans., 1995), 238.

3.  Wilbur J. Cohen to Lyndon B. Johnson (LBJ), Mar. 16, 1966, LBJ Papers, White House Central File (WHCF)-Aides Files (Douglass Cater), Box 20, Folder: Misc. Corres., Mar. 1966, LBJ Library (LBJL).

4.  Gardner's specific recommendations were intended to bring the benefits of better health care to children and the disadvantaged by empowering the secretary of health to be an advocate as well as an administrator, empowered to make grants to maternal- and infant-care agencies to cut the infant-mortality rate; to extend family planning services; to provide comprehensive health service (including dental and eye care) to children in low-income families; to fund the training of pediatricians; and to extend the Medical Assistance Program (Title XIX) to require states to provide children with periodic physical examinations. "Our economy has never been healthier. We can do the job in Viet Nam *and* regain domestic momentum," he wrote. See John W. Gardner to Bill Moyers, Aug. 4, 1966, WHCF-Aides Files (Cater), Box 15, Memos to Pres., Aug. 1966; Cater to LBJ, Aug. 4, 1966, ibid.

5.  Ibid.; Cater to LBJ, Aug. 4, 1966, in ibid.

6.  Selig Greenberg, "Promises and Pitfalls," *Nation* 202 (May 23, 1966): 617. Copy in LBJ Papers, WHCF-Aides Files (Fred Panzer), Box 380, Folder: Medicare, LBJL.

7.  Ibid.

8.  For Johnson's determination, see *New York Times,* May 30, 1966.

9.  Wilbur J. Cohen, "Oral History," 11–14, copy in LBJ Papers, AC 72–26, LBJL. See also Califano to HEW Secretary Anthony J. Celebrezze, July 28, 1965, ibid., WHCF-Confidential File, FG 155–20, Box 30, Folder FG 165/DHEW, 1964–1966; Harold R. Levy to Hayes Redmond, Nov. 5, 1965, ibid., Box 30, Folder: FG 165/H Health Insurance; Robert Kintner to Cater, May 28, 1966, in ibid.; Gardner to LBJ, May 23, 25, 27, 1966, ibid., WHCF-Aides Files (Cater), Box 14, Folder: Memos to the Pres., May 1966; Cater to LBJ, May 25, 31, 1966, ibid.; *New York Times,* May 30, 1966.

10.  "Presidential Remarks: Meeting with Medical and Hospital Leaders, June 15, 1966," LBJ Papers, WHCF-Aides Files (Cater), Box 15, Folder: Memos to the Pres., June 1966, LBJL.

11.  Ibid. See also William H. Stewart, M.D., "Civil Rights and Medicare," *JAMA* 156 (June 13, 1966): 175, copy in ibid.

12.  On June 29, two days before Medicare was to go into effect, Marvin Watson informed the president that the latest tally on the percentage of beds in southern hospitals that met the HEW requirement was essentially unchanged. Mississippi and Alabama were at the bottom, with only 30 percent compliance, and Texas, Florida, and North Carolina were at the top, with 90 percent. Virginia lagged behind at 47 percent. Despite two written requests, at least one personal contact, and one telephone call, HEW had reached the limits of voluntary compliance and was instructed to act swiftly to bring about full compliance. Medicare and civil rights are discussed in Gardner to LBJ, June 10, 23, 1966, and L. Peter Libassi to Cater, June 28, 1966, in ibid.; Marvin Watson to LBJ, June 29, 1966, and Libassi to Cater, July 7, 11, 1966, ibid., WHCF-FG 165 (June 28, 1966–Oct. 3, 1966), Box 240, Folder: FG 165, LBJL.

13.  Two lucid analyses of the problem of medical inflation are Allen J. Matusow, *The Unraveling of America* (New York, 1984), 228–231; and Paul Starr, *The Social Transformation of American Medicine*

(New York, 1982), 384–385. For a contemporary explanation, see Martin S. Feldstein, "The Welfare Loss of Excess Health Insurance," *Journal of Political Economy* 83 (Mar. 1973): 252; and Feldstein and Amy Taylor, *The Rapid Rise of Hospital Costs* (Staff Report of Council on Wage and Price Stability, Jan. 1977).

14. Martin S. Feldstein, "The Rising Price of Physicians' Services," *Review of Economics and Statistics* 52 (May 1970): 121–133. The role of Blue Cross is discussed in David Rothman, "A Century of Failure: Class Barriers to Reform," in *The Politics of Health Care Reform,* ed. James A. Morone and Gary S. Belkin (Durham, N.C., 1994), 14–17.

15. Matusow, *Unraveling of America,* 229.

16. Ibid., 229; Howard West, "Five Years of Medicare—A Statistical Review," *Social Security Bulletin* (hereafter, *SSB*), 34 (Dec. 1971): 18–19; Marian Gornick, "Ten Years of Medicare: Impact on the Covered," *SSB* 39 (June 1976): 12–15, 19.

17. So many gaps existed in Medicare's coverage that by 1970 state and local governments had to cover nearly one-fourth of all health care expenditures, mainly in the form of Medicaid payments. That in itself created a conundrum. Although Medicaid helped states pay for a wide assortment of medical expenses for welfare recipients and the medically indigent, it, too, was not immune to a variety of forces that included inflation, fraud, corruption, and unequal dispensing of services that eventually called the entire program into question. A useful overview of Medicaid's first ten years is in House, Committee on Interstate and Foreign Commerce, Subcommittee on Health and the Environment, *Data on the Medicaid Program: Eligibility, Services, Expenditures, Fiscal Years 1966–1977,* 95th Cong., 1st sess., 1977, Committee Print 95–10, 81; and Barbara S. Cooper and Mary F. McGee, "Medical Care Outlays for Three Age Groups: Young, Intermediate and Aged," *SSB* 34 (May 1971): 13. On Medicaid's problems, see the 1969 testimony of Dr. John Knowles, director of the Massachusetts General Hospital, in Senate, Special Committee on Aging, Subcommittee on Health of the Elderly, *Economic Aspects of Aging,* 91st Cong., 1st sess., 1969–1971, pt. 3: 582–584; House, Committee on Interstate and Foreign Commerce, Subcommittee on Oversight and Investigations, *Problems of Medicaid Fraud and Abuse,* 94th Cong., 2d sess., 1976, 58; *New York Times,* July 17, 1974. Also Theodore Marmor with James Monroe, "The Health Programs of the Kennedy-Johnson Years: An Overview," in *Toward New Human Rights: The Social Policies of the Kennedy and Johnson Administrations,* ed. David C. Warner (Austin, Tex., 1977), 173; Karen Davis and Roger Reynolds, "The Impact of Medicare and Medicaid on Access to Medical Care," in *The Role of Health Insurance in the Health Services Sector,* ed. Richard N. Rosett (New York, 1976), 393.

18. "Presidential Remarks."

19. Quoted in *Washington Post,* June 15, 1966, clipping in LBJ Papers, WHCF-Aides Files (Panzer), Box 379, Folder: Medicare. See also Cohen to LBJ, June 24, 1966, ibid., WHCF-Aides Files (Cater), Box 15, Folder: Memos to the Pres., June 1966, LBJL.

20. Cohen to Cater, June 24, 1966, in ibid.

21. Cohen to Cater, June 29, 1966, ibid., WHCF-FG 165, Box 240, Folder: FG 165, LBJL.

22. *TV Statement on Medicare,* draft of June 29, 1966, ibid., WHCF-Aides Files (Cater), Box 15, Folder: Memos to the Pres., June 1966. The news clipping of July 2, 1966 is in ibid., WHCF-Aides Files (Panzer), Box 379, Folder: Medicare, LBJL.

23. The Consumer Price Index in the first quarter of 1966 rose 2.3 points, to 113.3 percent of the July 1957–1959 average, but medical care in the same period rose 4 points, to a much higher 127.7 percent of the base. The major upward thrust occurred in the professional service part of the medical care total, observed a Labor Department official. This category, which excluded prescription drugs, had advanced 5 points since December 1965, to 133.9 percent of the 1957–1959 average. See *Wall Street Journal,* Aug. 24, 1966, news clipping in ibid., WHCF-Aides Files (Panzer), Box 379, Folder: Medicare.

24. Ibid. See also "A Report to the President on Medical Care Prices," attachment to "History of the SSA during the Johnson Administration, 1963–1968," in ibid., Administrative Histories, HEW, Social Security Administration, vol. 1, pt. 18, Box 9, Folder: Admin. Hist. of HEW, LBJL.

25. Julian E. Zelizer, *Taxing America* (Cambridge, UK, 1988), 261.

26. Ibid., 262.

27. Cater to LBJ, Sept. 10, 1966, LBJ Papers, WHCF-Aides Files (Cater), Box 15, Folder: Memos to the Pres., Sept. 1966; Cohen to Cater, Sept. 9, 1966, ibid. See also LBJ's memo of Oct. 4, 1966, in ibid., Box 15, Folder: Memos to the Pres., Oct. 1966, LBJL.

28. LBJ to Gardner, Sept. 29, 1966, ibid., WHCF-Confidential File, FG 165 (June 28, 1966–Oct. 3, 1966), Box 240, Folder: FG 165, LBJL.

29. Cater to LBJ, Nov. 5, 1966, ibid., WHCF-Confidential File, FG 155–20, Box 30, Folder: FG 155/DHEW, LBJL.

30. For the Gorham report, see HEW, *A Report to the President on Medical Care Prices,* Feb. 1967, ibid., DHEW, Box 16, SSA (Tabs 2–27), vol. 2, pt. IVe, LBJL.

31. HEW, *Report on the National Conference on Private Health Insurance,* Washington, D.C., Sept. 28–29, 1967, in ibid. See also HEW, *National Conference on Medical Costs: Chart Book,* July 1967, in ibid.

32. Cf. *Conference on Private Health Insurance.*

33. *Wall Street Journal,* Nov. 21, 1967, news clipping in LBJ Papers, WHCF-Aides Files (Panzer), Box 379, Folder: Medicare, LBJL.

34. Cf. Herbert Schandler, *Unmaking of the President* (Princeton, N.J., 1977).

35. Johnson, "Health in America," Mar. 4, 1968, 9–10, LBJ Papers, WHCF-Aides Files (Califano), Box 73, Folder: Office Files, Health, LBJL.

36. Ibid.

37. HEW, SSA, News Release, July 1, 1966; and Cater to LBJ, July 1, 1966, ibid., WHCF-Aides Files (Cater), Box 15, Folder: Memos to the Pres., July 1966, LBJL. See also HEW, SSA, "History of the Social Security Administration during the Johnson Administration, 1963–1968," 112–113.

38. Medicare and Medicaid relied ultimately on the equation that more medicine equaled better health. After 1965, death rates resulting from the major diseases dropped sharply, as did infant-mortality rates. Health reform advocates interpreted these trends as evidence that increased utilization of medical services by the poor and aged had paid off, but skeptics had their doubts. For a defense of Medicare and Medicaid, see Sar A. Levitan and Robert Taggert, *The Promise of Greatness* (Cambridge, Mass., 1976), chap. 4. For the skeptics' views, see Victor R. Fuchs, ed., *Essays in the Economics of Health and Medical Care* (New York, 1972), 15–18; John H. Knowles, ed., *Doing Better and Feeling Worse* (New York, 1977), 35–46, 57–80; and Fuchs, *Who Shall Live?* (New York, 1974), chaps. 1–2.

39. The exception to this generalization occurred in 1972 as a result of powerful interest-group lobbying and political horse-trading between the House and Senate tax-writing committees when Congress expanded Medicare benefits to include the disabled and those with end-stage renal disease. Jonathan Oberlander, *The Political Life of Medicare* (Chicago, 2003), 40–43, 47–53.

40. Ibid.

41. Gardner to Cater, Oct. 3, 1966; LBJ to Gardner, Sept. 29, 1966, LBJ Papers, WHCF, FG 165 (June 28, 1966–Oct. 3, 1966), Box 240, Folder: FG 165, LBJL.

42. News clipping in ibid., WHCF-Aides Files (Panzer), Box 379, Folder: Medicare, LBJL.

43. Lawrence D. Brown, "The Deconstructed Center: Of Policy Plagues on Political Houses," in *Health Policy and the Disadvantaged,* ed. Brown (Durham, N.C., 1991), 186–187.

44. A guide to the Nixon literature is Dale E. Casper, *Richard M. Nixon: A Bibliographic Exploration* (New York, 1988). An overall view of the Nixon presidency is presented in Richard P. Nathan, *The Administrative Presidency* (New York, 1983). Conservative thinking is examined in A. James Reichley, "The Conservative Roots of the Nixon, Ford and Reagan Administrations," *Political Science Quarterly* 96 (Winter 1981/1982): 537–550. For Nixon's electoral mandate, see Frank S. Meyer, "Mandate of 1968," *National Review* 20 (Nov. 20, 1968): 1170. On the "new federalism," see Robert K. Lekachman,

"Nixon's Program," *Commentary* 47 (June 1969): 67–72; "New Federalism," *Newsweek* 74 (Sept. 15, 1969): 24–25; and David Mars, "Nixon's New Federalism," *Nation* 210 (Apr. 15, 1970): 435–437.

45. In January 1969, Nixon had asked HEW to undertake a major study of health care problems and programs. The text, "A Report on the Health of the Nation's Health Care System," July 10, 1969, is reprinted in the *Weekly Compilation of Presidential Documents* 5 (July 8–12, 1969): 967. For Nixon's crisis statement, see *Public Papers of the Presidents of the United States: Richard Nixon, 1969*, 6 vols. (Washington, D.C., 1971–1975), 1: 505 (cited as *Public Papers: Nixon* [with year]).

46. The law conditioned state approval of hospital rates on their management practices, financially rewarding good management and penalizing poor management. Under the insurance scheme, employers were required to provide basic health insurance benefits: 120 days of semi-private, in-hospital care, 100 days of home care, hospital outpatient diagnostic services, and hospital outpatient care for accident, injury, or emergency illness. The cost to the employee was 2 percent of wages, or one-half of the cost of providing coverage. In appropriate cases, the state would contribute to meeting expenses that exceeded the financial caps for both employer and employee. A copy of Rockefeller's message is included as Appendix B-1 in the "Report of the Task Force on Health," Jan. 9, 1969, Nixon Presidential Materials Project (NPMP), Transitional Task Force Reports (1968–1969), Task Force on Health, Box 1, National Archives (NA) 2, College Park, Md. Subsequent references are to this report unless otherwise noted.

47. The money would come from the individual taxpayer's own pocket and would be deducted by him for taxes owed, rather than reimbursed to him or to the insurer by the federal government. The total amount would be used to maximum effectiveness by eliminating the loss that occurred in transit when first paid and subsequently returned as a grant. Curtis E. Montgomery, M.D., "Use of Federal Income Tax System," Report H, copy in ibid., Appendix B-2.

48. Rashi Fein, "A Proposal for the Financing of Medical Care via Income Tax Credit for Comprehensive Health Insurance," n.d., ibid., Appendix B-3.

49. Cf. "Proposed Revision of Title XIX of the Social Security Act," n.d., Appendix B-4; and "Proposed Changes in Title XVII of the Social Security Act, Made by the Blue Cross Association," n.d., ibid., Appendix C-2.

50. "Report of the Task Force on Health," Jan. 9, 1969.

51. Ibid.

52. Ibid.

53. Ibid. See also *Public Papers: Nixon, 1969*, Appendix C, 1092.

54. The report also called for more efficient and economical use of existing personnel; new programs to train health professionals, including medical education; and more money for medical research. Due to time constraints, the task force identified but made no recommendations regarding family planning, environmental pollution, accident prevention, generic versus brand-name drugs, and "the burdensome costs of prescribed drugs for older people." See "Report of the Task Force on Health," Jan. 9, 1969.

55. Ibid.

56. HEW, *Towards a Comprehensive Health Policy for the 1970's: A White Paper* (May 1971), House, Committee on Ways and Means, *National Health Insurance Proposals*, 92d Cong., 1st sess., 1971–1972, pt. 1, 56–109.

57. Quoted in Anderson to Sen. Fred R. Harris, Feb. 26, 1969, Fred R. Harris Papers, Box 150, Folder 13: Medicare, CAC-OU.

58. Butterfield to Ehrlichman, Mar. 20, 1969; *Washington Daily News*, Mar. 17, 1969, clipping in NPMP, White House Special Files (WHSF), White House Central Files (WHCF), Subject Files: Confidential Files, 1969–1974, Box 36, Folder: IS Accident-Hospital-Medical Health.

59. For Nixon's reaction, see Butterfield to Ehrlichman, Mar. 20, 1969, in ibid.

60. Kenneth R. Cole, Jr., to Ehrlichman, Mar. 21, 1969; memo, "Administration Position on Health Care Programs," Apr. 1, 1969; Ehrlichman to Nixon, Apr. 1, 1969, ibid.

61. Zelizer, *Taxing America*, 314–326.
62. Ehrlichman to Edmund Morgan, Dec. 17, 1969, in ibid. Ehrlichman's request took the form of an Action Memorandum from Cole to Morgan on Dec. 18, 1969. Copy in ibid.
63. "The $60-Billion Crisis over Medical Care," *Business Week,* Jan. 17, 1970, 50–64; "Our Ailing Medical System," *Fortune* 81 (Jan. 1970): 75–99. See also *New York Times,* Jan. 12, 1970; and "Medical Crisis and How to Meet It," *U.S. News* 67 (July 28, 1969): 34–36.
64. Starr, *Social Transformation of American Medicine,* 381; Leonard Woodcock to Carl Albert, July 14, 1970; Albert to Woodcock, July 24, 1970, Albert Papers, Legis. Files, Box 119, Folder 68, CAC-OU.
65. *New York Times,* Aug. 28, 1970.
66. Senate, Committee on Labor and Public Welfare, *National Health Insurance, Hearings on . . . S. 4323,* 91st Cong., 1st sess., 1970, pt. 1, 8–106; *New York Times,* Feb. 18, 1970; Aug. 28, 1970. The Butler memorandum and the subsequent account are from Starr, *Social Transformation of American Medicine,* 394–395.
67. Zelizer, *Taxing America,* 324–326.
68. "Health Care Financing Background Paper," Nov. 5, 1970, NPMP, WHSF, Staff Member and Office Files (SM&OF), Egil Krogh, 1969–1973, Alpha Subject, Box 13, Folder: Health.
69. Elliott Richardson, "Memorandum to the Members of the Domestic Council," Nov. 5, 1970, ibid.
70. These included, but were not limited to, an absence of clear administrative responsibility and accountability for the quantity, quality, distribution, and efficiency of existing health manpower and facilities; inadequate citizen health education; and federal support mechanisms that were too rigid, too complex, or inefficient. The last encompassed state barriers to licensure, malpractice laws, lack of incentives for preventive care, and the cost and duration of medical school education, which constituted a barrier to lower-class economic and racial groups. "Domestic Council—DHEW Presentation," Nov. 10, 1970, ibid.
71. Ibid.
72. *Public Papers: Nixon, 1971,* 170–186. Copies of Kennedy's remarks on introducing his bill and the Bennett bill may be found in the Fred R. Harris Papers, Box 12, Folder 52, CAC- OU.
73. Quoted in John K. Iglehart, "Prepaid Group Medical Practice Emerges as Likely Federal Approach to Health Care," *National Journal* 3 (July 10, 1971): 1444.
74. Edward L. Harper to Ehrlichman, June 8, 1971, NPMP, WHCF, SM&OF, E. L. Harper, Domestic Council Policy File, Box 8, Folder: DC-Meetings of Full Council.
75. *Public Papers: Nixon, 1971,* 764.
76. Domestic Council, "Major Domestic Proposals of the Nixon Administration," [Aug. 4?] 1971, NPMP, WHCF, SM&OF, E. L. Harper, Domestic Council Policy File, Box 10, Folder: Major Domestic Proposals.
77. A copy of Richardson's testimony is in ibid., WHCF, Subject Files: EX FG 33.21, Box 14, Folder: House Comms., Ways & Means, 1971–1972. See also "President's Health Strategy," n.d., ibid., WHCF, SM&OF, Edwin L. Harper, Domestic Council Policy Files—Chronology File, Box 8, Folder: Briefing Book.
78. Flanigan to Nixon, Jan. 17, 1972, ibid., WHSF, SM&OF, Egil Krogh, 1969–1973, Box 13, Folder: Patrick J. Buchanan, 1972 Election File.
79. *Public Papers: Nixon, 1972,* 384–396. Once more the president's request got caught up in election-year politics when *Time* reported that Democratic presidential candidate George McGovern supported compulsory national health insurance. Nixon campaign adviser Patrick J. Buchanan wrote: "The above should a) be costed out by OMB [Office of Management and Budget] and that figure attached to the McGovern program and b) conveyed to the nation's medical community, especially the doctors, whom one imagines are not yet committed to socialized medicine for the U.S." Buchanan's undated memo is in NPMP, WHSF, SM&OF, Egil Krogh, 1969–1973, Box 11, Folder: Buchanan, 1972 Election.

80. Edward D. Berkowitz, *America's Welfare State* (Baltimore, 1991), 69–72; Zelizer, *Taxing America,* 327–343.

81. Cook to William E. Timmons, Nov. 21, 1972, NPMP, WHCF: Subject Files, EX FG 33.21, Box 14, Folder: House Comms., Ways & Means, 1971–1972; Jennie Jacobs Kronenfeld, *The Changing Federal Role in U.S. Health Care Policy* (Westport, Conn., 1997), 160.

82. "National Health Insurance: Action Delayed in 1973," *Congressional Quarterly [CQ] Almanac* (1973), 508–509. A copy of the 1973 Kennedy bill is in the Carl Albert Papers, Legis. Files, Box 119, Folder 68, CAC-OU.

83. Weinberger to Nixon, Nov. 2, 1973, NPMP, WHSF, WHCF, Subject Files: Confidential Files, 1969–1974, Box 15, Folder: FG23 DHEW.

84. With the exception of the CEA, every executive branch agency had endorsed the revised bill. The CEA's Herbert Stein preferred not to mandate an employer-employee plan; wanted to limit health insurance to federal coverage of low-income persons; and wanted also to limit catastrophic protection to expenses below $25,000. Weinberger told Nixon, "We believe this approach would create major inequities between those covered with the Govt[.] Plan and those not." Nor would it have protected the growing number of individuals with medical expenses above $25,000. Weinberger hoped to resolve these differences when he met with Stein on December 13. See Weinberger to Nixon, Nov. 2, 1973, ibid.

85. David N. Parker to Dr. James Cavanaugh, Dec. 3, 1973, ibid.

86. Cavanaugh to Nixon, Dec. 7, 1973, in ibid.

87. *Public Papers: Nixon, 1974,* 132–140. See also "Brief Descriptions of and Major Health Insurance Programs Considered in 1974," *CQ Almanac* (1974), 388–389.

88. See, for example, "Health Insurance for All," *Time* 103 (Feb. 18, 1974): 67, and Alice M. Rivlin, "Agreed: Here Comes National Health Insurance," *New York Times Magazine,* July 21, 1974, 8–9.

89. A copy of the Mills-Kennedy joint statement accompanying introduction of the bill is in the Carl Albert Papers, Legis. Ser., Box 173, Folder 16: Ways & Means, CAC-OU. See also *New York Times,* Feb. 7, 1974, and *CQ Almanac* (1974), 386.

90. The bill also required co-payments of 25 percent and mandated that no individual or family would have to pay more than $1,000 in any year. *New York Times,* Apr. 7, 1974.

91. "Kennedy's Blow to Health Care," *Progressive* 38 (May 1974): 9. See also "Insuring the National Health," *Newsweek* 83 (June 3, 1974): 73–74; and *CQ Almanac* (1974), 387.

92. House, Committee on Ways and Means, "Press Release," Apr. 2, 1974, copy in Carl Albert Papers, Legis. Ser., Box 173, Folder 16: Ways & Means; *CQ Almanac* (1974), 388.

93. *CQ Almanac* (1974), 387; *New York Times,* May 21–23, 1974.

94. *New York Times,* June 8, 1974.

95. See "Health Insurance on Hold," *Wall Street Journal,* July 12, 1974, news clipping in Carl Albert Papers, Legis. Ser., Box 173, Folder 17: Ways & Means, CAC-OU.

96. Stephen E. Ambrose, *Nixon,* 3 vols. (New York, 1987–1991), 3: 596. The only major health care legislation passed during Nixon's term simply required company employee health plans with more than twenty-five employees to include at least one HMO option. See *CQ Almanac* (1974): 391.

97. Starr, *Social Transformation of American Medicine,* 405.

98. *Papers of the Presidents: Gerald Ford, 1974,* 6 vols. (Washington, D.C., 1975–1979), 1: 10.

99. *CQ Almanac* (1974): 391; Carl Albert to Samuel F. Miles, Oct. 16, 1974, Carl Albert Papers, Legis. Ser., Box 173, Folder 18: Ways & Means, CAC-OU.

100. *CQ Almanac* (1974): 386, 395. Ullman's bill had been floating around in various forms since 1973. See "Summary Sheet on H.R. 1 (Jan. 1973)" and Al Ullman to Carl Albert, Jan. 29, 1973, Carl Albert Papers, Legis. Ser., Box 173, Folder 15: Ways & Means, CAC-OU; Albert to Mrs. Dallas A. Lewis, Oct. 17, 1975, ibid., Box 212, Folder 12: Ways & Means, CAC-OU; Marie Gottschalk, *The Shadow Welfare State* (Ithaca, N.Y., 2000), 73–74.

101. Oberlander, *Political Life of Medicare*, 116–118.

102. Bill Clinton, "State of the Union," *Vital Speeches* 60 (Feb. 15, 1994): 258.

## CHAPTER 8. HEALTH CARE REFORM: THE POLITICS OF NEGLECT & REDISCOVERY

1. Few historians have turned their attention to the period after Watergate, leaving the field to journalists, economists, and political scientists. The Bureau of the Census offers a fine introduction to the period in its *Statistical Abstract of the United States* (114th ed., 1994). For insights into the period, see Jill Quadagno, "One Nation: Uninsured" (forthcoming), 169–188, 195–234; Lawrence D. Brown, "The Deconstructed Center: Of Policy Plagues on Political Houses," in *Health Policy and the Disadvantaged*, ed. Brown (Durham, N.C., 1991), 189; and Lawrence D. Brown, ed., *Health Policy in Transition* (Durham, N.C., 1987), which examines the central themes in health care and politics in the 1970s and 1980s. For general political coverage of the period, see A. James Reichley, *Conservatives in an Age of Change: The Nixon and Ford Administrations* (Washington, D.C., 1981); Burton I. Kaufman, *The Presidency of James Earl Carter, Jr.* (Lawrence, Kans., 1993); Haynes Johnson, *Sleepwalking through History: America in the Reagan Years* (New York, 1991); George Gilder, *Wealth and Poverty* (New York, 1981); and Frances Fox Piven and Richard Cloward, *Why Americans Don't Vote* (New York, 1988).

2. Carter's rise to political prominence is examined in Betty Glad, *Jimmy Carter: In Search of the Great White House* (New York, 1980).

3. On voter apathy, see *Wall Street Journal*, July 15, 1976; Aug. 27, 1976; Oct. 14–15, 1976; Nov. 2, 1976.

4. *New York Times*, Nov. 13, 1974.

5. Peter G. Bourne, *Jimmy Carter: A Comprehensive Biography from Plains to Postpresidency* (New York, 1997), 256–258, 278, 298; "Dilemma over National Health Insurance Delays Promised Carter Plan," *CQ Almanac* 36 (1978): 1770; *Wall Street Journal*, July 20, 1976.

6. *New York Times*, July 23, 29, 1978; Oct. 2, 10–11, 1978; Dec. 8, 10, 13, 1978.

7. William Shonick, *Government and Health Services* (New York, 1995), 327.

8. That figure was predicated on an annual growth rate of 5.5 to 6 percent in the GNP, which proved to be overly optimistic. Bourne, *Jimmy Carter*, 374–375; *Wall Street Journal*, July 12–13, 1976.

9. *CQ Almanac* (1979): 512; Elizabeth Wehr, "House Cost Control Rejected by One Panel, Weakened by Another," *CQWR* 37 (July 14, 1979): 1424–1425.

10. Bourne, *Jimmy Carter*, 426, 433.

11. "Health Plan Order, Presidential Directive/DPS-3, July 29, 1978," *CQWR* 36 (Aug. 5, 1978): 2059.

12. "Carter Lists 'Principles' of National Health Plan," ibid., 2058; *New York Times*, July 29–30, 1978.

13. *New York Times*, July 29–30, 1978.

14. Bourne, *Jimmy Carter*, 429–430.

15. Elizabeth Wehr, "Dispute over Poor Halts Health Insurance Markup," *CQWR* 37 (Nov. 10, 1979): 2542.

16. For example, the bill provided for universal coverage and a wide spectrum of services; eliminated cost-sharing; contained national as well as local annual budgets, reimbursement for hospitals according to negotiated fees, with no additional charges to patients; and continued Medicaid, but only for long-term care. Elizabeth Wehr, "Kennedy, Labor Coalition Outline Comprehensive National Health Plan," ibid., 37 (May 19, 1979): 970–971.

17. Elizabeth Wehr, "Corman Jumps Kennedy Ship," ibid., 37 (June 16, 1979).

18. The Health Care part covered 52 million people, 16 million on Medicaid, 14 million "near poor," and 22 million Medicare beneficiaries. Heavy cost-sharing was an integral feature of the Carter plan, with employers paying 75 percent of the premiums. Low-income workers, however, received partial subsidies for their share of the premiums, and maternal care and child care were totally covered. Pregnant women also received free prenatal, delivery, and postnatal care for one year after birth. Shonick, *Government and Health Services,* 327.

19. Wehr, "Dispute over Poor Halts Health Insurance Markup," 2542.

20. Patricia Roberts Harris, secretary of the newly established Department of Health and Human Services (HHS), was a vocal critic of the Kennedy-Waxman bill. See Elizabeth Wehr, "Harris Opens Attack on Kennedy Health Plan," ibid., 37 (Dec. 1, 1979): 2729.

21. *New York Times,* Nov. 11, 1977; Dec. 19, 29, 1977; Shonick, *Government and Health Services,* 327.

22. For Enthoven as a leading proponent of a market-oriented reform, see *Washington Post,* Jan. 26, 1992.

23. See, for example, Alain C. Enthoven, *Health Plan: The Only Practical Solution to the Soaring Cost of Medical Care* (Reading, Mass., 1980).

24. The growth rate of social expenditures, which had been 7.9 percent under Nixon and Ford, dropped to 3.9 percent under Carter. On Carter's social expenditures, see the study for the Urban Institute by D. Lee Bawden and John L. Palmer, "Social Policy, Challenging the Welfare State," in *The Reagan Record,* ed. John L. Palmer and Isabel V. Sawhill (Cambridge, Mass., 1984), 184, 228, 214.

25. Schlesinger's oft-repeated quote is cited in Vicente Navarro, *The Politics of Health Policy* (Cambridge, Mass., 1994), 8–9.

26. Kevin Phillips, *The Politics of Rich and Poor: Wealth and the American Electorate in the Reagan Aftermath* (New York, 1990), 49. The annual growth rate of social expenditures declined further during the Reagan administration, to 1.5 percent.

27. *New York Times,* Nov. 6, 1980.

28. On voter turnout and Reagan's election, see ibid., Nov. 9, 16, 1980.

29. *Public Papers of the Presidents: Ronald Reagan, 1981* (Washington, D.C., 1982), 1–4.

30. One in five children was being raised in a household whose income fell below the official poverty line. The economic impact of the Reagan years is discussed in John L. Palmer and Isabel V. Sawhill, eds., *The Reagan Experiment* (Washington, D.C., 1982); and Phillips, *The Politics of Rich and Poor.*

31. David Stockman, *The Triumph of Politics* (New York, 1986), 8.

32. Navarro, *Politics of Health Policy,* 162, 187.

33. Ibid., 36, 53, esp. nn. 168–173.

34. House, *An Act to Provide for Tax Reform, and for Deficit Reduction,* 98th Cong., 2d sess., 1984, H.R. 4170; Navarro, *Politics of Health Policy,* 35.

35. D. E. Altman, "What Do Americans Really Want?" *Health Affairs* 4 (Fall 1984): 139; W. Schneider, "Public Ready for Real Change in Health Care," *National Journal* 23 (Mar. 1985): 664; Navarro, *Politics of Health Policy,* 36.

36. Roger M. Battistella and Thomas P. Weil, "National Health Insurance Reconsidered: Dilemmas and Opportunities," *Hospital and Health Services Administration* 34 (Summer 1989): 139–156.

37. Ibid.

38. The literature is abundant, but see Nancy Amidei, "A Growing Hemorrhage," *Commonweal* 113 (July 11, 1986): 390–392; Kathleen McAuliffe, "Sick about America's Health Care," *U.S. News* 102 (June 11, 1987): 64; *Washington Post,* Apr. 3, 1988; May 24, 1988; Kenneth Thorpe et al., "Including the Poor, The Fiscal Impact of Medicaid Expansion," *JAMA* 265 (Feb. 17, 1989): 10003; Eli Ginzberg, "Health Care Reform—Why So Slow?" *New England Journal of Medicine* 322 (May 17, 1990): 1464–1466.

39. On the Catastrophic Coverage Act, see *Washington Post,* May 20, 26–28, 1988; June 3, 7, 9, 1988; July 2, 1988.

40. This account is drawn from Jonathan Oberlander, *The Political Life of Medicare* (Chicago, 2003), 5–73; Richard Himmelfarb, *Catastrophic Politics* (University Park, Pa., 1995), chaps. 1–7; and Julie Rovner, "Congress's Catastrophic Attempt to Fix Medicare," in *How Congress Shapes Health Care Policy*, ed. Thomas E. Mann and Norman Ornstein (Washington, D.C., 1995), 145–178.

41. Navarro, *Politics of Health Policy*, 37–38. Navarro's findings found support from other policy scholars. See, for example, Robert G. Evans, "Canada: The Real Issues," and William A. Glaser, "Universal Health Insurance That Really Works: Foreign Lessons for the United States," in *The Politics of Health Care Reform*, ed. James A. Morone and Geary S. Belkin (Durham, N.C., 1994), 463–486, 495–522.

42. Navarro, *Politics of Health Policy*, 37–38. See also Vicente Navarro, "The Arguments against a National Health Program, Science or Ideology?" *International Journal of Health Services* 18 (Nov. 2, 1988): 179–188.

43. Navarro, *Politics of Health Policy*, 38, 41; Thomas E. Kavanagh and Lorn S. Foster, *Jesse Jackson's Campaign: The Primaries and Caucuses* (Washington, D.C., 1984). Rodney D. Green and Finley C. Campbell argue that Jackson's health proposals would actually have left workers in a worse situation. See Rodney D. Green and Finley C. Campbell, "The Jesse Jackson Economic Platform of 1984: A Critique and an Alternative," in *The Social and Political Implications of the 1984 Jesse Jackson Presidential Campaign*, ed. Lorenzo Morris (New York, 1990), 102–105.

44. The text of the 1984 Democratic platform is in *CQ Almanac* (1984): 23.

45. Navarro, *Politics of Health Policy*, 84, 86.

46. For Jackson's efforts to build a multiethnic coalition, see Darryl S. Takeoff, "Jesse Jackson and the Rainbow Coalition: Working Class Movement or Reform Politics?" *Humanity and Society* 14 (May 1990): 158–173. On the Canadian model, see Rashi Fein, "A Model for Health Insurance, Can We Learn from the Canadian Example?" *Dissent* 38 (Winter 1991): 14ff.; Michael Walker, "Should We Adopt Canada's Health System?" *Consumers' Research Magazine* 73 (May 1990): 21ff.; "Canada's Health Plan Not for Importing," *Nation's Business* 78 (Sept. 1990): 34ff. In July 1991, congressional Democrats held a series of hearings comparing the U.S. and Canadian health systems. See *Washington Post*, July 23, 1991; Navarro, *Politics of Health Policy*, 83.

47. Navarro, *Politics of Health Policy*, 83.

48. For Jackson's national health care program and campaign platform, "The Revival of Hope," see Frank Clemente, ed., *Keep Hope Alive: Jesse Jackson's 1988 Presidential Campaign: A Collection of Major Speeches, Issue Papers, Photographs and Campaign Analysis* (Boston, 1989), 41–54, 143–151. See also *New York Times*, Mar. 31, 1988; Apr. 1, 3–8, 10, 14–16, 18–20, 1988.

49. *Washington Post*, Mar. 3, 1988; Apr. 14, 18, 22, 1988. Jackson's advisers were correct. See Glazer, "Universal Health Insurance That Really Works," 497–498.

50. On the primaries, see Penn Kimball, *Keep Hope Alive! Super Tuesday and Jesse Jackson's 1988 Campaign for the Presidency* (Washington, D.C., 1992); *Washington Post*, Apr. 26, 1988; Sept. 21, 1988; *New York Times*, June 19, 21, 27, 1988.

51. *New York Times*, June 13, 1988; July 10, 16–17, 19–20, 1988.

52. Jackson's July 19 address to the Democratic National Committee is in Clemente, *Keep Hope Alive*, 33–40. On the election and health care, see Lee Smith, "The Battle over Health Insurance, Without Getting into the Details or the Dollar Signs, Governor Dukakis Promises 'Health Care for All.' Vice President Bush Wants Government to Stay on the Sidelines," *Fortune* 118 (Sept. 26, 1988): 145–148.

53. See, for example, Julie Rover, "Broad Plans to Revise Health Insurance Offered," *CQWR* 47 (Feb. 4, 1989): 221; Thomas P. Weil, "Is It Time for National Health Insurance?" *Best's Review* 90 (Apr. 1990): 32–36; George D. Luneburg, "National Health Care Reform: An Aura of Inevitability Is upon Us," *JAMA* 265 (May 15, 1991): 2566–2567; Donald O. Natter et al., "Restructuring Health Care in the United States: A Proposal for the 1990s," ibid., 2516–2520; Andrew Kopkind, "Seizing the Historic Moment," *Nation*

253 (Dec. 16, 1991): 768–771; Theda Skocpol, "Is the Time Finally Ripe? Health Insurance Reforms in the 1990s," *Journal of Health Politics, Policy and Law* 18 (Fall 1993): 531–550.

54. Kevin Phillips, *Boiling Point: Democrats, Republicans, and the Decline of Middle Class Prosperity* (New York, 1993), esp. chaps. 8–9.

55. Congress, *An Act to Repeal Medicare Provisions in the Medicare Catastrophic Coverage Act of 1988*, 101st Cong., 2d sess., 1989. See also John D. Rockefeller IV, "A Call for Action: The Pepper Commission's Blueprint for Health Care Reform," *JAMA* 265 (May 15, 1991): 2507–2510.

56. *Washington Post*, Jan. 28, 1991; Mar. 22, 1991; May 25, 1991; June 6, 12, 16, 21, 1991; July 1, 1991; Sept. 3, 1991; Oct. 18, 1991; Julie Rover, "Mitchell, New Priority," *COIR* 49 (Feb. 16, 1991): 421.

57. Larry Martz, "The Scary Politics of Health: Bush and Congress Will Duck the Issue for '92," *Newsweek* 117 (June 24, 1991): 18; Max Gates, "Reform Needs a Push from a Reluctant Bush," *Automotive News*, Nov. 18, 1991, 48.

58. Wofford's campaign is discussed in Mary Matalin and James Carville with Peter Knobler, *All's Fair: Love and War and Running for President* (New York, 1994), 75–76. See also Arnold Birenbaum, *Putting Health Care on the National Agenda* (Westport, Conn.: 1995), 3.

59. *Washington Post*, Sept. 1, 1991; Nov. 17, 19, 1991; Susan Dentzer, "No More Patient Patients: What Pennsylvania's Vote Could Produce," *U.S. News* 111 (Nov. 18, 1991): 50–51; Julie Rover, "Congress and Health Care Reform 1993–1994," in *Intensive Care: How Congress Shapes Health Policy*, ed. Thomas E. Mann and Norman J. Ornstein (Washington, D.C., 1995), 181–182.

60. Jack Germond and Jules Witcover make this point in *Mad As Hell: Revolt at the Ballot Box, 1992* (New York, 1993), 73, but Allen Schick argues that health care reform was simply one of many agenda items of concern to voters. Allen Schick, "How a Bill Did Not Become a Law," 229, in Mann and Ornstein, *Intensive Care*, 229.

61. Rover, "Congress and Health Care Reform," 182, 196.

62. "Consumers Give Thumbs-up Sign to National Health Insurance," *Best's Review* 91 (June 1990): 20; Robert J. Blendon and Karen Donelan, "The Public and the Emerging Debate over National Health Insurance," *New England Journal of Medicine* 323 (July 19, 1990): 208.

63. Cathie Jo Martin, *Stuck in Neutral* (Princeton, N.J., 2000), 98–99. See also Martin, "Together Again: Business, Government, and the Quest for Cost Control," in *Politics of Health Care Reform*, ed. Morone and Belkin, 233–240.

64. Navarro, *Politics of Health Policy*, 196.

65. "Health Care Reform: Public versus Expert Perspectives," Henry J. Kaiser Family Foundation Background Briefing at the National Press Club, Prepared by Robert J. Blendon, Tracey Hyams, John Benson, Feb. 5, 1993, copy in Records of the Health Care Interdepartmental Working Group (HCIWG Records), Ira Magaziner Files, Box 1184, Folder: Drafts, National Archives II (NA II), College Park, Md. See also the same authors' "Bridging the Gap between Expert and Public View on Health Care Reform," *JAMA* 269 (May 19, 1993): 2573–2578, and *Washington Post*, Dec. 14, 1991; Jan. 6, 9–10, 30–31, 1992; Feb. 8, 1992.

66. Princeton University's Uwe Reinhardt, a leading voice among health policy analysts sympathetic to large employers, wrote that "[the root of the problem] is an entitlement mentality by American workers not shared by workers anywhere in the world." Quoted in Navarro, *Politics of Health Policy*, 208.

67. *Washington Post*, Oct. 9, 1991. Fried was a Wexler Group executive vice president with extensive experience in health care issues. Haynes Johnson and David S. Broder, *The System: The American Way of Politics at the Breaking Point* (Boston, 1996), 70. In many respects, this journalistic account remains the single best political analysis of the ill-fated Clinton effort to draft a comprehensive health care bill. For the Urban Institute's interest in health care reform, see John Holahan, Marilyn Moon, W. Pete Welch, and Stephen Zuckerman, "An American Approach to Health System Reform," *JAMA* 265 (May 15, 1991): 2537–2540.

68. "Senator Kerrey Introduces Socialized Health Plan," *Best's Review* 92 (Oct. 1991): 6; E. Richard Brown, "Health USA: A National Health Program for the United States," *JAMA* 267 (Jan. 22, 1992): 552–558; Robert Kerrey, "Why America Will Adopt Comprehensive Health Care Reform," *American Prospect* 6 (Summer 1991): 81–91. A succinct distillation of the major health reform plans before Congress in 1992 is contained in "Universal Public Coverage Plans," n.d., copy in HCIWG Records, Atul Gawande Papers, Box 1803, Folder: Drafting—Cong. Bills, NA II, College Park, Md.

69. Alain C. Enthoven, "The History and Principles of Managed Competition," *Health Affairs* 12 (Supple., 1993): 24–48. See also Mary Jane Fisher, "Tsongas, Managed Competition Key to U.S. Health Care," *National Underwriter Property and Casualty* (June 29, 1992), 3–4.

70. Enthoven's ideas were laid out in two influential articles. See Alain Enthoven and Richard Kronick, "A Consumer-Choice Health Plan for the 1990s: Universal Health Insurance in a System Designed to Promote Quality and Economy," 2 pts., *New England Journal of Medicine* 320 (Jan. 5, 1989): 29–37; ibid., Jan. 12, 1989, 94–101. See also Enthoven and Kronick, "Universal Health Insurance through Incentives Reform," *JAMA* 265 (May 15, 1991): 2532–2536.

71. Paul Starr, *The Logic of Health Care Reform* (Knoxville, Tenn., 1992), esp. chaps. 4–6. For a perceptive analysis of the use and misuse of the managed-competition concept, see David Himmelstein and Steffy Woolhandler, *Managed Competition: A Grimm Fairy Tale* (Cambridge, Mass., 1993). The press's role in promoting managed competition as the sole option is told in Trudy Lieberman, "Covering Health Care Reform, Round One," *Columbia Journalism Review* 32 (Sept.–Oct. 1993): 33–35.

72. Clinton discusses health care reform in *My Life* (New York, 2004), 224, 260, 496, 582, 592, 597, 610, 612, 629, 631, 641. See also *Washington Post,* Oct. 4, 1991; Johnson and Broder, *The System,* 77.

73. Johnson and Broder, *The System,* 77–78.

74. *New York Times,* Jan. 20, 1992; Johnson and Broder, *The System,* 75–76.

75. Bob Woodward, *The Agenda* (New York, 1994), 33–40, 91, 137–138, 193, 216; Johnson and Broder, *The System,* 78–79.

76. *New York Times,* June 20, 1992; Johnson and Broder, *The System,* 80–81.

77. Ibid.

78. Bill Clinton and Al Gore, *Putting People First: How We Can All Change America* (New York, 1992).

79. On the 1992 election, see Clinton, *My Life,* 417, 445; *New York Times,* July 16, 1992.

80. *Washington Post,* Feb. 7, 1992.

81. The efforts of Surgeon General Everett Koop to de-politicize health reform as a campaign issue failed. See Nancy Arvay to Saul Benjamin, Aug. 5, 1992, and attached copy of Koop's *New York Times* Op-Ed in HCIWG Records, Gawande Papers, Box 1803, Folder: Drafting—Cong. Bills, NA II. For Clinton's slippage in the polls, see Gawande to George S., James C., Bob R., Susan T., et al., Sept. 7, 1992, ibid.

82. On the basic campaign strategy, see Jack Ebler's informative memorandum to Gawande, Aug. 15, 1992, in response to Judy Feder's request for a review of the politics of health care reform and the Clinton campaign proposal, in Gawande Papers, Box 1803, Folder: Drafting—Cong. Bills, NA II.

83. Johnson and Broder, *The System,* 86–87.

84. Ibid., 88.

85. Clinton discusses universal coverage in *My Life,* 482–483, 492, 555–556, 601. See also Rover, "Congress and Health Care Reform," 183; Paul Starr, "What Happened to Health Reform?" *American Prospect* 20 (Winter 1995): 21.

86. *New York Times,* Sept. 25, 1992.

87. *Washington Post,* Nov. 4, 1992.

88. Soon after the election, a bipartisan group of legislators, including Senators Nancy Landon Kassebaum and John C. Danforth, and Representatives Dave McCurdy, Pat Roberts, and Dan Glickman, urged President-elect Clinton to support their proposal, "BasiCare," which combined some features of

Clinton's proposal but was more conservative. See their joint letter to Clinton, Nov. 25, 1992, HCIWG Records, Gawande Papers, Box 1802, Folder: Cong. Meetings, NA II.

89. Johnson and Broder, *The System*, 91–93.

90. Ibid., 94.

91. The transition team's work is delineated in the *Washington Post*, Nov. 27, 1992; Dec. 16, 1992; and in the memorandum of Gawande, Feder, and Thorpe to Hillary Clinton and Carol Rasco, Jan. 21, 1992, HCIWG Records, Gawande Papers, Box 1803, Folder: Task Force, NA II.

92. Ibid. For doubts that health care reform was achievable in the first "hundred days" of the Clinton presidency, see Victor Cohn's comments in the *Washington Post*, Dec. 8, 1992.

93. Gawande et al. to Hillary Rodham Clinton, Jan. 28, 1993, HCIWG Records, Gawande Papers, Box 1803, Folder: Task Force, NA II.

94. Ibid.

95. Ibid.

96. Ibid. See also *Washington Post*, Dec. 2, 1993.

97. Ibid.

98. Ibid.

99. *Washington Post*, Nov. 23, 1992.

100. For the transition team's budget analysis, see *Washington Post*, Jan. 23, 1993.

101. Ibid.

102. Johnson and Broder, *The System*, 109–110.

103. For the budgetary options, see Julie Kosterlitz, "O.K. Bill, It's Time to Pick Your Remedy," *National Journal* 23 (Jan. 1993): 200.

104. For the notion that Feder's team had been "set up," see ibid., 109–110; and Jacob S. Hacker, *The Road to Nowhere* (Princeton, N.J., 1997), 120.

105. See, for example, Walter Zelman, "Health Reform Technical Work Group on Market Restructuring and Cost Containment," Jan. 19, 1993, Walter Zelman Papers, HCIWG Records, Box 4001, NA II.

106. Rumors that Shalala intended to designate Feder and Thorpe as her deputies for health care issues made it unlikely that Clinton would entrust the assignment to HHS. Indeed, Shalala's alleged lack of familiarity with the issue enabled Clinton to bypass the agency in favor of a presidential task force. *Washington Post*, Jan. 22, 1993.

107. Gawande et al. to Hillary Rodham Clinton, Jan. 28, 1993, HCIWG Records, Gawande Papers, Box 1803, Folder: Task Force, NA II.

108. This is especially troubling because the task force was cognizant of the need to reach out to potential friends and allies. Its "Preliminary Work Plan" stated: "In addition to policy work, the task force should plan serious outreach activities. The policy work cannot be done in a vacuum." It also said, "We must also reach out to citizens' groups around the country to be sure that not only the most powerful and loudest lobbyists have impact on our process." With respect to allowing sufficient time for drafting the legislation, the plan's author stated: "We must have sufficient time to avoid sloppy drafting. Although some drafting flaws can be worked out in Congress, the administration could lose control of the process if drafting is not done thoroughly before the bill is submitted." [Magaziner?] "Preliminary Work Plan for the Interagency Health Care Task Force," HCIWG Records, copy in Zelman Papers, Box 4003, Folder: Task Force Beginnings, NA II.

## CHAPTER 9. "COMPETITION UNDER A CAP": THE CLINTON TASK FORCE

1. Hugh Heclo, "Clinton's Health Reform in Historical Perspective," in *The Problem That Won't Go Away, Re-forming U.S. Health Care,* ed. Henry J. Aron (Washington, D.C., 1996), 15–33; Jacob S. Hacker, *The Road to Nowhere* (Princeton, N.J., 1997), 117–118. Hacker's monograph is authoritative on Clinton's health plan.

2. Sidney Blumenthal, *The Clinton Wars* (New York, 2003), 78. On popular antipathy toward government and politics, see E. J. Dionne, Jr., *Why Americans Hate Politics* (New York, 1991); and Morris Fiorina, *Divided Government,* 2d ed. (Needham Heights, Mass., 1996).

3. *New York Times,* Jan. 19, 1993.

4. Celinda Lake, "Address," in *Beyond Gridlock: Prospects for Governance in the Clinton Years—And After,* ed. James L. Sundquist (Washington, D.C., 1993), 4–5; Charles O. Jones, "Campaigning to Govern: The Clinton Style," in *The Clinton Presidency, First Appraisal,* ed. Colin Campbell and Bert A. Rockman (Chatham, N.J., 1996), 21. Paul Starr's "Healthy Competition: Universal Coverage and Managed Competition under a Cap," *American Prospect* 12 (Winter 1993): 44–52, succinctly explains the ideas underlying Clinton's policy approach.

5. Bill Clinton's *My Life* (New York, 2004), 482, 499, 503, 515, 540, 547–548, 555, discusses and defends his wife's role as head of the task force. See also Hillary Rodham Clinton, *Living History* (New York, 2003), 148; *Washington Post,* Jan. 26–27, 1993.

6. Rodham Clinton, *Living History,* 143–154; "Health Care Task Force Headed by First Lady," *CQWR* 51 (Jan. 30, 1993): 225; *New York Times,* Jan. 27, 1993.

7. David Maraniss, *First in His Class: The Biography of Bill Clinton* (New York, 1995), 56; Tom Brazaitis and Eleanor Clift, *War without Bloodshed: The Art of Politics* (New York, 1996), 89.

8. For Magaziner's background, see *New York Times,* Feb. 26, 1993; Brazaitis and Clift, *War without Bloodshed,* 93.

9. For Clinton's use of the task force concept as governor of Arkansas, see Rodham Clinton, *Living History,* 149–152, 168, 182; *New York Times,* Jan. 26, 1993; Hacker, *Road to Nowhere,* 122.

10. "This is entirely my mistake, no one else's," Clinton later recalled, adding, "I probably made a mistake in not then going for a multi-year strategy, and not trying to say we've got to try to do it in 'ninety-four." See Haynes Johnson and David S. Broder, *The System: The American Way of Politics at the Breaking Point* (Boston, 1996), 122–128, 157.

11. On the link between the budget and health care reform, see Rodham Clinton, *Living History,* 150–153; "Crafting an Economic Package: A Reality Check for Bill Clinton," *CQWR* 51 (Jan. 16, 1993): 118–119; "Health Reform," ibid., 51 (Apr. 3, 1993): 813; Hacker, *Road to Nowhere,* 129–130.

12. Johnson and Broder, *The System,* 119–120.

13. *Public Papers of the Presidents, William J. Clinton, 1993,* 2 vols. (Washington, D.C., 1994), 1: 116 (cited as *Public Papers: Clinton* [with year]). See also Clinton, *My Life,* 547–549; *Washington Post,* Jan. 31, 1993; Feb. 19, 22, 1993.

14. *Public Papers: Clinton, 1993,* 1: 118, 120; *New York Times,* Feb. 18, 1993. See also Pat Towell, "More Money Comes in under Plan for 'Savings' in Budget," *CQWR* 51 (Feb. 20, 1993): 370–371.

15. For Byrd's influence, see Clinton, *My Life,* 492–493; Alissa J. Rubin, "The Process Debate," *CQWR* 51 (Mar. 13, 1993): 599; *Washington Post,* Mar. 14, 1993; Johnson and Broder, *The System,* 122–126, 157.

16. The best description of this process is in Johnson and Broder, *The System,* 112–113.

17. Rodham Clinton, *Living History,* 150–153.

18. Many of the papers from the Princeton conference of November 20–22, 1993, were published subsequently in *Health Affairs* 12 (Supple. 1993): 49–138. These included Walter Zelman's "Who Should

Govern the Purchasing Cooperative?"; Paul Starr's "Design of Health Insurance Purchasing Cooperatives"; James C. Robinson's "A Payment Method for HIPCs"; Shoshanna Sofaer's "Informing and Protecting Consumers under Managed Care"; and Richard Kronick's "Where Should the Buck Stop: Federal and
State Responsibility in Health Care Financing Reform." See also Starr's op-ed piece on health care reform in the *New York Times*, Feb. 4, 1992.

19. Rodham Clinton, *Living History*, 150–153; Paul Starr, *The Logic of Health Care Reform: Why and
How the President's Plan Will Work*, rev. and enlarged ed. (New York, 1994), xxiv.

20. Johnson and Broder, *The System*, 113.

21. Atul Gawande to Donna Shalala and Kevin Thurm, Jan. 28, 1993, HCIWG Records, Atul Gawande Papers, Box 1803, Folder: Task Force—Setting Up, NA II.

22. Ibid.

23. Pennsylvania Republican Representative William F. Clinger questioned Rodham Clinton's
policy-making role and also asked the GAO to review whether she was allowed to conduct any of the
task force's meetings in private. Shortly thereafter, the task force had to fend off a legal challenge from
two small groups of conservative physicians, the American Association of Physicians and Surgeons and
the American Council for Health Care Reform, along with the National Legal Policy Center, a conservative think tank. Together, they brought suit charging that the task force's clandestine activities had violated federal open-meeting laws. A U.S. District Court judge ruled on March 10 that Rodham Clinton
should be considered like any other "outsider" working for the White House, and therefore certain meetings of the task force she headed must be open to the public. The administration appealed the ruling,
contending that she was acting as a government employee; thus, the 1972 law requiring boards with
nonfederal employees to meet in public did not apply. A U.S. Court of Appeals panel ruled on June 22,
after the task force had disbanded, that it was not legally required to hold open meetings. The administration eventually did provide a roster of names to the press. *Washington Post*, Feb. 10; Mar. 4, 6, 11, 23;
June 24, 1993.

24. *Washington Post*, Feb. 24, 1993; Mar. 3, 27, 30, 1993; Vicente Navarro, *The Politics of Health Policy*
(Cambridge, Mass., 1994), 211.

25. Starr, *The Logic of Health Care Reform*, xxix–xxxi.

26. "Preliminary Work Plan for the Interagency Health Care Task Force," n.d., HCIWG Records,
Walter Zelman Papers, Box 4003, Folder: Task Force Beginnings; Ira Magaziner to Hillary Rodham
Clinton, Jan. 26, 1933, ibid., Ira Magaziner Papers, Working Group Files, Box 3305, Folder: Review
Groups, NA II.

27. "Guidelines for Meetings with the President to Discuss Health Care Reform Issues," n.d. [but
after March 10, 1993], ibid., Robert M. Kolodner Papers, Box 1468, NA II.

28. Some senior advisers also harbored private doubts that the Clintons had the resolve to tackle
the difficult economic and political costs of reform. See Johnson and Broder, *The System*, 115–117, 119.

29. Alissa Rubin, "Special Interests Stampede to be Heard on Overhaul," *CQWR* 51 (May 1, 1993):
1081–1084.

30. Quoted in *New York Times*, Sept. 18, 1994.

31. On the refusal of the Veterans Administration to cooperate with the health task force, see Vic
Raymond to Ira [Magaziner], n.d., HCIWG Records, Magaziner Papers, Box 3305, Folder: Toll Gates, NA
II. See also *Washington Post*, Apr. 9, 1993; Starr, *The Logic of Health Care Reform*, xxx–xxxi.

32. Navarro, *Politics of Health Policy*, 208ff.

33. Hacker, *Road to Nowhere*, 124.

34. *New York Times*, May 22, 1993; Johnson and Broder, *The System*, 129, 134–135, 137–139.

35. *New York Times*, Mar. 4, 1993. Hillary Rodham Clinton believed that because of demands on
their time, most legislators had only a rudimentary knowledge of the complexities of the health care
issue. Rodham Clinton, *Living History*, 232.

36. "Competition under a cap" is discussed in Walter Zelman's memo, "HIPC Strategies," to Ira Magaziner, Mar. 11, 1993, and Starr to Magaziner, May 17, 1993, HCIWG Records, Zelman Papers, Box 001, NA II.

37. See Starr's memo, "Rethinking Who Is 'In or Out of the HIPC,'" to Zelman and Magaziner, Mar. 10, 1993, in ibid.; Hacker, *Road to Nowhere,* 124–125.

38. Starr to Magaziner, May 17, 1993, HCIWG Records, Zelman Papers, Box 4001, NA II.

39. Ibid.; Alissa J. Rubin, "Are U.S. Taxpayers Ready for Health Care Reform?" *CQWR* 51 (Apr. 17, 1993): 955–959; *New York Times,* Apr. 15, 1933; Hacker, *Road to Nowhere,* 125.

40. CBO, *Estimates of Health Care Proposals from the 102nd Congress* (Washington, D.C., July 1993), 47–57; "Preliminary Work Plan for the Interagency Health Care Task Force," n.d., HCIWG Records, Zelman Papers, Box 4003, Folder: Task Force Beginnings, NA II. See also "HIPC Strategies," Zelman to Magaziner, Mar. 11, 1993, ibid., Box 4001; and Hacker, *Road to Nowhere,* 126.

41. David Cutler to Ira Magaziner, Feb. 20, 1993, HCIWG Records, Magaziner Papers, Box 3305, Folder: Materials Received, NA II.

42. Among the issues Cutler's group had to consider if a freeze were to be put in place were how long it should remain in effect, to which items and services it should apply, how to cope with "volume offset" tactics by physicians and hospitals attempting to mitigate the impact of controls, and how to manage the "ballooning" effect on medical costs once controls were lifted. See ibid.

43. Alain Enthoven to Ira Magaziner, Feb. 26, 1993, HCIWG Records, Starr Papers, Box 3210, Folder: Meetings with B.C., NA II.

44. Quoted in *New York Times,* Sept. 18, 1994.

45. Paul Starr to Ira Magaziner, Feb. 7, 1993, HCIWG Records, Starr Papers, Box 3210, Folder: Meetings with B.C., NA II.

46. Starr to Magaziner, Feb. 17, 1993, ibid., Zelman Papers, Box 4001, NA II; Hacker, *Road to Nowhere,* 126.

47. Bob Woodward, *The Agenda: Inside the Clinton White House* (New York, 1994), 197–200; Starr, "What Happened to Health Care Reform?" *American Prospect* 20 (Winter 1995): 24; Hacker, *Road to Nowhere,* 127.

48. Starr to Magaziner, Mar. 25, 1993, HCIWG Records, Starr Papers, Box 3210, Folder: Financing Choices/Costs, NA II.

49. Starr to Magaziner, Mar. 24, 1993, ibid.

50. Starr, "The Costs of Delay," Mar. 26, 1993, ibid., Starr Papers, Box 3206, NA II.

51. The Jackson Hole Group, using the model of the Securities and Exchange Commission, preferred a vertical integration of the health industry, as opposed to the traditional executive agency. Similarly, the size of the HIPC was an issue. Cf. "Federal Governance Structure," n.d., ibid., Zelman Papers, Box 4001, Folder: Governance; Starr to Magaziner, Mar. 22, 1933, ibid., Starr Papers, Box 3210, Folder: Financing Choices/Costs, NA II.

52. Starr, "Why Not Medicare-for-all? Here's Why," Mar. 25, 1993, and Starr, "Karen Davis' Alternative Model," Mar. 22, 1993, ibid., Starr Papers, Box 3210, Folder: Financing Choices/Costs, NA II. Davis was a critic of the managed-competition proposal espoused by Magaziner, Starr, Zelman, and the Jackson Hole Group.

53. Hacker, *Road to Nowhere,* 128.

54. The group was composed of forty-six physicians and nurses. Health Professions Review Group, "Synopsis of Policy Recommendations," May 5, 1993, HCIWG Records, Audit Groups, Box 3306, Binder: Health Professionals Review Group, NA II.

55. Navarro, *Politics of Health Policy,* 209.

56. *New York Times,* Mar. 23, 1993; Apr. 14, 16, 26, 1993; May 8, 12, 21, 1993.

57. Ibid., June 13, 1993.

58. *Washington Post,* Feb. 12, 24, 1993; Mar. 3, 5, 12–13, 1993.

59. Ibid., May 12, 1993; Johnson and Broder, *The System*, 128, 132–133, 139.

60. *Washington Post*, Apr. 3, 30, 1993; June 14, 1993.

61. Rodham Clinton, *Living History*, 158, 183. A good analysis of the First Lady's role in promoting health reform is in "Clinton Task Force All Ears on the Subject of Overhaul," *CQWR* 51 (May 22, 1993): 1293–1295.

62. "Accelerating New System Development," Mar. 24, 1993, HCIWG Records, Starr Papers, Box 3206, NA II.

63. "Health Care Deadline Set Back to June," *CQWR* 51 (May 22, 1993): 1301; *New York Times*, May 3, 1993; Johnson and Broder, *The System*, 141.

64. *New York Times*, Apr. 2, 1993; *Washington Post*, Apr. 30, 1993, Magaziner to Hillary Clinton, May 10, 1993, HCIWG Records, Magaziner Papers, Box 3307, Folder: Costs, NA II.

65. Quoted in *New York Times*, Sept. 18, 1994.

66. "Report of the Legal Review Group," May 28, 1993, HCIWG Records, Audit Groups, Box 3306, Binder: Legal Review Group, NA II.

67. Starr to Magaziner, May 9, 1993, ibid., Magaziner Papers, Box 3308, NA II.

68. See Megan Runty's memo, "Health Care Communications Policy," to Bob Boorstin, Feb. 2, 1993, ibid., Gawande Papers, Box 1803, Folder: Health Care Message, NA II.

69. Ibid.

70. Johnson and Broder, *The System*, 153–54.

71. Ibid., 143–145. No record of the debate or of Gawande's presentation is to be found in the task force files.

72. Ibid., 145–147; *Washington Post*, May 21–22, 27, 1993; *New York Times*, May 21, 1993.

73. *Washington Post*, June 22, 24, 1993; July 7, 1993; *New York Times*, Mar. 7, 1993; Apr. 6, 1993; June 3, 1993; Sept. 26, 1993.

74. Johnson and Broder, *The System*, 149–150.

75. Ibid., 155–156. For the budget, see *New York Times*, Aug. 6–7, 1993.

76. Johnson and Broder, *The System*, 157.

77. *Washington Post*, Aug. 17, 1993; Cathie Jo Martin, *Stuck in Neutral* (Princeton, N.J., 2000), 178–179.

78. *Public Papers: Clinton, 1993*, 2: 1388.

79. The other two agenda items were Vice President Gore's plan to reinvent government and ratification of the NAFTA agreement. See David Broder's column in the *Washington Post*, Sept. 8, 1993, and the paper's continuing coverage on Sept. 6, 15–16, 19, 1993.

80. Ibid., Sept. 20, 1993; Johnson and Broder, *The System*, 161–163.

81. *Public Papers: Clinton, 1993*, 2: 1558–1562.

82. *Washington Post*, Oct. 1, 1993; *New York Times*, Oct. 3, 1993.

83. *Washington Post*, Oct. 6, 9, 14, 16, 20, 1993.

84. Johnson and Broder, *The System*, 353.

85. *Washington Post*, Oct. 22, 28, 1993; Nov. 22, 24, 1993; *New York Times*, Oct. 11, 12, 1993; Nov. 11, 1993; Dec. 6, 1993.

86. *Washington Post*, Oct. 28, 1993.

87. "Health Care Debate Takes Off," *CQ Almanac* (1993): 338.

88. Rodham Clinton, *Living History*, 191–192, 228–229, 246; *Washington Post*, Nov. 24, 29, 1993; *New York Times*, Dec. 5, 1993; Johnson and Broder, *The System*, 318–326.

89. The following account is based on Cathie Jo Martin's excellent analysis in *Stuck in Neutral*, chaps. 5 and 7.

90. Marie Gottschalk, *The Shadow Welfare State* (Ithaca, N.Y., 2000), 137–141.

91. Ibid., 142–144.

92. Ibid., 145–146; *New York Times*, Dec. 11, 1993.

93. *Washington Post*, Nov. 22, 1993.

94. Rodham Clinton, *Living History*, 191–192, 228–229, 246. For criticism from conservative Republicans and business, see *Washington Post*, Nov. 22, 24, 29, 1993; *New York Times*, Dec. 5, 1993; Johnson and Broder, *The System*, 318–326.

95. Gottschalk makes this point in *The Shadow Welfare State*, 65, 158–159.

96. Jennifer Klein, *For All These Rights* (Princeton, N.J., 2003), 273, makes this point.

97. Cathie Jo Martin, "Together Again: Business, Government and the Quest for Cost Control," in *The Politics of Health Care Reform*, ed. James A. Morone and Gary S. Belkin (Durham, N.C., 1994), 253; Jennie Jacobs Kronenfeld, *The Changing Federal Role in U.S. Health Care Policy* (Westport, Conn., 1997), 125–126.

98. Hacker, *Road to Nowhere*, 149–151; Kronenfeld, *Changing Federal Role*, 126–128; Gottschalk, *Shadow Welfare State*, 149.

# CHAPTER 10. CLINTON, CONGRESS, & THE GREAT HEALTH CARE WAR

1. None of the major committee chairs—Democrats Moynihan, Kennedy, Dingell, or Rostenkowski—was a proponent of managed competition. California Democrat Pete Stark, the powerful chair of the House Ways and Means Health Subcommittee, was outspoken in his belief that competition saved nothing and increased costs.

2. *Washington Post*, Mar. 4, 1993; May 14, 1993; *New York Times*, Dec. 4, 1993.

3. Haynes Johnson and David Broder, *The System* (Boston, 1996), 301.

4. Alissa J. Rubin, "Two Ideological Poles Frame Debate over Reform," *CQWR* 52 (Jan. 8, 1994): 23; Jacob S. Hacker, *Road to Nowhere* (Princeton, N.J., 1997), 131–132.

5. Paul Starr and Walter A. Zelman, "A Bridge to Compromise: Competition under a Budget," *Health Affairs* 12 (Supple. 1993): 7–23.

6. *Public Papers of the Presidents: William J. Clinton, 1994*, 2 vols. (Washington, D.C., 1995), 1: 131 (cited as *Public Papers: Clinton* [with year]). Clinton later justified the veto pledge, saying: "Hillary argued that since we all felt that we wouldn't have done it right if we didn't do this [universal coverage], that in this case it was worth making the veto pledge." Connie Bruck, "Hillary the Pol," *New Yorker*, May 30, 1990, 90.

7. See, for example, the observation of Uwe Reinhardt of Princeton University in Alissa J. Rubin, "Uncertainty, Deep Divisions Cloud Opening of Debate," *CQWR* 52 (Aug. 13, 1994): 2344.

8. Paul Starr, "What Happened to Health Care Reform?" *American Prospect* 20 (Winter 1995): 26.

9. Education and Labor had only a marginal claim on Medicare and Medicaid and no jurisdiction over financing. Moreover, its members, who were well to the left of the House, were not likely to write a bill the leadership could take to the floor. Johnson and Broder, *The System*, 305–306.

10. Ever since entering the House in 1955, Dingell had introduced in each new Congress a national health insurance bill in memory of his father, John Dingell, Sr., the New Dealer who had been one of the earliest congressional advocates of universal health care and a cosponsor of the Wagner-Murray-Dingell bill. For Cooper's position, see *Washington Post*, Nov. 30, 1993; and Beth Donovan, "Spotlight on Cooper," *CQWR* 52 (Feb. 5, 1994): 250.

11. Beth Donovan, "Democrats as Divided as Ever on Eve of First Markup," *CQWR* 52 (Feb. 26, 1994): 475, 478.

12. *Washington Post*, Oct. 7, 1993; Dec. 6, 1993; Jan. 29, 1994; Johnson and Broder, *The System*, 313, 316.

13.  Bill Clinton's *My Life* (New York, 2004), 555–556, 576–578, 594–595, 601–602, discusses the opposition to health care reform. See also *New York Times,* June 17, 1994; Gary Wills, "The Clinton Principle," *New York Times Magazine,* Jan. 19, 1997, 34; Johnson and Broder, *The System,* 304–305.

14.  Dingell had even permitted his staff to leak an eight-page memo that included major concessions to small business to win over Cooper and other committee Democrats, but it proved fruitless. Alissa J. Rubin and Beth Donovan, "Moderate Democrats Shun Mandate on Employers," *CQWR* 52 (Apr. 30, 1994): 1067.

15.  For the Rowland-Bilirakis bill, see House, *A Bill to Reform the Insurance Market,* 103d Cong., 2d sess., 1994, H.R. 5228.

16.  Rubin and Donovan, "Moderate Democrats Shun Mandate on Employers"; Beth Donovan and Alissa J. Rubin, "Dingell Outline Softens Clinton Plan to Lure Energy Panel Democrats," *CQWR* 52 (Mar. 26, 1994): 738–739.

17.  The political maneuvering may be followed in Beth Donovan, "A Health Care Holdout," ibid., 52 (Apr. 23, 1994): 1007; Rubin and Donovan, "Moderate Democrats Shun Mandate on Employers," 1067; Rubin and Donovan, "At Every Turn, Clinton Plan Running into Roadblocks," ibid., 52 (May 7, 1994): 1124; Donovan, "A Disappointed Dingell," ibid., 52 (July 2, 1994): 1796; *Washington Post,* Feb. 15, 1994; Apr. 16, 1994; June 29, 1994; Oct. 11, 1994.

18.  For the White House's lingering concerns about Moynihan's commitment to health care reform, see *Washington Post,* Jan. 12, 1994. Mitchell's role is discussed in Beth Donovan and Elizabeth A. Palmer, "Panels Cutting through Clutter to Get to Heart of Debate," *CQWR* 52 (Apr. 23, 1994): 1005.

19.  Alissa J. Rubin and Beth Donovan, "Centrist Mood Won't Stop Work on Liberal Plans," *CQWR* 52 (Apr. 16, 1994): 891–892; Johnson and Broder, *The System,* 347–348.

20.  Beth Donovan, "Bipartisan Deal Gives Boost to Overhaul," *CQWR* 52 (May 21, 1994): 1298; Donovan, "Panel Strikes Surprising Accord with Benefits, Cost Concept," ibid., 1299–1300.

21.  During the Reagan and Bush presidencies, Dole had unsuccessfully urged Republicans to formulate a major health care initiative to counter the popular perception that the Republican Party cared less about health care—and, hence, about the average American—than did the Democratic Party. The Annapolis meeting is reported in Alissa J. Rubin, "GOP Seeks Unity to Bargain with Democrats," *CQWR* 52 (Mar. 5, 1994): 550; and in the *New York Times,* Mar. 4–5, 1994.

22.  Rubin and Donovan, "At Every Turn, Clinton Plan Running into Roadblocks," 1128.

23.  Alissa J. Rubin et al., "Rostenkowski Sets Markup to Get Panel on Track," *CQWR* 52 (May 14, 1994): 1221; Rubin, "Tension on Senate Finance Puts Panel in Holding Pattern," ibid., 52 (May 21, 1994): 1302–1303; *New York Times,* June 12, 1994; Johnson and Broder, *The System,* 369–374.

24.  The Kennedy bill softened the burden for small businesses by giving them the option of exempting themselves from the employer mandate. They might pay a payroll tax of 1 or 2 percent instead. Beth Donovan, "Details of the Kennedy Plan," *CQWR* 52 (May 14, 1994): 1222; Donovan, "Sen. Labor First out of Gate with Approval of Overhaul," ibid., 52 (June 11, 1994): 1522–1524; *Washington Post,* Mar. 15–16; June 10, 1994.

25.  Beth Donovan, "Betting Big on Public Backing, Clinton Stands Firm on Veto," *CQWR* 52 (May 25, 1994): 1703; *New York Times,* June 10, 21, 1994; Johnson and Broder, *The System,* 375–376.

26.  Alissa J. Rubin, "Finance Chairman's Bill Outline Becomes Bipartisan Flash Point," *CQWR* 52 (June 11, 1994): 1525. For Packwood's reversal on mandates, see Beth Donovan, "A Different Spotlight," ibid., 52 (June 18, 1994): 1613. See also *Washington Post,* June 20, 1994.

27.  Durenberger voiced his belief in market forces to reduce health costs as early as 1993. See David Durenberger, "Perspective: Government and the Competitive Marketplace," *Health Affairs* 12 (Spring 1993): 81–84.

28.  In 1991, 53 percent of people insured through their jobs were in traditional fee-for-service medicine. Three years later, the number had diminished to 35 percent, the rest being in some form of managed

care run mostly by for-profit companies. At least three-fourths of physicians and an even higher percentage of hospitals signed contracts in 1994 to reduce their fees for patients enrolled in managed care and accepted some degree of peer review of their diagnosis and treatment protocol by those administering the program. See *New York Times,* June 16, 1994; Johnson and Broder, *The System,* 381–382.

29.  Clinton, *My Life,* 594–595; Ceci Connolly, "Storming the Capital," *CQWR* 52 (July 23, 1994): 2042; *Washington Post,* May 24, 1994; June 12, 1994; *New York Times,* June 26, 1994; Johnson and Broder, *The System,* 382–387.

30.  Alissa J. Rubin, "GOP Sens. Backing Dole Plan," *CQWR* 52 (July 2, 1994): 1799; *Washington Post,* June 30, 1994.

31.  Alissa J. Rubin, "Senate Finance Panel Deals Blow to Universal Coverage Package," *CQWR* 52 (July 2, 1994): 1798; *Washington Post,* July 3, 1994; Broder and Johnson, *The System,* 373, 389–395.

32.  Alissa J. Rubin and Beth Donovan, "Leaders Tell Clinton Measure Must Have Slower Approach," *CQWR* 52 (July 23, 1994). For Mitchell's and Gephardt's bills, see Rubin, "Mitchell Aims for 95 Percent," ibid., 52 (Aug. 6, 1994): 2205; and Rubin, "Key Provisions of the Gephardt Plan," ibid., 52 (July 30, 1994): 2143. See also Rubin, "Leaders Using Fervent Approach to Convert Wavering Members," ibid., 52 (July 30, 1994): 2142, and Rubin and Donovan, "With Outcome Still Uncertain, Members Face Critical Vote," ibid., 52 (July 30, 1994): 2201–2204, 2208; *Washington Post,* July 30, 1994; Aug. 1–3, 1994.

33.  *New York Times,* Aug. 4, 1994; *Washington Post,* Aug. 3–5, 1994.

34.  Holly Idelson, "Clinton, Dems. Scramble to Save Anti-Crime Bill," *CQWR* 52 (Aug. 13, 1994): 2340–2343.

35.  Johnson and Broder, *The System,* 480–484.

36.  Ibid., 485; Alissa J. Rubin, "Uncertainty, Deep Divisions," *CQWR* 52 (Aug. 13, 1994): 2344–2345.

37.  David S. Cloud and Beth Donovan, "House Delays Health Care Debate As Leaders Plot Strategy," ibid., 52 (Aug. 13, 1994): 2349–2351; *New York Times,* Aug. 18, 1994; *Washington Post,* Aug. 23, 1994.

38.  Alissa J. Rubin and David S. Cloud, "Doubt Surfaces on Bill Passage as Senate Struggle Continues," *CQWR* 52 (Aug. 20, 1994): 2458–2460; *Washington Post,* Aug. 6, 12–16, 20, 1994; *New York Times,* Aug. 18–19, 1994.

39.  *Washington Post,* Aug. 19, 1994.

40.  Alissa J. Rubin, "Chafee Group Unveils Last-Minute Plan," *CQWR* 52 (Aug. 20, 1994): 2459.

41.  *New York Times,* Aug. 18, 20, 1994.

42.  *Washington Post,* Aug. 26, 1994; *New York Times,* Aug. 24, 27, 1994; Sept. 21–22, 27, 1994; Alissa J. Rubin, "Prospects for Major Overhaul Fade as Senate Goes Home," *CQWR* 52 (Aug. 27, 1994): 2486–2487; David S. Cloud, "Support Erodes as Key Backers Voice Little Hope for Passage," ibid., 52 (Sept. 17, 1994): 2571–2572; Rubin, "Chances for Limited Measure Slight as Congress Returns," ibid., 52 (Sept. 10, 1994): 2524.

43.  *New York Times,* Aug. 24, 27, 1994; Sept. 21–22, 27, 1994. The political fallout from failure to pass health care reform is discussed in Hillary Rodham Clinton, *Living History* (New York, 2003), 148–149, 153–154, 190.

44.  In Florida, Democratic Governor Lawton Chiles had proposed in 1992 that all employers be required to provide health insurance for their workers, but under pressure from large self-insured employers, he was forced to withdraw that plan. Two years later, the Republican majority in the state's upper chamber, in a bid to bring the budget under control, blocked his initiative to transfer $3.2 billion in federal Medicaid money over five years to a managed–health care program that would cover 40 percent of the state's 2.8 million uninsured. See *New York Times,* July 2, 1995; Deborah L. Rogal and W. David Helms, "State Models: Tracking States' Efforts to Reform Their Health Systems," *Health Affairs* 12 (Summer 1993): 27–30.

45.  Teresa A. Coughlin et al., "State Responses to the Medicaid Spending Crisis: 1988 to 1992," *Journal of Health Politics, Policy and Law* 19 (Winter 1994): 837–864.

46. In 1992 alone, 1.2 million families lost their insurance. Their plight focused intense public scrutiny on both the way American health care was delivered and its cost. Estimated to consume one dollar out of every seven of the goods and services produced in the United States, this was a higher proportion by far than any other nation. Peter Macpherson, "Health: Some Modest Proposals on Republican Table," *CQWR* 52 (Dec. 31, 1994): 3611–3613.

47. *New York Times*, Apr. 23, 1995; Peter Macpherson, "GOP Revives 1994's Hot Issue: Health Insurance Overhaul," *CQWR* 53 (Apr. 1, 1995): 944–946.

48. *New York Times*, Jan. 2, 7, 1995. See also Frank Barnes, "Balancing Act," *New Republic* 212 (Feb. 27, 1995): 10–11; and Joe Klein, "Calling Newt's Bluff," *Newsweek* 125 (Feb. 20, 1955): 35, for Senate Democrats' wariness of the balanced-budget amendment.

49. On Morris's influence, see Dick Morris, *Behind the Oval Office: Winning the Presidency in the Nineties* (New York: 1997), chaps. 4–6, 9; Elizabeth Drew, *Showdown: The Struggle between the Gingrich Congress and the Clinton White House* (New York: 1996), 63–67, 285–286, 298–299, 303–307, 312–313; James Carney, "The Republican in the Oval Office," *Time* 145 (June 26, 1995): 33–34.

50. Drew, *Showdown*, 69, 71.

51. Ibid., 77–78. Clinton discusses his second-term health care initiatives in *My Life*, 663, 669, 673, 680–682, and passim.

52. *New York Times*, Apr. 23, 1995.

53. Charles O. Jones, "Bill Clinton and the GOP Congress," *Brookings Review* 13 (Spring, 1995): 30–33; *New York Times*, Apr. 23, 1995.

54. *New York Times*, Jan. 31, 1995.

55. Like the Clinton health plan, what was driving the Republican charge were rising health costs and the web of electoral promises they had made to balance the budget in seven years while reducing personal and business taxes by nearly $400 billion. Medicare spending alone was projected to grow at an average annual rate of 9.1 percent over the next five years and to go broke by the year 2004. Sharyn Campbell et al., "The Challenge of Social Security and Medicare Funding," Employee Benefit Research Institute *Notes* 16 (Aug. 1995): 1–6. See also *New York Times*, Feb. 8, 12, 1995; Jeff Shear, "The Big Fix," *National Journal* 27 (Mar. 25, 1995): 734–738.

56. Mike Ervin, "Land of a Million Elephants," *Progressive* 59 (Feb. 1995): 39; Murray L. Weidenbaum, "A New Look at Health Care Reform," *Vital Speeches* 61 (Apr. 1, 1995): 381–384; *New York Times*, Feb. 12, 1995; Paul Magnusson, "Medicare: Now It's the GOP's Turn to Squirm," *Business Week* 59 (May 15, 1995): 59.

57. David Maraniss and Michael Weisskopf, *Tell Newt to Shut Up! Prizewinning Washington Journalists Reveal How Reality Gagged the Gingrich Revolution* (New York, 1996), 37–38. See also *New York Times*, Aug. 2, 1995; Sept. 15, 1995; Oct. 27, 1995; Lawrence Kudlow, "Cutting Edge," *National Review* 47 (Feb. 20, 1995): 28.

58. In one study, elderly and poor chronically ill patients enrolled in HMOs between 1986 and 1990 had worse physical health outcomes than similar people in fee-for-service systems in the same period. The authors of the study warned that current health care plans should carefully monitor the outcomes of these vulnerable subgroups. John E. Ware, Jr. et al., "Differences in 4-Year Health Outcomes for Elderly and Poor, Chronically Ill Patients Treated in HMO and Fee-for-Service Systems," *JAMA* 276 (Oct. 2, 1996): 1039– 47. See also David Hayes and Robert F. Black, "New Surgery for Health Care," *U.S. News* 118 (Feb. 27, 1995): 68–69; Marilyn W. Serafini, "Recipe for Reform?" *National Journal* 27 (Mar. 4, 1995): 546–549; Mike McNamee, "Give Medicare a Strong Dose of Managed Care," *Business Week*, Feb. 27, 1995, 44.

59. *New York Times*, Apr. 12, 1995.

60. Ibid., Apr. 23, 1995.

61. Ibid., Apr. 29, 1995.

62. Ibid., May 2, 1995.

63. *Public Papers: Clinton, 1995,* 1: 629–630; Susan Dentzer, "Medicare's Fine Fix," *U.S. News* 118 (May 8, 1995): 58–61.

64. Cf. House, Committee on Ways and Means, *Report of the Trustees of the Federal Hospital Insurance Trust Fund,* 104th Cong., 1st sess, May 2, 1995.

65. *New York Times,* May 3, 1995. Karen Tumulty, "Your Knife or Mine?" *Time* 145 (June 26, 1995): 34, discusses the debate within the Republican Party over budget cuts.

66. *New York Times,* May 3, 5, 8, 10, 12, 1995; "Medigrief," *Nation* 260 (May 22, 1995): 707–708; Suneel Rattan, "The Most Unkindest Cut," *Time* 145 (May 15, 1995): 37–38. On Domenici, see Gloria Borger, "A Moderate at the Revolution," *U.S. News* 118 (May 22, 1995): 39.

67. *New York Times,* May 10, 1995.

68. *New York Times,* May 16, 1995; Paul Magnusson, "Medicare: Now It's the Republicans' Turn to Squirm," *Business Week,* May 15, 1995, 59; Michael Petzer, "Medicare under the Knife: Radical or Cosmetic Surgery?" *Medical Economics* 72 (June 2, 1995): 170–172ff.

69. *New York Times,* May 19, 1995; Ann R. Dowd, "The Looming Budget Battle over Medicare," *Fortune* 131 (May 29, 1995): 20; Howard Glecksman, "Newt's Fingers Get Caught in the Showdown," *Business Week,* Nov. 27, 1995, 39.

70. Clinton's plan, like the Republicans', would have required major savings on Medicare ($124 billion) and Medicaid ($54 billion). James Carney, "The Republican in the Oval Office," *Time* 145 (June 26, 1995): 33–34; *New York Times,* June 14, 1995; Charles Krauthammer, "Clinton v. Congress: The Race Is Set," *Time* 119 (June 5, 1995): 42; "Clinton's Knife," *Nation* 261 (July 3, 1995): 1; James Popkin, "The Medicare Fight and the Budget War," *U.S. News* 118 (May 15, 1995): 44–45.

71. The timing was part of the centrist strategy proposed by Dick Morris, who told Clinton to focus on the swing voters—such as the Perot supporters—who would decide the election in 1996, rather than the party's left wing. The plan itself was chiefly the work of pollster Stan Greenberg and White House advisers George Stephanopoulos and Harold Ickes, who wanted to foreclose the prospect that Clinton would face a Democratic primary challenger for renomination in 1996. Gloria Borger, "Is It Survival or Cynical?" *U.S. News* 119 (July 3, 1995): 35; Michael Miller, "Kinder Cuts," *New Republic* 213 (July 10, 1995): 10–11.

72. Since February, the Republican-dominated Ways and Means and Commerce Committees of the House had been conducting periodic hearings on Medicare's future and the budget. See House, Committee on Ways and Means, *Medicare, Hearings on Controlling Costs and Improving Care,* 104th Cong., 1st sess., Feb. 6, 7, 10, 1995; *Saving Medicare and Budget Reconciliation Issues, Hearings...,* July 19, 20, 25, 1995; Committee on Commerce, *Future of the Medicare Program, Hearings...,* June 28, 1995; July 12, 18, 1995; Aug. 3, 1995.

73. Senior citizens who opted for a private plan that charged more than the Medicare rate would pay the additional premiums. A proposal for a federally supervised bazaar in which health insurers competed for business resembled the system of managed competition that many health experts and Clinton also had recommended in his ill-fated plan. *New York Times,* July 17, 1995; Norman J. Ornstein, "Flashback," *New Republic* 213 (July 3, 1995): 16.

74. *New York Times,* July 25–26, 1995; [Clinton], "Remarks on the 30th Anniversary of the Passage of Medicare, July 25, 1995," *Weekly Compilation of Presidential Documents* 31 (July 31, 1995): 1296–1299.

75. See the interview of Republican Senator Robert F. Bennett in "The Republican Rx for Medicare," *Medical Economics* 72 (Aug. 21, 1995): 137–138. See also Nancy R. Gibbs, "Medicare: Selling a Painful Cure," *Time* 146 (Aug. 7, 1995): 24–27, and *New York Times,* Aug. 4, 1995.

76. The effort to slash Medicaid to help balance the budget had been foreshadowed in a book coauthored by Republican pollster Frank Lutz: *The People's Budget: A Common Sense Plan for Cutting Washington Down to Size* (Washington, D.C., 1995). See also *New York Times,* Aug. 6, 8, 26, 1995; and James R. Cantwell, "Reforming Medicaid," *Policy Report, no. 197* (National Center for Policy Analysis, Aug. 1995).

77. Paul Starr, "Look Who's Talking Health Care Reform Now," *New York Times Magazine,* Sept. 3, 1995, 42.
78. Ibid., 43.
79. Ibid.
80. On Gingrich's plan, see Sidney Blumenthal, "Medicine Show," *New Yorker* 71 (Sept. 25, 1995): 7–8; Ramesh Ponnoru, "Medicare," *National Review* 47 (Sept. 25, 1995): 24; *New York Times,* Sept. 7, 10, 1995.
81. *New York Times,* Sept. 15, 1995.
82. Ibid., Sept. 16–17, 1995. See also William Schneider, "Spin Control on Medicare and Taxes," *National Journal* 27 (Oct. 21, 1995): 2672.
83. Ibid., Sept. 14, 1995; Colette Fraley and Alissa J. Rubin, "Opponents Solidify Stands on Health Care Proposals," *CQWR* 53 (Sept. 30, 1995): 2995–3001.
84. Gingrich bypassed the usual procedure of having the subcommittees of the Committees on Ways and Means and Energy and Commerce draft the initial Medicare and Medicaid proposals, appointing instead his own task force to write the bills. He also reached an understanding with Senate Majority Leader Dole that the Senate's bills would be substantially the same. *New York Times,* Sept. 15, 22, 1995; Johnson and Broder, *The System,* 586–587.
85. For details of the bill, see House, Committee on Ways and Means, *Medicare Preservation Act of 1995,* 104th Cong., 1st sess., H. Rep. 104–276, pt. 2, Oct. 16, 1995. The Republicans' bill effectively transformed Medicare from a "defined benefit" plan to a "defined payment" system, which no longer offered every recipient the same package of benefits. For analysis of the Republican bill, see "Medicare Reform: Pros and Cons," *Congressional Digest* 74 (Nov. 1995): 257–258; Tom Rosenstiel, "Buying Off the Elderly," *Newsweek* 126 (Oct. 2, 1995): 40–41, and "Do No Harm," *Commonweal* 122 (Oct. 6, 1995): 5–6.
86. For Democratic complaints of being excluded from Medicare reform, see the remarks of Representative Ron Klink of Pennsylvania, *Congressional Record,* 104th Cong., 1st sess., vol. 141, pt. 154 (Sept. 29, 1995): 9675–9676; and *New York Times,* Sept. 23, 1995.
87. CBO cost estimates are in House, Committee on Commerce, *Report on H.R. 2425, Together with Minority and Additional Views,* 104th Cong., 1st sess., 1995, pt. 2, 141–145. See also *New York Times,* Sept. 28, 1995.
88. Drew, *Showdown,* 315. For analysis of the benefits to the Republicans of threatening a budget train wreck, see Stephan Moore, "The Little Engine That Couldn't," *National Review* 47 (Sept. 25, 1995): 26; and Mortimer Zuckerman, "The Perils of Pauline—Again," *U.S. News* 118 (Sept. 25, 1995): 104.
89. *New York Times,* Oct. 3, 5–6, 1995.
90. Republican policy makers, for example, had sharply scaled back one proposal to allow the elderly to keep the savings generated if they chose less expensive medical coverage, after the AARP warned it could be used to exploit senior citizens into choosing cheap plans regardless of their needs. Ibid., Oct. 18, 1995.
91. Ibid.
92. Ibid.
93. House, Committee on Commerce, *Report on H.R. 2424,* 1995, pt. 2, 447–451. See also *Newport News (Va.) Daily Press,* Oct. 10, 12, 1995, and Jerelyn Eddings, "The GOP Cause Steps Forward," *U.S. News,* 119 (Oct. 30, 1995): 38–40.
94. Democrat Earl F. Hillard of Alabama reported the poll results in *Congressional Record,* 104th Cong., 1st sess., vol. 141, pt. 167 (Oct. 28, 1995): 9651–9652. For other Democratic criticism, see ibid., vol. 141, pt. 167 (Oct. 11, 1995): 9862, 9867–9870, 9874–9891. The AARP warning is in "G.O.P. Unveils Medicare Plan," *AARP Bulletin* 36 (Oct. 1995): 1, 13.
95. Drew, *Showdown,* 315–316.
96. *New York Times,* Oct. 15, 1995. By contrast, AMA leaders in December would express grave concern about Republican proposals to overhaul Medicaid under the proposed Medicaid Transportation

Act of 1995. This bill provided states with lump-sum grants and discretionary spending authority for health care for low-income people. The AMA wanted Congress to preserve a federal guarantee of health insurance for all low-income people. *Newport News (Va.) Daily Press*, Dec. 5, 1995.

97. Ibid., Oct. 12, 1995; Drew, *Showdown*, 318.

98. *Congressional Record*, 104th Cong., 1st sess., vol. 141, pt. 162 (Oct. 19, 1995): 10464.

99. *New York Times*, Oct. 22, 1995.

100. Ibid.

101. Ibid. Gingrich told a meeting of financial officials that he was prepared to shut down the government if Clinton did not agree to Republican demands for a balanced budget and tax cut. Congressional action was necessary to raise the federal debt ceiling before the Treasury could pay $25 billion in interest payments, due on November 15. He also warned that failure to raise the ceiling would create chaos in domestic and overseas financial markets. *Washington Post*, Oct. 22, 1995.

102. Montana Democrat Pat Williams declared, "Today, Medicare, tomorrow Social Security, programs they have always opposed and oppose today." Majority Whip Tom DeLay of Texas summarily dismissed Democratic amendments as "a joke wrapped in fraud and shrouded by farce." Gingrich terminated debate prior to the vote, insisting: "We want to solve problems for all Americans. We want no racial division. We want no class warfare. We want no conflict between generations. We want a solution to preserve and protect Medicare." See *Congressional Record*, 104th Cong., 1st sess., vol. 141, pt. 162 (Oct. 19, 1995): 10328–10385, 10455–10464. *Newport News (Va.) Daily Press*, Oct. 27, 1995.

103. Drew, *Showdown*, 316; Michael Kinsley, "Been There, Done It," *New Republic* 213 (Oct. 9, 1995): 12ff.

104. The Republican plan would have placed hard caps on how much the federal government could spend each year both on providers and on benefits. If costs rose faster than the amount the government proposed to spend, providers and beneficiaries would have to absorb the difference. The federal guarantee of adequate coverage for the elderly would, in essence, be removed. Worse still, no limits were placed on how much insurance companies could charge for supplemental policies to fill the gaps in coverage left by Medicare. See Drew, *Showdown*, 317; and John C. Goodman, "Second Opinion," *National Review* 47 (Nov. 27, 1995): 46–49, for a conservative comparison between the Republican and Clinton health plans.

105. Drew, *Showdown*, 317.

106. Ibid.

107. Less than 12 percent of the budget in 1995, Medicare was projected to account for 30 percent of the spending in the Republican budgets over the next seven years. *Congressional Record*, 104th Cong., 1st sess., vol. 141, pt. 162 (Oct. 19, 1995): 10386.

108. *1995 Board of Trustees Annual Report on the FHIA and Federal Supplementary Insurance Trust Funds*, dated June 6, 1995, is in the hearings before the Senate, Committee on Finance, 104th Cong., 1st sess., 1995. See also the remarks of North Dakota Democrat Byron L. Dorgan in *Congressional Record*, 104th Cong., 1st sess., vol. 141, pt. 168 (Oct. 27, 1995): 16067–16068; and *New York Times*, Oct. 20, 1995.

109. By the second decade of the twenty-first century, when the baby boomers retired, the CBO projected, Medicare would swallow such a large portion of the federal budget that there would be little left for other programs. In 1995, 4 workers were paying taxes for each person covered by Medicare; the proportion would fall to 2.5 workers in 2025. See *New York Times*, Oct. 20, 1995.

110. The budget reconciliation recommendations of the Finance Committee were reported as S. Rep. 104–34. Clinton's ire focused on two proposals affecting Medicaid recipients. One, found only in the House bill, would have repealed a 1988 law that required states to protect some income and assets of elderly people whose spouses were living in nursing homes. The other, found in both Senate and House versions, would have repealed the tough federal standards for nursing homes that Democratic Representatives John D. Dingell and Henry A. Waxman had written into law in 1987, after Congress

had documented unsafe and unsanitary conditions in scores of institutions. See *New York Times,* Sept. 30, 1995; Oct. 1, 1995.

111.   A Democratic amendment to scale back proposed cuts in Medicare to $89 billion was rejected on a fifty-three to forty-six vote. However, to hold the support of wavering moderate Republicans, the Senate leadership shepherded a last-minute package of changes in the bill that restored $10 billion for Medicaid and $2 billion for Medicare and partially restored the federal nursing home standards that had been slated for repeal. *Newport News (Va.) Daily Press,* Oct. 26–28, 1995; *Congressional Record,* 104th Cong., 1st sess., vol. 141, pt. 168 (Oct. 27, 1995): 16008–16009; pt. 169 (Oct. 30, 1995): 16201–16253.

112.   *Newport News (Va.) Daily Press,* Oct. 27–28, 1995.

113.   Health policy experts speculated that the Republicans' most enduring legacy might not be to curb health costs but to shift power over spending to the states, a realignment they feared might unleash new, unpredictable forces if the web of federal laws and regulations governing Medicare were swept away. See ibid.; *New York Times,* Oct. 29, 1995.

114.   *Public Papers: Clinton, 1995,* 2: 1628.

115.   Republicans were determined to shrink the federal government and reduce its presence in the lives of Americans. Clinton, too, regarded the deficit as serious, but he also was generally comfortable with the place of government in American life and was under pressure to follow through on his veto threat. "Medicare Showdown Near," *AARP Bulletin* 36 (Nov. 1995): 1, 13; *Congressional Record,* 104th Cong., 1st sess., vol. 141, pt. 178 (Nov. 10, 1995): 12088.

116.   *New York Times,* Nov. 11, 1955; Richard Lacayo, "Playing the Endgame," *Time* 146 (Sept. 25, 1995): 26–30; Drew, *Showdown,* 322–323.

117.   Maraniss and Weisskopf's *Tell Newt to Shut Up!* presents an excellent insiders' account of the budget negotiations with the White House, including Gingrich's problems with fellow Republicans. See also Bill Turque and Evan Thomas, "Missing the Moment," *Newsweek* 126 (Nov. 27, 1995): 26–29.

118.   Last-minute efforts at compromise are traced in Drew, *Showdown,* 334–338. The argument that Clinton would benefit from the closing down of government is discussed in Jacob Weisberg, "Counterrevolution?" *New York Magazine* 28 (Nov. 27, 1995): 40–41; and Stephen Budiansky, "Political Theater of the Absurd," *U.S. News* 119 (Nov. 27, 1995): 14–15.

119.   Drew, *Showdown,* 342–343; "Panetta's Moment," *New Republic* 213 (Nov. 6, 1995): 13–14; *New York Times,* Dec. 2, 7, 1995.

120.   *New York Times,* Dec. 7, 1995.

121.   The Medicare Report was released on June 5, 1996. See *New York Times,* June 6, 1996. On the Republican rewrite, see *Newport News (Va.) Daily Press,* Dec. 12, 1995. For efforts to reach a compromise, see *New York Times,* Dec. 8–15, 1995.

122.   "Newt's Fingers Get Caught in the Shutdown," *Business Week,* Nov. 27, 1995, 39. See also David Broder's column, "Gingrich's Fast Start Has Slowed Down Considerably," *Newport News (Va.) Daily Press,* Apr. 22, 1996; Maraniss and Weisskopf, *Tell Newt to Shut Up,* 188ff.

123.   For the adverse impact on Dole's presidential campaign in Florida, a state with large numbers of Medicare retirees, and on the Republican Party's political fortunes, see "Running 'Mediscared' in Florida," *Business Week,* Dec. 4, 1995; *New York Times,* Dec. 14, 17, 1995.

124.   For details of the *Health Insurance Portability and Accountability Act of 1996,* see PL 104–191, Aug. 21, 1996.

# CHAPTER 11. UNFINISHED BUSINESS

1. Congress passed the CHIP program in 1997 and allotted $4.2 billion to provide health insurance to children in low-income families. As of September 24, 2000, 45 percent of the funds ($1.9 billion) had remained unspent by forty states, with California and Texas (having 29 percent of the nation's 11 million uninsured children) accounting for half the unspent funds. Virginia, as late as February 2002, had forfeited nearly $56 million in federal matching funds. Under the law, the unspent allotment could be shifted to the ten states that did spend their money, beginning October 1, 2000. The states gave various bureaucratic justifications for not having spent their allotments, but as a spokesperson for the Children's Defense Fund declared after three years of the program's existence, "Get off the dime. Spend this money on what it's intended for." *New York Times*, Sept. 24, 2000; *Newport News (Va.) Daily Press*, Feb. 25, 2002. A Kaiser Family Foundation survey disclosed that 75 percent of those polled were unfamiliar with the CHIP program; 61 percent indicated they would be willing to enroll their children if they knew more about it. *National Survey on the Uninsured: April 2000* (Menlo Park, Calif., 2000), Fact Sheet and Charts 20 and 21.

2. *New York Times*, Aug. 9, 1998.

3. This was the conclusion of Robert Blendon, an expert on public opinion and health at Harvard. *New York Times*, Oct. 10, 1999.

4. *National Survey on the Uninsured*, Fact Sheet.

5. For physician criticism of managed care, see the AMA's report in the *Newport News (Va.) Daily Press*, June 11, 2000; and the report of Families USA in *New York Times*, June 20, 2000.

6. The Breaux commission's deliberations may be followed in Janet Firshein, "Medicare Panel Weighs Higher Eligibility," *AARP Bulletin*, Feb. 1999, 6, 17; Firshein, "Panel Grapples with New Medicare Idea," ibid., Mar. 1999, 40; *New York Times*, Mar. 17, 1999; *Newport News (Va.) Daily Press*, Mar. 28, 1999.

7. *New York Times*, Sept. 27, 1998; Jan. 24, 31, 1999; Mar. 15, 1999; *Newport News (Va.) Daily Press*, Sept. 10, 1998; Dec. 26, 1998.

8. *New York Times*, Feb. 21, 1999.

9. Ibid., Jan. 31, 1999; Feb. 21, 1999.

10. *Newport News (Va.) Daily Press*, Mar. 10, 1999.

11. The commission's proposal was modeled after the Federal Employees Health Benefits Program. This proposal instituted a "defined contribution" plan, with the federal government's contribution being 88 percent of the cost and the seniors' share totaling 12 percent, depending on ability to pay. Medicare would have been restructured, using the funds to create a choice of health plans for seniors. The 14 million seniors without drug benefits were to choose among the plans to find the right prescription drug benefit for them. The other 25 million Medicare recipients already had prescription drug benefits from Medicaid, retirement benefits provided by former employers, or privately purchased Medigap policies covering prescription drugs. *Newport News (Va.) Daily Press*, Sept. 24, 2000.

12. Clinton's concerns about prescription drug coverage were confirmed nearly a year later, when Medicare HMOs in the Philadelphia area cut all brand-name coverage from their zero-premium Medicare plans (though they continued to offer unlimited coverage for generic drugs). But his concerns also have led to confusion over what, in fact, are two distinct issues: one is the price of prescription drugs; the other is the long-term financial problems of Medicare. It is true that 14 million of the 29 million Medicare recipients in 2000 were without prescription drug coverage, which was a serious problem, but the larger issue was the perceived problem that pharmaceuticals were too expensive for everyone and their costs needed to be controlled. This problem has produced a dizzying array of solutions, ranging from block grants to states to re-importation of drugs from other countries to price controls. My point is that a stand-alone solution for the prescription drug issue for both Medicare and non-Medicare recipients,

either by following one of the above suggestions or by making prescription drug coverage a defined Medicare benefit, only delays the inevitable reform of the Hospital Insurance Trust Fund, which is projected to become insolvent in 2010. The AARP, which favors prescription drug coverage, also cautioned lawmakers that if they link the two issues, they should proceed cautiously to "do Medicare reform right." *Newport News (Va.) Daily Press,* Jan. 23, 2000; Sept. 24, 2000; "AARP to Congress: Do Medicare Reform Right," *AARP Bulletin* 41 (Mar. 2000): 2.

13.  On Jan. 19, 2000, Clinton proposed a $110 billion package of tax credits and subsidies to help 5 million people get health insurance over the next decade. The plan included a $3,000 long-term-care tax credit, costing $28 billion over ten years, a $76 billion "family care" plan to insure 4 million parents of children who receive health care under the Medicaid and CHIP programs, and a proposal to allow workers as young as fifty-five to buy into Medicare. Earlier, the head of the GAO noted that the president's proposal could undermine the remaining fiscal discipline associated with the self-financing trust fund concept. The director of the CBO believed prescription drug coverage would blow the budget and, by raising expectations, exacerbate Medicare's problems. *Newport News (Va.) Daily Press,* Jan. 20, 2000. See also David Broder, "Clinton Has Made the Medicare Problem Worse," ibid., Mar. 15, 1999.

14.  *New York Times,* Aug. 9, 1998; Feb. 20, 1999; Oct. 4, 1999; *Newport News (Va.) Daily Press,* Sept. 10, 27, 1998. The National Conference of State Legislatures reported that health care issues made up a greater proportion of bills in state legislatures than any other topic in 1999, about 27,000 bills out of about 140,000. *New York Times,* Jan. 23, 2000.

15.  Because of the protracted litigation inherent in allowing judges and juries—laymen struggling with a welter of conflicting expert medical testimony—to decide, a patients' rights bill would have resulted not in lower but higher costs, which HMOs would ultimately have passed on to employers and consumers. *Newport News (Va.) Daily Press,* Oct. 7, 9, 1999; Nov. 9, 1999; *New York Times,* Oct. 7, 1999.

16.  *New York Times,* Aug. 9, 1998; Oct. 10, 1999; Sept. 10, 2000.

17.  Steven Findlay and Joel Miller, *Down a Dangerous Path: The Erosion of Health Insurance Coverage in the United States* (Washington, D.C., May 1999).

18.  David Broder, "Presidential Candidates Ignore Health Care Crisis," *Newport News (Va.) Daily Press,* May 12, 1999; ibid., Sept. 29, 1999; Oct. 4, 1999.

19.  Bradley proposed to allow citizens to enroll in the same health plan as members of Congress and federal employees. He would ensure universal access to affordable health coverage by fully or partially subsidizing premiums for children and adults in low-to-middle-income families, offering everyone a tax break for premiums, and expanding Medicare by adding an optional prescription drug benefit with a $500 deductible, $25 premium, and 25 percent co-pay. Bradley estimated the total annual cost at about $65 billion, to be paid from program efficiencies and from the non–Social Security budget surplus. The latter was projected to be $82 billion in 2002, rising to $92 billion in 2005. *Newport News (Va.) Daily Press,* Sept. 29, 1999.

20.  Under Gore's plan, Washington would give the states more money to provide coverage for children; a 25 percent refundable tax credit for premiums for the self-employed; and a tax credit for long-term care. Ibid., Oct. 3, 1999. For the GOP proposals, see ibid., Sept. 29, 1999.

21.  Candidates Bush and Gore unveiled more-detailed health plans in September 2000. In a philosophical divide, Bush's plan focused on choice, whereas Gore promised higher subsidies. The Bush plan, costing $158 billion, would pay up to one-quarter of the cost of prescription drugs, whether seniors chose an optional new Medicare benefit program or a private plan. Gore's plan was more generous; it proposed to spend around $253 billion over ten years to add a prescription drug benefit to Medicare. Beyond this, a comparison of the two plans is difficult because the approaches are so different and there remained many unknowns about Bush's plan. Neither plan, however, would be as generous as what working people generally received. *Newport News (Va.) Daily Press,* Sept. 26, 2000; *New York Times,* Oct. 1, 2000.

22.  *Newport News (Va.) Daily Press,* Sept. 26, 2000; "Medicare Drug Wars: Battle Shapes Up in Congress," *AARP Bulletin* 41 (May 2000): 2.

23.  In Texas, 37 percent of low-income children remain uninsured as of 2000. A federal judge ruled in August 2000 that the state had failed to abide by a 1996 court order to provide appropriate health care for more than 1.5 million children eligible for Medicaid. *New York Times,* Sept. 10, 2000.

24.  Broder, "Trade-offs Necessary to Establish Health Care Policy," ibid., July 29, 1998.

25.  The ensuing discussion draws from Robert F. Rich and William D. White, "Health Care Policy and the American States: Issues of Federalism," in *Health Policy, Federalism, and the American States,* ed. Rich and White (Washington, D.C., 1996), 13–16, 25–27; and Thomas J. Anton, "New Federalism and Intergovernmental Fiscal Relationships: The Implications for Health Policy," *Journal of Health Policy, Politics and Law* 22 (June 1997): 691–720; Michael S. Sparer, "Leading the Health Policy Orchestra: The Need for an Intergovernmental Partnership," ibid., 28 (Apr.–June 2003): 246–248; and Jacob S. Hacker and Theda Skocpol, "The New Politics of U.S. Health Policy," ibid., 22 (Apr. 1997): 323–326.

26.  *Newport News (Va.) Daily Press,* Dec. 10, 2002.

27.  Ibid., Jan. 24, 2003; Feb. 11, 2003; Jack Hadley and John Holahan, "Covering the Uninsured, How Much Would It Cost?" *Health Affairs* 22 (June 4, 2003), available at http://healthaffairs.org/WebExclusives/Hadley_Web_Excl_060403.htm.

28.  Health Affairs Press Room, "New Study: United States Spends Substantially More on Health Care Than Any Other Country; Yet Does Not Provide Services," http://www.healthaffairs.org/press/may-june0301.htm.

29.  *Newport News (Va.) Daily Press,* Jan. 20, 2003; Feb 11, 2003; "Surging Health Costs Fuel Workers Unrest," *AARP Bulletin* 44 (Feb. 2003): 2.

30.  *Williamsburg Virginia Gazette,* Mar. 1, 2003.

31.  *New York Times,* Jan. 5, 2003; Mar. 2, 2003; Trudy Lieberman, "Bruised and Broken: U.S. Health System," *AARP Bulletin* 44 (Mar. 2003): 3–4.

32.  Gail Wilensky, "Thinking outside the Box: A Conversation with John Breaux," *Health Affairs* 22 (Mar./Apr. 2003): 15; Fred Brock, "Why a Centrist (No Fooling) Wants Universal Insurance," *New York Times,* Jan. 5, 2003.

33.  Ibid., Feb. 29, 2003; Nov. 23, 2003.

34.  Ibid., Mar. 2, 2003; *Newport News (Va.) Daily Press,* Jan. 24, 2003.

35.  *Newport News (Va.) Daily Press,* Jan. 18, Feb.10, 2003.

36.  Over the previous five years, claimants had prevailed in 186,300 cases, a success rate of 53 percent. *New York Times,* Mar. 16, 2003.

37.  Steven D. Gold, "Health Care and the Fiscal Crisis of the States," in *Health Policy, Federalism, and the American States,* ed. Rich and White, 118–120; Rich and White, "The American States, Federalism, and the Future of Health Care Policy," in ibid., 298.

38.  Together, the states and the federal government spent nearly $260 billion in 2002 on Medicaid, of which one-fifth was spent by states. The program's costs had risen 13 percent over the year. In Virginia in 2000 combined federal and state spending on Medicaid was $2.8 billion; in 2002, Medicaid absorbed $3.7 billion. *Newport News (Va.) Daily Press,* Feb. 24, 2003; Aug. 12, 2003; *New York Times,* Mar. 23, 2003; May 25, 2003.

39.  *Newport News (Va.) Daily Press,* Mar. 4, 5, 16, 2003.

40.  The Senate Finance Committee was scheduled in mid-June to begin voting on a Medicare plan that had broad bipartisan support and would make the most profound changes in the program's thirty-eight-year history. The $400 billion bill sought to foster a larger role for private health plans in caring for the elderly by relying on preferred-provider networks, which tend to be more popular than HMOs. The drug coverage envisioned in the plan would represent the largest expansion of Medicare benefits in the program's history by providing the first large-scale federal subsidy for elderly patients' prescription

drugs. The Senate Health, Education, and Labor Committee, at the same time, passed unanimously (and over the opposition of the Pharmaceutical Research and Manufacturers of America) a strengthening of a 1984 law intended to get generic drugs to market more quickly to save consumers billions of dollars. Cf. Patricia Barry, "Bush Drug Proposal Gets Cool Reception," *AARP Bulletin* 44 (Apr. 2003): 6–7; *New York Times,* Mar. 2, 2003; Nov. 23, 2003; *Newport News (Va.) Daily Press,* June 12, 2003.

41. *New York Times,* June 15, 2003.

42. *Newport News (Va.) Daily Press,* June 27, 29, 2003.

43. In fact, both the House and Senate bills exceeded President Bush's spending limits, which was likely to complicate efforts to reach a compromise. The CBO calculated the Senate-passed measure at $462 billion over ten years; the cost of the House-passed bill was pegged at $408 billion. Patricia Barry, "Stage Set for Final Battle over Drug Benefit in Medicare," *AARP Bulletin* 144 (July/Aug. 2003): 3; *Newport News (Va.) Daily Press,* July 1, 23, 2003.

44. Barry, "Stage Set for Final Battle over Drug Benefit in Medicare." See also *Newport News (Va.) Daily Press,* July 11, 2003.

45. *Newport News (Va.) Daily Press,* Oct. 12, 16, 31, 2003.

46. Ibid., Nov. 18, 2003.

47. Ibid., Oct. 29, Nov. 4, 13, 14, 16, 2003.

48. Ibid., Nov. 13, 17, 18, 2003.

49. *New York Times,* Nov. 22, 2003.

50. Ibid., Dec. 9, 2003; *USA Today,* Nov. 23, 2003; *Newport News (Va.) Daily Press,* Dec. 9, 2003.

51. *USA Today,* Nov. 25, 2003; *New York Times,* Dec. 7, 9, 2003; *Newport News (Va.) Daily Press,* Dec. 1, 2003.

52. Ibid.; see also the critiques of the bill by John Tierney and David Broder in *New York Times,* Nov. 30, 2003; Dec. 1, 2003, and by Rhode Island's Democratic Senator Jack Reed, a member of the Health, Education and Labor Committee, reprinted in the *Newport News (Va.) Daily Press,* Dec. 1, 2003.

53. *New York Times,* Mar. 13, 14, 21, 2004; *Newport News (Va.) Daily Press,* Jan. 30, 2004; Mar. 18, 19, 2004.

54. *Newport News (Va.) Daily Press,* May 26, 2004; June 25, 2004; July 1, 2004.

55. Ibid., June 22, 2004.

56. Ibid., Mar. 13, 2004; May 20, 26, 2004; June 22, 2004; *New York Times,* Mar. 14, 2004.

57. *Newport News (Va.) Daily Press,* May 14, 2004.

58. Ibid., Feb. 2, 2005.

59. Ibid., Feb. 2, 9, 10, 2005.

60. James A. Morone and Gary S. Belkin, eds., "Introduction," *The Politics of Health Care Reform* (Durham, N. C., 1994), 1–2; Jacob S. Hacker, "Health Care Reform: A Century of Defeat," *Harvard Health Policy Review* 1 (Fall 2000): 1–2.

61. Marie Gottschalk, *The Shadow Welfare State* (Ithaca, N.Y., 2000), 1.

62. Flint J. Wainess, "The Ways and Means of National Health Care Reform, 1974 and Beyond," *Journal of Health Policy, Politics and Law* 24 (Apr. 1999): 305–333.

63. Ibid.

64. Theodore R. Marmor et al., "National Health Reform: Where Do We Go from Here?" in *Health Policy, Federalism, and the American States,* ed. Rich and White, 278–281; John Watts, "It's the Institutions, Stupid! Why Comprehensive National Health Insurance Always Fails in America," *Journal of Health Policy, Politics and Law* 20 (Summer 1995): 330–372; Jill Quadagno, "One Nation: Uninsured" (forthcoming).

65. Jennifer Koella, "The Impact of Interest Group and News Media Framing on Public Opinion: The Rise and Fall of the Clinton Health Care Plan" (diss., University of Tennessee, 2001), 225–235.

66.  Ibid., 237, 326; Joseph White, "The Horses and the Jumps: Comments on the Health Care Reform Steeplechase," *Journal of Health Policy, Politics and Law* 20 (Summer 1995): 378; Jacob Hacker and Theda Skocpol, "The New Politics of U.S. Health Policy," ibid., 22 (Apr. 1997): 315–338.

67.  Paul Starr, "The Middle Class and National Health Reform," *American Prospect* 6 (Summer 1991): 7–12.

68.  Hacker and Skocpol, "The New Politics of U.S. Health Policy," 336–338; Hillary R. Clinton, "Now Can We Talk about Health Care?" *New York Times Magazine* (Apr. 18, 2004): 26–31, 54; *Newport News (Va.) Daily Press*, July 16, 2004.

69.  *New York Times*, Aug. 17, 2003; *Newport News (Va.) Daily Press*, Aug. 14, 2003. See also Neal R. Peirce, "Neither Health Plan Is the Right Prescription," ibid., Oct. 19, 2004.

# BIBLIOGRAPHICAL
# ESSAY

Health security affects a broad spectrum of interests that range from the consumer of health care to the physician and from health industry providers to politicians. Because so many entrenched interests are involved, it is often difficult to find objectivity when reading or discussing the subject. Moreover, the literature of the subject is so extensive that it would be foolhardy—and probably gratuitous—to attempt to list every letter and report, every document, every article, and every monograph from which I have drawn raw evidence, valuable leads, and interpretative ideas or organizing principles. The endnote citations attest to the specific kinds of materials I used. Here, I intend to discuss some of the more significant materials, primary and secondary, that were most useful to me and presumably would be most helpful to the serious reader.

## PERSONAL PAPERS

The Franklin D. Roosevelt Library, Hyde Park, New York, contains the papers of the thirty-second president of the United States. Although Roosevelt's private views on public policy and political issues often were guarded, the President's Personal File (PPF) and the Office File (OF) contain memoranda and correspondence that are useful for gleaning insights into the thinking of the president and his associates about social security and health issues. They should be supplemented with the Papers of Senator Robert F. Wagner, deposited in the Georgetown University Library, Washington, D.C. Wagner was a key participant in drafting national health insurance bills, and his papers illuminate the personalities, organizations, and politics of the New Deal and World War II years.

The Carl Albert Center, located at the University of Oklahoma, is a relatively unmined source of material on twentieth-century U.S. history. The Papers of Carl Albert, particularly the Legislative Files, the Andrew J. Biemiller Collection, the Page H. Belcher Papers, the Elmer Thomas Papers, the Toby Morris Collection, the Preston Peden Papers, and the Papers of George Howard Wilson are valuable for reconstructing the history of national health insurance from the immediate post–World War II period to the adoption of Medicare in the 1960s. They provide a wealth of information, including copies of bills and pamphlets, covering popular attitudes toward national health insurance, legislative efforts to bring it about, and conservative opposition, particularly by the AMA and Oklahoma's county medical societies. They should be read in conjunction with the Papers of Helen Gahagan Douglas, a congressional representative from California and a staunch New Dealer, which cover in rich detail the liberal health initiatives of the latter 1940s and early 1950s. The Papers of Oklahoma Democratic Senator Robert Kerr, coauthor of the Kerr-Mills health program, also shed light on the politics of health insurance prior to Medicare. The Fred R. Harris Papers contain somewhat less information on health insurance.

The Lyndon B. Johnson Papers, at the Johnson Presidential Library on the campus of the University of Texas at Austin, are indispensable for understanding both the political and legislative history of Medicare in 1965 and the problems of implementing the program immediately thereafter. Johnson's vice presidential papers, notably the Subject File, contain some information on health care reform, but it is the White House Central File (WHCF) that gives us an almost day-by-day picture of the evolution of the Medicare program in the context of the Great Society. The files of Johnson's legislative aides (Aides Files) Mike Manatos, Henry Hall Wilson, Fred Panzer, Richard Goodwin, Bill Moyers, Joseph Califano, and Jeremy Cater illuminate the delicate negotiations and compromises that had to be made with Wilbur Mills and other interested parties in order to enact Medicare and the early difficulties and successes in its implementation. These papers should be used in conjunction with the Department of Health, Education and Welfare, Social Security Administration's "History of the Social Security Administration during the Johnson Administration, 1963–1968," one of the several administrative histories summarizing the administration's major policies and actions to be found in the Johnson collection. The Papers of Wilbur J. Cohen, on deposit in the Johnson Library, also are important to understanding the transition from the Kerr-Mills program to Medicare.

The presidential and congressional papers should be supplemented with the oral history transcripts of President Truman's FSA administrator, Oscar R. Ewing, deposited in the Harry S. Truman Presidential Library and the Columbia University Oral History Collection. They provide useful insights into Truman's advocacy of national health insurance and the political obstacles it encountered.

## ARCHIVAL RECORDS

The official records of the National Health Survey, 1935–1936, are located in the National Archives in Washington, D.C., under the classification of Record Group 443, National Institutes of Health. They contain a wealth of raw data, including surveys, memoranda, and news clippings, documenting the state of the nation's health in the Great Depression. The survey findings provided important empirical evidence about the health status of the American people and became the basis for subsequent arguments of New Deal liberals for national health insurance.

Building upon the health inventory data are the Records of the Inter-Departmental Committee to Coordinate Health and Human Welfare Activities (IDC Records), deposited in the Franklin D. Roosevelt Library. The committee, whose chair was Treasury Department official Josephine Roche, was one of the earliest executive bodies to organize a national health conference (based on the findings of the 1935–1936 inventory) and to draft, in 1938, a national health plan. As such, it further helps us to comprehend the thinking and activities of both administration officials and New Deal liberals regarding the multifaceted problem of health care in the prewar period.

The Records of the Nixon Presidential Materials Project (NPMP), located in the National Archives II, in College Park, Maryland, are vital to understanding the attitudes and policies of the Nixon administration on health care, insurance, and HMOs. Particularly useful are the Transitional Task Force's 1969 Report on Health, the White House Central File's Confidential Subject Files, and the Staff Files of Egil Krogh.

The same archival location holds the records of President Clinton's health task force, more formally, the Records of the Health Care Interdepartmental Working Group. They comprise an exhaustive number of reports, memoranda, and printed materials documenting the state of the nation's health coverage as of the early 1990s. In some respects, however, the collection is disappointing. Besides finding the material in a haphazard state, the researcher is left with the impression that the most valuable information for reconstructing the task force's interaction with the White House and other political figures had been culled prior to the records' being deposited in the Archives in accordance with a court order. One searches the records in vain for the kind of confidential correspondence between the head of the task force, Hillary Rodham Clinton, the White House health care policy chief, Ira Magaziner, cabinet heads, congressional representatives, and the president that one would expect to find in order to understand the task force's thinking. Fortunately, staff reports and the working and occasional papers of individuals such as Kenneth Thorpe, Paul Starr, and Dr. Paul Ellwood make it possible to reconstruct the policy—if not the political—process.

## OTHER PUBLISHED SOURCES

The number of government publications touching upon all aspects of social and health security, including hospital construction and health care, insurance issues, Medicare and Medicaid, prescription drug coverage, managed care, and health legislation, churned out by the Government Printing Office is extensive. These take the form of congressional hearings, agency annual reports, special studies, and census data.

The starting point for any analysis of national health security is the innumerable hearings, committee prints, and reports of the House and Senate, particularly the Ways and Means Committee of the House, where all financial matters had to originate. A complete listing of the hearings relevant to this study may be found in the notes, but among the most significant on the House side of the aisle were U.S. House, Committee on Ways and Means, *Health Services for the Aged under the Social Security System, Hearings... on H.R. 4222*, 87th Cong., 1st sess., July 24–Aug. 4, 1961; U.S. House, Committee on Ways and Means, *Medical Care for the Aged, Hearings... on H.R. 3920*, 88th Cong., 1st and 2d sess., Nov. 18, 1963–Jan. 24, 1964; U.S. House, Committee on Ways and Means, *Medicare, Hearings on Controlling Costs and Improving Care*, 104th Cong., 1st sess., Feb. 6, 7, 10, 1995; U.S. House, Committee on Ways and Means, *Medicare Preservation Act of 1995*, 104th Cong., 1st sess., H. Rep. 104–276, pt. 2, Oct. 16, 1995.

In the Senate, various committees investigated health issues. Interest in European health systems dates to the late nineteenth century, when the upper chamber published John Graham Brooks's "Compulsory Insurance in Germany," *Fourth Special Report of the Commissioner of Labor*, 52d Cong., 2d sess., S. Exec. Doc. 66 (1893). Other Senate hearings relevant to this study include: U.S. Senate, Subcommittee on Problems of the Aged and Aging, *The Aged and Aging in the United State: A National Problem, Rept.... purs. to S. Res. 65*, 86th Cong., 2d sess. (Jan. 29, 1960), 1961; U.S. Senate, Committee on Finance, *Social Security, Hearings... on H.R. 6675*, 89th Cong., 1st sess., 1965; U.S. Sen., Select Committee on Aging, Subcommittee on Health of the Elderly, *Economic Aspects of Aging*, 91st Cong., 1st sess., 1969–1971; U.S. Senate, Committee on Labor and Public Welfare, *National Health Insurance, Hearings on... S. 4323*, 91st Cong., 1st sess., 1970. U.S. Senate, Committee on Commerce, *Future of the Medicare Program, Hearings...*, 104th Cong., 1st and 2d sess. (June 28, 1995; July 12, 18, 1995; Aug. 3, 1995), 1996.

Members of both houses also acted in concert on health matters. The Joint Economic Committee of Congress, for example, undertook specialized studies such as "Trends in the Supply and Demand of Medical Care," by Markley Roberts, Materials Prepared in Connection with Study of Employment, Growth and Price Levels, 86th Cong., 1st sess., Study Paper no. 5 (Nov. 10, 1959). In 1989, the 101st Congress, 2d session, when it passed *An Act to Repeal Medicare Provisions in the Medicare Catastrophic Coverage Act of 1988*, overturned a Reagan administration health bill.

Besides Congress, various governmental bodies, agencies, and commissions issued reports that have furthered our understanding of the different parameters of the health security issue. The Truman administration put national health security at the forefront of the nation's agenda in 1945 and continued to focus on it with the *Annual Report of the Federal Security Agency, 1951: Social Security Administration* (1952), even though by then the likelihood of national health insurance being enacted was remote. Nonetheless, the administration kept interest in the issue alive after Truman left office with the report, *Building America's Health: Report to the President by the President's Commission on Health Needs of the Nation* (1953). "The President's Health Security Plan," the complete text of the draft proposal on health care reform that emerged from President Clinton's presidential task force, and the White House Domestic Policy Council's final report, "Health Security: The President's Report to the American People" (October 27, 1993), were subsequently collected and published by the *New York Times* as a book: White House Domestic Policy Council, *The President: Health Security Plan* (New York, 1993). First Lady Hillary Rodham Clinton's foreword is an attempt to explain the complex issues and difficult choices behind the reform effort.

But it is the Social Security Administration that has, since its inception, regularly addressed the issue of health security in numerous published studies. One early analysis of the state of the social safety net that addressed health issues was the Social Security Board's Publication no. 20: *Social Security in America* (1937). Since then, the board has examined health issues from demographical, financial, and other perspectives. Medicare has been among the most intensively studied. The history of the program is carefully traced in Peter A. Corning's *The Evolution of Medicare* (1969) and published as DHEW Research Report no. 29 for the Social Security Administration's Office of Research and Statistics. In 1965, the Advisory Council on Social Security gave a boost to federally underwritten health insurance for the elderly in its report, *The State of the Social Security Program and Recommendations for Its Improvement: Report of the Advisory Council on Social Security, 1965* (Washington, D.C., 1965). The SSA's journal frequently published articles relating to specific aspects of Medicare that were useful for this study. These included: Howard West, "Five Years of Medicare—A Statistical Review," *Social Security Bulletin* 34 (Dec. 1971); and Marian Gornick, "Ten Years of Medicare: Impact on the Covered," *Social Security Bulletin* 39 (June 1976).

The Department of Health, Education and Welfare also lent its support to health coverage for Social Security recipients in 1961, when it conducted a White House Conference on Aging. The conference's findings and policy recommendations were published in 1961 as *White House Conference on Aging, 1961: Background Paper on Health and Medical Care* and *White House Conference on Aging, 1961: Policy Statements and Recommendations, February, 1961*. The Congressional Budget Office's interest in health issues derives from their impact on the budget. Whenever a major proposal is made, the CBO generally estimates the cost to the taxpayer in reports such as *Estimates of Health Care Proposals from the 102d Congress* (July 1993).

Congressional and agency documents should be used in concert with the *Public Papers of the Presidents of the United States*. The messages and statements articulate the aspirations of each president from Roosevelt to Clinton for the health care of the American people and the politics that enveloped those aspirations. The published presidential papers should be supplemented with the *Congressional Record*, an invaluable source for tracing the thoughts, words, and actions of legislators on each bill pertaining to health care. Its *Appendix* volumes often include reprints of news clippings and constituent petitions useful for shedding light on constituent thinking.

Besides governmental agencies, private organizations also have issued reports on matters of health security. Often their documents reveal more about their special-interest pleading than about the merits of the proposals being considered. But they are indicative of the period and circumstances in which they are written. For example, the Committee on the Costs of Medical Care's *Medical Care for the American People. The Final Report of the Committee on the Costs of Medical Care, Adopted October 31, 1932*, published by the University of Chicago Press in 1932, and its summary volume, *The Costs of Medical Care* (1933), edited by I. S. Falk, C. Rufus Rorem, and Martha D. Ring, were instrumental in focusing public attention on the inadequacies of the nation's health care and the need for reform in the late 1920s and early years of the Great Depression. By contrast, the AMA's pamphlet *Federalized Health Care for the Aged? A Critical Symposium* (1963) criticized federally underwritten health coverage for Social Security beneficiaries, and the May 1999 report by Steven Findlay and Joel Miller, *Down a Dangerous Path: The Erosion of Health Insurance Coverage in the United States*, for the National Coalition on Health Care, warned of the need to design solutions for the 43.4 million Americans who remained uninsured even in time of economic prosperity.

Recent insider accounts commenting on the Clinton health plan provide little new information. Hilary Rodham Clinton's *Living History* (New York, 2003) is a re-telling of the administration's effort to reform health care, but it reveals almost nothing about the inner workings of the presidential task force that she headed. *My Life* (New York, 2004), Bill Clinton's encyclopedic memoir, provides a disjointed and familiar defense of his efforts to reform the health care delivery system. His contention that the Republicans, particularly Senator Dole, were not serious about reform and transformed his proposed legislation into a partisan political issue may be accurate, but he minimizes his administration's missteps that made passage of the legislation virtually impossible. But again, much of his account is familiar. Sidney Blumenthal, a White House aide and author of *The Clinton Wars* (New York, 2003), links the collapse of the president's health care initiative to his larger failure to reverse an antigovernment sentiment fueled by the Republicans and the political Right, which since the 1960s had manipulated the media and the legal system and had obstructed the progressive political tradition.

Newspapers, of course, also provided extensive coverage of health issues and the political circumstances in which they were discussed. For the purpose of illustrating particular points, I found the following nationally circulated newspapers useful: the *New York Times*, the *Washington Post*, the *Wall Street Journal*, and the *New York Post*. A local newspaper, the *Daily Press* of Newport News, Virginia, provided good coverage of contemporary health legislation, including Medicare, insurance, and the Clinton administration's ill-fated health care initiative. These papers were supplemented with news clippings in relevant manuscript and archival collections.

## SECONDARY WORKS

The secondary literature on the politics of health security has grown exponentially over the course of time as a consequence of commercial and popular interest and the ubiquitous Internet. Much of the writing is dry, technical, or polemical, but among the more useful surveys of the subject in its multifaceted complexity are William Shonick's encyclopedic *Government and Health Services* (New York, 1995) and Jennie Jacobs Kronenfeld's *The Changing Federal Role in U.S. Health Care Policy* (Westport, Conn., 1997). Equally comprehensive is Princeton sociologist and Clinton presidential task force adviser Paul Starr's *The Social Transformation of American Medicine* (New York, 1982). Jill Quadagno brings valuable insights into why the United States has no national health insurance from the perspective of a historical sociologist in her forthcoming publication, "One Nation: Uninsured." Lawrence R. Jacobs, *The Health of Nations: Public Opinion and the Making of American and British Health Policy* (Ithaca, N.Y., 1993) provides a comparative context for understanding American thinking about health policy, although American health policy analysts and the public generally embarked upon a course, as Antonia Maioni notes in *Parting at the Crossroads: The Emergence of Health Insurance in the United States and Canada* (Princeton, N.J., 1998), that differed from European or Canadian models. These two works should be supplemented with the groundbreaking work of Carolyn Hughes Tuohy, *Accidental Logics: The Dynamics of Change in the Health Care Arena in the United States, Britain and Canada* (New York, 1999), which provides a rigorous conceptual and historical framework to explain why the three nations differ in their health policies. Oliver Garceau's *The Political Life of the American Medical Association* (Cambridge, Mass., 1941), although dated, offers useful insights into one of the key players in the health care industry. *The Politics of Social Policy in the United States* (Princeton, N.J., 1988), edited by Margaret Weir et al. is useful for thinking about health security in the larger context of social policy.

The decades from the 1890s through the 1920s were the formative years of American liberalism and the beginning of public interest in health security. Useful introductions to the economic and political events of this period are *Democracy in Desperation: The Depression of 1893* (Westport, Conn., 1998) by Douglas W. Steeples and David O. Whitten, and two older, but still authoritative, works on early-twentieth-century reform: George E. Mowry's *The Era of Theodore Roosevelt* (New York, 1958), and Arthur S. Link's *Woodrow Wilson and the Progressive Era* (New York, 1954). Beatrix Hoffman's *The Wages of Sickness* (Chapel Hill, N.C., 2001) is the definitive study of the politics of health insurance in the Progressive era.

Early interest in health security may be traced to the latter part of the nineteenth century with the publication of William F. Willoughby's *Workingmen's Insurance* (New York, 1898). Willoughby documents Americans' interest in the European movement for social security. In the early 1920s, Abraham Epstein draws the connection between the elderly and access to quality health care in *Facing Old Age* (New York, 1922). John Duffy's *The Sanitarians: A History of American Public Health* (Urbana, Ill., 1990) links health security to the broader public health movement, whereas James T. Patterson ties it to the fight against poverty in *America's Struggle against Poverty, 1900–1980* (Cambridge, Mass., 1981). The ambivalence of early-twentieth-century physicians toward universal health coverage is examined in *Almost Persuaded: American Physicians and Compulsory Health Insurance, 1912–1920* (Baltimore, 1978) by Ronald L. Numbers. Clarke C. Chambers's *Seedtime of Reform: American Social Service and Social Action* (Minneapolis, 1963) documents the continuing fight for social reform, including health security, at the state and local levels in the generally inhospitable atmosphere of the 1920s.

The literature on the Great Depression and the New Deal is extensive, but insight into the politics of the period may be gained from David Plotke's *Building a Democratic Political Order* (Cambridge, UK, 1996), which traces the course of American liberalism in the 1930s and 1940s; William E. Leuchtenburg's authoritative *Franklin D. Roosevelt and the New Deal* (New York, 1963); David M. Kennedy's sweeping *Freedom from Fear: The American People in Depression and War, 1929–1945* (New York, 1999); Frank Freidel's *Franklin D. Roosevelt: Launching the New Deal* (Boston, 1973); Arthur M. Schlesinger, Jr.'s *The Politics of Upheaval* (Boston, 1960); and *Voices of Protest: Huey Long, Father Coughlin, and the Great Depression* (New York, 1982), by Alan Brinkley. Jaap Kooijman's essay "Just Forget about It: FDR's Ambivalence towards National Health Insurance," in *The Roosevelt Years*, edited by Robert A. Garson and Stuart S. Kidd (Edinburgh, UK, 1999), examines Roosevelt's ambivalent attitude.

The construction of the social safety net was the work of many individuals, among whom one of the most influential was Arthur J. Altmeyer. His documentation of *The Formative Years of Social Security* (Madison, Wisc., 1968) is the standard account. I. S. Falk's *Security against Sickness* (Garden City, N.Y., 1936) is a landmark comparative study of health insurance in the United States and Europe, and it provided a rationale for broadening Social Security legislation to include national health insurance. Falk, like Altmeyer, remained a key player in the movement to make health security an integral part of the social safety net from the 1930s through the postwar period. Another key figure in the prewar movement for health security was New York's Senator Robert F. Wagner, whose activities are chronicled in J. Joseph Huthmacher's fine biography, *Senator Robert F. Wagner and the Rise of Urban Liberalism* (New York, 1968). For a longitudinal analysis of the public's perception of Social Security, see Michael E. Schiltz's *Public Attitudes toward Social Security, 1935–1965* (Washington, D.C., 1970). Daniel S. Hirshfield's *The Lost Reform* (Cambridge, Mass., 1970) looks at the revival of the campaign for compulsory health insurance in the 1930s and carries the story to 1943 with the defeat of the Murray-Wagner-Dingell bill. Michael R. Gray's *New Deal Medicine* (Baltimore, 1999) is a fine case study of the rural health programs of the Farm Security Administration.

The political atmosphere of the war years discouraged many American liberals, prompting them to reconsider their own commitment to an activist managerial state. Two books that played major roles in influencing popular and liberal thinking about the presence of government in virtually every area of American life are James Burnham's *The Managerial Revolution* (New York, 1941) and Friedrich A. Hayek's *The Road to Serfdom* (Chicago, 1944). They should be read in conjunction with Bartholomew H. Sparrow's *From the Outside In* (Princeton, N.J., 1996), which analyzes the buildup of the State in World War II; Nelson Lichtenstein's *Labor's War at Home* (Cambridge, UK, 1982), a study of the CIO; Lizabeth Cohen's *A Consumers' Republic* (New York, 2003), which links health care to the politics of mass consumption in the postwar period; and Meg Jacobs's article, "How About Some Meat?" *Journal of American History* 84 (Dec. 1997), which ties together the Office of Price Administration (OPA), consumption politics, and state building. Jennifer Klein's *For All These Rights* (Princeton, N.J., 2003) is magisterial in its scope, offering an incisive analysis of the roles of business and labor in shaping America's public-private welfare state. Alan Brinkley's *The End of Reform: New Deal Liberalism in Recession and War* (New York, 1996) brilliantly details how the liberalism of the early New Deal gave way to a postwar liberalism less hostile to corporate capitalism and more solicitous of individual rights, a transformation that had significant implications for postwar health policy debates.

William H. Chafe's *The Unfinished Journey: America since World War II* (New York, 1986) is a good overview of the postwar period, but it should be supplemented with the articles by Meg Jacobs and Julian E. Zelizer in Jacobs et al., *The Democratic Experiment* (Princeton, N.J., 2003), which discuss the struggles that have taken place over the roles of the federal government and representative democracy in forming the national polity. The two volumes of Truman's *Memoirs* (Garden City, N.Y., 1955–1956) set forth the postwar liberal agenda, and *Congressional Quarterly's* August 31, 1965, issue examines "Politics in America—1945–1964: The Politics and Issues of the Postwar Years." Eisenhower's dynamic conservatism is documented in Fred I. Greenstein's revisionist study, *The Hidden-Hand Presidency: Eisenhower as Leader* (New York, 1982).

Perhaps the best study of Truman's difficulties with Congress over health security legislation is Monte M. Poen's *Harry S. Truman versus the Medical Lobby* (Columbia, Mo., 1979). Although Truman was defeated on national health insurance, the author concludes that he planted the seed of what would become Medicare in 1965. Poen's study should be read in tandem with the series of articles in the *New Yorker* magazine on Medicare's historical antecedents in the 1950s and 1960s by Richard Harris, which were published subsequently as *A Sacred Trust* (New York, 1966), and Peter A. Corning's *The Evolution of Medicare*, cited above. Because the use of federal tax moneys was central to both the Kerr-Mills and the Medicare programs, John F. Manley's *The Politics of Finance: The House Committee on Ways and Means* (Boston, 1970) helps establish the central role of its chair, Wilbur Mills. Oklahoma Democratic Senator Robert S. Kerr's hostility to the New Deal welfare state and his coauthorship of the Kerr-Mills program are discussed in Anne H. Morgan's biography, *Robert S. Kerr: The Senate Years* (Norman, Okla. 1977). Senator Clinton P. Anderson, coauthor of the King-Anderson national health insurance bill, tells his story in *Outsider in the Senate: Senator Clinton Anderson's Memoirs* (New York, 1970). The pivotal role of Wilbur J. Cohen in bridging the gap between the Kerr-Mills program and Medicare is authoritatively examined in Edward D. Berkowitz's *Mr. Social Security: The Life of Wilbur J. Cohen* (Lawrence, Kans., 1995). The author draws extensively upon Cohen's papers, oral interviews, and archival records to document his contention that Cohen was a major legislative architect of the welfare state. It should be supplemented with the same author's *Robert Ball and the Politics of Social Security* (Madison, Wisc., 2003). Julian E. Zelizer's *Taxing America* (Cambridge, UK, 1998) is definitive on the influence of Wilbur Mills in shaping Medicare.

James L. Sundquist's *Politics and Policy: The Eisenhower, Kennedy and Johnson Years* (Washington, D.C., 1968) bridges the major policy issues linking the 1950s with the turbulent decade of the 1960s. A scholarly, comprehensive introduction to the decade is Allen J. Matusow's *The Unraveling of America: A History of Liberalism in the 1960s* (New York, 1984), which examines liberalism with a critical eye. Washington politics is commented on by longtime Kennedy adviser Lawrence F. O'Brien in *No Final Victories: A Life in Politics—from John F. Kennedy to Watergate* (New York, 1974). *Lyndon B. Johnson: The Exercise of Power* (New York, 1966) by Rowland Evans and Robert Novak is useful for understanding Johnson's ability to maneuver legislation, such as Medicare, through a sometimes-reluctant Congress. The Great Society is the subject of numerous studies; among the most helpful for understanding it are John A. Andrew III's *Lyndon Johnson and the Great Society* (Chicago, 1998), Bruce J. Schulman's *Lyndon Johnson and American Liberalism* (New York, 1995), and Doris Kearns Goodwin's award-winning *Lyndon Johnson and the American Dream* (New York, 1976).

Health security in the 1960s is surveyed in Theodore R. Marmor's essay written with James Monroe, "The Health Programs of the Kennedy-Johnson Years: An Overview," in *Toward New Human Rights: The*

*Social Policies of the Kennedy and Johnson Administrations,* edited by David C. Warner (Austin, Tex., 1977). The literature on Medicare specifically is extensive, but particularly useful to understanding the principles on which the program was founded and the compromises that had to be made to get the program enacted is Theodore R. Marmor's *The Politics of Medicare* (Chicago, 1973). It should be read in conjunction with the essay of Karen Davis and Roger Reynolds, "The Impact of Medicare and Medicaid on Access to Medical Care," in *The Role of Health Insurance in the Health Services Sector,* edited by Richard N. Rosett (New York, 1976). Sherri David's *With Dignity* (Westport, Conn., 1985) is another useful study of the origins of the Medicare and Medicaid programs. Medicare's promise and shortcomings are scrutinized in Victor R. Fuchs, *Essays in the Economics of Health and Medical Care* (New York, 1972) and *Who Shall Live?* (New York, 1974); Sar A. Levitan and Robert Taggert, *The Promise of Greatness* (Cambridge, Mass., 1976); and *Doing Better and Feeling Worse* (New York, 1977), edited by John H. Knowles. For understanding Medicare's vital role in the American social insurance state, *The Political Life of Medicare* (Chicago, 2003) by Jonathan Oberlander is indispensable.

The nation's growing conservatism arising out of the backlash against Great Society programs, the anti–Vietnam War protests, and escalating medical inflation affected how the political leadership of the 1970s approached the growing crisis in health care. As escalating medical costs extracted a toll on Medicare, Medicaid, and a host of other popular health programs, the number of Americans without insurance also rose. A good starting point for understanding the political temper of the times is A. James Reichley, *Conservatives in an Age of Change: The Nixon and Ford Administrations* (Washington, D.C., 1981). Richard M. Nixon, who first considered managed care as a cost-containment option, is examined in Stephen E. Ambrose's three-volume biography, *Nixon* (New York, 1987–1991). Dale E. Casper's *Richard M. Nixon: A Bibliographic Exploration* (New York, 1988) is a guide to the literature on Nixon and the Nixon administration. Two volumes look at the man who ran as a Washington outsider to become president in mid-decade: Betty Glad, *Jimmy Carter: In Search of the Great White House* (New York, 1980), and Burton I. Kaufman, *The Presidency of James Earl Carter, Jr.* (Lawrence, Kans., 1993). One of the more revealing analyses of how diminished expectations, woes, and confrontations with liberal Democrats and health reformers dogged Carter's presidency and paved the way for the presidential election of Republican Ronald Reagan in 1980 is physician Peter G. Bourne's *Jimmy Carter: A Comprehensive Biography from Plains to Postpresidency* (New York, 1997). *Health Policy in Transition* (Durham, N.C., 1987), edited by Lawrence D. Brown, brings together the writings of several authors who examined the interplay of health politics, policy, and law in the 1970s.

A significant but overlooked study of national health policy in the 1980s is Johns Hopkins public health specialist Vicente Navarro's *The Politics of Health Policy* (Cambridge, Mass., 1994). One does not have to subscribe to its Marxist perspective to agree with the author's conclusion that voters stayed away from the polls in the 1980s because neither political party was responsive to their real-life concerns. The Democratic Party leadership, with the exception of Jesse Jackson, who was largely marginalized, abandoned its historic New Deal base of support, instead parroting Reagan's economic ideas while ignoring the health needs of the poor and working poor, whose continuing support for national health insurance was documented in contemporary opinion polls.

Jesse Jackson was the only Democratic presidential candidate in the 1980s to espouse a platform that advocated national health insurance. Jackson's run for his party's nomination in 1984 is examined in Thomas E. Kavanagh and Lorn S. Foster, *Jesse Jackson's Campaign: The Primaries and Caucuses* (Washington, D.C., 1984), and his platform is analyzed in the essay by Rodney D. Green and Finley C. Campbell, "The Jesse Jackson Economic Platform of 1984: A Critique and an Alternative," in *The Social and Political Implications of the 1984 Jesse Jackson Presidential Campaign* (New York, 1990), edited by Lorenzo Morris. The 1988 campaign is recalled in Frank Clemente, editor, *Keep Hope Alive: Jesse Jackson's 1988 Presidential Campaign: A Collection of Major Speeches, Issue Papers, Photographs and Campaign Analysis* (Boston, 1989).

Reagan's successes as president were counterbalanced by a legacy of unsolved economic, social, and political problems for his successors. Haynes Johnson's *Sleepwalking through History: America in the Reagan Years* (New York, 1991) is a journalist's less-than-flattering account of the fortieth president. A starting point for examining the administration's accomplishments and failures is *The Reagan Record* (Cambridge, Mass., 1984), a collection of essays on policy issues edited by John L. Palmer and Isabel V. Sawhill. Critics accused Reagan's policies of contributing to the uneven economic fortunes of the rich and the poor, as in the two works of Kevin Phillips, *The Politics of Rich and Poor: Wealth and the American Electorate in the Reagan Aftermath* (New York, 1990) and *Boiling Point: Democrats, Republicans, and the Decline of Middle Class Prosperity* (New York, 1993), which examine correlations between political behavior and wealth, particularly the decline of middle-class prosperity. The economic problems of the poor and the working poor and the argument that the political system was nonresponsive to their needs, besides being treated in Navarro's study cited above, form the subject of *Why Americans Don't Vote* (New York, 1988), by Frances Fox Piven and Richard Cloward.

When George H. W. Bush entered the presidency in January 1989, it was clear that Americans and their political leaders would have to make difficult economic, social, and political choices in the final decade of the century. Political gridlock; Congress's inability to deal with economic and social problems, including sharply rising numbers of Americans without health insurance; growing antagonism toward "big government"; and voter alienation are discussed in E. J. Dionne, Jr., *Why Americans Hate Politics* (New York, 1991), and in *Mad as Hell: Revolt at the Ballot Box, 1992* (New York, 1993), by journalists Jack Germond and Jules Witcover. The rise and fall of the Medicare Catastrophic Coverage Act of 1988 is detailed in Richard Himmelfarb's *Catastrophic Politics* (University Park, Pa., 1995) and in Oberlander, cited above. Clinton's rise to the presidency in 1992 is recounted in Dick Morris's *Behind the Oval Office: Winning the Presidency in the Nineties* (New York, 1997), an account by a controversial former political adviser who conflates his own influence.

As evidence of a crisis in health care costs mounted in the 1980s and the early 1990s, health policy analysts examined alternatives to traditional fee-for-service medicine. The essays in *The Politics of Health Care Reform,* edited by James A. Morone and Gary S. Belkin (Durham, N.C., 1994), provide a good starting point. Other significant works include Clark C. Havighurst's *Deregulating the Health Care Industry* (Cambridge, Mass., 1982), advocating greater competition in the delivery of health care, and two influential works by Alain C. Enthoven: *Health Plan: The Only Practical Solution to the Soaring Cost of Medical Care* (Reading, Mass., 1980), and *Theory and Practice of Managed Competition in Health Care Financing* (Amsterdam, 1988). How to contain costs, expand access to coverage, and maintain quality is the conundrum addressed in *Reforming the System: Containing Health Care Costs in an Era of Universal Coverage* (New York, 1992), edited by Robert J. Blendon and Tracey S. Hyams. Sociologist Paul Starr's *The Logic of Health Care Reform* (Knoxville, Tenn., 1992 rev. edition) proposes universal health care with minimum federal standards, decentralized organization, private delivery of services, and state-established regional authorities to structure competition. But not everyone saw managed competition as the answer, as is evidenced in the critique by David Himmelstein and Steffy Woolhandler, *Managed Competition: A Grimm Fairy Tale* (Cambridge, Mass., 1993), for Harvard University's Center for National Health Program Studies.

The centerpiece of Clinton's legislative agenda in his first administration was health care reform, which came under intensive scrutiny. Perhaps the most meticulous reconstruction of the presidential task force's effort to write a universal health care reform bill is political scientist Jacob S. Hacker's *Road to Nowhere* (Princeton, N.J., 1997). It should be read in tandem with fellow political scientist Nicholas Laham's *A Lost Cause: Bill Clinton's Campaign for National Health Insurance* (Westport, Conn., 1999), which also offers a dispassionate analysis of why Clinton's legislation failed to pass muster with Congress. The fate of the Clinton reform initiative also is the subject of journalistic accounts, among which the most insightful are *The System: The American Way of Politics at the Breaking Point,* by Haynes Johnson and David S. Broder (Boston, 1996); *Showdown: The Struggle between the Gingrich Congress and the Clinton White House,* by Elizabeth Drew (New York, 1996); and *The Agenda: Inside the Clinton White House,* by investigative reporter Bob Woodward (New York, 1994). Filled with fascinating characters, shrewd insights, and telling details, these political reporters explain how the inner workings of Washington politics operated to stop dead in its tracks Clinton's plan for universal health insurance for Americans. Paul Starr's *The Logic of Health Care Reform,* cited above, is a reasoned defense of how and why the president's plan would work by one who helped to shape it. Despite its jargon and arcane methodology, Jennifer Koella's dissertation on interest groups and the liberal press, "The Impact of Interest Group and News Media Framing on Public Opinion: The Rise and Fall of the Clinton Health Plan" (University of Tennessee, 2001), makes some useful points.

The adverse impact on health care reform of Clinton's political difficulties with Newt Gingrich and the Republican-controlled 104th Congress is detailed in Drew's *Showdown,* cited above, and also in *Tell Newt to Shut Up! Prizewinning Washington Journalists Reveal How Reality Gagged the Gingrich Revolution* (New York, 1996), by David Maraniss and Michael Weisskopf. The fallout from political gridlock in the 1990s is the subject of essays arising out of a conference sponsored by the Brookings Institute, *Beyond Gridlock: Prospects for Governance in the Clinton Years—And After* (Washington, D.C., 1993), edited by James L. Sundquist. Morris Fiorina addresses the same problem in *Divided Government,* 2d edition (Needham Heights, Mass., 1996). The public's increasing hostility to bureaucratic government and liberal social spending is examined in Frank Lutz, *The People's Budget: A Common Sense Plan for Cutting Washington Down to Size* (Washington, D.C., 1995); and Theda Skocpol's analysis of the failed Clinton health plan, *Boomerang* (New York, 1997).

Labor's tortuous role in promoting health care reform from the postwar period through the Clinton administration's ill-fated health security bill is analyzed in the excellent study by Marie Gottschalk, *The Shadow Welfare State* (Ithaca, N.Y., 2000), whereas Cathie Jo Martin, in *Stuck in Neutral* (Princeton, N.J., 2000), challenges the conventional view that big business wielded enormous influence over America's political agenda and has been responsible for the relatively limited scale of the nation's social policies. Her dissection of the role of business in the failed Clinton health plan proposal is particularly illuminating.

Besides monographs, contemporary periodicals of both professional and popular nature devoted many articles and in some instances entire issues to the impact of health security upon American society. The obvious starting point to examine issues of public policy and health is *JAMA*, the *Journal of the American Medical Association,* whose editor throughout much of the period from the 1930s to the 1950s was the controversial Dr. Morris Fishbein. In addition to technical articles, *JAMA* reported regularly on political matters that touched on the medical profession. Its editorials staunchly defended fee-for-service medicine throughout much of its existence and commented, often unfavorably, on the progress of health insurance legislation, including Medicare. But it did open its pages to the explanation of new approaches to medical care, as in Alain Enthoven and Richard Kronick's 1991 article, "Universal Health Insurance through Incentives Reform."

*JAMA* should be supplemented with the prestigious *New England Journal of Medicine.* It too combined reporting on medical advances with medically related political news. Over the years, the latter has ranged from the scurrilously biting Morris Fishbein's 1939 article, "American Medicine and the National Health Plan," to the moderate, but no less critical, explanation by AMA president, Dr. Irvin Abell, "Attitude of the American Medical Association toward the National Health Program" (January 1939), to the equally partisan Eli Ginzberg's "Health Care Reform—Why So Slow?" (May 17, 1990). In between, the journal has published such dispassionate articles as Robert J. Blendon and Karen Donelan's "The Public and the Emerging Debate over National Health Insurance" (July 19, 1990).

Political officials from time to time also used medical and health journals to get across their particular viewpoints. In the 1930s, Josephine Roche utilized the *American Journal of Public Health* to rationalize the need for federal intervention in "Medical Care as a Public Health Function" (December 1937), as did Social Security official Arthur J. Altmeyer in "The National Health Conference and the Future of Public Health" (January 1939). Wilbur J. Cohen's "Reflections on the Enactment of Medicare and Medicaid" in *Health Care and Financing Review* (1985 Annual Supplement) allowed this former Social Security official an opportunity to respond to critics' attacks on these programs.

*Medical Economics,* as its name implies, looked at the economic implications for medicine of issues such as health insurance for the elderly in Robert L. Brenner's "Will Javits Bring on Social Security Medicare?" (vol. 38 [Nov. 20, 1961]: 195–196), "Why Not Let Blue Cross Handle Aged Care?" (vol. 40 [May 1963]: 120–122), and in 1995, when Medicare's financial future was in doubt, in the provocative article of Michael Petzer, "Medicare under the Knife: Radical or Cosmetic Surgery?" (June 2, 1995).

The health care crisis of the 1970s and 1980s forced a re-examination of universal coverage, long after the issue had been considered moot. Vicente Navarro, a Marxist physician at Johns Hopkins and the editor of the *International Journal of Health Services,* asked in that journal whether the arguments against a national health program were based on science or ideology ("The Arguments against a National Health Program: Science or Ideology," vol. 18 [Nov. 1988]: 179–190); and Roger M. Battistella and Thomas P. Weil addressed the dilemmas and opportunities in "National Health Insurance Reconsidered: Dilemmas and Opportunities," in the pages of *Hospital and Health Services Administration* (Summer 1989). By the 1990s, national health insurance was generating lively debate among physicians, insurance companies, economists, lawyers, and policy analysts. Theda Skocpol's 1993 survey of proposed reforms ("Is the Time Finally Ripe? Health Insurance Reforms in the 1990s," *Journal of Health Politics, Policy and Law* 18 [Fall 1993]: 531–550) was indicative of the optimism of many policy analysts that medicine's traditional fee-for-service approach was finally ripe for change. The *Journal of Health Politics, Policy and Law* is, perhaps, the leading scholarly periodical on contemporary and past issues of health policy. It is indispensable for studying national health care reform, comparative health care systems, and issues of cost containment, managed care, patient access, and the uninsured.

Other health journals also published regularly on the changes and debates that were occurring in the delivery and financing of medical care, as well as shifting public attitudes. *Hospitals* reported ("Survey Shows Voters Willing to Pay Tax for Health Care Plan," vol. 66 [June 5, 1992]: 10) the results of the Mildred and Claude Pepper Foundation survey revealing that voters were willing to pay a tax for access to better health coverage. *Health Affairs,* in its 1993 supplement, offered "A Bridge to Compromise: Competition under a Budget," by two experts who played major roles in formulating the Clinton reform initiative, Paul Starr and Walter A. Zelman; two years later (vol. 14 [1995]: 7–23), Robert J. Blendon, Mollyann Brodie, and John M. Benson asked rhetorically, "What Happened to Americans' Support for the Clinton Health Plan?" and then proceeded to tell readers.

Besides medical and medicine-related journals, the more traditional academic journals periodically touched on health issues. In November 1934, Edgar Sydenstricker examined "Health in the New Deal" in the pages of the *Annals,* a publication of the American Academy of Political and Social Science. In January 1951, I. S. Falk, a federal official involved in Social Security and health policy issues, discussed "Health Services, Medical Care Insurance, and Social Security" in the same journal. *Current History* also examined the nation's health in the Great Depression and New Deal with the publication in December 1932 of James A. Tobey's "Menace to National Health." In August 1963, Roy Lubove attempted to give readers of *Current History* historical perspective in "The New Deal and National Health."

By the early 1950s, health care for Social Security recipients was beginning to stir popular interest. Wilma Donahue et al. talked about the "Problems of Aging" in the August 1950 issue of the *University of Chicago Round Table.* With the passage of Medicare and the war in Vietnam, health costs became a pressing issue. In May 1970, University of Chicago economist Martin S. Feldstein analyzed medical inflation in "The Rising Price of Physicians' Services" in the *Review of Economics and Statistics.* Six years later Marian Gornick examined "Ten Years of Medicare: Impact on the Covered," in *Social Security*

*Bulletin* 39 (June 1976). By the 1980s, Jesse Jackson remained one of the few nationally prominent po-litical figures advocating national health insurance. In the May 1990 issue of *Humanity and Society,* Darryl S. Takeoff examined whether Jackson and the Rainbow Coalition was a true working-class move-ment or another, more traditional, manifestation of reform politics.

Clinton's health care reform initiative generated lots of attention and controversy. Trudy Lieberman's "Covering Health Care Reform: Round One" in the September–October 1993 issue of the *Columbia Journalism Review* was an attempt to gauge media coverage of the subject; Charles O. Jones examined the relationship between "Bill Clinton and the GOP Congress," in the spring 1995 issue of the *Brookings Review.*

Outside the health care industry and academia, every aspect of health security within the time pa-rameters of this study has come under scrutiny from the best-known to the most arcane of popular magazines and periodicals. *Survey, Survey Midmonthly, Time, Newsweek, U.S. News, Fortune, Business Week, New Republic, Nation,* and *Commentary,* representing both liberal and conservative points of view, were particularly useful for their coverage of health care during the Depression and New Deal years. In later years, Wilbur Cohen considered Richard Harris's four-part series on Medicare for the *New Yorker* magazine in 1966 to be the most accurate recounting of the origins of that program. Published subsequently as *A Sacred Trust,* as cited above, it greatly influenced my own thoughts on this important subject. The *AARP Bulletin* paid close attention to Medicare's cost problems, the plight of the uninsured, and other contemporary problems of the health care system.

Other special-interest magazines and trade journals, usually more narrowly focused and less known to the general population, periodically commented upon health security matters of specific concern to their readers. In the early 1990s, *Best's Review* covered national health insurance issues. In 1992, Mary Jane Fisher examined for *National Underwriter Property and Casualty* former presidential candidate Paul Tsongas's concept of managed care: "Tsongas, Managed Competition Key to U.S. Health Care" (June 29). Paul Starr's "Healthy Competition: Universal Coverage and Managed Competition under a Cap" and "What Happened to Health Care Reform?" for the *American Prospect* in the winters of 1993 and 1995 discussed Clinton's failed reform initiative. The *National Review* looked at the same topic, but from a distinctly conservative perspective. See, for example, Florence King's "The Misanthrope's Corner," *National Review* 46 (Jan. 24, 1994): 80, which is highly critical of the Clinton health plan, and Bruce Bartlett's "Low-Rent Health," ibid., 46 (May 2, 1994): 6, in which Barlettt draws an unflattering comparison between the adverse effects of the Clinton health plan and rent control pol-icies in America's cities.

Labor's take on health care tended to reflect the views of the prevailing Democratic administration, as in the *American Labor Legislation Review*'s 1938 article "Medical Politicians v. Medical Statesmen." The pages of the *ALLR* also became a forum for New Deal bureaucrats to promote their ideas, as in Jose-phine Roche's 1938 article, "The Worker's Stake in a National Health Program." The *American Federa-tionist,* the organ of the AFL-CIO, in the early 1960s endorsed Kennedy's health plan for Social Security recipients in James C. O'Brien's February 1962 article, "The Elderly Fight for Health Care," as did *Consu-mer Report* in 1965 in assessing the Johnson administration's "Medicare vs. the AMA's Latest Substitute." Among other journals that occasionally proved useful were *Progressive, Public Perspective, Reporter, In-dustrial Union Digest,* and the *Notes* of the Employer Benefit Research Institute, but these should be read along with Gottschalk's *The Shadow Welfare State,* cited above.

One would be remiss in not mentioning three journals that proved to be nearly indispensable for tracking the legislative history of health care issues from the 1970s through the end of the century. *Con-gressional Quarterly Weekly Report, Congressional Quarterly Almanac,* and *Congressional Digest* led this researcher through the maze that enveloped health bills as they made their way through the legislative process. The reporting of Alissa J. Rubin, Beth Donovan, Elizabeth Wehr, and Elizabeth Palmer was par-ticularly useful for unraveling the politics of Clinton's health plan.

Finally, with the demise of the Clinton health plan and the rise to power of conservative Republicans, attention began to shift to the role the states might play in the new politics of health care. *Health Policy, Federalism, and the American States* (Washington, D.C., 1996), edited by Robert F. Rich and William D. White, is a good starting point for examining health policy in the context of federalism and the politics of devolution.

# INDEX

DeBakey, Michael, 173
DeConcini, Dennis, 256
DeLay, Tom (Thomas), 291
Dellums, Ron (Ronald), 192
Democratic Advisory Council, 100
Democratic Party: conservative coalition, 3, 20, 38–39,
    51, 74; Democratic Advisory Council, 100; divisions
    within, 36, 73, 86, 92, 100–102, 202, 212–13, 238–49
    passim, 257, 299–301; DNC, 117; inflation, 172; Jesse
    Jackson, 199–202; voter alienation, 187–88, 195,
    200–202. See also individual presidents, legislators,
    and legislation
Dewey, Thomas E., 76
Dingell, John (Sr.): health insurance through Social Se-
    curity, 53, 90; Medicare, 154; postwar health legisla-
    tion, 63, 70, 79–82; Robert F. Wagner, 63
Dingell, John (Jr.), 149, 249–51
Dirksen, Everett M., 101
Dixiecrats, 77
Dodd, Christopher, 256
Dole, Bob (Robert): Clinton budget, 221; Clinton health
    plan, 221, 250, 252; conservative Republicans, 252,
    262, 274; Daniel P. Moynihan, 251; federal govern-
    ment, 273; health care reform, 233, 252; Medicare,
    262–63, 268, 273; minimalist insurance bill, 254;
    and Mitchell-Gephardt bill, 255; Newt Gingrich, 250,
    260, 273; presidential ambitions, 263, 273; Republi-
    can legislation, 250; Senate Finance Committee, 251;
    Senate Majority Leader, 221
Domenici, Pete V., 262, 274
Donnell, Forrest, 71–72
Douglas, Helen Gahagan, 71, 81
Douglas, Paul, 82, 107–8, 152–53
Drew, Elizabeth, 270–71
Dublin, Mary, 46
Dukakis, Michael, 201
Dungan, Ralph, 96
Dunn, Matthew A., 18
Durbin, Richard, 273
Durenberger, Dave, 253–54

Economic depressions: 1890s, 7; 1930s, 2, 12, 76, 187;
    1980s, 204–5, 246, 284–86, 303
Ehrlichman, John, 172–78
Eisenhower, Dwight D.: AMA, 91; disability benefits
    amendment, 93–95; divisions within administra-
    tion, 100–104, 112; Forand bill, 98, 100, 102; health
    insurance funded through Social Security, 91, 102;
    health reform, 91–92, 106; Kerr-Mills bill, 3, 109;
    New Deal, 91; presidency, 110; Reinsurance bill, 91–
    92; Richard M. Nixon, 102–3; White House Confer-
    ence on Aging, 112
"Eldercare," 142–44, 149
Elections: influence on Medicare legislation, 148, 271;
    presidency, 8, 12, 93, 133, 139, 159, 183–95 passim,
    282–84, 291, 297; Republican ascendancy, 257; voter
    apathy, 193–95, 200, 203
Eliot, Martha, 32

Ellenbogen, Henry, 21
Ellender, Allen, 44, 71
Elliot, Thomas, 20
Ellwood, Paul M., Jr., 174, 206, 222, 229, 240
Ely, Richard T., 8
Emergency Maternity and Infant Care Act (EMIC), 51,
    66
Employment Retirement Income Security Act (ERISA),
    278
Enthoven, Alain, 192, 206, 222, 229, 240
Etheredge, Lynn, 212, 214
Ewing, Oscar L.: DNC, 68; FSA, 73; health conference,
    74; health insurance funded through Social Security,
    88–89; National Health Insurance and Public Health
    bill, 87–88; Reorganization Plan, 82–83; report on
    health goals, 81; scaled-back health plan, 86–87;
    Truman health program, 73, 76, 79, 86

Fair Deal, 77–78, 91
Falk, Isidore S.: AALL, 8; CES, 15; communist issue, 72;
    experts in government, 65; health insurance in So-
    cial Security bill, 35, 63, 88; MAC, 18, 20; Medicare,
    97, 161; quoted, 6; Wagner-Murray-Dingell bill, 61
Farm Security Administration, 39, 49, 54
Feder, Judith, 205, 212–15, 222–23, 282
Federal Emergency Relief Administration (FERA), 15,
    28
Federalism, 29, 39, 44, 277–78, 284
Federal Security Agency (FSA), 63, 66, 71, 78. See also
    Ewing, Oscar L.
Federation of Women's Clubs, 80
Fein, Rashi, 170
Feldman, Myer, 99, 108, 125
Feldstein, Martin, 182
Finch, Robert, 169, 174
Fishbein, Morris, 31, 34, 51, 56, 79–80. See also Ameri-
    can Medical Association
Fisher, Irving, 14
Flanders, Ralph, 81
Flanders-Ives bill, 81, 85
Flannigan, Peter M., 178
Fleischer, Ari, 267
Flemming, Arthur, 100–102, 112, 262
Foley, Tom (Thomas S.), 249–56 passim
Folsom, Marion, 92, 98, 100, 112
Forand, Aime, 97, 99–108 passim. See also Cohen, Wil-
    bur J.; Eisenhower, Dwight D.; Kennedy, John F.;
    Johnson, Lyndon B.; Medicare; Mills, Wilbur
Ford, Gerald, 142, 184–87
Ford Motor Company, 287
Fowler, Henry, 147
Franks, Trent, 295
Fried, Bruce M., 205, 212
Friedman, Stephen, 289
Frist, Bill (William), 291, 304
Frothingham, Channing, 55
Fuchs, Victor R., 5
Fulbright, J. William, 151

Garamendi, John, 207–8, 223
Gardner, John W., 160, 164, 166
Gawande, Atul, 209–15 *passim*, 223, 236
General Electric Company, 287
Gephardt, Richard: Clinton transition team, 213; market competition, 192; Medicare, 262, 265; policy impasse between liberal and conservative Democrats, 221; Republicans, 256, 262; rescue bill, 255
Gergen, David, 237, 248–49
Germany, 2, 7, 38
Gingrich, Newt: balanced budget amendment, 259–62; Clinton health plan, 250, 255–56; Congress, 250; conservatism, 252–75 *passim;* Contract with America, 266, 271; crime bill, 255; Medicare, 258–65; Medicare Preservation Act, 268–74; misjudgment of Clinton, 265; political maneuvering, 261; Republican Revolution, 276; shutdown of government, 273–75; welfare bill, 275
Glenn, John, 256
Goldwater, Barry, 101–3, 133, 139
Gordon, Kermit, 147
Gore, Al (Albert Sr.), 107, 109, 132–36
Gore, Al (Albert Jr.), 220, 238, 282–83
Gorham, William, 166
Gramm, Phil, 250, 279
Grandy, Fred, 249
Grassley, Chuck (Charles), 291–92
Great Britain: Beveridge Plan, 51; congressional fact-finding tour, 83–85; Dellums-Corman bill, 192; health care, 7–8, 38, 78, 115; Margaret Thatcher, 195; single-payer system, 205; Westminster system, 300
Great Society: Johnson administration, 123, 128, 156; loss of momentum, 160; Medicare, 124, 139, 270; prosperity, 159; Vietnam War, 167
Green, William, 32, 54, 74
Greenberg, Selig, 160
Greenberg, Stan, 209, 211, 236

Griffin, Maurice F., 57
Griffiths, Martha W., 173, 176. *See also* Kennedy, Ted; Kennedy-Griffiths bill
Grunwald, Mandy, 211

Halleck, Charles, 134
Harper, Edward L., 177
Harris, Fred R., 152
Harrison, Burr, 103, 118, 121
Hartke, Vance R., 151–52
Hastert, J. Dennis, 291
Havighurst, Clark, 192
Hawley, Paul, 66, 68, 74
Hayden, Carl, 121, 128
Hayes, Charlotte, 212
Hays, Brooks, 104
Health: charity medical care, 3; documentation of poor health, 3, 27–29; employer-based health insurance, 3, 302; European health care systems, 2; FDR quote, 1; fee-for service medicine, 2; financing, 1–2, 4;

health care crisis of 1970s and 1980s, 3–4, 173, 187, 196–205 *passim*, 217, 282, 287; health security concept, 1, 3, 6, 299; inflation, 3–4; lack of social insurance, 2; market competition, 172, 174, 192, 202, 205–6, 222–23; "Means Test," 70, 150–51, 170; national health insurance, 76, 217, 301–4; need for federal intervention, 3, 277; numbers of uninsured, 4–5; pay-or-play, 205; political system, 1–2, 301–2; poverty, 6–7, 10; private sector medicine 3; restructuring by private system, 4, 278; single-payer system, 205–6; transition to mixed medical system, 3; treatment rationing, 278. *See also* Medicaid; Medicare; *other legislation*
Health, Education and Welfare (HEW), U.S., established, 91. *See also* Clinton, Bill; Flemming, Arthur; Forand bill; Health Maintenance Organizations; Hobby, Oveta Culp; Inflation; Medicare; Nixon, Richard M.; Shalala, Donna E.
Health care reformers: Breaux Commission, 279–80, 288; Brookings report, 75; Carter health plan, 188–89; CES, 15; class politics, 187–88; Clinton health plan, 211–12, 232–59 *passim*, 277–78; Congress, 301; conservative coalition, 63–64; divisions, 300–301; Eisenhower, 110–11; FDR, 59–60; George W. Bush's reform of Medicare, 289, 291–97, 300; Great Society, 169; health care options, 205–6; health crisis of 1980s, 198, 204; health security legislation, 23, 245; inflation, 165; Jesse Jackson, 199–201; Josephine A. Roche, 15, 23, 32, 35–37; Long amendment, 150; managed care, 192–93; means test, 70; media, 302; middle class, 302–3; Murray-Dingell bill, 52–55, 59–60; national health insurance, 217, 303–4; Nixon health plan, 244–45; patients' rights legislation, 281; Paul Starr, 223, 231; postwar period, 60–61; private insurance, 65–66; public funding of health care, 88; Robert F. Wagner, 38–48, 52–64; sanitarians, 9; separation of powers, 301; socialized medicine, 81; state government, 203; Ted Kennedy, 172–73, 181–83; Truman health message, 63–65
Health Insurance Association of America (HIAA), 127, 176, 184, 254
Health Insurance Portability and Accountability Act, 276–77. *See also* Clinton, Bill; Kassebaum-Kennedy bill
Health Maintenance Organizations (HMOs): Alain Enthoven, 192, 206, 222; business attitude towards, 278–81; Clinton health plan, 230, 232; George W. Bush's reform of Medicare, 284, 289–90, 295; HMO Act (1973), 174–75, 178–79, 188, 230; HMO Group, 281; managed competition, 174, 192; medical malpractice, 281; patients' bill of rights, 281; Paul Ellwood, 174; Republican policy, 175–76, 260, 266; Richard M. Nixon, 174–76, 188; Ronald Reagan, 196; Social Security, 175
Health Savings Account (HSA), 298
Health Security Act (1993), bill, 241–45, 257. *See also* Clinton, Bill; Clinton, Hillary Rodham; Labor (organized), Magaziner, Ira C.; National Federation of

Thompson, Lewis R., 24
Thompson, Tommy G., 289, 295
Thornburgh, Richard, 203
Thorpe, Kenneth: BBDG, 205; Clinton transition team, 212; presidential task force, 223, 234, 236
Thurmond, Strom, 77
Tibbits, Clark, 25
Topping, Worth M., 15
Townsend, Francis, 13
Truman, Harry S.: AMA, 62–63; background, 62; Clark Clifford, 70; cold war, 62, 66–73 passim; Commission on the Health Needs of the Nation, 89–91; Conference on Aging, 89; Congress (80th), 63, 68–76 passim; Congress (81st), 77–78, 85–86; critics, 63; Democratic platform, 76; Fair Deal, 77–78; Forland bill, 100; health conference, 75; health insurance through Social Security, 63, 89; health legislation, 65–66, 68, 79, 82–90; and health message, 63, 69; health security, 62, 64, 75–82 passim; Hill-Aiken bill, 82; Medicare-signing, 154; Oscar L. Ewing, 73–74, 79, 86; presidency, 62; presidential election (1948), 70, 74, 77; progressive leanings, 62, 65; Taft health bill, 71–72; Taft-Hartley Act, 82
Tsongas, Paul, 206–7
TXU Corporation, 287
Tyson, Laura D'Andrea, 227, 279

Ukockis, James R., 225, 229
Ullman, Al, 123, 129, 144
United Auto Workers, 243–44
United Health Group, 281
United Mine Workers, 96
United Presbyterian Church, 117
United Steel Workers, 96, 243–44
Urban Institute, 286, 293
U.S. Healthcare, 234
Uth, Gus, 41

Valenti, Jack, 154, 165
Veneman, John, 174, 176
Veterans' Administration (VA), 66, 68, 74, 225
Vietnam War, 151, 163, 166–67, 171
Virginia Health Care Foundation, 287

Wagner, Robert F.: Baruch proposal, 74; defeat of national health program, 60; FDR, 14; health coverage

for African Americans, 42; IDC, 38, 46; National Health Act (1939) bill, 38–48 passim; national health insurance, 14, 23, 31, 35, 39–40, 47–48; Medicare, 154; New Deal, 14; NHC, 31, 34; postwar health legislation, 63, 80; TCMC, 38–39; Wagner-Murray-Dingell bill, 52–70 passim; wartime hospital construction program, 45
Wagner-Murray-Dingell bill, 52–70 passim. See also American Medical Association; Dingell, John (Sr.); Murray, James E.; Wagner, Robert F.; Social Security Board
Ward, Donovan B., 144, 149
War on terrorism, 286
Warren, Earl, 76
Watergate scandal, 183
Watts, John, C., 124, 126–28
Waxman, Henry, 197, 249–50
Webb, James, 74
Weber, Adna F., 7
Weinberger, Caspar, 179–82
Wellstone, Paul, 245
West, Olin, 23, 62–63
Wexler, Anne, 205
Whitaker and Baxter, 78, 80
White, John, 191
White House Conference on Aging (1960), 112
Wickenden, Elizabeth, 151
Wilbur, Ray Lyman, 10
Williams, Harrison, 172
Willoughby, William F., 7
Wilson, George Howard, 73, 81–86
Wilson, Henry Hall, Jr., 123–42 passim
Wilson, Woodrow, 8–9
Withers, Garrett L., 79
Witte, Edwin, 15–18, 20
Wofford, Harris, 203, 211
Woodcock, Leonard, 173, 188
Works Progress Administration (WPA), 23
World War I, 9
World War II, 3, 45–50
Wright, Jim, 197

Young, Milton R., 132
Young, Whitney, Jr., 173

Zellman, Walter, 207–8, 223, 226